INTRODUCING CHRISTIAN ETHICS

Now in its second edition, *Introducing Christian Ethics* offers a and engaging introduction to the field suitable for beginners advanced readers. The field is divided into three distinct approaches: universal (ethics for anyone), subversive (ethics for the excluded), and ecclesial (ethics for the church). These three approaches present a fresh understanding of the field of Christian ethics, whilst providing a structure for thoughtful insights into the complex moral challenges facing people today. The text encompasses the field of Christian ethics in its entirety, surveying its history, and mapping and exploring the differences in all the major ethical approaches.

This new edition has been thoughtfully updated. It includes additional material on Catholic perspectives, ethics and social media, further case studies and a stronger pedagogical structure, including introductions and summaries. As well as discussing ethical issues and key thinkers, *Introducing Christian Ethics 2/e* provides a significant foundation for students by setting them in a framework that explores scripture, philosophy and church history. The text is structured so that it can be used alongside a companion volume, *Christian Ethics: An Introductory Reader* (Wiley-Blackwell, 2010), which further illustrates and amplifies the diversity of material and arguments explored here.

Samuel Wells is Vicar of St Martin-in-the-Fields, and a widely-known theologian, preacher, pastor, writer, and broadcaster. He is also Visiting Professor of Christian Ethics at King's College, London. He has published 25 books, including *Improvisation, God's Companions*, and *A Nazareth Manifesto*. He edited the partner book to this volume, *Christian Ethics: An Introductory Reader* (Oxford: Wiley-Blackwell, 2010).

Ben Quash is Professor of Christianity and the Arts at King's College London. He is the author of *Theology and the Drama of History* (2005) and is former Reviews Editor of *Studies in Christian Ethics*.

Rebekah Eklund is Assistant Professor of Theology at Loyola University Maryland in Baltimore, where she teaches theology, ethics, and Christian Scripture. She is the author of *Jesus Wept: The Significance of Jesus' Laments in the New Testament* (2015).

SAMUEL WELLS AND BEN QUASH WITH REBEKAH EKLUND

INTRODUCING CHRISTIAN ETHICS

SECOND EDITION

WILEY Blackwell

Registered Offices
John Wiley & Sons, Inc., 111 River Street, Hoboken, NJ 07030, USA
John Wiley & Sons Ltd, The Atrium, Southern Gate, Chichester, West Sussex, PO19 8SQ, UK

Editorial Office
9600 Garsington Road, Oxford, OX4 2DQ, UK

For details of our global editorial offices, customer services, and more information about Wiley products visit us at www.wiley.com.

Wiley also publishes its books in a variety of electronic formats and by print-on-demand. Some content that appears in standard print versions of this book may not be available in other formats.

Library of Congress Cataloging-in-Publication Data

Names: Wells, Samuel, 1965– author. | Quash, Ben, 1968– author. |
   Eklund, Rebekah, 1975– author.
Title: Introducing Christian ethics/Samuel Wells, Ben Quash, Rebekah Eklund.
Description: Second edition. | Hoboken, NJ : John Wiley & Sons, 2017. |
   Includes index.
Identifiers: LCCN 2016050483 (print) | LCCN 2016056613 (ebook) |
   ISBN 9781119155720 (pbk.) | ISBN 9781119155737 (pdf) | ISBN 9781119155751 (epub)
Subjects: LCSH: Christian ethics.
Classification: LCC BJ1251 .W453 2017 (print) | LCC BJ1251 (ebook) |
   DDC 241–dc23
LC record available at https://lccn.loc.gov/2016050483

Cover Image: Peter Horree / Alamy Stock Photo
Cover Design: Wiley

Set in 10.5/13pt Galliard by SPi Global, Pondicherry, India

10 9 8 7 6 5 4 3 2 1

For Harry Geoghegan

For Kathryn Chambers

For Lucia Eklund

Contents

Preface

This is a textbook for entry-level students in Christian ethics. It is designed for undergraduates and seminarians, in some cases pre-college students, and the elusive but much-coveted general reader. It is intended to be used in lay ministry courses, and a variety of educational and training courses, at diploma and informal levels. It sets out to do a number of things that are seldom done together.

It seeks to offer an overview of the whole field of Christian ethics. Some treatments offer a sequence of great authors in the history of the discipline. Others try to provide a taxonomy or typology or simply a list of the sometimes bewilderingly diverse and complex assortment of theories quoted and employed in the discourse. Others again work their way through a grab-bag of controversial issues and endeavor to present both balance and wisdom. This book has the temerity to attempt all three. Like any mapping exercise, it cannot pretend to be wholly objective; the classification and selection of issues examined, approaches explored, and authors extracted will be insightful and constructive to some, arbitrary and partial to others. Nonetheless we hope that, for those many who may disagree on some of the details, many more will enjoy and embrace the overall organization and presentation of the field.

The book rests on a broad division of Christian ethics into three approaches: universal (ethics for anyone), subversive (ethics for the excluded), and ecclesial (ethics for the church). It needs to be said that this distinction is not by any means generally accepted and adopted in the field, being simply the usage of one of the authors of this volume. This book may therefore be read as an extended road-test for the durability and comprehensiveness of this threefold distinction. But newcomers to the field who expect all subsequent interlocutors to recognize these approaches are likely to be disappointed.

The threefold distinction is designed to achieve a number of things. It is a tool for getting a handle on a huge subject, treating protagonists sympathetically but not uncritically. It is a means of distinguishing between the loudest voices in the field today, and the audiences and interests they perceive themselves as addressing. It is a way of showing unlikely correspondences between approaches that are sometimes perceived as opposites or antagonists. It is intended to balance description and critique, construction and analysis. It is not designed as a reductionist, watertight theory that diminishes the diversity and vitality of conversation across the discipline. There are many overlaps and anomalies in the field, as becomes clear in the last section of the book.

Not only does the book set out to discuss both approaches and issues (sometimes known respectively as theoretical and applied ethics), it is structured so as to bring the respective theories to bear on each issue. Once the threefold distinction of universal, subversive, and ecclesial approaches has been set out in the second part of the book, the third part examines fifteen pressing and abiding issues under each of these three headings. This not only amplifies the respective issues, it tests the respective approaches. The first part of the book may be read, among other things, as a long explanation of why the categories of universal, subversive, and ecclesial do not apply in anything like the same way before the era of Western modernity beginning around the early eighteenth century or even later. The birth of the discipline of Christian ethics as currently understood, and the plausibility of using these three categories, broadly coincide. They are both deeply related to the way ethics came to be pursued primarily in universities and only secondarily (and derivatively) in churches.

In addition to the three conventional kinds of introductions to Christian ethics cited earlier, a fourth kind presents a series of excerpts from significant works or on salient issues in the field, either in contemporary voice or across the historical tradition. Not content simply to synthesize the three earlier kinds of introductions, this project attempts this fourth kind as well. A sister volume to this one, *Christian Ethics: An Introductory Reader*, adopts exactly the same structure (not just in chapter titles but also in subheadings) and seeks to illustrate, amplify, and develop the diversity of material, voices, and arguments explored in this book. Thus, the companion volume deals with the tradition, the variety of approaches, and the range of issues, just as much as the textbook does. As far as we are aware, the bringing together of all four of these kinds of introductions to the field is unique to this project. The two volumes are carefully designed so that, while complementary and supplementary to one another, each can serve alone as an introduction to the subject, depending on the needs, opportunities, wishes, and budget of the student and teacher.

Any book that quotes ancient texts in English translation faces the difficulty of older conventions that used masculine pronouns for God and referred to people in general as men. We have decided to retain the original quotations without alteration, even where we might today have written "humanity" instead of "man." All Scripture quotations are New Revised Standard Version (NRSV) unless otherwise noted.

It may be asked whether the authors have a particular agenda in setting this project before the academy and reading public, beyond the customary humble disclaimers of hoping to be of some service and participating in the honored process of education and formation in Christian ethics. There is no doubt we have a close interest in the strand of ethics we are calling ecclesial. Some proponents of this strand have been associated with abrasive, not to say dismissive, regard for the other two strands as we are presenting them. But ecclesial ethics is not a monochrome approach, in style or in content, any more than subversive and universal ethics are. Thus aside from simply offering an accessible introduction to the field, part of the purpose of this book is to demonstrate beyond reasonable doubt that ecclesial ethics, when not in the mode of polemical stridency, is deeply respectful of, open to lively conversation with, and indeed profoundly indebted to, other approaches to ethics, and on many issues shares evaluations and commitments that resonate with subversive and/or universal approaches. It is not necessary to adopt the assumptions of ecclesial ethics to seek here an introduction to the dynamics and prospects of Christian ethics as a whole.

This book arises and derives from a number of friendships and collaborations. Most obviously, it has been shaped by a friendship between the two initial authors, Ben Quash and Sam Wells. We have collaborated on various projects in the past, academically and pastorally, with happy results; we have found our respective research interests complementary and stimulating, but most of all we simply enjoy one another's company, in laughter and in grief. It is a change of style, for each of us, to write a book together, but we hope it is no less a book for having two authors rather than one.

For the second edition, we have been joined by Rebekah Eklund, a third partner in scholarship, dialogue, enquiry, and friendship, and the joy of collaborating has been only increased by the greater wisdom and breadth of insight that a third heart, and mind, and soul, has brought. Among other improvements, the second edition includes a general introduction addressed to the reader, offers revised introductions to each of the three parts of the book, gives greater attention to Catholic and Orthodox ethics, revises and expands the section on the ethics of race to include more recent thinkers, and updates the section on media to incorporate the rapidly changing field of social media.

We have all been greatly enriched by the encouragement, imagination, and wit of Rebecca Harkin, whose vision for this project and depth of understanding of the issues and questions involved makes her a remarkable editor and publisher, and a rewarding creative partner. We are grateful to many wise colleagues, notably Hans Hillerbrand, Michael Goldman, Ebrahim Moosa, Kishor Trivedi, James Ong, Ellen Davis, Mary McClintock Fulkerson, John Kiess, and Fritz Bauerschmidt for guidance in waters where our judgments were unsteady. Jo Wells and Susannah Ticciati, among others, have offered perception in times of clarity and companionship in times of mystery.

Christian ethics is done in the communion of saints, and in this context Christians learn that they have living relationships with Christians past and future, departed and yet to come. The obligations and the joys traced by ethics bind the generations, and in this bond the memory of what has been takes the form of praise, and the anticipation of what will be is called hope. Rejoicing in this communion that binds the generations, and full of hope, we dedicate this book to two nieces and a nephew who make our lives richer, deeper, and truer.

Samuel Wells
Ben Quash
Rebekah Eklund

Introduction

We've written this book to give a student who is new to Christian ethics the ability to address issues and methods in the field in an informed and confident way.

To do that we believe a student needs three things:

1. a sense of what Christian ethics is, what its sources are, and how it has been practiced;
2. a framework for distinguishing between different styles of argument; and
3. discussion of the major topics that Christian ethics most frequently addresses, and an opportunity to apply the framework through exploring those topics.

These three elements constitute the three parts of the book.

The first part explores the four intertwining "stories" that contribute to the rich and complex story of Christian ethics today: the story of God as found in Christian Scripture; the story of the church from its origins in the first century through the present day; the stories of ethics in contexts outside Christianity, including in classical philosophy, in other religious traditions, and in present-day professional settings; and the historical development of Christian ethics as traced through its most influential figures.

In the second part of the book, we suggest that there are three major approaches to Christian ethics: universal, subversive, and ecclesial. (These terms, and the threefold division itself, are distinctive to this book and are not often found elsewhere in the field of Christian ethics.) The three chapters of Part Two describe in greater detail the origin and shape of these three major branches of Christian ethics. The first, universal ethics, assumes that ethics is for everybody. If it applies to one, it applies to all. Many of the conventional approaches to ethics fall into this category: deontological, consequentialist, natural law, and so on.

Introducing Christian Ethics, Second Edition. Samuel Wells and Ben Quash with Rebekah Eklund.
© 2017 John Wiley & Sons Ltd. Published 2017 by John Wiley & Sons Ltd.

The second approach challenges this universal assumption by considering the role of social location in ethics, asking who is excluded from this so-called "everybody," and focusing particular attention on questions of gender, race, and class. The branch of ethics we are describing as subversive is sometimes described as liberationist, since it is committed to the liberation of the oppressed and the empowerment of the voiceless or the dominated.

The third approach is a retrieval of the language of virtue, most associated with the classical Greek philosopher Aristotle, and also adopted in the thirteenth century by the Christian theologian Thomas Aquinas. It assumes that the primary context of Christian ethics is the church (the word "ecclesial" derives from the Greek word for church). It focuses on the shaping of character rather than on the moment of decision. Ecclesial ethics places Christian ethics into conversation with the church's specific theological commitments and practices, including the creeds and the sacraments.

This three-part structure is intended to be illuminating and not restrictive. We believe that it offers a useful way to identify different tendencies and methods within the broad field of Christian ethics, but it does not imply that we think individual thinkers often or always fit neatly into only one category. Instead, our hope is that the reader of this book will be trained to discern the methodological underpinnings of the texts and authors with whom they interact. Thus, one might come to read a document such as a papal encyclical, a university honor code, or a newspaper editorial and recognize a mix of methods and commitments in that one document. We have a particular interest in making more widely known the claims and possibilities of ecclesial ethics, but in general we seek to present each approach as clearly and charitably as possible.

The final part devotes five chapters to exploring the key issues and challenges addressed by Christian ethics. Here we meet a conventional list of ethical trouble-spots (abortion, euthanasia, war) as well as more general questions (the role of the state, environmental crises). In each chapter, we explore how the three "branches" of Christian ethics might typically approach these central ethical questions.

To avoid cluttering the text with footnotes or references, we have included the sources used in each chapter at the end of the chapter, alongside suggestions for further reading. Links to online documents are included where they are available. A selection of primary texts paired with each chapter is also available in the companion volume *Christian Ethics: An Introductory Reader*.

People often begin the study of Christian ethics hoping to find the right answers. Our approach focuses more on asking the right questions. Sometimes there are no easy answers: if there were, perhaps we would not need the church, a company of pilgrims with whom to share in discernment and practice. We have shared innumerable good disagreements in writing this book together, from which we have, we trust, become wiser and more humble. We hope the reading of the book will be as rewarding as the writing has been.

Part One
The Story of Christian Ethics

Christian ethics has three key sources: the written word of Scripture, the prayer and practice of the church, and the distilled wisdom and experience of the ages.

The document that shapes the identity of Christianity is the Bible, and it is impossible to begin studying Christian ethics without an understanding of the nature and content of the Scriptures and their role in the discipline. Thus, our first chapter begins with a consideration of Scripture and the nature of its authority and place in Christian ethics. It then considers the Bible in three parts – the People of God (the Old Testament), God in Person (the four gospels), and Following Jesus (the remainder of the New Testament).

The New Testament was written by the early church, and it was likewise the early church that determined the shape of the Bible as a whole. Christian ethics does not primarily refer to a sequence of significant authors or a collection of influential texts: instead it concerns a historical series of attempts to embody the instructions of Scripture, the good news of Jesus, and the example of his first followers. This historical series of attempts is called the church. Our second chapter therefore develops the story of Christian ethics by exploring the history of the church, again in three eras – Minority Status (the era before Christianity became the norm in the Mediterranean world), Christendom (the era when Christianity was the norm, while the Mediterranean world expanded its influence across the globe), and the Church in Modernity (the era when Christianity had ceased to be the norm, at least in the Western world).

Before Christians began to try to translate the heritage of Israel and Jesus into the habits and norms of personal and communal life, there had already long been a tradition, stretching back to ancient Greece, of reflecting on how human beings should live. Christian ethics has always been developed in relation to a conversation about what a person should do, and who a person should be, that went beyond the culture of the church. In fact it is only in relation to such conversation partners that the discipline of "Christian ethics" emerges at all. Christian ethics becomes the place where the heritage of Israel and Jesus, the practice and expectations of the church, and the disciplines and vocabulary of philosophical ethics, all meet. Hence our third chapter considers the emergence of "ethics" as a discipline in several key "non-Christian" contexts: in classical philosophy, in other religions, and in particular professional contexts.

Finally, these three strands – Scripture, history, and philosophy – come together to form the contemporary discipline of Christian ethics. Yet this discipline itself tends to trace its lineage less to the stories told in the first three chapters, and more to a story that emerges in relation to all three: that is, the sequence of great authors whose works form the canon of writings in this field. This fourth story is not so much the story of Christian ethics as a history of Christian ethicists. Many, perhaps most, of these figures did not explicitly think of themselves as ethicists (as distinct from theologians or philosophers), but it is in their tradition that most of those publishing work in the field of Christian ethics believe themselves to stand, as will become clear in the second and third parts of this volume.

Chapter One
The Story of God

Christians sometimes talk as if the Bible has all the answers to life's questions and problems. But a thorough reading of the Bible reveals various complexities. There are some ethical issues that the Bible does not specifically address. There are others where either the Bible seems to offer instruction (such as stoning wrongdoers) that is unpalatable to the contemporary world, or where the Scriptures seem to hold a worldview (such as ancient cosmology) that has since been largely abandoned. Finally, there are other issues where different verses or injunctions or stories seem to offer contradictory counsel.

For example, in the eighteenth and nineteenth centuries, especially in the American South, both abolitionists and slaveholders appealed to Christian Scripture to support their respective positions. According to the latter, Scripture clearly upholds the right of masters to own and discipline slaves; for the former, the Bible's trajectory of liberation and love categorically rules out any person owning another human being. The Bible continues to be invoked as a witness on both sides of many ethical debates, including same-sex marriage and war. What's seldom in question is the centrality of Scripture to Christian ethics; what's more complex is how that relationship plays out in practice.

The question of the relationship between Scripture and ethics necessarily involves one's understanding of what Scripture is in the first place. Christians, in fact, do not completely agree on what constitutes sacred Scripture. Orthodox, Catholic, and Anglican Christians include slightly different versions of the collection of books known as the Apocrypha in their Old Testament canons, whereas Protestant Bibles exclude the Apocrypha altogether. And then there is the nature of the text. Is the Bible a prescriptive code of conduct, a rulebook, a source of moral law? Is it a window into the heart of God, or a conduit through which the Holy Spirit shapes the moral imagination? Does it provide

Introducing Christian Ethics, Second Edition. Samuel Wells and Ben Quash with Rebekah Eklund.
© 2017 John Wiley & Sons Ltd. Published 2017 by John Wiley & Sons Ltd.

patterns for emulation or a clarion call to mend our ways? Is it a love song designed to woo humanity closer to God or a dash of icewater meant to awaken a sleepy conscience?

When it comes to describing the place of Scripture in Christian ethics, therefore, challenges abound; we will describe two of the most pressing here.

1. *Historical and cultural distance.* Reading the Bible is sometimes described as reading someone else's mail: these texts were written to and for other people in other times and places, often radically different from ours. The Bible does not explicitly address pressing contemporary issues like stem cell research or climate change. "The world of Leviticus is not the world of 1 Corinthians, and neither of these is our world" (Joel Green).

2. *The multivocity of Scripture.* While it is commonplace to talk about the Bible as if it were one book, it is instead a collection of books written by multiple authors and compiled by various editors over the course of thousands of years. It encompasses a wide variety of genres, some of which relate less obviously to ethics: in what sense is a poetic text an ethical one? Thus, describing the ethics contained within Scripture is itself fraught with tensions. New Testament scholar Richard Hays notes that careful, critical exegesis only heightens the problem by sharpening "our awareness of the ideological diversity within Scripture and of our historical distances from the original communities." He cites Oliver O'Donovan, who writes, wryly, "interpreters who think that they can determine the proper ethical application of the Bible solely through more sophisticated exegesis are like people who believe that they can fly if they only flap their arms hard enough."

And yet Christian ethics generally operates under the conviction that the ancient texts of Scripture nonetheless have enduring relevance and even binding authority over the lives of Christians in the present. (Some exceptions to this rule are taken up in Chapter Six.) But in what way are these texts authoritative? That is, where does authority reside when it comes to applying the Bible to ethical matters? There are three primary options.

*   Authority resides in the events *behind* the text of Scripture. That is, authority resides in God and in God's creating, saving, and liberating actions as narrated by the biblical books. For some, this has meant seeking to recreate as closely as possible the worlds and events described by the text, or to insist on the historicity of every event in the text (thus leading to long, heated battles over the historical character of the creation or the great flood in Genesis). For others, it has meant noting, more pragmatically, that Scripture is the best (or only) witness that we have to the Triune God. This leads to the next view.
*   Authority is inherent *within* the text itself, a position often associated with belief in the inspiration of Scripture. In this view, the Holy Spirit inspired each author (and perhaps editor) of the sacred books, and therefore the recorded

words themselves are holy. In this sense the text has a kind of derivative authority, since its authority comes from its divine author; but critics worry that this position makes the Bible itself a focus of worship, rather than a book that directs people to the worship of God.

A subset of this view focuses on the "final form" of the biblical books as we now have them, rather than on a reconstruction of the "original" text or the events described by the text, as the proper object of study. This approach is sometimes known as canonical criticism, which is a method that seeks to read all the books of the canon, Old and New Testaments, in relation to one another. Canonical reading reflects Augustine of Hippo's (354–430 CE) principle that Scripture interprets Scripture. Thus, the four gospels are to be read not only alongside one another, but in the context of Israel's story in the Old Testament and the early church's story in the rest of the New Testament as well.

- A third view locates authority *in front of* the text – that is, in the reader and the reading community. This view sometimes draws on postmodern literary theory, which proposes that texts themselves have no meaning until they are read and interpreted. Related to this is the view that sacred texts have no authority apart from the communities that interpret and adhere to them. Thus, authority resides in various interpreting communities: for Roman Catholics, this means the magisterium, or the apostolic teaching authority exercised by the bishops and the Pope; for some Protestants, authority is located in the local pastor or the local congregation. The approach sometimes known as liberationist ethics – described in this book as subversive ethics – tends to locate authority rather in the daily experience of the common people, especially the oppressed (more on this in Chapter Six).

One recent subset of this third view proposes that authority lies finally not in the reading of the text but in its communal embodiment – i.e., in faithfully "performing" or living out the Scriptures as members of a worshipping community. (This position is closely associated with ecclesial ethics, which will be taken up in Chapter Seven.)

Scripture also bears authority alongside what is typically called tradition, which includes summaries of Christian beliefs like the Nicene Creed and the ongoing teaching authority of the apostolic church. For Orthodox and Catholic Christians, Scripture itself is often viewed as an element of the church's tradition and therefore not finally distinguishable from a separate body of writings called "tradition." For example, in the Catholic Church, Scripture and tradition "flow from the same divine well-spring" and as such they both preserve and transmit the Word of God. For this reason Scripture and tradition are "accepted and honored with equal sentiments of devotion and reverence" (*Dei Verbum*). By contrast Anglicanism is associated with reading Scripture in creative tension with tradition and reason.

While most Protestants adhere to some version of the Reformation principle *sola Scriptura* (Scripture alone), almost every Protestant group uses written traditions such as the Augsburg Confession (the central statement of faith for the

Lutheran tradition), or unwritten traditions such as the perspicuity of Scripture (the idea that Scripture has a single, plain meaning), as important but less authoritative guides to interpreting Scripture. In practice any view that looks to Scripture for moral guidance must decide how to adjudicate differences in the interpretation of that Scripture – for example, when the slaveholder and abolitionist both appeal to the biblical text.

The diversity of the biblical material in relation to ethics can be a significant challenge. Yet it can also enliven the ethical imagination, if this diversity is taken as a gift rather than a problem – as a prompt to creative faithfulness in new situations. This depends on discerning an underlying unity threading through the complexity of the scriptural texts – a coherent story about God. We now turn to a brief account of that story, in all its diversity.

The People of God

What Christians call the Old Testament is a collection of books that record the faith and the experience and the insights of God's people Israel from earliest times until around 300 years before the birth of Jesus. The Old Testament is made up of three largely distinct kinds of literature. The first is Law, in Hebrew *Torah*, which refers to the first five books: Genesis, Exodus, Leviticus, Numbers, and Deuteronomy. The Law is not simply a series of injunctions, although there are thought to be 613 positive and negative rules spread across these books; instead the Law offers a foundational narrative that provides a context for the covenant made between God and Israel, of which these laws are an expression and symbol – rather as a wedding ring is an expression and symbol of a marriage covenant. The *Torah*, sometimes also known as the Pentateuch, begins with the stories of creation and fall, of flood and of Babel. It then introduces Abraham as the patriarch of Israel and bearer of God's promise that through his descendants many peoples will find a blessing. Abraham enters the Promised Land, but famine takes his descendants to Egypt, where God has already sent Abraham's great-grandson Joseph to protect them. Generations later, however, they fall into slavery, and God calls Moses to lead them out of Egypt and through the Red Sea. They come to Mt. Sinai, where God gives Moses the Ten Commandments and many other instructions. They wander in the wilderness for forty years. The Pentateuch ends with the death of Moses, just as the Israelites are on the brink of entering the Promised Land.

The second major collection of literature in the Old Testament is the Prophets. Just as the Law does not simply contain laws, so the Prophets does not simply contain prophecies. The Prophets includes all the books that take the story of Israel from the entry into the Promised Land under Joshua to the exile in Babylon. Many of these are in narrative form – notably the so-called "Deuteronomistic history." The Deuteronomistic history traces how Joshua took the Israelites into the land, how a series of ad hoc rulers known as judges galvanized the twelve tribes at moments of crisis, and how eventually the prophet Samuel anointed Saul as Israel's first king. Saul was followed by David, and David by Solomon, during a period that marked the zenith of Israel's power and prestige. The kingdom split after Solomon's death, with the ten tribes of the northern kingdom (Israel) ruled separately from the two southern tribes (Judah). The northern kingdom was overrun by the Assyrians (ca. 722 BCE), and finally the southern kingdom was invaded by the Chaldeans, the empire known in the Old Testament as Babylon, around 300 years after Solomon (586 BCE). The history concludes with a great number of people being taken into exile in Babylon. This long history is "prophecy" because it identifies the action of God as a living influence in the present as in the past; God is an active participant in the story. The books of Isaiah, Jeremiah, and Ezekiel, together with the twelve shorter prophetic books, interweave pronouncements and declarations of God's role and purpose in these events, particularly the later ones, while generally presupposing the broad outline of the narrative.

The third main part of the Old Testament is the Writings. These include most notably the Psalms, which mix narrative incantation with praise and lamentation, and Proverbs, a distillation of the wisdom of sages. But they also incorporate several narrative books such as Ruth and Chronicles. The narrative books affirm that there is a future for Israel after the catastrophe of exile – a future that lies in the reconstruction of Jerusalem (Ezra and Nehemiah), the wit and imagination to live under foreign rule (Esther), and the cosmic future plans of God (Daniel).

Approaches

Given that the central figure in Christianity is Jesus Christ, and that Jesus Christ does not appear in the flesh in the first 77 percent of the Bible known by Christians as the Old Testament, the ethical and theological significance of the Old Testament is always going to be a controversial question for the Christian tradition. There are three broad approaches to the Old Testament from the point of view of Christian ethics.

1. *Separation.* This view assumes the Old Testament should be considered independently of the New Testament. It comes in two quite distinct forms, resting on either the hearty embrace of Judaism or its outright rejection.
    a. One view regards the "Old Testament" as something of a Christian construction. It tends rather to use the term "Hebrew Bible" to refer to the books of the Law, Prophets, and Writings. It notes that for most Jews, this collection of thirty-nine books has never had a fixed or settled character. The Law has a unique status for most Jews. But the Hebrew Bible as a whole comprises a relatively small part of what Jews today might regard as their sacred canon. It would also include the *Mishnah*, compiled around 200 CE, the *Tosephta*, recorded 100 or more years later, and the *Gemara*, which were found in Jerusalem and Babylon and were completed by

around 850 CE. The whole corpus, known as the *Talmud*, is a significant part of Jewish tradition largely untouched by Christians. There is a huge body of moral instruction found in *Halakhah*, or classical Jewish religious law. The argument goes that if the point of consulting the Old Testament is to be listening to what God has said to Israel, then that listening has to include what God has said to Israel since Jesus, not just before Jesus. It follows that the Old Testament should be read not so much as part of the Christian Bible, in the context of the New Testament, but as part of the accumulation of Jewish tradition, in the context of the Talmud and Halakhah.

b. The second view is a much less subtle and much older view. It is that the God of the New Testament is fundamentally different from the God of the Old Testament. It is often supposed, for example, that the God of the Old Testament is a God of war, whereas the God of the New Testament is a God of peace; or that the Old Testament God is obsessed with law, whereas the New Testament God is full of love; or again that the Old Testament is largely concerned with rituals through which one can attain purity, whereas the New Testament is concerned with grace through which one can receive life. Likewise it is sometimes suggested that the Old Testament offers a host of laws but no fundamental change of heart, whereas with the New Testament comes the Holy Spirit and genuine repentance and conversion. The earliest name associated with this view is Marcion of Sinope (ca. 110–ca. 160 CE). Marcion argued in the early second century that the creator God of the Old Testament was chiefly concerned with the law. Jesus came to displace the God of the Old Testament and inaugurate an era of love. Marcion's Bible had none of the eventual Old Testament and only parts of Luke and Paul in it. By rejecting Marcion's proposal (he was excommunicated in 144 CE) and agreeing on a canon of sixty-six books, including thirty-nine that Christians call the Old Testament, the early church made a decisive move against the rejection of Israel's God.

Nonetheless the tendency to assume the New Testament replaces the Old has never gone away. It often focuses on "wrathful" passages such as the dashing of babies' heads against rocks (Ps 137:9) or the ethnic cleansing of the settlement period (Joshua 6:21). It can be seen not too far from the surface in the work of Martin Luther (1483–1546), the great sixteenth-century Reformer. Luther describes Judaism in stark terms, identifying it with justification by works; the gospel, as he sees it, is utterly different, seeing justification as only by grace through faith. Here already we see one particular hesitation that Protestantism has often had with the whole notion of Christian ethics: it looks too much like letting law back in by the side door. When a person claims that they have no need for Christian ethics because "Jesus has always been enough for me," they are expressing an antinomian view – a conviction that faith abolishes the law.

2. *Seamlessness.* This view takes the opposite stance from the "separation" approach. It sees overwhelming continuity between the Old Testament and the New. Perhaps the theologian most associated with this view is another great sixteenth-century Reformer, John Calvin (1509–64). It has two broad dimensions.

    a. The Old Testament offers a series of anticipations, prefigurements, and prophecies of the revelation to come in the New Testament. The relation of Old to New Testament is thus one of promise and fulfillment. This construal of the more widely held conviction that God does not change led proponents of the seamlessness view to argue that the great figures of the Old Testament may not have had a clear notion of what lay in store, but God did. The laws, the priests, the sacrifices, the temple, the kings, and the prophets of the Old Testament were all fulfilled in Jesus. The "anticipation" view is often accompanied by an assumption that the Hebrew ethic was earthy and tangible, whereas the Christian ethic was spiritual: for example, the Old Testament looks on the Promised Land as the New Testament looks on heaven.

    b. When it comes to the more troubling passages, the Spanish Jewish scholar Maimonides (1138–1204) offered in his work *The Guide of the Perplexed* (ca. 1190 CE) what became a very influential distinction. He argued that the Torah laws were centrally about preserving Israel from its two main enemies: idolatry and ill health. The Italian Dominican friar Thomas Aquinas (1225–74) took up Maimonides' argument and distinguished between the moral laws and the ceremonial (and civil) ones. The moral laws were part of natural law, and thus remained binding. The ceremonial laws applied specifically to ancient Israel and had no abiding authority. Thus, circumcision ceased to be binding on Christians, and many of the severe punishments could be softened; the Ten Commandments remain in place. This view dominated Reformation discussions, and is often quoted today. However, it is not always clear where the line between moral and ceremonial lies: for example, is the Sabbath law moral or ceremonial – is it still binding or not?

3. *Creative tension.* This third view is inclined to take a more generous view of Judaism in general and the Old Testament in particular. It rejects false polarities such as law–gospel or material–spiritual. It sees significant continuities between the character of God revealed in the Old Testament – abounding in steadfast love (*ḥesed*), faithfulness (*emunah*), justice (*mishpat*), and compassion (*rahmim*) – and the God of Jesus Christ. This approach covers a spectrum from the cautious to the more sanguine.

    a. The more cautious approach is to distinguish between precept and example. It is suggested that the Old Testament is of limited use as precept, or instruction. One can subdivide precepts between rules, such as the Ten Commandments, which apply in every situation, and principles, such as "act justly, love mercy, and walk humbly with your God" (Mic 6:8), which provide general moral frameworks. But the primary value of the Old Testament in Christian ethics is as a collection of salutary stories, challenging prophecies, and distilled wisdom. These are sometimes called paradigms (narratives of exemplary or reprehensible conduct) or symbolic worlds (broad parameters for understanding the action of God or the human condition). This does not mean the stories merely illustrate truths found elsewhere: the Old Testament is still regarded as revelation. The real task involves taking the rich store of engagements with such issues as freedom for the oppressed, justice for the poor, compassion for the outcast, and regard for the whole earth, and interpreting them in a society that looks very different from ancient Israel.

b. The more sanguine approach is to regard the New Testament as like a drama, and the Old Testament as providing the stage and setting for the drama. Here the difference between the two remains significant, but the Old Testament is regarded as indispensable in explicit ways: the New Testament is incomprehensible without the Old. A similar view employs a term such as "people of God" to underline the continuities between Israel and the church. This is always at risk of supersessionism, the assumption that the church has simply replaced Israel; nonetheless it focuses on the efforts of God's people to imitate the faithfulness of God as the single unchanging strand across both testaments, while still acknowledging the genuine newness of Christ's incarnation, death, and resurrection.

Characteristics

The Old Testament presents a polyphony of voices, and it is a little dangerous to generalize too swiftly about its contents. We may, however, identify three characteristics that cover the corpus as a whole, each of which has a significant bearing on Christian ethics.

1. The Old Testament is about *God*. There are books that notoriously keep God largely or wholly invisible (Esther and Ecclesiastes). However, the most striking thing about the Old Testament is that it is always centrally about God. It is essentially a theological history of Israel, with God as the initiator, hidden hand, or engaged observer. God chooses Israel, not because Israel is great, but because God is gracious. The significance for Christian ethics is that an ethic that addresses the Old Testament must always be theological – that it must always see human flourishing in relation to the nature, purpose, and revelation of God. God is never to be regarded as a neutral observer, mere creator, or passionless demiurge. God is passionate, jealous, and often angry – totally involved in creation.

2. The Old Testament is about God's *people*. From Genesis 12 onwards, the Old Testament is a long conversation about Israel's freedom and flourishing, how it was attained, how it should be enjoyed, how it could be (and was) lost,

how deeply God is involved in its achievement, shaping, maintenance, loss, and restoration, and how significant it is for the whole world. The key word here is holiness, because holiness names the unique character of God, which God bestows on Israel (Ex 19:6) and which is to be a blessing for the other nations. Holiness requires a certain separation between Israel and the nations, but this is for the sake of the nations, not just for the sake of Israel. The heart of the Old Testament is the covenant between God and Israel, definitively expressed at Mt. Sinai, and the events of liberation and law that precede and follow – and are inseparable from – that covenant.

3. The Old Testament is about the *story* of God's people. In recent decades there has been increasing focus on the fact that, despite the idiosyncrasies of the Old Testament and the diversity of its literature, it does tell a broad, coherent story in relation to which the rest of the material finds its context. Some have argued that this shows that the category of narrative has always been vital for understanding ethics. Others see the term narrative in a narrower sense, as an integral part of a single, particular narrative incorporating Jesus and the church, around which everything in Christian ethics must circle. Both of these views are kinds of narrative ethics, a term that is much in use in recent years and will be explored in Chapter Seven.

Themes

Because the Old Testament is such a rich and diverse collection of literature, the elucidation of themes is itself a significant act of interpretation. Relatively few writers in Christian ethics have shaped their models and theories from Old Testament foundations, wholly or even largely; thus, the Old Testament has more often been used to illustrate, exemplify, or underwrite convictions formed on other grounds. In other words, ethicists tend to find in the Old Testament what they go looking for.

1. *Kingship and law.* For those writers assuming or aspiring to a settled hierarchical social model, the tendency has been to see David as the central figure in the Old Testament. All that precedes him leads up to him: Moses, Joshua, and Saul. All that follows him is decline: the kingdom's split, the destruction of Jerusalem, the exile in Babylon. Despite all the turmoil described in the Old Testament, those interested in building or sustaining some kind of godly commonwealth have invariably seen the period of the kingdom in the united Israel as some kind of template. The ruler is seen as the key (anointed) instrument of God's rule, and the ideal is for a godly people to live holy lives subject to that rule. The degree to which Jesus and the New Testament might challenge conventional structures of authority is seldom discussed. Instead, Jesus is seen as the true King of Israel and the fulfillment of God's covenant with David. Alongside this focus on the kingdom comes an emphasis on law. The Ten

Commandments emerge as the epitome of Old Testament instruction: simple, transferable, and an explicit statement of what is required of lay Christians. Amongst the myriad of Old Testament laws, those concerning human sexuality and the family often come to prominence in these treatments.

2.   *Liberation and prophecy.* For those writers seeking to challenge settled hierarchical models of society, the focus has invariably been upon God's action in bringing Israel out of slavery and offering freedom through covenant. Liberation is the paradigm for all such readings of the Old Testament. The exodus shows not just God's power but God's purpose. It is not just a moment in time: it comes alive whenever it is recalled, especially at Passover, but also in the agony of exile.

The key question for the rest of the Old Testament is therefore, "Can Israel keep the freedom it has been so graciously given?" The Deuteronomistic history rests on this question. The prophets become highly significant, particularly Isaiah, Amos, and Micah, for they call Israel's attention to the way care for the poor, the alien, the orphan, and the widow embodies Israel's faithfulness to the covenant God made with Moses (for Israel was once a slave itself). The denunciations of the rich and the oppressors have a contemporary ring when placed in a context of extreme wealth differentials today.

3.   *Worship and community.* Those who see ethics as primarily about forming faithful communities, rather than shaping stable society or liberating the oppressed, tend to identify most quickly those parts of the Old Testament that are concerned with liturgy and common life. The Psalms are an important dimension of the Old Testament, for here law and history and reflection are turned into song and prayer and worship. The Psalms do not describe a society that has fixed boundaries between government and law and worship and private life. Those who see worship and ethics as integrally linked would begin here.

Just as it is possible to see the Old Testament as centrally about government and legislation, or centrally about freedom and social critique, so it is possible to see the Old Testament as a lengthy meditation on how to live as a faithful community under God. It is sometimes pointed out that individual salvation was not the obsession for Israel that it has been for many Christians: the salvation that Israel sought was inherently one that had to be shared. It is also noted that the Old Testament is based on a covenant, rather than a contract or rights in the way that many contemporary relationships assume.

Other ethical lenses could also be highlighted – for example, the overarching themes of creation (thus focusing on God's sovereignty over and care for all nations) and covenant (thus tracing the mutual obligations of God and Israel in their covenant relationship). Some ethical thinkers approach the text more critically, noting that the Old Testament poses a particular set of challenges for Christian ethics regarding violence, broadly conceived. First is the apparent sanctioning of violence by certain Old Testament texts, including the narratives that describe the conquest of Canaan (the "Promised Land") by the Israelites. Similarly, Christians have debated whether and under what conditions they ought to pray the imprecatory psalms, or the psalms that curse and wish violent retribution upon the enemy, in light of Christ's commands to love and bless the enemy and the persecutor. Finally, and most specifically, feminist scholars like Phyllis Trible (b. 1932) point to the "texts of terror" in the Old Testament that describe violence against women – such as the rape of Dinah or the sacrifice of Jephthah's daughter. All these cases highlight further the apparent tensions between the two testaments. (The question of violence is discussed in relation to ecclesial ethics in Chapter Seven and in relation to war in Chapter Eight.)

God in Person

Jesus of Nazareth was a controversial figure in late Second Temple Judaism, who was crucified on a charge of insurrection by the Roman governor in Judea around 30 CE. This is practically all the hard historical evidence available: the rest is largely dependent on sources within the New Testament, whose reliability it is not possible to assess conclusively by modern standards. Nevertheless we can summarize Jesus' context, ministry, death, and resurrection as a preliminary to identifying his significance for Christian ethics.

Jesus' context was dominated by the occupation of the land of Israel by the Romans. It had been 600 years since the Jews had run their own affairs in Jerusalem. While the Persian king Cyrus had ended the exile in Babylon, the Jews had remained under first Persian, then Greek, then eventually Roman rule, minus a brief period of independence after the successful Maccabean revolt (142–63 BCE). Various parties within Israel took different approaches to these circumstances: some, such as the Sadducees, largely cooperated with the status quo; others, such as the Pharisees, saw renewal primarily in the common people keeping the Jewish law; others again, such as the group that later coalesced as the Zealots, sought the violent overthrow of the Romans; and yet another group, the Essenes, withdrew to seek holiness in secluded community. There were outspoken prophets, such as John the Baptist, and some level of anticipation that the world might soon end. The birth narratives in Matthew and Luke are largely concerned to locate Jesus within this context of exile and expectation.

The ministry of Jesus, as recorded in the Gospels, begins with his baptism by John and his calling of twelve disciples, representing a renewed Israel (since Israel in the Old Testament had twelve tribes). While teaching his disciples in story and discourse, he also attracted and engaged with a second segment of society, a crowd of outcasts – rich tax-collectors, unclean lepers, shunned prostitutes, and those made poor by sickness, subjection, or circumstance. His teaching and his ministry of healing and miracle brought him into controversial interaction with the Jewish leadership of the time, and these conversations make up a third dimension of his career. Jesus announced that the kingdom (or reign) of God was at hand. God's inrushing justice would reverse the current assumptions about holiness and power, with the humble and faithful exalted and the regnant and rich laid low. Like the prophets before him, he pointed to God's deeper purposes and criticized those who were content with superficial appearances. His loyalty to the temple was strained when he saw activities in the temple directing the energies of the people away from God.

Two factors led to Jesus' crucifixion. One was his relentless criticism of the Jerusalem leadership, by action and word, through cleansing the temple and through healing on the Sabbath, through claiming to forgive sins and through comparing authorities to unfaithful keepers of the vineyard. The other was his refusal to take up armed struggle. His presence in Jerusalem at the Passover festival and his overturning of the merchants' tables in the temple was a provocation the Jerusalem leadership could not ignore and an opportunity they could not miss. Meanwhile his talk of the kingdom and dramatic miracles quite naturally led many to consider him as one who sought to be king. And when arrested, he refused either to fight or to proclaim his innocence.

And, the gospels tell us, God raised Jesus from the dead. Jesus appeared, mysteriously but tangibly, to his dispirited disciples. He forgave, recommissioned, and inspired them. He prefigured the new creation at the end of time, and the judgment and resurrection of all people. Very soon after his death, a vibrant movement known as the church began to spread with the conviction of his message and the power of his defeat of death.

Is Jesus Normative for Christian Ethics?

The gospels present narratives of Jesus' birth, life, death, and resurrection. What is the relationship between the life that Jesus lived and the life that the Christian is to live? Is Jesus the *definitive* human, such that he is a model for human action and, if so, in what precise respect? Is Jesus the *exemplary* human, illustrative of all that human values might seek? Or is Jesus the *divine* human, unique in every way, such that the details of his ministry and passion are unrepeatable and significant largely or wholly for the new world they make possible? This is one of the most important questions in Christian ethics. There are broadly four answers to this question, depending on which aspect of Jesus one regards as most significant: his incarnation and birth, his ministry and teaching, his passion and death, or his resurrection and ascension.

Each answer can be seen in two ways. Jesus can be understood as illustrating truths also available elsewhere, such as the worthiness of equality, kindness, and justice. Or Jesus can be portrayed as establishing norms that could not and cannot be perceived without his unique person and/or work. For those who take the former, *illustrative* view, Jesus is an example of things that would have been right and good and true even if he had not come. For those who take the latter, *normative* view, all knowledge is subject to that which is only accessible in the new reality brought about in and by Jesus.

1. *Incarnation and birth*
    a. **Illustrative.** Many writers and preachers have seen the incarnation as God's unconditional affirmation of humanity and of creation. It is good to party, because Jesus went to parties; it is good to be physical, to enjoy one's body, because Jesus came as a fully human being; it is good to strive for the noblest human ideals and the highest human achievements, because in sharing our heart and mind and soul and strength Jesus affirmed the dignity of human aspiration. In short, he came that we may have life, and have it to the full. This is an illustrative conviction because it seldom deals with the specifics of the time and place of Jesus' incarnation – it is generally more concerned with God's broad affirmation of humanity, a conviction that might have been arrived at without Jesus coming to Bethlehem, Nazareth, and Jerusalem.
    b. **Normative.** "For He was made man so that we might be made God." So writes Athanasius of Alexandria (ca. 293–373 CE), who represents the Eastern Orthodox view that in the incarnation God healed and restored sinful human nature by uniting with it, thus making humanity capable of taking on divine characteristics (a concept also known as *theosis* or divinization). Likewise, Irenaeus of Lyons (d. ca. 202 CE): "The Word of God, our Lord Jesus Christ, … did, through His transcendent love, become what we are, that He might bring us to be even what He is Himself." For Orthodox ethics, the incarnation is the unique act by which God enables and invites people not only to be good but to take on the very likeness of God.

        Reformed theologian Karl Barth (1886–1968) presents another example of a normative approach to Christ's incarnation. For Barth, ethics deals fundamentally with the *command* of God – creator, reconciler, and redeemer. Jesus is the declaration that God expects complete obedience from God's people, and Jesus is the embodiment of that complete obedience. God's command is not an ideal – whether an obligation or a permission – but a *reality*. That reality is the person and work of Jesus Christ. Jesus is not just the ground, not just the content, but also the *form* of God's command. The center of Christian ethics is not our action but God's action in Jesus. Barth's theology has a circularity about it because it always loops back to God's definitive action in Christ as the purpose and expression of all things. Divine command ethics will be treated in Chapter Five, and Chapter Seven will examine Barth's theology in greater detail.

2. *Ministry and teaching*
    a. **Illustrative.** It is frequently said that Jesus was a great moral teacher. For some, Jesus' principal significance lies in his ethical instruction, such as the Sermon on the Mount (Matt 5–7). They appeal to summary passages such as his articulation of the greatest commandment, "You shall love the Lord your God with all your heart, and with all your soul, and with all your mind" and "You shall love your neighbor as yourself" (Matt 22:37–40) or his

words to the woman caught in adultery, "Has no one condemned you? ... Neither do I condemn you. Go your way, and from now on do not sin again" (John 8:10–11). It is not always clear whether Jesus said such things because they are binding, or whether they are binding because he said them.

A different way of putting this would be to say that the ethical significance placed on Jesus' moral teaching depends largely or entirely on the theological significance placed on his birth. Those who regard Jesus as the incarnate fully human, fully divine second member of the Trinity tend to take the view that Jesus' words are true because Jesus said them: everything Jesus said was true because of who he was. Those who are more skeptical about Jesus' divinity tend to evaluate Jesus' teaching in the light of other ethical norms. This last is the context in which the phrase "great moral teacher" is invariably used.

Sometimes it is not so much Jesus' teaching but the quality of relationships he made that is highlighted. Attention is commonly drawn to the counter-cultural way Jesus related to women, for example. Jesus talked with a notorious woman in the open air in the heat of the day (John 4:6–9). He allowed himself to be corrected by a woman in the course of a disagreement (Mark 7:27–9). He mixed easily with women who were not members of his family (Luke 10:38–42) and was prepared to touch women whom others would shun (Mark 5:22–43). Meanwhile Jesus spoke easily with children, lepers, and prostitutes. And Jesus rejected relationships of domination in favor of servant ministry (Mark 10:35–45).

Some would put the emphasis not so much on the teaching or the relationships but more generally on the new community that Jesus brought into being. Most famously the New York Baptist Walter Rauschenbusch (1861–1918) founded his understanding of the Social Gospel on a notion of the new society gathering around Jesus' earthly community. There was real hope that the society that Jesus had described could be translated into social and industrial relations in America and elsewhere. In the view of the Roman Catholic theologian Elisabeth Schüssler Fiorenza (b. 1938) the gospel accounts of Jesus' ministry are windows into the life of the earliest Christian communities. She sees these communities as reformed elements within first-century Judaism, viewing God's reign as a present embodiment of a gathering of equals, incorporating all marginalized people, and anticipating a time beyond death, suffering, and injustice.

Those who concentrate on the quality of relationships and those who trace the emergence of an egalitarian community both have a broadly illustrative approach to Jesus' life. This is because each seems to be working with a model of relationship or community that is grounded in the highest aspirations of contemporary culture rather than the language and culture of first-century Palestine. Jesus is a key figure but his significance is that he is an outstanding example of wisdom that is available elsewhere.

b. **Normative.** The historical figure most associated with seeing Jesus' life as normative for ethics is the Italian friar St. Francis of Assisi (ca. 1181–1226). Francis encouraged his followers to imitate Jesus in every respect: to go barefoot, to have no fixed home, to keep a vow of poverty, to be with the poor, the sick, and the socially marginalized, and to engage in manual labor. Many aspects of Jesus' life and ministry have been presented since Francis as suitable for imitation: celibacy, the life of a carpenter, spending time in deserts or on mountaintops, the retreat period of forty days, the gathering of twelve close followers, the use of parables. All have seemed to some to epitomize Jesus' ethic.

While accepting the normative status of Jesus' life and teaching, two notes of caution have been prominent and widespread. The first is the argument that Jesus' life and teaching made and make perfect sense for simple rural face-to-face relations, but that when it comes to more conventionally political contexts, the marketplace, the houses of government, and industry, a more complex ethic must prevail. This view is particularly associated with Reinhold Niebuhr (1892–1971), long-time professor at Union Seminary in New York, in his work *Moral Man and Immoral Society* (1932), which argues that when one transfers from the personal to the political, something beyond the ethic of Jesus is required.

The other cautionary note customarily directed at a wholesale imitation of Jesus is associated with the German-French theologian and humanitarian physician Albert Schweitzer (1875–1965). In Schweitzer's view Jesus' whole program assumed that the end of the world was coming very soon. Jesus expressed no interest in the careful work of establishing institutions and social practices and creating wealth because he assumed all was shortly to pass away, but in fact such institution-building and wealth generation are exactly what is required for a stable and healthy society. Thus Jesus' relevance for Christian ethics is very limited. Schweitzer's thesis has been criticized as implausible given that the Gospels were written down up to fifty years after Jesus spoke words apparently assuming an imminent end. But it has nonetheless been very influential.

3. *Passion and death*
   a. **Illustrative.** The theologian Reinhold Niebuhr strongly rejected the Social Gospel movement of the early twentieth century. He believed it had far too shallow an understanding of human sin. For Niebuhr the cross of Jesus illustrated the fundamental reality of the human condition. This reality was flawed by original sin. Humanity, according to Niebuhr, is caught between two rival poles, finitude and freedom – between the aspiration to reach great ideals and the inevitability of becoming knotted in sin. Even the "man without sin" had been cruelly executed, because human nature could not reach the impossible possibility of a life under grace. Niebuhr frequently quotes Romans 7:18–19: "I can will what is right, but I cannot do it. For I do not do the good I want, but the evil I do not want is what I do."

b. **Normative.** The alternatives to Niebuhr are of broadly two kinds: those who see the cross as a cosmic victory over sin and death, and those who see the cross as a specific event whose place and time have vivid significance.

For many, the significance of Jesus is primarily that in his death he overcame all that separates humanity (or creation) from God. He vanquished the devil, or alternatively paid in his body whatever price was necessary to restore fellowship with God. The importance of such a view for ethics is that overcoming sin makes it possible for Christians to live faithful lives in the power of the Spirit. No longer must one be resigned to being dragged down by the anchor of sin or to hoping naïvely in the power of education and effort to withstand human weakness. Now, through the grace of God, through repentance and forgiveness in the cross of Christ, new life is genuinely possible: the commands of God can be kept, and the church can live in the bonds of peace. Hence ethics means believing in the redeeming power of the cross, ceasing to try to find righteousness in one's own resources, and holding fast to the guiding hand of the Spirit through temptation and setback. The perennial danger in such a rendering of ethics is that it has relatively little connection with the Gospel accounts of Jesus' ministry and passion. Jesus simply came to die: why it had to be a cross, why it had to be first-century Palestine, why he called disciples, told parables, performed healings – these details remain unclear. Thus, vital as Jesus' death is, it yields little in the way of a specific ethic that makes Jesus normative.

The modern theologian most concerned to overcome the abstraction of the cross in ethics is the American Mennonite John Howard Yoder (1927–97). Yoder insists on the normative quality of Jesus' life and death. He makes the simple claim that the New Testament does enjoin the imitation of Jesus, but not in a general way. It commands the specific imitation of Jesus in relation to encounters with enmity and power. Jesus rejected the quietism of the Essene movement: he was not tempted to withdrawal. The other two key temptations rejected by Jesus were on the one hand that of establishment responsibility (the Sadducees), colluding with the Romans in the oppression of Israel, and on the other hand that of the crusade (the later Zealots), joining the struggle in taking up arms against the occupying power. Instead, Jesus took up the way of the cross.

What is required of the disciple, Yoder argues, is to follow the trajectory of Jesus' decision. The emphasis on Jesus' life and his journey to the cross only makes sense if Jesus is seen as not only the fully human, fully divine son of God but also the one who rose physically from the dead. In this case, cross and resurrection emerge as the "grain of the universe," the force that fundamentally shapes history in a way that armies and markets are usually taken to do. Thus, the disciple who renounces the sword and the gun does so not because such weapons are too dangerous but because they are too weak. Yoder resists every method of making the cross an abstraction – such as the pastoral observation that we "all have our cross to bear" – and insists on the call to walk the way of the cross as the specific command that characterizes Christian ethics today. We will discuss Yoder's approach to ethics in more detail in Chapter Seven.

4. *Resurrection and ascension*
    a. **Illustrative.** Once again the distinction between illustrative and normative approaches to Jesus' resurrection are doctrinal ones – that is to say, those who insist on Jesus' physical resurrection are inclined to a more normative reading and those who maintain some form of spiritual resurrection tend to a more illustrative reading. The figure perhaps most associated with an illustrative reading of the resurrection is Rudolf Bultmann (1884–1976). For Bultmann, the resurrection is essentially found in the proclamation ("kerygma") of the apostles after Jesus' death. This proclamation called people from inauthentic existence (Bultmann's notion of sin) to authentic existence (a life resting on grace). Resurrection faith means obedience in which the self renounces its striving for self-righteousness, and its corresponding anxiety, and receives the good news of God's righteousness – making it free and open to the future. Bultmann's ethics are much more concerned with wresting the Christian's imagination free from anxiety than on specific engagement with the details of particular lives. They also remain somewhat detached from the precise details of Jesus' life (which is why they belong in the resurrection section). But they do emphasize in characteristically Lutheran style the sharp contrast between sin and grace.
    b. **Normative.** If the physical resurrection is accepted as a historical event, albeit one without parallel, then its significance for ethics is enormous, perhaps definitive. The contemporary figure whose reading of ethics is most explicitly founded on the resurrection is Oliver O'Donovan (b. 1945). O'Donovan maintains that "Christian ethics depends upon the resurrection of Jesus Christ from the dead." The resurrection transforms hope for redemption *from* creation into hope for redemption *for* creation. "When the gospel is preached without a resurrection … then, of course, the cross and the ascension, collapsed together without their centre, become symbols for a gnostic other-worldliness."

    O'Donovan's central contention is that the resurrection overcomes any false distinction between the "ethics of creation" – reflection on the natural order – and the "ethics of the kingdom" – reflection on the inrushing new life brought by Christ with the promise of a dramatic climax in the coming eschaton. "In the resurrection of Christ creation is restored and the kingdom of God dawns." He goes on:

    > When the resurrection is distinguished from the ascension (as it is by Saint Luke and indirectly by Saint John – cf. 20.17) it looks backwards. It is a recovery of the lost. … Death, the enemy of mankind, is conquered. … From

> this aspect the emphasis of the resurrection narratives is on the physical reality of the restored body. ... When, however, the resurrection is presented alone without the ascension (as it is by Saint Mark and Saint Matthew) it looks forwards. Already Christ is transformed. ... Humanity is elevated to that which it has never enjoyed before, the seat at God's right hand which belongs to his Son.

The resurrection of Jesus is thus about overcoming sub-natural enslavement to sin and death and about anticipating supernatural destiny. Ethics is the same.

Following Jesus: The New Testament and Christian Ethics

The ethics of Jesus turn into New Testament ethics at the point where one recognizes that we know almost nothing about Jesus of Nazareth except what we are told by the records left by the early church. The New Testament canon represents those texts the early church regarded as comprehensive and authoritative.

New Testament scholar Richard B. Hays (b. 1948) outlines four distinct tasks to be addressed in studying New Testament ethics: descriptive, synthetic, hermeneutical, and pragmatic.

1. *The descriptive task.* The student must first gain an understanding of the breadth and variety of the New Testament canon. Each of the books has its own particular preoccupation and emphasis: to understand their ethics one needs to gain some understanding of the communities in which and for which each book was written. Some scholars have concluded that the literature in the New Testament is so diverse that no overall ethic can or should be attempted. This diversity is on the structural level: the narrative gospels are very different documents from the letters of Paul and others, and the book of Revelation may appear to defy ethical exegesis. But it is also on the level of particular instruction: for example, the activity of women in ministry and worship seems in one place to be assumed, in another forbidden; divorce is excluded wholesale in one place, allowed under certain conditions in another; the state seems to be God's servant in one place, God's enemy in another.

2. *The synthetic task.* This is the attempt to bring together the different New Testament writings and elucidate a distinctive and coherent ethic from them. As Hays notes, many interpreters have tried to isolate a single great principle, such as love, that holds together the whole of the New Testament's moral teaching. The term "love," however, is notably absent from the Acts of the Apostles, and largely absent in other texts such as Hebrews and Revelation; thus to employ the term love as the epitome of the New Testament breaks the terms of the descriptive task described above. Similar criticisms could be made about the catch-all term "liberation": allusive as it is in its reading of the exodus story and its attention to contemporary social and economic realities, it hardly

does justice to Matthew's emphasis on obedience or the pastoral epistles' regard for order, and it is always in danger of prioritizing human action over the prevenience of God's grace. Hays himself distills the grand narrative of Christ's birth, ministry, death and resurrection, and the Spirit-filled life of the early church, into three themes: community, cross, and new creation.

3.   *The hermeneutical task*. This names the chasm between the political, social, economic, technological, and cultural circumstances of the first century CE and those of today. Hays makes it clear that interpretation is always an act of imagination: "with fear and trembling we must work out a life of faithfulness to God through responsive and creative reappropriation of the New Testament in a world far removed from the world of the original writers and readers." This has often been regarded as the primary task of the preacher: coining metaphors and painting pictures through which the text comes vividly alive in the contemporary circumstances of the church. But the issue is how to do this while being faithful both to the descriptive task – doing justice to the polyvalent voices of the New Testament – and to the synthetic task – hearing the New Testament speak with one clear voice.

4.   *The pragmatic task*. The final task is to embody the text in the life of a faithful community. Attention to detailed exegesis, broad coherence, and imaginative correlation culminates in pragmatic application. "The value of our exegesis and hermeneutics will be tested by their capacity to produce persons and communities whose character is commensurate with Jesus Christ and therefore pleasing to God." Hays acknowledges that the hermeneutical and the pragmatic tasks cannot properly be separated. One is the conceptual application, the other is the enacted application: but "there can be no true understanding without lived obedience, and vice versa."

The Gospels and Christian Ethics

The remainder of this chapter will take up what Hays calls the descriptive task, and will seek to outline the variety and breadth of New Testament ethics, beginning with the Gospels.

1.   *Matthew*. For Matthew, Jesus is primarily a teacher. The key figure whom Jesus fulfills is Moses. Matthew's Gospel is made up of five substantial teaching discourses interspersed by significant actions – rather as the Torah is made up of five books. Jesus fulfills the Law of Moses – he calls for his disciples not just to be holy, but to be perfect: not just to love Israelites but to love enemies, not just to avoid divorce but to avoid lust, not just to avoid murder but to avoid malicious anger (Matt 5:17–48). Jesus' teaching inspires awe (Matt 7:27), but it is not an explicit list of rules. Whereas the focal point of Moses' teaching is the Ten Commandments, the epitome of Jesus' teaching is the Beatitudes (5:3–12). "Blessed are the peacemakers, for they will be called children of God" is allusive, profound, but far from specific teaching. In some ways Matthew's

Gospel maintains a tension between the call to perfection and the call to compassion, but the overwhelming emphasis is that Jesus' compassion is his perfection. Twice Matthew quotes Hosea 6:6, "I desire mercy and not sacrifice," and constantly Jesus interprets this to mean the inclusion of sinners and a generosity in seeing mercy as the true heart of the Law.

Instead of explicit rules, Matthew's Gospel offers a handbook for an aspiring community of disciples. Their common life of discipline and mercy is guaranteed by the promise that "where two or three are gathered in my name, I am there among them" (18:20). The paradigmatic parable is the final teaching before the passion narrative begins (25:31–46): the true community finds in retrospect that it has ministered to Jesus in the face of the hungry, the sick, and the prisoner. It did not realize it was ministering to Jesus: it was concentrating more (if it was following the Sermon on the Mount in chapters 5–7 and other similar passages) on putting aside violence, hypocrisy, anxiety over material possessions, as well as anger, lust, and pride, and on taking on the love of enemies, a readiness to forgive, and generosity in supporting those in need. Jesus' final parable is told in the context of final judgment. Matthew's Gospel is poised between the certainty of Jesus' return and its perhaps somewhat unexpected delay. Thus, Jesus counsels his disciples not just to be ready for the coming king but also to act justly and mercifully to foster faithful community in the meantime. Matthew is sustained by the presence of Jesus in the church – from the announcement in Joseph's dream that Jesus' coming means "God is with us" (1:23) to the final assurance from the ascending Lord that "I am with you always, to the end of the age" (28:20).

2. *Mark.* Mark has almost none of Matthew's extensive teaching material. Mark's story is, in fact, three interwoven stories. First of all, there is Jesus' creation of a new community, based around the messianic hopes of his preaching. He calls around him twelve disciples and commissions them to spread the fire of his kingdom. The disciples falter and stumble, out of fear of the cross, lack of imagination, and cold betrayal. But in Mark's account of the resurrection there is promise of a restored community in Galilee. The second story is Jesus' mission to the crowd, the teeming mass of poor and oppressed whom Mark mentions thirty-eight times in his Gospel. This is a ministry of healing, exorcism, and liberation, through story, announcement, and gesture. On Palm Sunday the crowd seem to have taken up the cause of liberation, but by Good Friday they have chosen the terrorist Barabbas instead. The third interwoven story is Jesus' confrontation with the powers that held Israel in a stranglehold. One by one Jesus takes on the Pharisees, the scribes, the Herodians, and the Sadducees. He dismantles their authority and challenges their control, but eventually the veil of pretense is pulled aside and behind emerges the real power in Israel, the power that toys with all other powers – the iron fist of Rome. It is the nails and wood of Roman execution that finally destroy Jesus – only for him to dismantle even Rome's control over life and death.

These three stories, of disciples, crowds, and authorities, are interwoven in Mark's Gospel like three strands in a rope. Each finds its climax in the account of Jesus' passion. The three stories in the end comprise one story. And that story is the sending of Jesus by the Father, crystallized in the Father's words at Jesus' baptism, "You are my Son, the Beloved" (1:11), epitomized in the Father's words at the transfiguration, "This is my Son, the Beloved" (9:7), and climaxing in the centurion's words at the cross, "Truly this man was God's Son!" (15:39). There is almost no mention of love in Mark's Gospel. Jesus' intimacy with the disciples, his mission to the crowd, and his confrontation with the authorities are drawn together not in an abstract ideal but in a concrete command to follow – to the cross.

3. *Luke (and the book of Acts, which forms a continuous narrative with the Gospel of Luke).* The Holy Spirit is a much more significant part of Luke's story than of Matthew's or Mark's. Jesus is blessed by the Spirit in baptism, led by the Spirit into the wilderness, and anointed by the Spirit to bring good news to the poor. Whereas Matthew's notion of prophecy is to predict the Messiah's coming, Luke's understanding of prophecy is to call for justice. Jesus' final words are "Father, into your hands I commend my spirit" (23:46). The Acts of the Apostles portrays the Spirit as making Jesus present in the church. The gift of the Spirit is a sign of the "last times" as the events of Pentecost display. The Spirit is not just for the apostles but for all whom God calls. Those called become prophets, establishing communities of repentance, forgiveness, liberation, and justice. Their reward is to imitate Jesus: Peter does so in healing Dorcas as Jesus healed Jairus' daughter; Stephen does so in facing martyrdom while forgiving his persecutors; and Paul does so in going up to Jerusalem to be arrested. In the power of the Spirit, believers can do all things.

The church, proclaimed in Luke and practiced in Acts, is at the center of Luke's ethics in a number of ways. As N. T. Wright (b. 1948) has insisted, Jesus' ministry of gathering in outcasts, sinners, and strays is a depiction of the renewed Israel, ending 500 years of exile stretching back to the destruction of Jerusalem six centuries before. This is the bold expectation set up by the birth narratives and by John the Baptist's preaching. And in the early chapters of Acts there are two descriptions of how the new community fulfills the covenant ordinances of Deuteronomy 15 ("There will, however, be no one in need among you … open your hand, willingly lending enough to meet the need, whatever it may be"). Luke's blessings and woes (6:20–26) are specifically oriented to wealth and poverty in a way that Matthew's beatitudes are not. And Luke's sense of judgment on the hard-hearted wealthy who refuse to enter this new covenant community is epitomized in the parable of the rich man who is tortured on account of his neglect of the poor Lazarus at his gate (16:19–31). Zacchaeus offers a suitable contrast by distributing his tax-farmed earnings (19:1–10). But there is another dimension to the church: a society that stands as a rival to the empire, with its own king. On the surface the church appears respectful and courteous to its Roman governors, but in one city after another its quiet discipleship and subversive worship make the community ungovernable. The world is being turned upside down: one reversal follows another, from the exaltation of the lowly Mary to the reappearance of the crucified Lord. The empire surely will be next.

4.   *John*. The Fourth Gospel has a mystical quality that sets it apart from the three Synoptic Gospels. Jesus was with the Father in glory before the creation of the world. He is not *of* this world. And yet, decisively, the pre-existent Word became flesh. He is *in* this world. John's Gospel has a different sense of time from the other gospels: judgment does not lie ahead, in the return of Jesus – it has already come, in the arrival of the light in the world, which shows up deeds of darkness. Eternal life has already begun for believers: those who live and believe will never die.

John's Gospel repeatedly dwells on the identity of Jesus, particularly in the frequent "I am" sayings and the intimacy between Jesus and the Father. The heavenliness of Jesus is constantly in tension with his earthly surroundings throughout the Gospel. Sometimes it seems Jesus is simply supernatural: he performs telling signs and disappears from dangerous situations, and he paints a vivid contrast between the life of those who abide in him and those who are of the "world." At other times he appears very human, weeping over the death of a close friend, facing up to the dirt of his disciples' feet, and asking for a drink.

John's Gospel has little specific ethical instruction. The central command is to love one another, but there is no implication that this love extends to those outside the believing community. This love, enacted in washing feet, is the principal way the world will recognize Jesus' disciples. Love may lead to laying down one's life for the community. Believers are strengthened by the presence of the Holy Spirit in the community, which leads them into all truth. It is widely supposed that John's Gospel and the epistles of John were composed in a Christian community made up largely of Jews who had recently been expelled from the synagogue. This would account for the heavy emphasis on the disciplines of mutual care and the antagonistic relationship between the beloved community and the "world." It also provides a background for the castigation of the "Jews," particularly the Jerusalem leaders who claim before Pilate that they have no king but the emperor (19:15).

The Ethics of Paul and his Followers

The thirteen letters that immediately follow the Acts of the Apostles in the New Testament are attributed to Paul the Apostle. Much research and speculation have gone into identifying whether, for instance, Ephesians or 1 and 2 Timothy and Titus belong to the same corpus, given their differences in style, vocabulary, and argument from the other letters. More important for our purposes is the significance of these letters for Christian ethics. We shall look in turn at their style, their theological emphases, and their ethical method.

The letters cannot be described as either systematic theological treatises or thorough ethical expositions. Instead they respond to crises in the early churches, discussing local problems in such a way as to bring together saving revelation with practical wisdom. Most representative perhaps is 1 Corinthians, sometimes known as the beginning of Christian ethics, where Paul proceeds through a sequence of pressing questions, including incest, lawsuits among believers, divorce, eating food previously sacrificed to idols, covering the head in worship, equal distribution of food at the Lord's Supper, and speaking in tongues. Paul engages with his readers in an intense and often deeply personal way, holding himself up as an example for imitation but being honest about his trials and travails, often pleading with them to make personal and financial sacrifices or berating them for their foolishness. The parallel between Jesus' journey around the Holy Land to arrest in Jerusalem and Paul's own journey around the Mediterranean to captivity in Rome is not lost on Paul.

Paul's theological emphases can be outlined by describing where he perceives his readers to stand in relation to world history. In the (relatively recent) past lies the overwhelming event of Christ's cross; behind it lies the still very significant relationship of God to Israel. In the (perhaps near) future lies the completion of God's work begun in creation and fully expressed in Christ. In the present lies the church, a reality most fully emphasized and explored in Ephesians, but assumed throughout the Pauline letters. These three themes require closer examination.

1. *What God has done.* Unlike the gospels, Paul's letters do not dwell on the historical circumstances surrounding Jesus' crucifixion under Pontius Pilate. Instead, the cross is the definitive historical event without parallel. It has a number of meanings, of which perhaps three stand out. In the first place, the cross demonstrates that, however unfaithful Israel may be, God is thoroughly true to Israel even to the point of utmost agony. Nothing can therefore separate us from the love of God. Second, humanity's sin is not sufficient to overcome God's faithfulness: through his death on the cross, Christ atones for the sins of God's people and vindicates the righteousness of God. This is sometimes portrayed as a scene in a court of law, where Jesus shoulders the punishment due to God's people. The cross not only addresses past sin, but creates a new relationship between God and Israel that makes it possible for even Gentiles to live according to the righteousness of God – a transition embodied in baptism. Hence Paul can say, "I have been crucified with Christ; and it is no longer I who live, but it is Christ who lives in me" (Gal 2:19–20). And third, the cross is a paradigmatic example of what it means to be dedicated to God. Christ's death not only demonstrates the life God requires of the church, it makes that life possible.

    This third dimension is perhaps the most significant for Paul's ethics. He consistently calls upon his readers to be obedient in the way Christ was obedient.

The most vivid example of this appeal comes in Philippians 2, which describes how Christ made himself nothing, taking the form of a servant, and humbled himself by becoming obedient to death – even death on a cross. Paul suggests that his readers follow a similar path of humility and self-offering, epitomized by the cross. He points out that this is exactly what he himself has done – for he renounced whatever claims he had as a Pharisee and a blameless law-keeper in order to place his destiny in "the righteousness from God based on faith." He goes on, "I want to know Christ and the power of his resurrection and the sharing of his sufferings by becoming like him in his death" (Phil 3:10). He has no hesitation in asking his readers to imitate him – because he is imitating Christ.

2. *What God will do*. Paul describes himself and his readers as those "on whom the ends of the ages have come" (1 Cor 10:11). In other words, the church occupies the overlap between the "sufferings of this present time" in which the creation is in "bondage to decay" and "groaning in labor pains" (Rom 8:18, 21–2), and the coming "freedom of the glory of the children of God" (Rom 8:21). Just as the sufferings of Christ came immediately before the wonder of his resurrection, so the hardships and trials of Paul and his readers presage the coming of the new creation.

    Paul steers a path between those who on the one hand hope in Christ "for this life only" (1 Cor 15:19) and those who on the other hand believe the new age is already in full swing (1 Cor 4:8). In one metaphor he describes the Holy Spirit as a "first installment" or a downpayment, an instantiation of the new age, not a full realization of the new creation but a guarantee that it is coming (2 Cor 1:22; 5:5). Sometimes it seems the final eschatological revelation is wholly different from present circumstances and will come suddenly and overwhelmingly (1 Thess 4:16–17). In other places it seems the transformation is more gradual and incremental, and that it has already begun – indeed, today is the day (2 Cor 6:2).

    The new age comes about through *God's* initiative not human endeavor. Yet it is a transformation of *this* world, not an escape to another. Its imminent coming *intensifies* the significance of faithful and sacrificial discipleship in this world – it does not negate it. Easy as it would be to imagine the hope of future glory disabling any commitment to godly living in this era, that is not the perspective of Paul. He stirs his readers to action that anticipates the final disclosure of God, and encourages his readers to withstand suffering that is preliminary to the coming of God.

3. *What God is doing*. Paul urges his readers to faithful living in imitation of Christ and in anticipation of his return. The essential environment for this new way of life is the church. The church is that community of people, filled with the Holy Spirit, alive with prayer, the use of spiritual gifts, and mutual upbuilding, which demonstrates the new unity between God and humanity by embodying unity through reconciliation amongst its members.

Perhaps most telling is Paul's discussion about speaking in tongues (1 Cor 14). He insists throughout that the Corinthians bear in mind what builds up the church. Gifts are not good in themselves – they are given that the whole church be edified. And why is the building up of the church so significant? Because the church has become the point of reconciliation between God and the world: "Do you not know that you are God's temple and that God's Spirit dwells in you?" (1 Cor 3:16). The "you" in each case is plural: this is a high claim for the corporate importance of reconciled Christian community. Such community is no less than the "body of Christ" (1 Cor 12:27). The key act that brings together Christ's death, the promise of his return, and the present life of the body of Christ, is baptism (Rom 6:3–11).

Paul frequently talks about slavery. The transformation brought about by Christ's death and resurrection transfers the "ownership" of the Christian from sin to God. Those who were once slaves to sin now become slaves to righteousness. Meanwhile membership of the body of Christ is a similar endeavor – Paul tells the Galatians that they must use their freedom in Christ to become "slaves to one another" (Gal 5:13). Christian obedience fundamentally means imitating the definitive obedience of Christ in sacrificial obedience to one another in community. Theology and ethics are inseparable.

The Letter to the Ephesians is the high water mark of the New Testament understanding of the church. Christ's death has inaugurated a new humanity: the dividing wall between Jew and Gentile has been demolished, and the church embodies the reconciled destiny of the entire cosmos with God. Understanding its heritage, receiving gifts, and living a redeemed life synthesize to achieve one goal: equipping the saints for ministry, "for building up the body of Christ, until all of us come to the unity of the faith and of the knowledge of the Son of God" (Eph 4:12).

So the church lies between the dying of the old era, identified in the cross, and the rising of the new era, anticipated in Jesus' resurrection and to be fulfilled in the coming eschaton. One feature of the Pauline letters that seems to fit less comfortably within this scheme is the lists of instructions that resemble Hellenic morality of the day, including the so-called *Haustafeln* or household codes. These occur in Eph 5:21–6:9, Col 3:18–4:1, Titus 2:1–10, and also later in the New Testament in 1 Pet 2:18–3:7. Other passages similarly incorporate contemporary moral expectations into spiritual instruction, for example, the counsel on the conduct of an overseer (1 Tim 3:4–5), or appear to have negative messages for the role of women in the church (1 Cor 14:34–5). Such passages have been seen as troubling because they appear to harness New Testament ethics to a particular set of conditioned social norms. Such norms, while facilitating the life of the emerging first-century church, may not be fully appropriate either to the transformation brought by Christ or to the somewhat different social context of the twenty-first-century church.

These passages have evoked huge debate in the history of the church, especially in recent times. Some have seen them as grounds to exert far-reaching patriarchal control over the domestic and sometimes political sphere; others have viewed their apparent social conservatism as grounds for seeing the New Testament as irredeemably time-bound and thus for questioning its value for ethics. Many modern scholars question the genuine Pauline authorship of all these letters (with the exception of 1 Corinthians), arguing that a later and more conservative author than Paul penned them. Others again have sought through close textual analysis to establish whether passages such as 1 Cor 14:34–5 were added later to the original letter, or whether certain words might be translated differently from the way they traditionally have been; others again have pointed out that many of these passages (e.g., Eph 5:21–33) are deeply theological and have a profound understanding of human interdependence unknown in the Hellenic culture amidst which they were written.

The Diversity of New Testament Ethics

Besides the four gospels and Acts and the letters from Paul and his followers, the New Testament canon includes a number of other books, each of which has a bearing on the ethics of the New Testament.

The book known as the Letter to the Hebrews is notoriously not by Paul, quite possibly not written to the Hebrews, and does not take the form of a letter. Hebrews asserts that the new covenant inaugurated by Christ fulfills and surpasses the old covenant given to Moses. Christ is the great high priest whose tradition stretches back to but surpasses Melchizedek. Hebrews enjoins hospitality to strangers, solidarity with those suffering, the sharing of resources, and obedience to leaders, but its emphasis is primarily on the inadequacy of the sacrifices made in the Jerusalem temple, and on the sufficiency of the sacrifice made by Christ the great high priest, who now stands ready at the throne of grace to receive prayers and provide help in the time of need.

The Letter of James is rooted in Jewish piety, with counsel concerning prayer, particularly with the sick and those experiencing hardship, the life of Christians in community, and the need for control of the tongue and for humility in the face of God. One could see James lying in continuity with the wisdom tradition of the Old Testament: there is no explicit sign of its reasoning being shaped by the unique event of Jesus Christ. One noticeable feature is the explicit warnings against wealth, pleas for justice, and commendation of charity toward the poor.

First Peter is very different from James. It explicitly grounds a wide-ranging vision of faithful Christian discipleship in the life, death, resurrection, and ascension of Jesus. It has an important role for the church, which offers to an often hostile world a model of hope, generous social action, and integrity in spite of suffering. The church inherits the distinctive vocation of Israel to be holy, as God is holy. At the heart of the letter lie these words: "But even if you do suffer for doing what is right, you are blessed. ... Always be ready to make your defense to anyone who demands from you an accounting for the hope that is in you" (3:14–15). Second Peter and Jude are more concerned with internal dissent and false teaching than with withstanding threats from outside the church.

Perhaps the most controversial book in the whole canon is Revelation. Full of vivid symbolism and significant numbers (such as seven and twelve), Revelation is apocalyptic literature, which operates on the imagination like a cosmic parable. It is deeply concerned with the nature of current suffering and the promise that God will intervene to vindicate the saints. It claims that this climax of history will come soon. This world is in the hands of the enemy, and God will overturn the status quo by remaking reality – finally bringing a new heaven and a new earth. There is a stark and uncompromising contrast between good and evil, light and darkness, God and Satan, church and world. The book, which is also a letter to seven churches in Asia Minor, addresses those facing persecution for their faith at the hands of the Roman Empire, and aims to shake those who are comfortable or affluent into facing the realities of their faith. There is no trace of engagement with – let alone compassion toward or love for – the enemy. Yet at the center of the book stands Jesus, described twenty-eight times as the "Lamb who was slaughtered." There is much mention of war, and the expectation is that the saints will face martyrdom, confident that the victory of the Lamb will become theirs. Revelation abounds with songs, but those songs perhaps sound somewhat different depending on the social context of those hearing them. For the persecuted and suffering, they ring out with hope. For the complacent and compromising, they offer a strident call toward greater faithfulness and passion, so as not to be spit out of God's mouth (3:16).

Summary

In this chapter we have met the following key themes. First, the Old Testament is made up of Law, Prophets, and Writings. Some have seen it as less authoritative than the New Testament, others have seen it as equally authoritative, while many have seen the two testaments in a creative tension.

Second, the gospels tell of the incarnation and birth, ministry and teaching, passion and death, and resurrection and ascension of Jesus. Those who draw on Jesus for their notion of ethics tend to focus on one of these four dimensions of who Jesus is. We have seen that there is a significant distinction between those who see Jesus (or the Bible in general) as *illustrative* of values that can be discovered through other sources, or as *normative*, that is, a unique display of information and example that is not available elsewhere and is ultimately without comparison to other sources of knowledge.

Third, the New Testament contains a significant diversity of viewpoints and perspectives. To hold to the "authority of Scripture" is not to be able to read off an answer for every issue one faces; it is to regard the conversation already taking place within the pages of Scripture as decisively shaping ongoing ethical reflection on themes that subsequently arise.

References and Further Reading

Joel Green's comment about the worlds of Scripture is from the introduction to the *Dictionary of Scripture and Ethics* (Joel B. Green, ed.; Grand Rapids, MI: Baker Academic, 2011), page 1.

For Richard Hays' discussion of our distance from Scripture, including his quotation of Oliver O'Donovan, see Richard B. Hays, *The Moral Vision of the New Testament* (San Francisco, CA: HarperCollins, 1996), page 3.

For the Catholic understanding of the relationship between Scripture and tradition, see especially *Dei Verbum* (Dogmatic Constitution on Divine Revelation), formulated at the Second Vatican Council. The sections quoted above are from *Dei Verbum* 9. Available online at http://www.vatican.va/archive/hist_councils/ii_vatican_council/documents/vat-ii_const_19651118_dei-verbum_en.html.

The reference to "creative faithfulness in new situations" is indebted to Allen Verhey, *The Great Reversal: Ethics and the New Testament* (Grand Rapids, MI: Eerdmans, 1986), page 171.

For a more detailed discussion of the normative character of the incarnation in relation to *theosis* in Orthodox ethics, see Vigen Guroian, *Incarnate Love: Essays in Orthodox Ethics* (2nd edn; Notre Dame, IN: University of Notre Dame Press, 2002), chapters 1, 2, and 4; and Stanley S. Harakas, *Toward Transfigured Life: The Theoria of Eastern Orthodox Ethics* (Minneapolis, MN: Light and Life Publishing Company, 1983), chapters 2, 8, and 10. The specific quotations related to *theosis* are as follows: Athanasius, *On the Incarnation of the Word*, in Philip Schaff and Henry Wallace, eds, Nicene and Post-Nicene Fathers, Second Series, vol. 4 (Peabody, MA: Hendrickson Publishers, 1994), 54.3, page 65; Irenaeus, *Against Heresies*, in Alexander Roberts and James Donaldson, eds, *Ante-Nicene* Fathers, vol. 1 (Peabody, MA: Hendrickson Publishers, 1994), Book V, Preface, page 526.

In reference to the life of Jesus and illustrative ethics, Reinhold Niebuhr's key work is *The Nature and Destiny of Man* (Louisville, KY: Westminster/John Knox Press, 1996).

Cited just after Niebuhr as an example of the way Jesus is normative for ethics is material drawn from chapters 1, 5, 7, and 12 of John Howard Yoder, *The Politics of Jesus* (2nd edn; Grand Rapids, MI: Eerdmans, 1972, 1994).

The heart of Rudolf Bultmann's ethics may be found in his influential work *Theology of the New Testament* (Kendrick Grobel, trans.; Waco, TX: Baylor University Press, 2007).

Oliver O'Donovan's exploration of the significance of the resurrection is found in *Resurrection and Moral Order* (2nd edn; Leicester, UK; Grand Rapids, MI: Eerdmans, 1994). Specific quotations are from pages 13, 15, and 57.

The fourfold typology for New Testament ethics listed above is distilled from Richard Hays, *The Moral Vision of the New Testament*, particularly pages 1–11. This work is a masterly analysis, but is perhaps not the place to begin for a basic introduction.

N. T. Wright's theology of the church is best found in *The New Testament and the People of God*, vol. 1 of his multi-volume work *Christian Origins and the Question of God* (Minneapolis, MN: Fortress Press, 1992–).

Helpful introductory texts to the place of the Bible in Christian ethics include:
- John W. Rogerson, Margaret Davies, and M. Daniel Carroll R. *The Bible in Ethics.* Sheffield: Sheffield Academic Press, 1995.
- Thomas W. Ogletree. *The Use of the Bible in Christian Ethics: A Constructive Essay.* Philadelphia, PA: Fortress Press, 1983.
- J. I. H. McDonald. *Biblical Interpretation and Christian Ethics. Cambridge: Cambridge University Press, 1993.*
- Bruce C. Birch and Larry Rasmussen. *Bible and Ethics in the Christian Life.* Minneapolis, MN: Augsburg Fortress, 1989.

Works that treat ethics in the Old Testament include:
- John Barton. *Ethics and the Old Testament*, 2nd edn. London: SCM Press, 2003.
- Bruce C. Birch. *Let Justice Roll Down: The Old Testament, Ethics, and Christian Life.*

Louisville, KY: Westminster/John Knox Press, 1991.

- Walter C. Kaiser Jr. *Toward Old Testament Ethics*. Grand Rapids, MI: Zondervan, 1983.
- Christopher Wright. *Old Testament Ethics for the People of God*. Leicester: InterVarsity Press, 2004.

A basic introduction to NT ethics is Frank Matera, *New Testament Ethics: The Legacies of Jesus and Paul* (Louisville, KY: Westminster/John Knox Press, 1996). Some more advanced treatments, beside that of Richard Hays, include:

- Charles E. Curran and Richard A. McCormick, eds. *The Use of Scripture in Moral Theology*. Ramsey, NJ: Paulist, 1984.
- Stephen Fowl and Gregory Jones. *Reading in Communion: Scripture and Ethics in Christian Life*. Grand Rapids, MI: Eerdmans, 1991.
- Brian Brock. *Singing the Ethos of God: On the Place of Christian Ethics in Scripture*. Grand Rapids, MI: Eerdmans, 2007.
- Allen Verhey. *The Great Reversal: Ethics and the New Testament*. Grand Rapids, MI: Eerdmans, 1984.
- Brian K. Blount. *Then the Whisper Put on Flesh: New Testament Ethics in an African American Context*. Nashville, TN: Abingdon Press, 2001.

Selections from the following works are quoted in the corresponding chapter of *Christian Ethics: An Introductory Reader*.

- Tertullian. *Adversus Marcionem*. Ernest Evans, ed. Oxford: Oxford University Press, 1972. Available at www.tertullian.org/articles/evans_marc/evans_marc_00index.htm.
- Karl Barth. "Israel and the Church." *Church Dogmatics*. Volume 2, Part 2. Edinburgh: T & T Clark, 1949.
- John Howard Yoder. *The Original Revolution: Essays on Christian Pacifism*. Scottdale, PA: Herald Press, 1972.
- Oliver O'Donovan. *The Desire of the Nations: Rediscovering the Roots of Political Theology*. Cambridge: Cambridge University Press, 1996 (reprinted 2002). Pages 21–9.
- *Calvin: Institutes of the Christian Religion*. 2 vols. John T. McNeill, ed.; Ford Lewis Battles, trans. The Library of Christian Classics 20. Philadelphia, PA: Westminster Press, 1960. Excerpt from Vol. 1, Books II–III. Also available online at http://www.ccel.org/ccel/calvin/institutes/.
- Stanley Hauerwas. *The Peaceable Kingdom: A Primer in Christian Ethics*. Notre Dame, IN: University of Notre Dame Press, 1983.
- Dietrich Bonhoeffer. *The Cost of Discipleship*. London: SCM Press, 2001, 2004.

Chapter Two
The Story of the Church

Human action and behavior are shaped not only by stories but also by communities. In the previous chapter we looked at the story of God – the Bible. In this chapter we look at the community that tells God's story – the church, with its historical series of attempts to be true to that story in new contexts. The church in responding to the story of God has its own story. And we are concerned with how that history, even though it is often neglected, is intrinsic to the story of Christian ethics.

The church is the community in which Christian people allow their identity to take form – and be transformed. It is a community that makes sense of who its members are and how they act. The content of its ethics involves claims about a kingdom, which fulfills the purposes of God by creating a sanctified people. But the way the church goes about this shaping of ethical lives has varied from place to place and from era to era. Three broad periods of time are identified in the present chapter:

1. Minority status: the period before Christianity became the official religion of the Roman Empire under Constantine, during which Christianity was a minority religion centered largely around the Mediterranean and was often persecuted.
2. Christendom: the period between Constantine and the time of the European wars of religion and the Enlightenment, during which Christianity was the dominant religion of the Mediterranean and then the European world. This period also marks the divergence of the Eastern and Western Churches into distinct branches of Christianity.
3. Modernity: during which Christianity in the West has faced a series of challenges to its intellectual and social centrality, and has had to find a way of

Introducing Christian Ethics, Second Edition. Samuel Wells and Ben Quash with Rebekah Eklund.
© 2017 John Wiley & Sons Ltd. Published 2017 by John Wiley & Sons Ltd.

relating to multiple worldviews – some religious and some anti-religious – in a less Eurocentric world. Meanwhile Christianity in the global South has undergone increasingly rapid growth.

We begin with the time of the church's minority status.

Minority Status

Marks

What were the characteristic marks of the ancient church as an ethical community? We may look in broad terms at two significant areas: the internal life of the community, and its relations to people outside the circle of believers.

1. *Internal.* The pagan polemicist Celsus (ca. 180 CE) commented on the close-knit structure and coherence of the Christians as a social group. He attributed this in part to the way that their "social dissidence" and their "fear of outsiders" bred a particularly powerful sense of unity. This explanation is of course framed by a critic, but by social dissidence he meant something that was actually very important to the Christians: their rejection of the cults of the pagan gods of Rome (to which later would be added the emperor cult), cults which Celsus saw as an integral part of the social fabric of the empire. The Christians generally also refused to undertake military service during this period; there is no record of any Christian serving in the imperial armies until about 170 CE. Their lives were characterized by secrecy, withdrawal, and non-participation in public entertainment and spectacles such as gladiatorial combats. Celsus saw all of this as subversive. But his sense of the close-knit structures of the churches was borne out by their highly effective pastoral care of their own: Christians cared for the poor in their midst, supported widows and orphans, visited and offered help to prisoners. Church members in many places benefited from the generous provision of such "welfare" within their communities.
2. *External.* The Christian "fear of outsiders" commented upon by Celsus was partly their justified fear of persecution. For certain periods in the first three centuries of the church's life, and in certain regions, this persecution was brutal. Christians often had to hide, and even the slightest hint of Eucharistic wine on the breath of a Christian could lead to betrayal. But even in calmer times, there was a concern on the part of the first Christians not to be unnecessarily misunderstood (e.g., as communities of antinomianism or moral license), let alone to be thought guilty of the wilder charges of human sacrifice and cannibalism that were occasionally leveled at the church. So Celsus' talk of fear of outsiders may also refer to this circumspection. Certainly, we find the Epistle to Titus insisting that decorous behavior will help prevent the Word of God being brought into disrepute (Titus 2:5), and

Paul had written to the Corinthians that they should have an eye to the unfavorable impression their disorderly behavior in worship might have on "outsiders or unbelievers" (1 Cor 14:23–5). However, Christians also had more active forms of relationship with outsiders; the scope of the church's charitable work was not always restricted to the company of believers. The early Christian communities were marked by a developed concern to provide charitable assistance and practical help to their non-Christian neighbors when in need. This may have been one of the most potent causes of the success of Christianity. For example, Christians tried to help those condemned to the "living death" of labor in the mines, and they were prominent in responding to calamities like famine, earthquake, pestilence, or war with practical help for the victims.

Tensions

A number of divisive issues precipitated the ethical reflection of the early church. They included the difficult question of how to relate to their religious inheritance (Judaism) as well as their dominant religious environment (paganism – although the use of the word "pagan" to denote non-Christian heathens dates only from the fourth century). They included questions of how to relate to the power of the state (the Roman Empire) and the facts of economic life. There was also the vital matter of how in ongoing history to live out Jesus' radical message of preparation for the end of days, amidst the continuing institutions of marriage, the family, money, and so on.

1. *Religious inheritance and environment.* What made Christians distinctive in relation to Jews and pagans? Ought they to remain virtually indistinguishable from Jews in their life and worship? Could they justify borrowing from pagan ideas and values, and to what extent?
    a. **Judaism.** We find St. Paul in Romans 14–15 and in 1 Corinthians 10 discussing what was a profoundly serious dilemma for his converts: whether or not to abstain from meat sacrificed to pagan gods. Jews of Paul's day would have regarded such abstention as one of the minimum requirements for fidelity to the true God; and the principle was endorsed by the most authoritative council we know of in the church's first decades, the apostolic synod described in Acts 15. On the other hand, there was a growing recognition that the sacrifice of Christ had put all the laws of ritual purity in question. This affected the church's attitude to circumcision (the requirement for which it rejected) and to the dietary laws of the Jewish community (which it likewise set aside fairly rapidly). In the case of food sacrificed to idols, urban converts in Mediterranean cities, negotiating the practical complications of their lives, were under particular strain as they sought to shop for food in markets where the meat on sale had often been "offered" in this way.

Paul's arguments give us an insight into how the primitive church dealt with such issues. Unlike dietary laws and circumcision, where Jewish practice was eventually set aside, in this case the scruples Christians shared with Jews were to some extent respected. As Rowan Williams has pointed out, "Paul is fighting on two fronts at once. He warns, in Romans 14, of the risks of the 'pure,' the ultra-conscientious, passing judgement on the less careful, at the same time as warning the less careful against causing pain to the scrupulous by flaunting their freedom in ways that provoke conflict or, worse, doubt." What emerges for Paul as the key ethical principle in this area is the importance of bearing one another's burdens, including the burden of conscience. In the Corinthian text, the theological rationale for his advice is that decisions should be guided by the imperative of building the body of Christ more securely – as a form of imitation of God's own selflessness.

b.   **Paganism.** Christians shared some of the habits and mores of the Hellenistic world of their time (e.g., aspects of its attitudes to women and slaves). They also, from a very early stage, drew on its philosophical traditions and ideas when those ideas seemed to clarify or commend Christian teaching and moral discipline. Notable figures who borrowed from Hellenistic thought in the first years of the church's life were Clement of Alexandria (145–215 CE) and Origen (182–251 CE). Origen, amongst other things, adapted to Christian purposes the concept of natural law, which he saw as available to reason, higher than local human-made laws, and provided by a "legislator God" for all human beings to obey. Clement skillfully drew on the inherited classical traditions of ethics in a quest to draw the church into line with the prevailing culture of Greco-Roman civilization. Both Clement and Origen were much affected by Stoicism. The Stoic tradition had a particular influence within early Christian moral thought, since its view of ethics as living in harmony with nature resonated with the Christian affirmation of God's creation. Nonetheless, despite these borrowings from the schools of the philosophers, a great many aspects of pagan belief and practice were deeply offensive to Christians.

Tertullian (160–225 CE), writing in the late second and early third century, was one of the most forceful voices on this issue, emphasizing the need for Christians to estrange themselves from their surrounding culture. He and many other Christian writers saw the worship of the gods of the pagans as idolatrous, crude, and barbaric – for these gods were manifestly immoral, sexually predatory, and violent. Tertullian refers in his *Apology* (ca. 197 CE) to the "madness of the circus," the "immodesty of the theatre," and the "atrocities of the arena," all of which were associated with pagan religious ritual. He also notes the readiness of pagans to abandon their children or kill them by exposure.

2. *The State.* "The paradox of the church," writes Henry Chadwick, "was that it was a religious revolutionary movement, yet without a conscious political ideology; it aimed at the capture of society throughout all its strata, but was at the same time characteristic for its indifference to the possession of power in this world." As the Christian church worked out its attitude to the state during the period of its minority status, it repeatedly faced a tension between two extremes of provocation and compromise.

    a. **Provocation.** The temptation to provoke was born out of a rigorist strand of Christian thought that has asserted itself at intervals throughout Christian history, and that in this period was exemplified by the great controversialist whom we have just met: Tertullian. Tertullian was driven by the conviction that there could be no compromise with what he saw as the polluting morals and the idolatry of Roman society. He emphasized the need for separation from that society, including from its institutions; he thus became one of the key voices to denounce military service. He perceived that the blood of the martyrs was the seed of the church and argued that in the last resort Christians should be happy to embrace death when resisting the power of the state (as they were often given no choice but to do in times of active persecution).

        The opposition that Tertullian's views provoked in Carthage eventually led him to enter the sect known as Montanism, marked by intense eschatological expectation, asceticism, and emphasis upon the immediacy of the Holy Spirit's operation in phenomena such as ecstatic prophecy. The Montanists' belief that Christian individuals and communities were perfectible reinforced his sectarian view of the church, and challenged the more institutional ecclesiology that he had himself espoused earlier in life.

        Another rigorist figure, who was influenced by Tertullian's writings, was the Roman presbyter Novatian (eventually consecrated bishop of Rome as rival to a perceived compromiser with paganism), who himself suffered martyrdom under the Emperor Valerian in 257–8 CE. Novatian's rejection by the church at Rome in 251 CE effectively marks the defeat of rigorism. There were early Christian rigorists who operated at levels less intellectually impressive than those attained by Tertullian and Novatian, many of whom made martyrdom something to be actively sought in confrontational and macabre ways. The mainstream church quickly condemned such seekers after martyrdom as mere suicides deserving no recognition.

        Nonetheless, martyrdom was an important dimension of Christian interaction with the Roman state. It was a clear statement that the Christian kingdom was not of this world – that Christians lived within a different aeon and under a different authority from their pagan rulers. In many ways martyrdom brought together questions of authority, idolatry, and eschatology. Martyrdom seemed the most visible way to bear witness to Jesus' own willingness to deny himself and take up his cross.

b. **Compromise.** Many Christians perceived opportunities for accommodation with existing social institutions and ideas, and saw the value of state power at least as a restraint on lawlessness and chaos. Jesus himself, it seemed, had taught that it was possible to render due service to Caesar as well as to God (Matt 22:21). Most Christians were not keen to adopt an attitude of zealous resistance to the Roman state. Jewish Christians in Jerusalem fled the city when nationalist Jews helped to trigger the war in 66 CE. Christians paid their taxes dutifully, and Paul, himself a Roman citizen as well as a citizen of Tarsus, was of the view that magistrates were to be respected as ministers of divine justice in the restraint of crime. The *Pax Romana* – established and enforced by Augustus – was seen by some early Christian historians in the mid-second century as an instrument of God's providence, designed to assist the spread of Christ's own gospel of universal peace and goodwill. As we have seen, the problem that Christians had with the state in these early decades was with its paganism. On the other hand, the state turned violently on Christians at certain traumatic intervals including the so-called "Great Persecution" (250–1 CE) under the Emperor Decius, and Christians had a strong sense of having a higher allegiance than that to their political masters. On April 21, 247 CE, there were cultic celebrations of Rome's millennium. Coins proudly proclaimed *Roma Aeterna*, advertising Rome's thousand-year achievement under the aegis of the old gods. Christians abstained from participating in the celebrations, and this became the cause of protest and hostility in parts of the empire.

3. *Eschatology and daily life.* It seems that many of the very first Christians were expecting the imminent return of the Lord Jesus, the end of days, and the final judgment of all people. As they rapidly adapted to the fact that they might not see this in their own lifetimes, and that they still had to live in the world, they had to make decisions about how to relate to material possessions and slaves, about what attitudes to adopt to sex, and about the respective roles of women and men, while still preserving their sense of having already, in some sense, entered into the new and eternal life of the kingdom inaugurated by Jesus. (As the *Letter to Diognetus* from the later second century puts it, "It is true that they are 'in the flesh,' but they do not live 'according to the flesh' ... they busy themselves on earth, but their citizenship is in heaven.") Direct applications of the teaching and example of the Savior did not always provide an adequate answer to all issues.

a. **Money and slaves.** The early church rejected the dualist theologies of Marcion and others, which denied the importance of material reality for Christians (seeing matter as nothing to do with the God of Christianity, and understanding Christ entirely "spiritually"). Ever since then, Christian ethics has worked itself out in the belief that the physical universe and all the objects within are to be related to God's creative and redemptive purposes. This led the early church to devote a great deal of careful consideration to the relationship between rich and poor. There is a strong appreciation in the writings of many of the church's first moral thinkers that wealth is a source of spiritual and moral danger, but also a resource for building and sustaining communities and expressing practical love. As the *Didache* says, "If you have what is eternal in common, how much more should you have what is transient!"

This did not mean that the early church generally practiced a sort of proto-communism; the writings of the first two centuries suggest that the onus to give fell on individuals and their personal acts of charity. Even if sharing found a degree of institutionalized expression, it remained voluntary. Justin Martyr (100–65 CE) writes: "Those who prosper, and who so wish, contribute, each one as much as he chooses to. What is collected is deposited with the president, and he takes care of orphans and widows, and those who are in want on account of sickness …, and those who are in bonds, and the strangers who are sojourners." Clement of Alexandria argued that Christ's statement about camels going through eyes of needles (Mark 10:25) did not *literally* mean rich people could not be saved; it simply referred to those whose lives were centered on material wealth to the point that it became more important to them than God – and therefore idolatrous.

Slavery, meanwhile, is perhaps surprisingly rarely criticized in this period given its challenge to Christian ideals of community and fraternity. Writers like Ignatius of Antioch (ca. 35–ca. 107 CE) were more likely to enjoin the obedience of slaves to masters "so that they may obtain from God a better freedom" – though Christian slaveowners too are sternly commanded not to be harsh. The church in this period was not able, it seems, to question an institution that was such an important fact of economic life in the Roman world, as it had not yet considered an economic ethic for society as a whole.

b. **Sex and marriage.** There appears to have been considerable sexual license in the cultures surrounding the early church. Thus, Christian teaching required much stricter standards than were generally to be found in the wider society – making sexual self-discipline a necessary part of spiritual wholeness. St. Paul's teachings on sexual continence are frequently quoted in this period. Lust, fornication, and adultery are the focus of particular condemnation, but there are also clear rejections of same-sex relations.

The early Church Fathers could not bring themselves to deny that the institution of marriage was good, but almost all of them relegated it to a secondary good, after the celibate state. Widowed partners ought not to marry again (although allowances were made between Christians); neither ought divorcees, except perhaps if their partner had subsequently died. Even within marriage, ideals of chastity were articulated. Spouses must "follow God's will and not the promptings of lust" (Ignatius of Antioch): wedded chastity consisted in transforming sexual intercourse from a satisfaction of desire to a necessary duty (e.g., when the act was undertaken for the generation of children).

As for the relationship between husband and wife, the Fathers discuss it with a conservatism that derives from St. Paul (e.g., 1 Cor 14:33–6) but which also shows itself in sympathy with prevailing secular opinion, there being very few obstacles to reconciling the two attitudes. In marriage, asserts John Chrysostom (ca. 347–407 CE), the wife must not be considered an equal partner with her husband, for man was ordained to regulate woman, and his duty is to mold her and form her while she is still young and timid. There is little doubt that a married woman's worst personal disadvantages were mitigated by the more considerate and respectful treatment that she generally received as a "sister" in the Lord – and the instruction to husbands in Ephesians places a good deal of emphasis on mutual love and respect, as of one's own body. John Chrysostom, for example, writes, "Supply her with everything. Do everything and endure trouble for her sake." Nevertheless, the fact of subordination in marriage very clearly remains and, if anything, is reasserted after the first century of the church's life, for as Chrysostom also asserts, "where there is equal authority [in marriage] there can never be peace."

c. **Women.** The church wrestled with the role of women as it developed its earliest forms of ministry. On the one hand, it labored under the patriarchal inheritance of Judaism, and the predominantly patriarchal character of the Hellenistic secular culture. On the other hand, it struggled with the implications of the freedom in Christ it had begun to proclaim within its own communities – a freedom from traditional distinctions that St. Paul had summed up when he said that there is now no longer Jew nor Greek, slave nor free, male nor female (Gal 3:28). There is clear evidence of a variety of important women's ministries in the early church, including in Paul's own letters: Paul names several women as his co-workers in the gospel, including Prisca, Phoebe, Mary, and Junia (Romans 16).

Because it was precisely within private households that the church had its life and roots, and because women were mainly responsible for the households and hospitality of that day, they were quite naturally in the forefront of providing the context for Christian life and growth, and the spread of the gospel. This was all the more true in situations where women had their own households and financial means but no husbands to restrict their Christian activities. Luke gives us such a figure in the person of Tabitha, also called Dorcas, who is described as a female disciple. In her ministry of good works for the congregation, we seem to have some sort of precursor to the later ministry of women, which was to be focused in the order of deaconesses. This can be deduced from references in the New Testament (1 Tim 5:3; 1 Tim 3:11) but only comes into clear focus in the *Apostolic Tradition* attributed to the early Christian writer and presbyter Hippolytus (ca. 170–235 CE), in which we are told of a ceremony of laying on of hands for deaconesses that is an exact duplicate of the ceremony for deacons. In the

Syrian *Didascalia Apostolorum* originating at about the same time there are a considerable number of references to deaconesses, amongst which they are said to have the responsibility of instructing new female converts in how to live a Christian life. It seems, then, that certain women enjoyed liberties and privileges during the days of the early church that were characteristic of the new way of life proclaimed by Paul and Luke, within certain limits.

Nevertheless, neither the New Testament authors nor patristic writers went so far as to suggest that social norms ought to be completely over-turned. There were many ways in which Christianity made itself suspect and unpopular in the first three centuries of its existence – as we have seen, it rejected the emperor cult and sometimes military service. It was impera-tive, therefore, for Christians to appear to be good citizens in the few areas where they *could* endorse the values of their society. These areas were chiefly in obedience to governing authorities and the endorsement of abid-ing family norms. We seem to witness, therefore, a development toward greater conformity with the patterns of the dominant secular culture. This trend begins with the Pastoral Epistles' strong concern for the opinion of contemporary society, in which the "good" that older women are to teach younger women involves conventionally acceptable female behavior – chastity, domesticity, kindness, and submissiveness to husbands, so "that the word of God may not be discredited" (Titus 2). Later patristic teaching contains similar emphases. Clement of Alexandria calls for sobriety amongst women: "Love of display is not for a lady, but a courtesan. Such women care little for keeping at home with their husbands … they become lazy in house-keeping, sitting like painted things to be looked at, not as if made for domestic economy." Augustine advocates "more orderliness and more decency" in domestic affairs. Here, the Church Fathers choose to emphasize domestic and civic values that are far from adventurous.

Monasticism before Constantine

A final key way in which the eschatological imperative found embodiment in the early church was in the form of monasticism. The eschatological character of the monastic lifestyle in this period was impelled by the belief that Christians are not in the end made for this world. Whether in the eremitic (reclusive) life of solitary anchorites or (later) in the cenobitic (communal) monasteries, a clear distinction was drawn between the visible "world" on the one hand, and the society of the holy who live in detached readiness for the second coming of Christ on the other. When the Lord had disappeared in the cloud of his glory, the apostles kept their eyes raised to heaven. A reawakening of this primitive expectation was unmistak-able in the early phase of monasticism, and continued to characterize it, in both East and West, such that it is still quite apparent in the Middle Ages – for example, the greatest number of sermons left by Bernard of Clairvaux (1090–1153) are on the ascension, more even than on the passion.

So, too, in the beginnings of monastic withdrawal into the Egyptian desert in the third century, everything was judged according to its relationship with the final consummation of the whole of reality. Antony of Egypt, around the year 270 CE, heard the words in the Gospel of Matthew by which Jesus called the would-be disciple to relinquish everything he had and to give it to the poor (Matt 19:16–24). As Athanasius of Alexandria (296–373 CE) recounts it, "[Antony] considered while he walked how the apostles, forsaking everything, followed the saviour, and how in Acts some sold what they possessed and took the proceeds and placed them at the feet of the apostles for distribution among those in need, and what great hope is stored up for such people in heaven." This anticipation of death and the hope of heaven, combined with an intense desire to follow Christ, can be recognized as the basic motives of Antony's adoption of the desert life, and of all the monks and nuns in subsequent generations who were taught to look upon him as the "father of all monks" and as their exemplar in his radically reconfigured relationship with the world. He was not the first to do it, but he became an icon of the solitary life.

Despite the subsequent interest and emulation that Antony's life was to inspire, it would be wrong to see his decision in isolation from the context of Egyptian asceticism, and indeed the underlying interests of the Mediterranean world. Those involved sought to be perfect (*teleios* in Greek) – a word and a quest found in pagan thought as well as in Christian and Jewish. While Antony looked back to Elijah for his prototype, his way of life resonates with aspects of Greek philosophy and religion – especially that of the Stoic school, whose influence we have already noted. (Stoicism is explored in more depth in Chapter Three.) His move to the desert emphasized the detachment necessary to this quest for perfection in the most forceful way.

The basic precepts of Antony's life were propagated and expounded by Athanasius as follows: "He worked with his hands, spent what he made partly for bread, and partly on those in need. He prayed constantly." Athanasius adds that "he mortified the body and kept it under subjection, so that he would not, after conquering some challenges, trip up in others." The primary object of his planting and tilling was to make himself physically self-sufficient. We should not underestimate the importance for a monk like Antony of the desire not to be a burden to others, so as to be entirely freed from the bonds of economic (and therefore worldly) obligation. Thus, we find Athanasius describing the intent with which he had begun to plant and till the soil at his distant oasis, "rejoicing because he would be annoying no one because of this." But a secondary object of his planting and tilling was that "the visitor might have a little relief." Here we see the pattern set for subsequent monasticism. Prayer and physical labor combine with a sense of the duties of hospitality, and the necessity of strict control of the body's impulses. It is important to remember that no dualism is implied here: the body was seen as part of a whole human being. The human being *as a totality* was fallen, so restoration of a spiritual way of life must involve physical restoration too. Antony's body is recorded as having been made perfect, and virtually incorruptible, at the same time as he wins his spiritual battles.

The first monks were not ecclesiastics, nor were they rich, cultured, or learned. In seeking this highly empirical way of defining and quantifying their Christian discipleship, they displayed impulses that can be equated with the impulse to martyrdom. The parallel is very often drawn in the literature of the time. In his description of some very provocative behavior by Antony toward the pagan officials when in Alexandria, Athanasius tells us that "Antony also prayed for martyrdom. He seemed, therefore, like one who grieved because he had not been martyred." The monks were "bloodless martyrs" – their lives making bold statements about where their true treasure lay in a way comparable to the martyrs. The need for such clear demarcation was to seem all the more acute to many after Christianity became the official religion of the empire.

Christendom

The Constantinian Church

The world changed decisively for Christians and non-Christians alike when the Emperor Constantine became the senior ruler of the empire in 312 CE, and made himself Christianity's champion. Toleration and imperial favor for the Christian faith followed, as did a far greater imperial concern for the internal affairs of the church, for Constantine's instincts were to tie imperial state and Christian church together as closely as he could. In a way that has marked the Byzantine world ever since, he thought not in terms of two "societies," sacred and secular, but in terms of a single society, with the emperor's earthly role mirroring that of God's heavenly one. His involvement in adjudicating the Donatist controversy between 313 and 316 CE, and his summoning of the Council of Nicaea in 325 CE to settle the Arian dispute, are examples of this new involvement.

Many other consequences flowed from Constantine's commitment to Christianity. From the fourth century onwards, Christian churches acquired a "public" style of architecture and became recognizable as such. Policy and legislation took on a strongly Christian character – the criminal law and the law of debt were made more humane, the conditions of slavery were mitigated, grants were made to support poor children and thus discourage the exposure of unwanted babies, and certain financial obligations were lifted from clergy and celibates. In 321 CE Constantine ordered that Sunday should become a public holiday. Positions of church leadership became positions of real public status and wide social influence, to which the worldly and not only the religiously devout might aspire. Many local churches acquired substantial property and land holdings. By the end of the fourth century, from one perspective, the church seemed virtually to have captured society – though, as a good many have argued, the capturing was not all one way, and it was not long before the church began to realize that in many respects it now enjoyed less freedom and self-determination than it did before. Christian scholars today disagree over whether the Constantinian legitimization of Christianity was a blessing for the church – in that it allowed the church to flourish as never before – or a disaster – in that it diminished the church's witness to a way of life marked not by dominating power but by self-giving love. Meanwhile Christians in parts of the world outside the reach of the Roman Empire – for example, in India and Persia – never enjoyed the shift from persecution to relative power.

In the immediate post-Constantinian period the church's new confidence and influence were accompanied by an intellectual flowering. Some of the key thinkers here were – in the East – John Chrysostom and the so-called "Cappadocian Fathers": Basil of Caesarea (330–79 CE), Gregory of Nazianzus (ca. 330–ca. 390 CE), and Gregory of Nyssa (ca. 335–94 CE), as well as Basil and Gregory of Nyssa's sister Macrina (ca. 330–79 CE). In the West there were Ambrose of Milan (339–97 CE) and Augustine of Hippo (354–430 CE). None of these thinkers was concerned with a special area of interest we can separate off and identify as "ethics" – and they were certainly not interested in writing a systematic or comprehensive account of Christian ethical life – but all of their writings touch naturally upon the practical and social demands of the Christian faith in particular spheres.

Monasticism after Constantine

The threat of persecution and the possibility of martyrdom having receded, devout Christians looked for other ways to keep alive their sense of not being wholly of this world – to mark their boundaries with the world, and preserve an intensity of discipleship appropriate to those whose true citizenship was in heaven. It was in 313 CE that Antony had carried his eremitic manner of life to the interior mountain where he was to remain. Shortly afterwards, in 320 CE, a monk named Pachomius founded a community of anchorites at Tabennesis, also in Egypt. Here was something of a different model, although springing from the same impulses. Antony, according to Athanasius, had certainly attracted followers, who had associated themselves with him and lived nearby, but more in a confederation of solitaries than in a structured community. By contrast, Pachomius' community sought to do God's perfect will collectively, rather than seek to be perfect each in his individual life and largely independent of the others. As the community grew, and came to include a convent of women begun by his sister Mary, Pachomius drew up a rule for them, composed from Scripture, giving guidance for achieving balance in clothing, food, and sleep. In this, a pattern was laid down that was to be copied, translated, and spread across the Mediterranean world, influencing later rules of monastic life, even in the sixth-century French city of Arles. At the time of Pachomius' death in 346 CE, his rule encompassed nine monasteries for men and two for women. From there the Pachomian monasteries multiplied and filled, so that they eventually counted their monks and nuns by the thousands. It was this model of communal asceticism that eventually won the important endorsement of Basil of Caesarea and came to have the greatest influence in the later history of monasticism.

There were substantial social as well as ethical implications to this development. The monks of fourth-century Egypt stood as a challenge to a situation of near-hunger and dependence on the marketplace that characterized Near Eastern society. The greatest battles that Antony and those like him had fought were with the stomach, and this came to seem a microcosm of the battle against the "world" and all that it stood for: the unceasing cycles of marriage, birth, and death. In an analogous way, the fourth-century Egyptian monks were wrestling with the "world" of the settled areas, which seemed condemned to live in powerless subjection to the demands of food production and consumption, eking out a living from agriculture and trade. The Pachomian monasteries grew to such an extent that they were larger and more populous than many towns and villages around them – indeed, one of the first four of the monasteries was actually called "The Village." They provided a vast workforce at strategic times of the year, notably at harvest, spreading into the whole surrounding region before returning again to the monastery – bestowing their good will on the surrounding society while still free from economic or social obligation to it. Pachomius had shown that it was possible to found a monastery that functioned as an alternative village in the midst of the settled world.

A need to clarify borders or boundaries was as clear as ever – more pressing perhaps when the monastery lacked the geographical and partly mythic distinction of being deep in the desert, like the cells of the anchorites. The monastic rule was part of this definition, and emphasized the passing over to a new pattern of living, in which one dressed in a regulation tunic with the sign of the cross on it to demonstrate that this life was discipleship of Christ. The monasteries had vast enclosing walls, also to emphasize their boundaries. Later, by the end of the fourth century, there are also increasing signs of a preoccupation with sexual separateness, growing, perhaps, out of an experience of morally lax behavior amongst the monks. Boundaries had to be emphasized in terms of one's physical and social relationships after the transfer to the monastic lifestyle, and this emphasis can be seen to have grown more explicit in the cenobitic monasteries by the beginning of the 400s CE.

The distinction between the churches of the cities and the humble retreats of the desert could be blurred, and we find bishops like Ambrose, Theophilus of Alexandria, and John Chrysostom advocating the virtues of monasticism in their urban contexts, and turning to monks and to monasteries when making ecclesiastical appointments. There is no denying that monasticism underwent significant modifications during this process. Antony had been an illiterate layman, and the majority of Egyptian monks much the same. As the monastic ideal spread, it became fueled by wealthy individuals and intellectuals and filtered west via them, returning in some forms to the cities (so that we find John Chrysostom setting forth an ideal of the Christian household as a lay monastery, closed against the profane world). Monasteries for women were often founded by women of wealth and noble birth, such as Paula (d. 404 CE), who was a close companion of Jerome, and Melanie the Younger (385–448 CE). Writers and thinkers were increasingly drawn into the monastic life. The two communities founded by Augustine at Hippo show an intellectually sociable monasticism that is theologically alert, open to new questions, and keen on discussion. As monks were drawn on to fill high-ranking ecclesiastical posts, the monastic system became definitively ecclesiastically oriented. Nevertheless, the continuity with Antony and the desert is never forgotten in the minds of the later monks of both East and West, and the early traditions remain the avowed model for all the developments and adaptations that follow.

The Medieval Period

There was a remarkable continuity of Christian influence even as the Western half of the Roman Empire gave way to the power of assorted Germanic tribes following the sack of Rome in 410 CE. The Goths, Vandals, Visigoths, Franks, and Burgundians who overran the imperial territories converted to catholic Christianity, attracted by it as they were attracted by the glory of the empire they had taken. In *The City of God*, Augustine had developed the thesis that the church was a pilgrim reality whose fate was formally distinct from that of the centers of earthly power. This thesis was allowed to prove itself as Rome fell. The Western Church succeeded in weathering the storm of the empire's disintegration, and continued to think catholically – giving a now fragmented world spiritual ways to think beyond the political changes it was undergoing. This sense of catholicity represented a more universal perspective that offered Christians a still viable way to think about the world's unity and purpose under God.

In the Eastern portion of the fallen empire arose the Byzantine Empire, which survived for another thousand years and in which the Eastern Church continued to thrive, with Constantinople as its heart. Christians in the East were increasingly occupied with issues different from those taken up in the Western Church – for example, the controversy over whether it was proper to venerate icons, and the clashes with Islam, which began in the seventh century and culminated in 1453 with the fall of Constantinople to the Ottoman Empire.

In 1054, simmering tensions between the Eastern and Western Churches came to a head and led to a schism, or a mutual split, over differences that had to do with theology, ecclesiastical practices, and political power. The largely Latin-speaking West formalized its tendency to look to Rome as its center of authority, and the Greek-speaking East formalized its tendency to look towards Constantinople. The Eastern Orthodox and Roman Catholic Churches were born.

Other centrifugal forces were at work too, which laid the foundations for much of the church's global diversity even today. Christianity had established itself in India as early as the first century, long before many Western European areas had been evangelized, and it remained a continuous presence there until waves of Catholic and subsequently Protestant missionaries arrived to found new churches from the fifteenth century onwards. Another major branch of Orthodoxy is represented by the ancient Coptic Church of Ethiopia, which was established at least by the fourth century and perhaps as early as the first. These venerable traditions of Christian life and witness are a crucial part of the story of the church. However, in tracing the development of Christian *ethics* in the church we need to turn back to the Christian West, for the story of ethics owes a particular debt to some highly influential thinkers in the European Middle Ages. Of these, the foremost figure to emerge is Thomas Aquinas (1225–74), whose thought will be explored in depth in Chapter Four.

Confession and penance

In the transition to the medieval period, the stage was set for new considerations of how to characterize and commend moral purpose.

A key way in which the church sought to foster the "good life" in believers was through the evolving practices of confession and penance. As has already been indicated, the monastic movements continued to generate enormous creative energy in the centuries after Constantine, and to exert great influence in shaping both social and economic patterns of life, and also the devotional lives of individual Christians. They were also one of the most significant factors in encouraging the growth of practices of individual auricular confession in the medieval period. The spiritual heroism depicted in the stories of saints was often explicitly an expression of a religious life that ordinary lay Christians could not aspire to emulate – but they could at least try to ensure that they did not lose all hold on the way of perfection, and they could do so by the regular, careful, and accurate examination of their sins and receiving of the church's medicinal sacramental ministry. The model of spiritual direction of novices and monks by their superiors increasingly offered a model for lay as well as religious people, and from the sixth century onwards manuals came into being to assist confessors in their task of hearing confessions and prescribing penances.

The purpose of these may partly have been to ensure a certain uniformity of practice, and to address the urgent need to give a basic moral education to Christian converts in otherwise quite barbaric contexts. But one curious effect of these penitential books, their codifications of morality, and the practices they supported was that the sorts of fundamental questions of the good and the right ordering of desire that are such a high achievement of Augustine's theology sometimes went unaddressed. While they show some interest in the intentions of the penitent, it is largely secondary. In some cases they tend toward making morality a sort of transaction in which the offense (considered in abstraction from the person of the offender) is paid for by a given penance. Ethics is principally on this approach about actions and not agents – and above all about those actions that are to be avoided or corrected rather than those that are to be aspired to. Making the penance fit the sin was the confessor's art, and it is perhaps not surprising that such a transactional approach did in due course lend itself to expression in financial terms, as money was exchanged in lieu of any other penalty, and in payment for objectively quantified sins (this was called "commutation"). But there were intellectual developments in the church of the medieval period that offset the concentration of the penitential manuals on actions over agents – especially the revival, following Aristotle, of conceptions of virtue by key figures like Thomas Aquinas. These redressed the balance in favor of the habits that made an agent a *holy* agent.

Social ethics

The social and political roles of the church in this period were remarkably settled. There was no crisis of belief of the kind that confronted the early church (although there were disturbances: the Albigensians, or Cathars, being one ruthlessly suppressed Manichean sect with wide appeal especially in southern France). This stability permitted a more reflective synthesizing of Christian moral commitments, although (we may note in retrospect) the attempt to articulate natural laws and to claim for them a continuity with eternal mandates could often lead to the justification of culturally and historically particular assumptions as though they were timeless. Most church thinkers of the period reinforced a sense of the divine underwriting of a feudal social order. Monarchy in particular was seen as a part of the natural order.

In other areas we find similar concern to legitimate the status quo. The teaching of this period continues, on the whole, to prefer virginity to marriage, and the contemplative to the active life – though this privileging of the religious calling is resolutely coordinated with a vision of the good of the temporal order, as the merits and prayers of the religious are seen to serve the ("supernatural") good of the whole of Christian society. On the subject of sexual difference, we find Aquinas affirming that the image of God is as much woman's as man's, but also claiming that "the good of order would have been wanting in the human family if some were not governed by others wiser than themselves. So by such a kind of subjection woman is naturally subject to man." Here too the church is of its era, appealing to an inherited notion of the natural.

War

Generally the church in this period argued that war could be waged as a necessary evil (here too Augustine's influence remains strong), but in carefully defined circumstances. It must be waged under authority of the sovereign, the cause must be just, and the intention must be rightful (i.e., "the advancement of good, or the avoidance of evil"). Moderation of the traditional Christian hostility to war was one factor that helped permit a prominent feature of the period: the succession of religious Crusades into the Holy Land that were intended to wrest control of those territories in the Eastern Mediterranean from Muslim into Christian hands. These Crusades were given legitimacy by church pronouncements that helped establish a rationale for them not unlike that given to pilgrimage. Crusading expeditions abounded between 1095 and 1464, although from the 1290s onwards enthusiasm for them declined as other ways of spreading the gospel were initiated and commended – for example, the preaching of the friars. They also marked a nadir of relations with the Orthodox

Churches – especially in light of the Fourth Crusade's deliberate targeting of Christian Constantinople (1199–1204).

The Crusades presented unfortunate opportunities too for the vilification and persecution of Jews both at home and abroad. Jews were regularly accused of poisoning water sources, murdering Christian children in blood rituals, profaning the Eucharistic host, and being an insidious force for the corruption of Christian society. Such anti-Judaism in the medieval period was further fueled by the Black Death in 1348–9, for which Jews were widely blamed. Rarely secure for any long period, the great centers of European Jewish life in Spain, France, Germany, and elsewhere gradually disappeared. Many Jews migrated toward Eastern Europe.

Money

Usury – the practice of lending money at interest – continues to be widely condemned (including by Aquinas, who allows that Christians can *pay*, but not charge, usury). Individual ownership of property is defended, for essentially practical reasons, because people are more likely to care for that which is clearly their own to care for, and less likely to argue over it. This plays into a very live debate in the Middle Ages about dominion. In the early fourteenth century, the radical Franciscan ethic of poverty (or non-proprietorship) was countered by a papal move to justify enforceable legal property rights on the basis that rule over the human and non-human creation was part of Christ's perfect humanity. Both sides appealed by analogy to the *divine life* to make their case:

- for the Franciscans, the rejection of all possessions was an *imitatio Christi* (an imitation of Christ);
- for the papal side, Christ was thought to have enjoyed universal and immediate lordship over property in a way that those now "in Christ" could share.

The papal position was to have a significant influence on a subsequent secular tradition of natural rights theory and its exaltation of the proprietary will, but it obscured the teaching that human "lordship" is always to be exercised in the service of God and the neighbor. Aquinas himself kept this concern clearly in mind, for in affirming the right of property, he nonetheless insisted that in its *use* human beings "ought to possess external things, not as [their] own, but as common, so that … [they are] ready to communicate them to others in their need."

The Reformation

Despite the relatively settled state of Christendom in the Middle Ages, there were signs in the early fourteenth century that its organic unity was not unassailable. In the East, the Byzantine Empire struggled against the rise of Islam for several centuries. In the West, the conception of a Holy Roman Empire with perfectly integrated temporal and spiritual realms was challenged by:

- the rising power of individual monarchies and states (whether emerging nation-states like those of France and England, or city-states like those vying with one another in Italy); and
- the fracture in papal authority that followed its years of exile in Avignon (1309–77), during which rival popes were elected for a time.

Spiritual and temporal centers of power themselves competed for political supremacy and there were debates about whether the authority of monarchs needed ratification by ecclesiastical authority or came directly from God (Dante [ca. 1265–1321], amongst others, argued for the latter). There were also early signs in the writings and activity of the Englishman John Wycliffe (1325–84) and the Bohemian John Hus (1372–1415) that papal authority could be challenged on theological grounds. "A man is not bound to believe the sayings of the saints which are apart from Scripture," wrote Hus, "nor should he believe papal bulls, except in so far as they speak out of Scripture." Hus was executed for his views.

In the early sixteenth century the Protestant Reformation brought many of these forms of change and unrest – theological, ecclesiastical, and political – to a decisive head, as large parts of Christendom threw off papal control (and an inherited model of the unity of the Western Church), and with the support and protection of particular monarchs and princes developed theologies with new emphases on the centrality of Scripture and the radical priority of grace in Christian life. Augustine remained a key influence on the architects of the Protestant Reformation as he had been on so much medieval thought, but, as has famously been said, it was as though in the Reformation his theology of grace triumphed over his theology of the church. Concern for the church's unity was subordinated to concern for a scripturally legitimated doctrine of grace. The towering thinkers in this period are Martin Luther (1483–1546) and John Calvin (1509–64), with more "radical" versions of Reformation thought finding expression in the growth of Anabaptist and other groups, and significant responses being stimulated in the Catholic humanist tradition in the work of Erasmus (1466–1536) and Thomas More (1478–1535), as well as in the so-called Counter-Reformation (or Catholic Reformation) initiated at the Council of Trent (1545–63).

The key ethical themes of Reformation thought include the following:

1. *Works and the will.* The Reformation churches insisted on the relative importance of agents over actions in a way even more radical than the virtue ethic of Aquinas had allowed, because the great Reformers were so suspicious of any conception that salvation could be won by external works. Good works, and the moral precepts to which they are accountable, are radically relativized in Reformation theology; the Christian is free from enslavement to such external, objective constraints, and is wholly dependent on (and liberated by) God's grace. Nonetheless, the response of the believer to this prevenient grace might well be a life in which good works abound. This view marked both Lutheran and Calvinist churches. Protestant Christians started to examine

themselves for signs of the regeneration consequent upon election – an election they could not earn. Some have argued that this issued in a new religious intro-spection quite as developed as that fostered by the confessional manuals of the medieval period (though without any practical outlet).

The Anabaptists and certain other strands of the so-called Radical Reformation had in some respects a more activist and optimistic attitude to the will. Many felt that any human being could, if he or she willed to, respond to God, and therefore that baptism must express the conscious choice of the believer. An emphasis upon the inward spirit and its relation to God manifested itself in the seventeenth-century Quakers' intuition-based model of personal and commu-nal moral discernment.

2.   *Social order.* The mainstream Reformers were keen to assert the dignity of secular life, and not to compare it unfavorably with some allegedly more privi-leged vocational sphere where ecclesiastical hierarchy or monasticism could be located and given special honors. They were not, however, social revolutionar-ies, and thought that most people ought to remain true to their social stations and hereditary callings. The sober, even sombre, views about human nature characteristic of Protestant thought meant that the Reformation churches tended to insist that state power had a crucial role in stopping human beings from "devouring" one another. Evil had to be restrained. Both Luther and Calvin opposed the pacifism of the Anabaptists. The opening words of Romans 13 were enormously influential:

> Let every person be subject to the governing authorities; for there is no authority except from God, and those authorities that exist have been instituted by God. Therefore whoever resists authority resists what God has appointed, and those who resist will incur judgment. For rulers are not a terror to good conduct, but to bad. Do you wish to have no fear of the authority? Then do what is good, and you will receive its approval; for it is God's servant for your good. But if you do what is wrong, you should be afraid, for the authority does not bear the sword in vain! It is the servant of God to execute wrath on the wrongdoer. (Romans 13:1–4)

Critics, particularly from the Radical Reformation tradition, have sometimes observed that these words were read by the magisterial Reformers in isolation from the preceding chapter, Romans 12, where Paul develops a more sustained account of the church and calls it not to "be conformed to this world" (Romans 12:2).

3.   *Money.* Luther's condemnation of the peasants' uprising in 1524–5 included the denial that there was any case to be made for the compulsory socialization of goods on the basis of baptism. Calvin too defended the right to own prop-erty, even while emphasizing that property is to be understood as held in trust for God (a doctrine of the stewardship of material things), and to be used to

glorify God. This enables us to draw a contrast between both Luther and Calvin, on the one hand, and the more "communist" Protestant sects of the early Reformation period, on the other. The latter had an interesting later manifestation in the seventeenth-century Digger movement in England. The Diggers went one step further even than their contemporaries the Levellers (who deployed natural law arguments in service of a strongly egalitarian political vision but held off from undermining property rights). The Diggers explicitly sought greater economic equality and the holding of property in common, describing "all the riches of the Earth" as "a Common Stock." The mainstream Reformation churches did not espouse such a radical program. Indeed, while counseling frugality, caution about the excessive enjoyment of material things, and a readiness to bear poverty "peaceably" if required, the new Christian communities they established proved compatible with a certain sort of active entrepreneurialism and economic productivity that some have linked with the growth of capitalism.

The German economist and sociologist Max Weber (1864–1920) developed an influential thesis in his 1905 book *The Protestant Ethic and the Spirit of Capitalism*. Weber coined the term the "Protestant work ethic." He identifies the way the legacy of Calvin made perpetual labor appear to be a sign of a person's membership of the elect. Weber argues that for Catholicism, salvation was guaranteed by the blessing of the clergy and by participation in the sacraments. But Protestants lacked any such assurance. They poured their religious zeal into their labor, but had few appropriate ways of spending their rewards. Purchasing church adornments was demoted by the Protestant emphasis on looking to the Bible alone. Almsgiving to the poor was disdained because the poor should be encouraged to work harder. Personal luxury spoke of greed. Weber cites this culture as fertile soil for the growth of mass production, for industrial staple products suited the emphasis on stylistic understatement. Thus, Weber argues, surplus capital was invested, and capitalism took hold.

The Protestant Reformation inevitably had effects on the thought of Catholics as well as its own adherents. Erasmus of Rotterdam was concerned, against Luther, to retain an understanding of grace in which the will still had genuine freedom, and human reason could still be counted on to discern the good and direct human creatures towards it. Thomas More (above all in his work *Utopia*) attacked many of the corruptions and abuses he saw in his own Catholic Church, but at the same time optimistically and attractively depicted a humanity capable of living in an orderly way with the help of natural law, and not laboring in need of some radical cure (like those being put forward in Protestant doctrines of grace). The Roman Catholic Church's so-called Counter-Reformation asserted itself in the renewed affirmation of the importance of works alongside faith in the salvation of human creatures made by the Council of Trent (1545–63). The Council also reaffirmed the necessity of auricular confession, the church's continued power to absolve through its priests, and its right to grant indulgences. Meanwhile the establishment of the Society of

Jesus, or Jesuit order, by Ignatius of Loyola (1495–1556) spearheaded a rigorous renewal movement within the Roman Catholic Church that sought to deepen and cleanse its life, reinvigorating the missionary impulse of the church and eventually founding universities around the world. The Spanish Jesuit Francisco de Suarez (1548–1617) was Catholicism's most influential theologian during this period, though he remained largely indebted to the thought of Thomas Aquinas.

The Church in Modernity

The origin of modernity can be located any time between 1439, with Gutenberg's adoption of moveable type, and 1789, when the French Revolution occurred; likewise 1520 (and Luther's rebellion against church authority), 1648 (and the end of the Thirty Years' War), or the 1680s (with Newton's creation of modern science) are oft-cited beginnings. Whichever way we date it, certain key intellectual shifts take place in the West as a result of the confluence of Reformation, Renaissance, and Enlightenment ideas, and many of these are the result of new discoveries and historical experiences. Nature, society, and the human self are all reconceived in fundamental ways. Where traditionally God was seen in all of them, and all of them were understood in relation to ideas of God, many thinkers in the modern period bracketed out reference to God and did not feel the bracketing to have any serious consequences – indeed in some ways they regarded the excision of God as an advantage, particularly as a liberation from superstition. While the nation-state was emerging as the key political entity in place of the church, the wars of religion between Protestants and Catholics in Europe were interpreted as a sign of the devastating injuries to human flourishing that certain forms of religious commitment could inflict. This interpretation of religion's dangerous effects on the unity and peace of societies has continued to have wide currency ever since. At the same time, the "New Worlds" being colonized made it possible to experiment with new political and economic forms of life. Together, these changes radically affected the church's place in the world, and its self-understanding.

Key factors in the rise of modern consciousness included the development of mechanistic and mathematicized approaches to knowledge, the search for regular laws and causal explanations, and the exaltation of empirically verifiable knowledge. There was a widespread quest for "clear and distinct" ideas. All of this had an impact on Christian understandings of God's presence and work in creation. Other factors included an increasing historical awareness, drastically enlarged historical and geographical horizons, and a new relativism about the status of time-specific cultural settlements or perceptions of religious, moral, or aesthetic kinds. The biggest impact upon Christianity was perhaps on its attitude to its sacred scripture, the Bible, and how to read it – with a new historical-critical approach accentuating the cultural specificity of Jesus (but often detached from his Jewishness) and questioning the literal truth of many of the miraculous events associated with his life. But there was also a widespread rejection of the authority of tradition and the church. Moreover, greater historical awareness prompted questions about God's goodness in history in relation to suffering and evil.

The church in the modern West has not been able to remain untouched by (or uninterested in) such modern questions – including its descriptions of who and what human beings are, and of how they should act (whether Kantian, Freudian, Darwinian, Marxist, or other). At the same time, it has rarely been able to speak from any privileged platform or with the unequivocal backing of any of the significant political powers of the modern period (despite some vestiges of its former dignity and role), and its voices and perspectives have had to compete for recognition with many others.

Furthermore, the West itself has ceased to be the place where the greatest concentrations of Christians live. The success of the missionary movements in the heyday of European colonial expansion (roughly, 1750–1950) introduced Christianity to new territories, and added new strains of Christianity to places where there had been ancient Christian churches from earliest times (like those in Syria, Ethiopia, and India). One effect has been to engender what is today a thriving and diverse non-European Christianity, in close proximity to other major world religions. This has created new forms of Christian thought and practice. For example, Jesuit missionaries provoked more than one controversy for their tendency to encourage or allow the blending of Christianity with local cultural and religious traditions, such as the veneration of ancestors in China. Sometimes Western Christian ethics has been slow to respond to such traditions, and incorporate their insights.

It is in the modern period that we see the emergence of a self-conscious area of thought called "Christian ethics" (the preferred term in broadly Protestant traditions) alongside a similarly more specialized strand of Roman Catholic thought called "moral theology." Many of the significant individual thinkers who have played their part in articulating Christian moral and ethical ideas in the modern period will be dealt with within that framework. Here we concentrate on a more general outline of what happened in "the church's story," especially as it touches on questions of the great ethical challenges of the modern era.

Reasonableness and Fervor

One of the greatest underlying debates of the eighteenth and nineteenth centuries in the context of Europe and North America was between the "reasonable religion" of figures like Bishop Joseph Butler (1692–1752) of the Church of England, and the piety and zeal of a variety of revival movements including John Wesley's Methodism, the Great Awakenings of the American colonies, and the German Pietism that became a new force within continental Lutheranism from the 1670s onwards. Joseph Butler is an example of how the church responded to the so-called "Age of Reason," and tried to come to terms with a more empiricist and humanist basis for knowledge that avoided any claims about special revelation in particular traditions or to particular individuals.

The religious reactions to this (and other) "reasonable" constructions of Christian religion recovered, in various ways, an emphasis upon the atonement and its effects in the radical transformation of a believer's life. In England the combination of these movements came to be described as the Evangelical Revival, which began in 1737. Leading figures in the North American "Awakenings" included Jonathan Edwards (1703–58); and in England, meanwhile, John Wesley (1703–91) and George Whitefield (1714–70) led the way in fostering a new spiritual and moral discipline in their converts to the new traditions of Methodism. Another spiritual renewal movement, known as Pietism, first took root in Germany in the late seventeenth century and later spread into the state Lutheran churches in Scandinavia. German Pietists such as Philipp Jakob Spener (1635–1705) sought to breathe new life into the established Lutheran church by insisting that religion must descend from the head into the heart. Pietist sermons became more concerned with the devotional life of congregations, and the laity were encouraged to form devotional societies for prayer and study (like the class meetings of Methodism, or – in pre-Reformation times – the oratories). This had a huge effect on German life, both in the church and in wider society. It brought a new enthusiasm for missionary work, for German Pietists (like Methodists) stressed the liberating possibility of overcoming human limitations by the experience of conversion. Due to its emphasis on inner transformation, it has often been criticized as politically and socially quietist – distrusting worldly concerns in the name of inward-looking faith. In its original manifestations, however, it insisted that new life in Christ express itself in works of charity and social benevolence in addition to evangelistic mission. For example, Pietist forefather August Hermann Francke (1663–1727) founded a school for poor children, an orphanage, and a medical clinic.

Revolutions, Global Expansion, and a Plural World

Four dimensions express the Western Church's encounter with a fast-changing world in the modern period.

1. *Industrialization and mission.* In England and Scotland the "dissenting" churches (Methodism foremost among them) proved to be better at responding to the Industrial Revolution than the established churches (the Church of England and the Church of Scotland, respectively) – rapidly and flexibly creating new networks for preaching and pastoral provision. The growth of industry increased the proportion of those who (having moved away from small towns and villages to new urban centers) had little or no contact with church life. It took a while before any systematically effective religious provision was made for them, and the shift was a key stage in the British churches' loss of influence in the nation's imagination and moral thinking. With its parallels elsewhere in Europe, this loss is often identified as a key factor in what has been called "secularization," by which is generally meant the development of social institutions and a shared social imaginary that (either intentionally or by default) exclude Christian reference points and the influence of the churches.

Interestingly, North America's industrialized and urban society continued – and continues even today – to resist the "secularization" thesis, although in its public life it is ideologically committed to refusing social privileges to any particular organized religious group. Paradoxically, at the same time as industrial developments created problems for the churches in their traditional European heartlands, the huge energy and confidence of the newly industrialized societies led to a new missionary energy overseas, which saw Christians working in parallel with the technological advances of the times, inspired by the vision that they would bring an end to want (and, as they saw it, to error) worldwide, and bring in a new and universal well-being.

2. *Mission and the shift away from Western Europe and North America.* As we have seen, Christianity's global numbers and its global spread have increased in the modern period. There are ambiguous aspects to this, not least the link between this growth and the expansion of Western economic and military power. We may also note the insensitive ways in which indigenous churches were often patronized or ignored by missionary churches. Any story told about this spread from a Western point of view would look significantly different if told from a Latin American perspective, or from the vantage point of the Indian subcontinent, or of Japan, China, Africa, or the Middle East. But it has been a positive development that in the wake of the enlarged global presence of Christianity, increasingly numerous Christian voices from the Two-Thirds World have been able to force the Western churches to think harder about the economic and social disadvantages of large parts of the world in comparison with the privileges of the industrialized West. And they have been able to ask what the teachings of Christianity about sin and redemption might have to say about such issues of structural inequality.

Liberation theologies are one of the results of these new perspectives from outside Europe. After the Second Vatican Council (1962–5), also known as Vatican II, the Roman Catholic Church realigned itself in a new openness to popular movements that have actively confronted repressive regimes of both left and right (though it has been cautious about the association of some liberation theologies with Marxism, especially in Latin America). Alongside sharp questions about justice, the growth of non-European Christianity has posed insistent questions about the extent to which Christian life can take new cultural forms – the issue of "inculturation." In worship, preaching, doctrine, and ethics, there has been pressure to accept indigenous expressions of Christian commitment, and after an initial tendency to offer Christianity to non-Europeans in a strictly European idiom, most of the Western churches have become more open to what Pope John Paul II (1920–2005) called "the incarnation of the Gospel in native cultures" and to welcome the introduction of these cultures into the life of the church as a whole.

3. *Ecumenism and other faiths.* Their closer encounters with other traditions of belief and practice as a consequence of missionary expansion – and the benefits of cooperating inter-denominationally in new contexts – also made the various churches work harder to express their unity through ecumenical initiatives. These bore fruit in the establishment of the World Council of Churches (WCC) in 1948, and (important in ethical terms) the inter-denominational body established in 1925 to address issues of "Life and Work" (which paralleled the "Faith and Order" initiative established in 1927). "Life and Work" was concerned to relate the faith of the churches to the society around them.

    Missionary encounters with other traditions of faith also laid the foundations for a new openness to learning from non-Christian religious perspectives on ethics – some of which have gained fresh strength in recent decades in interfaith alliances that have argued for greater protection for the environment, or against abortion. Here too, in Roman Catholicism, Vatican II issued in a new openness in official teaching. Although the WCC remains Protestant-dominated (with some participation from the Eastern Orthodox churches), post-Vatican II Catholicism has been more willing to enter into and to recognize the importance of ecumenical partnerships, and to acknowledge elements of truth in other faiths.

4. *Political and theological liberalism.* The politics of "liberalism" were, for some time afterwards, associated closely with the experience of the horrors of the French Revolution's violent excess. This bred in many nineteenth-century European churchpeople a distrust of any liberal agenda. Such distrust extended to the call for fraternity as well as for liberty and equality, and ensured that emerging socialist movements that asserted the brotherhood of all people against oppressive inherited institutions and systems did not often meet with a ready hearing in the churches. This to some extent changed as the nineteenth century gave way to the twentieth. Even though Marxist forms of socialism have been consistently opposed by Catholic and Protestant churches alike on the grounds of their reductive economic materialism and restriction of the expression of personality (especially noticeable here are a series of papal encyclicals, several of which are discussed in Chapter Nine), the Western church in most of its branches has nonetheless now endorsed the rhetoric of liberty and equality, and has to a significant degree espoused the idea of human rights. Liberalism also came to designate a theological movement with ethical consequences that drew heavily on the new biblical criticism of nineteenth-century Germany to depict a demythologized Jesus whose teaching could speak directly to the concerns of modern humanity with the idea of a universal "brotherhood of man."

There was an end to many received certainties in this time of massive social and intellectual change. Some of the early responses to it in the church's life were quests for certainty that had a conservative flavor: the anti-modernist emphasis on papal authority of the First Vatican Council in 1870, as much, perhaps, as the growth of fundamentalism in the United States in a series of conferences from the 1870s onwards. But many forms of the recovery of tradition released energy for fresh pastoral engagement and valuable social critique too – as in some aspects of the renewal of Catholic liturgical and pastoral practice in the Church of England (which produced a great many parish priests energized for service in deprived areas and with great love of their flocks). A watershed in the twentieth century that represents not so much a grasping for earlier fixity as a creative response to new circumstances was Vatican II – which in 1965 produced a document of great ethical importance called *Gaudium et Spes* (the Pastoral Constitution on the Church in the Modern World). This made strong assertions about the dignity of the human person, linking that dignity to freedom and the social circumstances that made such freedom possible. It continued the Catholic transition to solid support for democratic political systems rather than politically authoritarian ones, supporting, as it did, the idea that "the largest possible number of citizens" should "participate in public affairs with genuine freedom." If the twentieth century in the West has been a century whose politics have been dominated as never before by totalitarian political ideologies on left and right, then the churches – both Catholic and Protestant – have had developed resources to critique and resist such ideologies. For many Christians, including some of its most notable ethical thinkers (like Dietrich Bonhoeffer [1906–45], who lived in Germany under the Third Reich), this resistance has entailed martyrdom.

The past hundred years have seen unprecedentedly rapid changes in what human beings can achieve for good as well as for ill. The possibility of air travel has been followed quickly by the successes (and equally dramatic failures) of space travel. There have been phenomenal advances in medicine and genetic science, opening up thorny new questions in relation to bioethics. New global epidemics, like HIV-AIDS and the SARS virus, have challenged the capacities of modern medicine. Global communications systems have become faster and more sophisticated than could ever have been conceived a few decades ago, creating the conditions for the burgeoning of social media platforms that are transforming the way people relate. It has become possible to make energy with nuclear technology, but the same technology has heralded an era of weapons of mass destruction. There have been terrible wars on a huge scale. There has been continued urbanization at a vast pace and terrible poverty as a consequence. The growing threat of environmental crisis has mocked the confidence of human technologies in managing the effects of industrial expansion. There has been rapid population growth accompanied by mass migrations which nation-states cannot easily manage. Such volatility has been exacerbated by the destabilizing actions of radical movements, like the so-called Islamic State group, which are displacing huge populations while exporting a new strain of fanatical terrorism worldwide.

What the church has been able to say in the face of all these overwhelming developments has often been limited. Its statements have now to compete with many other theories and proposals for action, and it has stood on the margin of many of the most dramatic changes in modern Western history. Individual thinkers of the modern period have continued to make significant contributions to moral and ethical thinking in the nineteenth and twentieth centuries, but the institutional weight of the churches has not been as great as in previous centuries. The complexity of many of the ethical issues of modernity has sometimes made it hard for the churches to pronounce on them with any particularly deep understanding. On the other hand, Christians have retained, on the whole, a clear sense that they know *how* and *why* to value what they value, in a world where imported and often highly artificial efforts to quantify all value in quasieconomic (or "market") terms have been common. This may often mean Christians have more to say when they are at one remove from "applied" moral decision-making (in the area sometimes now called "meta-ethics"), for the Christian ethical tradition equips them here in a way that many non-religious ethicists cannot match. In addition to which – *outside* as well as inside the churches – there is now a widespread distrust of reductively materialist ways of handling moral issues. Science and humanism have not unequivocally delivered the goods their advocates once hoped they would. Christianity may be facing new opportunities to influence issues of economics and the environment, politics, and peace. Its history equips it with a breadth of vision and a depth of critical insight that merit such an influence.

Summary

This chapter has given a broad shape to the story of the church, with a particular emphasis – in looking at the medieval and modern periods – on the *Western* Church, for it is here that the contemporary discipline of Christian ethics has its principal roots. The telling of this story has seen expansions and contractions of the *reach* of the church's influence on Christian lives and their surrounding environment – sometimes focused largely on the home and the congregation; sometimes addressing emperors and presidents, magistrates and generals, economists and scientists. The narrative has also traced expansions and contractions of the *ambition* of the church's teaching – in both domestic and societal settings. Sometimes these ambitions have seemed to challenge or deny the ordinary ways of the world – as in the highly influential practices of monasticism, or the bold experiments of the Radical Reformation. Sometimes they have sought to find ways to harness and transform them through close and sympathetic understanding – as when Thomas Aquinas or Martin Luther gave cooperative advice to Christian princes, or the papal encyclicals of the late nineteenth and twentieth centuries addressed all people of good will. Whether conciliatory or rebarbative, source of blessing or reproof, adopting the stance of priest, ruler, or prophet (and often combining these roles), the church has been a key agent in the world's history – sometimes for good; sometimes for ill. By the way it has sustained and transmitted its practices, it has been both a teller of God's story and an interpreter of the world which it believes is God's possession.

References and Further Reading

For general introductions see J. Philip Wogaman, *Christian Ethics: A Historical Introduction* (Louisville, KY: Westminster/John Knox Press, 1993); and Diarmaid MacCulloch, *Christian History: An Introduction to the Western Tradition* (Peterborough: Epworth, 2006). This chapter is indebted to both for their capable overviews of Christian history (and in Wogaman's case the history of Christian ethics in particular), and both give more detail than is possible in this short chapter. Wogaman is an especially good source on the ethics of the early church. The discussion of the origins of the modern period in this chapter follows Stephen Toulmin's account in his book *Cosmopolis: The Hidden Agenda of Modernity* (New York: Free Press, 1990).

For basic introductions to the history and spread of global Christianity, see Douglas Jacobsen, *The World's Christians: Who They Are, Where They Are, and How They Got There* (Oxford: Wiley-Blackwell, 2011); and Robert Louis Wilken, *The First Thousand Years: A Global History of Christianity* (New Haven, CT: Yale University Press, 2012).

Minority Status

The thought of Celsus and his polemics against the early Christians may be found in Origen's *Contra Celsum* (Boston, MA: Brill, 2001).

Rowan Williams' discussion of ethics in the early church, quoted above, is to be found in his thought-provoking essay, "Making Moral Decisions," which was first delivered to the Lambeth Conference of Anglican bishops in 1998, and is now reproduced in *The Cambridge Companion to Christian Ethics* (Robin Gill, ed.; Cambridge: Cambridge University Press, 2001).

Origen talks of God as the legislator of the law of nature in *Against Celsus* V.37, which can be found in *The Ante-Nicene Fathers* (Alexander Roberts and James Donaldson, eds; Grand Rapids, MI: Eerdmans, 1978–81), vol. 4, pages 559–60.

Tertullian's disapproving comments on pagan culture are from his *Apology*, chapter 38, in *The Ante-Nicene Fathers*, vol. 3, pages 45–6.

Henry Chadwick's exploration of the early church's relationship to the state is drawn from *The Early Church* (Harmondsworth: Penguin, 1967), page 69; and the first part of this chapter is indebted to that book more widely as well.

The quotation about Christians' true citizenship is from the *Letter to Diognetus*, also known as *The Epistle of Mathetes to Diognetus*, which may be found at www.earlychristianwritings.com/text/diognetus-roberts.html; a portion of this letter is also contained in the corresponding chapter of *Christian Ethics: An Introductory Reader*.

The *Didache's* comment about sharing possessions in common is from *Didache* 4.12; see www.earlychristianwritings.com/text/didache-roberts.html.

In the discussion on the early church and money, Justin Martyr's *First Apology* is quoted, which can be found in *Early Christian Fathers* (Cyril C. Richardson, ed.; New York: Macmillan, 1970); and the discussion of Clement of Alexandria is based on *Who is the Rich Man That Shall Be Saved?* XI–XV, available at www.earlychristianwritings. com/text/clement-richman.html.

On slavery, Ignatius of Antioch's remarks can be found in his *Letter to Polycarp* 4.2. The same letter is the source of the quotation dealing with chastity (*Letter to Polycarp* 5.1–2). Available online at www.ccel.org/ccel/schaff/anf01.v.viii.iv.html.

John Chrysostom's views on women and marriage are taken from *Homily XX (On Ephesians)*, where we find his discussion of Ephesians 5:22–4. See www.ccel.org/ccel/schaff/npnf113.iii.iv.xxi. html.

Clement's remark on sobriety among women is from his *Paedagogus (The Instructor)*, 3:2, in *The Ante-Nicene Fathers*, vol. 2, page 272; Augustine commends orderliness and decency in *Letter 262* in Augustine, *Letters 211–270* (John E. Rotelle, ed.; Hyde Park, NY: New City Press, 2005), pages 203–8.

Athanasius' account of the desert monk Antony's life is in his *The Life of Antony* (London: SPCK, 1980). The specific quotations are from pages 31–6, 66, and 69. A valuable source on monastic practice in the early church is Derwas J. Chitty, *The Desert a City* (New York: St. Vladimir's Seminary Press, 1966), though this should be supplemented by Peter Brown's *The Body and Society*, mentioned below.

Peter Brown's magnificent study of attitudes to the body in early Christianity, and the relation of these attitudes to their Hellenistic context, can be found in *The Body and Society: Men, Women, and Sexual Renunciation in Early Christianity* (2nd edn; New York: Columbia University Press, 2008). This book can be supplemented by four other works by Peter Brown: *Augustine of Hippo: A Biography* (Berkeley, CA: University of California Press, 1967, 2000); *Society and the Holy in Late Antiquity* (London: Faber and Faber, 1982); *The Rise of Western Christendom* (2nd edn; Oxford: Blackwell, 2003); and *Poverty and Leadership in the Later Roman Empire* (Waltham, MA: Brandeis University Press, 2002).

On early urban Christianity, see Wayne Meeks, *The First Urban Christians: The Social World of the Apostle Paul* (2nd edn; New Haven, CT: Yale University Press, 2003).

The following works are quoted in the corresponding chapter of *Christian Ethics: An Introductory Reader.*

- *The Epistle to Diognetus* (cited above).
- Perpetua, "Martyrdom of Perpetua." From *In Her Words: Women's Writings in the History of Christian Thought*. Amy Oden, ed. Nashville, TN: Abingdon Press, 1994. [Also available at www.newadvent.org/fathers/0324.htm]
- Clement of Alexandria, *Who is the Rich Man That Shall be Saved?* (cited above).

Christendom

Thomas Aquinas' claim about "the good of order" is from *Summa Theologica* (5 vols; Notre Dame, IN: Christian Classics, 1948), Prima Pars [First Part], Question 92, Article 1; also available at www.ccel. org/ccel/aquinas/summa.html. Aquinas on the right of property can be found in *Summa Theologica*, Secunda Secundae [Second Part of the Second Part], Question 66, Article 2.

John Hus writes on papal authority in *The Church* (Westport, CT: Greenwood Press, 1915, 1974), page 71.

The following works are quoted in the corresponding chapter of *Christian Ethics: An Introductory Reader.*

- Eusebius of Caesarea. "A Speech on the Dedication of the Holy Sepulchre Church." Pages 58–65 in *From Irenaeus to Grotius: A Sourcebook in Christian Political Thought 100–1625.* Oliver O'Donovan and Joan Lockwood O'Donovan, eds. Translation adapted from E. C. Richardson, *Nicene and Post-Nicene Fathers.* Grand Rapids, MI: Eerdmans, 1999.

- *The Rule of St. Benedict.* Caroline White, trans. New York: Penguin Books, 2008. [Available online in multiple versions at www.osb.org/rb/.]

- John Howard Yoder. *The Priestly Kingdom.* Notre Dame, IN: University of Notre Dame Press, 1984.

Modernity

Pope John Paul II's definition of inculturation can be found in the 1985 papal encyclical *Slavorum Apostoli*, §21; see www.vatican.va/holy_father/ john_paul_ii/encyclicals/documents/hf_jp-ii_ enc_19850602_slavorum-apostoli_en.html

The following works are quoted in the corresponding chapter of *Christian Ethics: An Introductory Reader*:

- Ernst Troeltsch. *The Social Teaching of the Christian Churches.* Vol. 1. Olive Wyon, trans. New York: Macmillan Company, 1931.
- H. Richard Niebuhr. *Christ and Culture.* New York: HarperCollins, 1951, 2001.

Chapter Three
The Story of Ethics

Philosophical Ethics

The story of ethics is widely assumed to begin in the classical Greek era around the fourth and fifth centuries BCE. This is not to say that significant moral reflection did not take place elsewhere at this time or even earlier. For example, Confucius, the influential Chinese moral philosopher, was born around 551 BCE. Nor is it to ignore that the Greek tradition is taken by many to have its roots in African Egyptian thought. Nonetheless the Western tradition, within which Christian ethics was to take its place, is generally acknowledged to begin in Athens in the fifth century BCE. From the fourth century CE onwards, with the advent of the Christian Empire, moral philosophy and theology can be said to dovetail in most respects. But with the coming of modernity from the seventeenth century onwards and the onset of the set of developments subsequently called the Enlightenment, there begins to be a decisive parting of the ways, and recent centuries have seen the story of philosophical ethics emerge as separate from, and sometimes in specific opposition to, the story of Christian ethics.

Plato

Plato and Aristotle were not the first Greek philosophers. The earliest figure whose work is still discussed today is Thales of Miletus, who was born in 640 BCE. But Plato and Aristotle are the two giants of classical philosophy. It is vital to grasp the heart of their respective programs and the significance of their differences.

Plato (428–348 BCE) was an Athenian aristocrat inspired by the wisdom, character, and courage of Socrates, who was put to death in Athens in 399 BCE, accused of corrupting the city's youth and interfering with civic religion. Plato's early

Introducing Christian Ethics, Second Edition. Samuel Wells and Ben Quash with Rebekah Eklund.
© 2017 John Wiley & Sons Ltd. Published 2017 by John Wiley & Sons Ltd.

works (*Euthyphro* and *Crito*) center on dialogues between Socrates and his conversation partners, in which Socrates asks a series of questions that dismantle widely assumed notions about human life, society, and the gods. In *Euthyphro*, Socrates denies that moral rectitude lies in pleasing the gods, because he instead assumes that "the good" has its origin outside the whim of the gods. In *Crito*, while awaiting his execution Socrates discusses the morality of escaping his imprisonment, and concludes that no citizen should evade the laws of the state even when those laws have been unfairly applied.

Ethics is at the heart of Plato's philosophy. His parable of the cave illustrates this well. In *The Republic*, Socrates describes the experience of being in a deep cave, one that slopes downhill. Near the bottom of the cave is a group of people. The people are facing the back wall of the cave at its deepest point. Above and behind them, nearer the cave entrance, is a fire, which provides all the light in the cave. Between the people's backs and the fire is a puppeteer. The puppeteer moves around puppets depicting animals, plants, and other things, and these shadow images are reflected on the back wall, which becomes like a cinema screen. This is the only reality the people in the cave know. Things change if and when a person leaves the cave. The person is initially blinded by the sun, but quickly realizes the new world is more real than the old one. But if the same person returns to the cave, he or she may be dismissed by the cave-dwellers as blind because he or she can no longer see the reflections as well as before. Plato's concern is to train people not to be overwhelmed by the unreality of the material world. To see the real requires a transformation of the self – like leaving the cave.

Plato argued that the world as it is apparent to the human senses – the realm of the "many" – is transitory. Being thus subject to change, and liable to pass away, it is not the location of fundamental reality. The fundamental realm is the level where things are eternal and unchangeable. This higher realm is the level of *essence* or "being." It contrasts with the lower realm, which is the realm of *existence* or "becoming." Every earthly creature or object is an inadequately realized manifestation of its *form*, or ideal. Goodness means correspondence to the appropriate form. The gap between a particular cat and the ideal of catness, or between a particular tree and the ideal of treeness, is called evil. Philosophy is the quest for an understanding of the ideal forms. Because humans are inherently intellectual beings – this is what distinguishes them from the other animals – goodness for humans means contemplating the forms and thus discerning the nature of being.

Plato's Socratic dialogues are directed towards describing and realizing virtue. In his *Republic* Plato establishes what would later be called the four cardinal virtues. He begins by distinguishing between the rational and the passionate parts of the human soul.

- The *rational* aspect enables a person to apprehend truth and perceive goodness: to do this a person requires the virtue of wisdom.
- The *passionate* aspect can itself be subdivided between the *spirited* dimension and the *sensuous* dimension.

- The spirited dimension refers to the will: and this evokes the virtue of courage.
- The sensuous dimension refers to desire: and this evokes the virtue of temperance.
- For Plato there is an ideal state of being that displays a hierarchy: reason governs spirit, which in turn governs desire; this good order discloses the fourth virtue, that of justice.

Plato discusses the origin and nature of evil actions in the light of his conclusions about virtue. Evil arises when humans fail to realize their humanness – and their humanness means a just pattern of wisdom, courage, and temperance. When the soul is disordered, evil arises because desire and will and reason are out of correct relation to one another. Plato regards evil as inherently unreasonable – that is, something one could never intend if wisdom were appropriately governing one's will and desire.

The ultimate goal of philosophy is knowledge of the form of the good – a knowledge that is not within everyone's reach. This profoundly affects Plato's view of politics. The correct hierarchy of virtues in society reflects the ordering of virtues in the human person. Thus the rational persons should be the legislators, who should be wise; the spirited ones should be the soldiers and teachers, who should be courageous; and the sensuous ones should be given over to commerce and material provision – these should be temperate. The result of appropriate contributions of each class to the social good should be justice. Character, aptitude, and interest thus determine class. Plato assumes that ethics requires politics – there is no morality that does not presuppose a corresponding social order.

Aristotle

Plato's pupil Aristotle (384–323 BCE) is perhaps the key figure in pre-Christian ethics. Aristotle based his philosophy on four causes – material, efficient, formal, and final. These may be illustrated in relation to a statue.

- The material cause is the substance out of which the statue is made (bronze).
- The efficient cause is the force which brings the statue about (the chisel or sculptor).
- The formal cause is the shape into which the statue is made (a leader riding a horse).
- The final cause is the purpose for which the statue is made (the decoration of the square, or the glorification of the model).

For Aristotle, the forms were not ideals, but specific objects accessible to sense experience. For him, the key distinction was not between ephemeral existence and eternal essence, but between actual form and material potential. The actuality of an object is what that object has if its potential is realized: a poppy seed has the potential to become a flower. A lump of bronze has the potential to become a statue. Matter is that which has potential to become actual. The lump of bronze is material – it is unrealized matter. The statue is actual – it has realized its actuality. Thus, whereas Plato's philosophy focuses on the ideal, Aristotle's focuses on the actual.

Life is therefore about realizing actuality – reaching one's full potential. And one's full potential is happiness. Happiness is more than pleasure, which animals can share, and more than honor, which says more about the bestower than the recipient. Happiness is worth pursuing for its own sake – unlike money-making – and is satisfying in itself. It is not a state but an activity – either following a moral principle or perceiving one, in other words either doing or thinking. *Thinking*, which Aristotle calls contemplation or theoretical wisdom, is superior to *doing*, which he calls practical wisdom. The life of contemplation is therefore the highest human activity, in which humans imitate the gods and indeed become immortal by fulfilling their true potential. Most attention is given today to Aristotle's *Nicomachean Ethics*, but in his *Eudemian Ethics* he suggests that the chief end of human life is "to serve and contemplate God."

The moral life – the life of practical wisdom – has thus a secondary place. But it is nonetheless a source of well-being. It is a healthy recognition that humans are bodies and not just minds. And it makes the life of contemplation possible: the good legislator brings about the material and political conditions for theoretical wisdom, and the strong character by subduing the passions brings about the personal conditions for such happy reflection.

Aristotle's understanding of the shape of the moral life is provided by his discussion of virtue. Virtue shapes the moral life because it enables the human person to realize his or her actuality. Again he is more interested in activity than static being. Thus, virtue is acquired by pursuing activities that avoid excess and defect, and by pursuing pleasure in appropriate moderation. Good actions produce good habits; good habits and moral training create good dispositions; virtue names the ways good habits become inscribed on a person's character. Aristotle's understanding of virtue is that it is a state of character (and thus the will) determined by a rational principle (and thus the intellect) that lies in a mean. For example, courage is a mean between recklessness (or the enjoyment of danger for danger's sake) and cowardice; temperance is a mean between the self-indulgent and the numb (i.e., those who are insensible, or deficient with regard to pleasure). Aristotle looks closely at justice, which is the sum of all virtue. Justice comes in two kinds: distributive justice, which ensures each citizen has his or her due, and rectifying justice, which is concerned not with punishment but the restoration by the perpetrator of what the victim has lost. Aristotle also considers reciprocal justice. This accommodates inequalities in commercial exchange by introducing the notion of money.

For Aristotle, ethics is simply part of politics. Humans are political animals, who can realize their potential only in communal settings. Thus, his idea of the state is as an inherently moral project, oriented that its members live well and thus happily. Aristotle's thought plays a key role in ecclesial ethics, which will be explored in depth in Chapter Seven.

Epicureans and Stoics

Two other Greek traditions are essential to note. Epicurus (340–270 BCE) rejected Plato's pursuit of ideal knowledge and Aristotle's quest for the realization of potential. He excluded any consideration of a divine element in human behavior. He concentrated entirely on material reality. There had been no creation and there would be no final destiny: there were only atoms that combined and separated to shape every object and event. This is known as atomic materialism. There was nothing to fear in death, because for those that exist there is no death, and for those that are dead there is no existence.

Unlike Aristotle's rejection of pleasure in favor of happiness, a notion more oriented to final fulfillment, Epicurus had no hesitation in asserting that the highest good was pleasure. The Greek philosopher Aristippus (435–356 BCE), a pupil of Socrates, argued that the only genuine pleasure was the satisfaction of the appetites in the present – for neither remembering past pleasures nor anticipating future ones was truly real. Epicurus accepted Aristippus' emphasis on pleasure, but concentrated on duration rather than intensity. For Epicurus, the height of pleasure was the calm serenity that abides when the soul is at peace. It is very important to distinguish between Epicurus' notion of pleasure and the sensual indulgence that has become associated with his name in later times. Pleasure for Epicurus meant the absence of pain in the body and trouble in the mind. Since gratifying the appetites in the present tended to make for pain in the future, Epicurus encouraged his followers to avoid sensuality. Falling in love and sexual exchange are too disturbing to peace to be entertained, and even politics is best avoided. It is best to live unseen. Virtue is worth pursuing because it helps to avoid circumstances that could involve pain or discomfort.

Stoicism also traced its roots back to Socrates through his pupil Antisthenes (444–365 BCE), who highlighted his master's dutiful self-possession in even the most trying circumstances. Stoicism sought a way of life that steered between the extremes of complete freedom and complete determinism. Its adherents sought to develop a will that was in accord with nature, and thus free of destructive emotions. From 301 BCE Zeno of Citium (333–264 BCE) began to teach in the *stoa poikile* (painted walkway or portico), and in due course Stoicism became the most influential moral philosophy among the Greco-Roman ruling classes. It was thus the soil, in addition to Judaism, in which early Christian ethics grew. The notion of *apatheia* was very significant: this is a state of mind where one becomes indifferent to what is out of one's control (health, reputation, love, death, and so on). After the high ideals of the Roman Republic had been displaced by the bureaucratic pragmatism of the Roman Empire, Stoicism became the definitive way for respectable office holders to describe and conceive of their lives. It became a noble internal politics in an era when external politics was becoming increasingly disreputable.

The biggest difference between Epicureanism and Stoicism is that God is very significant in Stoicism. For the Stoics, God is omnipresent and settles the destiny of all things. Fate and providence are therefore identical. The place of humankind is to assent to the all-pervasive will of God, which is also known as nature and sometimes as the *logos*. Human beings flourish by bringing their will into alignment with God's will. Virtue is the practice of doing so. Virtue is knowledge of God's will (vice is ignorance of God's will), and nothing else matters. Nonetheless, some things that do not matter are still worth seeking, like beauty, health, and honor. Stoics concentrate only on that which is in their power, and that means giving their assent to God's will. This means that, while they have a positive view of feeling, they shun any emotion that may distort truth by opening them up to pain: in the face of even the greatest suffering, they must be able to say that this is the will of God. Ethics is the highest branch of philosophy, and must be pursued with ascetic discipline, including contemplation of death. Because all people derive from the same universal spirit they should show filial love toward one another across conventional boundaries of class and ethnicity. Even slaves are to be treated well. Thus in Stoicism lies the root of ideas such as universal reason and natural law, two key themes whose significance we shall explore in more detail in Chapter Five.

Plotinus

The last great Greek philosopher, Plotinus (ca. 204–70 CE), bookends the classical era by returning to the concerns of Plato seven centuries earlier. Plotinus is the most prominent exponent of an era now commonly known as Neoplatonism – a development of Plato's thought that was influential on early Christian theologians, particularly Augustine. The tendency in Neoplatonic thought is to take Plato's theory of the forms in a more mystical direction. In other words, for Plotinus and others the bodily world of sense experience, the realm of becoming, is thoroughly secondary to the realm of being, of eternal forms. Whereas Plato saw evil as no more than the privation of the good, Plotinus often spoke of matter in general and the body in particular as though they were evil in themselves. Whereas Plato had believed human thought could ascend from particularity to more and more abstract notions, and thus by stages attain an understanding of the real, for Plotinus there is a significant duality between matter and the ideal (or form) of goodness.

At the heart of all things for Plotinus is the One, a concept beyond description and indeed beyond being. From the One proceed emanations, first of all Mind (like Plato's forms), secondarily Soul (both the life force in general and the individual soul in particular), and finally Matter (which has no form). Humans are poised between soul and matter, and the yearning of their souls inclines them toward their true fulfillment in the One. The goal of human life is to return to the One, through detachment from the body, transcendence of the intellect, and cultivation of the soul.

Plotinus affirmed the tradition of the virtues, endorsing Plato's four cardinal virtues. However, because the virtues shaped the complex life of the body, they were of secondary interest to the "simple" life of the soul. Living a good life in society is not the principal aim: instead, life is a quest for the soul to become divine. The legacy of Plotinus to Christian ethics is evident wherever the interior life is prized above social interaction, and wherever the body is distinguished from the soul and seen as of less worth than, even a hindrance to, the soul's flourishing.

Religious Ethics

We have seen that Christian ethics emerges in relation to an existing and ongoing tradition of philosophical ethics. We now suggest that Christian ethics takes shape alongside and in a significant degree in the context of the developing ethics of the different world religions. Before considering the specific ethics of these major traditions, it is worth pausing to assess the competing judgments concerning how these traditions might interact with one another and with the discipline of ethics.

- In the first place there is the disputed notion of religion itself. In its mild form this is an attempt at a descriptive, sociological term that seeks to bring together all aspects of global society that involve such typical indicators as ritual, notions of divinity, worship, doctrine, faith, devotion, and so on. There is room for significant variety but there appear to be broad similarities in terms of observable behavior and central texts. However, this mild form sometimes narrows to a stricter definition of religion, which seeks to articulate and identify common denominators of religion and then use such a normative model as a way of assessing and quantifying religions new and old. This can yield sweeping generalizations such as "all wars stem from religion."

  In response to such reductionism, it is common for members of particular traditions to note that such a notion of religion comes from secular observation and is not internal to any of the specific traditions. There has sometimes been a tendency for Christianity to be seen as a template onto which other traditions are mapped; this pattern has been opposed not only by many from other traditions, but also by some from within Christianity who have objected to the tendency to reduce Christian doctrines and ethics down to simpler, transferable categories.

- Another set of approaches regards religion as being more or less identical with ethics. In its mild form this recognizes the practical aspect of the major traditions of faith, and the reality that the founders of many of the great world traditions were themselves historical figures with pressing personal and political issues to address. It has more than one extreme form. One would be the tendency within some traditions to suggest that those without faith and religious conviction cannot exhibit or embody goodness, virtue, or right living. This would be to say without religion, there can be no ethics.

An alternative extreme would be to say that there is nothing that can be said within the tradition of a religion that could not be said as well or better by a broadly based, largely philosophical ethic. In other words, this view assumes that there is something fundamental that can be called ethics of which the different religious traditions are but varied exemplifications. This appears to rest on a rather narrow definition of religion, shrunk to fit a notion of ethics that is slow to name its own provenance and assumed story. Such a view sometimes presents itself, as in the case of Immanuel Kant (1724–1804), as a rational solution to the problems created by irrational religion. Kant will be studied in detail in Chapter Five.

- Another more pragmatic approach seeks to find common ground among the various ethical traditions in order to address pressing social issues. In this view, the matter at hand is so urgent that it requires all religious traditions to marshal their respective resources and together bring them to bear in order to effect change. For example, in his 2015 encyclical *Laudato Si'* (On Care For Our Common Home), Pope Francis called for the religions of the international community to engage in dialogue with one another and with the sciences to address the serious problem of climate change and environmental degradation. Other recent efforts have focused on human rights, violent conflict, and global migration.

Religious ethics is thus a much-disputed discipline. Even if no presuppositions are made about the priority of a notion of "religion" or "ethics" before embarking on such a study, for a full understanding of Christian ethics some understanding of ethics as understood in other major faith traditions is essential. It may be helpful to distinguish between the so-called Abrahamic faiths, those arising in the Indian subcontinent, and those arising elsewhere.

The Abrahamic Faiths

One could call Judaism and Christianity siblings (perhaps the latter a prodigal son and the former an elder brother); and one might call Islam and Christianity cousins. Whatever their filial relationship, the ethics of the three Abrahamic faiths are relatively easy to set alongside each other, because they share significant common assumptions. By contrast the other major world traditions share fewer, if any, common assumptions with Christianity.

Jewish ethics
Two themes stand out in Jewish ethics.

- The heart of Jewish ethics lies in the *covenant* between God and Israel, definitively established on Mt. Sinai and narrated in the book of Exodus. The covenant is the way God demonstrates holiness and Israel becomes holy. Israel inhabits the abundant life of God, enjoys the freedom of God's service, and shows its gratitude for its deliverance from slavery by guarding and keeping the commandments. These commandments concern relationships both between human beings and between God and Israel. They seldom differentiate explicitly between ritual and ethical actions. For example, Deuteronomy 24:19 says, "When you reap your harvest in your field and forget a sheaf in the field, you shall not go back to get it; it shall be left for the alien, the orphan, and the widow, so that the LORD your God may bless you in all your undertakings." This ties ethics to worship. Adhering to the commandments is inseparable from the liturgical and ritual recitation of them ("Oh, how I love your law! It is my meditation all day long" Ps 119:97).

The emphasis on law reflects the desire to embody moral ideals in the life of a community and to expect adherence of each member. A particular emphasis of the covenant tradition is the significance of mercy and justice for the widow, the orphan, and the sojourner. The way Israel shows its gratitude to God for delivering it from Egypt is in the way it treats those who are figuratively still in Egypt. The process of bringing controversies before a priest or a judge (Deut 17) led to the evolution of a vast series of recorded wisdom and decisions encoded from 200 to 500 CE in the *Mishnah* and the *Gemara* (which is a commentary on the *Mishnah*), as we described in Chapter One.

This tradition of recorded wisdom arose in earnest after the destruction of the Second Temple in 70 CE. This catastrophic event shifted the location of worship from Jerusalem to the local synagogue and of authority from priest to rabbi. Whereas priestly authority had been rooted in prayer and sacrifice, rabbinic authority rested in the interpretation of texts. The rabbis introduced the concept of precedent, recorded their proceedings (including minority opinions), and made reason the principal instrument for legislation. Thus, they made Judaism into something it had not been before. This is a transformation generally lost on Christians, who tend to ignore the degree to which Judaism has changed since gospel times. With the exception of the Reform movement (which, as the name denotes, embodies a radical departure from traditional Judaism), the importance of rabbinic literature far outweighs that of biblical in Jewish ethics.

- Set alongside the covenant tradition is the *creation* tradition. It is primarily found in Genesis, but recurs elsewhere: "The heavens are telling the glory of God; and the firmament proclaims his handiwork" (Ps 19:1). A key aspect of this creation dimension is Genesis 1:27: "God created humankind in his image." This gives rise to the notion of the sanctity of the life of every human being. There is also a strong tradition that "whatever was created in the first six days requires further preparation" (*Genesis Rabbah* 11:3): in addition to requiring male circumcision, this opens the way to medical intervention, certain forms of contraception, and a general orientation toward actively preserving life. Judaism's sense of the human (and Jewish) task is explicitly interventionist. God creates people for the task of completing creation.

In addition the description of each moment of creation as *tov* ("mighty fine") encourages a perception of the material world as good, a general absence of the dualistic assumption sometimes found in Christian ethics that spirit is superior to matter, and a continued emphasis on land as essential to salvation. The creation and covenant traditions come together in the Ten Commandments, which are both a covenant and a new creation, in the sense that they create a people and an everlasting relationship with God.

Two other traditions require attention. One is the *prophetic* tradition. The prophets such as Hosea, Amos, and Micah called people back to the terms of the covenant, and in particular its dimension of social justice. A second is the *wisdom* tradition. Centering on the book of Proverbs, the wisdom writers develop themes in the creation tradition that elicit guidance for life from the pattern of God's ways. Each of these traditions has been influential in Christian ethics.

From the medieval period onwards, Jewish "ethics" began to emerge as Judaism interacted with other ethical lines of thought, notably classical philosophy and Christianity. Moses Maimonides (1138–1204) sought to uphold Aristotle's golden mean but he continued to assume inter-human relationships are dependent on divine–human ones. Maimonides' *Mishneh Torah* gathered together all the binding laws from the Talmud with the judgments of the early medieval Jewish scholars. Joseph Karo (1488–1575) also became immensely influential. His *Shulchan Arukh* (Prepared Table) was a short digest that listed what a Jew should do in every circumstance of life. Its publication coincided with the arrival of the printing press and this helped bring it to wide attention.

Since Kant, with his hugely influential emphasis on universal (or universalizable) principles (see Chapter Five), Jewish ethics has been divided on whether it should stress or soften its particularistic emphasis. But other developments, notably Hasidism (beginning in the eighteenth century) with its mystical, pietistic fusion of the divine–human and inter-human relationship, offer a rich tradition for reshaping understandings of law, covenant, creation, and holiness.

Muslim ethics

Muslim ethics centers on, but is not limited to, the Qur'an, which began to be read in the late seventh century CE. The Qur'an urges its readers to live good lives, but generally assumes the readers already know what the good is. There is no notion of original sin, unlike the Augustinian Christianity to be explored in Chapter Four: human beings, through reasoning and reflection, can discern the good. The Qur'an calls on them to do exactly that, and give God the obedience that God is owed. This is a matter for individuals: the day of judgment will be an accounting of agents, not peoples. Perhaps the most significant general feature of Islamic ethics is the paradox that Muslims are enjoined to act well but are seldom instructed specifically in what the good life entails, besides the basic binding duties of the five pillars, described below.

The Qur'an does not distinguish between doctrine and ethics. On the one hand there are instructions toward charity and justice, with associated eternal rewards; there are encouragements to give money to family, orphans, the poor, the prisoner, and the beggar, and to trade fairly; there are expectations about promise-keeping, endurance in times of trial, and humility; and there are injunctions against disposing unwanted children, wasting goods, adultery, and unwarranted killing. On the other hand there are accounts of the nature of God and worship. But these are not distinguished from one another.

A Muslim's minimal religious duties (the "five pillars") are as follows:

- faith in one God;
- worship five times a day;
- fasting during the month of Ramadan;
- almsgiving;
- at least one pilgrimage to Mecca.

Whether the additional duty of *jihad* means outer warfare or inner struggle is highly controversial.

Islam as a whole stresses adherence to the *Shari'a* (law), but this law is not restricted to the Qur'an. Additional sources of Muslim ethics include the *sunna* (practice) of Mohammed. The Prophet's example of good character is highly regarded, and the *hadith* record accounts of his actions and remarks on a range of subjects. A third source of authority is the *ijma* – the community consensus – and a fourth is *qiyas* or analogy. The latter largely refers to teachings emerging in the earliest centuries of the Muslim era.

While *Shari'a* is translated as "law" in European languages thanks to the colonial encounter between the West and Islam, *Shari'a* is actually a system of ethical doctrines and practical elaborations. The major doctrinal divide is between those who espouse the stance that something is good or bad because revelation says so, and those who argue that good and bad are determined by reason. (See Chapter Five for a similar distinction in Christian ethics.) The latter is largely a Shi'a position, the former a Sunni position – although Sunnis argue that reason confirms divine assessments of good and bad.

Social historians have sometimes highlighted the significance of the nomadic culture into which Islam came. This brought with it a deep emphasis on hospitality, together with warrior virtues of courage, honor, endurance, and loyalty to the tribe – virtues that were largely incorporated into Islamic culture. For example, polygamy, slavery, and warfare are all taken for granted by the Qur'an, but are placed within a framework of Muslim observance. Many Muslims, however, would dispute this socio-cultural reading of Muslim ethics.

Islamic ethics are not monolithic: there is significant variation among the four Sunni schools and the Shi'a school. Sufism, a more mystical branch of Islam, introduces an emphasis on the inner life rather than on outer conformity, highlighting a tension common in Christian ethics. There has also always been considerable variation in patterns of assimilation of external thought, whether classical (Aristotle reached the West through Muslim translators) or Enlightenment (modernists distinguished between the Qur'an's eternal truths and its cultural conditions).

Perhaps the most important factor in contemporary Islam is the rise of fundamentalism, which in its Shi'a form has tended toward political revolution and the introduction of *Shari'a* as national law. Sunni fundamentalism can be revolutionary but can also be highly conservative. The tendency in both cases is to reject the culture of modernity in general and the West in particular.

Ethics Beyond the Abrahamic Faiths

While Hinduism, Buddhism, and indigenous religions, including those originating in Africa, China, and among the native peoples of North America, have an important and increasingly valued part to play in contemporary ethical discourse, it is important to recognize that they have a much smaller part to play in the story of Christian ethics because they do not share many of the foundations Christianity shares with Judaism and to a large extent with Islam, and because the cultural exchange brought about in the colonial era came after the Catholic, Orthodox, and Protestant fault-lines of Christian ethics had been well set. Interaction with non-Abrahamic religions also raises the question of whether to speak of "ethics" means to map onto such traditions a structure that sits uneasily at best. It may be that "ethics" is an ancient Greek philosophical notion that must be applied with caution to specific religious traditions.

Another issue raised by so-called comparative religious ethics is the degree to which the discussion is governed by texts. For example, African religious traditions are unquestionably extensive, ancient, and diverse, and undoubtedly have substantial ethical dimensions, but bringing those dimensions into conversation with other global traditions is problematic. While there are written historical texts, scholars from Western backgrounds have not always been quick to engage with these traditions on a textual level. Some have generalized about an African moral outlook as concerned with such qualities as truthfulness, industry, moderation, generosity, patience, and respect for elders and community, but here the work is closer to anthropology than to ethics as generally understood in the academy.

Christianity has profound roots in Africa and Asia, as we saw in Chapter Two. But at this point it is time to identify the non-Christian Asian and especially South Asian traditions that have come to be the most visible dialogue partners for Christianity.

- Hinduism broadly recognizes four principal goals of life:
  - *Dharma* represents righteousness, duty, and moral and social laws. *Dharma* comes first, indicating that the other three goals cannot be fulfilled without fulfilling the obligations of *dharma*.
  - *Artha* refers to the honest acquisition of wealth or worldly property. It is needed to maintain one's own physical body and to satisfy the needs of the family and other dependants.

- *Kama* means desire and pleasure within the limits of *dharma*. This is to satisfy the mind and intellect.
- To satisfy the soul, one must attain liberation (*moksha*) from the cycle of birth and death, known as *samsara*, by achieving union with God. *Moksha* is the final goal of life. Different schools of philosophy provide different paths to achieving *moksha*. These are devotion and surrender to God, self-less work, true knowledge, or meditation.

In contemporary Christian ethics, Hinduism is admired for its tolerance, with its respect for considerable diversity of thought and practice. Through the influential practice of Mohandas (Mahatma) Gandhi (1869–1948) it is seen as offering a model of nonviolence. And through its reverence for life, particularly the life of animals and plants, it has been seen as an example in ecological discussions.

- Jainism arose in India in the sixth century BCE. It takes its name from the conquerors who have reached spiritual perfection. Escaping the wheel of rebirth is achieved by following five principles – nonviolence (*ahimsa*), truthfulness, not stealing, non-possessiveness, and chastity. The term *ahimsa* was very influential on Mahatma Gandhi. It means protecting all living beings from harm. In other words Jains extend nonviolence from living beings to soil, sand, oceans, fires, insects, microbes, and plants. They are fruitarians – they eat only fruit, milk, and nuts, which are acceptable because they are not living beings but only by-products of living beings.
- The heart of Buddhism lies in four basic insights into the human condition that dawned upon Siddhartha Gautama (the Buddha, ca. 560–ca. 483 BCE) in the course of attaining enlightenment (*nirvana*). The first of these so-called Four Noble Truths is that all existence is suffering. In the fourth Noble Truth, the Buddha lays down the Noble Eightfold Path as the way out of this suffering. The Noble Eightfold Path is a set of guidelines for ethical conduct that cultivate the virtues of wisdom and compassion. They range from the practice of meditation to precepts against lies, slander, harsh words, idle chatter, taking life, and stealing, and against trade in weapons or living beings (slavery, butchery, or prostitution). In adhering to the first five of the 227 precepts, Buddhists avoid harming living beings, taking things not freely given, engaging in sexual misconduct, taking intoxicants, and speaking falsely. The attitude of compassion pervades Buddhism as love (*agape*) pervades Christianity.

  The two main branches of Buddhism are the smaller Theravada tradition and the larger Mahayana tradition. Compassion receives its clearest articulation in later schools of the Mahayana tradition. These shifted the goal of Buddhist practice from awakening in general to awakening for the benefit of all sentient beings. This has spawned an influential ethical tradition within Buddhism that centers on the ideal of the *bodhisattva*, beings who possess the six virtues or perfections (*paramitas*) – generosity, morality, patience, energy, meditation, and wisdom – and use these virtues to help other sentient beings attain their own enlightenment.

In Christian ethics appeal is made to Buddhism in respect of its tradition of discipline and training, monastic life, its rejection of class systems and inequality and consequent openness to issues of social justice, and its record of having triggered no religious wars – although recent violence beginning in 2012 against the Muslim minority Rohingya in Buddhist Myanmar raised international concerns.

- Confucianism, originating in but not limited to the writings of Kongzi, or Confucius (551–479 BCE), is oriented toward good government and an ordered society, allowing for a minimum of engagement with metaphysical or doctrinal claims. (It is thus unclear whether Confucianism should be called a "religion.") Confucian ethics in some ways corresponds to classical and Christian virtue ethics, in that it concentrates on developing character rather than identifying principles or prescribing rules. Harmony takes the place in Confucianism that compassion takes in Buddhism or love in Christianity. The Five Relationships offer a pattern of priorities for the good life and a prescription for harmony: they consider lord and vassal, father and son, older and younger brother, husband and wife, and friend with friend. In Japan the first of these seems most important, in Korea the last, and in China those in between.

Chinese religion is by no means restricted to Confucianism: Daoism has been a major tradition since it became organized in at least the second century BCE. Many environmentalists look to Daoism for a renewed relationship to nature, and many feminists admire the longstanding prominence of women in leadership roles in the tradition.

Professional Ethics

This section of the chapter identifies a third context for Christian ethics, in addition to classical philosophy and non-Christian religions. This third context is the professional and disciplinary ethics so preponderant today. This is in some ways a throwback to the classical era, as we shall now explain.

If the story of ethics starts in earnest in the world of Plato and Aristotle, then it begins in a world where the great minds addressing issues of the good and of right action appear to be isolated eminences. They are notable because they are thinking in advance of or in distinction to the prevailing thought world of their day. The ethical thought of the Constantinian, medieval, and early modern periods – in Europe at any rate – presents itself to our eyes as having a far less individualist character. In other words, such thought was part of a comprehensive, unifying vision of Christian life in a Christian civilization: of citizens serving the Christian God in societies that honored that God, whose structures mirrored divine authority and channeled divine providence. The corporate life of the church at the heart of Christian societies embraced and set the context for ethical thought – which was always in any case not a separate area of intellectual enquiry, but part of thought about relationship to God in all its aspects (in prayer, sacraments, the search for divine truth, the acknowledgment of divine beauty). In this context it was possible for ethical thought (thought about the *good*) to aspire also to being *true*, inasmuch as it nested within a unified vision of how the world hung together: a worldview.

In the modern period in the West there has, in a sense, been a return to the Platonic and Aristotelian state of things. There is no longer an ethics coterminous with a unifying worldview. There are many worldviews and many versions of ethics. There is a now a department of specialized thought called "Christian" that is identifiably different from other definable areas or traditions of thought, and even more specifically there is a department of specialized thought called "Christian ethics." The Christian ethics of the late modern period in particular does not know for sure that it makes much of a difference to wider society. It could be argued that what it now tries to do, given that it can no longer straightforwardly and with common consent claim to be *true*, is try to be *useful*.

As a result, Christian ethics becomes a discipline that seeks to find particular issues for itself – many of them with technical or professional specifications – in order to comment upon them, or make its contribution to them. This means that the church is no longer the definitive location for Christian ethical thought (as a seamless part of Christian worship, thought, and activity). By contrast Thomas Aquinas' (1225–74) thought, which we shall explore in Chapter Four, was framed by daily attendance at the Eucharist, and John Calvin's (1509–64) thought, which we shall also explore in Chapter Four, assumed the shaping of a godly Geneva. Christian ethicists in the modern era emerge as individual spokespersons once again, operating in a fragmented environment, in which there is an incentive to follow an agenda imposed from outside (e.g., by "the professions," which become quasi-churches, with their own agenda-setting corporate concerns and priorities). Modern ethicists have been cut off from the roots and soil that gave their thought much of its rationale and context.

In the section that follows we will examine a sample of these areas of "specialized ethical interest" in the modern environment, in which the voice of the Christian ethical thinker has been more that of a respondent than that of an initiator. These moral communities – or, at least, communities of interest – are not ecclesial, even though they may often include and at times be addressed by Christian thinkers. Some of the issues below are treated in more detail in Part Three (work, business, and management are taken up in particular in Chapter Nine), but they are offered here as a sample of where the field stands today.

Business and Management Ethics

The technological advances of the nineteenth and twentieth centuries have made available phenomenal new powers of production of material goods, in terms of both the speed with which, and the quantities in which, they are made. These powers of production have assisted a rapid economic expansion in all parts of the developed world, which brings new moral challenges in its wake. Trade in industrially manufactured goods has also been joined now by a more "virtual" trade in finance capital, as more sophisticated information technology makes it possible to speculate on stock markets all round the world, to trade in interest rates and buy bonds or currencies on one exchange for sale at a profit on another.

Concern with the relation between politics and economics was a dominating mark of the twentieth century – and this concern remains a central one as we advance further into the new millennium. More specifically, the world after the "Great War" of 1914–18 has had to be increasingly concerned with the relation between the nation-state and an emerging global economic system. Global economics raises issues of high ethical (as well as technical) complexity. In the same way that feudal economies, based around households, were overtaken by national (often industrial) economies managed by governments, so in turn the rise of a new set of transnational economic networks has tested the power of nation-states to shape and coordinate them. States have faced the problem of how to retain some direction and control of industrial and commercial developments, and of how to manage their consequences.

Acknowledging the fact that they cannot do this unilaterally, many national governments have been active in setting up new international bodies to try to stabilize and regulate the complex forces of global economics: the World Bank, International Monetary Fund (IMF), and World Trade Organization (WTO) are all examples of such bodies. They recognize that they must address ethical concerns in the overall context of what they do, and that industrial and commercial developments have ecological and social effects that need attention (directly relating to levels of world poverty, for example, and to human rights issues). They also recognize that businesses can only work effectively if there are at least minimal levels of trust, probity, and good practice across very different cultural boundaries, and are concerned to analyze, understand, and promote these business-specific "virtues." Increasingly, the threat of climate change has brought business and economic interests into conversation with environmental ones.

The contributions of explicitly religious traditions of ethics to such discussions (Christian ethics included) have often been invisible or marginal in recent decades. The modern strands of Christian ethical thinking that have seemed best fitted for use by those engaged in the management of global economics arguably stem from the sociological analysis of Ernst Troeltsch (1865–1923) and from the discussion of the "orders of creation" offered by Emil Brunner (1889–1966), as well as from the Roman Catholic encyclical tradition from Leo XIII (1810–1903) to John Paul II (1920–2005). There was also a vigorous flowering of thought about economics in the English "Christian Socialist" tradition in the mid-twentieth century, though this inevitably had limited practical effects in a world economy fast becoming global. All of these strands of thought sought to make connections between Christian tradition and the transformation of concrete social conditions in their environment that would benefit Christians and non-Christians alike. These themes will be revisited in Chapter Four and the final section of Chapter Five.

One important offshoot of "business ethics" is the ethics of *management*. Market practices have generated this area of specialist expertise, and it has taken on increasing importance in the modern developed world. The expertise in question aims at the maximization of efficiency (and regularly also transparency – though this too in the service of efficiency) in any particular corporate undertaking. Part of management's influence in the contemporary environment is that its virtues are viewed as almost limitlessly applicable to any area of organized human activity (healthcare, sport, education, town planning), even if the primary matrix that gave it birth is business. This makes it a set of techniques that is regularly construed as *abstractly* important to all *particular* endeavors. Early advocates of "scientific management" techniques like Frederick Taylor (1856–1915) and Harrington Emerson (1853–1931) in the first decades of the twentieth century equated management with moral wisdom because of the way it seemed to promise the delivery of social unity.

As with modern business practices, Christian ethicists have been divided about whether to commend or to criticize the art of management, and how. There is a body of literature about how a Christian may be a good manager, acting in the interests of others in the work environment to ensure that what they do is not wasted (the work of a Christian being a form of service of God), and that there is truthful and fair recognition of the value of gifts, skills, labor, and so on. At the same time, voices are raised to ask whether management will always seek efficiency over excellence, because its abstract procedures cannot recognize the particular goods of particular activities. Management may be blind to the goods proper to, say, the provision of higher education, or care of the elderly. Those goods may best be determined within their respective fields, by those who are not themselves professional managers – or, indeed, by religious traditions of thought. Management may be open to serving any master – and is in practice more likely to recognize and serve an economic master, whose "good" is the maximization of profit.

Medical Ethics

Key issues

The ethics of medicine began life specifically in relation to the practice of doctors, or physicians, until in the nineteenth century a distinct nursing profession also emerged, with its own codes of conduct. Since the 1960s and 1970s there has been an expanding range of new issues in medicine that seem to require ethical adjudication. The rapid development of biomedical science appears to offer multiple possibilities of dealing technically with human problems, but few ways of judging between these possibilities. Society has increasingly looked to medicine to resolve questions that have seemed beyond medicine's ability to answer. The variety of problems that have surfaced in biomedicine have entailed a broader conception of medical ethics (as "bioethics"), incorporating questions concerning organ transplantation, new reproductive technologies, genetic engineering, abortion, and the prolongation or curtailment of life; and also including professional–patient relations (such as privacy, confidentiality, and what permission is needed for research involving human subjects or organs), and issues of justice surrounding public health provision. Those in the latter list have provoked less distinctively Christian debate than those in the former.

Many of the new issues raised are raised because of unprecedented technological advances; many, perhaps more, are the result of shifts in public consensus about what constitutes a good life, a good death, and human entitlements and dignity. It is new technology, for example, that has intensified debates about the ethics of organ and tissue transplantation, in which biological material from one body (often dead, sometimes living) can be transferred to another person's body. This can be seen as an act of charity (or "neighbor love"), but can also provoke concern that due honor is not being given to the human cadaver. Sharp distinctions are made between the practice of willing organ donation, on the one hand, and the conscription or marketing of body parts, on the other, because the latter seem to commodify the human body.

Ethical debates about genetic engineering are likewise principally a consequence of technological advances. Critics worry especially about the risks of a new "eugenics," that is, a program of selective "breeding" aimed at improving the human race, in which genetic interventions in the name of "gene therapy" try to enhance human qualities like intelligence or physical strength.

Technology has also made it a great deal easier to preserve physical life for long periods of time after there has been a cessation of most (or all) brain function. Breathing and heartbeat are no longer so obviously an indication of life, and this has entailed a fierce debate about when and if medical treatment should be withdrawn in such cases.

Other areas of acute ethical debate are not the direct result of new technology (though such technologies may increase the availability and efficiency of certain procedures), but reflect shifts in attitude amongst significant numbers of people. This is the case in attitudes to active euthanasia, assisted suicide, and abortion. Abortion procedures have become more widely used and accepted since the mid-twentieth century, laws against euthanasia have been relaxed or abolished, and the debates about whether such terminations of life are right or wrong are accompanied by discussions about whether it is right to maintain those inherited professional norms and legal rules that prohibit or restrict these acts. There is also lively discussion about whether sufficient resources and imagination are being dedicated to exploring effective alternatives to euthanasia and assisted suicide (e.g., palliative care).

A final vigorous area of discussion in the wide field of medical ethics overlaps with the previous domain of professional ethics we looked at: management ethics. This has to do with the just allocation of limited healthcare resources. And connected with the ethics of decisions made at the "sharp end" of resource allocation are larger questions about access to healthcare (whether it should be seen as a universal right, for example), and justice (what, for example, is the moral relevance of factors like age and lifestyle in patients whose needs are being weighed against each other?). Complex judgments about need, likelihood of success, patient merit, and so on ask to be made here.

Key principles

In Chapter Eleven we will be concerned with a more detailed examination of Christian ethical comment on debates about contraception, abortion, euthanasia, stem cell research, and so on. Here we may simply outline some of the key principles that Christians have sought to bring to the emerging field of Christian medical (or "bio-") ethics. Overall, the debates can be situated within the terrain of a theological anthropology, which asks when human beings are most human, when and how they reflect God's image, and (thus) when and how they are to be valued and protected. These concerns informed the attitudes of initial defenders of developing medical technology, for example, Joseph Fletcher (1905–91), who saw the use of technology to modify "natural" processes of human reproduction as a proper exercise of the human vocation to control nature through reason. But they have also informed those who view the manipulation of natural processes as intrinsically inhuman, and unnatural, in particular Roman Catholic teaching in relation to reproductive technology.

The metaphors that inform one's view of the origin and value of human life have immense implications for any practical decision that is made about life, death, reproduction, or medical intervention. In Christian terms these metaphors are likely at the very least to inculcate a view of life as a divine gift – and, in some cases, more strongly as divine *property* – viewing the body as God's "handiwork" (Ps 139:13) or "temple" (1 Cor 6:19), for example. More relational language may qualify this – as when human beings are characterized as God's children or servants, suggesting a proper faculty of response or self-determination. In any case, such understandings prohibit actions that make the human person the object of limitless manipulation, that "instrumentalize" bodies for the purposes of research, or that will contemplate terminating a human life for the supposed greater happiness of that of another human being.

On the other hand, the new powers of medical science to extend the dying process through the use of sophisticated technology risk going to the other extreme, and idolizing life. This amounts to seeing it as more than a gift; rather, as a commodity to be safeguarded at all costs. Here, much of the tradition of Christian ethical thought will assert the importance of accepting mortality and finitude as part of what God has given in and with the gift of life. In some of the debates about cloning, both tendencies coexist: advocates of cloning evidence a willingness both to instrumentalize one person's body for the sake of another person's happiness and, at the same time, to idolize the perpetuation of life in exactly replicable forms. The latter is a process from which contingency has been eliminated, and in which the triumph of science (a bio-utopia) has replaced the reign of God.

Professional Ethics

There are of course a number of other spheres of specialized professional activity where ethical debate goes on today, and in which Christian ethicists seek to contribute their own perspectives even though the discourse in question is not specifically Christian. The list might be extended to include, for instance, the ethics of military activity, the ethics of sport, the ethics of government, and the ethics of journalism. Although not all of them are dealt with here (the list is highly extendable), many receive treatment elsewhere in this book (e.g., in discussion of war, the state, and the media – all of which occur in Part Three). There are, however, some recurring themes that characterize discussions about "professional ethics," especially when there is perceived to be some sort of duty of care for others in the profession in question. We have already dealt with medical ethics, where that duty of care is obvious; it is also a basic aspect of the work of teachers, lawyers, psychotherapists, counselors, clergy, social workers, police officers, and many others. When these areas of activity become ethically self-conscious, they bring their "practical wisdom," or professional expertise, into dialogue with traditions of philosophical (and, more rarely, theological) thought in order to come to greater clarity about their goals and standards. The understandings that emerge are usually then embodied in codes of professional practice, systems of certification and licensing to safeguard high standards of competence, and practices of self-policing to weed out impropriety and incompetence.

Common issues across such professions, in which the professional is regarded as a figure of trust by virtue of her specialized knowledge or experience, include what obligations are entailed by the superiority of her knowledge. To what extent must a professional make a client aware of all the information she has; to what extent may she make decisions on a client's behalf without fully informed consent (which in specialized or complex cases may be difficult to obtain)? Conversely, how obliged must a professional be to maintain the confidentiality of a relationship with a client, when she is privy to information about that client that the client might not want others to know? Even if she adheres to a principle of confidentiality, is she *absolutely* bound by it, or can she override it in order (for example) to prevent harm to others? Is there such a thing as "role morality," in which an individual operates by a different ethical code when operating professionally from when she is acting as a private person – as, for example, when a lawyer works to gain the best result for a client whose innocence she may doubt? Might concepts of the public good require systems whereby professional help is made available for free (or at artificially low cost) to the poorest in society? And should professionals allow concepts of public good to override obligations to individual clients in certain cases? All of these questions and more are the subjects of lively discussion in a range of disciplines today.

The Relation of Legislation to Morality

Christian tradition contains a wide variety of views about whether the civil law should be used to promote or enforce moral values – and these have further varied depending on whether Christian communities have dominant or minority status in the societies where they are. Whenever law has been seen as directly mirroring the ordinances of God then, conceptually, there has been little to distinguish law from morality. On the other hand, certain Christian precepts have never been adopted in civil law, such as the injunction to love one's enemies and the command not to covet.

The debate about how legislation should relate to morality is not of course restricted to Christians. It is certainly a live topic in modern liberal societies, which must continually ask themselves whether the fact that certain behavior is widely regarded as morally wrong should be a reason for it to be illegal. Areas of particular contestation arise in relation to drug use, sexual behavior, marriage, abortion, and euthanasia. Liberal tradition, following the British philosopher John Stuart Mill (1806–73), has tended to invoke the so-called "harm condition" whereby it is supposed that there should only be a legal prohibition against an individual's chosen behavior if that behavior harms others. But even if this premise is accepted, gauging what constitutes "harm" is not easy. A working distinction between the morality of "universal" values (without which a society cannot function) and the morality of "tastes and conventions" does not deal with the fact that tastes and conventions can create an ethos that affects even those not immediately exercising their moral autonomy in a given situation. For example, a climate of drug use or disregard for the natural environment may have harmful effects on whole communities and societies. These effects are not likely to be reducible to active or conscious choice by individuals. On this basis, legislation may be used to enshrine certain of a society's moral ideals – and thus be "ethos-promoting" – as well as simply to enable legal intervention and deterrence in relation to specific actions. This is harder to achieve, however, when (as in most post-Christendom societies) there is little agreement on a common set of values.

Historically, Christian attitudes to legislation have at times relied heavily on the idea of natural law, to which human laws are meant to approximate wherever possible. This is especially prevalent as an idea in Catholic tradition, as we shall see in Chapter Five. The Calvinist tradition has followed its founder in identifying a use of law that readily translates into civil legislation, its purpose being to denounce wrong, exercise discipline, and administer punishment – thus reining in those who without the imposition of sanction would have no regard for justice. Because of this use of the law, Christians are obliged to respect the authority of those who administer the state's systems of justice.

Nonetheless, most Christian tradition acknowledges, with Paul in his letter to the Romans (8:3–4), that the law in itself is powerless to make people good, even if it has a role in restraining evil.

Seed Beds of Ethical Thought

Modern Western societies tend now to describe themselves as *pluralist*, in the sense that they have many intermediate institutions or groups operating within them – coalitions around values, interests, or forms of critical enquiry which can in turn be influential political forces – but no single agreed-upon authority structure. In practice pluralism can be exaggerated: few if any people live a plural ethic; such an ethic may not even be possible. But pluralism names a general willingness to tolerate a variety of ethical communities and their practices. Some intermediate bodies develop new ideas, some promote agendas for social action or intervention, and some are communities for the formation of character – and there are many overlaps between these functions. Think tanks, pressure/campaign groups, and universities are all examples of such intermediate bodies. They are the products of a modern "organizational revolution" which gained pace in the eighteenth century, and in which there was an increased separation of powers in most Western societies. This revolution brought the antislavery movements; the organization of dissenting minorities, ethnic groups, and women; trade unions; neighborhood associations; scientific and professional societies; missionary societies; libraries; and much else.

Such bodies have parallels with the churches (indeed, many were inspired and sponsored by the church), and can often ally with them, inasmuch as they are associations with an interest in:

1. critically examining the practices and preconceptions that make our social world what it is;
2. engendering or affecting public opinion; and
3. resisting or promoting social change.

At the same time, they can interact with the churches and with each other in conflict as well as in cooperation, and create a "bear pit" of competing interests that is characteristic of life in many liberal societies. They are often a subject of interest for contemporary Christian ethicists, and sometimes also of approbation in an era when the state has seemed inclined to take back more centralizing power and increase its regulation of voluntary organizations and intermediate institutions. This is perhaps because they display the way that virtue is fostered by habitual association. It is also because they display the fact that moral character is socially formed, in contrast to models where everything is reduced to the interaction of autonomous individuals and government regulation. Alasdair MacIntyre (b. 1929), a figure we shall examine in Chapter Seven, has been a key exponent of this insight.

Postmodernism

Postmodern thought arose in the late twentieth century as a form of intellectual resistance to the hegemony of the "grand narratives" of Enlightenment tradition – the possibility of universal reason, the supremacy of the democratic political system, the myth of human progress, the possibility of disinterested science, and so on. It has owed much to the rise in the nineteenth century of a recognition that social location plays a significant role in the origins of values, practices, and truth-claims (as we shall explore in detail in Chapter Six). It is in some ways a historicizing move, in that it accentuates the contingency of propositions, institutions, and political settlements. It seeks to expose the irrational, paradoxical, and playful forces whose traces it discerns below the surface of the modern mind's ordered presentation of its experience, and thus to challenge the justifications modernity gives for its activity. It deconstructs the meanings modern minds give to the objects of their understanding by showing how they only have meaning that is relative to other (equally relative) interpretations of what is real or true. Just as the meaning of every word in a dictionary can only be explained by the use of other words, so all concepts are simply signposts to other concepts. Thus, postmodernism opens up the possibility of an infinite deferral of final meaning. But at this point, history itself as a field of enquiry becomes opaque and interest-ridden, so that postmodern thought finds its skepticism turning back on its own premises, and at these points it can seem impenetrable and circular.

The creativity of postmodernism (e.g., in the arts) has been in its readiness to celebrate unexpected juxtapositions that transgress the normal categories of inherited rational science. Meanwhile it questions the standardization and rigidity of modernity – exemplified for many postmodern thinkers by modernity's mass production methods. Postmodernism tends to regard the claims of the dominant (Western) cultural model as implicitly totalitarian. That model is simultaneously political, economic, military, and intellectual. Some Christian ethicists who see modernity as bequeathing an unhealthy and damaging legacy (in the form, for instance, of militarism, rapacious capitalism, environmental damage, and social oppression) see subverting that legacy as key to their enterprise. Thus postmodernist and Christian thinkers have found common cause in questioning the normative reference points of our societies.

Summary

The first three chapters have described the three key contexts for Christian ethics – Scripture, history, and philosophy. Philosophy is far from a straightforward term. In Chapter Five we will look extensively at ways philosophy has overlapped with and been integrated into Christian ethics. Here we have considered three aspects that have remained more distinct from Christian ethics: philosophical ethics, religious ethics, and professional ethics.

Classical philosophy is distinct for historical reasons: it simply emerged before the Christian era. Plato, Aristotle, the Epicureans, the Stoics, and Plotinus nonetheless shaped the philosophical world in which Christianity emerged, and no understanding of Christian ethics can exist without them.

Christianity is today one religion amongst many world faiths. It grew out of Judaism and has much in common with Islam. But Christians must remember that Judaism has developed significantly since New Testament times. Most Jews do not recognize their beliefs and practices in the ways they are often portrayed by Christian stereotypes. Likewise fear of violent fringe tendencies in contemporary Islam has inhibited many Christians from engaging seriously with the depth of the Muslim tradition in ethics. There are also important resonances and dissonances with Christian ethics outside the Abrahamic family of faiths.

In the contemporary Western world ethics is frequently associated with professional standards of conduct and with dilemmas that arise in medical practice. These are increasingly investigated outside the assumptions of a Christian worldview. The relationship of ethics to legislation remains an unresolved but important area. Meanwhile postmodernism has a lively following in some ethical circles, despite the fear in some parts of the church that it tends to diminish the language and concept of truth.

References and Further Reading

Philosophical Ethics

Plato's writings as cited in this chapter include *The Republic* (R. E. Allen, trans.; New Haven, CT: Yale University Press, 2006); and *Euthyphro* and *Crito*, which may be found in *Four Texts on Socrates: Plato's Euthyphro, Apology, and Crito, and Aristophanes' Clouds* (Thomas G. West and Grace Starry West, trans.; Ithaca, NY: Cornell University Press, 1998).

Aristotle's discussion of the four causes may be found in his *Physics*, section II.3 (Oxford; New York: Oxford University Press, 1996). Additional writings of Aristotle noted in this chapter are *Nicomachean Ethics* (Cambridge; New York: Cambridge University Press, 2000); and *Eudemian Ethics*, in vol. 20 of the Loeb Classical Library (Cambridge, MA: Harvard University Press, 1952). The quotation about serving and contemplating God is from *Eudemian Ethics* VIII. iii.16–17.

Plato's *Republic* and Aristotle's *Nicomachean Ethics* are also quoted in *Christian Ethics: An Introductory Reader*, and are available online at http://classics.mit.edu/Plato/republic.html and http://classics.mit.edu/Aristotle/nicomachaen.html, respectively.

The thought of Epicurus may be found in *The Epicurus Reader* (Indianapolis, IN: Hackett, 1994). Selections from Plotinus' writing are collected in *The Essential Plotinus: Representative Treatises from the Enneads* (Elmer O'Brien, trans.; 2nd edn; Indianapolis, IN: Hackett, 1964, 1984).

There are a number of accessible guides to classical philosophical ethics. They include:

- Tom L. Beauchamp. *Philosophical Ethics: An Introduction to Moral Philosophy.* New York: McGraw-Hill, 1982.
- Martin Cohen. *The Essentials of Philosophy and Ethics.* London: Hodder Arnold; New York: Oxford University Press, 2006.
- John Sellars. *Stoicism.* Berkeley, CA: University of California Press, 2006.
- Stanley Grenz. *The Moral Quest: Foundations of Christian Ethics.* Downers Grove, IL: Inter-Varsity, 1997. See chapter 2, "The Greek Ethical Tradition."

Religious Ethics

The two most accessible overview texts on ethics in the world religions are probably the following:
- Peggy Morgan and Clive A. Lawton, eds. *Ethical Issues in Six Religious Traditions.* 2nd edn. Edinburgh: Edinburgh University Press, 2007.
- William Schweiker, ed. *The Blackwell Companion to Religious Ethics.* Malden, MA: Blackwell, 2005.

For comparative religious ethics, see Charles Mathewes, Matthew Puffer, and Mark Storslee, eds, *Comparative Religious Ethics* (Routledge, 2016), Volume 1: Comparative Religious Ethics: Defining a Field by Comparison; Volume 2: The "Human" in Comparative Religious Ethics; Volume 3: Meaning and Understanding in Comparative Religious Ethics; Volume 4: Practical Ethics and Everyday Life.

Useful texts for Jewish ethics are:
- Elliot Dorff and Jonathan K. Crane, eds. *The Oxford Handbook of Jewish Ethics and Morality.* New York; Oxford: Oxford University Press, 2012.
- Eugene B. Borowitz and Frances Weinman Schwartz. *The Jewish Moral Virtues.* Philadelphia, PA: The Jewish Publication Society, 1999.
- Sol Roth. *The Jewish Idea of Ethics and Morality.* New York: The Michael Scharf Publication Trust of the Yeshiva University Press, 2007.
- Barry Holtz, ed. *Back to the Sources: Reading the Classic Jewish Texts.* New York: Summit Books, 1984.
- Joseph Soloveitchik. *Halakhic Man.* Trans. Lawrence Kaplan. Philadelphia, PA: Jewish Publication Society of America, 1983.
- Alan L. Mittleman. *A Short History of Jewish Ethics: Conduct and Character in the Context of Covenant.* Oxford: Wiley-Blackwell, 2012.

Works that explore Muslim ethics include:
- M. A. Draz. *The Moral World of the Qur'an.* Trans. Danielle Robinson and Rebecca Masterton. London; New York: I. B. Tauris, 2008.
- Dwight M. Donaldson. *Studies in Muslim Ethics.* London: SPCK, 1953.

- Tariq Ramadan. *In the Footsteps of the Prophet: Lessons from the Life of Muhammad.* New York; Oxford: Oxford University Press, 2007.
- Amyn B. Sajoo, ed. *A Companion to Muslim Ethics.* London; New York: I.B. Tauris Publishers, 2010.
- Mona Siddiqui. *The Good Muslim: Reflections on Classical Islamic Law and Theology.* Cambridge: Cambridge University Press, 2012.

Introductions to ethics among the non-Abrahamic faiths include:
- Balbir Singh. *Hindu Ethics: An Exposition of the Concept of Good.* New Delhi: Mayfair Press, 1984.
- S. Cromwell Crawford. *The Evolution of Hindu Ethical Ideals.* Asian Studies of Hawaii no. 28. 2nd edn. Honolulu, HI: The University of Hawaii Press, 1974, 1982.
- H. Saddhatissa. *Buddhist Ethics: Essence of Buddhism.* 3rd edn. Somerville, MA: Wisdom Publications, 1997.
- Peter Harvey. *An Introduction to Buddhist Ethics: Foundations, Values, and Issues.* Cambridge: Cambridge University Press, 2000.
- Ken Jones. *The New Social Face of Buddhism.* Somerville, MA: Wisdom Publications, 2003.
- Dale S. Wright. *The Six Perfections: Buddhism and the Cultivation of Character.* Oxford: Oxford University Press, 2011.

The following works are quoted in relation to religious ethics in *Christian Ethics: An Introductory Reader*:
- Sumner B. Twiss. "Comparison in Religious Ethics." Chapter 16 in *The Blackwell Companion to Religious Ethics.* William Schweiker, ed. Malden, MA: Blackwell, 2005.
- Mohandas K. Gandhi. *An Autobiography: The Story of My Experiments With Truth.* Mahadev Desai, trans. Boston, MA: Beacon Press, 1957.
- His Holiness The Dalai Lama. *Ethics for the New Millennium.* New York: Riverhead Books, 1999.

Professional Ethics

Among introductory guides to professional ethics are:
- Tom L. Beauchamp and James F. Childress. *Principles of Biomedical Ethics.* 5th edn. Oxford: Oxford University Press, 2001. An excerpt from

this work is included in the corresponding chapter of *Christian Ethics: An Introductory Reader.*
- Robert Frederick, ed. *A Companion to Business Ethics.* Malden, MA: Blackwell, 1999. Thomas F.

McMahon's article "A Brief History of American Business Ethics" from this volume is in the corresponding chapter of *Christian Ethics: An Introductory Reader*.

In addition to the above, Max L. Stackhouse has written authoritatively on "Business, Economics, and Christian Ethics" in *The Cambridge Companion to Christian Ethics* (Robin Gill, ed.; Cambridge: Cambridge University Press, 2001). The section of this chapter dealing with business ethics draws on his work.

The section on management ethics draws on Michael Hanby's essay "Interceding: Giving Grief to Management," in *The Blackwell Companion to Christian Ethics* (Stanley Hauerwas and Samuel Wells, eds; Oxford: Blackwell, 2004). "Professional Ethics" is discussed as well by David Fletcher in the *New Dictionary of Christian Ethics and Pastoral Theology* (David J. Atkinson and David H. Field, eds; Leicester: InterVarsity Press, 1995), and this chapter is indebted to his article too.

Other further reading on professional ethics includes William F. May, *Beleaguered Rulers: The Public Obligation on the Professional* (Louisville, KY: Westminster/John Knox Press, 2001), as well as his earlier *The Physician's Covenant: Images of the Healer in Medical Ethics* (2nd edn; Louisville, KY: Westminster/John Knox Press, 1983, 2000).

Chapter Four
The Story of Christian Ethics

This chapter offers a historical introduction to the discipline called *Christian* ethics, against the background of the story of *ethics* told in the last chapter. It will look at the creative interplay between Scripture, philosophy, and circumstance that has shaped Christian moral thinking over the past 2000 years.

We should note, however, that the category of "Christian ethics" is itself problematic. It may seem to imply that there is a general thing called "ethics" that is then qualified by the particular descriptor "Christian." But for most of the church's history, there was no supposedly universal concept of "the ethical" – which is to say, a set of principles about right and wrong action against which the claims of particular traditions of thought and practice could be measured and evaluated. No one claimed such an overview. Nor was "ethics" used to denote the service of a transcendent "good" that floated free of the specific terms of humanity's history with God: salvation history.

Moreover, as we noted toward the end of Chapter Two, for most of the church's history there was not a special category of Christian theological enquiry called "ethics," nor any special department of Christian practice called "the ethical." The implications of the confession of Christian faith were assumed to shape action and thought together (in the context of a worshipping community), and both action and thought were understood as having been transformed by the action of God in Christ, by which God had redeemed the faithful. There is, of course, a lot of moral guidance and instruction in the Bible, and in centuries of church teaching and preaching. But until the modern period this did not involve Christians saying: "and now I am going to take a moment to do ethics." Discipleship in the church was a whole context of worshipful practice: the following of God. That it generated and informed particular forms of behavior did

Introducing Christian Ethics, Second Edition. Samuel Wells and Ben Quash with Rebekah Eklund.
© 2017 John Wiley & Sons Ltd. Published 2017 by John Wiley & Sons Ltd.

not mean that this needed analysis in a special field of its own, distinguished from the study of liturgy or doctrine.

Things became somewhat different in the Enlightenment era, as we have had cause to note in the last two chapters (and will see again in Chapter Five). It was in this period that the idea of "universal ethics" (an ethics that can supposedly be acknowledged by "anyone") was invented. Immanuel Kant (1724–1804), whose thought and influence will be explored in Chapter Five, was its chief architect. Kant sought to found moral obligation upon reason alone. Such tradition-rejecting ethics asserted its autonomy with respect to any external instruction – for example, by a religious tradition of thought. The ground of ethics was found in the human subject realizing him- or herself *as* a subject by acting in accordance with universal laws. So it was that the self-proclaimed autonomy of the Enlightenment subject went hand in hand with the assertion of the autonomy of ethics – its freedom from any historical or religious determination.

The modern period increasingly saw the metaphysical and historical presuppositions of premodern Christianity being called into question – for example, by the development of Newtonian science and critical historical scholarship. As a consequence, those who still wanted to give a rationale for Christian practice and truth-claims did so by trying to find a generally acceptable basis for them that could be shared by Christians and non-Christians alike. Their aims were to secure relevance and consensus. In other words, they followed a Kantian lead. For example, some strands of liberal Protestant theology in Germany, and later in America, argued for Jesus' importance on the grounds of his moral excellence, employing measures of moral excellence that were not particular to the church. Under the influence of Albrecht Ritschl (1822–89) and Ernst Troeltsch (1865–1923), Americans like Walter Rauschenbusch (1861–1918) argued theologically for the social importance of Jesus' teachings, but reduced them to principles barely different from Kant's: the dignity of the individual and the "brotherhood of man."

It is in this way that "Christian ethics" emerged as a special discipline, commending itself in the marketplace of ideas, and scarcely rooted in ecclesial life and activity. This detachment from the soil that gave it life has in turn meant that the discipline of "Christian ethics" has played into the widespread view of its surrounding environment that "ethics" is about universal laws and rights on the one hand, and individual decision-making on the other, rather than being about the formation of character through a rhythm of corporate practice. This is why, in the present chapter, the move from the premodern era to the modern period is a move from a story whose chief characters have their center of gravity in the church (and who might evoke the reaction: "I never really thought of that person as an *ethicist*"), to a story whose chief characters have their center of gravity in the academy – working in a field that can be distinguished if not isolated from the liturgical life, daily habits, and elementary practices of the church.

Nonetheless, this chapter uses the heading "Christian Ethics" – self-conscious about the anachronistic nature of the term – to denote more than that recently emerged special discipline. The "Christian ethics" whose story is told in this chapter includes the many ways in which particular Christian thinkers in the two millennia of the church's history have sought to work out the faith they confess in relation to questions of character, right action, and the good.

We begin by looking at key representatives of ethical thought in the first centuries of the church's life.

Foundations

We saw in Chapter Two how the early church devoted a great deal of thought to how to keep its own house in order (e.g., by avoiding public scandal), and how to reflect its relation to a generous God in practices of generosity – many of which constituted what we might today call a welfare system for those within (and sometimes those outside) the church. For as long as the church did not wield power or have large-scale public responsibilities, community ethics was its natural concern. The church's early teachers and preachers gave a great deal of careful consideration to the relationship between rich and poor, to the ethics of sex and marriage, and to how to relate to civil authority. We look here at just some representative individuals amongst them. They fall into three strands: the early Fathers, Augustine, and Thomas Aquinas.

The Early Fathers

1. *Justin Martyr.* Justin Martyr (100–65 CE) is the first "Father" of the Greek Church, most famous for his *Apology* (in two parts, published toward the end of his life) in which he defended the Christian faith to the emperor and his counselors, and to the cultured pagans of his day. He was martyred in Rome.

    The purpose of the *Apology* is to prove the injustice of the persecution of the Christians, who are the representatives of true philosophy. Christians are the true worshippers of God, the Creator of all things, and their following of Christ's teaching leads them to perfect morality. The doctrine of Jesus as the eternal Logos is specially emphasized – and, by Logos, Justin meant the rational activity of God in the created order, or the divine reason itself. Overcoming the deceitful work of demons (false pagan gods), Christian righteousness is manifested in lives lived in accordance with reason. Reason involves response to God's prompting and enlightening work, and so a good life involves participation in God's purpose and activity.

2. *Tertullian.* As we noted in Chapter Two, Tertullian (ca. 160–ca. 225 CE) was a forthright advocate of strict Christian discipline, and of austerity in the Christian life. The gospel for him was a "new law," given to assist Christians in holy imitation of God. Where Justin had attempted to show *continuities* between Christianity and the intellectual culture of his day (arguing, for example, that Plato's teaching prefigured that of Christ), Tertullian highlighted Christianity's

points of *conflict* with and necessary *opposition* to the world of classical learning and moral instruction. This reluctance to find common cause with the ethics of his pagan environment set him apart from the more apologetic strands in Christian thought at the time (not only Justin, but Clement of Alexandria, Origen, and others). He comprehensively attacked many aspects of Roman civilization including its public amusements and – as he saw it – the license given to its women. Like many of the other African Fathers, he is thus easily identifiable as a rigorist in the context of the early church. Such views may have been what led him to adopt Montanism, which was a tradition of spiritual and ascetic enthusiasm that believed in the continuance of prophetic gifts and the imminence of Christ's second coming. His first major work was the *Apology*, and was written around 197 CE.

Tertullian's belief that Christians should abstain from the theater or the amphitheater was based on his conviction concerning their polluting power: we should not look at or listen to others doing what we may not ourselves do; the sight of polluted things pollutes. He thought that the atrocities of the arena offended all principles of modesty, purity, and humanity, and were underwritten by appeal to deities who themselves committed appallingly immoral acts. Tertullian regarded the unmarried state as higher than the married (and thought that married couples should be celibate), and he argued from scriptural texts in the Pauline tradition for the need for both unmarried and married women to keep their heads covered – and for all women to dispense with jewelry. He regarded second marriage as a form of adultery. In the later part of his life he was an unqualified opponent of military service by Christians, even though in his earlier writings he had insisted on their duty to pray for the emperor (as one whose rule must have been ordained and given by God).

3. *The Cappadocians.* Basil of Caesarea (330–79 CE), Gregory of Nazianzus (ca. 330–ca. 390 CE), and Gregory of Nyssa (ca. 335–94 CE) were educated in the Hellenistic philosophical, literary, and cultural norms of their day, and came from well-off Christian backgrounds in what is today Turkey. To these three theologians we should add Macrina (ca. 330–79 CE), elder sister of Basil and Gregory of Nyssa, whom Gregory calls the Teacher in their *Dialogue on the Soul and the Resurrection*. They are amongst the greatest theologians of the early church, most famous for their conceptual articulation of a Trinitarian theology to explain the divine relations within the Godhead. Basil in particular also became one of the first theologians to draw up a detailed model of the rules and regulations that ought to govern the monastic life, following his own embrace of that vocation. The Rule of St. Basil continues to guide the life of Orthodox monastic communities today.

These celebrated thinkers of the Eastern Church are particularly significant in the story of Christian ethics for their reflections on economic issues. For all of them, money given to the poor is an eternal investment. Basil was highly critical of social inequalities and was active, as a bishop, in setting up institutions that would meet the needs of those economically disadvantaged through illness, disability, or unemployment. He wrote: "Man, indeed, is a political and social animal. Now, in social relations and in common life, a certain disposition to share one's goods is necessary in order to assist the needy." He reinforced the traditional rejection of usury. Gregory of Nyssa, meanwhile, wrote forcefully against slavery, and on deeply theological grounds – for it is "vain," as he puts it, "to put a price on persons created in the image of God."

4.   *Ambrose of Milan.* Ambrose (339–97 CE) was a Roman governor prior to his baptism and designation as a bishop; he was a confident political practitioner, learned in classical tradition, and is perhaps the main architect in the West of the concept of an orthodox empire from which religious error would be excluded (or where lack of orthodoxy would at least reduce a person to the status of a second-class citizen). This did not make him blindly servile to the state. On one celebrated occasion he required the emperor to accept public penance before restoration to communion, thus demonstrating that the church was as concerned with illegality and immorality as with its own interests. He reflected at length on issues of justice as necessary to the holding-together of society, and saw the accumulation of wealth ("to buy more land and be the richest of all") as an economic *in*justice: an offense against nature and God's decrees. He was characteristic of his age in no longer writing as a pacifist, although he believed violence should only be used in the defense of others. He was a significant figure in the conversion and formation of Augustine.

Augustine

Augustine (354–430 CE) was bishop of Hippo in present-day Algeria. There is no other thinker whose influence in Western (Latin) Christian thought is as great as his. He addressed major questions about the nature of evil, the freedom of the will, the meaning of history, and the doctrine of God which still set a framework for theological discussion centuries later. Some of the key themes in his thought follow here.

1.   *Sin.* Underpinning much of Augustine's ethical teaching is a fundamental commitment to the idea that evil is the *privation* of good, not an opposite and/or equal force to it. He held decidedly to this view once he had put behind him his decade-long involvement with the Manichean sect, which regarded the material order as evil and saw the world as a site for an ongoing and primeval conflict between light and dark principles. All being, for Augustine, has its source in God, and is therefore intrinsically good, but the disordered affections and will of fallen humanity are attracted to lesser goods in ways that deny God (in relation to whom all things are properly loved), and this is evil. Such misplaced desire is also a path away from true human well-being, which is to say from salvation.

So Augustine's ethical writings are centered on a theological analysis of the human will and its need of grace, which is an absolute need. He confronted the relative moral optimism of Pelagian ideas, which set a high premium on what could be achieved by the efforts of the human will using its native capacities. By contrast, Augustine emphasized that after the Fall only God gives this power, by drawing the will back to God. In doing so, however, God restores true freedom to the Christian believer, as liberation from attachment to falsity and from self-love. Augustine's emphasis on grace and concern for church unity also led him to oppose the Donatist schismatics in his native North Africa. The Donatists sought to carve out a pure church from whose midst any morally compromised ordained ministers were excluded (their sacramental activity being declared invalid). Augustine thus became the architect of the principle that the unworthiness of particular ministers does not in any way damage the validity of the sacraments at which they preside. The church catholic is an inclusive community, not a sect for the ethically unblemished.

2. *Sex.* Augustine defended marriage against those who regarded it in a quasi-Manichean way as a sort of failure, albeit a tolerable one. He argued for the possibility of sex prior to the Fall. God *could* have found an alternative to sexual intercourse, creating some other way for new generations to follow upon previous ones. There was nothing necessary or inevitable about sexual intercourse as the means to this end. Nevertheless, God *did* create sex, and he did so to permit obedience to the injunction to be fruitful and multiply. Augustine articulates three goods of marriage: the having of children, the sanctifying pledge of faithfulness between partners, and the sacramental mirroring of Christ's permanent union with his church. He associated the friendship between man and woman in marriage with the last of these three. He saw such human friendship as facilitating friendship with God. Nonetheless, Augustine's sexual ethic does not abandon the widespread patristic view that the life of celibacy is to be preferred as a better way than any other, and he does not believe that sexual intercourse can escape being a sinful expression of sexual lust – even if the act of conception is not intrinsically evil. He associated sexual desire with the sin of Adam; the act of intercourse conjures up for him the rebellion in the Garden of Eden. The tradition has, somewhat unfortunately, tended to ignore Augustine's identification of sex as a created good, and has focused almost exclusively on Augustine's perception of sex after the Fall, wherein the act of procreation is always affected by evil, and becomes a vehicle for the very transmission of sin through the generations. Though not to be equated with original sin itself, it is the mechanism by which all human beings are born into the condition of original sin.

3. *War.* Augustine emphasizes peace as the original and final good of humankind – its true happiness. All nations desire peace, he argues, which is the ordered harmony of authority and obedience between citizens. In this respect,

earthly peace echoes in an imperfect way the highest peace of the heavenly realm, in which the harmonious communion of those who find their joy in God will be found. But at the same time Augustine pioneers a Christian doctrine of just war in various discussions throughout his writings. A society may have to go to war precisely to secure peace. It must be a last resort, however, and only when required to prevent or punish aggression (or heresy), when pursued by rightful authority, when driven by love, and when undertaken with mercy and restraint. Christians, for Augustine, are called to be peacemakers even when they are at war – and by observation of these principles they should seek to make any war (which must only be undertaken by a legitimate authority) into the servant of a better peace.

4. *The City of God*. Rome fell to the Goths in 410–11 CE, and many who fled the city came to North Africa. In 413 CE Augustine began to write his *City of God*, a theological interpretation of history in which we also see his political ethic set out in its greatest detail. In the work, he is showing in a hopeful way that the church does not fall even when earthly cities are overthrown. He is also arguing against those who blamed the sack of Rome on the empire's embrace of Christianity. To the contrary, he argues: the ruin of the empire was caused by pagan vices.

It is important to note that the city of God is not strictly the visible, historical church; it is the community of the elect, whose pure form will only fully be disclosed at the eschaton. Until then, it exists alongside its earthly counterpart, and even intermingles with it – and the visible church itself will share in this mixture of the righteous and the unrighteous.

Augustine contrasts the way that the city of God is determined by the worship of God with the city of earth's depravity and its focus on transitory things. The two cities are thus identified by the objects of their respective loves. The contrast is not wholly to be understood as an attack on worldly political order, however; even though the city of earth will ultimately fail, it has a role in God's providence in realizing a certain measure of temporal well-being. The city of God can "enjoy the peace of Babylon … the temporal peace which the good and the wicked together enjoy." Nonetheless, he holds fast to the conviction that Rome – and all earthly empire – is in the end in thrall to the sinful love of glory, and is the inheritor of the mantle of Babylon (that ancient enemy of God's people). Even its manifestations of order are corruptions of God's providential gift of *true* order, which can only be based on the worship of God.

It was not until the medieval period – and pre-eminently the work of Thomas Aquinas – that a concerted attempt would be made to re-establish a positive view of worldly political life as serving the ultimate good of humanity. As the next great colossus in the story of Christian ethics, we now turn to look at his thought.

Thomas Aquinas

The friar Thomas Aquinas (1225–74), a member of the recently established Dominican Order of Preachers, is the foremost representative of an extraordinary new intellectual energy in Christian thought in the early medieval period. He brought his philosophically sophisticated belief in God into deep conversation with the thought of the classical world. The most explicitly ethical writings of Thomas are to be found in his *Commentary on the Nicomachean Ethics* of Aristotle (whose thought influenced him deeply), as well as in the *Disputed Questions*, the *Commentary on Lombard's Sentences*, the third book of the *Summa Contra Gentiles*, and the second part of his most famous work, the *Summa Theologica*.

Aquinas shared with Augustine a basic conviction that all things are good by virtue of having existence at all, but he also supposed that every existent thing is properly understood only in relation to its end (or *telos*), the fulfillment of which is its truest good. The ultimate *telos* of human beings lies beyond this world in the beatific vision (the perfect contemplation of God).

Human beings have higher, rational powers like intellect and will; they also have lower capacities like sense cognition and bodily appetites. The best possible use of these various powers is what makes a good life, and the genuinely good life is accomplished when right reason is allowed to control the lower capacities. Natural law provides principles with which reason can discern what is right and wrong, as it shapes the body's appetites and activities – though the fall of human-kind means that we now need more than natural law to help us to achieve virtue. Aquinas therefore teaches that there are three other dimensions to law than those immediately discernible by the natural powers of human observation and reflec-tion. We look at these below, in the context of his overall conception of law.

1. *Virtue*. For Aquinas, the achievement of the human end of contemplating God is served by habits – or dispositions of the will – which orient persons to that ultimate end. There is more to the moral life than acts. The potential for doing good acts resides in the will and its dispositions, which can become developed in us as our reason learns to shape its appetites. Virtue, writes Aquinas, is "a habit which is always referred to good." The cardinal virtues (prudence, justice, fortitude, and temperance) are "proportioned to human nature" and are in the Christian worldview to be fulfilled by the three theologi-cal virtues of faith, hope, and love (*caritas*), which are made known to us "by divine revelation, contained in Holy Scripture." These lift our eyes even beyond the moral teachings of the classical tradition, and lift our wills to God.

2. *Law*. The four forms of law that Aquinas specifies are as follows: the natural, the divine, the human, and the eternal.
    *   *Natural law* is not a self-evident truth but takes its place in relation to the other three forms of law. We have noted already how natural law, even though divinely appointed, is available to be understood by all people of

reason (not just believing Christians), just as it was understood by the pre-Christian philosophers of old. Aquinas believes that it can be seen at work in the created order and learned about from there.

- *Divine law* meanwhile must complement natural law (as revelation complements reason). The fallen condition of human beings means that they can err and be mistaken in their appropriation of natural law, and so distort it. Divine law (which is revealed, as the codes of law given to the people of Israel were revealed) corrects such distortions, and it also directs us to our supernatural good, which natural reason cannot discern unaided (this sits in something of a tension with Aquinas' desire to ground an ethic in universal reason).
- *Human law* is what is administered by civil authorities – monarchs and other duly appointed officials – and is the application of natural law to the circumstances of human social life.
- The *eternal law* is in a sense the highest form of law, as it is simply the mind and will of God, which is then mirrored and applied in all other forms of law.

Aquinas' work gives us the most influential meditations on moral law in the whole medieval period. His attention to law shows that his teleological (or end-oriented) approach to ethics as outlined in the previous section does not preclude prescription. Yet law itself has a *telos*, namely, as an articulation of the "divine wisdom ... moving all things to their due end."

3.   *Politics.* Aquinas affirms that human life must be social. He holds that society depends on mutual service and interdependence, but at the same time – for him – the system is irreducibly hierarchical. Nature itself, he believed, gives us examples of hierarchical government, and we can deduce the "duties of a king" from such examples. Aquinas' view of the state (of which the family is a microcosm) is thus one in which the ruler has a proper coercive power over his subjects. A ruler exercises his responsibility to bring unity to the multitude, safeguard peace, ensure all have what is necessary in order to lead a good life. In short, he is there to benefit the common good of the people in a way that is answerable to God and accords with natural law. In contrast to the later teaching of Martin Luther, Aquinas did not maintain that a tyrant's authority must necessarily be accepted. Although princely government directs the lives of individuals according to natural law, it is itself subordinate to divine law; and tyrannical law, not being according to reason, is not law at all in the true and strict sense.

Aquinas' belief that human beings can sometimes add to the natural law allowed him to justify the existence of slavery. Poverty and wealth are not virtuous or wrong in themselves, but either can be taken to excess, and in departing from the measure of reason they may take on an evil aspect. His development of Augustine's just war principles continues to be widely influential. Aquinas assumed the inevitability of wars, but did not think it right for the clergy to fight in them because of war's incompatibility with their contemplative and sacramental roles.

Aquinas was clearly not of the Augustinian opinion that the sexual act was always sinful by its inevitable association with lust, or "concupiscence." He saw sex as a natural good in accord with divine providence. Nevertheless, Aquinas shared with Augustine the view that procreation was sex's primary purpose, and was typical of his time in holding that celibacy was a higher condition of life than marriage.

Revisions

The relatively unitary world of the Western Middle Ages disintegrated from the Reformation onwards. This brought about substantial revisions of the Augustinian–Thomist foundation, largely along three lines, as follows.

Martin Luther

It might be said that Aquinas' thought had made the doctrine of God fundamental, such that the Christian must "think towards" other doctrines from this starting point. In the work of the great Reformer Martin Luther (1483–1546), to whom we now turn, it is a different doctrine that has priority for all theology (and thus all ethics): the doctrine of salvation. The fact of salvation, known in the experience of the Christian believer, is the basis of all that can be said about God and about the life of humanity in relation to God.

At the center of Luther's thought is the doctrine of justification by faith alone (*sola fide*). But for Luther the consequence of faith – even though it cannot itself be a work – is gratefully and lovingly fulfilling the true intent of the law in good actions. "Thus," writes Luther, "from faith flow forth love and joy in the Lord, and from love a cheerful, willing, free spirit, disposed to serve our neighbour voluntarily, without taking any account of gratitude or ingratitude, praise or blame, gain or loss." The obedience of Christians is infused and motivated by thankfulness. The unmerited forgiveness they are assured of in faith liberates them to turn toward their neighbors and serve them. Gospel ethics is thus based upon the "divine indicative" of God's love rather than the "divine imperative" of law.

Luther believes that there is a proper divine ordering of creation, and this conviction established itself in later Lutheran theology as the principle of *Schöpfungsordnungen* or "orders of creation." For Luther, these orders include political ones (e.g., governments) and domestic ones (e.g., marriage), as well as ecclesiastical and economic ones. They are ordained by God to preserve the postlapsarian (post-Fall) world from even worse chaos than it already experiences – and to perform this task they do not necessarily have to be made Christian. Luther thus gives a status to "secularity" that was to be highly influential in the later history of the West – while at the same time his affirmation of the life of everyday people meant that mundane tasks, relationships, and responsibilities could be seen as vocational, and fully a part of divine service. For Luther, Christians did not endanger their salvation by marrying or engaging in secular pursuits, and for many this was a liberating insight.

In his *The Freedom of a Christian* Luther begins with the paradox of Christian life: "A Christian is a free lord, subject to none. A Christian is a perfectly dutiful servant, subject to all." In other words, as forgiven children of God, Christians are no longer forced to keep God's law; nonetheless, they freely and joyfully serve God and their neighbors. Thus, Luther balances the notions of freedom *from* and freedom *to*.

Luther condemned the idea that rulers could ever be deposed – even if they were tyrants – except in cases of real insanity. A tyrant's punishment would be God's business in due course, and in the meantime even a tyrant could not hurt a person's soul. He advised rulers that they had a right to defend their subjects by military action – though with mercy and due regard for the innocent. Derived as it is from his belief in the orders of creation, Luther's theology of the state as a necessarily stern instrument in the government of the world forms one part of his "two kingdoms" theology, in which the interdependence but also the proper differentiation of the roles of church and state are laid out:

> For this reason these two kingdoms must be sharply distinguished and both be permitted to remain; the one to produce piety, the other to bring about external peace and prevent evil deeds; neither is sufficient in the world without the other.

God is the ruler of the whole world and rules in two ways: the earthly or left-hand kingdom is ruled through secular government, by means of law or force, and the heavenly or right-hand kingdom (the church) is ruled through grace. It is worth noting that here Luther brings his notion of authority into the doctrine of God. He was not in this sense a social revolutionary (even though in practice his thought changed the world!). He does not think the Christian's social task is to overturn the political status quo. Social structures are normally to be accepted as God's providential dams for the containment of sin.

John Calvin

The Frenchman John Calvin (1509–64), who was to become the chief Reformer of Geneva, shared Luther's attitude to moral effort as always a response to grace and never the achievement of the human will in independence of the divine sovereignty. Human beings are incapacitated by sin; God's moral law demonstrates this incapacity, at the same time as it shows the utter righteousness of God. God's will determines who will be able to respond to the divine offer of grace and who will not. Our corrupt wills do rightfully incur God's wrath, so God's damnation is not somehow unfair on God's part. But in God's free and loving grace some are enabled to love God and do God's will. This could appear to take away any impetus to moral effort, and breed an ethical fatalism, but Calvin would have argued that his is a proper counterblow to all forms of ethics that are secretly a type of self-seeking rather than being wholly God-centered.

Despite his radical view of human dependence on God, Calvin had a great deal to say about social order as he developed his model of a Christian society in Geneva. In his *Institutes of the Christian Religion* he treated sanctification prior to justification, and thus opened out a role for holiness that Luther lacked. This made more space for developing a commitment to human institutions. All callings can be made a form of service to God's sovereign will, but the depth of human evil means that these insights cannot be expected to safeguard a polity without institutional backup. There must be civil government and jurisdiction; they are part of the divine order. Magistrates are bearers of divine authority. Calvin describes the role of government in this way:

> Civil government has as its appointed end, so long as we live among men, to cherish and protect the outward worship of God, to defend sound doctrine of piety and the position of the church, to adjust our life to the society of men, to form our social behaviour to civil righteousness, to reconcile us with one another, and to promote general peace and tranquillity.

He accepted the occasional need for war as a last resort and when a defense against aggression. His attitude to economics was innovatory in that it gave some permission to the charging of interest on loans – though he insisted that this interest must not be excessive, and for just that reason should not be charged on loans to the poor.

Calvin had a greater readiness than Luther to allow an ongoing purpose for "imperatives" in Christian life – rather than simply making Christian ethics a matter of response to the "indicatives" of grace. In his account of the three uses of the law, he talked not only of:

1. its power to display sin and provoke repentance; and
2. its role in maintaining civic order; but also
3. its continued place in the Christian life as a stimulus to purer obedience and knowledge of the divine will. Law can lead a person to Christ by showing them the righteousness of God.

The Radical Reformation

For some European Christian communities, the reforms of Luther and Calvin and their followers did not go far enough – and a more radical form of counter-cultural living seemed to be required by the Christian gospel. These movements and sects pulled in the opposite direction from the more moderating tendencies of Catholic humanism and the Counter-Reformation.

One of the most lasting forms achieved by this more radical reforming zeal was the Anabaptist tradition, comprising a variety of specific traditions in sixteenth-century Europe whose adherents made great play of being strangers and sojourners in the world, and thus of the need at all times to be ready to resist and renounce the world. This made their ecclesiology an altogether different thing from that of the magisterial Reformers (i.e., Luther and Calvin), who defended the church's place in the world by appeal to God's providence. They had a high view of scriptural authority, and this led to their especial concern with the moral teachings of the New Testament, believing passionately that ideas of grace were not to be a *substitute* for works. To be a Christian one had to be a *disciple* – to make a conscious choice to realign one's whole life and behavior. This underpinned the Anabaptist emphasis on "believer's baptism." In 1527 the Anabaptists issued the Schleitheim Confession, which was a statement of some of their key principles. It emphasized the central importance of morally disciplined living, including the rejection of violence. Another key Anabaptist statement was that of Hans Denck (d. 1528), who wrote that "No one can know Christ except by following him in life."

Jacob Hutter (d. 1536) led the Anabaptist communities who found asylum in Moravia and modeled a common ownership of property. Their descendants are known as Hutterites. In the year Hutter died, the first Reformer of the Netherlands, Menno Simons (1496–1561), renounced his Catholic priesthood and joined the persecuted Anabaptist cells in their radical disciplines. The Mennonite tradition takes its name from him. He argued that conversion and regeneration lead to transformation of life. Believer's baptism opens the way into the community of the obedient (and often persecuted) faithful. In imitation of Christ, this new community will necessarily involve two central practices:

- a commitment to nonviolence; and
- the sharing in simplicity of goods and resources (even one's life and blood).

One of the notable ways in which nonviolent sanctions were applied within Anabaptist communities was the practice of "banning." This was a form of community ostracism intended to secure the sinner's repentance and reform. The key scriptural passage is the model of fraternal correction laid out in Matthew 18:

> If another member of the church sins against you, go and point out the fault when the two of you are alone. If the member listens to you, you have regained that one. But if you are not listened to, take one or two others along with you, so that every word may be confirmed by the evidence of two or three witnesses. If the member refuses to listen to them, tell it to the church; and if the offender refuses to listen even to the church, let such a one be to you as a Gentile and a tax collector. (Matt 18:15–17)

A key reason why infants could not be baptized was that they could not be subject to such a process of fraternal correction.

The characteristic pacifism of the Anabaptist tradition did not prevent it from being the victim of fierce repression by both Catholics and Protestants. This was perhaps provoked by the moral and spiritual challenge they represented. Nonetheless, the movement expanded to various parts of Europe and, in due course, North America. Some – like the Hutterites – have experienced huge growth there in modern times.

Legacies of Division

In the "modern" period, by which we mean from the seventeenth century onwards, there was an increasing distinction between official "church teaching" and the arguments and views of particular Christian writers. The modern university was emerging during this period as something quite different from the medieval schools, freer of church control, and by the nineteenth century it was possible to conceive of a secular university. Many of those who have written about Christian ethics in the modern period have held posts in universities rather than positions in the church. We shall consider six denominational traditions in this period.

Luther's Legacy

The contemporary scholar Robert Benne identifies four main themes in the broad field of Lutheran ethics.

1. A sharp distinction between salvation offered by God in Christ, and all human efforts. Ethics, politics, education, and therapy are desacralized and relativized, since they are attempts to improve the human condition, not matters of salvation. "No one was with Christ on the cross to die for our sins. Or viewed differently, everyone was with Christ on the cross but only as passive inhabitants of his righteous and suffering person."

2. A focused and austere doctrine of the church and its mission. "Its calling is to proclaim and gather a people around the gospel, forming them through the Spirit into the body of Christ. No other community has that calling, no other will promote the gospel if the church fails in its task." Thus works of charity, justice, or public service are important but secondary.

3. The twofold rule of God through law and gospel. If the law is made into the gospel, "the demands and operation of the law are viewed as redemptive, which makes Christ unnecessary." If the gospel is made into the law, "little account is taken of the power of sin and evil in the world, and society becomes vulnerable to the most willful agencies of evil." The former secularizes the gospel while the latter sentimentalizes it. This tension between law and gospel is the foundation for the worldly callings of disciples, and thus for the strong Lutheran tradition of the sacredness of secular vocations.

4. A paradoxical view of human nature and history. Human beings "have a capacity for freedom, love, and justice. Yet they use their freedom to fasten to lesser things, creating a hell for themselves, other human beings, and the world around them. They are a paradox of good and evil, manufacturing idols of the good things they are given. They cannot solve this predicament on their own." Because they look to God to resolve this paradox, they "are freed from trying to manage history according to great schemes. Instead [they] must strive for relative gains and wait on God. [They] must work for reform without cynicism's paralysis or idealism's false hope."

Five figures may be taken to represent aspects of this legacy.

1. *Kierkegaard.* The Danish philosopher-theologian Søren Kierkegaard
    (1813–55) was captivated by the otherness of God and the unique vocation of
    the church (one the Danish Lutheran Church of his time sorely neglected).
    He was vehemently opposed to the Hegelian suggestion that all basic opposi-
    tions were in principle resolvable in the medium of thought: in other words,
    to Hegel's intellectualism. In particular, he thought that to subject the
    Christian religion to such an approach was to domesticate its radical existential
    challenge, which requires individuals to act and choose in the face of an "infinite"
    that defies circumscription by any human faculties of knowledge. Kierkegaard's
    writings revolve repeatedly around ethical questions, but many of these are
    written under pseudonyms, and adopt stances that are not compatible with
    each other (let alone representing something we can identify as his own construc-
    tive program of ethics). The various proposals he puts forward must therefore be
    considered in some distinction from each other.

    One of the key ideas he puts forward in his first major work, *Either/Or*
    (1843), is the distinction between aesthetic and ethical existence. The aesthetic
    stage of existence is one we all begin at, but it is a starting point that should not
    become a way of life because in this mode we live only in the immediacies sur-
    rounding us, pursuing pleasure and enjoyment but essentially being determined
    from outside ourselves (so that the aesthetic can also designate mere conform-
    ity to social custom or etiquette). The ethical stage, by contrast, is one in which
    we make our own decisions and thus actualize our personhood in freedom and
    responsibility. It is the stage of our personal "becoming" through a positive
    exercise of our will.

    But Kierkegaard's writings undertake a relativization of the ethical too, in a
    religious moment epitomized by God's command to Abraham that he sacrifice
    Isaac. In *Fear and Trembling* (1843) Kierkegaard calls this moment the "teleo-
    logical suspension of the ethical." Kierkegaard's pseudonymous author here
    ("Johannes *de silentio*") seems to want to question any theory that pretends to
    define the meaning of human existence exhaustively (for instance, Hegel's
    concept of *Sittlichkeit*, or "ethical life"). In this sense the ethical too can be a sort
    of idolatrous final horizon of meaning that underwrites a false social conformity,
    obscuring the fact that the individual ultimately stands in a direct, unmediated
    relation to God that is irreducible to anything else. The "universal" (e.g., a general
    notion of the good) cannot be allowed to subsume the "particular" (each
    individual in his or her own absolute relation to the absolute). This needs to be
    so even if the individual may return to the ethical in the wake of its suspension,
    and resume ethical life. If he or she does so, it will be with a new sense of the
    relative and not absolute validity of the "ethical."

    Kierkegaard's diverse writings are in constant conversation with Christian
    concepts. They acknowledge the profound importance of ideas of sin and grace,
    whose capacity to undermine complacent rationalism Kierkegaard relishes.

They explore the paradoxes of faith in a God-man, Christ, who called human beings to radical self-sacrificial love. A consistent theme is that the individual must acquire independence from what are taken to be the normal ways of the world, must refuse to swim with the social tide, and must be ready to face the rejecting judgment of other people.

2. *Ritschl.* In contrast to Kierkegaard's concentration on the individual, Albrecht Ritschl (1822–89) made the idea of community central to his theology, and thus laid a key foundation for later developments in social ethics in the nineteenth and twentieth centuries. The gospel, argued Ritschl, was addressed to communities and not individuals; the subject of divine revelation and the recipient of redemption was the church, whose relations he frequently conceived as analogous to familial bonds. So justification, or the forgiveness of sins, is to be looked for in morally integrated human community. The ultimate form of such integrated community is the kingdom of God, which is the final purpose of God for redeemed humanity. The so-called "Ritschlian School" inspired by his writings is marked by its emphasis on community and its stress on ethical questions in preference to metaphysical ones, which it repudiated.

3. *Troeltsch.* Ernst Troeltsch (1865–1923) was a key figure in the growth of the sociological study of religion. His seminal book, *The Social Teaching of the Christian Churches* (1912), laid a foundation for subsequent social ethics – as well as for the emerging discipline of sociology of religion. He made a powerful case for the way in which theological ideas translate into social forms at different periods of history, as well as acknowledging that social, political, and economic forces shape religion. According to Troeltsch, Christianity has tended to veer toward one of three archetypal forms at different times in its past: a "church-type," which views Christianity as an all-encompassing social framework or civilization; a "sect-type," which gathers a company of the faithful out of what is perceived to be a fallen world, and demands costly and committed discipleship from them; and "mysticism," which focuses not on institutions or groups but on individual experience as the site of encounter with God.

4. *Niebuhr.* Reinhold Niebuhr (1892–1971) epitomizes the convictions noted by Benne in his third and fourth themes listed above. He grew up as a Lutheran in a denomination that later united with Reformed traditions and eventually formed part of the United Church of Christ in 1957. He viewed the power plays and varieties of self-interest in the political sphere as intractable aspects of human life, and had a developed doctrine of original sin. He thought it made little sense to talk about love at the level of institutions and political organizations until one had first addressed the need for justice – even if the highest aim of the Christian ethic remains selfless love. He was a great advocate of the advantages of participative democracy in countering the human tendency to injustice and the abuse of power. He was a ferocious critic of bourgeois individualism.

One result of Niebuhr's so-called "realism" about sin was an articulate critique of pacifism, forged in response to the onset of World War II. Living by the law of love for him could never be a simple possibility in human history. Even if one insists that warfare must never be accepted too readily, one should not therefore slip too easily into the acceptance of injustice as the price of avoiding war.

5.   *Bonhoeffer.* Dietrich Bonhoeffer (1906–45) travelled to the USA planning to study under Reinhold Niebuhr. Having learned less than he had hoped from Niebuhr, he returned to Germany. His second visit to the USA was curtailed when he returned to Europe in order to join the resistance to Hitler. His corpus is small because of his untimely death at the hands of the Nazi regime. His key work is perhaps *The Cost of Discipleship*, which distances itself from the Lutheran tradition by its heavy emphasis on discipleship, traditionally more of a Radical Reformation theme. Bonhoeffer's other key ethical work – *Ethics* – was published posthumously. In it he develops a more characteristically Lutheran distinction between "ultimate" and "penultimate" things (see Benne's second theme above). He explores how the *ultimate* (God's perfected kingdom at the end of time, to which the church points) relates to the *penultimate* (our life in time and in human flesh, looking toward what is to come but not pretending it is already here). Bonhoeffer explored this in a famous passage on the tension between radicalism and compromise:

> Radicalism sees God as Judge and Redeemer; compromise sees God as Creator and Preserver. In Radicalism the end is rendered absolute; in compromise, things as-they-are are rendered absolute. Radicalism hates time; compromise hates eternity. Radicalism hates patience; compromise hates decision. Radicalism hates wisdom; compromise hates simplicity. Radicalism hates moderation and measure; compromise hates the immeasurable. Radicalism hates the real; compromise hates the Word.

We may summarize what Bonhoeffer is saying here as follows:

- The ultimate can be made the enemy of the penultimate. That is radicalism in Bonhoeffer's sense.
- The penultimate can be made the enemy of the ultimate. This happens when material institutions and forms of human life like family, work, and the state become ends in themselves. That is compromise and that is a risk the church constantly faces, tempted as it is to baptize the status quo and go for the most comfortable option.
- But God's will is that the ultimate and the penultimate be allowed to serve each other. The penultimate takes on significance and definition from what it is moving towards; the ultimate gives space and time to the created order for its response. Penultimate things should be referred beyond themselves to the God they are meant to serve, the God from whom they derive their real meaning.

Calvin's Legacy

By the early seventeenth century, Reformed Protestantism in the Netherlands was in profound dispute over the teachings of Jacob Arminius (1560–1609) and his followers, the Remonstrants. Arminius differed with Calvin's view of predestination and God's prevenient grace. In response, the Synod of Dort (1618–19) adopted the famous Five Points of Calvinism (TULIP): total depravity, unconditional election, limited atonement, irresistible grace, and perseverance of the saints.

Contemporary scholar Douglas Ottati points out a number of subsequent themes in Reformed ethics.

1. A broad understanding of the sources of wisdom. While Calvin and the Westminster Confession of 1647 had a high view of the uniqueness of Scripture, Ulrich Zwingli (1484–1531) and Calvin both made significant use of early creeds and the writings of the Church Fathers. Calvin believed the moral law was the testimony of natural law and conscience; Roger Williams (1603–83) believed Jews and Muslims had such a conscience, and Jonathan Edwards (1703–58) wrote that "to find out the reasons of things in natural philosophy is only to find out the proportion of God's acting."
2. A high view of human possibility. Despite the radical derangement brought about by sin, "God continues to uphold in fallen persons impressive abilities in the arts and sciences, as well as certain basic social affections and a rudimentary sense of justice or fairness." Meanwhile well-being and well-doing are restored by grace and the Spirit, and are demonstrated in piety toward God and charity toward neighbor.
3. A positive view of law. Moral behavior and good works should stem not from prudence (to keep on good terms with neighbors or to attain salvation), but from thankfulness for God's goodness and grace. The most important purpose of law is to guide and exhort the faithful in their efforts to do good.
4. The relationship of God and world. Sovereignty is the chief issue for Reformed ethics, in the same way that justification is the center of Lutheran ethics. For the Dutch theologian and statesman Abraham Kuyper (1837–1920), the root principle of Calvinism is "the Sovereignty of the Triune God over the whole Cosmos, in all of its spheres and [dominions], visible and invisible." The conviction that "every dimension of living, both inward and outward, should be reordered and redirected toward God and God's glory" underpins the large investment Reformed ethics has tended to have in ordering and governing civil society.

Three figures may be taken to illustrate the legacy of Reformed ethics.

1. *Edwards.* The legacy of Reformed ethics may be identified with its most prominent figures. Jonathan Edwards, the New England Puritan and prophet of the first Great Awakening, expressed the first, second, and fourth of the

above themes in his integration of European philosophy and Calvinist heritage. In *The Nature of True Virtue* (1765), Edwards defines Christian love as an unearned gift, which was not limited or partial, was steady not episodic, and was always uniting creatures both to God and to one another. For Edwards, virtue is essentially benevolence, extended to all things. Such benevolence involves a consent to, a propensity to, or a union of the heart to God, the Supreme Being, and thence to all other beings (being-in-general). This is what it means to speak of general good will. Virtue is thus the form God's love takes when it is imparted to God's creatures. For Edwards, humans did indeed possess a natural capacity for following an internal moral sense. But this kind of morality was no more than prudential action, designed for pragmatic purposes. It was not the same as true virtue, which was primarily about love for God.

2.   *Kuyper.* Abraham Kuyper lived what he wrote about. A theologian who was for a period prime minister of the Netherlands, his theology wove together creation, history, the cosmic work of the Holy Spirit, and public theology. He is known for his articulation of common grace. For him, Calvinism honors humanity because it is made in the image of God, and honors the world as the creation of God. It balances a particular grace that brings about salvation with a common grace by which God maintains the life of the world, mitigates the curse that burdens it, and halts its process of corruption. This balance creates the space for the development of human life in which it comes to glorify God. Instead of distinguishing between nature and grace, Kuyper preferred to talk of creation and re-creation. This positive view of the world under God's sovereignty underwrote his theology of engagement. He did not believe in a national church, but he did believe in the possibility of a Christian nation. A Christian nation would, he believed, come about when particular grace in the church and among Christians influenced common grace so profoundly that common grace came to attain its highest development.

3.   *Barth.* We will meet Karl Barth (1886–1968) once again in relation to divine command ethics (Chapter Five) and ecclesial ethics (Chapter Seven), but he cannot be omitted from any account of Calvin's legacy. Already profoundly influenced by religious socialist ideas, Barth's world was shaken by the experience of world war and the totalitarian pretensions of the Nazi state. Against this background he returned more deeply to the radical descriptions of a world of sin and grace he found in the "strange world of the Bible." He became the most influential and prolific Protestant theologian of the twentieth century, and the pivotal figure in ending the dominance of liberal Protestant theology in Europe.

Barth emphasized the radical command of God, which breaks in from outside and overturns all existing cultural and social norms. He is in part a disciple of Kierkegaard in this relativization of national identities, ecclesiastical structures, and moral assumptions. Other key commitments in his ethical thought include the formulation that "ethics is dogmatics and dogmatics ethics." In other words, the "subject matter" of theology – that is to say, the disclosure of God's all-encompassing relation to the human person in freedom and love – *necessitates* a total reorientation of the human being in correspondence to what has been revealed. The revelation has not really happened, and the "subject matter" has not really been understood, unless there is this reorientation. Theology cannot articulate its core truth (God-in-humanward-action) unless it is also ethics (humans-in-Godward-action). The need for the dramatic intervention of God's revelatory self-disclosure to show this truth is what underlies Barth's vociferous rejection of natural law thinking – a tradition which he sees as compromising God's freedom to "give" Godself by proposing that God can be "found" by our existing faculties of enquiry and knowledge.

In an Augustinian vein, Barth emphasizes the simultaneity of freedom and obedience in the Christian life: we are only genuinely free when God makes it possible for us to hear the divine command and obey it (in joy!). Until that point, we may feel we have great autonomy but in practice are in thrall to pride, sloth, and falsehood. The truth of our created natures is found in redeemed, reconciled, and faithful obedience to God. A final key category for Barth is covenant. From the foundation of the world, God intended covenant fellowship with the creation (expressed in the fellowship of Christ with the church); in other words, covenant was what creation was *for*, all along. In light of this, the human task is to respond to this gracious intention for fellowship, in every realm of created life. Morally significant patterns in the created order – disclosed and affirmed by revelation – include the man–woman relationship, and the state, which can have a provisional role in preserving civility and allowing the church to proclaim the gospel message until the eschaton is fully realized.

Anglican and Methodist Themes

The Anglican tradition originated in the establishment of the Church of England in 1534 as a state church independent of Rome's authority; the Methodist tradition began as a renewal movement within the Church of England in the early eighteenth century. It benefits both Anglicanism and Methodism to study their developments in the light of one another. Thus we can see the truly sacramental character of Wesley's thought and the way Anglicans were dragged into rethinking their social ethics partly by the example of Methodist adaptation to the new industrial world.

John Wesley (1703–91) was a cradle Anglican (his parents having rejected their dissenting background in favor of the established church). Nevertheless, he was deeply influenced by the devotional traditions of certain independent Protestant traditions, including the Pietist spirituality of the Moravians, with its strong appeal to experience. His part in fostering the spiritual discipline of the Oxford-based "Holy Club" from 1729 involved not only the encouragement of theological study, fasting, and frequent reception of the sacrament of Holy Communion, but also regular visits to the poor, sick, and imprisoned. An emphasis on social involvement would remain central to Methodism.

Central to Wesleyan preaching was the universal love and grace of God, and a key part of their vision was the possibility of Christian "perfection" as an outworking of this grace. Perfection for Wesley meant the life of holiness that was the proper goal of every believer, a holiness whose expression would naturally entail love of neighbor as well as love of God. His doctrine of perfection did not mean that the Christian never again erred or suffered. He was clear that perfection was as much a gift of grace as faith was, and never a *property* of the believer. But the doctrine of perfection expressed his belief that in *cooperation* with the Holy Spirit human discipline really led to growth in holiness. So we may say that if Luther's concern had been with how righteousness was *imputed* (divinely attributed) to the believer, Wesley held that one had to look for the ways righteousness was also *imparted*. Only in sanctification is the final aim of justification realized – not only in the salvation of individual souls, but in "social holiness" too. Thus, when one's neighbor was in material or social need, then that need should be met, whether in the form of homes, free health clinics, food, clothing, coal, or prayer. Even though Wesley himself may not have been a more than superficial analyst of the complex underlying forces at work in the early Industrial Revolution, his movement was energetic in responding to some of its immediate symptoms. Such energy issued in the establishment of Sunday Schools and no-interest loan funds, and in promoting cottage industries. He was also an unrelenting opponent of the slave trade and of slavery, and (though not a pacifist) he was eloquent about the evils and stupidities of war.

A key figure in adapting American Methodism to its particular cultural context was Borden Bowne (1847–1910). Bowne set out to refute the materialism and naturalism of the prevailing scientific and secular environment. In his book *The Immanence of God* (1905) he identified the undivineness of what he called "the natural" and the unnaturalness of what he called "the divine." He regarded both as disastrous ways in which popular thought had lost its divine resonance. For Bowne, what he called *personality* was at the heart of a new way of talking about God. The person is prior to the universe. This is because the significance of the universe lies in the person who experiences it. Jesus Christ was the revelation of God as an infinite person. Religious experience is the central foundation of this natural theology. Only God has inner freedom, the indispensable key to reality and truth. Thus, Bowne harmonized the Methodist themes of personal salvation, renewal of true humanity, and human freedom. The emphasis on the immanence of God appealed to the Methodist emphasis on the possibility of moral development through the Holy Spirit. Bowne looked at the problems of philosophy and believed he had solved them in the conscious unity, identity, and free activity of personality. Perhaps his most lasting legacy in late twentieth-century ethics consists in his influence on the thinking of Martin Luther King Jr., who studied with Bowne's student Edgar Sheffield Brightman (1884–1953) at Boston University.

Unlike Roman Catholicism, the churches of the Anglican Communion do not have a single authoritative body of moral teaching, though they have inherited a modest tradition of canon law. Richard Hooker (1554–1600) ensured that a strand of natural law thinking derived principally from Thomas Aquinas continued in the Church of England, and reproduced Aquinas' basic typology of natural, positive, divine, and eternal law. Anglican evangelicals – especially in the eighteenth and nineteenth centuries – used scriptural arguments that verged on the crudely literalistic to argue for social reforms, amelioration of the hardship and injustice that were consequent upon the Industrial Revolution, and the abolition of slavery.

A key Anglican figure in the modern period is the Englishman F. D. Maurice (1805–72), who asserted the ethical implications of the doctrine of the incarnation for the way that social problems were addressed and handled. Against the other-worldly, atonement-centered evangelicalism of his day, he believed that Christians had an urgent duty to improve their social environment. He rejected the doctrine of original sin as incapacitating, and affirmed the responsibility and ability of Christians to make a difference in the world. He was one of the founders of Christian socialism, looking to advance a cooperative spirit to deal with economic and social problems. Maurice and others engendered a more incarnationally grounded Christian socialist tradition which has had its disciples ever since. They were gripped by the vision of a Christian society that embodied "the science of partnership," in which people worked with, and not in competition with, each other. This, for them, was what "socialism" *meant*. Charles Gore (1853–1932) had his prophetic spirit nurtured in this tradition. He went on to edit the influential work *Property, Its Duties and Rights* (1913) and to write his own *Christ and Society* (1928), as well as to found the Interdenominational Conference of Social Service Unions.

In the twentieth century a prominent figure was Kenneth Kirk (1886–1954), Professor of Moral and Pastoral Theology at Oxford, whose greatest book, *The Vision of God* (1931), explored the intrinsic relationship between ethics and worship, and argued that it is in the activity of worship that Christians will find the key resources they need for addressing their ethical problems. He was also a great modern exponent of the idea of conscience. William Temple (1881–1944) inherited Gore's passionate social concern, and through writings like *Christianity and Social Order* (1942) is one of the people credited with creating a climate of opinion that made possible the social legislation of the post-war period in England, including the establishment of a welfare state.

In recent decades, the General Synod of the Church of England has issued several reports that are concerned with the social responsibility of Christians – with successive focus on the city and the countryside. The other autonomous provinces of the worldwide Anglican Communion have done analogous social responsibility work through similar bodies. Some of the most arresting voices in contemporary Anglican ethics are described in Chapter Seven under the category of "ecclesial ethics" – foremost amongst them being Oliver O'Donovan (b. 1945) and John Milbank (b. 1952). Anglicans in South Africa were some of the key architects of the movement of theological protest (e.g., the 1985 Kairos Document) that helped bring an end to apartheid, as well as of the nation's post-apartheid Truth and Reconciliation Commission. But both within the Church of England in particular, and across the Anglican Communion as a whole, there are profound divisions today about a variety of ethical issues, notably sexual ethics, and little consensus about the value of natural law approaches as compared with biblically derived imperatives or appeals to human experience. Many of the fault-lines in the current debates are shared with other denominations.

Roman Catholic Moral Theology

From the seventeenth century onward, modern Catholic ethics (or moral theology, as the Catholic tradition typically refers to it) is influenced by several factors. It takes its shape in part as a response to the galvanizing forces of the Protestant Reformation. Like the other streams of Christian ethics described here, it also responds to the pressures of the Enlightenment. In other ways, unlike the Protestant traditions described above, it continues to be dominated by the earlier emphases of the medieval era.

From the late sixteenth century until the Second Vatican Council in 1962–5, manuals of moral theology were the main medium for Roman Catholic ethical instruction. The need for the manuals originated in two key developments: the rise of the modern university, which began in the thirteenth century and culminated in the eighteenth century, and the establishment of seminaries, which emerged from the deliberations of the Council of Trent (1545–1563), held in large part as a response to the Protestant Reformers.

The manuals, which were mainly developed as a resource for the education of priests, have important similarities to a body of writings known as the "penitentials," or penitential manuals, which arose in the sixth century alongside the increasing practice of priests hearing private confessions and assigning penance (see also the discussion of penance in Chapter Two). By giving priests guidelines regarding the appropriate acts of penance to assign for particular sins, the penitentials sought to prevent priests from assigning penance in an arbitrary or inconsistent way, but they have often been criticized for their lack of reflection on the role of intention and circumstances, and for their restriction of the priest's flexibility in relation to the exercise of prudence. This shift in Catholic thinking away from catechesis (preparation for baptism) and toward penance would have long-standing consequences for Catholic ethics, not least because they shape the character of the manuals of moral theology in the Reformation and modern eras.

Like the penitentials, the manuals were oriented especially toward the hearing of confessions and the sacrament of penance. The prototype for all subsequent manuals was the syllabus for moral theology (*Institutiones morales*) developed by the Spanish Jesuit Juan Azor (1536–1603), which divided moral theology into four main sections: human acts, conscience, laws, and sins. The manuals also focused on the practice of casuistry, or moral reflection on specific cases where there appeared to be a conflict between different moral principles or laws.

Casuistry was particularly associated with the Jesuit order, which was founded in 1540 and whose central document for Jesuit education (*Ratio studiorum*) included a section on the study of moral cases. Though casuistry was by no means a Jesuit preserve, it was a tradition of moral reasoning used extensively by them in the confessional, provoking suspicion and attacks from some (like Blaise Pascal in 1656–7) who thought that Jesuit casuists were manipulating it to wink at the sins of wealthy donors. Some Jesuit casuists famously promoted the doctrine of "mental reservation," by which a certain withholding of the truth, or deliberate deception, was legitimated in cases where it was judged that one's interlocutor was not owed the full truth.

Another controversial approach related to the casuistry of the manuals was probabilism: the view that if a significant minority of authorities taught that a moral law was not binding, one could adopt that position even if it was more probable that the law *was* binding. Although many Jesuits used probabilist reasoning, the idea originated with a Spanish Dominican, Bartholomew of Medina (1527–80). Probabilism was vigorously criticized as a path to moral laxity, and the controversy was only settled at the end of the eighteenth century through the compromise of the Catholic bishop Alphonsus Liguori (1696–1787), who argued that one may be released from a moral obligation only if the arguments in favor of freedom from the obligation are at least equal to the arguments in favor of keeping the law.

A perception that the tradition embodied in the manuals was overly extrinsic, legalistic, and focused on the choices and responsibility of individuals was one of the motivations for a "neo-Thomist" movement (a revival of Thomas Aquinas' thought) in the twentieth century. This movement focused on the encompassing category of *the good* as embedded in nature and in human life. A central figure in this revival was Servais-Théodore Pinckaers (1925–2008), a theologian and member of the Dominican order. Pinckaers argued that the Franciscan William of Ockham (c. 1295–1349) restructured all subsequent moral theology through his notion of nominalism, which gave rise to a morality of obligation or duty-based ethics in the place of Thomas's virtue-based ethics. Pinckaers and other neo-Thomists rejected "nominalistic" suggestions that any particular deed is good simply because it is commanded, and they urged a return to Thomistic, virtue-based ethics rather than the duty-based ethics that arose in the fourteenth century and that dominated moral theology, including the manuals, until Vatican II. This retrieval of virtue ethics has analogies in Protestant ethical thinking and will be examined in depth in Chapter Seven.

The nineteenth and twentieth centuries have seen a huge energy in Roman Catholic moral theology, which will be summarized briefly here and which is explored throughout this book – both in the chapter on universal ethics that follows this one, and also throughout the last five chapters of the book, which deal with specific ethical issues. Other significant elements in contemporary Roman Catholic ethics, notably proportionalism, will be addressed in the next chapter.

In the nineteenth century, Catholic moral theology (as well as Protestant ethics) adapted in order to address the challenges raised by Enlightenment thinkers like Immanuel Kant, John Stuart Mill, and Friedrich Nietzsche. It also took on a new character due to the need to address an increasingly pluralist world – often by appealing to the principle of natural law. It is in this context that a body of official church writings known as Catholic social teaching emerges in the late nineteenth century, beginning (one could argue) with the papal encyclical *Rerum Novarum* (On Capital and Labor, 1891). Catholic social teaching is characterized not only by its communal ethic and concern for the poor (these had always been part of Catholic teaching), but by its arguments on the basis of natural law that certain aspects of human flourishing such as health or human dignity are intrinsically good and should be upheld by all peoples and governments, whether Christian or not. The principle of the "common good" has thus been a keystone of Catholic social teaching.

In the mid-twentieth century, the Second Vatican Council (1962–65) sought a renewed attention to the distinctiveness of the Christian life in relation to the universal concerns of natural law ethics. The writings of Pope John Paul II – for example, the 1994 encyclical *Veritatis splendor* (The Splendor of Truth) – evince the ongoing effort in Catholic ethics to balance between a universal ethic, rooted in natural law and binding on all people, and a distinctively Christian ethic rooted in following and imitating Christ. Vatican II also recognized the limitations of the manuals of moral theology and called for moral theology to be more deeply nourished by Scripture, more closely linked to dogmatic theology, and more thoroughly grounded in the insights of science and philosophy.

The Second Vatican Council's strong impetus to a renewed engagement with Scripture changed the character of Catholic moral theology accordingly. The Scriptures were affirmed as the "soul" of all theology, and the effects of this turn are still evident in recent papal encyclicals, which are frequently exegetical. At the same time, Catholic thinkers found themselves freer to engage with modern currents of philosophical thought; a scholastic paradigm such as that used by Aquinas was no longer the exclusive basis for moral (or any other) theology. For example, the Jesuit priest and theologian Karl Rahner (1904–84) drew deeply on traditions of idealism to argue that there is an intrinsic, self-transcending openness to God built into the structures of human subjectivity. This has offered a more conducive framework than the manuals ever provided for thinking about growth and development in the moral life.

A complex debate also emerged in the twentieth century over the so-called twofold end of action, or the two ends of the human creature: a person's end as a created being (nature), and her end as a person in Christ (grace). (This debate mirrors the tension named above between natural law and revealed Christian truth.) As Augustine claimed, "our heart is restless until it rests in [God]"; human beings find their true fulfillment through resting in God and thus, paradoxically, can only fulfill their true created purpose by exceeding their nature, through the "supernatural" gift of God's grace. Yet some argued that if the longing for God is written into human nature, then this blurs the line between nature and grace. Others, like the Jesuit Henri de Lubac (1896–1991), appealed to Aquinas' teaching that "grace does not destroy nature but perfects it" and insisted on humanity's inherent, universal desire for God. The previously dominant dualism between the natural and the supernatural has largely dropped away in favor of views, like de Lubac's, that celebrate a grace-infused nature. From this vantage point, "pure nature," a theoretical state in which humans perfectly fulfill the end of their existence in relation only to their nature and not through participation in God, is only *formally* conceivable apart from grace (in order to show that grace is a free gift and not a necessity or a "right" of the creation) but in fact it has never existed independently of it.

At the same time, there have been energetic developments of "personalist" thought in modern Roman Catholic ethics, with a high view of the dignity and freedom of the whole human person (this was a powerful concern of Pope John Paul II, and fired much of his passionate resistance to communism). Greater emphasis on the person has worked in tandem with renewed interest in the theme of character and virtue, and has linked moral theology more closely with liturgical and sacramental theology.

Finally, Catholic political and liberation theologies have drawn from a variety of non-traditional philosophical sources, including Marxism, to stress the importance of praxis (practice) and of orthopraxis (right action) alongside theory and orthodoxy. Some of the most arresting voices in modern Christian ethics have been those of the liberation theologians of Latin America, and the great majority of these have been Roman Catholic, most notably the Peruvian theologian and Dominican priest Gustavo Gutiérrez (b. 1928). While official church pronouncements have historically been less warm to liberation theology, largely due to its association with Marxism, the installation of the Jesuit Argentinian Jorge Mario Bergoglio (b. 1936) as Pope Francis in 2013 has led to a certain new openness in the Vatican to liberationist approaches. Liberation theologies will be dealt with in detail in later chapters, especially in Chapter Six.

Eastern Orthodox Ethics

Eastern Orthodox thought diverged from Western theology and ethics long before the modern era. Whereas Western ethics draws on Augustine as one of its primary wellsprings, Orthodox ethics finds its roots in the Eastern Fathers, including the Cappadocians, Maximus the Confessor (ca. 613–662 CE), and John of Damascus (ca. 670–749 CE). Maximus was both a monk and a mystic; there is in Orthodox ethics a greater openness to the insights of the mystical tradition than is usually found in Western ethics. John of Damascus is generally regarded as the last of the great Fathers of the East; the third part of his *Fount of Wisdom* (the *Exposition and Declaration of the Orthodox Faith*) is a systematic exploration of Christian doctrine, including a defense of the veneration of icons that is rooted in the doctrine of the incarnation.

For modern Orthodox ethics, the incarnation and God's nature as Trinity are perhaps the two key doctrines from which all else flows. This demonstrates the close connection between doctrine and ethics in the Orthodox traditions, which have retained the premodern church's reluctance to see ethics as in any way an area of Christian enquiry or activity separate from worship and the teaching of doctrine. Worship, doctrine, and ethics are all about the impartation of the divine reality to human creatures, and about creatures being drawn into ever deeper participation in the divine life in both thought and deed. The "energies" of the triune God make that God actively present in human life, and human life can only come to fulfillment with their powerful assistance. The *telos*, or end, of human life is written into its beginning; as humans are created in God's *image*, so through God's grace do they take on God's *likeness*. God-likeness was the vocation of humanity from the very beginning; it was denied by Adam at the Fall but perfectly taken up by Jesus Christ in the incarnation. The Fall, then, is viewed less as a radical corruption of the natural goodness of humanity and more as a diminishment of humanity's capacity for communion with God, a capacity restored by Christ's incarnation, which healed human nature. The process of growing in God's likeness is known as *theosis*.

For Orthodox ethics, *theosis* is inextricable from the nature of God as Trinity – as inexhaustible, self-giving communion – and therefore as love, or *agape*. The self-emptying and uniting character of love was perfectly enacted in the incarnation, by which divine and human nature were united in Christ. The vigor of the doctrine of the Trinity in Orthodoxy helps to undergird a vision of love that exceeds mere mutuality and passes over into communion and union, after the pattern of the relation between the divine Persons.

Key contemporary figures whose work has had an impact in the English-speaking world include the Russian theologian and political theorist Sergei Bulgakov (1871–1944) – much of whose thought has been mediated to the West by contemporary Anglican theologian Rowan Williams – and John Zizioulas (b. 1931). Bulgakov was a prominent Orthodox priest in Russia who was eventually exiled by the Bolshevik government and died in Paris; his views on the Virgin Mary were highly controversial and subjected him to charges of heresy, which were later dropped. The work of Zizioulas, who is Metropolitan of Pergamon in Turkey, has largely focused on the theme of communion, in *Being as Communion* (1985) and *Communion and Otherness* (2007), and on the theme of eschatology in *Remembering the Future: An Eschatological Ontology* (2008).

In the United States, the leading voices in Orthodox ethics are Stanley Harakas (b. 1932) and Vigen Guroian (b. 1948). Harakas is a theologian and priest of the Greek Orthodox Archdiocese of America; his book *Toward Transfigured Life: The Theoria of Eastern Orthodox Ethics* (1983) is often considered the first major work in specifically Orthodox ethics (rather than Orthodox theology). Guroian, an Armenian Orthodox lay theologian, has taken up Harakas's work and extended it in his own writing, especially *Incarnate Love: Essays in Orthodox Ethics* (1987, updated 2002).

Pentecostalism

At the turn of the twenty-first century, the most rapidly growing Christian tradition in the world was also the newest. Pentecostalism took root in a series of revivals in the United States in the early 1900s, when small groups of Christians became convinced that they had experienced a new descent of the Holy Spirit, similar to the day of Pentecost described in the book of Acts. The Pentecostal movement emerged in part from a branch of Methodism known as the Holiness movement, which insisted on the necessity of a "second blessing" constituted by a baptism in the Spirit. Pentecostal Christians similarly emphasized a baptism by the Holy Spirit accompanied by spiritual gifts such as the ability to speak in tongues, to prophesy, and to heal the sick. Whereas early Pentecostal leaders like William Seymour (1870–1922) saw the breaking down of interracial barriers and the preaching of women as signs of a new movement of the Spirit, conflict swiftly erupted over both issues, and these then-radical stances proved difficult to maintain. Over time, the movement coalesced into several distinct denominations such as the predominantly African-American Church of God in Christ, and spread rapidly to Africa and Latin America through the efforts of missionaries. Pentecostal ethics today face several challenges, including the role of personal experience in relation to doctrine, the rapid pace of growth that often outstrips ecclesiastical structures, and its association in some regions with the so-called prosperity gospel, which equates God's blessing with material wealth.

Summary

What we have seen in telling this story about the evolution of Christian ethics is how the church's claims about who God is and about what the world is made for, as well as the moral disciplines that have accompanied those claims, have constantly interacted with their social and historical environment. Christian ethics has both *made differences* and *had differences made to it* in the course of this history. At some times and in some places, Christian thought about moral issues has been a minority voice in a world where other descriptions, other ways of thinking, and other ethical reference points have been dominant. This was especially true in the first three centuries of Christianity's life, and has been again in the modern period. In such circumstances, Christian ethics has had to resist, or try to commend itself to, these dominant stories. It has sometimes assimilated itself to them. At other times and places, perhaps above all in the period of medieval Christendom, Christianity was itself the dominant story, and provided the shared environment for thought and action within which others had to find their place. At such moments, Christianity has done ethics not just for an embattled few, not just for a minority community, not just in matters of "internal regulation," but has thought with confidence about every level of human life in the world, from the bedroom to the throne room. The distinctive emphases and contributions of different denominations are a reminder that the story of Christian ethics does not have a single plot, but has variegated and overlapping strands of development. And the huge shifts it has undergone at certain points, under the influence of the Roman Empire's sponsorship of Christianity in the fourth century, or the revolutionary changes of the Reformation, or the impact of Kant's thought, are just vivid examples of a more general truth: that Christian ethics never stands still.

References and Further Reading

A valuable source throughout the chapter has been J. Philip Wogaman, *Christian Ethics: A Historical Introduction* (Louisville, KY: Westminster/John Knox Press, 1993). This is a helpful book for any reader wanting a more expansive overview of the history of Christian ethics than is possible in this chapter.

In its early sections this chapter has made use of Henry Chadwick, *The Early Church* (Harmondsworth: Penguin, 1967). The following texts by Peter Brown are also authoritative sources for understanding ethics in the first Christian centuries: *The Body and Society: Men, Women, and Sexual Renunciation in Early Christianity*

(2nd edn; New York: Columbia University Press, 2008); *Augustine of Hippo: A Biography* (Berkeley, CA: University of California Press, 1967, 2000); *Society and the Holy in Late Antiquity* (London: Faber and Faber, 1982); *The Rise of Western Christendom* (2nd edn; Oxford: Blackwell, 2003); and *Poverty and Leadership in the Later Roman Empire* (Waltham, MA: Brandeis University Press, 2002).

For a general introduction to Western church history, see Diarmaid MacCulloch, *Christian History: An Introduction to the Western Tradition* (Peterborough: Epworth, 2006).

Foundations

Justin Martyr's *First Apology* can be found in *Early Christian Fathers* (Cyril C. Richardson, ed.; New York: Macmillan, 1970); available online at at http://www.ccel.org/ccel/richardson/fathers.x.ii.html.

Tertullian's most important early writing is his *Apology*, which can be found in Vol. 3 of *The Ante-Nicene Fathers* (Alexander Roberts and James Donaldson, eds; Grand Rapids, MI: W. B. Eerdmans, 1978–1981). His later pronounced opposition to military service can be found in *On Idolatry*, 19, also in *The Ante-Nicene Fathers*, Vol. 3, page 73.

For Gregory of Nyssa's views on slavery, see his *Homily on Ecclesiastes* in *Social Thought* (Peter C. Phan, ed.; Message of the Fathers of the Church 20; Wilmington, DE: Michael Glazier, 1984), page 128.

The quotation from Basil about humanity as a political and social animal comes from his *Homily on Psalm XIV*, I, in *Message of the Fathers of the Church: Social Thought* (Peter Phan, ed.; Wilmington, DE: Michael Glazier, 1984), page 110.

The discussion of Ambrose of Milan's reflections on justice and economics quotes from his *Duties of the Clergy*, I.28, in *Nicene and Post-Nicene Fathers*

(Philip Schaff and Henry Wace, eds; Grand Rapids, MI: Eerdmans, 1978–9), Vol. X, page 23.

A key work for Augustine's thought is *The City of God* (Henry Bettenson, trans.; New York: Penguin Books, 1972, 1984); see especially Book XIX; Augustine discusses war and peace in Book XIX, chapters 1–14, and the quotation about the role of the earthly city is from Book XIX, chapter 26. *The City of God* is available online at www.ccel.org/ccel/schaff/npnf102.toc.html. A selection from *The City of God* is included in the corresponding chapter of *Christian Ethics: An Introductory Reader*.

Thomas Aquinas' magisterial work is *Summa Theologica* (5 vols; Notre Dame, IN: Christian Classics, 1948), also available at www.ccel.org/ccel/aquinas/summa.html. Aquinas discusses virtue in the Prima Secundae [First Part of the Second Part], Questions 61–2; his outline of the four forms of law is from Prima Secundae, Questions 93–6. His discussion of war is from Secunda Secundae [Second Part of the Second Part], Question 40, a portion of which is quoted in the corresponding chapter of *Christian Ethics: An Introductory Reader*.

A helpful general source for this chapter is *Message of the Fathers of the Church: Social Thought*, edited by Peter Phan (see above).

Revisions

Martin Luther's thought may be found in *Martin Luther's Basic Theological Writings* (Timothy F. Lull, ed.; Minneapolis, MN: Fortress Press, 1989). The quotation "from faith flow forth love and joy in the Lord" is from Luther's work *Concerning Christian Liberty* (1520). Luther's idea of the "freedom of a Christian" is also from *Concerning Christian Liberty*, which may be found in *Readings in Christian Ethics: A Historical Sourcebook* (J. Philip Wogaman and Douglas M. Strong, eds; Louisville, KY: Westminster/John Knox Press, 1996). Luther's exposition of the "two kingdoms" can be found in "Temporal Authority: To What Extent it Should Be Obeyed," in *Martin Luther's Basic Theological Writings* (Timothy F. Lull, ed.; Minneapolis, MN: Fortress Press, 1989). A selection from this treatise may also be found in the corresponding chapter of *Christian Ethics: An Introductory Reader*.

John Calvin's quotation about civil government is from *Institutes of the Christian Religion* (Chicago, IL: Encyclopaedia Britannica, 1990), IV.xx.2–3; and his discussion of the three uses of law is from *Institutes* II.vii.6–12.

The Hans Denck quotation ("No one can know Christ …") is from his treatise "Whether God is the Cause of Evil" (Augsburg, 1526), and is reproduced in *Spiritual and Anabaptist Writers* (George H. Williams and Angel M. Mergal, eds; Philadelphia, PA: Westminster Press, 1957), page 108.

Menno Simons' discussion of "banning" can be found in "A Kind Admonition on Church Discipline," in *The Complete Writings of Menno Simons* (Leonard Verdiun, trans.; John Christian Wenger, ed.; Scottdale, PA: Herald Press, 1956); and is also in the corresponding chapter of *Christian Ethics: An Introductory Reader*.

In addition to the above, the following is also included in *Christian Ethics: An Introductory Reader*: John Wesley, "The Use of Money," in *The Works of John Wesley* (Vol. VI: *Sermons on Several Occasions*; Grand Rapids, MI: Zondervan, 1958), available online at http://wesley.nnu.edu/john-wesley/the-sermons-of-john-wesley-1872-edition/sermon-50-the-use-of-money/.

Legacies of Division

The section on Lutheran ethics draws on Robert Benne, "Lutheran Ethics: Perennial Themes and Contemporary Challenges," pages 11–30 in *The Promise of Lutheran Ethics* (Karen L. Bloomquist and John R. Stumme, eds; Minneapolis, MA: Fortress, 1998).

Two of Søren Kierkegaard's important ethical works are *Either/Or* (Howard V. Hong and Edna H. Hong, trans.; Princeton, NJ: Princeton University Press, 1987) and *Fear and Trembling* (C. Stephen Evans and Sylvia Walsh, eds.; Sylvia Walsh, trans.; Cambridge; New York: Cambridge University Press, 2006).

Albrecht Ritschl's most influential work is *The Christian Doctrine of Justification and Reconciliation: The Positive Development of the Doctrine* (H. R. Mackintosh and A. B. Macaulay, trans.; Eugene, OR: Wipf & Stock, 2004). See also *Three Essays: Theology and Metaphysics; Prolegomena to the History of Pietism; Instruction in the Christian Religion* (Philip J. Hefner, trans.; Eugene, OR: Wipf & Stock, 2005).

Ernst Troeltsch's ethics are found in *The Social Teaching of the Christian Churches* (Vol. 1; Olive Wyon, trans.; New York: Macmillan, 1931); for his summary of the three "types" (church, sect, mysticism), see the conclusion to that work, especially the section entitled "Results of this Survey."

The main references to Reinhold Niebuhr's thought here have been from *Moral Man and Immoral Society: A Study in Ethics and Politics* (New York: Charles Scribner's Sons, 1932), chapter 10, "The Conflict Between Individual and Social Morality." A selection from this chapter may also be found in the corresponding chapter of *Christian Ethics: An Introductory Reader*.

Dietrich Bonhoeffer's quotation about radicalism and compromise is from his *Ethics* (Eberhard Bethge, ed.; New York: Macmillan, 1955), page 128.

The section on Reformed ethics draws on Douglas Ottati, "The Reformed Tradition in Theological Ethics," in *Christian Ethics: Problems and Prospects* (Lisa Sowle Cahill and James F. Childress, eds; Cleveland, OH: Pilgrim Press, 1996).

Karl Barth's phrase the "strange world of the Bible" is from the preface to *Epistle to the Romans* (London; New York: Oxford University Press, 1968); the source for his claim that ethics is dogmatics is from *Church Dogmatics* I.2 (Edinburgh: T & T Clark, 1975), page 782.

Borden Bowne's thought may be discovered in *The Immanence of God* (Boston, MA: Houghton Mifflin; Cambridge: Riverside Press, 1905).

William Temple's discussion of ideas relating to a welfare state is in *Christianity and Social Order* (London: SCM Press, 1950), chapter 4, "Christian Social Principles," a portion of which is also included in the corresponding chapter of *Christian Ethics: An Introductory Reader*.

For a general introduction to Roman Catholic moral theology, see Romanus Cessario, *Introduction to Moral Theology* (Washington, DC: Catholic University of America Press, 2001).

The section on Roman Catholic moral theology is also indebted to Frederick Christian Bauerschmidt and James J. Buckley, *Catholic Theology: An Introduction* (Wiley-Blackwell, 2017), especially chapter 9, "The Good Life"; and Servais Pinckaers, *The Sources of Christian Ethics* (Mary Thomas Noble, trans.; Washington, DC: Catholic University of America Press, 1995). Pinckaers' work may also be found in shorter, more accessible form in *Morality: The Catholic View* (Michael Sherwin, trans.; South Bend, IN: St. Augustine's Press, 2001).

Augustine wrote about the restlessness of the human heart in his *Confessions* (Henry Chadwick, trans.; Oxford: Oxford University Press, 2009); and Aquinas discussed the perfection of nature by grace in *Summa Theologica* (5 vols; Notre Dame, IN: Christian Classics, 1948), Prima Pars [First Part], Question 1, Article 8; also available at www.ccel.org/ccel/aquinas/summa.html.

For an introduction to the writings of Karl Rahner, see *The Content of Faith: The Best of Karl Rahner's Theological Writings* (Karl Lehmann and Albert Raffelt, eds; Harvey D. Egan, trans.; New York: Crossroad, 1993).

The Pontifical Council for Justice and Peace assembled a summary of Catholic social teaching in the 2004 *Compendium of the Social Doctrine of the Church*, available at http://www.vatican.va/roman_curia/ pontifical_councils/justpeace/documents/rc_pc_ justpeace_doc_20060526_compendio-dott-soc_ en.html.

For Eastern Orthodox ethics, Vigen Guroian's thought may be explored in *Incarnate Love: Essays in Orthodox Ethics* (2nd edn; South Bend, IN: University of Notre Dame Press, 2002). Stanley Harakas has written several introductions to Orthodox ethics, including *Wholeness of Faith and*

Life: Orthodox Christian Ethics (3 vols; Brookline, MA: Holy Cross Orthodox Press, 1999). The section on Orthodox ethics draws from both these writers. One might begin an acquaintance with Sergei Bulgakov's thought with *A Bulgakov Anthology* (James Pain and Nicholas Zernov, eds; Philadelphia, PA: Westminster Press, 1976). Anglican theologian Rowan Williams also provides an introduction to Bulgakov's thought in *Sergii Bulgakov: Towards a Russian Political Theology* (Rowan Williams, ed.; Edinburgh, T & T Clark, 1999). For John Zizioulas, see *Being As Communion* (Crestwood, NY: St. Vladimir's Seminary Press, 1985).

For an introduction to historic and contemporary Pentecostalism, see Harvey Cox, *Fire from Heaven: The Rise of Pentecostal Spirituality and the Reshaping of Religion in the Twenty-first Century* (Reading, MA: Addison-Wesley Publishing Company, 1995).

Part Two
The Questions Christian Ethics Asks

The variety of theories offering themselves as models for ethics in general and Christian ethics in particular can seem bewildering to the newcomer. But the argument of this book is that these many theories can be grouped under three broad headings. What determines each heading is *for whom* each theory assumes its ethical deliberation is being conducted. *For whom* do the respective approaches assume they speak? There are three broad answers to this question, and these answers shape this section of the book.

The first answer is, "Ethics is for everybody." That is, what is right for one person is right, in principle, for everyone else. Of course circumstances may change, but then appropriate behavior may change too. The point is, all people are assumed to be fundamentally the same, with the same relationship to command, or duty, or consequence, or society, or rights, or whatever is deemed to be the normative means of assessing the good. Thus, ethics is not so much about people as about the quandaries they find themselves in and the decisions they make. The problem with focusing on people is that people differ from one another in personal characteristics, commitments, and circumstances. Decisions, by contrast, appear to be common to everybody. We may call this strand of ethics "universal ethics," because it has no doubt that what applies to one applies to all. For similar reasons it has a particular relationship to government and legislation, for as soon as one assumes one can establish what is good for all, independent of any particular considerations, one is faced with the question of whether and how that good can be demanded, expected, encouraged, or permitted from a populace. If one were to sum up universal ethics in one word, that word would probably be "decision." This is the subject of Chapter Five.

The second answer is, "But whom are you leaving out when you say *everybody*?" In simple terms, Christian ethics, like history, has tended to be written from a certain social location, namely that of the economically secure, Caucasian, North Atlantic, heterosexual male. Such a person could be described as the "winner" of almost all of Christian history. But is not Christianity inherently concerned with those who are not and have not been the "winners"? Is not the God of Jesus Christ the God of the widow, the orphan, the alien? Is not the paradigmatic story of the Bible, the story that shapes the Old Testament and provides the prototype for the New, the narrative of the exodus from Egypt? Is not God's story the story of a people being brought from slavery to freedom? And an ethic that forgets this not only falls under the power of privileged social elites, but meanwhile assimilates constructions of society and what it means to be human and to flourish that have little or nothing to do with Christianity and much to do with maintaining those elites' stranglehold on power. This is the perspective of what we may call "subversive ethics." This is an approach concerned to expose and interpret the interests and power-bids of agents – and equally concerned with the empowerment of those who are often denied a voice by such agents. If one were to sum up subversive ethics in one word, that word would probably be "liberation." This is the subject of Chapter Six.

The third answer is, "Christian ethics is for the church." This approach we may call "ecclesial ethics." It shares with subversive ethics a skepticism concerning the assumptions of universal ethics. It is inclined to tell a particular story of the emergence of Christian ethics. Such a story begins with Christians being a minority community in the Roman Empire, one whose assumptions and values made it at best a curiosity and at worst, from Rome's perspective, a threat. When the emperor became a Christian in the fourth century, Christians began to think in universal terms. In the process many of them lost the distinctiveness of their ecclesial practice and their ethic. In the Reformation the great Reformers – Martin Luther, John Calvin, Ulrich Zwingli, and so on – largely maintained "universal" assumptions, although the Radical Reformers did not (see Chapter Four for more on the Reformation). With the rise in the seventeenth and eighteenth centuries of two powerful themes, the individual and the nation-state, it was all too easy for Christianity to be subsumed into such demanding agendas. Many contemporary writers in Christian ethics lament the way over the past 200 years it has become rare to identify a Christian perspective that was distinct from the good of the family or the state – or a narrow protection of one denomination's corporate interests. Ecclesial ethics is a call for a renewal of the visibility of the church and for an emphasis on the distinctiveness of Christian ethics, particularly in relation to the person of Jesus. Such a distinctive ethic may have something to offer those beyond the church – but that is not to be taken for granted; nor is it healthy to limit reflection about what is right for Christians to what can be expected of or legislated for everybody. Ecclesial ethics is less about the decisions everyone takes, and more about the distinctive character of those making the decisions. If one were to sum up ecclesial ethics in one word, that word would be "character." This is the subject of Chapter Seven.

These three categories are not watertight. Few authors fit wholly and entirely in one strand; most draw on more than one, and in some cases on all three. Martin Luther King Jr. is a celebrated twentieth-century figure who turns to each of the three strands at different moments. The medieval theologian Thomas Aquinas has both universal and ecclesial shades to his arguments. But this is a textbook, and the point of a textbook is to help the student navigate a sometimes daunting myriad of authors and approaches, identifying salient themes and learning to formulate arguments of various kinds. We trust identifying these broad styles of argument will help the student comprehend the diversity of Christian ethics while perceiving the most marked varieties in approach, audience, and assumptions.

Chapter Five
Universal Ethics

Universal ethics is seldom a name any strand of ethics would give itself. It is usually a name given by others who question the assumption of universality on the part of those who claim or dare to speak or decree or legislate for everybody. Many, perhaps most, of those who aspire to speak for everybody would not imagine there was any other way to speak. That is an indication of the power of the arguments made by the key figures in this strand, and the way their assumptions have come to be so widely taken for granted.

What distinguishes different approaches to ethics *within* this strand is not their audience or constituency but their respective understandings of where the good is fundamentally located. There are broadly three universal approaches to ethics, each of which assumes it applies to everybody but which differ in their understanding of the moment or place that is the key to the discipline.

1. Perhaps the most obvious is the first approach, which sees ethics as concerning right *actions*, linked inextricably to right intentions. It is obvious because the popular understanding of morality tends to assume it is about doing good things rather than bad things. The means are everything, and a good end cannot justify the use of dubious means to bring it about.
2. By contrast the second approach sees ethics as concerning right *outcomes*. In this case what is good is whatever produces the right result. The ends do – or at least may – justify the means.
3. The third approach gathers together a number of concerns not adequately addressed by the previous two approaches. It concentrates on right *relationships*. Here the priority is a good and healthy society, rather than right actions by or right outcomes for particular individuals. The third approach does not necessarily invalidate or even differ from either of the first two,

Introducing Christian Ethics, Second Edition. Samuel Wells and Ben Quash with Rebekah Eklund.
© 2017 John Wiley & Sons Ltd. Published 2017 by John Wiley & Sons Ltd.

but it places its emphasis elsewhere, in the well-being of the community rather than the decisions of the individual.

We shall look at each approach in turn.

Right Actions

Ethics that focuses on right action is most commonly known as deontological ethics, after the Greek noun *deon* meaning duty or obligation. Deontological ethics has many dimensions, and here we shall look at the scriptural tradition of the divine command, the ancient tradition of natural law, and the hugely influential categorical imperative of Immanuel Kant. These theories may be categorized by what they respectively take to be the source of the law – God, nature, or the conscience.

Divine Command

The so-called divine command theory of ethics is that actions are required, good, permissible, bad, or evil simply because God decrees them so. God holds people morally accountable for their actions, and there will be some kind of judgment or reckoning after death or at the end of time. The Ten Commandments, recorded in Exodus and Deuteronomy, appear to represent this kind of ethic, and have undoubtedly been received as such in many Christian households, congregations, and traditions.

The Ten Commandments, or Decalogue, include the following injunctions.

- You shall have no other gods before me.
- You shall not make for yourself an idol.
- You shall not make wrongful use of the name of the LORD your God.
- Remember the sabbath day, and keep it holy.
- Honor your father and your mother.
- You shall not murder.
- You shall not commit adultery.
- You shall not steal.
- You shall not bear false witness against your neighbor.
- You shall not covet anything that belongs to your neighbor.

For many Christians, these have constituted the essence of the divine command. While the New Testament contains no such list of injunctions, it still seems to endorse the principle of ethics being founded on God's unambiguous command: in Jesus' words, "'You shall love the Lord your God with all your heart, and with all your soul, and with all your mind.' This is the greatest and first commandment. And a second is like it: 'You shall love your neighbor as yourself.' On these two commandments hang all the law and the prophets" (Matt 22:37–40).

In answer to the question "Are morally good acts willed by God because they are morally good, or are they morally good because they are willed by God?" the proponent of the divine command theory will respond with the latter answer. God's will is thus discernible in the decrees of direct revelation, rather than in the traces of God's ways found in creation and experience. This argument maintains a strong emphasis on God's sovereignty (rather than human freedom) and on the personal, rather than abstract, character of God.

The question "Does God command this particular action because it is right, or is it right because God commands it?" is sometimes known as Euthyphro's dilemma. Plato records a conversation between Euthyphro and Socrates after it comes to light that Euthyphro is prosecuting his own father for the murder of a servant. Socrates asks Euthyphro a question along these lines. Philosophers have long been troubled that the latter answer makes ethics arbitrary. If God commanded something widely regarded as morally repugnant, it would nonetheless be obligatory, since God commanded it. The command to Abraham to sacrifice his son Isaac (Gen 22) is often cited in this regard. Many Christians and non-Christians have reacted strongly against this apparent arbitrariness, finding it intolerable, because it seems to portray God as a rule-maker, but not a rule-keeper. Others have modified the abrasive quality of saying "things are morally good simply because God says so." For example, some, such as Thomas Aquinas (1225–74), have suggested (at the risk of limiting God's sovereignty) that moral principles bind God in the same way that logical principles do – that it is impossible to imagine God acting outside them. Others might use a phrase (at the risk of putting too many demands on the word "love") like "Any action is ethically wrong if and only if it is contrary to the commands of a loving God." Others might question whether the God being discussed here bears any regular resemblance to the God made known in Jesus Christ. Others again might say that it is precisely the Father's sending the Son to the cross that constitutes the most dubious ethical command of them all.

Natural Law

Classical accounts
Natural law emerges for the first time in the later tragedies of ancient Greek drama. In these plays characters find that their ordinary actions have cosmic significance. When they go against a fixed code of obligation, terrifying forces are let loose – even if this was far from the characters' own intention. The Stoic philosophers, beginning with Zeno and Chrysippus in Athens in the third century BCE, saw natural law as the necessity for humanity to conform itself to the realities of existence (Stoicism was previously presented in Chapter Three). There are simple building blocks of life that are firm and unchanging, and following natural law means not trying to manipulate or alter these foundations but simply adhering to them.

While the Greeks perceived the nature of things, the Romans saw how that nature turned into law. Natural law for them was not the passive acceptance of the givens of the universe but the active employment of the insights of reason, intelligence, and experience. From the time of Cicero (106–43 BCE) onwards there was a greater sense of a morally lawful universe in which all evils are eventually set straight. In the second century CE the Roman jurist Gaius (ca. 130–ca. 180 CE) distinguished between the law of nations (*ius gentium*) and the law of custom (*ius civile*). The *ius gentium* was a kind of universal law, found in almost every culture – although Gaius did not speak of it as binding. In the following century Ulpian (ca. 170–223 CE), another Roman jurist, largely accepted Gaius' categories, although his view of the *ius gentium* was rather more explicitly a human construction. Ulpian, however, crucially added the notion of natural law, *ius naturale*, which he saw as the law that bound both humankind and the animals. Ulpian's view had much less of a role for human reason and intelligence, beyond what was required to perceive the realities of nature. To follow the helpful argument of Timothy O'Connell in his *Principles for a Catholic Morality*, the difference between Gaius and Ulpian is this: Does natural law name humankind's difference from the animals (Gaius) or its similarity (Ulpian)? Is humankind fundamentally an intelligent species that sets out to stamp its limitless mark on the world or is it essentially a form of animal that must accept its place within a closed system? This question runs through perpetual debates thereafter. One can, for example, immediately recognize its significance for ecological questions today, as we shall see in Chapter Twelve.

Medieval accounts

The medieval notion of natural law emerged from this debate, mediated by Isidore of Seville (560–636 CE). Isidore accepted Ulpian's three categories of law. He agreed that natural law is a given, and not simply a result of human construction. But he had no interest in aligning humankind with the animals. Instead he saw natural law as characterized by human reflection on natural circumstances. It was a position somewhere between Gaius and Ulpian, and opened the way to the formulations of the scholastic era (ca. 1100–1500).

This tension – between natural law as fundamentally about reason or fundamentally about nature – runs through the work of the most significant contributor to the natural law tradition, Thomas Aquinas. The Fourth Lateran Council held in 1215 had decreed that pastoral work should be shaped around preaching and the hearing of auricular confessions. Shortly afterwards the Order of Preachers was commissioned to take up these two tasks under the leadership of St. Dominic. A series of books emerged to support the ministry of Dominican preachers and, especially, confessors. It was in the context of trying to ensure that the pastoral work of the Dominicans retained its theological, rather than merely practical, character that the *Summa Theologica* of Thomas Aquinas was written.

Aquinas learned from Aristotle, whose *Nicomachean Ethics* was newly available in Latin translation, that created things have their own nature and each may find its own perfection, or fulfillment. He also derived from Aristotle a confidence that human reason, reflecting on sense experience, was a sound source of knowledge about the world. Thus, he distinguished between natural knowledge, which could be attained by reason, and supernatural knowledge, which required revelation from God. Because of the disparity between creator and creature, the created order is unable to realize the divine goal; when sin is added, that difference between humanity and God becomes even starker. However, all things came from God and will finally return to God, so the dissimilarity is not total. God is the beginning, the end, and the means of human existence. Most famously, Aquinas affirms that "grace does not destroy nature, but perfects it."

His *Summa Theologica* is divided into three parts: concerning God (I), the advance of the rational creature to God (II), and Jesus (III). In the second part Thomas lays out his moral teaching. It is significant for the history of ethics that this second part has often been read in separation from the more explicitly theological parts (I and III). The aspects of part II that concern virtue are described in Chapter Seven; here we shall consider Aquinas' understanding of natural law. His understanding of natural law comes within his treatise on law. Aquinas retains the ambiguity noted above going back through Isidore of Seville to the active "Roman" notion of Gaius and the more passive "Greek" notion of Ulpian. He sees human beings as shaped by reason, and he is aware that right action may not be the same for all or equally known by all (although the principle of natural law is simple: "good is to be done and pursued, and evil is to be avoided"). But he also refers to natural law as common to all animals and to the need for humans to accept their givenness as animals.

Aquinas' hugely influential description of natural law assumes three orders of precepts. (A precept is a more specific dimension of a law.) There is the precept shared with all beings, that of self-preservation. "Whatever is a means of preserving human life, and warding off its obstacles, belongs to the natural law." Next there are the precepts shared with all animals, "such as sexual intercourse, education of offspring and so forth." Thirdly there is a uniquely human precept, an inclination to good – "to know the truth about God, and to live in society … for instance, to shun ignorance, to avoid offending those among whom one has to live" and so on. None of these precepts gives clear guidance except as they come to be articulated through particular laws.

Early modern accounts

This vivid description of natural law remained highly significant into the modern era. It is sometimes supposed that the magisterial Reformers – those leaders of the Reformation whose movements were endorsed by governing authorities – rejected all sense of the knowledge of God or the good outside revelation, but this is not entirely the case. Martin Luther (1483–1546), John Calvin (1509–64), and their contemporaries insisted that knowledge of God as creator, which is partly available through human observation and experience, is not to be confused with knowledge of God as redeemer, which is only available through revelation. But the supernatural knowledge of salvation available through Scripture does not, for them, invalidate the rather different natural knowledge available through reason.

Perhaps the most significant of the Reformers in relation to natural law is Richard Hooker (1554–1600). Hooker's principal work, *Of the Laws of Ecclesiastical Polity*, sets out to defend the practical reason on which the constitutional establishment of the Church of England rests against moderate Puritan criticisms. He follows Luther and Calvin (and before them Augustine and Aquinas) in arguing that after the Fall, humankind retained the (natural) desire to be happy, but lost the ability to bring its desire about. Reason desires God, but cannot find God. Thus Hooker says that there are two forms of government: that which would have been in a free creation, and that which is now, after the Fall. But he affirms that natural law still comes from God:

> Since God alone is the source of all good, you must not doubt, that whatever truth you anywhere meet with, proceeds from Him, unless you would be doubly ungrateful to Him. ... Philosophy is, consequently, the noble gift of God, and those learned men who have striven hard after it in all ages have been incited thereto by God himself, that they might enlighten the world in the knowledge of the truth.

The philosophers associated with the early Enlightenment period introduced a new dimension into natural law thinking. Whereas for the medieval thinkers natural law existed as part of a pattern of eternal, divine, and human laws, now speculation grew that no longer took eternal and divine law for granted. The work of Thomas Hobbes (1588–1679) emerged out of the chaos of the English Civil War. In his book *Leviathan* he vividly describes the dangerous existence of humankind in its natural condition. Hobbes thus derives self-protection from natural death as the highest necessity. A great deal of his argument is given over to demonstrating the necessity of a powerful central authority to avert the evil of civil war. That strong central government was obliged to maintain the conditions of security above all else.

Hobbes expounds several laws of nature:

- Everyone ought to endeavor peace, as far as they have hope of obtaining it; and for peace, and defense of themselves, to lay down their right to all things; and be content with so much liberty against others as they would allow others against themselves.
- They should keep their covenants, for the definition of injustice is the non-performance of a covenant.
- If someone receives grace from another, they should endeavor that the one who gives it have no cause to regret it.
- Everyone should strive to accommodate themselves to the rest, and pardon those who repent, not seek revenge, declare no hatred or contempt of another, and acknowledge others as their equal by nature.

The significance of Hobbes' version of natural law is witnessed by the abiding resonance of his phraseology in contemporary discussions.

Joseph Butler (1692–1752), a bishop in the Church of England first of Bristol and later of Durham, was a natural law opponent of Hobbes. In his *A Dissertation of the Nature of Virtue* he showed his debts to the philosophies of Aristotle, the Stoics, and John Locke, as he commended the moral capacities of human nature when properly governed by rational principles of self-love and benevolence. He did not see a necessary conflict between ideas of moral duty, on the one hand, and self-interest, on the other. Both involve following nature, whose author is God, and the fact that one principle is oriented to the good of society and the other to the good of the individual only confirms the fact that they should therefore coexist harmoniously, for "we were made for society." He thus utterly dismissed Hobbes' claim that selfish impulses are the basic motivation for most human actions. Butler makes very few explicit appeals to theological principles, but in his high view of the role of conscience he clearly supposes that the directives of conscience are coincident with the will of God.

More recent accounts
A number of intellectual developments led to natural law thinking falling out of fashion in the nineteenth and twentieth centuries. The simplicity with which some of the medieval writers assumed nature could be "read off the page" of observation was profoundly questioned by a series of wholesale challenges. If human beings were animals, no one before Charles Darwin (1809–82) had supposed they were *just* animals. But Darwin's theory of natural selection implied precisely that. The study of human goods belonged, according to this logic, with the study of animal behavior. And in the hands of B. F. Skinner (1904–90) and other radical behaviorists, this logic extended to the abolition of conventional notions of freedom, and it becomes difficult to speak of the good in any conventional sense at all. Meanwhile for Karl Marx (1818–83) what restricts human freedom is the network of power relations in society. Human beings are subject to their own self-deceptions and to the largely economic forces that govern human interaction. For Sigmund Freud (1856–1939) the fault lies not in society but in our own selves. We are subject to the unconscious drives that operate within us, and freedom lies in coming to terms with these drives rather than in striving hopelessly to control them.

Roman Catholic moral philosophers such as John Finnis (b. 1940) and Germain Grisez (b. 1929) have stimulated something of a revival in natural law thinking in recent decades. Their approach is sometimes known as basic goods theory. It suggests that there are a number of goods inherent to human life – but these goods are so different from one another in kind that one cannot sacrifice or substitute one for another. They must all be accepted in their concrete plurality. Any act that attacks one of these goods – even if it simply sacrifices one good for another – is intrinsically evil. Finnis offers seven such goods, which can never conflict with one another: life, knowledge, play, aesthetic experience, sociability (or friendship), practical reasonableness, and religion. (Grisez adds personal integration.) This is a list derived from experience and reflection and is not designed to be exhaustive.

These goods may inevitably be neglected, but they may never be attacked. Finnis also adds what he calls the "first moral principle," which is: "in voluntarily acting for human goods and avoiding what is opposed to them, one ought to choose and otherwise will those and only those possibilities whose willing is compatible with integral human fulfilment."

Immanuel Kant and the Categorical Imperative

To understand the sources and significance of the ethics of Immanuel Kant (1724–1804) it is first necessary to understand the moral and philosophical catastrophe constituted by the religious wars of the sixteenth and seventeenth centuries in Europe. The medieval ideal was of a unified Europe, drawn together by a single church, united in praise of God, with a harmonious universe ordered in social and ecclesial hierarchies. Thomas Aquinas' view of the benign dovetailing of eternal, divine, natural, and human law perfectly expresses this confidence. But the wars of religion that followed the Reformation dismantled this harmonious ideal. As his late 1795 essay *Perpetual Peace* makes clear, Kant was searching for a grounding for truth and meaning and morality that would lead toward peace rather than endless conflict. He found it by accepting the Enlightenment's characteristic "turn to the subject": in other words, like many of his contemporaries, he made human sensibilities and potentialities, rather than God's character and revelation, the center of his enquiries. The starry heavens above could evoke, but only the moral law within could evince guiding truth. Unlike those who investigated divine or natural law, he did not see truth as fundamentally "out there" but rather "in here" – in the individual's intuition of the moral law. His life reflected his introverted philosophy in that through all his eighty years he never traveled more than a hundred miles from his native Königsburg (then in Prussia, now in Russia). His *Critique of Pure Reason* (1781) argued that God, immortality, and freedom are beyond knowing. But he later described them as "postulates of reason," that is, assumptions that must be made if reason was to proceed. He identified God with the moral law that he regarded as fundamental. His assumptions about historic Christianity are amply expressed by the title of his 1793 work, *Religion within the Limits of Reason Alone.*

Kant's work in moral philosophy is largely contained in three books, *Groundwork for the Metaphysics of Morals* (1785), *Critique of Practical Reason* (1788), and *Metaphysics of Morals* (1797). He regards morality, the limitation of oneself by refusing to engage in certain activities, as the most significant expression of freedom. Freedom, in this sense, is the state of being outside the influence of external forces. To be subject to such desires as hatred or greed or ambition or revenge is to be heteronomous. Such desires are genuine, but they are external to the will, because they are irrational. Instead, Kant sought for the will to be subject only to its own nature – its mind and rational thought. This was true freedom, or autonomy. Freedom and rationality are essentially the same thing.

Kant's project is therefore to articulate a rule of morality that is binding yet ensures both the individual and morality itself remain autonomous, independent of history, tradition, or religious conviction. This means that the rule can only concern the *form* of morality, not its *content*. If the rule were to trespass into the content of morality it would be making assumptions about matters the individual subject had an interest in (God, happiness, honor, or whatever). But that would interfere with the subject's autonomy. A rule that depends on the subject's prior interests and commitments is a *hypothetical* imperative – hypothetical because it starts with an assumption of what the subject wants to bring about. Hypothetical imperatives begin with the word "if"; thus, "If you wish to inherit the earth, you must be meek." What Kant is seeking is a *categorical* imperative – a rule that is binding *whatever* the subject desires or whatever outcome the subject has in mind – a rule that takes nothing for granted and makes no assumptions.

Starting with a hypothetical imperative (the subject's prior commitments) leads to defining the moral in terms of the good. (The moral is something that can be defined without reference to particular commitments, whereas the good is always partial to specific beings.) Kant insists that instead we start with the categorical imperative, independent of personal commitments and judgments, and thus define the good in terms of the moral. Only the priority of the moral, in this sense, can preserve the will from being controlled by desires and thus keep the subject autonomous. Kant suggests there are three ways of arriving at ethical judgments; he rejects the first two and argues for the third:

- He rejects moral *mysticism*, which is seeking or sensing the approval of God or some other supernatural force. Moral mysticism bears some relation to divine command theories as outlined above.
- He also rejects (even more firmly) moral *empiricism*, which seeks to evaluate good and bad outcomes by observation, often based on pleasure. Moral empiricism is related to consequentialism, which we shall explore later in this chapter.
- Instead he advocates moral *rationalism*, which means abstract reflection on the degree to which an action arises from the right *motivation* – and the right motivation is duty. In this sense Kant differs from the divine command and natural law theories discussed above. All three are deontological theories, but the former two are focused on right actions, whereas Kant's is more concerned with right dispositions.

So what is this fundamental duty that Kant sees as an end in itself? He gives three formulations of his categorical imperative.

1. Act only according to that maxim whereby you can at the same time will that it should become a universal law.

    This is the principle of universalizability. By "maxim," Kant means the logic or reason behind a person's actions. It is the combination of their action and their motivation – hence "I will invest money in a company (action) on the basis of profit alone (motivation)." If one can imagine a world in which every-one acted according to such a maxim and there was no irrationality or contra-diction in so doing, then acting according to that maxim would be required, or at least permitted.

This has more of a negative than a positive implication. It is not that every action that could be universalized should be enacted, but rather that every action that could not be universalized should be avoided. The liar always assumes a world in which their falsehood is an exception to others' truth. Kant simply eliminates such exceptions. He regards some principles as impossible to universalize, such as the commitment not to keep any promise or never to help others. One cannot oneself break a rule one would expect others to keep in relation to oneself. (This comes very close to the Golden Rule of Matthew 7, "In everything do to others as you would have them do to you.") Thus lying is never permissible, even to save a person's life from someone who means them harm.

2. Act in such a way that you treat humanity, whether in your own person or in the person of any other, always at the same time as an end and never simply as a means.

    It would be absurd never to treat people as a means, for if so no one could ever hire another person to do a job, but to treat another *merely* as a means – to neglect their welfare or humanity – is ruled out. This formulation is perhaps the most influential statement in ethics today. Countless movements for social jus-tice take this principle for granted, whether they trace their origins to Kant or not. It is interesting that for Kant humanity includes one's own humanity, and thus one cannot ever commit suicide, because to do so would be to treat life as a means to a further end, such as happiness, comfort, or at least absence of pain. Kant assumed that this second formulation was logically identical with the first, but many have noted that here Kant appears here to talk about the good and not just the moral, thus breaking his principle of addressing only form and not content.

3. All rational beings must so act as if they were through their maxims always legislating members in the universal kingdom of ends.

    To be legislating members is a way of saying that all one's actions could be turned into universal laws. To abide in the universal kingdom of ends means to treat others always as ends, and never only as means.

    Thus, Kant's third formulation draws together his first and second. One should behave as though everyone shared this code of morality, even though one knows that not everyone does, and not everyone that shares it actually keeps it. One should not simply act as a member of such a community, but should act as a leader should act, setting an example and pondering the univer-sal implications of all actions.

It is hard to overestimate the significance of Kant for Christian ethics. One impor-tant strand is the way Albrecht Ritschl (1822–89), the most famous of the German liberal theologians of the nineteenth and early twentieth centuries, blended Kantian ethics with the more familiar theological notions of the historical Jesus and the kingdom of God. Christian ethics became the establishment of a "kingdom of ends," in which no one was ever to be treated simply as a means, and in which all actions that applied to Christians should apply just as much to everyone else. This tradition was maintained vividly by the Social Gospel movement in America, in works such as *Christianizing the Social Order* (1912) by Walter Rauschenbusch (1861–1918). Another strand leads to the political philosopher John Rawls (1921–2002), whose work we shall consider later in this chapter, and the critical theorist Jürgen Habermas (b. 1929). It is simply impossible to enter a discussion of deontological ethics without accepting Kant's achievement in relation to universalizability and his emphasis on autonomy, particularly his insistence on never treating persons simply as means to a further end. Whenever a parent says to a child, "What if everybody scribbled on the walls of other people's houses?" or a union member says to an employer, "You can't treat people like that," they are, whether they know it or not, deeply in debt to Immanuel Kant.

Right Outcomes

Ethics that focuses on right outcomes is most commonly known as consequential ethics. It represents a shift away from assuming that some things are simply set in stone, and toward a view of humanity as the shaper of its own destiny. It is common, for example, to hear someone aspire "to leave the world a better place than I found it." But this presupposes that one has significant control over the outcomes of one's actions. This assumption may be described as a characteristic of the modern era. "Consequentialism" is a term that was coined by the philosopher Elizabeth Anscombe in 1958. It refers to a family of theories that hold in common their rejection of deontological ethics, whether divine command, natural law, or Kantian in character. The theories differ on their answer to three questions: What counts as a good outcome? Good for whom? And who decides? However, the history of consequentialism is by no means as long as that of deontological ethics. It begins in earnest with the utilitarianism of the late eighteenth century. Most other views, which we shall consider thereafter, define themselves in relation to utilitarianism.

Utilitarianism

Jeremy Bentham
Jeremy Bentham (1748–1832) was an English legal and social reformer living through a time of enormous social and political change. He had many views that would seem more in keeping with those widely held two centuries later than with those prevalent in his own day – notably on the equality of women, the legalization of homosexuality, the welfare of animals, the permissibility of divorce, the

abolition of slavery, the prohibition of corporal punishment, and the introduction of pensions, health insurance, and inheritance tax.

He brought his legal facility to his vision for social improvement. Resolving the complexity of human experience into two poles, pain and pleasure, he sought to maximize pleasure among the maximum number of people. He aspired to a complete code of law based on the "greatest happiness principle," which, borrowing a phrase from the philosopher Francis Hutcheson (1694–1746) a century earlier, he originally called "the greatest happiness of the greatest number." Bentham's confidence in the application of mathematics and science to morality was such that he developed what he called a felicific calculus (after the Latin for happiness; also known as the hedonistic calculus, derived from the Greek for pleasure), which he believed could determine the morality of any proposed decision. Six dimensions determined the degree of pleasure within an individual, and a seventh determined the number of individuals involved. They included intensity of pleasure, duration, likelihood, propinquity (how soon), fecundity (the likelihood of repetition or extension), and purity (the likelihood of bringing about opposite sensations). Thus, it was simply a matter of calculating whether pleasure was likely to exceed pain across these criteria to establish the appropriateness of a course of action.

Bentham took a number of things for granted that his successors found problematic. He regarded pleasure as a measurable commodity, and he regarded his own estimate of what constituted pleasure as normative. But pleasure has seldom seemed in the hands of later ethicists the uncomplicated value it always appeared to Bentham. Meanwhile he had extraordinary confidence in his and others' ability to predict the outcome of events. One simply never knows what might have been – world and personal history is brimming with "what ifs" – and one cannot tell if the adult whose life one sacrifices to save the children when the oxygen is running out might have lived to find a cure for cancer.

John Stuart Mill

Bentham's most significant successor was his student John Stuart Mill (1806–73). It was Mill who coined the term "utilitarianism" as the title of his 1863 book. He regarded utilitarianism as an empirical, or experience-based, form of ethical reflection, as opposed to the intuitive and categorical ethical systems of Kant and others. His understanding was that morality was founded on utility, or the greatest happiness principle – that is, actions are right in proportion as they tend to promote happiness, wrong as they tend to produce the reverse of happiness. By happiness is intended pleasure, and the absence of pain; by unhappiness, pain, and the privation of pleasure.

Mill refines Bentham's account of pleasure by distinguishing between the lower, bodily, sensual pleasures and the higher, intellectual, mental pleasures. The former can evoke contentment, but only the latter can genuinely lead to happiness. Mill famously summarized this distinction with the words, "It is better to be a human being dissatisfied than a pig satisfied; better to be Socrates dissatisfied than a fool satisfied." He had a high view of the value of education, and believed that better education led people to seek higher pleasures. It was in order to encourage the release of these higher capacities that Mill took such a strong stand on liberty, with the famous words, "The only purpose for which power can be rightfully exercised over any member of a civilized community, against his will, is to prevent harm to others." This led Mill, among other things, to the rejection of censorship.

Mill does not overcome all of the weaknesses in Bentham's theory. It remains difficult to rest the whole of ethical deliberation on a single thread, pleasure. One only has to imagine the heart-searchings of a family around the bedside of a dying relative to sense that pleasure cannot bear the weight of all the dimensions of human good. And even if pleasure is divided into higher and lower, it is not straightforward to distinguish the difference between the two, and not easy to distinguish between different forms of "higher" pleasure. Mill's account of liberty is often thought of as a deontological defense, but it is in fact subject to utilitarianism, because liberty fundamentally brings about the greatest happiness of the greatest number.

Henry Sidgwick
The next major development in utilitarian thinking came through Henry Sidgwick (1838–1900), notably in his book *The Methods of Ethics* (1874). He criticized what he called psychological utilitarianism, by which all persons seek their own pleasure, and instead advocated ethical hedonism, by which every individual should seek the common good and happiness of all. He rejected Mill's claim that utilitarianism was based on empirical observation. He put forward three self-evident truths of ethics. One was prudence – the ability to defer the gratification of smaller pleasures in anticipation of greater future pleasures. Another was justice – which resembled the Golden Rule in proposing that we should treat others as we would wish to be treated ourselves. And the third was benevolence – seeking the good of others as much as one seeks one's own.

Realism and Non-realism

At this point it becomes clear that consequentialism in general and utilitarianism in particular run into a number of issues that deontological theories tend to avoid. Deontological theories tend to take for granted that there is an objective standard of truth and thus morality against which all ethical judgments can be established. Early utilitarian theories, such as Bentham's, tend to concur with this assumption. But once Bentham's approach came to be criticized as subjective, the question arose about whether in fact every ethical system was subjective – and indeed whether there could be any such thing as "objective" ethics – ethics for everybody – at all. While this is a matter for all ethical (and philosophical) discussion, and is not simply a matter for consequentialism, it is in the context of the questions raised by and about consequentialism that the issue most naturally arises, so it is appropriate to discuss it here.

Realists regard morality as an objective matter. There is only one moral truth (or set of moral truths) and the task of philosophy and ethics is to get as close to it as possible. This rests on a *correspondence* notion of truth – the assumption that statements describe states of affairs that are real and true whether the statement had been made or not. Thus, to say a table has four legs is to assume that the notions of "table" and "four" are in no sense arbitrary but are simply givens that exist in an unchanging realm of reality. While realism insists that reality is unchanging, it has to accept that human perception of reality can change and develop – and thus realism is particularly tied to discoveries in natural and social science that enhance its picture of truth.

- Some moral realists are *naturalists*, who assume that all ethical systems are based on properties or characteristics in the natural world that can be discovered by observation, experience, or experiment. This view was famously criticized by Cambridge University philosopher G. E. Moore (1873–1958), who used the term "naturalistic fallacy" to argue that one can never assume it is possible to derive an "ought" (a moral statement) from an "is" (a statement about nature).
- Moore was a consequentialist who took the alternative realist view, *intuitionism*. Intuitionism simply means that there are objective truths and falsehoods, but that these are not to be read off the page of nature by observation. Instead they are self-evident to every human being through common sense. (When the founding fathers of America stated that they held life, liberty, and the pursuit of happiness to be self-evident, they were speaking as intuitionists.) Early intuitionists referred to an additional, sixth sense by which human beings can identify right and wrong; later their successors made much of the analogy between morality and aesthetics, maintaining that just as everyone has an eye for beauty, so everyone has an eye for morality. It is easy to see how an objective theory that assumes everyone has the same intuitions can lead to controversy and dispute when not everyone agrees what these intuitions are.

Non-realists regard morality as a subjective matter. They regard truth as essentially a matter of human construction, emerging over time within languages, cultures, and societies. This rests on a *coherence* notion of truth – the recognition that there are no free-standing facts but that all truth is like a piece of a jigsaw puzzle that is evaluated by whether it fits with other recognized truths. Non-realism covers a spectrum from thoroughgoing relativism to a position almost as objective as realism. Some non-realists maintain that ethical statements are subjective claims – in other words that morality lies in the eye of the beholder. This is a view made popular by cultural anthropology. Anthropologists observing a wide variety of cultures came to the conclusion that while there are particular customs, there is no general morality. The logic of this position is to refuse to favor any one ethical conviction over another, perceiving such a preference as a form of cultural imperialism. It is a position that makes passing on a tradition from one generation to another within a multicultural society deeply problematic, and adjudicating legally between traditions equally so. One attempt to counter the dangers of moral relativism, while accepting its philosophical starting point, is to speak of the ideal observer. The ideal observer is the person who is fully informed, wholly rational, and yet suitably compassionate and imaginative. When one has accepted the relativist perspective this is as close to an objective view as one can get.

Non-cognitivism

Not all non-realists regard themselves as moral relativists. A significant movement in twentieth-century moral philosophy is known as non-cognitivism. Non-cognitivism is similar to G. E. Moore's intuitionism; that is, it shares Moore's view that morality cannot be grounded on observations that can be made about the natural world "out there," but it differs from Moore in that Moore was a cognitivist (who regarded his intuitive morality as nonetheless objective), whereas non-cognitivists have given up on the claim that ethical judgments can be simply true or false. Two particular kinds of non-cognitivism have been widely influential.

- The first is *emotivism*, which emerged in the eighteenth century. Hume (1711–76) argued in his book *Enquiry Concerning the Principles of Morals* (1751) that approbation or blame is a work of the heart, not of judgment, and that it involves active feeling or sentiment rather than simply evaluating propositions. In other words, the statements "monogamy is good" or "lying is bad" express the emotions of the speaker and are therefore not objective moral claims.
- Meanwhile the influential philosophical movement known as *logical positivism* from the late 1920s assumed that philosophy is concerned simply with verifying the truth or falsehood of propositions. The movement only accepted two kinds of statements as valid propositions – analytical, which are inherently true, and might be called tautologies ("all parents have children"), and synthetic, which require empirical evidence ("eating carrots helps you see in the dark"). Because ethical statements (along with aesthetic and theological ones) are not of either kind, such statements, according to logical positivists, are "meaningless," which means not nonsensical but unprovable.

In his 1944 book *Ethics and Language* C. L. Stevenson (1908–79) developed Hume's views alongside those of the logical positivists. He saw ethics as more a matter of expression of feeling than assertion of fact. He was particularly interested in the magnetic power of ethical vocabulary to commend and persuade persons of certain courses of action. Persuasion, he said,

> depends on the sheer, direct emotional impact of words – on emotive meaning, rhetorical cadence, apt metaphor, stentorian, stimulating, or pleading tones of voice, dramatic gestures, care in establishing *rapport* with the hearer or audience, and so on. ... A redirection of the hearer's attitudes is sought not by the mediating step of altering his beliefs, but by *exhortation*, whether obvious or subtle, crude or refined.

For Stevenson, an ethical statement comes in two parts: one declares the speaker's attitude (or values) and the other declares an imperative to correspond with it. Thus, "It's drafty" is a declaration of the speaker's disposition toward temperature and wind control, while "Close the door" is an imperative that mirrors the declaration. The speaker supports this imperative with reasons, but these reasons are invariably indications of the likely consequences rather than proofs as such. Stevenson seems to reduce ethics to those conversations that seek to change or influence the attitudes of others, which, many have suggested, describes only one dimension of ethics as a whole. The Scottish-born philosopher Alasdair MacIntyre (b. 1929), whose work we shall consider in Chapter Seven, criticized emotivism in language that echoes Kant when he claimed that emotivism entails the "obliteration of the distinction between manipulative and non-manipulative social relations." In other words, for emotivism others are always means, never ends.

An alternative kind of non-cognitivism is *prescriptivism*. R. M. Hare (1919–2002) developed his notion of prescriptivism in relation to the influential debate over emotivism. His book *The Language of Morals* (1952) harmonizes some of the assumptions of emotivism with the commitments of Kant. Hare accepts the logical positivists' assumption that ethical statements cannot be statements of fact. He divides ethics into two strands, descriptive and non-descriptive (or evaluative). Evaluative statements work rather as Stevenson had portrayed them – they prescribe both attitude and behavior. In this sense prescriptivism has much in common with emotivism. But Hare goes beyond Stevenson in arguing that evaluative statements ("Lying is wrong") not only offer magnetic emotional force, they are genuine imperatives, because they express not just a view on behalf of the individual speaker but a vision for all times and places. This echoes Kant's universalizability principle, and for this reason Hare's theory is often called universal prescriptivism. Hare regards every use of the word "ought" as an indication of prescriptivism.

Some Developments in Consequentialism

Because consequentialism has been so closely identified with utilitarianism, on the one hand, and been supposed to open the door to non-realism in general and moral relativism in particular, on the other, it has often fallen into disrepute, particularly in Roman Catholic circles. However, traditions have been developed or emerged, particularly within Roman Catholic moral theology, that seek to harness some of the insights of consequentialism to a realist, largely natural law perspective.

One tradition that goes back to Thomas Aquinas is the principle of the double effect. In some ways it can be traced to the words of the Hippocratic Oath, originally composed around the fourth century BCE: "First, do no harm." It faces the reality that some actions, for example in medicine and in war, are likely to have multiple effects, some good and others not. It assumes there is a difference between on the one hand promoting some good in such a way that one realizes that one will at the same time cause harm as an anticipated side-effect, and on the other hand deliberately causing harm while seeking thereby to achieve good in the longer term. There are four criteria to be met in carrying out the proposed action according to the principle of the double effect.

- The action itself must be good, or at least indifferent.
- The intention must be to bring about a good outcome.
- The good outcome must not be the direct outcome of the bad effect (e.g., the end of suffering must not simply come through killing the patient).
- The resultant good must exceed the incurred harm.

One very common application of this principle is to permit physicians to prescribe powerful painkilling medications – ones which may, for example, damage the liver so much that they would in due course kill the patient – in cases where the patient is not in any case expected to live very long. The principle of double effect enables the physician to distinguish this treatment from euthanasia. Perhaps the most controversial example of the employment of the principle is to justify the dropping of the atomic bombs on Japan to bring an abrupt end to World War II; strictly speaking, unless there was a munitions factory in Hiroshima, there was no double effect justification for dropping the bomb there.

The principle makes many assumptions: that it is possible to describe acts as good or bad without regard to context; that it is never possible to engage in a worthwhile activity without some negative outcomes; and that there can ever be as few as two effects, rather than countless ones, arising from any action. The principle is sometimes paraphrased as "the end does not justify the means." But this rests on an ambiguity about the meaning of the word end. If "end" means purpose, intention, or goal, then this is in keeping with the principle of double effect. But if "end" means actual final outcome, then the implication is somewhat different. If the final outcome really is a great and admirable one, then it could be taken to justify any proportionate means. This links the principle of double effect to the heart of consequential ethics.

The connection is made clearer by the late twentieth-century movement in moral theology known as proportionalism, most explicitly stated in Bernard Hoose's 1987 work *Proportionalism*. Proportionalism seeks to steer a path between deontology and consequentialism. It sides with natural law against divine command in insisting that acts are forbidden because they are wrong, not wrong because they are forbidden. But it sides with consequentialism in affirming that acts are judged not just by intention, but by outcome. And the key to that outcome is the degree to which they contribute to human flourishing and fulfillment. Proportionalism recognizes that actions invariably have both good and bad effects, and thus both contribute to and detract from human fulfillment. They are not to be evaluated as to whether they are perfect, but as to whether the good they bring about is proportionate to the harm they do. This is considered an appropriation of Thomas Aquinas' (and Aristotle's) virtue of prudence, which the former regarded as the key to ethics. It is a decisive move away from exceptionless norms – the assumption that what is good has always been good and always will be. It acknowledges that some goods change over time, and may change in the future in ways that cannot be anticipated. It becomes impossible to speak of acts that are intrinsically evil. Proportionalism was decisively rejected in the 1993 papal encyclical *Veritatis Splendor* (The Splendor of Truth).

Situation Ethics

One consequential theory that takes its rejection of deontology to an extreme is situation ethics. In his book *Situation Ethics* (1963), the Episcopal priest Joseph Fletcher (1905–91) presented his model of ethics as a mean between what he called legalist (natural law and divine command) and antinomian (entirely spontaneous and unprincipled) ethics. He saw all laws as merely useful to the extent they could bring about love, and he regarded his ethic as embodying the love commandment of Jesus – although he later renounced Christianity. The central purpose is *agape* – which Fletcher defined as loving one's neighbor as oneself.

Fletcher gave several examples of extreme situations in which the demands of love ran contrary to the expectations of law. In one, a young woman found herself in a time of war. Her government wanted her to seduce and sleep with an enemy spy in order to be able later to blackmail him. Would it be worth breaking her usual values in order to save thousands of lives and bring the war to an end? In another, at the close of World War II in Europe a German mother found she could only be released by her Russian captors and reunited with her family if she were pregnant. She asked a camp guard to impregnate her and, on becoming pregnant, she was sent back to Berlin and found her husband and children. Fletcher pointed out that these examples were extreme to show that in normal circumstances principles would apply whereas in extreme ones they might not – but these examples contributed to the growing assumption that ethics largely concerns the practice of decision-making in extremely challenging situations.

Fletcher developed four working and six fundamental principles. The working principles were:

1. pragmatism (the course of action must succeed in bringing about love);
2. relativism (one can never say "never" – Fletcher insisted this relativized the absolute, but did not absolutize the relative);
3. positivism (which, for Fletcher, meant everything depends on adherence to the Christian notion of *agape* love, and no logic can prove its unique status);
4. personalism (all laws exist to work for the good of people).

The fundamental principles were:

1. the only thing that is intrinsically good is love – no action is intrinsically right or wrong independent of circumstances;
2. Christianity means self-giving *agape* love, and the Ten Commandments and other laws are subservient to *agape* love;

3. love and justice are the same thing – justice is simply adapting love to the needs of distribution;
4. love is unconditional – it attends to the neighbor regardless of whether the neighbor is likeable or loves in return;
5. only the end (love) justifies the means (this is close to utilitarianism, although here "love" replaces "happiness");
6. love's decisions should be made in freedom – entirely in the context of the situation – and not in law.

Situation ethics captured the mood of an era. It had a remarkable confidence in the human ability to identify and practice love without self-deception. It had no fear that in opening the door to actions like euthanasia it might ever be difficult to close the door again. It had great assurance of human beings' ability to predict the outcomes of unusual courses of action. In these ways it was widely and loudly criticized. But shorn of its extremes, it has made itself a significant element in consequential thinking, and is not so different from the theory of proportionalism, which has gained much more support in "respectable" ethical circles.

Right Relationships

Both deontological and consequential theories of ethics have a habit of focusing on the individual as the center of ethics. In the period following the Enlightenment, however, two significant developments contributed to the emergence of what we might describe as a third strand in universal ethics, one with significant aspects in common with each of the first two. In the modern era, by which we mean the era bequeathed by the Enlightenment, it was no longer possible for Europeans to imagine the world as a seamless Christian whole, in the way that had been more common in the medieval period. Not only was there a split between Catholics and Protestants, there were increasingly vocal elements who rejected a theological frame of reference as a ground for ethics in at least the public sphere, and sometimes in the personal sphere too. Meanwhile, as we saw in Chapter Two and Chapter Four, huge economic, social, and political changes were taking place across Europe, to which churches, theologians, and philosophers were seeking to adapt.

To make the journey from Kant's emphasis on individual choice to a concern for society understood as a whole requires passing through two influential philosophers who dominated the nineteenth century. G. W. F. Hegel (1770–1831) owed much to Kant's emphasis on mind as the location of ultimate reality, a view known as idealism. Hegel saw history as a gradual development involving *Geist* (the collective or universal mind or "spirit" in which all rational human beings share). *Geist* first posits concepts, then finds apparent incompatibilities between them, and, finally, in seeking to overcome these incompatibilities, moves toward ever greater self-understanding. This threefold process is known as Hegelian dialectic.

In specifically ethical terms, Hegel is keen to think beyond the limitations of very abstract principles of the rightness and wrongness of actions themselves (abstract right), which cannot give an adequate account of the role of the agent as one who chooses and is responsible for his or her actions. But he is also critical of a Kantian approach to obligation and responsibility (morality), which tries to posit universalizable rules for action that are valid for *any* rational agent while failing to take account of the particular character and circumstances of *specific agents*. Instead there needs to be a greater attention to the changing social and cultural settings in which people act, and this – Hegel argues – requires the category of ethical life (*Sittlichkeit*). Ethical life is the arena where we find the concrete institutions that frame and shape human action – like family, civil society, and the state. These basic social units are distillations in actual historical circumstances of the concepts of the good and of human well-being that are current in their time. We do not necessarily choose these institutions, even though we may interact creatively with them from within – and this marks a profound difference between Hegel's ethics and the more voluntarist, or choice-based, models of ethics associated with a Kantian tradition.

Karl Marx (1818–83) outlined a vision of the world order that he thought must characterize the ultimate stage in the development of humanity in history. He took from Hegel a belief that human freedom is not the property of individuals, but is best understood as the activity of a self-realizing whole. By participating in the judgments and liberating forces at work in historical process, humanity as a *whole* will realize itself as a universal and free society. History's final stage is one in which self-centered and group-centered activity will transcend itself, finding true fulfillment in the service of universal humanity. This stage will mark an end to human exploitation. Every human being will contribute freely and rationally to society, and receive what he or she needs from it. Marx's belief in the possibility of freedom through political struggle has been a powerful motivator of liberation movements ever since – including Christian liberation theologies that have borrowed analytical tools from Marx in their critique of the ideology of privilege and their exposure of social exploitation. We shall examine these further in Chapter Six.

One of the great achievements of Marx's thought was to show how ideas (including ethical ideas) are social products. In other words, ideas do not simply exist – they are created by particular people in particular circumstances. Moreover, he contended, they are often particularly influenced by class interests, or by economic relations in which there is unequal power. The powerful have especially good opportunities to sponsor morality that will serve their requirements in any given set of economic conditions. In this respect, Marx's thought is anti-ethical, because it rejects the idea that any philosophy of human behavior is normative; for him, ethics masks power. On the other hand, his is a morally passionate (though anti-religious) philosophy. This is one of its paradoxes.

The Marxist vision of community without private property argues for much more than the sharing of property practiced in the early church of Acts 2–4; it argues for shared ownership of *the means of production themselves*. Moreover, it is intrinsically critical of models of shared ownership that are limited to particular communities or groups, such as the church, because of its vision of a society that encompasses the whole human species.

Marx's understanding that human existence is an unfolding drama, whose dynamic is human relationship to production, is known as "historical materialism." It has come to constitute one of the principal alternatives to a Christian worldview in the modern era. One of the key questions Christian ethicists have put to Marxist thought is what room it has for articulating the obligations and aspirations of interpersonal relationship. Can the specifics of life in community with other human beings be articulated and valued adequately in the terms provided by Marx's thought, or will humanity always only be describable as productive labor, and community in functional terms as cooperative solidarity in that labor?

Three themes emerged from the legacy of Hegel and Marx that have come to hold important places in contemporary conversations in Christian ethics: responsibility, rights, and justice. While the writings and traditions that embody these themes vary in their acceptance or rejection of Hegelian and Marxist themes, they all share a commitment to the communal – rather than merely individual – aspect of the ethical life.

Responsibility

As an ethical theme, responsibility focuses on the obligations that members of a society have toward one another. It asks the scriptural question, "Am I my brother's keeper?" and wonders about the ways in which we are responsible for the well-being of those around us, especially the most vulnerable. The theme of responsibility takes shape in a number of different areas throughout the twentieth century, including in the Catholic social teaching embodied in the papal encyclicals, the Social Gospel that flowered in American Protestantism, and Anglican social thought.

Papal encyclicals

During the papacy of Leo XIII (1810–1903, pope from 1878), there began a series of encyclicals, or open letters, from the Vatican that acknowledged the changing social and economic circumstances of the modern era, and sought to address these new conditions with an approach based around natural law. From 1963 the popes recognized a need to speak not just to Roman Catholics but to the world community. Each encyclical is known by the opening words of its Latin edition. The first encyclical was *Rerum Novarum* (On Capital and Labor, 1891), followed forty years later by *Quadragesimo Anno* (On the Reconstruction of the Social Order, 1931), and then, in turn, *Mater et Magistra* (On Christianity and Social Progress, 1961), *Pacem in Terris* (On Establishing Universal Peace in Truth, Justice, Charity, and Liberty, 1963), *Dignitatis Humanae* (Declaration on

Religious Freedom, 1965), *Populorum Progressio* (On the Development of Peoples, 1967), *Octogesima Adveniens* (On the Eightieth Anniversary of *Rerum Novarum*, 1971), *Laborem Exercens* (On Human Work, 1981), *Sollicitudo Rei Socialis* (For the Twentieth Anniversary of *Populorum Progressio*, 1987), *Centesimus Annus* (On the Hundredth Anniversary of *Rerum Novarum*, 1991), *Evangelium Vitae* (On the Value and Inviolability of Human Life, 1995), *Deus Caritas Est* (On Christian Love, 2006), *Caritas in Veritate* (Charity in Truth, 2009), and *Laudato Si'* (On Care for Our Common Home, 2015). Several of these are treated at greater length in Part Three of this book.

A number of themes run through this social encyclical tradition.

- Most visible is the sanctity of life and the dignity of the human person. This begins from the moment of conception and ends with death – thus, racism and similar forms of discrimination are opposed; abortion, euthanasia, and the death penalty are ruled out; and just war principles, with their assumption of war as a last resort, must be followed. The basic unit of society is the family, and through communities, nations, and the global society, every person has a place in a kind of family.
- There is a varying degree of coolness toward socialism, whose methods of analysis are sometimes commended but whose materialism and atheism are intolerable, and toward capitalism, whose commitment to private property is endorsed but whose tendency to exacerbate class struggles is noted. There is no confidence that an entirely free market is capable of yielding justice: "Just as the unity of human society cannot be founded on an opposition of classes, so also the right ordering of economic life cannot be left to a free competition of forces. For from this source, as from a poisoned spring, have originated and spread all the errors of individualist economic teaching" (*Quadragesimo Anno*).
- The principle of subsidiarity expresses a concern that all state decisions should be taken as close to the level of the common people as is practicable.
- The popes make significant use of rights language. Everyone has a right to life and the necessities for a full and flourishing life, such as medical care, education, employment, and a living wage. Everyone has the right to property, but the right to use the world's resources comes with a duty to attend to those who lack access to basic goods: this stance is sometimes known as the social mortgage.
- Catholic tradition already recognized *commutative* justice (arithmetic equality, among individuals), *distributive* justice (proportionate share of goods and burdens, across society), and *legal* justice (obligations to society); the encyclical *Quadragesimo Anno* introduced the notion of *social* justice, a preferential commitment to the poor in word, prayer, and deed, and an invitation to social organization to achieve the common good. (The term "social justice" was first coined by the Jesuit Luigi Taparelli [1793–1862].) The rights of workers include that of forming trade unions and enjoying safe working conditions. A

quotation from *Rerum Novarum* gives a flavor of the language in which these sentiments are expressed: employers must not "look upon their work people as their bondsmen, but … respect in every man his dignity as a person ennobled by Christian character."

- Since the 1960s there has been an increasing recognition that social problems are global in nature, and that just lending arrangements and care for the natural environment as God's creation are vital dimensions of human solidarity. These words from *Pacem in Terris* are typical: "We exhort our people to take an active part in public life, and to contribute towards the attainment of the common good of the entire human family as well as to that of their own country." This theme gained in prominence and urgency with the 2015 encyclical *Laudato Si'*, which asserts that the earth is like a sister who "now cries out to us because of the harm we have inflicted on her by our irresponsible use and abuse of the goods with which God has endowed her," and which calls on all the religions and nations of the earth to engage in an international dialogue concerning the present environmental crisis.

The Social Gospel

It was not just the Roman Catholic tradition that adapted to the challenges of the modern world by stressing the theme of communal responsibility. Two other contributions stand out. One was the Social Gospel movement in the United States in the early years of the twentieth century. Washington Gladden (1836–1918), a Congregational pastor in Columbus, Ohio, and Walter Rauschenbusch (1861–1918), a German Baptist pastor in New York, are generally seen as the center of the movement. Rauschenbusch was particularly influenced by the novelist Charles Sheldon (1857–1946), especially his novel *In His Steps* (1897), which coined the phrase "What Would Jesus Do?". The Social Gospelers concentrated on Jesus' proclamation of the kingdom of God, which they saw as truly realizable on earth in the foreseeable future. There was great confidence in human progress, as a result of humankind following God's initiative, and in the capacity of education to introduce a law of love that would eradicate the sin of selfishness from individuals and institutions. One significant document was *The Social Creed of the Churches* (1912), which advocated conciliation and arbitration in industrial disputes, the abolition of child labor, a reduction in working hours, and a living wage. The movement was roundly criticized by Reinhold Niebuhr (1892–1971) as naïve and lacking an understanding of sin.

Reinhold Niebuhr served thirteen years as an Evangelical German Lutheran pastor in Detroit before moving to Union Seminary in New York in 1928. While initially sharing the pacifism and optimism of the Social Gospelers, he came to renounce such views and developed instead an approach he called Christian realism. In *Moral Man and Immoral Society* (1932) he makes a distinction between individual face-to-face relations, which have the capacity to be unselfish, and interactions between one group and another, where such unselfishness is virtually impossible. In *An Interpretation of Christian Ethics* (1935) he describes love as an "impossible possibility," and suggests justice as a more suitable term for economic and political discourse. Thus, "Man's capacity for justice makes democracy possible; but man's inclination to injustice makes democracy necessary." In the *Nature and Destiny of Man* (two volumes, 1941, 1943) Niebuhr focused more explicitly on the question of sin, arguing that the doctrine of original sin is the only empirically verifiable doctrine of the Christian faith. It is the limitation imposed by sin that keeps humanity in the finite and prevents it realizing its destiny in the infinite. Niebuhr regarded the *agape* love of Jesus as a religious ideal that could not be treated as a normative ethic. The cross was a tragic moment in history that illustrated the selflessness in human destiny but not the selfishness that lies in human nature. Thus, justice would require coercion to balance out social disparities and resist tyranny. The following sums up his notion of realism:

> Man's concern for some centuries to come is not the creation of an ideal society in which there will be uncoerced and perfect peace and justice, but a society in which there will be enough justice, and in which coercion will be sufficiently nonviolent to prevent his common enterprise from issuing into complete disaster.

Anglican social ethics
Anglican theology has a significant tradition of social thought in this same "responsibility" line. At the head of the tradition in the modern era is F. D. Maurice (1805–72), who lost his chair at King's College London when he denied the doctrine of everlasting punishment in hell. Maurice and Charles Kingsley (1819–75) described Christian socialism as the science of partnership. They foreswore competition and strove to promote the kingdom of God as an existing reality. They were an inspiration for the cooperative movement, which sought to protect workers in the face of the newly mechanized economy, and later for the Christendom Group, which aspired to the medieval ecology of church, nation, and social order. The most celebrated member of this tradition was William Temple (1881–1944, archbishop of Canterbury 1942–4). He saw the incarnation and the sacraments as the ground on which material reality was valued, and thus the lens through which reflection on economics and politics was required. In January 1941 Temple presided at the Malvern Conference, a gathering that particularly considered the relation of the church to economic life. He elucidated the principle, first coined by J. H. Oldham (1874–1969), of "middle axioms" – guiding principles that could take a middle place between general theological goals and specific political policy. Temple's best-known work is *Christianity and Social Order* (1942). He first used the term "welfare state" and was a crucial figure in inaugurating the era of social reform in post-war Britain.

Rights

There are a number of sources for the tradition of human rights. For example, the Code of Hammurabi, found in Mesopotamia, and dating back to around 1800 BCE, recognizes to some degree the rights of women, children, and slaves; and the

Cyrus cylinder, found in 1879 and dating back to 539 BCE, shows how Cyrus of Persia abolished slavery in his empire and promoted freedom of religious expression. But the tradition of human rights in the West begins in earnest in the debate about the status of the native peoples conquered by the Spanish in South America in the sixteenth century.

Bartolomé de Las Casas (1484–1566), Dominican friar and bishop of Chiapas in southeast Mexico, was horrified by the conquistadores' atrocious treatment of the indigenous peoples of what became known as Latin America. He advocated the self-determination of peoples, believing that power resides in the populace, and that rulers should serve the people and gain their consent when implementing significant actions. He believed the indigenous peoples were free people under natural law, were fully rational, and should be evangelized without coercion. In 1550–1 in Valladolid he engaged in a celebrated debate with the Jesuit Juan Ginés de Sepúlveda, who argued that the Amerindians were natural slaves. Initially Las Casas argued that Africans should be brought to the New World to carry out slave functions, but he later changed his view on this.

The notion of natural rights was taken up by Hugo Grotius (1583–1645). Prior to Grotius, reference to rights was always (as in the English Magna Carta of 1215) in relation to social roles. From Grotius onwards comes the notion of inalienable rights, which became so significant in the US Declaration of Independence. Grotius explicitly stated that it was possible to ascertain certain moral necessities without belief in God; these included freedom, equality, and the pursuit of peaceable cooperation in society. The right of governments was secondary to these natural individual rights – governments simply oversaw the security and distribution of property and the arrest and punishment of offenders. Thomas Hobbes assumed, as we have seen, that natural rights were identical with self-interest. The state of nature was one in which everyone was entitled to claim everything from everybody, ensuring misery and danger for all. The inevitable result was the emergence of an absolute central authority, one of whose roles would be to restrict the exercise of natural rights to just one: the right to self-preservation. John Locke saw natural rights lying not in simple self-interest but in a recognition of the wrongness of inflicting harm on others and the rightness of helping others in distress. On these foundations, governments guarantee the right to hold property and to protection from arbitrary force or oppression.

Locke was a significant influence on Thomas Jefferson, and thus the notion of rights played a large part in the American Revolution of 1776. The Declaration of Independence announces it is "self-evident" that all persons "are created equal, that they are endowed by their creator with certain unalienable rights, that among these are life, liberty, and the pursuit of happiness." One figure who was significant in the age of revolution was Thomas Paine (1737–1809), who wrote, "individuals themselves, each in his own personal and sovereign right, entered into a compact with each other to produce a government: and this is the only mode in which governments have a right to arise, and the only principle on which they have a right to exist." His views also shaped the Declaration of the Rights of Man and of the Citizen, issued in Paris in August 1789, which claimed that certain individual and collective rights were due not only to the people of France but to all people everywhere. Paine published *The Rights of Man* in 1791, which largely echoed the US Declaration of Independence.

A generation later Henry David Thoreau (1817–62) wrote "Civil Disobedience" (originally published as "Resistance to Civil Government") to explain his non-payment of taxes. Words like these influenced the later civil rights movement immensely:

> "Under a government which imprisons unjustly, the true place for a just man is also a prison. ... A minority is powerless while it conforms to the majority; it is not even a minority then; but it is irresistible when it clogs by its whole weight. If the alternative is to keep all just men in prison, or give up war and slavery, the State will not hesitate which to choose. If a thousand men were not to pay their tax bills this year, that would not be a violent and bloody measure, as it would be to pay them, and enable the State to commit violence and shed innocent blood. This is, in fact, the definition of a peaceable revolution, if any such is possible.

Perhaps the high water mark of human rights aspirations was the Universal Declaration of Human Rights adopted by the United Nations General Assembly in 1948. These rights were later, in 1966, divided into civil and political rights, and economic, social, and cultural rights. Specific rights named include the rights to life, liberty, security, equality before the law, the absence of enslavement or torture, freedom of conscience and religion, education, work (in healthy conditions), leisure, and freedom of movement. Subsequent international legislation has sought to defend women, children, and those vulnerable to racism, genocide, or torture. The work of Amnesty International and other campaigning organizations has made human rights a central and popular global social cause.

Not everyone has proven to be a supporter of human rights. It is common in Islam to regard human rights as a secularized form of Judeo-Christian ethics, and thus to resist the universal claims generally associated with the tradition. Major figures in the utilitarian and virtue strands of ethics, such as Jeremy Bentham and Alasdair MacIntyre, respectively, have criticized the human rights tradition as based on a fiction that has no objective reality. Others note that there is no easy way to tell whose rights take priority when the rights of different groups come into conflict – for example, when the right to free speech clashes with the right to public safety. However, the accumulation and momentum behind international rights legislation are hard to dismiss so easily.

Justice

Alongside rights, perhaps the most common word in contemporary debates about universal ethics is justice. Justice has two broad connotations – distributive and retributive. The latter, concerning punishment and rehabilitation, is not the concern here. Instead, we shall consider influential understandings of distributive justice. Each is concerned with the questions of what is to be distributed, to whom it is to be distributed, and what the appropriate level of distribution should be.

1. An ancient notion of justice is that of *just desert*, or "rendering to each their due." There are broadly three kinds of just desert theories. They vary on the criteria by which the distribution is made.

    - One assumes the distribution should be made according to merit, and that a combination of ability and hard work entitles some to a greater share of resources than those who lack such ability and/or withhold such intense labor. This is known as meritocracy.

    - Another view sees need as the central criterion, and begins with the distribution of necessities such as food, clothing, shelter, and medical supplies. This echoes the words of Acts 2:44–5, "All who believed were together and had all things in common; they would sell their possessions and goods and distribute the proceeds to all, as any had need." These in turn are reflected in Henri de Saint-Simon's words, taken up by Karl Marx, "From each according to his ability, to each according to his needs."

    - A third view assesses the goods due to a person by the quality or extent of their past, present, or future contribution to the general social benefit.

2. A very common notion in ethics is to see justice in terms of *equality*. Equality cannot and does not mean that people are the same, since they evidently are not, but that they should in significant ways be treated the same. In which ways? A number of answers are given to this question.

    - One is that they should be treated equally under the law, and have equal rights, for example to receive a fair trial or to vote.

    - Another is that they should have an equal distribution of goods. This is not likely to last for very long, since some people will quickly trade tangible goods for intangible ones, others will save, others again waste, others invest and gain, others invest and lose; thus, a further answer is that people with fewer goods should be treated with equal respect, and not have to put up with exclusion, disregard, or humiliation.

    - Perhaps the most common aspiration is equality of opportunity, particularly to education, employment, and social advancement; however, such equality may simply be a cover for meritocracy, and it quickly exposes the tensions to be found between equality and other notions of justice, such as the meeting of appropriate needs.

3. The description of justice as *fairness* was made more widely known by the publication in 1971 of the book *A Theory of Justice* by the Harvard philosopher John Rawls (1921–2002). Rawls outlines what he calls the "original position," which in some ways resembles the "state of nature" often recalled by Enlightenment thinkers. In the original position, human beings were self-interested, equally able to propose models of society, rational, equally in possession of the relevant facts,

and, crucially, under a "veil of ignorance" about their future station in life, wealth, character, and abilities. This veil of ignorance ensures mutual benevolence, because no one would wish to make an enemy of a person they might later badly need as a friend. It excludes utilitarianism, because no one would take the risk that theirs would be the happiness that would be sacrificed for that of the greatest number. Hence Rawls derives two principles of justice.

- *Liberty*: each person should have equal access to the most extensive total system of equal basic liberties compatible with a similar system of liberty for all.
- *Difference*: social and economic inequalities are to be arranged so that they are both (a) to the greatest benefit of the least advantaged, and (b) attached to offices and positions open to all under conditions of fair equality of opportunity.

4.   Finally, the notion of justice as *entitlement* is associated with another Harvard philosopher, Robert Nozick (1938–2002). His most famous work is *Anarchy, State and Utopia* (1974), although he qualified some of his claims in his later work, *The Examined Life* (1989). If Joseph Fletcher may be regarded as offering a theory characteristic of the 1960s, Nozick offers a theory characteristic of the 1980s. He criticizes theories of social justice such as Marxism and utilitarianism that seek to impose a pattern on society and ignore the pragmatic making-do by which societies actually run. Nozick claims every person is entitled to what they own, earn, or acquire so long as they do so legally. He sees two main patterns at work in a just society: (1) just acquisition, or procurement; (2) just transfer, or sale. If either of these trespasses outside the law, there is a possible third principle, that of rectification. Whether one approves of the way a person acquires goods or disposes of them is irrelevant. Meanwhile all attempts to redistribute goods according to an ideal pattern, without the consent of their owners – for example, redistributive taxation – are theft.

We shall meet ideas of justice again in Chapter Eight.

Summary

Ethics is often portrayed as a dogfight between deontological approaches, which focus on action and intention, and consequential approaches, which focus on outcomes. This chapter has demonstrated the complexities within each of these two approaches but noted that they agree more significantly than they differ, and it has added a third "universal" approach, which we have termed right relationships.

Within deontological ethics we considered first divine command and then natural law strands. Both of these are "ethics for everybody," but the former locates authority in God's expressed will, whereas the latter finds authority in human nature and reason. (The two overlap where the natural law is itself seen as an expression of God's divine law.) We then saw that Kant's categorical imperative was an attempt to find incontrovertible ground in right intention.

Within consequential ethics we saw the significance of utilitarianism and the way it promises to be able to calculate the right thing to do. We surveyed other theories, noting but not endorsing the common anxiety that consequentialism undermines the whole notion of right and wrong.

Finally we considered a number of recent strands in ethics that have focused less on moments of individual decision and more on the formation of a good and healthy society. It is an acute awareness of those who have most frequently been excluded from the benefits of such a society that gives rise to the concerns of our next chapter.

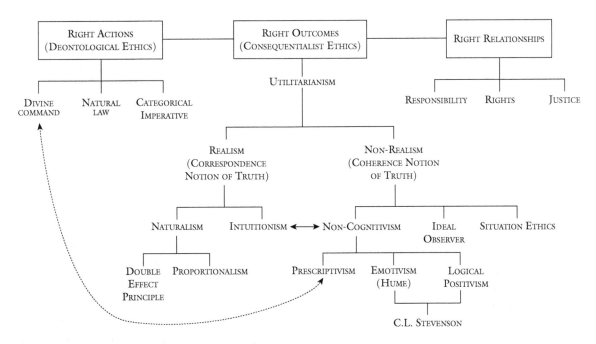

Figure 5.1   Universal ethics tree.

References and Further Reading

Right Actions

Euthyphro's dilemma may be found in *Plato*, Vol. 1: *Euthyphro, Apology, Crito, Phaedo, Phaedrus* (Loeb Classical Library; Cambridge, MA: Harvard University Press, 1938), pages 35–41. Plato's *Euthyphro* is also available online through the Internet Classics Archive at http://classics.mit.edu/Plato/euthyfro.html.

In reference to natural law, Timothy O'Connell examines the thought of Gaius and Ulpian in *Principles for a Catholic Morality* (rev. edn; San Francisco, CA: Harper & Row, 1990), chapter 13, pages 135–7.

Thomas Aquinas explores God's natural and supernatural knowledge in two key places in *Summa*

Theologica (5 vols; Notre Dame, IN: Christian Classics, 1948), Prima Pars [First Part], Question 25, Articles 5–6; and Prima Pars, Question 105, Article 6. His quotation about grace perfecting nature is in *Summa Theologica*, Prima Pars [First Part], Question 1, Article 8, Reply 2. The three orders of precepts within natural law are from *Summa Theologica*, Prima Secundae [First Part of the Second Part], Question 94, Article 2. The *Summa Theologica* is also available online in the Christian Classics Ethereal Library at www.ccel. org/ccel/aquinas/summa.html.

Richard Hooker treats natural law in Book 1 of his 1593 work, *Of the Laws of Ecclesiastical Polity* (Vol. 1; Cambridge, MA: Harvard University Press, 1977). Hooker quotes John Calvin on the natural law ("Since God alone is the source of all good …") in his *A Christian Letter* (contained in *Of the Laws of Ecclesiastical Polity* [Vol. 4; Cambridge, MA: Harvard University Press, 1982]).

For Thomas Hobbes' reflections on natural law, consult his *Leviathan: Authoritative Text, Backgrounds, Interpretations* (New York: W. W. Norton, 1997); especially the section "On Man"; Chapter XIV, "Of the First and Second Natural Laws, and of Contracts." Excerpts from this section are in the corresponding chapter of *Christian Ethics: An Introductory Reader*. *Leviathan* is also available online at http://ebooks.adelaide.edu. au/h/hobbes/thomas/h68l/.

For Joseph Butler's opposition to Hobbes in his *A Dissertation of the Nature of Virtue*, see *Butler's Fifteen Sermons Preached at the Rolls Chapel; and, A Dissertation of the Nature of Virtue* (London: SPCK, 1970), pages 147–54.

The seven goods of Catholic philosopher John Finnis are to be found in *Natural Law and Natural Rights* (Oxford: Clarendon Press; New York: Oxford University Press, 1980), chapter 4.

Key texts for Immanuel Kant's ethical thought are *Critique of Practical Reason* (Mary Gregor, trans. and ed.; Cambridge; New York: Cambridge University Press, 1997); and *Groundwork for the Metaphysics of Morals* (Arnulf Zweig, trans.; Thomas E. Hill Jr. and Arnulf Zweig, eds; Oxford; New York: Oxford University Press, 2002). Kant's discussion of "postulates of reasons" is in the section "Dialectic of Practical Reason" in Part I of *The Critique of Practical Reason*. The categorical imperative is in *Groundwork for the Metaphysics of Morals*, the Second Section: "Transition from Popular Moral Philosophy to a Metaphysics of Morals," which is also quoted in the corresponding chapter of *Christian Ethics: An Introductory Reader*. Kant's *Groundwork for the Metaphysics of Moral* is also available online at http://www.earlymoderntexts. com/assets/pdfs/kant1785.pdf.

The continuation of Kant's legacy in the thought of Albrecht Ritschl may be seen in *The Christian Doctrine of Justification and Reconciliation* (H. R. Mackintosh and A. B. Macaulay, eds; Clifton, NJ: Reference Book Publishers, 1966).

In addition to Hobbes and Kant, the following are quoted in the corresponding chapter of *Christian Ethics: An Introductory Reader*:

- Karl Barth. *Church Dogmatics*. Volume 2, Part 2. Edinburgh: T & T Clark, 1949. From "Ethics as a Task of the Doctrine of God"; "The Command as the Claim of God."
- Thomas Aquinas. *Summa Theologica*, Prima Secundae [First Part of the Second Part], Question 94, "The Natural Law," Article 2. Available at www.ccel.org/ccel/aquinas/summa.html.

Right Outcomes

Key texts for Jeremy Bentham's moral philosophy, including the greatest happiness principle, are *Introduction to the Principles of Morals and Legislation* and *A Fragment on Government*, both in volume 1 of *The Works of Jeremy Bentham* (John Bowring, ed.; New York: Russell & Russell, 1962).

The summary of John Stuart Mill's thought is drawn primarily from *Utilitarianism* (Roger Crisp, ed.; Oxford: Oxford University Press, 1998), chapter 2, an excerpt of which may be found in the corresponding chapter of *Christian Ethics: An Introductory Reader*. *Utilitarianism* is also available online at www.utilitarianism.com/mill1.htm.

The naturalistic fallacy is explained in more depth in G. E. Moore's 1903 book *Principia Ethica* (New York: Courier Dover Publications, 2004), pages 13–20.

David Hume's description of emotivism is from his book *Enquiry Concerning the Principles of Morals* (Tom L. Beauchamp, ed.; Oxford: Clarendon Press; New York: Oxford University Press, 1998).

C. L. Stevenson is quoted from his *Ethics and Language* (New Haven, CT: Yale University Press; London: H. Milford, Oxford University Press, 1944), page 139.

Alasdair MacIntyre critiques emotivism in *After Virtue* (2nd edn; Notre Dame, IN: University of Notre Dame Press, 1981, 1984), chapters 2 and 3; see particularly page 25 for the specific quotation.

The account of R. M. Hare's notion of prescriptivism may be found in *The Language of Morals* (Oxford: Clarendon Press, 1952); see especially chapters 1 and 10.

Bernard Hoose describes proportionalism in *Proportionalism: The American Debate and Its European Roots* (Washington, DC: Georgetown University Press, 1987).

The thought of Joseph Fletcher may be found in his *Situation Ethics: The New Morality* (Louisville, KY: Westminster/John Knox Press, 1997). An excerpt is also quoted in the corresponding chapter in *Christian Ethics: An Introductory Reader.*

In addition to the above, a portion of the following is included in the corresponding chapter of *Christian Ethics: An Introductory Reader*: Richard A. McCormick, *Ambiguity in Moral Choice* (Milwaukee, WI: Marquette University Press, 1973).

Right Relationships

G. W. F. Hegel's ethical thought lies principally in *Phenomenology of Spirit* (A. V. Miller, trans.; Oxford: Clarendon Press, 1977). The philosophy of Karl Marx may be explored in *The Communist Manifesto* (with Friedrich Engels; David McLellan, ed.; Oxford; New York: Oxford University Press, 1992). What came to be known as historical materialism is articulated in the preface to *A Contribution to the Critique of Political Economy* (Maurice Dobb, ed.; S. W. Ryazanskaya, trans.; New York: International Publishers, 1970).

The papal social encyclicals are available on the Vatican's website at www.vatican.va/phome_en.htm. The 1891 encyclical *Rerum Novarum* is quoted in the corresponding chapter in *Christian Ethics: An Introductory Reader.*

For an introduction to the Social Gospel movement and its theology, consult Walter Rauschenbusch, *Christianizing the Social Order* (New York: Macmillan, 1923) and *A Theology for the Social Gospel* (Louisville, KY: Westminster/John Knox Press, 1997).

Reinhold Niebuhr's description of love as an "impossible possibility" is in *An Interpretation of Christian Ethics* (San Francisco, CA: Harper & Row, 1963, 1987), page 37. His explanation of "Man's capacity for justice" is in *The Children of Light and the Children of Darkness* (New York: Scribner's, 1944), page ix. The quotation of his notion of realism is from *Moral Man and Immoral Society* (New York:

Continuum International, 2005), page 16. Another key ethical work is his *Nature and Destiny of Man* (2 vols; Robin W. Lovin, ed.; Louisville, KY: Westminster/John Knox Press, 1996).

Key writings for Anglican social ethics as described in this chapter are William Temple's *Christianity and Social Order* (Harmondsworth, UK; New York: Penguin Books, 1943); Kenneth Kirk's *The Vision of God: The Christian Doctrine of the Summum Bonum* (2nd edn; London; New York: Longmans, Green, 1932); and F. D. Maurice, *The Kingdom of Christ* (4th edn; London: Macmillan, 1891).

The thought of Bartolomé de Las Casas is recorded in his *History of the Indies* (Andrée Collard, trans. and ed.; New York: Harper & Row, 1971). Selections from the Prologue are in the corresponding chapter in *Christian Ethics: An Introductory Reader*; portions are also available online at www.columbia.edu/acis/ets/CCREAD/lascasas.htm.

The notion of natural rights in Hugo Grotius may be found in *De Jure Praedae (Commentary on the Law of Prize and Booty)* (Gwladys L. Williams with Walter H. Zeydel, trans.; New York: Oceana; London: Wildy, 1964); and *De Jure Belli ac Pacis (On the Law of War and Peace)* (Francis W. Kelsey, trans.; New York: Oceana, 1964).

The quotation from Thomas Paine on government is from *The Rights of Man* (page 467), in *Thomas*

Paine: Collected Writings (New York: Library Classics of the United States, 1995), pages 431–661.

Henry David Thoreau's explanation of his non-payment of taxes is from his essay "Civil Disobedience," which may be found in *Walden, Civil Disobedience, and Other Writings* (3rd edn; William Rossi, ed.; New York: W. W. Norton, 1966, 2008), page 236.

The Universal Declaration of Human Rights is available at www.un.org/Overview/rights.html, and is also included in the corresponding chapter in *Christian Ethics: An Introductory Reader*.

The slogan "From each according to his ability, to each according to his needs" is from Karl Marx's 1875 *Critique of the Gotha Programme* (with Friedrich Engels; Moscow: Foreign Language Publishing House, 1959).

John Rawls' notion of justice, including the "original position," is articulated in John Rawls, *A Theory of Justice* (rev. edn; Cambridge, MA: Belknap Press, 1999), chapter 1, "Justice as Fairness." The corresponding chapter in *Christian Ethics: An Introductory Reader* quotes from this section of Rawls.

Robert Nozick's views on just acquisition and just transfer are laid out in *Anarchy, State and Utopia* (New York: Basic Books, 1974), especially pages 150–82.

In addition to the primary sources listed above, the following are introductions to some of the key thinkers in this chapter:

- George C. Kerner. *Three Philosophical Moralists: Mill, Kant, and Sartre: An Introduction to Ethics.* Oxford: Clarendon Press; New York: Oxford University Press, 1990.
- Enrique D. Dussel. *Beyond Philosophy: Ethics, History, Marxism, and Liberation Theology.* Lanham, MD: Rowman & Littlefield, 2003.
- Thomas Winfried Menko Pogge. *John Rawls: His Life and Theory of Justice.* Trans. Michelle Kosch. Oxford: Oxford University Press, 2007.

Chapter Six
Subversive Ethics

Subversive ethics names a cluster of approaches to ethics that emerges in response and reaction to what we have called universal ethics. That does not mean that the agenda of subversive ethics is limited to response and reaction to what in varying ways it perceives as universal assumptions. Each strand of what we are calling subversive ethics develops its own constructive models that go well beyond critique. Perhaps the most quoted scriptural verse in subversive ethics is Galatians 3:28: "There is no longer Jew or Greek, there is no longer slave or free, there is no longer male and female; for all of you are one in Christ Jesus." This explicit identification of race ("Jew or Greek"), class ("slave or free"), and gender ("male and female") roots issues of difference at the heart of the gospel, and raises the central question of whether difference is fundamentally something to be enjoyed or to be overcome.

While there are a number of alternative approaches to ethics that could identify with the themes addressed in this chapter, we limit ourselves to a discussion of four strands. Each strand argues that the nature of truth, and therefore of the good, looks different depending on where one is standing. This perspective is sometimes known as social location. Of the variety of social locations, three recur in ethics repeatedly, and a fourth has an emerging voice, as follows.

1. *Class.* This covers a range of concerns, including most specifically the exclusion and oppression of the poor, but it also refers to issues concerning class struggle and the influence of questions of power and economics on ethics in general.
2. *Race.* Again this most specifically refers to the way certain races have been subdued, suppressed, and exploited by certain other races, but it also refers to the way questions of nation and ethnicity have had a bearing on the nature and practice of ethics.

Introducing Christian Ethics, Second Edition. Samuel Wells and Ben Quash with Rebekah Eklund.
© 2017 John Wiley & Sons Ltd. Published 2017 by John Wiley & Sons Ltd.

3. *Gender.* This begins with a concern for the subservient status of women both within Christianity and across the human race as a whole for most of its history in most parts of the world, but it also refers to minority forms of sexual orientation and gender identity and the bearing these perspectives have on ethics.
4. *Disability and age.* The question in this case is whether justice is best understood as giving each person the same, or giving all persons their due – and thus whether rights language is sufficient to meet the particular and diverse needs of those whose "difference" is age or disability.

We shall look at each of these in turn.

Class

The movement that has made the particular theological location of the poor the most explicit is that of Latin American liberation theology; and so our examination of class concentrates there. There then follows a consideration of other locations, approaches, and dimensions of the ethics of class. It is of course possible to be of a higher class and yet poor, or of a lower class and yet not poor; thus, class is generally seen as a more comprehensive category for ethics than poverty.

Latin American Liberation Theology

The colonial and postcolonial history of South and Central America in the nineteenth and twentieth centuries has been one of a heavy hand. The military dominance of the Spanish and Portuguese conquerors was accompanied by a tight form of religious control that saw faith in otherworldly terms, an economy that kept the many in poverty, and a political structure that kept the few, often military dictators, in power. The countryside was full of landless farmers harvesting cotton or coffee beans under a merciless sun for a pitiful wage, while malnourished children combed city dumping grounds for scraps of food or clothing. The economies were in the hands of transnational corporations who dominated the mining and manufacturing industries, and oligarchies who monopolized rural landholdings. Protest, in the form of developing self-help communities or organizing labor, was brutally suppressed. The culture seemed a long way from the thoughtful imperatives of Immanuel Kant or the careful calculations of Jeremy Bentham described in Chapter Five; for some it required a new approach to ethics.

A number of influences brought a new spark to the Latin American churches' response to poverty in the 1960s.

- One was the 1959 revolution in Cuba led by Fidel Castro (b. 1926) and Che Guevara (1928–67).
- Another was the growth of basic ecclesial communities, consisting of around twenty households, supported by clergy, gathering once or twice

weekly to articulate their troubles, reflect on Scripture, and support one another in addressing their oppression.

- A third was the growing organization and politicization of Catholic university students.
- A fourth was the impetus for ecclesial renewal brought about by the Second Vatican Council (1962–5), particularly the approach known as "reading the signs of the times" found in the pastoral constitution *Gaudium et Spes* (the Pastoral Constitution on the Church in the Modern World, 1965). The official origins of liberation theology are sometimes traced to a subsequent gathering of Catholic Church leaders, the 1968 Conference of Latin American Bishops in Medellín, Colombia, where the bishops denounced social injustices and declared the church's solidarity with the poor and oppressed.
- And a fifth was the program of conscientization practiced in Brazil and Chile by the educator Paulo Freire (1921–97). Freire saw literacy as the key to the poor becoming agents of their own destiny, but he also regarded as equally significant their becoming aware of the ways their oppression had dismantled their own creative potential. His work *Pedagogy of the Oppressed* (1968) was highly influential in identifying the heart of liberation theology in the educational process.

What emerged was an approach to theology and ethics that made reflection a second, rather than a first, step.

Praxis

The assumption of most theological and philosophical reflection has been that ethics emerges in putting together authoritative sources, notably Scripture, the tradition of the church, and philosophical enquiry. In some cases the contribution of human experience is incorporated. But nowhere is a particular personal (and political) commitment assumed – indeed for many, such as Kant, it is explicitly ruled out. For the liberation theologians of South and Central America, human experience arising out of a particular commitment is exactly the substance of ethical reflection. This is rooted in a conviction that God is on the side of the oppressed and thus following God means sharing God's commitment, known as the "preferential option for the poor." Such experience based on commitment, which transforms the participant in the process of addressing injustice, is known as "praxis." Differences of social status, the struggle for daily survival, and an emerging new self-understanding among the poor create diversity in moral theology where universal ethics sees only uniformity. When one reflects on the source of such commitment, and on the simultaneous transformation from fatalism to engagement, it becomes difficult to separate praxis from reflection; thus, the emphasis on the priority of praxis becomes less about where one starts and more about the necessity of reflection being grounded in commitment.

Praxis originates historically in Aristotle's threefold distinction between:

- *theoria* (theory, or knowledge about that which cannot be other than it is, in the study of which Aristotle considered the happiest life to lie);

- *praxis* (doing, or political conduct, resting on practical wisdom); and
- *poiesis* (making, or enjoying).

Many of those who later became liberation theologians had been educated in an intellectual environment that assumed contemplation (*theoria*) was superior and prior to *praxis* (although such a sequential distinction between theory and practice was unknown to Aristotle). Hence the significance of their rejection of this heritage in the face of the profound poverty they were encountering. For G. W. F. Hegel (1770–1831) in his work *The Phenomenology of Spirit* (1807), when a slave is making objects for a master, the slave is simultaneously aware of both his or her alienation and his or her creativity. Recognizing this tension and in due course overcoming this alienation while asserting this creativity is a process Hegel calls *dialectic*, as we saw in Chapter Five. In the view of Karl Marx (1818–83), this dialectic assumed a particularly sinister character in capitalist societies, because the worker became isolated from his or her product, labor, and fellow-laborers. Praxis has two senses for Marx. It describes an appropriate, legitimate form of work that enables people to meet their needs while developing and expressing their humanity. But it also refers to the revolutionary transformation of the economic and political status quo that suppresses human flourishing.

The praxis approach to ethics runs broadly as follows. A problem emerges from the praxis of the poor or the theologian. For example, it comes to light that workers are routinely being laid off just days before they become eligible for formal hiring and the receipt of health benefits. The problem is then analyzed in relation to its causes, the parties concerned, and the impact on the poor and on others. Then there is scriptural or theological reflection on one aspect of the problem. Eventually the process results in a new understanding of theological method, Christian faith, or praxis. Praxis thus comes to be used as something of a code term in liberation theology. While in theory it means any form of ethical conduct that takes social disadvantage and particularly poverty seriously, its use tends to assume activities such as the following:

- community organizing, particularly in the form of basic ecclesial communities and neighborhood associations;
- the introduction of educational programs, designed to help people name their reality, denounce exploitation, and announce more humane structures;
- political gestures, particularly against oppression, including bishops' letters expressing protests against governments or policies;
- sometimes the facing of harassment, torture, and even death from hostile forces both inside and outside the country; and
- in some cases, violent resistance movements.

These commitments offer a critical lens through which to understand pronouncements previously regarded uncritically as authoritative. Before accepting any authority, liberation theologians first question what kind of praxis it embodies, endorses, or encourages.

Ethical emphases

While insistence on the preferential option for the poor and the priority of praxis are significantly different from the assumptions of universal ethics, many of the particular components of the liberationists' ethical program resemble the concerns we noted under the "right relationships" section of Chapter Five. When liberation theologians speak of the reign of God, they often invoke values such as human rights, liberty, the dignity of the individual, and the common good. They begin with the right to life, which for many of those they serve is constantly threatened by hunger, disease, and violence; they move to the restoration of goods stolen and compensation for injuries inflicted; then they consider the right to free speech, assembly, and social organization. Such rights take precedence over the assumption (again drawn from universal tradition, for example, John Locke [1632–1704]) that the right to property always prevails. One liberation ethicist, Enrique Dussel (b. 1934), calls what we have in this book been calling universal ethics "morality," and regards it as a "peaceful remorseless conscience" that endorses the assumptions of global capitalism. Meanwhile he calls his vision – of engaged discipleship based on praxis – "ethics."

Liberation theologians consider there to be no such thing as a theological statement that is not at the same time an ethical one. For example, much of liberation theology works with a realized eschatology – that is, it challenges the widespread view that the kingdom of God is an otherworldly realm of rewards for faithful individuals, and instead insists that the reign of God is advanced and indeed brought about by divinely inspired and divinely empowered acts of love and justice. The kingdom of God is not an individual relationship but a society entered when one person helps another transform the inhumane, undignified, and depressed conditions of their lives. The kingdom of God is a genuinely historical event, the time of its coming is now, and the agents of its coming are those who usher it in with sacred acts that enfranchise and unite persons who have labored under oppression.

For liberation theologians, ethics cannot be considered without social analysis. All knowledge is socially situated. For example, when Brazilian brothers Leonardo Boff (b. 1938) and Clodovis Boff (b. 1944) consider the US economy, they distinguish between functionalist and dialectical analysis. Functionalist analysis assumes a healthy organism, seeing such issues as unemployment and crime as dysfunctions of a basically sound system, and assuming a continuous line from underdevelopment to a thriving economy integrated in the global system. This is the conventional language of economic development. Dialectical analysis sees the conflictual quality inherent in and between complex societies, especially along the lines of race, class, and gender. It sees poverty not as backwardness but as oppression. Such an approach disclaims the idea of value-neutral social analysis, identifies with the perspective of the poor, and offers an agenda for structural and sometimes revolutionary change.

Scripture

The early liberation theologians tended to see the story of the exodus as the key to the whole of Scripture. They saw in that story that God hears the cry of the oppressed and intervenes in history to set the captive free. (Critics have noted that this overlooks significant aspects of the story – such as the long dwelling in Goshen, the wilderness time, and the later enslavement of the Canaanites.) As the movement developed, the exodus story came to be read in more complex ways. For example, biblical scholar Jorge Pixley (b. 1937), a professor in Puerto Rico, in Mexico, and more recently in Nicaragua, sees the exodus story as a paradigm of class struggle and regards the precise details – of Jewish ethnicity and the conditions of slavery – as secondary. This exhibits a tendency in some aspects of the liberation tradition to see Jesus as simply representing and exhibiting the already established trajectory of exodus and kingdom. Yet gradually other parts of the Bible came to be incorporated in the liberationists' vision, and the Scriptures came to be seen as offering resources beyond the transformation of people's awareness of God's action amidst their oppression. Above all liberation theology is about ordinary, often illiterate, laborers discovering that the Bible is their reality. In the words of the Dutch Carmelite Carlos Mesters (b. 1931):

> In the past we members of the clergy expropriated the Bible and got a monopoly on its interpretation. We took the Bible out of the hands of the common people, locked it with a key and then threw the key away. But the people have found the key and are beginning again to read the Bible. And they are using the only tool they have at hand: their own lives, experiences and struggles.

Notable in this broader reading of Scripture is the work of perhaps the most famous liberation theologian, the Peruvian Dominican Gustavo Gutiérrez (b. 1928). Already in his original groundbreaking work, *A Theology of Liberation* (1971), he saw liberation as concerning not just the elimination of the causes of poverty and injustice, but also the opportunity for the poor to develop themselves freely and in dignity. This meant liberation from selfishness and sin, and restoration of right relationships. For Gutiérrez, liberation has always involved a particular understanding of spirituality. Where others refer to commitment, he prefers the term conversion. He refers often to justice, but increasingly in the context of the gratuitous overflow of God's love. His books *We Drink from Our Own Wells* (1983), *On Job* (1986), and especially *Las Casas: In Search of the Poor of Jesus Christ* (1993) underline his vision of the unity of spirituality and ethics.

Criticisms

Liberation ethics has been criticized in a number of areas. Some critics object to the insistence on a prior bias to the poor as a fundamental criterion of ethics. Others see the use of Marxist social analysis as dubious, given the hostility of

Marxist commitments toward Christian presuppositions. Still others suggest the liberationists are too selective in their use of Scripture, or point out that the distinction between theory and praxis does not do justice to the Aristotelian notion of practical reason. And some identify liberation ethics with one or another kind of the universal theories we examined in Chapter Five, such as the situation ethics of Joseph Fletcher (1905–91) or the utilitarianism of Jeremy Bentham (1748–1832) and John Stuart Mill (1806–73). Although liberation theology has long been treated with caution by the Vatican, largely because of its association with Marxism, the Argentinian Pope Francis (who became Pope in 2013) has signaled a new openness to the insights of liberation theology at the highest levels of the Catholic Church.

Liberation Theology Around the World

While liberation theology is most frequently associated with South and Central America, similar movements appeared independently and contemporaneously in other parts of the two-thirds world. In 1976, twenty-two representatives from Africa, Asia, and Latin America, and one black theologian from the USA met in Dar es Salaam, Tanzania, for an "Ecumenical Dialogue of Third World Theologians" to explore with one another theological developments in their respective traditions – Catholic, Protestant, and Orthodox. A declaration made at this gathering sums up the mutual concerns of many of these contextual theologies, and bears quoting at length.

> The theologies from Europe and North America are dominant today in our churches and represent one form of cultural domination. They must be understood to have arisen out of situations related to those countries, and therefore must not be uncritically adopted without our raising the question of their relevance in the context of our countries. Indeed we must, in order to be faithful to the gospel and to our peoples, reflect on the realities of our own situations and interpret the Word of God in relation to those realities. We reject as irrelevant an academic type of theology that is divorced from action. We are prepared for a radical break in epistemology which makes commitment the first act of theology and engages in critical reflection on the praxis of the reality of the Third World …
>
>   We call for an active commitment to the promotion of justice and the prevention of exploitation, the accumulation of wealth in the hands of a few, racism, sexism and all other forms of oppression, discrimination and dehumanization. Our conviction is that the theologian should have a fuller understanding of living in the Holy Spirit, for this also means being committed to a life-style of solidarity with the poor and the oppressed and involvement in action with them. Theology is not neutral. In a sense all theology is committed, conditioned notably by the socio-cultural context in which it is developed. The Christian theological task in our countries is to be self-critical of the theologians' conditioning by the value system of their environment. It has to be seen in relation to the need to live and work with those who cannot help themselves, and to be with them in their struggle for liberation.

While the movements that broadly cluster under the heading "postcolonial" will be reviewed later, at this point it is our concern to look at two further dimensions of liberation ethics that have an essentially class character.

Minjung theology

Minjung theology arose in South Korea in the 1970s. Minjung theology is generally thought to have emerged out of the human rights movement in Korea, during the time of significant social oppression; minjung theologians, along with workers, students, and peasants, are those whose theology has been shaped by this experience. Their theology looks not just at contemporary experience, and not just at Korean church history, but at the entire socio-economic history of Korea. Most particularly these theologians have tried to listen to and learn from the *minjung*, the "mass of the people" (understood as a dynamic organism), and to see reality from their perspective.

A key term in minjung theology is *han*. Han is a collective feeling that expresses both the experience of oppression and the rising tide of rebellion. It could, inadequately, be translated as "righteous indignation." Significantly, when missionary Protestants translated the Bible in the late nineteenth century they used Korean, the language typically written and read by the minjung, rather than the Chinese that was the preferred language of writing among the educated classes. Similarly, Christians in Korea have always played a prominent role in the struggle for independence from Japan; some Japanese were said to detest the books of Exodus and Daniel, which were at the center of the Korean sense of the scriptural story.

One dimension of minjung theology that has made it especially controversial to some Christians is that it is in some respects syncretistic. It has drawn together not just Christian elements but messianic Buddhism and the local Donghak religion. Here is a feature minjung theology has in common with some of the postcolonial theologies we shall address later. Most significantly for Christian ethics, minjung theology explicitly disavows universal claims; it is deeply contextual, and not designed for export.

Dalit theology

Meanwhile in the very different cultural climate of India, another class movement that offers a liberation ethic is dalit theology. Dalits, or untouchables (known by Gandhi as *harijan*, or children of God), make up 20 percent of the Indian population – thus around 200 million people. Dalits constitute about 70 percent of the Christians of India, partly because Christianity offered improved social status and a way out of the caste system. Many, however, found caste discrimination in the churches as well as outside them, with few dalits holding leadership roles until the late 1990s. Dalit ethics reflects the need to find a theological expression to help dalits in their daily struggles with hunger, poverty, suffering, injustice, and illiteracy. It is a rejection of the Brahmanic (upper-caste) dominance of Indian theology.

Like minjung theology, dalit theology gives a vital place to the recovery and articulation of woundedness, pain, and anger, and the renarration of Indian history with dalits now regarded as subjects. Unlike minjung theology, dalit theology has so far steered away from syncretistic elements. It concentrates on acts of solidarity and liberation – and this includes liberation from "self-captivity." The incarnation of Jesus is seen fundamentally as God's act of solidarity with humankind. Jesus is the ultimate dalit, the cross is the ultimate experience of what it means to be a dalit, and thus God is a dalit God – a suffering servant. The story narrated in Deuteronomy 25:6 of how a wandering Aramean (Abraham) became a great nation, of how what was once no people became a people, takes the role in dalit theology that the exodus narrative holds in many liberation theologies. Rather than emphasize the entering of the Promised Land, the key element in salvation is of attaining the image of God, in all its glorious liberty.

Race

A branch of ethics that has long been dominated by black theology, the ethics of race have grown increasingly diverse in the twenty-first century. Theology done *for* a particular people and *from* a specific social location is sometimes called contextual theology (or contextual ethics), and this is especially true for theologies that examine ethics from the perspective of a minority racial or ethnic group. Here the line often blurs between race and class (as in black liberation theology) and between race and gender (as in womanist theology). Attention has increasingly focused on the history of "race" as a constructed category, and on the theological problem of whiteness.

Black theology stands in relation to the theology and ethics of race rather as Latin American liberation theology stands in relation to the theology and ethics of class: that is to say, it by no means exhausts the agenda and the literature, but its concerns significantly shape the whole field. Historically, black theology arose from two particular contexts of historic oppression: the African American experience of slavery, and the long walk to freedom in South Africa. We will consider them in turn.

African American Theology

Between the fifteenth and nineteenth centuries an estimated 30 million people were captured in Africa, shipped in dire conditions to America, and enslaved. They were largely regarded either as property or as beings somewhere between humankind and the animals. A significant controversy arose among the peoples who held slaves about whether the slaves should be evangelized, since for a slave to accept the gospel seemed to make it evident that the slave was a full human being – and thus would expose what later came to be recognized as the crime of slavery. Evangelism to the slave populations began in the early eighteenth century, but arguments continued to be used to justify slavery, whether by reading the curse on the sons of Ham in Genesis 9:20–27 as applying to Africans, or by reading Paul's injunctions to slaves as an endorsement of slavery, or by seeing the bringing of Africans to America as giving them a chance to hear the gospel. Preaching encouraged slaves to focus on the glories to come in heaven and not to dwell on the troubles of life on earth. But slaves began to establish their own (often secret) congregations within two generations, restricted as their place was in white churches. Songs known as spirituals developed as a code for talking about liberation from slavery.

From the mid-nineteenth century through the mid-twentieth century, a number of figures and themes emerged as African Americans found a public theological and political voice, and it is these figures and themes that laid the foundation for contemporary African American theology.

- Nat Turner (1800–31) was a firebrand preacher who sought freedom through violent revolt.
- Frederick Douglass (1818–1895) was a former slave who became a vocal abolitionist and civil rights advocate. His autobiography *The Narrative of the Life of Frederick Douglass* (1845) sold 5000 copies in its first four months, and remains one of the most eloquent and widely read accounts of American slavery.
- Booker T. Washington (1856–1915) was perhaps the dominant voice in the African American community from 1890 to 1915, promoting education and economic advancement and advocating against confrontation with the white majority.
- W. E. B. Du Bois (1868–1963), a more radical thinker than Washington, founded the National Association for the Advancement of Colored People (NAACP) in 1909, and became the most visible leader of African American public opinion prior to the civil rights movement. His book *The Souls of Black Folk* (1903) was and continues to be enormously influential, showing how race is inscribed into every aspect of American public and domestic life, advocating for higher education for black people and thus helping to establish the foundations of a black middle class, and tracing a global color line. In his essay "Of Our Spiritual Strivings," Du Bois coined the term "double consciousness," by which he meant the constant awareness of being both American and black, "two warring ideals in one dark body" – and of being constantly observed "in an amused contempt and pity."
- Marcus Garvey (1887–1940) was a Jamaican-born black nationalist who advocated a return to the African homeland, particularly Liberia, and the establishment of an independent black capitalist economy.
- Howard Thurman (1900–81) was Dean of the Chapel at first Howard University and then Boston University, and had many foreign interlocutors, notably Gandhi. His influential book *Jesus and the Disinherited* (1949) made numerous connections between the African American experience and Jesus' context – for example, that the Jews' minority relationship with the Romans resembled the African experience within the USA.

- Martin Luther King Jr. (1929–68) was a Baptist minister and the most prominent leader of the civil rights movement. King articulated the call to and possibility of nonviolent liberation in a way that captured the imagination of a generation. King saw all humankind as siblings, and he saw the incoming tide of God's justice as inexorable, if not rapid. He had a profound faith in the principles underlying the American Revolution and Constitution; he often blended appeals to civil law and the Bible in his speeches and sermons. Unlike those who called for violent uprising or separation, King insisted that only the redemptive power of love for the enemy could transform the oppressor and lead to true justice. His nonviolent strategies drew both from Jesus' Sermon on the Mount, which he read as a deeply political text, and from the work of Mahatma Gandhi.
- In the late 1960s and early 1970s the Black Power movement emerged out of the experience of the depth and intractability of white racism and the obstacles to black people entering the circles of power. Stokely Carmichael (1941–1988) was a Trinidadian-American civil rights activist who is often credited with coining the term "black power"; he later changed his name to Kwame Turé and became a champion of the global Pan-African movement. In contrast to King's movement, the Black Power advocates encouraged the establishment of black political and cultural institutions to advance black interests, values, and autonomy, and in some cases rejected the approach of nonviolence.

Such constitutes a brief sketch of the backdrop to contemporary black theology.

Black liberation theology

The founder and most vocal proponent of black liberation theology is James Cone (b. 1938), an African American Methodist and since 1970 professor at Union Theological Seminary in New York City. Growing up in Arkansas during the segregation era, Cone experienced the constant diminution of his human dignity that characterized the African American experience. In *Black Theology and Black Power* (1969) Cone argues that both these evocative terms – black theology and black power – aspire to help black people find freedom through a new dignity and self-determination. The black churches have largely neglected this key dimension of black power, becoming passive and quiescent in the face of racism. For Cone, blackness is a physiological characteristic, referring to black skin. But it is also a status of being – attained by those participating in the struggle of black people for liberation from oppression. By contrast whiteness denotes sickness and oppression. In this second sense, because God is still concerned for the injustice against God's people (a concern consistent since the time of the exodus), God is black.

Cone's view of Jesus is that Jesus is fully divine, fully human, and fully committed to liberating the oppressed. Jesus is black – because God becomes present in a form that restores the image of God among the oppressed of the earth. Jesus' resurrection demonstrates the divine commitment to and human possibility of throwing off oppression. Like the Latin American liberation theologians, Cone has a realized eschatology that sees salvation as a present and attainable social reality, to be reached out for by people infused with God's Spirit. Cone does not rule out violence: instead he insists that we must refocus our attention on the violence of the oppressor rather than condemn the violence of the oppressed. He takes a line similar to the view we described in Chapter Five as proportionalism, suggesting that slavery, hunger, and exploitation are all forms of violence and may need to be thrown aside by violence if there is no better way.

Like many liberation theologians, Cone draws on the thought of Karl Marx, but he does so primarily for Marx's analysis of the social nature of knowledge. Other black theologians such as philosopher Cornel West (b. 1953) speak for a generation that no longer regards Marxist thought as inherently associated with America's Soviet enemy. West calls for black theology and Marxism to converge, and to join in dismantling capitalism and imperialism. He laments the neglect of economic justice in black theology, seeing class alienation as a profound social disease, much as race oppression is. Those keeping poor whites and African Americans in subservience are the same people. West finds in his Baptist roots the long tradition of prophecy in the face of oppression, and appeals to the Christian aspiration for the development and flourishing of each individual – a vision that contradicts all discrimination. He aspires to a synthesis of Marxism and Christianity in a true socialist society.

In response to those who worry that black theology has defined itself too much in opposition to white dominance, or "white theology" – and thus that is in danger of replicating the patterns of those it criticizes – Cone replies that such criticisms come from those who insist on the universal note of Christianity but who cannot see the way their notion of universal masks their own particular social interests. "As long as they can be sure the gospel is *for everybody*, ignoring that God liberated a *particular* people from Egypt, came into a *particular* man called Jesus, and for the *particular* purpose of liberating the oppressed, then they can continue to talk in theological abstractions." For Cone, such talk only becomes gospel when it is related to practical steps to set the downtrodden free.

Nonetheless black theology continues to wrestle with the tension between the particular and the universal in its formulations. In the words of Samuel K. Roberts in his *African American Christian Ethics* (2001),

> Can we contemplate a theological (and subsequently ethical) vision that takes seriously the experience of black people without incurring the narrow exclusivism that was indicative of so much of black theology in its classic stage? Is there a way of constructing a theology that is able to account for the singularity of the black religious experience without presuming that it has legitimate claims to exclusive normative status among other viable theologies? How can we account for the universality of God and the peculiar favor God bestows on human beings in the midst of their peculiar experiences?

Some twenty-first century thinkers have praised Cone's work for its groundbreaking significance but have also suggested that it fails to be radical enough. It is to these voices that we now turn.

The theological problem of whiteness

For several decades, Cone's thought dominated the shape of black theology. Shortly after the turn of the century, however, new voices arose that both extended and challenged the important work of Cone: most prominently, J. Kameron Carter (b. 1967) and Willie Jennings (b. 1961). Among the themes shared by Carter and Jennings are a retrieval of premodern thinkers and themes, the importance of the body (especially black bodies) in contrast to docetic or Gnostic theologies, a sharp critique of Enlightenment thought, and an insistence that the church lost its way once it ceased to understand itself in relation to Judaism.

Indeed Carter traces the origins of the modern racial imagination precisely to "Christianity's quest to sever itself from its Jewish roots." This was accomplished in two steps: Jews were imagined as a distinct race (Orientals) and were then deemed inferior to Christians of the West (Occidentals). Carter's shorthand for this racial imagination is "the theological problem of whiteness." Carter locates the genesis of modern racial reasoning in the thought of Immanuel Kant, due to the way that Kant detached Christ from his Jewish identity, but also names it as a newer manifestation of a much older problem – that of Christian supersessionism, or the view that God has replaced Israel with the church in the divine plan of salvation.

For Carter as for Cone, whiteness signifies not merely skin color but an entire system of intellectual, political, and economic domination that diminishes and oppresses the racialized other. Carter's critique of Cone's work is that it is not radical enough when it construes blackness as a site of power; while brilliant, Cone's approach nonetheless unwittingly participates in modern racial reasoning and leaves the problem of whiteness itself unresolved. Carter instead appeals to two different aspects of the past to imagine a new way forward: first, the premodern theological tradition as represented by Irenaeus of Lyons (anti-Gnostic intellectual), Gregory of Nyssa (abolitionist intellectual), and Maximus the Confessor (anti-colonialist intellectual); and second, writings of Briton Hammond, Frederick Douglass, and Jarena Lee, chosen as representatives of "New World Afro-Christian faith" in North America before the Civil War.

Carter draws on the first set of thinkers to find in aspects of the Christian tradition deep resources for an alternative theological imagination, one which envisions the Christian life as participation in Christ, whose body must always be remembered as Jewish, covenantal flesh. For example, Carter positions Irenaeus' refutation of the Gnostics as an affirmation of Christ's body as "intrahuman, intraracial, mulatto flesh" – retrieving and repurposing a word (mulatto) that once meant a person with mixed black and white ancestry. The patristic thinkers are placed into resonant conversation with the writings of Hammond, Douglas, and Lee, who for Cone display the truth that "success in destabilizing race as a founding and grounding category of existence is tied to how one imagines the passion of Christ." Carter sees in all these respective writers a trajectory, tragically diverted during the Enlightenment, toward a vision of Christian identity that rejects racial purity in favor of a "mulattic" existence modeled on Christ. Brian Bantum (b. 1975) extends Carter's conception of the place of the "mulatto" in Christian thinking in his 2010 *Redeeming Mulatto: A Theology of Race and Christian Hybridity*, in which he uses the Chalcedonian Definition (451) of Christ's consubstantial humanity and divinity alongside the Orthodox concept of divinization to imagine Christian existence as a mulattic or hybrid blend of body and spirit, modeled on Christ's own life.

For Jennings, as for Carter, the Western Christian theological imagination has been warped by deeply faulty racial reasoning; Jennings locates the origins of this warping not in the Enlightenment but in colonialism. Jennings invokes Alasdair MacIntyre's definition of tradition to argue that traditioned Christian existence in the West became fundamentally changed through colonialism as Christians assumed hegemony in the so-called New Worlds. Like Carter, Jennings traces the deepest roots of the problem back long before the colonial era to the supersessionist impulse within Christianity, which led first to the church detaching itself from the particularity of God's covenantal relationship with Israel and from the Jewish Jesus, and inexorably led second to European Christians articulating racial difference in a ranked system from white (linked to beauty, intelligence, European-ness, the capacity to become good Christians) to black (linked to ugliness, stupidity, alien-ness, and a resistance to Christian ethics).

Jennings critiques what he sees as two mistakes that, while opposite, are also two sides of the same coin: the universal or Docetic mistake is an incarnational denial, a failure to discern the divine presence in new spaces, rooted in a prior failure to accord the divine entrance into history its specific social and political contours. On the other side, the contextual or adoptionist mistake creates a cultural nationalism that imagines God present with *any* people without the "disciplining presence" of God present with Israel and in Christ. What unites both mistakes is a tragic twofold turn, away from reckoning with God's specific presence with Israel, and away from God's unique and concrete presence revealed in the Jewish Jesus, both of which should press Christianity toward intimate joining with others – just as the Gentiles were united to the children of Israel. In common with other subversive ethics, then, Jennings resists the universal, but alongside Carter he also proposes that the contextual is just as flawed. Instead he calls for a renewal of the Christian intellectual imagination through two acts of reclamation: Christians must reread themselves and the story of Jesus *as Gentiles*, and they must recover a sense of their own creatureliness, their rootedness in specific places and lands. It is only then that they can imagine a new identity and a new space for both Jew and Gentile where they are joined by the Spirit and embody a new cultural politic.

Black Lives Matter

In the American context, the Black Lives Matter movement launched in 2012 by Alicia Garza, Patrisse Cullors, and Opal Tometi has provided a particular focus for African American theology and ethics around the issues of police violence toward African Americans, the deaths of young black men like Trayvon Martin and Freddie Gray, and the lingering effects of slavery in the white supremacist structures of American society. It originated as a social media hashtag

(#BlackLivesMatter), demonstrating the power of social media platforms to galvanize social movements, but quickly grew into a national conversation and coalition. While it draws on universal principles such as human dignity and civil rights, it is subversive in its unremitting attention to racial injustice and the particular dangers posed to black lives in contemporary America.

South African Theology and Ethics

Black theology took a significantly different turn in South Africa, in the context of apartheid rather than slavery. Its earliest proponents to get a public hearing were white – people like Anglican priest and later archbishop Trevor Huddleston (1913–98), known especially for his book *Naught for Your Comfort* (1955), and the Reformed Afrikaner Beyers Naude (1915–2004). After Steve Biko (1946–77) formed the Black Consciousness Movement in 1977, black theologians came to the fore, articulating an ethic of justice and liberation. These "contextual theologians" included the Zulu Lutheran bishop Manas Buthelezi (b. 1935), the Xhosa Anglican archbishop Desmond Tutu (b. 1931), the Cape Colored Reformed theologian Alan Boesak (b. 1945), the Pentecostal pastor Frank Chikane (b. 1951), and the white Dominican Albert Nolan (b. 1934). Their key institutional instrument was the South African Council of Churches, chaired in turn by Tutu, Naude, and Chikane.

A landmark moment in the contextual theology movement was the publication in Soweto in 1985 of the *Kairos Document*. It delineated three political positions in the South African church.

- One was "state theology" – "the theological justification of the status quo with its racism, capitalism and totalitarianism." State theology inappropriately regarded Romans 13:1–7 as applying even to an unjust state, and made a false assumption that obeying the state is a requirement of obeying God. It labeled anything that stood against it as "communist," and invoked the name of a false god in the 1983 South African Constitution – "a god of teargas, rubber bullets, sjamboks (whips), prison cells and death sentences" – "the devil disguised as Almighty God."
- A second was "church theology," associated with the English-speaking churches, notably the Anglicans, Lutherans, and Methodists. These churches habitually called for reconciliation, but did not expect repentance. They called for justice, but did not realize some changes required more than piecemeal reform. They called for nonviolence, but did not appreciate that state violence makes individual nonviolence impossible. All of these calls rested on an otherworldly spirituality. Thus, the *Kairos Document* insisted, "When Jesus says that we should turn the other cheek he is telling us that we must not take revenge; he is not saying that we should never defend ourselves or others." Here the document's connections with Latin American liberation theology and its call for social analysis are clear.

- In place of state and church theology the *Kairos Document* commends "prophetic theology." This is not an ethic for all times and places, but precisely for this context. It is a call for "repentance, conversion and change," anticipating persecution and confrontation, but rooted in joy and hope. Prophetic theology traces a continuous thread from God's hearing the cries of the oppressed in Exodus, to his defense of Israel against her enemies and persecutors, through to Jesus' embodying God's will as the suffering servant dying to save the oppressed. Social analysis makes it clear this context goes beyond pious discipleship: "It is therefore not primarily a matter of trying to reconcile individual people but a matter of trying to change unjust structures so that people will not be pitted against one another as oppressor and oppressed."

  Appealing to a tradition that goes back to John Calvin's *Institutes of the Christian Religion* (1560), the document argues that a tyrannical government loses the blessing of God and the right to expect its people's obedience. "A regime that has made itself the enemy of the people has thereby also made itself the enemy of God." In this context, the requirement to love the enemy means as follows: "the most loving thing we can do for *both* the oppressed *and* for our enemies who are oppressors is to eliminate the oppression, remove the tyrants from power, and establish a just government for the common good for *all the people*." Thus the document calls on the churches to join the struggle that is already going on, and become involved in campaigns and civil disobedience.

The most notable fruit of the *Kairos Document* in particular and the contextual theologians' work in general was the Truth and Reconciliation Commission (TRC; 1996–8), chaired by Desmond Tutu. The TRC used amnesty as a method for establishing the truth about the apartheid past, and was not designed as a court to issue punishments. It had three committees – a Human Rights Violations Committee, which investigated human rights abuses that occurred between 1960 and 1994; a Reparation and Rehabilitation Committee, which sought to restore victims' dignity; and an Amnesty Committee, which considered applications from individuals who applied for amnesty in cases where the crimes were politically motivated, proportionate, and there was full disclosure by the person seeking amnesty.

While South African theology has gained significant global attention, other contextual ethics have flourished in sub-Saharan Africa and more recently in the Asian-American context.

African Theology and Ethics

The Kenyan Anglican John Mbiti (b. 1931) speaks of the particular experience of an African Christian. In the process he rejects the assumption that God's revelation of Christ is principally to those who have been exposed to the Christian gospel – a notion sometimes called "special revelation." He sees the traditional Western distinction between "special revelation" and "general revelation" to be inadequate. He says: "The missionaries who introduced the gospel to Africa in the past 200 years did not bring God to our continent. Instead, God brought *them*. They proclaimed the name of Jesus Christ. But they used the names of the God who was and is already known by African peoples." These are names such as Mungu, Mulungu, Katonda, Ngai, Olodumare, Asis, Ruwa, Ruhanga, Jok, Modimo, Unkulunkulu. For Mbiti, these are not empty names. They are names of one and the same God, the creator of the world, the Father of Jesus Christ.

Mbiti identifies the central commitment of African theology: to recover and honor the distinctively African experience of God. Desmond Tutu described the African Christian experience as follows:

> With part of himself he has been compelled to pay lip service to Christianity as understood, expressed and preached by the white man. But with an ever greater part of himself, a part he has often been ashamed to acknowledge openly and which he has struggled to repress, he has felt that his Africanness was being violated. The white man's largely cerebral religion was hardly touching the depths of his African soul; he was being redeemed from sins he did not believe he had committed; he was being given answers, and often quite splendid answers, to questions he had not asked.

There were around 9 million Christians in Africa in 1900; there were around 380 million in 2000. This growth is partly due to the work of overseas and indigenous missionaries, of schools and Bible translations; but it is also grounded in the existing practice of prayer, thanksgiving, and sacrifice in African spirituality. Yet Africa remains complex: as Tinyiko Maluleke notes, Nelson Mandela's inauguration as president of South Africa in 1994 coincided with genocide in Rwanda. Maluleke argues that "the African poor are pouring scorn at 'liberation-rhetoric' regardless of the quarters from where it emanates because long after independence they remain poor if not poorer – if they have not been killed off by disease or the guns of the more powerful." Charles Villa-Vicencio hints at a model of "reconstruction" that goes beyond the language of liberation and inculturation, and takes seriously the task of rebuilding cultures, particularly in the South African context. Maluleke, while acknowledging the danger of the glorification and romanticization of African culture, summarizes many of the contemporary initiatives in African theology, particularly by women, as converging on the recognition of Africans as agents – actors, not just victims, in their own society's drama.

> A careful analysis of the newest offerings in African theology – from the work of Lamin Sanneh and Kwame Bediako, through that of [Mercy] Oduyoye and her sisters in the circle of Concerned African Women Theologians, [Jesse] Mugambi and [Charles] Villa-Vicencio's reconstruction theology, [Itumeleng] Mosala and [Takatso] Mofokeng's quest to understand how black Christians may and do intend to "use the Bible to get the land back without losing the Bible," [Desmond] Tutu's theology of forgiveness … to Robin Peterson's riveting attempt to discover "what really goes on" in African Independent Churches (AICs) – reveal[s] a rediscovery of the agency of African Christians in the face of great odds.

One of the challenges faced by African ethics is the popularity in many African churches of the prosperity gospel, which proclaims that scriptural verses like 2 Corinthians 8:9 ("Yet for your sakes he became poor, that you by his poverty might become rich") and Deuteronomy 8:18 ("God gives you the power to get wealth to establish his covenant") refer to the material blessings God promises to all the faithful and thereby offer a prescription for contemporary ethics.

Asian American Ethics

This is perhaps the newest branch of subversive ethics considered in this chapter, as indicated by the fact that the first book-length study of Asian American Christian ethics was published in 2015. While practitioners acknowledge the heterogeneity of the term "Asian American," and there is not always universal agreement on where the boundaries of that term lie, a relative commonality in approach exists. Grace Y. Kao and Ilsup Ahn, the editors of the 2015 volume *Asian American Ethics*, outline two sometimes overlapping approaches: (1) an agency- or advocacy-centered approach, as described by Kao, in which the work of Asian American Christian ethics should be "about us," "by us," "for us," and "near us"; and (2) a method of "cocritical appropriation," explained by Ahn as "a critical excavation and appropriation of rich and diverse sources of Asian and Asian American history, culture, and tradition alongside of a similar process of critical appraisal and selective retrieval of more mainstream and other contextualized ways of doing ethics." The topics addressed by the eleven essays in the volume, all "by us" (that is, by self-identified Asian Americans), range from gender and sexuality to peace and war, from health and immigration to the environment and cosmetic surgery.

Postcolonial Ethics

There are several strands of ethics that self-consciously address the postcolonial era as their specific social location. To some respect, many of the ethical approaches described above can be understood as postcolonial ethics, and thus to categorize only the ethics below as postcolonial is an artificial distinction. Jennings, for example, engages in postcolonial analysis in his conceptualization of Christian intellectual history; and the black theology of South Africa is clearly postcolonial in its engagement with the Dutch masters of apartheid. On the other hand, there are also subversive approaches to race and class that are not primarily focused on a colonial and postcolonial history.

Postcolonial theory arose largely as a literary, cultural, and political discourse whose primary aim was, and is, to account for and resist the effects of colonialism. Christian ethicists who incorporate postcolonial theory share an abiding concern for naming and overcoming the effects of subjugation under European colonial powers, for example by restoring the authentic voices and agency of the marginalized or "subaltern." We highlight Caribbean theology as one major branch of postcolonial ethics.

Caribbean theology

The sense that white people had long seen their God through white spectacles, and thus that black people should start to see their God through their own spectacles, fostered the culture in which Rastafarianism appeared in Jamaica. Focusing on the crowning of Ras Tafari Makkonnen (later Haile Selassie) in 1930 as emperor of Ethiopia, Rastafarianism emerged as a form of black messianism, perceiving the black and African world as human and the white colonialist world as inhuman, with the British queen personifying the whore of Babylon and Ethiopia representing a literal heaven. Unlike many liberation movements, Rastafari does not have an explicit program for social and economic change. Instead it makes space within the current political system for people to discover liberation in mind and body from the experience of being a slave.

Caribbean life is beset by profound poverty, a deep cultural alienation, and a culture of dependence rooted in its history of colonialism and slavery, the legacy of which has been a constellation of issues around class and gender as well as race. While the Caribbean context has much in common with the African American and African experience – notably that after 400 years of oppression, it is hard to disentangle Christianity from colonialism and slavery – there is one significant difference. In the Caribbean those people who were displaced and brought across the Atlantic to a life of slavery are now, in many places (notably Jamaica, though not in Trinidad or Guyana), in the significant majority. Thus the situation is not just one of exodus but of being in exile where the exiled are the principal occupants of the land.

In the 1970s Jamaican theologian William Watty suggested three themes for Caribbean theology.

- One was divine sovereignty – for the colonialists had justified their hegemony by claiming divine providence. Watty retorted that there is no continuity between God's rule and earthly rule – often quite the opposite: God's power is invariably "manifested not in the power but in the tribulation of the elect."
- A second theme was salvation history, and the affirmation (as we saw in relation to African theology) that the Old Testament assumes God is at work in nations other than Israel. This means that every people's history is potentially salvation history.
- The third theme is eschatology. Aside from rejecting merely otherworldly conceptions of redemption, Watty points out that the power of God relativizes all other powers – and thus that even the most overwhelming oppressor and far-reaching empire has within it the seeds of its own decay.

Caribbean theology has followed African theology in reaching back to traditions, intuitions, and cultural signs into which the Christian gospel came as a new story. In its own estimation, it has sometimes struggled to balance reflections on the particularity of the Caribbean context with the particularity of God's identity, and it has had difficulty incorporating the experiences of the region's diverse populations. Caribbean theology was relatively quiet in the two decades following

Watty's analysis but saw a significant revival in 2010 when Jamaica Theological Seminary hosted an ecumenical Forum on Caribbean Theology. While the legacy of colonialism and its attendant poverty and violence remained central, several new contexts also garnered attention, most notably the challenges of globalization and the 2010 earthquake that devastated Haiti. In addition to Watty's themes, the new generation of Caribbean theologians focuses on justice, Caribbean identity, and the growing challenge of the prosperity gospel, among other themes.

Gender

The theologian Susan Parsons (b. 1945) describes a feminist as "one who takes most seriously the practical concerns of women's lives, the analysis and the critique of those conditions of life, and the ways in which women's lives may become more fulfilling." Feminist Christian ethics has in the past half-century become a very large dimension of the discourse in Christian ethics as a whole. With the ethics of class and race, it shares a far-reaching critique of universal ethics. That critique dwells on the misuse of the Bible, the false association of divine qualities and universal rationality with maleness, and the devaluation of women's projected and genuine capabilities, callings, and spheres of influence. Further critiques have emerged as the initial generation of feminist theologians has been examined for its own race and class location. The constructive dimensions of feminist Christian ethics have varied in the degree to which they see the task as incorporating women into a universal paradigm, restoring a universal paradigm, or rejecting the universal project in ethics.

Feminism and the Bible

The Bible is often at the center of feminist Christian ethics, because the Bible is often taken to affirm patriarchy. Thus, crucial to feminist Christianity have been those readings that have questioned conventional interpretations of key texts and unearthed neglected passages and patterns. No text is more significant than Genesis 1–3. The conventional reading is that God created Adam as the climax of creation; Eve was created out of Adam to help him, but her weakness in the face of the serpent brought about creation's fall. Feminist readings question every aspect of this powerful tradition. When humanity is made in the image of God (Gen 1:27), not only is humanity not male but the word for God, *Elohim*, is a plural form. If woman was created last as in the Genesis 2 account, why is she not seen as the climax of creation? Why is Eve seen as a "helper" when the word could equally mean "partner" (or even "savior")? Why is Eve seen as weaker because she talked with the serpent, rather than more intelligent? Why is she not seen as independent, reflective, and assertive, and why is Adam not seen as passive, silent, and quiescent, let alone greedy, thoughtless, and inept? Why is it assumed that Adam was absent when Eve was debating with the serpent, and why is the blame put on her rather than on both of them? Why are the punishments handed out by God – the sufferings of childbirth and the dominance of man over woman – regarded as "natural" conditions of human existence, when they seem clearly to be an evil?

Two other aspects of the scriptural reference to women could be described as key texts for feminist ethics. One is the identity of those Jesus chose to be his closest followers and thus those who became the leaders of the earliest churches. Again the conventional reading is that the twelve disciples were all men and that women held no significant leadership roles. Feminist readings question such selective reception of the tradition. After all, the first person to meet the risen Christ is, in each gospel account, a woman. Women were among Jesus' inner circle – consider Mary of Bethany (Luke 10:38–42 and John 11). The faithfulness of a woman is explicitly contrasted with the unfaithfulness of a male disciple in the account of Jesus' anointing (Mark 14 and John 12) – to such an extent that Mark's Gospel has been seen by some as a thoroughgoing critique of male leadership. A third key set of texts are those in the epistles referring to the guidelines for liturgical (1 Cor 14:34–5) and domestic (Eph 5:21–33) propriety. These appear in general to assume a subservient role for women, but, in view of the radical nature of many claims also found in the epistles ("there is no longer male and female," Gal 3:28) and the naming of women in leadership roles, they can hardly be taken as an unequivocal demand for male headship.

Among the many passages neglected by conventional scriptural overviews but brought to attention by feminist and sympathetic scholars, perhaps the most famous are the disturbing narratives invoked by Phyllis Trible (b. 1932) in her *Texts of Terror* (1984). Trible describes the way Hagar, Tamar, an unnamed concubine, and Jephthah's daughter experience horrifying crimes including rape, murder, abuse, and exploitation as victims of a culture that assumed the priority of men's sexual, dynastic, and honor needs. These women have important but forgotten roles – Hagar is the first to name God, while Jephthah's daughter is an astounding witness to a love that withstands betrayal and death. Moreover these texts echo with the piercing, unresolved, and often unnamed wrestlings of faith. Less distressing than the stories named in Trible's work but equally neglected in the scriptural canon are the cases of prominent women such as Deborah and Esther, along with Judith and Susannah in the Apocrypha. Esther in particular is portrayed in the Bible as the savior of her people, and thus as a type of Jesus – yet she is almost overlooked in many traditions and lectionaries.

Perhaps the key figure in feminist interpretation of the Bible is Elisabeth Schüssler Fiorenza (b. 1938). Her book *In Memory of Her* (1983) develops a "hermeneutic of suspicion" for reading the Bible in the light of its authors' commitments. A hermeneutic of suspicion is a form of interpretation that begins with a mistrust of both the social location of a text's author and the dominant historical ways such a text has been read. She points out that:

> since the Gospels were written at a time when other New Testament authors clearly were attempting to adapt the role of women within the Christian community to that of patriarchal society and religion, it is all the more remarkable that not one story or statement is transmitted in which Jesus demands the cultural patriarchal adaptation and submission of women.

She also develops a model of historical reconstruction that recasts the New Testament as promoting a reform movement within Judaism that envisaged and practiced the discipleship of equals.

Feminism Throughout Christian History

Male theologians throughout Christian history have typically, although not universally, associated male attributes and pronouns with God, and have likewise tended to associate rationality, along with other such qualities as autonomy, independence, and transcendence, with masculinity. Among the influential writers of the early centuries, Tertullian (160–225 CE), Origen (182–251 CE), John Chrysostom (ca. 347–407 CE), and Jerome (347–420 CE) all assumed women were the weaker sex. Nonetheless all believed in the sacred possibilities of virginal life and martyrdom for women. And all believed that in such ways women could attain a status in the church and before God at least equal to men. Augustine (354–430 CE) is often regarded especially negatively in feminist theology. He had a very dim view of the positive qualities of sexual intercourse, and like his contemporaries he took male headship for granted, but he saw the goods and responsibilities of marriage as owing to and owed by both partners. Likewise Thomas Aquinas (1225–74) assumed women's inferiority in regard to strength and rationality, and indeed in everything other than childrearing and friendship with God; while he was concerned to protect their well-being in the domestic sphere, feminist ethics typically regards this concern as a form of paternalism.

The Middle Ages, despite these significant constraints, were not a desert for women's discovery and articulation of faith and ethics. Women came to the fore in the realm of mysticism and as recipients of revelatory words and visions. Julian of Norwich (1342–ca. 1416), Teresa of Avila (1515–82), Hildegard of Bingen (1098–1179), Catherine of Siena (1347–80), and Mechtild of Magdeburg (ca. 1210–ca. 1282) were prominent among the spiritual awakenings of the period. Meanwhile convents offered women opportunities for education and an alternative to a life of subordination – opportunities that were lost in Protestant regions after the Reformation. On the fringes of the Reformation emerged a host of radical groups, some of which believed in and practiced gender equality – of which the Quakers have been the most long-lasting. Of the magisterial Reformers, Martin Luther (1483–1546) saw gender inequality as a result of the Fall (although he did not challenge it), while John Calvin (1509–64) also saw a much broader purpose for marriage than simply childrearing, one in which the sanctification of the couple took a significant place.

These scriptural and historical debates provide the backdrop to what we shall now explore as three broad constructive approaches within contemporary feminist Christian ethics.

Maintaining but revising a universal paradigm
One significant strand in feminist Christian ethics accepts a good deal of society's prevailing and emerging social norms, but seeks equality for women through legal

and political reform. Standing in the liberal political tradition that emerges from the Enlightenment, it has confidence in the individual woman, through her behavior and decision-making, to bring about a gender-equal society without social revolution. Like many movements rooted in the Enlightenment, it attributes social ills to superstition, false religion, outdated science, and obscure tradition, and it retains a profound social optimism that such ills can be removed, and once rid of them, society will flourish as never before. The key terms are rights, equality, and the dignity of the human person. This liberal model has tended to concentrate on flagship legal achievements, such as the right for women to vote; the right to equality in education, in the workplace, and in remuneration; the right to abortion; and the right not to have to endure sexual harassment. For example, Beverly Wildung Harrison says:

> We have a long way to go before the sanctity of human life will include genuine regard and concern for every female already born. ... We desperately need a desacralization of our desire to reproduce and at the same time a real concern for human dignity and the social conditions for personhood and the values of human relationship.

In the late eighteenth century the debate was led by those who maintained that gender difference was more a matter of nurture than nature – notably Mary Wollstonecraft (1759–97). In her *A Vindication of the Rights of Woman* (1792) she argued that society teaches men morals, requiring education and understanding, while it teaches women manners, which any automaton could grasp. It encourages women to develop evasive and manipulative characteristics, and it turns female virtues – notably gentleness – into vices such as obsequiousness. Susan Parsons, whose perceptions have guided many of our reflections on feminism, helpfully summarizes the Enlightenment assumptions shaping such a new way of thinking:

> Underlying Wollstonecraft's argument is a belief that the rational mind is capable of transcendence, being basically independent of the body and its environment. Some aspect of this mind is able to rise above physical conditions as well as received beliefs, in order to question, to ascertain the deeper truth which lies beyond these realities, and to discover there the salient features of the good human life. Through the use of our rational capacity, human beings are able to detach themselves from present situations and from confinement to physical conditions. Reason is thus characterized by suspicion, doubt and challenge until that which may not be questioned or doubted appears. The mind has thus the human capacity to transcend, and, through its functioning, human beings are independent and free. Such activity becomes the highest expression of human possibilities and of the real essence of humanness which lies at the heart of each one of us. From this central recognition comes the affirmation of a basic human dignity established by reason.

Here already are all the ingredients of what we are calling the revised universal paradigm. Human dignity resides in transcendent reason, which delivers persons from the particular and contingent to the universal and ultimate. God lies at the summit of this mountain of reason. Through reason one may discern a universal ethic, in many cases assumed to rest on a Kantian moral law, in other cases reflecting natural rights; in either case, universal ethics includes women as much as men. Reason is inherently an individual capacity, and so individual qualities such as honesty, integrity, and freedom of thought and expression are central. Gender, in the exercise of reason, is thus irrelevant. The emphasis instead is on unfettered, rational choice. In Letty Russell's words, "feminist theology strives to be *human* and not just *feminine*, as other forms of theology should strive to be *human* and not just *masculine*."

These themes are strong in contemporary feminist Christian ethics. The logic of the revised universal paradigm is to see the program of Christianity as one of stripping away the irrational accretions of the centuries (the centuries of Israel initially, and now also the centuries of the church) that have kept the individual, reasoning spirit in bondage. Jesus' mission is therefore one of a liberator. Jesus, however, is problematic because he is limited in time and space, limited to the perspective of one person, and limited by being of one gender only, the male one. His maleness has no ultimate significance: what distinguishes him is his self-emptying of patriarchy. The strengths and weaknesses of this view of feminist Christian ethics are summarized by Rosemary Radford Ruether:

> Liberal feminism too readily identifies normative human nature with those capacities for reason and rule identified with men and with the public sphere. It claims that women, while appearing to have lesser capacities for these attributes, actually possess them equally; they have simply been denied the educational cultivation of them and the opportunity to exercise them. Opening up equal education and equal political rights to women will correct this and allow women's suppressed capacities for reason and rule to appear in their actual equivalence to men's. ... Liberalism does not entirely recognize the more complex forms of women's psychological and economic marginalization that result in only token integration of women into "equal" roles in the public sphere. ... Once women are allowed to enter the public sphere, liberalism offers no critique of the modes of functioning within it.

Restoring a universal paradigm

What we are calling a restored universal paradigm rests on the assertion that there are indeed profound differences between men and women, and the problem lies not in the differences but in the ways "male" tendencies and characteristics have been exalted and "female" ones demeaned or neglected. The differences are related to the bodily distinctions between men and women: they shape social roles appropriately, and male and female psychological development is accordingly different. Such an approach, sometimes called "romantic" in the way the previous one is called "liberal," has a much greater appetite for the heritage of theological reflection than other feminist approaches.

Whereas the revised paradigm or "liberal" approach relates to the Kantian and rights universal traditions, the restored or "romantic" version appeals more explicitly to a particular notion of natural law. It sees nature as intrinsically linked to the body, and thus biology and psychology play an important role in understanding its contours. It sees reproduction not as accidental to human nature and differentiation but as foundational. Goodness lies in fulfilling the function "that nature intended." When God is seen as creator, a seamless transition can be made from "as nature intended" to "as God wills." Rather than being social constructions, gender roles and interactions are in large part written into a largely unchanging architecture of life itself. There is a serious issue about who gets to decide what is natural; it does not take close examination of historic definitions to surmise that the judges have invariably been men, and the bias has invariably been in a direction that seems, to many today, to serve men. And it must be said that the biological necessities of life tend in this tradition to be accorded disproportionately to women rather than men.

In the following chapter we shall look more closely at teleological ethics, the notion of morality governed by a final destiny or goal. But we may anticipate a little here and note that the restored (or romantic) paradigm is in some ways a teleological ethic, because it seeks the realization of latent characteristics within each person and expressed through the development of character. It sees a continuity between what God intends and what natural science discovers – and thus commits what some criticize as the naturalistic fallacy, the confusion of what ought to be with what observably is. The two conventional ways of developing appropriate generalizations about the two sexes' inherent natures – theological tradition and natural scientific research – each have a long and widely criticized heritage of presuppositions undermining women. One unresolved question is thus whether they retain any claim to be trusted.

Such arguments are often extremely controversial, because they seem to undermine the ethos and gains established by the liberal branch of feminism. Among the wide variety of "restored universal" approaches to feminist ethics, we shall briefly note three, which may be termed feminine, maternal, and radical.

- The best known proponent of the feminine approach is Carol Gilligan (b. 1936). Gilligan's book *In a Different Voice* (1982) examined Lawrence Kohlberg's influential six-stage process of moral development. Kohlberg traced how children move from (1) obedience to (2) limited reciprocity to (3) seeking to please to (4) duty to (5) utilitarian law-keeping to (6) a self-legislated Kantian principled universalism. But in Kohlberg's analysis, while men often reached stages four and five, women seldom progressed beyond stage three. What Kohlberg missed, argued Gilligan, was that women reasoned in a "different voice" – one she described as an "ethics of care." This ethics of care was different from the (male) ethics of justice that focused on rules and rights. It had three levels – one, where women overemphasize their own interests; two, where women overemphasize the interests of others; three, where women weave together their own and others' interests. This model affirms that women's ethical reasoning is generally (though Gilligan stresses not always) relational rather than individual, collaborative rather than isolated, a synthesis of body, mind, and spirit rather than a detached, desiccated cerebral process. Hence relationship, rather than rule, action, or outcome, becomes central to ethics. Feminist criticisms of Gilligan have centered not so much on whether women are indeed different from men, but on whether it is prudent to make those differences the foundation for ethics, given that it tends to reinforce stereotypical images of women.

Successors to Gilligan such as Nel Noddings and Fiona Robinson have extended the logic of the ethic of care into the public sphere, arguing that duty, rights, and utilitarian theories have failed to address successfully issues such as global poverty – largely because they are too abstract and not sufficiently grounded in relationships. What is required, argues Robinson, is for the affluent to appreciate the connections between others' poverty and their own wealth, and to realize that simple charity cannot offset the problems that lie in economic, political, and social injustice.

- The maternal view is represented, among others, by Sara Ruddick. In her book *Maternal Thinking* (1989) Ruddick promotes the key virtue of attentive love. Attentive love enables a mother to see her child as the child actually is – however unpalatable the reality turns out to be, and in spite of internal pressures to see only a fantasy of the child. Such realistic attentive love then becomes the lens through which persons make judgments about other things such as war. War is not primarily about noble goals or even primal urges, but about destroying a child whom someone has spent years rearing. The key dimensions to rearing a child are preserving, fostering growth, and training. Preserving means doing what is necessary to feed, clothe, and shelter a child – including ensuring the well-being of the mother in order to do so. Fostering growth means offering a child maternal stories that show the child he or she is deeply loved whatever his or her shortcomings; it does not mean assuming a given outcome for the child's personal development. Training means balancing maternal values that seek the uniqueness and flourishing of a child's individuality with social values that often seek to make the child conform to fashions or expectations that might threaten his or her integrity. These and other maternal views of ethics are sometimes criticized for overemphasizing one relationship above all others and reinforcing a restricted perception of the role of women in society.

- The radical feminist view is that the roots of women's oppression lie squarely with men. Radical feminism posits a "fall" at some point in the past, when men, due to weak egos or unruly violence, overthrew egalitarian social orders and used their strength to monopolize control. Women have distinct values and culture – aesthetics, priorities, perceptions – but these have been suppressed by men. This regime is called patriarchy. Egalitarianism is only possible under matriarchy; only when patriarchy is ended will racism, capitalism, and imperialism be eradicated. In the meantime women should form enclaves for support and nurture – recognizing that heterosexuality in general and marriage in particular underwrite male supremacy. There is no significant political program other than such withdrawal.

The most renowned exponent of radical feminism in relation to Christian ethics is Mary Daly (b. 1928). Her works, including *Beyond God the Father* (1973) and *Gyn/Ecology* (1980), articulate the destructive force of a "phallic morality" of domination and control, restore women's awareness of their own fundamental goodness, and coin a vocabulary for post-patriarchal ethics. This last ability, to create a new language, is central to her project, since she notes, "Women have had the power of naming stolen from us." She seeks a more profound truth, one in which the relational dimension of feminism rediscovers that everything is connected, and that beyond, behind, beneath patriarchy there is "an unquenchable gynergy." Her most famous claim is that "If God is male, then the male is God. The divine patriarch castrates women as long as he is allowed to live on in the human imagination." The radical feminist approach certainly posits a restored universal paradigm, but its universal is clearly one that has no place for men.

Rejecting the universal paradigm

Mary Daly's female universalism stretches universalism to its breaking point. For a great many feminists, including significant thinkers in Christian ethics, feminism has to abandon the idea of a universal paradigm for ethics: it has to recognize the inherently conflictual nature of human life, particularly the institutional power relationships shaped by gender, and cease to hold to the fantasy that if the right theory emerged with the right application, a peaceable existence would break out.

At the sources of this strand of ethical feminism lies Betty Friedan's hugely influential book *The Feminine Mystique* (1963). Friedan identified what she called "The problem that has no name" – which was "the fact that American women are kept from growing to their full human capacities." She vividly described the situation of middle-class women of her era:

> It was a strange stirring, a sense of dissatisfaction, a yearning that women suffered in the middle of the twentieth century in the United States. Each suburban housewife struggled with it alone. As she made the beds, shopped for groceries, matched slipcover material, ate peanut butter sandwiches with her children, chauffeured Cub Scouts and Brownies, lay beside her husband at night, she was afraid to ask even of herself the silent question: Is this all?

Friedan argued that women had been lured into slavery by succumbing to the feminine mystique. Her method of analyzing popular culture, particularly the advertising industry, and of perceiving the links between power and the struggle for economic survival and mastery, set the model for many successors by demonstrating the convergence of social and economic forces with cultural myths. Susan Parsons again identifies the heart of this approach to ethics, which she calls "social constructionist":

> Instead of pointing to a transcendent source of value, in this paradigm, values are understood to be the products of social institutions, within which they serve particular functions. The context for individual insight and choice is the social world,

comprised both of structures in which individuals act and interact, and of the language and ideology with which individuals comprehend themselves and the world and communicate with others. [This] … is to affirm the fundamentally social nature of human beings, and to understand that in all moral deliberation, social realities and language are intrinsic.

The separation of fact and value assumes that consensus is built by establishing straightforward facts that are free from value judgments. The distinction between fact and value is integral to the Enlightenment project. Radical feminism challenges this distinction. For the revised universal (or "liberal") model, the individual is basic, and the rational individual can be extricated from his or her social context in order to make judgments derived from universal principles. But once the social context becomes basic, rights and wrongs are evaluated within networks of relationships and in relation to the various groups and roles that have a claim on one's life. This social context has a narrative, which can be identified for critical examination. It is not dependent on an outside or transcendent reality for its meaning or purpose. Meaning is found not in an external source of existence or in an abstract rational realm of principles, but in the investigation of power, language, and patterns of relationships within the narrative. There is no set ideal of society, either to be restored from the past or to be reached in the future; in each generation the marginalized and silenced voices provide the social creativity to imagine new forms of relationship and power distribution. Hence feminism is closely aligned with support of other vulnerable groups such as the disabled, the elderly, the chronically sick, children, and so on.

The claim that "the personal is political" suggests that areas such as sexual reproduction are quite as publicly significant as areas such as industrial production. This implies that the balance of power in society is up for negotiation. In this context it is up to those whose values and experiences have been demeaned and devalued to place those identities as the subject for public debate. Once this happens the norms of society are vulnerable to reconstruction. This is a broad description of the social agenda of postmodernism. It is an approach characterized by suspicion toward all ideologies that claim to have a purchase on a natural or rational order of things. Gender becomes an instrument by which one can peel back the veneer of society's surface to reveal the power relations and assumptions lurking beneath. Meanwhile sacred stories, standard interpretations, and governing narratives are constantly ripe for analysis and new readings. (However, the logic of postmodern feminism is to distrust any single explanation of women's experience or indeed any single notion of what it means to be a woman – since such linear, rational explanations are inherently male.)

This kind of examination, sometimes known as deconstruction, can of course be turned inward on feminism itself. Notable within this approach are three movements that in different ways have pointed out that ethical feminism has been narrower and more blind to its covert commitments than it has been prepared to realize: womanism, lesbian ethics, and ecofeminism.

Womanism

Womanism is a term articulated by Alice Walker (b. 1944) to describe the experience of women of color – particularly African American women. It emerged not only in response to developments in feminist theology but also in relation to the growing influence of black theology. Delores Williams (b. 1937) defines the movement as a prophetic call to attend to the well-being of all African Americans, not just women. But it specifically seeks to help black women "see, affirm, and have confidence in the importance of their experience and faith for determining the character of the Christian religion in the African American community." Meanwhile it challenges oppressive forces inhibiting black women's struggle for survival. It strives for "a positive, productive quality of life conducive to women's and the family's freedom and well-being."

Delores Williams identifies the black woman's experience with that of Sarah's slave Hagar, mother of Abraham's son Ishmael. Whereas white women may identify with Sarah, and the status motherhood bestows on them in the world, black women are more likely to identify with Hagar, whose motherhood is coerced and who is exploited by both a woman (Sarah) and a man (Abraham). White feminists have continually neglected or ignored the role of white women in exploiting black women. Hagar survives in the wilderness with only God to help her, and remains homeless. This wilderness experience characterizes what it means to be an African American. Williams concludes: "It is God's continuing work in the African American community's ever-present struggle for economic justice, for physical and emotional survival and for positive quality of life that forms 'the stuff' of black Christians' doctrines of resistance."

Among the most noted figures in this field are bell hooks, Emilie Townes, and Katie Cannon. Gloria Jean Watkins (b. 1952), who writes under the name bell hooks, notes the inspiration she received from Sojourner Truth (1797–1883), an African American born into slavery who, after gaining freedom in 1826, became a renowned campaigner for women's rights and the abolition of slavery. Truth's most famous speech included the words:

> Then that little man in black there, he says women can't have as much rights as men, 'cause Christ wasn't a woman! Where did your Christ come from? Where did your Christ come from? From God and a woman! Man had nothing to do with Him.

The title of Truth's speech lent its name to hooks' first book, *Ain't I a Woman? Black Women and Feminism* (1981), which examined the history of sexism and racism, the devaluation of black womanhood, the necessity of cultural criticism, and the neglect of race and class issues within white middle-class feminism. In recent years hooks has adopted a conversational literary style, believing the highly academic style of feminist discourse alienates the intellectuals from their popular base.

Katie Geneva Cannon's (b. 1949) *Black Womanist Ethics* (1988) distinguishes between ethics for the dominant and ethics for the dominated. In America the dominant class for many decades prided itself on self-reliance, frugality, and freedom, while withholding the facility for such expression from African Americans. The ethical imperative for black people is to defy such rules or laws that degrade black people in order to affirm their validity and purge them of self-hate. Likewise Emilie Townes (b. 1955) has no hesitation in calling womanist ethics biased. Working for love and justice amid the fallenness of class, race, and gender oppression is inevitably biased: there is no neutral place to stand. Womanism cannot simply stand by and assume the dominance of Eurocentric theological ethics.

In a similar way, Ada María Isasi-Díaz (1943–2012) coined the term *mujerista* to describe those who focus on the particular experiences of Latina women and who work toward their liberation. *Mujerista* ethics emerged in part as a challenge to perceived racism in feminist ethics and perceived sexism in liberation theology, again demonstrating the overlap of race and gender in subversive ethics.

Lesbian Ethics

Lesbian approaches to ethics stretch the rejection of a universal paradigm to a further logical conclusion. Their most far-reaching challenge is to question the conventional meaning and use of the term "good." The goods held up for women by patriarchal culture – sacrifice and self-denial – should be replaced by values such as self-creation, freedom, and liberation. Sarah Lucia Hoagland and Marilyn Frye are among those who expose whose interests are truly served by conventional notions of good. It is a male assumption that one should not only be regarded as good but also position oneself to make others good like oneself. Women have no interest in accepting or imitating such a conception of right action. Lesbians have no stronghold from which to shape society around their notion of the good – nor have they any desire to do so. Free from the responsibility of the deadly seriousness of universal approaches to ethics, some lesbian ethicists emphasize the opportunity for playfulness – for adventure and curiosity. This affirms the creative possibilities that are gained by letting go of the need to do ethics for the whole human race at one go. There are links here to the wider agenda of what is known as queer theology – the exploration of the possibilities of theology and ethics outside a heterosexual paradigm.

Lesbian ethicists reject the heart of what they see as the inherently masculinist project of ethics as a whole. However, lesbian ethics still makes assumptions that some ethical approaches would regard as "conventional" – namely, the assumption that ethics is fundamentally about choice.

Ecofeminism

Rosemary Radford Ruether describes "deep ecology" as the "study of the symbolic, psychological and ethical patterns of destructive relations of humans with nature and how to replace this with a life-affirming culture." Ruether sees ecofeminism as the intersection of ecology with the third kind of feminism we have been exploring. She foresees collaboration between historians of culture, natural scientists, and social economists who would all share a perception of the connection between domination of women and the exploitation of nature. Alongside these groups would need to be "poets, artists and liturgists, as well as revolutionary organizers, to incarnate more life-giving relationships in our cultural consciousness and social system" – to support relations of mutuality, rather than competitive power. Ecofeminism rests on identifying women with nature and males with culture. It also identifies and challenges the assumption that nature is a reality below and separated from "man," rather than a realm in which humanity itself is inseparably embedded. Ruether articulates the narrative that drives the movement:

> It is from the perspective of this male monopoly of culture that the work of women in maintaining the material basis of daily life is defined as an inferior realm. The material world itself is then seen as something separated from males and symbolically linked with women. The earth, as the place from which plant and animal life arises, becomes linked with the bodies of women from which babies emerge. The development of plow agriculture and human slavery very likely took this connection of woman and nature another step. Both are seen as a realm, not on which men depend, but which men dominate and rule over with coercive power. Plow agriculture generally involves a gender shift in agricultural production. While women monopolized food gathering and gardening, men monopolize food production done with plow animals. With this shift to men as agriculturalists comes a new sense of land as owned by the male family head, passed down through a male line of descent, rather than communal land-holding and matrilineal descent that is often found in hunting-gathering and gardening societies. The conquest and enslavement of other tribal groups created another category of humans, beneath the familiar community, owned by it, whose labor is coerced. Enslavement of other people through military conquest typically took the form of killing the males and enslaving the women and their children for labor and sexual service. Women's work becomes identified with slave work. The women of the family are defined as a higher type slave over a lower category of slaves drawn from conquered people. In patriarchal law, possession of women, slaves, animals and land all are symbolically and socially linked together.

Ruether points out that the Protestant Reformation largely removed the positive value of nature as a window into the divine. The result of this was to render nature dangerous and demonic. Meanwhile the scientific revolution a century later made a firm distinction between transcendent intellect and dead matter. These are the seeds of the ecological crisis. Sallie McFague takes these insights a stage further and, particularly in her books *The Body of God* (1993) and *Super, Natural Christians* (1997), sees the world as God's body, a model that for her overcomes the tensions between the immanence of God in this present world and the transcendence of God in the world beyond. She also recasts the Trinity as mother, lover, and friend.

Ecofeminism thus requires a new conception of human life, overcoming the dualism between mind and matter. It requires a new conception of God, as the present and tangible source of life that sustains the whole planetary community.

And it requires a new conception of salvation, as a continual conversion to a healthy relation to nature and one another.

Much as womanism extends feminist concerns to the experiences of black women, so also ecowomanism incorporates questions of race into ecofeminist conversations. Ecowomanist writers tend to focus on environmental issues that display the convergence of race, class, and gender – highlighting, for example, the way that pollution and hazardous waste sites disproportionately affect lower-income and minority communities and place an especially heavy burden on those women and their children.

Feminism and Church Practices

We began the section on gender by considering feminism in relation to Scripture; we conclude by looking at an emerging stream of feminist ethics that approaches the church and its practices using the methods of practical theology.

The term practical theology originally referred to the subfield of theology devoted to training future clergy in skills such as preaching and leading worship. It evolved in the early 1990s into a distinct field (sometimes called empirical theology) that uses the social sciences to explore the interplay between the beliefs and practices of religious communities. Don Browning (1934–2010) of the University of Chicago Divinity School was a key proponent. Practical theology shares with liberation theologies an interest in praxis; and it shares with ecclesial ethics an interest in the virtue of wisdom (or *phronesis*, a kind of practical wisdom) and in the collective life of the church community. For example, Presbyterian ministers and theologians Mary McClintock Fulkerson and Marcia Mount Shoop examine the Eucharist in relation to the racialized assumptions and white privilege of many mainline Protestant congregations. While the ethics that arise from practical theology are not exclusively feminist, many of the practitioners of practical theology are attentive to the ways in which gender (and race) influences religious practice.

Age and Disability

The literature of subversive ethics clusters around questions of class, race, and gender. But the logic of subversive ethics stretches to other social groups whose "difference" has historically been seen negatively or is frequently seen today as related to social disadvantage. The relative paucity of literature in these areas perhaps speaks for itself about the degree of social exclusion involved – although disability has received greater theological attention in the twenty-first century. One other feature sets this area of subversive ethics aside from the other branches considered in this chapter: unlike many other marginalized groups, ethicists who focus on age and disability tend to speak on behalf of others rather than out of their own experience (with a few important exceptions), departing from the "by us" and "for us" emphasis that is characteristic of other subversive ethics. We shall here look briefly at the issues raised in three areas: disability, the elderly, and children.

Disability

The secular ethics debate about disability centers around the medical model and the social model. Does disability lie primarily in the body or mind of the impaired person or primarily in the discriminatory perceptions and the exclusive social structures brought about by the non-disabled person?

- The *medical* model of disability assumes it is a physical (or mental) condition, intrinsic to the individual, which places the individual at a significant disadvantage (hence the term "handicap"). Such disability makes that person's life different and less desirable than the norm. It puts the responsibility on society and the medical profession to respond with initiatives aimed at cure or future prevention. Many activists point out the unvaryingly negative portrayal this model offers: the only positive options are eradication or cure, both of which have sinister undertones.
- In its place has emerged the *social* model, which tends to prefer the term "impairment," and locates the problem not so much in the body of the disabled person as in the narrow social attitudes and unjust lack of infrastructure that accompany disability: hence "My impairment is the fact that I can't walk; my disability is the fact that the bus company only purchases inaccessible buses." Disability in the social model is an issue for every member of society and is not restricted to people with disabilities and those in health care. The logic of the social model is to make generalizations about disability undesirable – and simply to see mental and physical difference as a universal aspect of human diversity, with few common interests or concerns among those adversely affected. Yet one common concern is that whenever rationality is considered essential to ethics, those with developmental disabilities are always in danger of being regarded as subhuman; and whenever utilitarian considerations are in vogue, people with disabilities are always in danger of having their well-being sacrificed for the happiness of the majority.

The tendency of the social model is to focus attention on those whose disabilities are physical and those whose social issues are largely concerned with acceptance and access. The perspective of those whose disabilities are mental and those facing profound pain tends to be less visible. Those whose work in Christian ethics has attracted most attention in regard to disability have concentrated on the neglected areas in the secular discourse – although of all the authors discussed below, only one has a disability. The first three authors discussed below incorporate themes more common to ecclesial ethics, such as the power of narrative and the character of Christian communities.

Hans Reinders, in his *The Future of the Disabled in Liberal Society* (2000), argues that what people with disabilities need is more than liberal society can give. Liberal society is drawn to two approaches – increasing access for disabled people to offer them a full participation in public life, and genetic screening to eradicate disability at its source. The two approaches conflict, because it seems inevitable that preventative uses of human genetics will threaten the welfare benefits that help support disabled people and their families. Reinders shows that what is required is the narratives of those parents who have been enriched by the lives of their disabled children: such stories question the assumptions of what constitutes a good and fulfilling – and free – life at the heart of liberal society.

Jean Vanier (b. 1928) is the founder of L'Arche, an international organization that creates communities in which people with developmental disabilities and those who assist them share life together. He explores in works such as *Community and Growth* (1989) the ways disability both inhibits and enables the expression and reception of the vulnerable areas in the lives of both the developmentally disabled and those who assist them. His L'Arche communities are one of the greatest living examples of the engagement of Christians with an issue that requires a life-transforming personal response.

Stanley Hauerwas (b. 1940), whose work will be considered at greater length in the next chapter, points out, for example in *Suffering Presence* (1986), how issues around disability expose the most profound assumptions about why people have children and what aspirations people have for their lives. He challenges an ethic of parenting that regards children as consumer items that can be picked up or altered at will, and shows how the neediness that often arises among children with disabilities and their parents is part of what makes the church possible and necessary. Echoing themes raised in regard to gender and race by Rosemary Radford Ruether, James Cone, and others, he points out that the suffering and death of Christ demonstrate that God is not removed from the story of people with disabilities – indeed, God's face is their face.

Nancy Eiesland (1964–2009) likewise identifies God with disability by arguing that the wounds in the risen Jesus' body reveal God as "the disabled God" (a phrase which was also the title of her 1994 book). Eiesland's reflections arose in part out of her own experience of disability: she had a painful congenital bone condition that necessitated multiple surgeries and restricted her mobility. For Eiesland, a liberatory theology of disability arises from those who have disabilities; like Asian-American ethics, it is a theology done "by us" and "for us." Her reconstrual of God as the "Disabled God" also resonates with Cone's portrait of God as black, inasmuch as both imagine God's radical identification with their own non-privileged social location.

Finally, Pentecostal theologian Amos Yong (b. 1965) re-reads several biblical texts through the lens of disability. While Yong does not himself have a disability, he writes out of his experience of living for many years with a brother diagnosed with Down syndrome. He aims to unveil how traditional theological understandings of disability have marginalized those with disabilities and excluded them from churches. He approaches biblical texts with a hermeneutic of suspicion that he terms a "disability hermeneutic," one which questions "normate assumptions," or the unexamined prejudices of the non-disabled. His discussion of scriptural texts – including Leviticus, Job, selected healing stories in the gospels, and Pauline texts that discuss weakness – underscores his argument that the Bible is more liberative for those with disabilities than it first appears, when read with a non-normate lens. Like Eiseland, he rejects the notion that disability has no place in God's new creation.

The Elderly

In many ways the elderly point up the tensions in universalist ethics as sharply as any other "different" or excluded group. The absurdity of "difference" lies in the fact that most of those who might act in a way prejudicial to elderly people might expect one day to become elderly themselves. And yet elderly people, particularly the frail elderly, offer to society in a focused way many pervasive concerns. These concerns include suffering, death, the need to feel and look good, together with the personal fears of losing autonomy, being a burden, developing dementia, and the social costs, in Western societies, of an aging population. There is a tendency to regard the aging process itself as a kind of suffering. It sometimes seems that old age is the one illness that perversely resists the contemporary inclination to view all adversity through the lens of cure or therapy.

As with issues concerning disability, the secular discourse tends to focus on issues of justice, and on the different notions of distributive justice – merit, equality, fairness, and so on – that we discussed in Chapter Five. Euthanasia is complex, as we shall see in Chapter Eleven, because it represents a clash between two universal principles – autonomy and the sanctity of life. Christian ethics can sometimes struggle with issues of old age; advanced years do not fit with the notion of a militant church and a martyred Christ. Some, though, have begun to challenge the technological efforts to interrupt the aging process or to extend life by extracting consciousness from the body; for example, ethicist Gilbert Meilaender (b. 1945), while not dismissing the goodness of extended life, also names what he sees as the significant losses of the project to extend life indefinitely – but he does so largely from an ecclesial or virtue ethics approach.

Many of the questions about old age resemble those concerning disability, and contrast the concern for autonomy found in much secular discourse with the role of the church that will be discussed in the next chapter. Growing old is a challenge to universal ethics, because it pushes against assumptions about rationality and autonomy; but it also pushes against some assumptions of subversive ethics, because arguably some of the most marginalized persons in society are so not because of their race or class or gender, but because of their age and infirmity. For example, Michael Banner names the social isolation and even abandonment of the elderly as a pervasive problem for which the Christian tradition has rich resources, not least the rite of gathering around a common table to eat together.

While Banner identifies Alzheimer's and other forms of dementia as an exacerbating factor in the isolation of the elderly, John Swinton (b. 1957) seeks to develop a practical theology of dementia that redescribes the stories of people with dementia within the larger counter-story of God. In God's story, human identity and value are rooted not in our capacities but in the God who created and sustains them. Swinton likewise places the problem of memory loss within the larger story of God remembering *us*: as his book's subtitle claims, we live "in the memories of God." This is a subversive ethic inasmuch as it does ethics *for* a group of people whose voices are lost, ignored, or silent, but it can rarely if ever be a theology done *by* those very people. One of the deepest challenges of dementia is that people with dementia cannot always (or often) do ethics on their own behalf, a dilemma that links the theology of dementia to that of mental disability. Swinton's work is also an ecclesial ethic in that it names key practices of the church that "have the potential to bring healing out of the brokenness of dementia," including lament and hospitality among strangers.

Children

A similar range of issues arises in relation to children as to elderly people and those with disabilities. Many advocates for children concentrate on what we have called a universal ethical paradigm. This leads them to look at drawing up charters of rights for children, seeing children as vulnerable to social exclusion through class, race, and gender, but also due to their age. Among areas where these concerns are especially acute are the risks of being a child in relation to physical, emotional, and sexual abuse and neglect.

However, a growing number of practitioners and theorists have developed approaches that challenge the liberal Enlightenment notion of a child as a rational being in embryo. These take approaches broadly corresponding to the restorationist/romantic and the social constructionist views of feminism, respectively. The romantic strand tends to see children as having an innate spirituality. Inspired by the work of the educationalist Maria Montessori (1870–1952) and advocated by the Roman Catholic Sofia Cavalletti (1917–2011) and the Episcopalian Jerome Berryman (b. 1937), the church has been presented with a challenge that, given appropriate conditions, children may gain an insight into and intimacy with God that adults seldom find. The social constructionist perspective is given to much concern over the effects of early childhood experiences and environments on later adult development. Children, like very elderly people, may face dangers and experience exclusion in challenging ways, ones that may be exacerbated by issues of class, race, and gender. But children may also, like very elderly people, have virtually no way of voicing such perspectives, even to one another. This challenges the way that subversive ethics often elevates the principles of autonomy and self-advocacy.

Summary

The point of this chapter is not to aggregate together a host of social groups and suggest that what is interesting about them is their oppression, still less their difference from a white Western male perspective. What the diverse perspectives brought together in this chapter have in common is that they make social location the starting point for ethical reflection, and thus deny the universal assumptions of the approaches examined in Chapter Five. This is what makes them subversive. The issues of class and of children, discussed at the beginning and end of the chapter, differ from the other themes raised in that they are not inherently fixed states. It is difficult but possible to change one's class. A child is likely to grow into an adult. Thus, subversive ethics is not fundamentally about expressing identity but about locating the action of God in the experience of the oppressed.

Liberation theology focuses on the key term "praxis," which comes to mean not only a style of theology that makes action and commitment the first step, but also some particular styles of social commitment. The various theologies of race differ significantly, largely in relation to the social histories from which they emerge – slavery and segregation in the United States, for example, and apartheid in South Africa. Feminism comes in several strands, and some of its determining features have come to relate to the areas where it overlaps with the ethics of class and race. Finally in the areas of disability, the elderly, and children we see themes emerging, such as the critique of autonomy, that anticipate the ecclesial emphases of the next chapter and that highlight otherwise hidden similarities between universal ethics and some forms of subversive ethics. These kinds of critiques will form the heart of our next chapter.

References and Further Reading

Class

Paulo Freire's program of conscientization is found in his *Pedagogy of the Oppressed* (30th anniversary edition; Myra Bergman Ramos, trans.; New York: Continuum, 2000).

Aristotle's threefold distinction between *theoria*, *praxis*, and *poiesis* is in Book VI of his *Nicomachean Ethics* (Cambridge; New York: Cambridge University Press, 2000).

G. W. F. Hegel's description of dialectic may be found in *The Phenomenology of Spirit* (A. V. Miller, trans.; Oxford: Clarendon Press, 1977). Hegel himself uses the phrase "speculative reason" rather than dialectic.

A key work for Karl Marx's philosophy of praxis is his *Theses on Feuerbach* – see *Karl Marx: Selected Writings* (Kenneth Winkler, ed.; Indianapolis, IN: Hackett, 1994).

One may find Enrique Dussel's distinction between morality and ethics in *Ethics and Community* (London: Burns & Oates, 1988), pages 34–9.

Leonardo and Clodovis Boff provide a helpful sketch of liberation theology in *Introducing Liberation*

Theology (Paul Burns, trans.; Maryknoll, NY: Orbis Books, 1987). Their explanation of functionalist and dialectical analysis is on pages 26–7.

Jorge Pixley's reading of the Exodus story is in *The Bible, The Church and the Poor* (Paul Burns, trans.; Maryknoll, NY: Orbis Books, 1989), especially pages 21–7 and 96–8.

Carlos Mesters' comment on the Bible in the hands of the common people is from his essay "The Use of the Bible in Christian Communities of the Common People," pages 119–33, in *The Bible and Liberation: Political and Social Hermeneutics* (Norman K. Gottwald, ed.; Maryknoll, NY: Orbis Books, 1983), page 125.

Liberation theologian Gustavo Gutiérrez's most central work is *A Theology of Liberation: History, Politics, and Salvation* (rev. edn; London: SCM Press, 1988; translation copyright 1988 by Orbis Books). An excerpt from chapter 13 ("Poverty: Solidarity and Protest") is quoted in the corresponding chapter in *Christian Ethics: An Introductory Reader*. His other works include *We Drink From Our Own Wells: The Spiritual Journey of a People* (Matthew J.

O'Connell, trans.; Maryknoll, NY: Orbis Books; Melbourne, Australia: Dove Communications, 1984); *On Job: God-Talk and the Suffering of the Innocent* (Matthew J. O'Connell, trans.; Maryknoll, NY: Orbis Books, 1987); and *Las Casas: In Search of the Poor of Jesus Christ* (Robert R. Barr, trans.; Maryknoll, NY: Orbis Books, 1993).

The 1976 declaration of the Ecumenical Dialogue of Third World Theologians is quoted in full in Theo Witvliet, *A Place in the Sun: Liberation Theology on the Third World* (John Bowden, trans.; Maryknoll, NY: Orbis Books, 1985), page 27. Witvliet's work also provides a very helpful introduction to African, Caribbean, Latin American, and Asian theologies.

Further primary source readings on the theologies explored in this section include:

- Alfred T. Hennelly, ed. *Liberation Theology: A Documentary History.* Maryknoll, NY: Orbis Books, 1990.
- R. S. Sugirtharajah, ed. *Voices From the Margins: Interpreting the Bible in the Third World.* 2nd edn. Maryknoll, NY: Orbis Books, 1995.

Race

W. E. B. Du Bois' term "double consciousness" is found in "Of Our Spiritual Strivings," chapter 1 of his work *The Souls of Black Folk* (Oxford; New York: Oxford University Press, 2007), page 3.

Howard Thurman's *Jesus and the Disinherited* (Richmond, IN: Friends United Press, 1976, 1981) explores the connection between African American experience and Jesus' context.

The ethical thought of Martin Luther King Jr. may be found in his speeches – see *A Call to Conscience: The Landmark Speeches of Dr. Martin Luther King, Jr.* (Clayborne Carson and Kris Shepard, eds; New York: IPM with Warner Books, 2001) – and in *Strength to Love* (Philadelphia, PA: Fortress Press, 1963, 1981).

James Cone articulates a black liberation theology in *Black Theology and Black Power* (Maryknoll, NY: Orbis Books, 1997) and *God of the Oppressed* (rev. edn; Maryknoll, NY: Orbis Books, 1997). An excerpt from Cone's *A Black Theology of Liberation*

(Twentieth Anniversary Edition; Maryknoll, NY: Orbis Books, 1986) is quoted in the corresponding chapter in *Christian Ethics: An Introductory Reader*. Cone replies to criticism of his claim that "Christ is black" in the article "Black Theology and Ideology: A Response to My Respondents," *Union Seminary Quarterly Review* 31.1 (Fall 1975): 82–3.

Cornel West's work may be explored in *Cornel West: A Critical Reader* (George Yancy, ed.; Malden, MA: Blackwell, 2001).

Samuel Roberts' words on black theology come from *African American Christian Ethics* (Cleveland, OH: Pilgrim Press, 2001), page 23.

J. Kameron Carter's seminal work is *Race: A Theological Account* (Oxford: Oxford University Press, 2008); quotations from pages 4, 6, 256, and 192. Brian Bantum extends Carter's work in *Redeeming Mulatto: A Theology of Race and Christian Hybridity* (Waco, TX: Baylor University Press, 2010).

Willie Jennings' exploration of race and Christian theology is *The Christian Imagination: Theology and Origins of Race* (New Haven, CT: Yale University Press, 2010).

The *Kairos Document* is available at https://kairossouthernafrica.wordpress.com/2011/05/08/the-south-africa-kairos-document-1985/.

John Mbiti's perspective on African Christianity quoted above is in "The Encounter of Christian Faith and African Religion," *Christian Century* 97, no. 27 (Aug. 27–Sep. 3, 1980): 817–18.

Desmond Tutu's famous description of the African Christian experience may be found in his essay "Black Theology/African Theology – Soul Mates or Antagonists?" in *Third World Liberation Theologies: A Reader* (Deane William Ferm, ed.; Maryknoll, NY: Orbis Books, 1986), pages 257–8. This volume also contains readings on a variety of Third World and liberation theologies.

Tinyiko Maluleke's analysis of African theology is found in his essay "The Rediscovery of the Agency of Africans," in *African Theology Today* (Emmanuel Katongole, ed.; Scranton, PA: University of Scranton Press, 2002), pages 154 and 161. Charles Villa-Vicencio's model of "reconstruction" may be discovered in his *A Theology of Reconstruction* (Cambridge: Cambridge University Press, 1992).

The first book-length study of Christian ethics from Asian American perspectives is Grace Y. Kao and Ilsup Ahn, eds, *Asian American Christian Ethics: Voices, Methods, Issues* (Waco, TX: Baylor University Press, 2015); quotations from pages 11–12 and 14.

William Watty's exploration of Caribbean theology is to be found in *From Shore to Shore: Soundings in Caribbean Theology* (Kingston, Jamaica: Golding Print Service, 1981).

Papers given at the 2010 Forum on Caribbean Theology were published with other invited essays in Garnett Roper and J. Richard Middleton, eds, *A Kairos Moment for Caribbean Theology: Ecumenical Voices in Dialogue* (Eugene, OR: Pickwick Publications, 2013).

In addition to the above, Theo Witvliet's book *A Place in the Sun: Liberation Theology in the Third World* (John Bowden, trans.; Maryknoll, NY: Orbis Books, 1985) guided much of the material in this chapter's section on theologies in the developing world.

Gender

This section of the chapter draws several times on Susan Parsons' introduction to Christian feminist ethics in her book *Feminism and Christian Ethics* (New York: Cambridge University Press, 1996). Parsons' description of a feminist is from page 8; her observations about Mary Wollstonecraft are from pages 18–19; and her explanation of Betty Friedan's social constructionism is on page 75.

Phyllis Trible explores the troubling stories of biblical women in *Texts of Terror* (Philadelphia, PA: Fortress Press, 1984).

Elisabeth Schüssler Fiorenza examines the social location of the Gospels in her book *In Memory of Her* (New York: Crossroad, 1983), page 247.

Beverly Wildung Harrison's comment on the sanctity of life is quoted from page 213 of her article "Theology and Morality of Procreative Choice," in *Feminist Theological Ethics: A Reader* (Lois K. Daly, ed.; Louisville, KY: Westminster/John Knox Press, 1994).

Mary Wollstonecraft's early feminist work *A Vindication of the Rights of Woman* is available in *Mary Wollstonecraft's A Vindication of the Rights of Woman; and, The Wrongs of Woman, or, Maria* (Anne Mellor and Noelle Chao, eds; New York: Pearson Longman, 2007).

Letty Russell's description of feminist theology quoted above is from *Human Liberation in a Feminist Perspective* (Louisville, KY: Westminster/John Knox Press, 1974), page 19.

Rosemary Radford Ruether's summary of liberal feminism may be found in her *Sexism and God-Talk: Toward a Feminist Theology* (Boston, MA: Beacon Press, 1993), pages 109–10; portions of this book may also be found in the corresponding chapter in *Christian Ethics: An Introductory Reader*.

Carol Gilligan's approach to feminist ethics is articulated in her book *In a Different Voice: Psychological Theory and Women's Development* (Cambridge, MA: Harvard University Press, 1993).

Sara Ruddick addresses the virtue of attentive love in *Maternal Thinking: Toward a Politics of Peace* (2nd edn; Boston, MA: Beacon Press, 1995), pages 119–23.

Discussed in Mary Daly's *Beyond God the Father: Toward a Philosophy of Women's Liberation* (Boston, MA: Beacon Press, 1985) are the "power of naming" (page 8) and the famous phrase "If God is male, then male is God" (page 19). The phrase "unquenchable gynergy" is from *Gyn/Ecology: The Metaethics of Radical Feminism* (Boston, MA: Beacon Press, 1990), page 34.

Betty Friedan's description of middle-class American women is quoted from the opening words to chapter 1 of *The Feminine Mystique* (New York: Norton, 2001).

Delores Williams defines womanist theology in her article "Womanist Theology: Black Women's Voices," *Christianity and Crisis* 47, no. 3 (March 2, 1987): 66–70. An excerpt from this article is also quoted in the corresponding chapter of *Christian Ethics: An Introductory Reader*.

Sojourner Truth's famous speech, "Ain't I a Woman," may be found online at www.feminist.com/resources/artspeech/genwom/sojour.htm. The title of the speech is drawn on by feminist bell hooks in her *Ain't I a Woman: Black Women and Feminism* (Boston, MA: South End Press, 1981).

Other womanist theologians treated in this chapter are Katie Cannon (*Black Womanist Ethics* [Atlanta, GA: Scholars Press, 1988]) and Emilie Townes (see, e.g., *Womanist Justice, Womanist Hope* [Atlanta, GA: Scholars Press, 1993]).

Rosemary Radford Ruether's narration of ecofeminism is quoted from the essay "Ecofeminism: Symbol and Social Connections on the Oppression of Women and the Domination of Nature," in *Ecofeminism and the Sacred* (Carol J. Adams, ed.; New York: Continuum, 1993), pages 13, 15–16.

Additional perspectives on ecofeminism are Sallie McFague's *The Body of God: An Ecological Theology* (Minneapolis, MN: Fortress Press, 1993) and *Super, Natural Christians* (Minneapolis, MN: Fortress Press, 1997).

For a definition of ecowomanism, see Melanie Harris, "Ecowomanism: An Introduction," *Worldviews: Global Religions, Culture, and Ecology* 20, no. 1 (2016): 5–14.

One example of a feminist practical theology is Mary McClintock Fulkerson and Marcia W. Mount Shoop, *A Body Broken, A Body Betrayed: Race, Memory, and Eucharist in White-Dominant Churches* (Eugene, OR: Cascade Books, 2015).

In addition to the above, a selection from the following is quoted in the corresponding chapter of *Christian Ethics: An Introductory Reader*: Ada María Isasi-Díaz, *Mujerista Theology: A Theology for the Twenty-First Century* (Maryknoll, NY: Orbis Books, 1996).

The following sources provide further helpful material in addition to the above list:

- Ann Loades, ed. *Feminist Theology: A Reader*. London: SPCK; Louisville, KY: Westminster/John Knox Press, 1990.
- Lois K. Daly, ed. *Feminist Theological Ethics: A Reader*. Louisville, KY: Westminster/John Knox Press, 1994.

Age and Disability

Hans Reinders addresses the question of disability in *The Future of the Disabled in Liberal Society* (Notre Dame, IN: University of Notre Dame Press, 2000).

The issue of developmental disability is explored from a gentle, Christian perspective by Jean Vanier in *Community and Growth* (rev. edn; Bombay: St. Paul, 1991). Sections of this work (from chapters 3 and 5) appear in the corresponding chapter in *Christian Ethics: An Introductory Reader*.

Stanley Hauerwas also explores a Christian response to mental disability in *Suffering Presence* (Notre Dame, IN: University of Notre Dame Press, 1986).

Nancy Eiesland constructs a theology of disability in light of her own disability in *The Disabled God: Toward a Liberatory Theology of Disability* (Nashville, TN: Abingdon Press, 1994).

Amos Yong reads biblical texts through the lens of disability in *The Bible, Disability, and the Church: A New Vision of the People of God* (Grand Rapids,

MI: Eerdmans, 2011); quoted phrases are from pages 10 and 13.

For Gilbert Meilaender's exploration of the project of life-extension, see *Should We Live Forever? The Ethical Ambiguities of Aging* (Grand Rapids, MI: Eerdmans, 2013).

Michael Banner considers the question of aging and dying in chapters 5 and 6 of *The Ethics of Everyday Life: Moral Theology, Social Anthropology, and the Imagination of the Human* (Oxford: Oxford University Press, 2016).

For John Swinton's practical theology of dementia, see *Dementia: Living in the Memories of God* (Grand Rapids, MI: Eerdmans, 2012).

Chapter Seven
Ecclesial Ethics

Ecclesial ethics names a strand that has always been present in Christianity, but has attracted particular attention in the last generation under the leadership of some of the foremost names in contemporary theology. Whereas universal ethics concentrates on what is right for anyone and everyone, and subversive ethics points out the particular perspective of the marginalized and excluded, ecclesial ethics suggests that Christian ethics should first of all be concerned with the life made possible in Christ for Christians. It is not that Christians are better or more deserving of attention than others; it is that Christians are (or should be) those who look first to the transformation brought in Christ, rather than the contours of human society, for the sources of ethics.

It would be hard to ignore the polemical nature of much of the recent writing in this strand. Prominent writers have set out grand and far-reaching arguments suggesting (in most cases) that the current ethical establishment represents a loss of crucial commitments and assumptions from an earlier era, the recovery of which is indispensable for articulating and embodying a Christian ethic. Most of these arguments rest on complex historical narratives, and an examination of these narratives forms the first part of this chapter.

One key point of consensus for ecclesial ethics is that ethics in general, and Christian ethics in particular, has tended to concentrate on moments of decision and thus to neglect other significant issues. The description and evaluation of these other issues form the constructive dimension of ecclesial ethics. The second section of this chapter traces the connections between such regularly employed terms as practices, habits, and virtue.

While the most prominent advocates of ecclesial ethics are often associated together, there are in fact some significant differences between their respective emphases. In particular the role of Jesus in ethics is seen as normative by some but

Introducing Christian Ethics, Second Edition. Samuel Wells and Ben Quash with Rebekah Eklund.
© 2017 John Wiley & Sons Ltd. Published 2017 by John Wiley & Sons Ltd.

not by all, and this question among others has far-reaching implications for ethics. The third section of this chapter investigates some of these important differences and enquires whether ecclesial ethics forms a genuinely coherent field.

Persuasive Narratives

Several of the most notable writers in the field of ecclesial ethics capture the imaginations of their readers with a story that goes broadly as follows. Western society is coming to the end of an era known by many names, the most common of which is modernity. Modernity describes a prevailing ethos and system of thought that gradually replaced an earlier consensus, stretching back to the medieval period or beyond. The key features of modernity for Christian ethics are:

- that it tends to put humanity, particularly the individual person, at the center of enquiry – rather than God and the ways of God;
- that it tends to achieve consensus by avoiding public discussion of truth and purpose, thus privileging the technocratic facility of getting things done; and
- that it justifies its understanding and practice of authority by the more or less evident alternative of violence and chaos.

For some writers the emergence of postmodernity, with its relentless suspicion of established systems, privileged narratives, and confident authorities, constitutes a significant challenge to modernity; for others, postmodernity is simply an outworking of one aspect of the logic of modernity. In this context, the narratives outlined by those associated with ecclesial ethics have a backward- and a forward-looking aspect. They look back to a time when communal and institutional life was shaped around particular practices derived from and dependent on particular perceptions of truth. And they look forward to the reassertion of confidence in those institutions – notably the church – that survive but which are currently shorn (or losing sight) of the practices that give their continued existence meaning.

We shall examine six persuasive narratives that accept this broad shape. Two – those of Alasdair MacIntyre and John Milbank – may be said to define the field. A further three – those of Karl Barth (and his interpreter George Lindbeck), Stanley Hauerwas, and Oliver O'Donovan – offer significant dimensions and modifications. Finally, we consider the work of Jennifer Herdt, for her charitable critique and extension of these narratives, and the parallel retrieval of virtue ethics in Catholic moral theology. We begin with Karl Barth, who lays the foundation for much that follows.

Karl Barth

If ecclesial ethics is associated with one name above all it would be the Swiss theologian Karl Barth (1886–1968) – and such criticisms as are raised of ecclesial ethics are generally related to criticisms of Barth's overall theological project.

His theological revolution, begun in his *Epistle to the Romans* (1922) and continued through his magisterial *Church Dogmatics* (14 volumes, 1932–68), originates in his horror at the way his liberal Protestant German teachers capitulated to the Kaiser's militant policies in Germany prior to and during World War I. This ethical failure was rooted, he perceived, in a theological wrong turn. This wrong turn was to accord independent and abiding validity to any cultural or moral norms: such a mistake had led to the uncritical acceptance of national identity, particular regimes, ecclesiastical structures, and cultural assumptions that had paved the way to 1914 (and were later to pave the way for Hitler's rise to power). For Barth, there was no so-called "rational necessity" – such as racial identity – that could inhibit the authority and freedom of the command of God. This insistence gave Barth the clarity to draw up the Barmen Declaration (1934) denouncing the heresy of Hitler's regime.

Barth's early period is sometimes known as dialectical theology because of his insistence on the infinite qualitative distinction between God as creator and human beings as creatures. For Barth the difference between God and human beings was not quantitative – as if God were a very big person. It was qualitative – God and humanity were altogether different beings. And this qualitative difference was infinite: God and human beings are utterly different.

Many philosophers and theologians followed G. W. F. Hegel (1770–1831) in seeing human history as an emerging cultural narrative wherein theses contrasted with antitheses resulting in eventual syntheses: Karl Marx's proposal of the emergence of the communist utopia through the clash between the bourgeoisie and the proletariat fits this pattern. Barth, by contrast, followed Søren Kierkegaard (1813–55), who rejected the idea that a synthesis would always overcome an antithesis. Sometimes all one has is a paradox – an unresolved thesis and antithesis. The incarnation of Jesus, as both God and a human being, is such a paradox. For Barth, such paradoxes are the heart of theology, which concerns the way eternity entered time and the infinite became finite. The ultimate choice is God's choice never to be except to be for us in Jesus Christ – and thus Jesus Christ is the fundamental ground and norm for ethics. God makes demands on us to conform to God, God makes possible the fulfillment of this command, and God vicariously suffers the judgment and punishment that lack of conformity brings upon us. Barth's actual treatment of ethical issues and concerns takes a Trinitarian shape: he divides his material under the headings of creator, reconciler, and redeemer. Thus, under the heading of creator, Barth discerns a fourfold pattern in human life – shaped by relationships to God, to other people, to the self, and to the natural limits of life.

Barth's precise ethical method and conclusions have been influential, but more significant for ecclesial ethics has been the broad sweep of his rejection of cultural necessity and his assertion of the unbridled command of God expressed in Jesus Christ.

Among Barth's many interpreters, perhaps the most significant for the self-understanding of ecclesial ethics has been George Lindbeck (b. 1923). Lindbeck has been prominent alongside Hans Frei (1922–88) in the so-called Yale School, which has become the tradition most closely associated with the assimilation of Barthian theology into mainstream Protestant theology outside the Reformed tradition. Lindbeck outlines his theological perspective in his *The Nature of Doctrine* (1984). Rather than offer a historical narrative as such, this book offers a threefold typology that presupposes a historical narrative, and in doing so locates the abiding legacy of Barth's work for ecclesial ethics in the third of the three types outlined.

Lindbeck identifies the approach to theology that has pervaded the church until recent centuries as "cognitive-propositional." This strand assumes that doctrines operate as direct truth claims about objective realities. Theology stands therefore alongside science and philosophy – that is, as a system of thought that puts forward quantities of information that offer meaningful renderings of the world. Here Lindbeck's typology assumes a historical narrative – one in which, prior to the Enlightenment, it was possible to posit earthly, transient realities as indicators of heavenly, eternal truths. We may call this the preliberal era. The second strand emerges out of the response made by Friedrich Schleiermacher (1768–1834) to the breakdown of the cognitive-propositional approach, particularly at the hands of Immanuel Kant (1724–1804). (This is a reading of Schleiermacher that Lindbeck owes to Barth.) Schleiermacher's work earmarks a turn toward what Lindbeck calls "experiential-expressivism," an approach for which doctrines are "noninformative and nondiscursive symbols of inner feelings, attitudes, or existential orientations." This era, which we may call the liberal era, represents the implications of the Enlightenment's turn to the subject. Value, meaning, and reality take place fundamentally within a person's experience, rather than having some more significant external purchase – and thus God is centrally a reality within human experience. In place of these two approaches, Lindbeck proposes what he calls a "cultural-linguistic" approach. It is this vision that he hopes will usher in what he calls a "postliberal" era. The term postliberal has often subsequently been associated with ecclesial ethics, particularly in its Protestant varieties.

A cultural-linguistic view sees doctrines "not as expressive symbols or truth claims, but as communally authoritative rules of discourse, attitude and action." In other words, doctrine is more like a language and like the rules or manners that shape a culture than it is like a science manual or an account of religious experience. Being religious means interiorizing a set of skills derived from a community and enhanced by practice and training. Lindbeck's account owes much to the philosophy of Ludwig Wittgenstein (1889–1951) and the anthropology of Clifford Geertz (1926–2006), but behind it lies the long shadow of Karl Barth, whom Lindbeck sees as charting a way for theology to escape experiential-expressivism. He is profoundly concerned with truth, but unlike the cognitive-propositional approach he does not believe there can be a form of truth that can be advocated in the absence of its embodiment in forms of human community, particularly if it is contradicted by patterns of human action.

Lindbeck appeals to Aristotle's notion of rationality as a matter more of skill than of universal principle. In Aristotle's view, rationality is not innate but acquired; it lies not in the mind but in intelligible practices, which must be learnt. "Reasonableness in religion and theology, as in other domains, has something of that aesthetic character, that quality of unformalizable skill, which we usually associate with the artist or the linguistically competent," says Lindbeck. "Intelligibility comes from skill, not theory, and credibility comes from good performance, not adherence to independently formulated criteria." There is no neutral high ground from which to adjudicate truth. The only criteria for assessment come from within theology itself. A sentence may be true within its appropriate context: abstracted from that context it is neither true nor untrue; it is simply meaningless. The point is not that there is no such thing as propositional truth. The point instead is that theological truth demands response and participation, and its merits cannot be investigated any other way. For Lindbeck, the proposition "Jesus is Lord" is true, but the only way to assert its truth is to act accordingly. The preliberal approach to truth tended to privilege history and science. But Lindbeck's postliberal approach favors liturgy, preaching, and ethics. It is in these activities that one aligns oneself with what one takes to be most important in the universe – and thus claims the truth.

Already we can see a number of features of ecclesial ethics. There is the restoration of theological confidence, as represented by the prominence of Barth and Thomas Aquinas (1225–74). No longer does theology constantly have to adapt to the changing fashions and demands of contemporary knowledge; instead, contemporary knowledge is judged through the lens of theological perception. There is the narrating of a story that problematizes the assumptions of liberal modernity. There is the reconception of truth in theology. And there is attention to the way theology and practice are formed in communities that develop their own "grammar," or linguistic habits and manners. Our next key figure picks up several of these themes from outside the world of Protestant theology.

Alasdair MacIntyre

Alasdair MacIntyre (b. 1929) is a Scottish-born philosopher who has been based in the United States since 1970. Much of his early work reflected Marxist sympathies. But for the sake of describing the emergence of ecclesial ethics, the decisive period of his writing is 1981–99, with the publication of his four major works, *After Virtue* (1981/1984), *Whose Justice? Which Rationality?* (1988), *Three Rival Versions of Moral Enquiry* (1990), and *Dependent Rational Animals* (1999). These books retain his earlier antagonism to liberal capitalism, but ground his constructive alternative in a restoration of the assumptions made about ethics by Aristotle and Thomas Aquinas. In the background lies his emerging loyalty to a Roman Catholicism derived from Aquinas, but this commitment remains implicit rather than explicit in his work.

The opening and closing passages of *After Virtue* are among the most celebrated rhetorical flourishes in modern philosophy. MacIntyre begins his landmark work by lamenting the incoherence of ethical debate today. He paints an imaginary picture of enlightened people trying to restore the discipline of science after it had fallen into such disrepute that almost all laboratories, textbooks, and research had been destroyed or lost. The discipline would be reconstructed from fragments of the periodic table, hazy memories, and mysterious equipment. Such is the state of moral discourse today, argues MacIntyre. Ethics is characterized by interminable disputes between irreconcilable parties who neither understand one another nor share a common ethical vocabulary – such as the contesting parties in the abortion debate. "Detached from the theoretical and social contexts in terms of which these conceptions were originally elaborated and rationally defended, the assertions of each of these rival positions … have characteristically and generally become no more than expressions of attitude and feeling." This impasse constitutes the failure of secular moral philosophy, a situation MacIntyre describes as "emotivism."

MacIntyre traces the roots of this condition to the failure of what he calls "the Enlightenment project." Thinkers like Hume, Bentham, Diderot, and Kant set out to replace traditional and (in their view) superstitious forms of morality with a new universal morality that would elicit the assent of any rational person. The legacy of their various attempts is a set of rival models that all claim to be the only rational approach – as witnessed in endless disputes between Kantian deontologists and utilitarian consequentialists (see Chapter Five). This impasse invites the rejection of rational approaches in favor of emotivism, which perceives moral preference in terms of attitude and feeling. Another legacy, according to MacIntyre, is the emergence of "a set of moral concepts which derive from their philosophical ancestry an appearance of rational determinateness and justification which they do not in fact possess." These include human rights and utility or welfare, which MacIntyre calls "useful fictions."

Emotivist ethics presupposes compartmentalized lives and manipulative social relations, and modernity calls this manipulative mode "managerial effectiveness." This notion "presupposes the availability of a set of social scientific laws, knowledge of which will enable managers to control social reality; but we do not in fact know any such laws" – for social reality has an ineradicable unpredictability that bureaucracies are embarrassed to acknowledge. Friedrich Nietzsche (1844–1900), more than anyone else, identified that moral assertions were little more than masks protecting undisclosed purposes and motivations. In doing so Nietzsche let loose the mode of skeptical enquiry that has characterized postmodernism. MacIntyre offers a rival history to that provided by Nietzsche in the latter's *Genealogy of Morals* (1887). MacIntyre sees the failure of the Enlightenment project (and the missing ingredient in Nietzsche's genealogy) as the rejection of Aristotle's ethics and politics in the previous two centuries. MacIntyre provides his own history tracing the portrayal of the virtues from Homer to medieval Europe. Such virtues are qualities developed over time without which social goods are not sustainable; virtues are also required to enable human lives to realize their purpose or *telos*, and this unity of a human life requires a narrative structure. This narrative structure only emerges in relation to the individual's embeddedness in social traditions.

The later medieval era failed to sustain the tradition of the virtues, and Aristotelian ethics and politics were rejected in the upheaval of the Reformation. The later Enlightenment period witnessed through Kant a revival of virtue (in the singular), but today we live "after virtue" in a time of unresolvable disputes and dilemmas. MacIntyre concludes that only a return to Aristotle avoids the critique that Nietzsche directed against both deontologists and consequentialists – and he famously brings his account to a climax by advocating withdrawal to secluded communities, like the monks of the fourth and fifth centuries, to await a new but different St. Benedict, for the barbarians are not simply at the gates – they have been ruling over us for some time.

MacIntyre's subsequent works all assume the narrative outlined in *After Virtue*, although they develop its argument in different ways. For example, *Three Rival Versions of Moral Enquiry* sets the Enlightenment project (which MacIntyre entitles "encyclopaedia," after its attempt to encompass all things) alongside Nietzsche's revision (which MacIntyre calls "genealogy," following Nietzsche's term for the tracing of the sources of ethics), and then sets them both alongside the philosophy of Thomas Aquinas (which MacIntyre calls "tradition"). In advocating the ethics of Aristotle as interpreted by Aquinas, MacIntyre is assuming the story he narrates in *After Virtue*. Likewise *Dependent Rational Animals* seeks to redress the balance in ethics and philosophy by regarding human beings not only as rational but as dependent and as animals. This is a corrective to the assumption of Aristotle (and many other philosophers) that rationality is the key to human identity. Again MacIntyre takes for granted that only a recovery of a broad Aristotelian ethos can save contemporary society from a politics that is really civil war by other means.

John Milbank

Like MacIntyre, John Milbank (b. 1952) offers an ambitious historical narrative. In his *Theology and Social Theory* (1990) and elsewhere, he recalls how theology has lost its sense of its own place and has taken on a false humility, allowing itself to be located by the social sciences, rather than itself locating them. This tendency is characteristic of a theological sensibility known as Radical Orthodoxy, with which Milbank is often associated. The characteristically Anglican emphasis on Christ's incarnation encourages Milbank, together with colleagues including Graham Ward and Catherine Pickstock, to see revelation as primarily a matter of an emerging historical story. It goes as follows.

Once there was no secular. Every aspect of life was defined by its relationship with the transcendent sphere of existence – the creator God. There was thus no such thing as a material world of "nature": instead, all was "creation," what Milbank describes as a charged immanence. In other words even the material world was bursting with the energy given to it by the transcendent God. Thus, there was no objective, autonomous reason, no state, no public or private realm – and no form of existence that was not inherently ordered toward creaturely praise of the creator. Creation is for communion: creatures are made for harmonious interaction and friendship with God and one another, with conflict and opposition as a secondary intrusion, not a necessary or inevitable state of being. Whereas so much of what we have called the "universal" approach regards difference between people and between other entities and forces as troubling and dangerous, Christianity is precisely shaped to embrace and enjoy difference. Indeed Christianity is "the coding of transcendental difference as peace." Christianity is all about the reconciliation of God and humanity and consequently the reconciliation of humanity with itself and with its surroundings. To talk of creation means to rule out a dualism that regards spirit as superior to matter (Gnosticism), and equally to exclude a materialism that reduces the world to spiritless immanence (positivism). The story of grace-infused creation runs from Plato to Gregory of Nyssa to Augustine to Thomas Aquinas.

But the harmony of participation in this seamless universe was broken, and the name for this fracture is "modernity." This transformation began with the medieval theologian John Duns Scotus (1266–1308), who detached the immanent world from the transcendent heaven. Duns Scotus talked about earthly things without assuming that all earthly things were participating in a divine story. This created a new realm. This new realm was one of neutral, objective, autonomous universal reason, described by Milbank as the "univocity of being." Instead of a harmonious communion of enriching friendships, reality was constructed from the starting point of an isolated individual subject – the thinker of René Descartes, who became also the autonomous subject of Immanuel Kant, the owner of inalienable rights of John Locke, and the competitive aggregate of self-interested preservation instincts of Thomas Hobbes and Adam Smith. In place of participatory communion there was now self-interest; in place of worship there was now fundamental antagonism. As the philosopher James K. A. Smith summarizes it: "The modern subject became a parody of God, the modern state became a parody of the Church, the modern city became a parody of the new Jerusalem, modern social theory became a parody of theology."

Postmodernism is upon us, and it is founded on Friedrich Nietzsche's profound questioning of interests and ability to trace genealogies of power. However, postmodernism's nihilism – its thoroughgoing skepticism that finds no resting place for suspicion and doubt – is no more than an extension of modernity's assumptions about the "univocity of being" – that is, the restriction of philosophy to considering the secular, detached from the divine. A true postmodernism would correct this philosophical error and return to contemplating and acting in a universe suffused with the transcendent and thus presuming that difference is good rather than dangerous.

The inspiration for Milbank's seminal book, and in many ways for the whole movement of Radical Orthodoxy it spawned, is Augustine's *City of God*. Just as Milbank writes in the context of the emergence of postmodernism and the predicted demise of modernity, Augustine writes in the wake of the sack of Rome by Alaric the Goth in 410 CE and the impending demise of the empire. As Augustine distinguishes the City of God from the Earthly City, so Milbank highlights the difference between the participatory, liturgically shaped universe of the Middle Ages and the univocal, immanent world of modernity. As Augustine argues there can be no true justice without right worship, so Milbank outlines how the inherently conflictual, antagonistic character of modernity can be traced to a fundamental theological mistake that left behind the presupposition of harmonious difference.

Just as Milbank imitates Augustine, he also attempts to subvert Nietzsche. *Theology and Social Theory* tries to out-genealogize Nietzsche's genealogy, by narrating a story within which Nietzsche's assumptions emerged, and pointing out that the moves Nietzsche shared in common with modernity were more significant than the ways in which they differed. Meanwhile Milbank also owes much to Alasdair MacIntyre, since vestiges of MacIntyre appear in Milbank's narrative. One notable difference is that Milbank highlights the inherently violent assumptions of Aristotle's notion of virtue, which, he argues, is locked into the paradigmatic role of the soldier. Milbank does not believe MacIntyre's reliance on Aristotle is compatible with a fundamental commitment to the configuration of difference as peace.

Stanley Hauerwas

Stanley Hauerwas (b. 1940) draws together the story told by Karl Barth with the story told by Alasdair MacIntyre, and then brings these two stories into conversation with the very different story told by the Mennonite theologian John Howard Yoder (whose story will be told below). Hauerwas flirts with the grand declension narratives of MacIntyre and Milbank, which trace the decline of philosophy and theology from a long ago time when they got things right. He also pays attention to revisionist historical accounts that question, for example, the way the immanent universal ethics of the Enlightenment arose out of the discrediting of religious perspectives after the brutal Thirty Years' War (1618–48). But he never hangs his theological flag on any specific historical mast. Instead we can trace three narratives that shape Hauerwas' project, one being his own, another for which he offers a broad outline, and a third that we may infer.

- The first context is that of American Methodism. For Hauerwas, Methodism is rooted in a sustained and disciplined quest for holiness, through regular meetings, Scripture study and exposition, worship, and a personal pursuit of perfection inspired by the Holy Spirit. Yet American Methodism has tended to be dominated by revivalist influences – what Hauerwas sees as the ephemeral, self-absorbed nature of the conversion experience, the lack of connection to historic tradition or wider church practice, and the vulnerability to become captive to whatever prevailing ideologies dominated the notion of Christianity in each era.

  Hauerwas connects these shortcomings to the flaws in contemporary ethics, which is similarly obsessed with the moment of decision, similarly detached from historic tradition and wider church practice, and similarly captive to prevailing ideologies – notably liberalism, the "story that we have no story." For Hauerwas, liberalism means those forces in society that, in the name of individual freedom, dismantle the resources by which morality can be the shaping of character in community. Thus, they turn ethics in particular and life in general into a series of insoluble dilemmas made up of arguments and agents that not only cannot be reconciled but cannot even find a vocabulary with which to interact. The heart of Hauerwas' concern is that the church has lost its identity: hence his claim that the first social duty of the church is to be the church.

- The second narrative is the story of Christian social ethics in America. One can tell this story in four generations.

  - First comes Walter Rauschenbusch (1861–1918) and the Social Gospel movement in the early decades of the twentieth century. This represented a broad and somewhat uncritical harmonization of the social program of Jesus and the emerging human and industrial relations of America.

  - Then follows Reinhold Niebuhr (1892–1971) with a wholesale critique of the Social Gospel, largely shaped around a renewed and profound awareness of the significance of sin. Reinhold and his brother Richard Niebuhr between them set the agenda of Christian ethics in twentieth-century America, and all subsequent contributors have had to adapt to the reality they articulated.

  - The third generation is that of figures such as the Princeton scholar Paul Ramsey (1913–88) and the Yale ethicist James Gustafson (b. 1925), figures whose constructive work both reflects the assumptions of their forebears and begins to adapt to a world that no longer shares the assumptions of a broad Christian (in fact, largely liberal Protestant) benevolence.

  - In this story Stanley Hauerwas emerges as a leading, if not *the* leading, figure in a fourth generation that includes James McClendon (1924–2000) and John Howard Yoder. This generation argued that, in Hauerwas' words, the subject of Christian ethics in America has never been the church: it has always been America. America was taken to be the body that Christian ethics was designed to serve.

  Thus, Hauerwas is prominent among a generation of those in theological ethics who castigated their forebears for making the church invisible in Christian ethics, and for constantly replacing the church with America. Though it is not significant in Hauerwas' early work, the church is crucial to Hauerwas' theological ethics because it becomes the political, social, and most importantly *imaginative* alternative to enable people to enter the world of discipleship inspired and empowered by the definitive figure of Jesus.

- The third perspective is the story of the church and academy in twentieth-century America. Here Hauerwas' significance is more debatable, but perhaps even more far-reaching than in relation to ethics alone. One can tell a story in which what we are calling universal ethics was once dominant. This was a period when most of the major institutions in America were in the grip of a liberal Protestant elite, when women had a largely hidden social role, and when African Americans were in many cases excluded from walking the corridors of power and privilege. It seemed that one could write about the nature and destiny of "man," as Reinhold Niebuhr did, and not acknowledge or even realize how narrow that notion of "man" in fact was.

The subsequent period (loosely known today as "the sixties") both gradually and in some cases dramatically broke or blew apart the narrowness of that "man" that had been taken to be an unquestioned universal. We are calling the style of ethics that arose from this period subversive, because its principal objective is to critique and correct the universal project, particularly through the now-privileged perspective of those formerly ignored or excluded on such grounds as gender, race, and class.

Hauerwas' achievement, along with but perhaps unmatched by others, has been to describe a third approach – the approach that we are calling ecclesial ethics. While universal ethics sees itself as ethics for anyone and subversive ethics sees itself as ethics for the excluded, ecclesial ethics simply sees itself as ethics for the church. Hauerwas endorses much of the critique that subversive ethics makes of universal ethics. Many of his critics overlook this, and thus often speak of him as allying with or opening the door to conservative religious, social, or political movements. This criticism is misplaced – as Hauerwas reminds his critics, no such conservative movements claim him. But Hauerwas also distances himself from subversive ethics by arguing that universal ethics and subversive ethics tend to share many of the same assumptions. Furthermore he is concerned with a positive program of shaping people of character through disciplined communal practices centered on performing and embodying the one apparently particular but in fact truly universal story.

It is perhaps in imagining, describing, and inspiring such a way to do ethics and be the church beyond conventional liberal–conservative divisions that his greatest significance may come to lie.

Oliver O'Donovan

Oliver O'Donovan (b. 1945) seeks to identify and articulate the distinctively political character of Christianity and the uniquely Christian character of politics. What he has in common with the preceding figures is that he sees ethics in largely teleological terms. That is, he sees ethics as concerned with the eschatological fulfillment of the created order. He also seeks to recover the scriptural roots of Christian ethics. Like Milbank he seeks to reinvest the human with the divine: he sees politics "not as a self-enclosed field of human endeavour but as the theatre of the divine self-disclosure": for O'Donovan, *The Desire of the Nations* (the title of his 1996 book on political theology) is Christ.

Where O'Donovan differs is that he does not dwell on a historical narrative that imagines some kind of loss of theological or moral transparency or coherence. For

O'Donovan, "historicism," as he calls it, is a danger. History discloses the unavoidable unpredictability of outcomes, but it does not offer an ideal model emerging from the clash of lesser, or contrasting, models. The other key difference is that O'Donovan sees no fundamental distinction between church and world. The sources of Christian ethics are available to everybody and binding on everybody, and yet they are derived from authorities that only Christians recognize. O'Donovan sees himself as an evangelical, because his ethics are founded on "what God has done for the world and for humankind in Jesus Christ," but also as a realist, because "purposeful action is determined by what is true about the world into which we act." Hence O'Donovan is a kind of bridge figure between ecclesial ethics and universal ethics.

In his *Resurrection and Moral Order* (1986/1994) O'Donovan distinguishes between order conceived as final eschatological purposes or "ends" and order conceived as "kinds" that transcend time and place. In this he is steering between two extremes. The first is an ethic based wholly on revelation, which is oriented to ends that are inaccessible to the non-believer. The second is an ethic based wholly on reason, which takes away any need for revelation. The former he calls "voluntarism" and the latter he calls "nominalism." O'Donovan is always striving to synthesize these two extremes. The resurrection of Jesus is the key synthesizing moment. It vindicates the created order but inaugurates the kingdom of God which proves that creation is not a lost cause. This makes O'Donovan more sympathetic to natural law perspectives than most figures in the world of ecclesial ethics.

In *The Desire of the Nations* O'Donovan steers between "liberals," who divide theology from politics (and are driven by a corrosive and trust-reducing suspicion), and "historicists," who unite theology and politics but at the unacceptable price of wholesale skepticism. O'Donovan's own approach is to render Israel's scriptural politics under four broad headings: salvation (God's mighty acts), judgment (government), possession (the tokens of God's promise, especially law and land), and Israel's response in praise.

In *The Ways of Judgment* (2005) O'Donovan investigates the theological ideas out of which political science grew. He perceives the profound ways in which human sinfulness jeopardizes the legitimacy and efficiency of all human institutions. He sees political society as ordained by God to make normative judgments about when "to limit freedom in order to realize it." The central political task – judgment itself – derives from God's judgment (and not from human consent or contract); but it is radically questioned by Christ's "counter-political" command to "judge not."

Jennifer Herdt

Jennifer Herdt (b. 1967), professor of Christian ethics at Yale Divinity School, offers a charitable critique and extension of ecclesial ethics in her own distinctive key. She identifies MacIntyre and Hauerwas especially as generative conversation partners, incorporates several of Barth's key insights, and explores the Aristotelian virtue ethics of Augustine and Aquinas. Her work has been wide-ranging but two particular aspects concern us here. First is her insistence that Christian practices (especially liturgical ones) warrant close reflection for the way they can both form and malform. Second, and more complex, is her emphasis on the cooperation of human and divine agency in the formation of virtuous character; this relates to her call for the particularism of ecclesial ethics to be what she terms comprehensive rather than exclusive. And it finally includes a plea for Christian ethics to retrieve a generous, humanist understanding of pagan and secular virtues not as splendid vices (as Augustine famously termed them) but as true virtues, such that Christian ethics may be oriented both toward the *telos* of fellowship with God and service to the common good.

Herdt engages with what she calls the liturgical turn in Christian ethics, the turn toward construing worship as ethics epitomized by *The Blackwell Companion to Christian Ethics*, edited by Stanley Hauerwas and Samuel Wells (2004, revised 2011), and by Wells' book *God's Companions* (2006). When Hauerwas and Wells note, "Christians may get their worship of God wrong," Herdt affirms this caution and further explores its significance in relation to the genuine power of the liturgy to form character. While she applauds the focus on practices over theory, Herdt also suggests that ecclesial ethics must analyze not simply a single idealized liturgy but the multiple and diverse liturg*ies* enacted in specific churches for the ways they "succeed and fail, heal and warp." Her expansive definition of liturgy includes not only baptism and Eucharist, prayer and doxology, but also an afternoon at the food bank or a Saturday morning at the local baseball diamond.

In her book *Putting On Virtue* and elsewhere, Herdt seeks to overcome what she views as the false dichotomy between human agency ("putting on" virtue through mimesis, or imitation) and divine agency (God's transforming grace), a dichotomy related to the theological distinction between acquired and infused virtues. She identifies key resources in the thought of Desiderius Erasmus (ca. 1466–1536) and the early Jesuit dramatic tradition for their "positive account of virtue as simultaneously acquired through mimetic action and infused through divine grace." Likewise, she reads the work of Hauerwas and Wells approvingly as "an effort to articulate the non-competitive character of divine and human agency."

The mimetic action Herdt has in mind is first and foremost imitation of Christ as the exemplar of virtue. In this and other ways, her work aligns with the irreducible particularity of ecclesial ethics, its insistence on rooting itself in the specific narratives of Israel, Jesus, and the church. Yet one feature of this tilt away from the universal and toward particularity worries Herdt. She appeals to Karl Barth's Christocentrism – his belief in the cosmic, all-encompassing scope of what God has done in Christ – as an example of what she calls comprehensive particularism, or the conviction that "from within one's first-order theological commitments one may offer an account of the significance of narrative or virtue or performance or liturgy ... and affirm that we can speak adequately only from these first-order commitments." By contrast she sees exclusive particularism as the aim "to remain wholly within first-order theological categories, to dwell within the God-given, revealed narratives and practices and virtues that compose the Christian life, and *eliminate* non-particularist categories." Her analysis of Hauerwas' writings concludes that Hauerwas often employs the rhetoric of exclusive particularism while regularly including themes that distance him from it.

For Herdt the dangers of exclusive particularism, with which she believes ecclesial ethics occasionally flirts, are threefold: (1) it tends toward an avoidance of reflection on practices such that they cannot be corrected should they become false or sinful (bringing us full circle back to our first point in this section); (2) it risks impoverishing Christian ethical reflection when it refuses to draw on second-order theological activities such as natural law and casuistry; and (3) it bears within it a potential "excuse for withdrawal from the tasks of living out God's love in the world," that is, an avoidance of civic friendship and cooperation for the sake of the common good. She points to the work of Eric Gregory (b. 1970), Charles Mathewes (b. 1969), and Luke Bretherton (b. 1968) as counter-balances to this tendency, praising their commitment to both the particularity of the Christian witness and a truly public theology.

Earlier we pointed to Herdt's redefinition of the liturgy as including participation in public life and other mundane or worldly actions. For her, "One of the most important tasks facing us is powerfully to affirm – and actively to embody – the fact that Christian formation, formation for fellowship with God in Christ, is at the same time formation for service to the common good." It is this emphasis that also characterizes, at least in part, the retrieval of virtue ethics in Catholic moral theology.

The (Re)Turn to Virtue in Catholic Moral Theology

While Catholic ethicists have revived virtue ethics in ways partially analogous to the Protestant retrieval, they have done so largely through the lens of Thomas Aquinas and, to some extent, MacIntyre. We have already briefly described in Chapter Four the retrieval of Aquinas and his adaptation of Aristotle's virtue ethics by twentieth-century Catholic ethicists such as Servais Pinckaers (1925–2008). At a time when Catholic ethics was largely focused on natural law and the prescriptions of the manuals of moral theology, Pinckaers and others called for a renewed attention to the contributions of Aquinas to moral reasoning and the formation of virtuous character. Likewise Jean Porter (b. 1955) appeals to Aquinas's theory of morality in order to revive an account of human virtue in relation to the moral law. While Porter adopts MacIntyre's diagnosis of the diverse and competing nature of contemporary moral discourse, she disagrees with his view that Christian ethics ever truly had or can recover a unified moral tradition, a point on which she also criticizes Hauerwas. Her concern for the moral act as well as the human agent leads her to resist the dichotomy drawn between "quandary ethics" (i.e., decisionist ethics, described below) and virtue ethics.

Meanwhile an abiding concern for the common good and the universality of the moral law has led Catholic social teaching and the ethical instructions of the Vatican to retain a strongly universal character. For example, Pope John Paul II's 1993 encyclical *Veritatis splendor* (Splendor of Truth) is addressed to the Catholic bishops, but it aims to defend the moral norms of Christianity – which are "universal and unchanging" – not only on behalf of the church but for all humanity, for the good of "society as such."

A New Aristotelianism

For all the energy and interest evoked by Milbank's project and that of his Radical Orthodox colleagues and followers, and for all the wisdom and sober judgments of O'Donovan, neither of these programs has issued in the extent of sustained ecclesial movement ignited by the cluster of work emerging from MacIntyre and Hauerwas, and to a large extent characterized by Lindbeck. It is possible to describe a broad consensus that has emerged within this territory – one that may be generally recognized by those who have an interest in identifying ecclesial ethics, but one whose constructive agenda is largely detachable from its polemical articulations, many of which are set within wide-ranging historical narratives. What follows is an attempt to draw together the overlapping themes that are found in MacIntyre, Hauerwas, and Lindbeck in such a way that portrays an ecclesial ethic that might be recognized even by this emerging tradition's most ardent critics.

People, not Decisions

Perhaps the key move accepted by the core thinkers in ecclesial ethics is their decisive break with universal ethics (see Chapter Five). Universal ethics – whether grounded in right intentions, right actions, right outcomes, or right relationships – tends to focus on the moment of decision as the central question in ethics. Ecclesial ethicists point out a number of flaws in this approach. They argue it offers an inadequate description of an ethical situation if the circumstances, commitments, and characters of those most closely involved are not taken into account. Indeed, neglect of such details discloses an assumption that human beings are essentially isolated individuals. Conventional, universal ethics narrows the range of relevant material to identify a decision that needs to be made, a dilemma that is being faced, and a moment in which it is focused. It separates the presenting fact from the value that is presumed to lie behind it, locating ethics in the detached "value," and never questioning that such a separation not only can but must be done.

Subversive ethics (see Chapter Six) redescribes that moment and that decision by pointing out the power relationships and unspoken assumptions hidden within the decision and (in some cases) the whole construction of the need for and nature of the decision. It questions the separation of fact and value, and asks whether there are indeed value-free facts, pointing out why it might be so convenient for universal ethics to imagine that there were. Ecclesial ethics seeks to broaden the perspective so that all the information excluded by universal ethics becomes relevant again. Universal ethics excludes such information because it seems particular, and thus must be excluded if ethics is to concentrate on phenomena that have been or could be replicated in many other contexts. Ecclesial ethics points out that it is precisely this particular information, which universal ethics shuns, that makes ethics comprehensible.

We might illustrate this with a common, though emotive, example. A pregnant woman is considering an abortion. Universal ethics considers whether abortion is always wrong, is sometimes permissible, is likely to produce positive or negative outcomes for the woman and for society, and so on. Subversive ethics points out that the gender, race, and class and other such information about the woman make a huge difference to the judgments involved, quite possibly a decisive difference. Ecclesial ethics agrees, but highlights yet another dimension. What are the things that the woman and those close to her are taking for granted? Are abortions routine in her world, or catastrophic? How did the pregnancy come about, and did it arise from habitual behavior or a turn of events that was out of character? Is the woman part of a community in which these events are connected with a story larger than her own?

"Decisionist" ethics has two principal weaknesses, from this point of view.

- The first is that most people live most of their lives by habit rather than by choice. They do what they do not because they decide to do so, but because of the kind of people they are. If ethics is to concern the whole of life, and not just the momentary crisis, it has to address the way people shape their whole lives. The convictions that go so far toward making people what they are do so by forming a person's descriptions of the world and determine the shape of such dilemmas as present themselves.
- The second weakness of decisionist ethics is that those decisions that do come along are not made in a vacuum. They arise out of existing commitments – so much so that those who appear to have made noble decisions are sometimes almost unaware of having done so, because their convictions simply ruled out alternative courses of action.

In short, ethics becomes a matter less of making good decisions than of making good people. For it is good people who make good decisions. It is very common in contemporary culture to hear someone say, "He was a good kid who just made some bad choices." While no doubt sharing the sense of mercy and compassion behind such a statement, ecclesial ethicists would tend to be highly skeptical of its content. Good kids, in this tradition, do not make bad choices. Good kids are those who have been so schooled, so formed, so trained that they have learned to take the right things for granted. The moral life is partly about hedging inevitable aspects of temptation and human frailty with regularized patterns of activity, accountable authority, intimate support, and clarity of purpose, such that what would otherwise seem irresistible seems instead to be irrelevant. This is what is meant by character, perhaps the most used word in ecclesial ethics. Character is a kind of power that is developed and strengthened by certain kinds of activities and commitments, and leaves one far from impregnable but certainly not defenseless in the face of inevitable sin, abiding temptation, and agonizing decision.

Character emerges as a theme in ethics as a mean between two extremes. One is the indeterminist idea that the human will can choose to do whatever it likes, and is the only factor in moral decision-making. The other is the determinist idea that humans have no independence of will but are entirely shaped by factors such as environment, genes, and diet. Character emerges as a way of talking about human action and decision-making (together known as "agency") in a way that acknowledges human situatedness in given contexts but still recognizes the reality of human freedom.

Thus, it is character, rather than decision, that emerges as the center of ecclesial ethics. And because character directs attention to the ways people are formed to take the right things for granted, attention in ecclesial ethics moves to focus on these ways. The philosopher Iris Murdoch (1919–99) is reputed to have said, "We resort to decisions when we have tried everything else." Character ethics refers to that "everything else."

Virtue and Practices

When Plato and Aristotle spoke of those powers that enabled persons to maintain their integrity and character in the face of temptation and oppression, they spoke the language of virtue. In his *Republic* Plato lists four cardinal virtues, based on his threefold division of the human soul between appetite, spirit, and intellect. Appetite yields the virtue of temperance, spirit that of fortitude, while intellect yields the virtue of prudence. Justice orders these three other virtues in a hierarchy that places intellect, and its virtue of prudence, at the top. Plato believed in the unity of the virtues: anyone who embodied one of them should necessarily embody all of them. There could be no true justice that did not require courage and temperance, for example.

Aristotle's account of virtue in his *Nicomachean Ethics* is widely, though not universally, accepted in ecclesial ethics circles. Some have noted that his description of virtue applies only to a small, privileged class of men, and have sought to adapt his insights for a wider context. Aristotle sees three dimensions of the human soul – passions, faculties, and states of character. "Passions" refer to desires and feelings; these arise involuntarily in response to circumstances, and are not the cause of praise or blame, and are thus not virtues. "Faculties" refer to natural capacities or abilities, which again attract praise or blame only when suitably applied. "States of character," by contrast, are dispositions to act in particular ways in particular circumstances – and it is here that virtue resides. But not all states of character are virtues. Here the key term is the "mean." Virtues, in the most influential (but not the only) description offered by Aristotle, are those states of character that lie at the mean between excess and deficiency. To be a person of virtue is to have learned to steer a course between being too forward and too withdrawn, too passionate and too cool, too prodigal and too thrifty. Courage steers between the excess of rashness and the deficiency of cowardice; temperance steers between the excess of intemperance and the deficiency of insensibility; magnanimity is a mean between the excess of vanity and the deficiency of timidity.

Augustine is more informed by Plato than by Aristotle, but is more open than Plato to distinctions among the virtues. These arise, for him, not because of a lack of unity of the soul but because of a diversity in the range of contexts wherein the virtues are exhibited. Meanwhile Augustine recognized, in addition to the four cardinal virtues, three theological virtues: faith, hope, and love. Augustine inverted the relationship between love and the cardinal virtues, by describing virtue as perfect love of God. Thus, all four cardinal virtues were forms of love:

> temperance is love keeping itself entire and incorrupt for God; fortitude is love bearing everything readily for the sake of God; justice is love serving God only, and therefore ruling well all else, as subject to man; prudence is love making a right distinction between what helps it towards God and what might hinder it.

Instead of love being a function of the virtues, the virtues become functions of our love for God. Virtue is thus "rightly ordered love." Thomas Aquinas, who followed Augustine closely in relation to these matters, yet incorporated most of Aristotle's understanding of virtue, described love as the form of the virtues.

It is this language that MacIntyre seeks to recover in the constructive argument of *After Virtue*. To understand what MacIntyre is looking for in invoking the term virtue requires an introduction to three subsidiary terms that together constitute the notion for MacIntyre.

- The first of these terms is *practice*. The term "practice" refers to "any coherent and cooperative form of socially established cooperative human activity through which goods internal to that form of activity are realized in the course of trying to achieve those standards of excellence which are appropriate to, and partially definitive of, that form of activity, with the result that human powers to achieve excellence, and human conceptions of the ends and goods involved, are systematically extended." MacIntyre offers examples such as farming, fishing, football, and chess, together with science and the arts. His key point is that Aristotelian (and to some extent medieval) politics was a practice, whereas modern politics is not.
- The second term is *telos*. If one imagines the moral life as a quest, with a particular destination in mind, then the virtues are those qualities that enable one to sustain the quest until one reaches or realizes the goal, or (in Greek) *telos*. The

telos is the final end, the ultimate purpose of life. MacIntyre notes that this quest for the good enables one to order all other goods in relation to it. And, as is common with medieval quest stories, the journey is as important as the goal: "a quest is always an education both as to the character of that which is sought and in self-knowledge." Sometimes consequential ethics, which evaluates alternative courses of action according to their likely outcomes, is known as teleological ethics. But here ecclesial ethics claims "teleological" to mean not just outcome but final goal: the timeframe and scope of the question are entirely different. One example of a teleological approach is the motto of the Scots-American Presbyterian pastor Peter Marshall (1902–49): "It is better to fail in a cause that will finally succeed than to succeed in a cause that will finally fail." The motto arose in the context of the Northern Irish Troubles and led to actions – such as attempts to bring together terrorists and families of those they had killed – that would seldom have been commended within a consequential approach.

- The third term is *tradition*. Virtues are qualities required to sustain and replenish ongoing social traditions. For MacIntyre, a living tradition is a healthy form of ongoing conflict. It is "an historically extended, socially embodied argument, and an argument precisely in part about the goods which constitute that tradition." Meanwhile traditions are sustained and strengthened, weakened or destroyed, in large part by "the exercise or lack of exercise of the relevant virtues." What destroys traditions is precisely lack of courage, lack of justice, lack of truthfulness. There can be no justice without just people to implement just laws and keep just customs. Stanley Hauerwas develops his notion of the virtues alongside MacIntyre and employs these key terms in similar ways. What Hauerwas adds that MacIntyre omits is a specific conception of sin. For Hauerwas sin resides in seeing character and virtue as an achievement rather than a gift. It is "the positive attempt to overreach our power as creatures," and its fundamental form is self-deception. The heart of sin is "the assumption that we are the creators of the history through which we acquire and possess our character." Thus, sin is rooted in unbelief – distrust that one is the creature of a gracious creator.

The terms *telos*, practice, and tradition are closely interrelated. Practices, for example, both sustain and are nourished by traditions; and the repetition of practices can shape the practitioner toward a specific *telos*. And all three are needed to understand the notion of virtue.

Habits and Formation

How do people come to take the right things for granted? Proponents of ecclesial ethics talk extensively about the formation of character, and among this literature four themes stand out.

Traditions of the kind that MacIntyre describes are fostered in *communities*, and character is formed by being reared or shaped within such a community.

Thus, moral convictions become like the sea in which a fish learns to swim. Community is the place where one learns the significance of language; indeed language, in its invisibility and yet its integral relation to community, is a common theme in ecclesial ethics, particularly in those more Protestant strands influenced by Lindbeck. Learning a language is an analogy for being formed by a moral community, but it is also a demonstration of the way one can be taught to see new things in new ways, by allowing oneself to be clothed with the culture of a people. Because of the emphasis on stable communities with deep roots and carefully ordered practices, links have been made between ecclesial ethics and both communitarian political commitments and ecological agrarian movements. Writers more influenced by Hauerwas and Lindbeck than by MacIntyre have tended at this point to make more explicit the distinctions between community in general and church in particular, and highlight the significance of the latter while accepting and in some cases welcoming analogies and common themes with the former.

Character is formed by the regular and disciplined performance of practices that after long exercise emerge as *habits*. Aristotle distinguished between those capabilities acquired through nature and those skills developed through practice. Here he hints at a similarity between growing in virtue (notably justice, temperance, and bravery) and developing skills in the arts (especially building and playing the lyre). He goes on to distinguish between the internal state of virtue and the external actions of virtue. And the key point here is that one may cultivate the internal state by practicing the external actions. This is highly significant because many would describe such behavior – to do something good that one does not feel – as hypocrisy. By contrast those influenced by Aristotle and commending ecclesial ethics would say that it is precisely by training in virtue (or pretending) that one becomes virtuous – what Herdt describes as "putting on" virtue. As Aristotle says, "by being habituated to despise things that are terrible and to stand our ground against them we become brave, and it is when we have become so that we shall be most able to stand our ground against them." Thus, anyone might do a virtuous deed, but only a person trained in virtue would do such a deed virtuously.

The analogy with the arts and the shift from locating ethics primarily in actions or outcomes brings to the fore the moral *imagination*. The early writing of Hauerwas is much influenced by the philosophy of Iris Murdoch and its emphasis on vision. In Murdoch's view, we act in the world that we see, and thus moral training is concerned with learning to see aright. In this sense conversion is like putting on a new set of spectacles – or taking off a pair of blinkers. Hauerwas and MacIntyre are much interested in the role of the novel, especially in authors such as Anthony Trollope (1815–82) and Jane Austen (1775–1817). They see fiction as a significant way in which one can probe a number of likely outcomes and explore the formation, depths, and complexities of character. While the moment of decision is undoubtedly (in universal ethics) one that calls upon the full extent of the agent's imagination, proponents of ecclesial ethics are more likely to locate the key aspect of imagination in the period of formation. The aim is to shape the imagination of persons by so training them in community through habit-formation within a tradition that they learn to take the right things for granted and thus at the moment of decision act apparently effortlessly without anxiety or dismay. All the moral "effort" has taken place previously.

In recent writing this concern for formation of the imagination has focused on the significance of worship in honing the habits and moral imagination of Christians. Ecclesial ethics has taken a turn toward stressing the liturgical shape of the moral life, one framed by prayer, shaped by sacrament, inscribed by scripture reading, renewed by confession and reconciliation, and displayed by practices such as footwashing and preaching. In Hauerwas' words:

> Baptism and eucharist are not just 'religious things' that Christian people do. They are the essential rituals of our politics. Through them we learn who we are. Instead of being motives or causes for effective social work on the part of Christian people, these liturgies *are* our effective social work. For if the church *is* rather than has a social ethic, these actions are our most important social witness.

Narrative

For MacIntyre, what makes it possible to think of human lives having a *telos* is the fact that they are already structured as a narrative. Human beings are essentially storytelling animals. And these stories are inextricably interwoven with one another: "I can only answer the question 'What am I to do?' if I can answer the prior question 'Of what story or stories do I find myself a part?'" Meanwhile manners, culture, and social roles are embedded in narratives: "There is no way to give us an understanding of any society, including our own, except through the stock of stories which constitute its initial dramatic resources."

Narrative has become a pervasive theme in contemporary theology. Its widespread use tends to mask some significant variations in the way the term narrative is employed and understood. In relation to ecclesial ethics, there are broadly four uses of the term, and they help to distinguish different emphases within this emerging tradition.

- The first identifies the ways the self (or agent) is situated in a context, or rather a number of contexts, from which it cannot simply be abstracted for the purpose of coming to a moment of decision. There is no "real self" outside the relationships and stories that embed the self in a context. This is broadly MacIntyre's notion of narrative. To ask, in the crisis moment, "What should I do?" may well miss the more significant "Who (or what) am I?" and thus the more obviously narratival "How have I come to be here?"
- The second use credits narrative with the ability to make a coherent whole out of separate events and realities in one's life: an individual who can do this has established an identity; a community that can do this has established a tradition.

This tends to be the emphasis of Stanley Hauerwas' writing prior to 1981. He points out that conventional ethics tries to study the self outside such a narrative setting, and thus overlooks most if not all of what "matters" about the self. These two claims about narrative are formal ones – that is to say, they characterize ethics in a general sense, and would belong as a subdivision of universal ethics.

- The third use of the term refers to the way MacIntyre and Milbank especially, but a number of imitators after them, have traced a "declension narrative" from a time when ethics made some kind of sense, to a period (today) when it no longer does. These stories of decline have such polemical power that they have come to characterize the whole field, even though many in the field would dispute or even reject them.

  For example, Oliver O'Donovan is profoundly concerned to avoid identifying the truth of God with any process of outworking over time, a tendency he connects particularly with Hegel and, as we have noted, calls "historicism." So, for O'Donovan, even though he laments the loss of the rich tradition of political theology represented at its apex by Hugo Grotius (1583–1645), there is no "fall" by which the fruits of this tradition are in any damaging form inaccessible today. O'Donovan is deeply opposed to what he describes as "voluntarism" – the assumption that ethics is a matter of somewhat arbitrary choice, command, and commitment, rather than being woven into the fabric of God's creating purpose. This opposition arises largely because he sees no way to stop such assumptions turning into wholesale moral relativism. Thus, as we have already seen, O'Donovan is a kind of bridge figure, with one foot in ecclesial ethics (because of his emphasis on particular revelation) and another in universal ethics (because of his insistence on universal application).

- The fourth sense of narrative, which eventually becomes dominant in Hauerwas' thinking, is explicitly about Christian ethics in particular. It marks the difference between teleology, which is about orienting actions toward an ultimate (but humanly attainable) goal, and eschatology, which is about acting in the light of a final destiny that can only be received as a gift from God. In his *With the Grain of the Universe* (2001) Hauerwas argues that the cross and resurrection of Jesus are in fact a natural theology, because of the claim that these unique events disclose the character and action of God in such a way that they constitute "the grain of the universe." Reading the Bible though the lens of cross and resurrection discloses what the grain of the universe means in narrative form. This includes the covenant with Israel, its recapitulation in Jesus, and its display and performance over again in the history of the church. What accords with and amplifies these events – notably the witness of martyrs who have died rather than deny their Lord – portrays what it means to live with the grain of the universe. What does not accord with these events – notably war and violence – goes against the grain, and is thus in a fundamental way unnatural. Obedience to Christ is thus participation in the very nature of God.

This is provocative because it is nothing less than a reconstruction of the term "natural" as used in ethics. Previously ecclesial ethics (with the exception of O'Donovan, who, as we have seen, is a far from central figure in this tradition) has kept something of a distance from the term natural, seeing it as a password into universal ethics. But Hauerwas develops the full philosophical implications of ecclesial ethics by recognizing how the notion of nature needs to be redescribed once the cross and resurrection are placed at the center of history.

This last move threatens to split ecclesial ethics apart as a coherent tradition, in ways we shall now examine.

The Christological Turn

The theologian who inspired Hauerwas' turn to grounding ethics in the definitive narrative of Christ, Israel, and the church was the Mennonite John Howard Yoder (1927–97). Yoder's early theological engagements were largely concerned with Anabaptist history and with the ecumenical movement. The second half of his career was directed toward the themes that make his work so challenging for ecclesial ethics – namely, his insistence that pacifism is a central, if not *the* central, Christian practice.

A shadow hangs over Yoder's legacy. It has emerged that Yoder seriously misused his power in pursuing sexual relationships with and harassing as many as one hundred women over more than thirty years. This raises two questions about his theology. The first is a general one: is the work of a theologian who is discovered to have profound moral flaws to be accordingly set aside? The tradition with errant clergy has been that the failure of the priest does not invalidate the sacrament; the same principle may be said to apply to theologians and their publications. Yet, while perhaps not wholly discredited, Yoder's legacy is nonetheless deeply damaged.

The second question is more specific: are Yoder's failings inextricably related to his ethics? In short, how could a pacifist so abuse power in relationships with so many women? Karen Guth (b. 1979), who teaches at the College of the Holy Cross in Massachusetts, calls for ecclesial ethicists who follow Yoder to develop a pacifism that incorporates the insights of feminism, especially feminist analysis of patriarchy and the societal structures that enable gendered violence, and that attends not only to the violence of war but to sexual violence as well: "… a Christian witness of peace cannot be limited to resisting war." In response to Yoder's actions, Guth draws on both ecclesial (what she calls "witness") and subversive (feminist) traditions to map out a restorative-justice approach, with an emphasis on truth-telling and communal responses to all forms of violence.

The abiding validity of Yoder's work depends on whether he fell far short of his own vision, or whether his whole account of ethics is flawed beyond redemption. David Cramer, Jenny Howell, Jonathan Tran, and Paul Martens take the former view, suggesting that Yoder's pacifism itself articulates precisely what was wrong with his actions. They cite Yoder's own definition of the word violence, offered in an unpublished essay:

> 'Violence' is thus meaningless apart from the concept of that which is being violated. That which is violated is the dignity or integrity of some being. ... As soon as either verbal abuse or bodily coercion moves beyond that border line of loving enhancement of the dignity of persons, we are being violent. The extremes of the two dimensions are of course killing and the radical kind of insult which Jesus in Matthew 5 indicates *is just as bad*. I believe it is a Christian imperative always to respect the dignity of every person: I must never willingly or knowingly violate that dignity.

Jesus as Normative for Ethics

In the opening chapter of his book *The Politics of Jesus* (1972/1994), Yoder confronts the catalogue of reasons put forward to explain why the life of Jesus is seldom considered normative by those concerned with Christian ethics. It is said (1) that Jesus was assuming an interim period, before the final eschaton, which he expected to be very brief. "The rejection of violence, of self-defense, and of accumulating wealth for the sake of security, and the footlooseness of the prophet of the kingdom are not permanent and generalizable attitudes toward social values." The survival of society thereby "takes on a weight which Jesus did not give it." It is said (2) that Jesus was a simple agrarian figure whose ethic only makes sense in a village sociology of face-to-face relations. Or, it is said (3) that Jesus was operating in a world over which he and his followers had no control, and the church must adapt to different circumstances where it is a powerful social force. Or, it is said (4) that Jesus was concerned with the spiritual not the social, with matters of the heart rather than movements of history, with the infinite not with the mundane. Or, it is said (5) that he came to die, to atone by his death for human sin, to transform humanity's place before God – not to prescribe a particular ethic. Among other arguments are (6) historical-critical skepticism about whether the text provides sufficiently accurate witness to the reality of Jesus' words and deeds; (7) skepticism that a single coherent ethic can be elicited from diverse and sometimes divergent texts; or (8) the desire to balance the particular activity of the Son with the more general considerations and commitments evoked by the Father and the Holy Spirit.

Yoder notes that the conventional alternatives to the life of Jesus are drawn from themes such as nature, reason, creation, and reality. He observes that advocates of each seem to claim that its meaning is self-evident; that each is hard to define precisely for ethical guidance, especially in regard to dissent; that each appears to differ in substance from the ethic propounded by Jesus; and yet that each seems to be granted a higher or deeper authority than Jesus. Yoder dismisses most of these assumptions as falling victim to the early heresy known as Ebionism; that is, they fail to do justice to the divinity of Christ. Meanwhile he criticizes those assumptions that make the person (and life) of Jesus subordinate to his saving work on the cross as falling into the trap of the early heresy known as Docetism; that is, they fail to do justice to the humanity of Christ.

Instead Yoder maintains that Jesus faced the same issues and pressures that Christians do today. Like his contemporary followers, he cared for the downtrodden and oppressed, longed for justice to roll down, and could see the potential of attaining political power. He chose servanthood and forgiveness as his path – and Yoder proposes that this is a path not just for Jesus, but for all who follow him. In drawing on Jesus' life as a paradigm for Christian ethics, Yoder steers a path between two mistaken poles. On the one hand there are those who advocate a step-by-step imitation of Jesus' lifestyle. Yoder sees no call to Christians to wander barefoot without regular sources of income, to renounce property wholesale, to adopt an artisan or single life, or to spend significant time on mountains or in the wilderness. Meanwhile there are those who select one rather arbitrary and abstract feature of Jesus' ministry – such as love or humility or faith – for translation into Christian life. Neither of these offers a concrete political alternative to what Yoder calls "Caesar" – the governing political authority of the time. Imitating Jesus instead means one thing above all: the voluntary suffering of the cross in the face of enmity and power.

Yoder explains that the cross was not a painful sickness or sudden inexplicable catastrophe (as suggested by the phrase "we all have our cross to bear"); nor was it an emblem of every variety of suffering. It was not the path of quietism and withdrawal (the Essene way). It was not the path of conservative social responsibility (the Sadducee way). It was not the path of violent revolution or crusade (Barabbas' way). It was the climax of a freely chosen path that refused violence but instead insisted on loving the enemy, demonstrating to the world the reality of the realm to come. This path led to the cross – and it still does.

Discipleship and Constantinianism

What Yoder is asking of ethics in general and ecclesial ethics in particular is an alteration in its understanding of what constitutes politics. For a theologian like O'Donovan the practices of the church that arise from faith in cross and resurrection – confession and reconciliation, for example, or footwashing – are socially significant but could not be described as politics. Milbank, by contrast, would agree with Yoder that forgiveness constitutes the heart of Christian politics. Yoder maintains that such practices are what politics means, and invites a comparative study of the politics of "Caesar" with the politics of the church. For Yoder politics is not about the inevitably impoverished practices of distribution of limited goods by compromised officials – even if those officials are restored as MacIntyre would have them be by an Aristotelian notion of virtue. Instead politics becomes the art of what the imagination makes possible when set free from the dominance of armies, markets, and the fear of death.

Yoder himself has a kind of declension narrative, because he privileges the social location of the early church. The conversion of the Emperor Constantine at the start of the fourth century marks the turn for the worse in Christian social ethics. In two sentences in his book *The Priestly Kingdom* (1984), Yoder sums up what this fall meant:

> Before Constantine, one knew as a fact from everyday experience that there was a believing Christian community but one had to "take it on faith" that God was governing history. After Constantine, one had to believe without seeing that there was a community of believers, within the larger nominally Christian mass, but one knew for a fact that God was in control of history.

Eschatology, the study of the end-times, and ecclesiology, the study of the church, swapped places. Now attention shifted from what was mandatory for all believers to what was possible for rulers. In his *The Christian Witness to the State* (1964) Yoder outlines a variety of historical perceptions of social ethics. Each is Constantinian: they all assume the options are either "responsibility" or "withdrawal." The law of non-resistant love, which most interpreters have regarded as the gospel's distinctive ethic, is displaced in favor of an autonomous moral absolute such as responsibility, creation, or natural law. These approaches claim Christlike authority yet call people to do things that Christ does not call them to do.

For Yoder, therefore, it is discipleship, not responsibility, that is at the center of Christian social ethics. He does not take it for granted that Christianity has access to power or even to a majority of those in a society – quite the opposite, in fact. He asks two questions that demonstrate the way his notion of ethics differs from that of those who assume Christians have a stake in the world's survival in more or less its current form.

> Instead of asking about one's action "If I do this, how will it tip the scale … ?", one rather asks "in a situation in which I cannot tip the scales, on what other grounds might I decide what to do?" … If everyone gave their wealth away, what would we do for capital? If everyone loved their enemies, who would ward off the Communists? … Such reasoning remains ludicrous wherever committed Christians accept realistically their minority status. Far more fitting than "What if everybody did it?" would be its inverse, "What if nobody else acted like a Christian, but we did?"

Nonviolence as the Key

For John Howard Yoder and the later work of Stanley Hauerwas, nonviolence becomes the key to Christian ethics. All the perceptions of neo-Aristotelian ethics described above – virtue, character, habits, practices, formation, narrative – need to be reassessed. That reassessment takes place from the vantage point of the two central decisions – God's decision to be fully revealed in the fully human and fully divine Christ, and God's decision in Christ to face the world's rejection and enmity by going voluntarily to the cross rather than responding with conformity or violence. For Yoder and Hauerwas nonviolence is not a clever tactic that harnesses public relations and mass movements and thus resolves conflict more effectively; it may do this, but sometimes it will actually make the world a more violent place. Yet it is faithful simply because it is following the way of Christ, and is thus in line with the grain of the universe.

Yoder and Hauerwas are not the only ones to have raised questions about the capability of Aristotelian virtue to translate into a Christian ethic. John Milbank, although not himself a pacifist, highlights in his *Theology and Social Theory* the way the soldier becomes the paradigm of virtue in Aristotle's scheme, and thus the way the whole notion of virtue presupposes violence. By contrast for Aquinas, as Hauerwas acknowledges, the paradigm of virtue is the martyr. Elsewhere the distinction between antique and Christian virtue has been drawn between the hero (a term never cited in the New Testament) and the saint (mentioned sixty-four times in the New Testament, always in the plural).

It is above all nonviolence that makes ethics ecclesial – not, again, because only ecclesial ethics can be nonviolent (there are other rationales for nonviolence, in Christianity, in other faiths, and in philosophical ethics) – but because nonviolence requires the kind of disciplined training and constant practice that only a committed community can foster. For Hauerwas and Yoder, pacifism creates politics, because it is constantly shaping and searching for practices that enable the resolution of conflicts that avoid the resort to violence.

Because pacifism requires such an intentional community, it will constantly be at risk of being described as sectarian. There is no criticism that Hauerwas rejects more vehemently, since he sees the term "sectarian" as indicating an assumption that the fundamental unit of Christian morality is the state – whereas for him it is the church. He insists that Christians should participate in public activities and offices and responsibilities, so long as they do so as Christians. It is unlikely, for example, that they will be elected to public office more than once, since speaking of final ends, seeking nonviolent resolutions, and refusing to tell lies will make them uncomfortable leaders.

In his more polemical moments Hauerwas maintains that it is not the church that is sectarian, for it has no walls and crosses every barrier. On the contrary it is the nation-state that is sectarian, for it demands that one Christian should be prepared to kill another Christian for the sake of an abstract ideal such as freedom or self-determination. For Yoder, the key question for a Christian is, "How can I be a reconciling presence in the life of my neighbor?" This may yield a diversity of responses dependent on context, but it is hard to see how it can ever involve killing.

Nonviolence – and its explicitly Christological derivation – emerges as the fault-line that runs between two overlapping, but fundamentally distinct, traditions in ecclesial ethics.

- On the one hand there is the tradition represented most explicitly by Alasdair MacIntyre, which prizes the classical tradition of the virtues and sees narrative and the church in largely generic categories as part of the vocabulary and practice of generating people of character who can engage in the public sphere while seeking goods that have a genuinely teleological, or ultimate, dimension.

- On the other hand lies John Howard Yoder, for whom there are no general categories, only the specific revelation of the cross and resurrection of Jesus as the axis of history, and the political manifestation of Jesus' journey to the cross as the definitive response of Christians to conflict and violence.
- In between lie the inheritors of Barth, notably George Lindbeck, whose general approach endorses Yoder's attention to the specificity of Jesus but whose broad categories seem to have more space for the self-disclosing purposes of creation, and Jennifer Herdt, who aligns herself with Barth in her commendation of comprehensive particularity. Similarly Oliver O'Donovan emphasizes the significance of Christ but sees Christ's resurrection as above all affirming the created order – and regards Yoder's approach as offering no defense against relativism.
- Meanwhile John Milbank also occupies a position between these two poles, offering a rhetoric apparently as distinctive as Yoder's, but assuming like O'Donovan that a Christianity that permeates the public sphere cannot begin with nonviolence.
- Finally there is Stanley Hauerwas, avowedly seeking to unite the Catholic vision lying within the arguments of MacIntyre and Milbank with the emphasis on revelation of Barth and O'Donovan, but with the subversive tone and commitments of Yoder. It is perhaps Hauerwas who most successfully harmonizes the diverse themes of ecclesial ethics, and who is most repeatedly criticized by those who believe such diverse themes are incapable of harmonization.

Fundamentally ecclesial ethics is not about a constellation of influential theologians but about relocating Christian ethics from the academy to the church, from the theories of philosophers to the practices of disciples, from the dilemmas of the textbook to the habits learned in Sunday school. Its claim is that it is in sacrament and sermon, in food kitchen and at hospital bedside, in daily prayer and in annual church finance meeting, rather than in John Rawls' original position or Immanuel Kant's categorical imperative, that the heart of ethics truly lies.

Critiques and Future Promise

There is a tendency for the key figures of ecclesial ethics to be Western, white males – a fact that limits its credibility in the view of some. While many of its adherents view themselves as living and working in contexts where Christianity has a reduced or minority social status, it still rather often resonates with a superior rhetorical tone. Perhaps the greatest evidence of its durability and importance is the fruit it has begun to bear as a second generation of Christian ethicists engage and extend the work of Hauerwas, Lindbeck, Milbank, MacIntyre, and O'Donovan, as we have already seen in the constructive work of Herdt, and which one can see in other projects such as William Cavanaugh's description of the Eucharist as the church's response to torture and disappearance in Chile. The variety of essays considering ethical issues in light of Christian practices in *The Blackwell Companion to Christian Ethics* (2004) also bears witness to the way that some ethicists have incorporated subversive concerns into their ecclesial reflections – for example, when Willie Jennings pairs baptism with racial identity, and when Lauren Winner considers the act of kneeling in prayer alongside gender roles.

Others have taken the integration of subversive and ecclesial ethics further. In her 2015 book *Christian Ethics at the Boundary: Feminism and Theologies of Public Life*, Karen Guth has sought to weave them together by placing representatives of three often isolated and sometimes antagonistic ethical approaches in conversation with one another: "realist" theology (Reinhold Niebuhr, whom we discussed in Chapter Five), "witness" theology (John Howard Yoder), and feminist theology (Martin Luther King Jr., who represents a feminist and womanist "politics of love").

Summary

Ecclesial ethics is not a term in wide current usage. This chapter has described it as a movement that shares many of the criticisms of universal ethics made by subversive ethicists, adds a few of its own, and then builds a constructive ethic centered around the practices of the church. But this description has not been widely articulated. The theologians highlighted in this chapter are diverse in style, in subject matter, and in choice of dialogue partners. For example, Hauerwas and MacIntyre are comfortable talking with Aristotle and Thomas Aquinas, but seldom venture into contemporary European philosophy in the way Milbank constantly does.

Nonetheless the thinkers examined in this chapter represent much of the dynamism in Christian ethics today. The narratives explored in the first section of the chapter have set a trajectory, and almost all writing in the field of Christian ethics has had to take note. The constructive agenda laid out in the second section of the chapter has a genuine claim to a place in ethical discussion, alongside conventional theories such as natural law, the categorical imperative, and utilitarianism. In the end, perhaps the most significant question posed by ecclesial ethics of other approaches (and of itself) is this. Is Jesus, in the example of his life and death, really the foundation of Christian ethics? This question is a suitable place to conclude Part Two of this book, since it goes back to a question voiced near the beginning of Part One.

It is now time to see how universal, subversive, and ecclesial ethics respond when faced with some of the most pressing issues and questions of our time.

References and Further Reading

Persuasive Narratives

Karl Barth's influential and magisterial work is the fourteen-volume *Church Dogmatics* (Edinburgh: T & T Clark, 1949). A helpful introduction to Barth's work is George Hunsinger's *How to Read Karl Barth* (New York: Oxford University Press, 1991).

George Lindbeck's threefold typology is laid out in *The Nature of Doctrine* (Philadelphia, PA: Westminster Press, 1984); see especially pages 16–19. Lindbeck's appeal to Aristotle's notion of rationality ("Reasonableness in religion and theology ...") is from page 130; the proposition "Jesus is Lord" is dealt with in pages 63–4.

A key work for Alasdair MacIntyre's thought is *After Virtue: A Study in Moral Theory* (2nd edn; London: Gerald Duckworth, 1990), a section of which is also included in the corresponding chapter of *Christian Ethics: An Introductory Reader*. His description of emotivism ("Detached from the theoretical and social contexts ...") is found on page 70 of his own summary of *After Virtue* provided in *The MacIntyre Reader* (Kelvin Knight, ed.; Cambridge: Polity Press, 1998). MacIntyre further explores emotivist ethics in chapters 2 and 3 of *After Virtue*. He continues to develop his argument in *Three Rival Versions of Moral Enquiry: Encyclopedia, Genealogy, and Tradition* (Notre Dame, IN: University of Notre Dame Press, 1990) and *Dependent Rational Animals* (Chicago, IL: Open Court, 1999).

John Milbank's key ambitious work is *Theology and Social Theory: Beyond Secular Reason* (2nd edn; Oxford; Malden, MA: Blackwell, 2006), a portion of which appears in the corresponding chapter of *Christian Ethics: An Introductory Reader*. Specific sections cited in the chapter are: "the coding of transcendental difference as peace" (page 6) and "univocity of being" (pages 303–4). James K. A. Smith describes Milbank's view of creation as "charged immanence" in *Introducing Radical Orthodoxy: Mapping a Post-Secular Theology* (Grand Rapids, MI: Baker, 2004), page 88, and his summary of the modern (as parody) is from page 89. Milbank's treatment of Nietzsche is most focused on pages 282–90; and his discussion of virtue (vis-à-vis Alasdair MacIntyre) is from pages 326–79.

Stanley Hauerwas' oft-quoted claim that the first task of the church is to be the church can be found in *The Peaceable Kingdom: A Primer in Christian Ethics* (Notre Dame, IN: University of Notre Dame Press, 1983), page 99. The same claim is previously made in *A Community of Character* (Notre Dame, IN: Notre Dame Press, 1981), page 84, where he also gives a description of liberalism as the "story that we have no story." His observation that in America the subject of Christian ethics has always been America is in *Against the Nations* (San Francisco, CA: Harper and Row, 1985), page 31. An excerpt from *The Peaceable Kingdom* is included in the corresponding chapter of *Christian Ethics: An Introductory Reader*. Samuel Wells provides a constructive introduction to Hauerwas' thought in *Transforming Fate into Destiny* (Eugene, OR: Cascade, 1998, 2004).

Oliver O'Donovan's key works are *The Desire of the Nations* (Cambridge; New York: Cambridge University Press, 1999); *Resurrection and Moral Order: An Outline for Evangelical Ethics* (2nd edn; Leicester, UK: Apollos; Grand Rapids, MI: Eerdmans, 1994); and *The Ways of Judgment* (Grand Rapids, MI: Eerdmans, 2005). O'Donovan's description of politics as "the theatre of the divine self-disclosure" is on page 82 of *Desire of the Nations*. His self-description as an evangelical and a realist is on pages vii, ix of the prefaces to *Resurrection and Moral Order*. His notions of voluntarism and nominalism may be found on pages 49–50 in *Resurrection and Moral Order*. The quotations from *The Ways of Judgment* are on pages 52–3 (limiting freedom) and page 233 (Christ's counterpolitical command to judge not).

Jennifer Herdt engages with liturgical ethics in her Afterword to *The Blackwell Companion to Christian Ethics*, Stanley Hauerwas and Samuel Wells, eds (2nd edn; Oxford: Wiley-Blackwell, 2011); quotations from pages 41 (see also 541) and 543. Her sustained study of Aquinas and the virtues is *Putting on Virtue: The Legacy of the Splendid Vices* (Chicago, IL: University of Chicago Press, 2008); quotation from page 223. Herdt's consideration of divine and human agency, and her analysis of the two types of particularism, may be found in "Hauerwas Among the Virtues," *Journal of Religious Ethics* 40, no. 2 (2012): 202–227; quotations from pages 209, 218, and 222. Finally, her reflections on virtue and the common good is in her essay "Back to Virtue," *Scottish Journal of Theology* 65, no. 2 (2012): 222–26; quotation from page 226.

The (Re)Turn to Virtue in Catholic Ethics

For Jean Porter's retrieval of Thomas Aquinas's virtue ethics, see *The Recovery of Virtue: The Relevance of Aquinas for Christian Ethics* (Louisville, KY: Westminster/John Knox, 1990); and *Moral Action and Christian Ethics* (Cambridge: Cambridge University Press, 1995).

The encyclical *Veritatis Splendor* is available at http://w2.vatican.va/content/john-paul-ii/en/encyclicals/documents/hf_jp-ii_enc_06081993_veritatis-splendor.html.

A New Aristotelianism

Plato describes the four cardinal virtues in *The Republic* (R. E. Allen, trans.; New Haven, CT: Yale University Press, 2006), Book IV, Section 3.

Aristotle's account of virtue is found in *Nicomachean Ethics* (Cambridge; New York: Cambridge University Press, 2000), Book II, chapters 5–9. His discussion of skills developed through practice and the quotation about bravery is found in *Nicomachean Ethics*, Book II, chapter 2.

Augustine describes the four cardinal virtues in *Of the Morals of the Catholic Church*, at the beginning of chapter 15 (available at www.logoslibrary.org/augustine/morals/15.html). Augustine also discusses the four virtues in *The City of God* (Henry Bettenson, trans.; New York: Penguin Books, 1972, 1984), Book 19, chapter 4, pages 853–7. The notion of virtue as "rightly ordered love" may

be found in *The City of God*, Book 15, chapter 22, page 637.

MacIntyre's ideas around practices, tradition, and narrative are in *After Virtue*, chapter 15. His definition of a practice is on page 207; his notion of the quest is particularly explored on page 219; his definition of a living tradition is on page 222; and the questions and comment quoted about stories in the chapter above are on page 216.

Hauerwas' view of sin may be found in *The Peaceable Kingdom*, pages 30–4 and 46–9; he also discusses baptism and Eucharist in *The Peaceable Kingdom*, pages 107–11. Hauerwas explores the cross and resurrection and natural theology in *With the Grain of the Universe* (Grand Rapids, MI: Brazos Press, 2001); see especially pages 15–17.

The Christological Turn

Karen V. Guth proposes a restorative justice approach to Yoder's actions in her essay "Doing Justice to the Complex Legacy of John Howard Yoder: Restorative Justice Resources in Witness and Feminist Ethics," *Journal of the Society of Christian Ethics* 35, no. 2 (2015): 119–39.

David Cramer, Jenny Howell, Jonathan Tran, and Paul Martens discuss Yoder's legacy at http://theotherjournal.com/2014/07/07/scandalizing-john-howard-yoder/.

John Howard Yoder lists the reasons why Jesus is not considered normative for ethics on pages 4–11 of his *Politics of Jesus* (2nd edn; Grand Rapids, MI: Eerdmans, 1994); a selection from this book is also quoted in the corresponding chapter of *Christian Ethics: An Introductory Reader*. Yoder's exploration of the imitation of Jesus is found especially on pages 112–33.

Yoder discusses Constantine in *The Priestly Kingdom* (Notre Dame, IN: University of Notre Dame

Press, 1984), page 137. He further explores what he calls Constantinian social ethics in *Christian Witness to the State* (Newton, KS: Faith and Life Press, 1964); see, e.g., page 56. Yoder's two questions (about acting like a Christian) are from *The Priestly Kingdom*, page 139. His key question ("How can I be a reconciling presence …") is in *What Would You Do?* (Scottdale, PA: Herald Press, 1983), page 40.

John Milbank critiques Aristotle's paradigm of virtue and Alasdair MacIntyre's use of it in *Theology and Social Theory*, pages 331–3, 347–53, 359–62. Hauerwas' discussion of Milbank's critique is in *Christians Among the Virtues: Theological Conversations with Ancient and Modern Ethics* (with Charles Pinches; Notre Dame, IN: University of Notre Dame Press, 1997), pages 61–8.

Critique and Future Promise

Ecclesial themes are prominent in William Cavanaugh's *Torture and Eucharist: Theology, Politics, and the Body of Christ* (Oxford: Wiley-Blackwell, 1998).

Karen Guth places feminist and ecclesial ethics in conversation with one another in *Christian Ethics at the Boundary: Feminism and Theologies of Public Life* (Minneapolis, MN: Fortress Press, 2015).

The following are additional readings on ecclesial ethics:

- Samuel Wells. *Improvisation* (London: SPCK; Grand Rapids, MI: Brazos Press, 2004); and *God's Companions* (Oxford; Malden, MA: Blackwell Publishing, 2006). A selection from *Improvisation* is also included in *Christian Ethics: An Introductory Reader*.

- Stanley Hauerwas and Samuel Wells, eds. *The Blackwell Companion to Christian Ethics*. Oxford; Malden, MA: Blackwell Publishing, 2006.
- Stanley Hauerwas. *The Hauerwas Reader* (John Berkman and Michael Cartwright, eds; Durham, NC: Duke University Press, 2001).

The following work is also quoted in the corresponding chapter of *Christian Ethics: An Introductory Reader*:

- Thomas Aquinas. *Summa Theologica*. 5 vols. Notre Dame, IN: Christian Classics, 1948. Also available at www.ccel.org/ccel/aquinas/summa.html. From Prima Secundae [First Part of the Second Part], Question 55, Question 61, and Question 65.

Part Three

The Questions Asked
of Christian Ethics

The first part of this book set the *context* for the discipline of Christian ethics, establishing the *history* and *traditions* within which those writing and exploring ethics today sit, whether they know and acknowledge it or not. The second part discussed the *method* and *audience* of Christian ethics, recognizing that there is no single approach, nor even one single group of approaches, but several – at least three – overlapping and contrasting approaches to the discipline, which vary in their estimation of what ethics is and for whom it is practiced.

This third part looks at the *subject matter* of Christian ethics, namely those issues and questions that present themselves to Christians and others as pressing and controversial. These are issues on which people of good conscience disagree, and yet because they are, or have a close bearing on, what Augustine called "common objects of love," they are matters on which careful deliberation is necessary if not vital for personal and communal well-being. Because ethics has, since classical times, deliberated on the nature and nurture of the good, each of the following chapters is designed as an examination of the good in relation to different aspects of human existence.

We begin in this chapter with "Good Order," taking the ancient Greek assumption that the well-being of the individual depends on the prior well-being of the social organism of which the individual is inevitably a part. The issues considered here are all ones of what is generally called the "state," inasmuch as they deal with government, law and order, and warfare.

We then move in Chapter Nine to what we term "Good Life." This refers to questions that, while they clearly involve the state and they clearly involve the individual, lie somewhere between the interests of the two: questions of economics, wealth, and poverty; issues of work and the workplace; and the possibilities and perils of communication and the media.

Next we have two chapters – "Good Relationships" (Chapter Ten) and "Good Beginnings and Endings" (Chapter Eleven) – which, while obviously having wider dimensions, including in some cases legislative aspects, are generally regarded as bearing on more personal concerns. Chapter Ten considers questions related to friendship, marriage, and sexuality; while Chapter Eleven looks at the complex area known as bioethics or medical ethics.

Chapter Twelve is entitled "Good Earth." This has the broad canvas of the chapter on good order but also the intermediate quality of the chapter on good life, for the issues involved in dealing well with the environment have to be addressed at so many levels. They are matters that require state policies and both international and civic cooperation, but they are also matters of personal responsibility and relationship.

Each chapter considers three distinct but overlapping issues. Each issue is introduced by an overview of the historical and scriptural dimensions most frequently cited. Of course, as demonstrated in Part Two, the very description of each issue itself contains its own presuppositions and claims – for example, as soon as one chooses to use the term "prostitute" rather than "sex worker," one has made a significant moral judgment. Nonetheless, these introductory treatments seek to be as even-handed as possible. Each issue is then considered under the respective approaches of universal, subversive, and ecclesial ethics. In some cases universal and subversive approaches look similar; in some cases subversive and ecclesial approaches look similar; in other cases ecclesial and universal approaches look similar; sometimes they all look very different from one another.

In almost every case, however, the threefold approach to the issue brings to the surface perspectives and convictions that not only shed light on the issue, but reflect back on the respective methods employed. The point is not to see the three approaches as mutually exclusive, but to recognize the underlying commitments of the respective approaches. One writer might take an essentially ecclesial approach while still adopting insights from the subversive strand; another might blend a universal with an ecclesial outlook. Thomas Aquinas, for example, draws from both the universal and the ecclesial; Pope Francis displays sympathy with all three approaches. In practice, few figures fit neatly or exclusively into one single approach; nonetheless, clearly naming and describing the respective approaches can clarify otherwise unstated commitments.

Chapter Eight
Good Order

The State

Scripture

Jesus submitted to worldly government, but he reminded government that its power was not arbitrary human will but "a gift from above" (John 19:11). This tension between the obligations of citizenship and the clear-sighted referral of human dominion to God's higher judgment has underlain all Christian reflection about good order. In most periods, Christians have sought to varying degrees to relativize the authority of the state, its laws and its power. They have looked at the power of the state in the light of the cross, which reveals humanity's radical denial of God in the name of violence and basic self-interest. Only in that context have Christians then appraised the necessity of human rule for continued life in creation. Life may still need to be under government, but government is best when it knows that the roots of its validity lie in the ultimate rule of God over all things; government which is both established and judged by the priority and ultimacy of God's government, under which it stands. The church stands first and foremost under the sovereignty of God, and only in *that* relation does it stand also under the authority of earthly rulers, earthly laws, and earthly swords.

The roots of this chastened view of state authority go back all the way to the earliest days of kingship in ancient Israel, where the monarchy was subjected to constant critique. A central authority figure having been called for by the people because of the moral anarchy that reigned under the judges (a regime in which everyone suited themselves), the monarch was subsequently presented as a very ambiguous blessing. The biblical model of constrained monarchism insisted that the king is not to exalt himself over others in the community, and is daily to subject

Introducing Christian Ethics, Second Edition. Samuel Wells and Ben Quash with Rebekah Eklund.
© 2017 John Wiley & Sons Ltd. Published 2017 by John Wiley & Sons Ltd.

himself to the teachings of Torah. In the New Testament, Jesus models a comparably limited kingship. It is a servant kingship that neither abdicates authority nor grasps after control. And he leaves for his church this pattern of a vulnerable authority that all the time makes itself transparent to the authority of God.

Tradition: Continuities between Early and Late

The category of the *state* may be distinguished from the idea of *society*:

- State usually denotes an institution in which political power and authority are seated.
- Society is not straightforwardly an institution at all (though it may contain and engender institutions).

It is commonplace today to think of the life of a society as being ordered and directed by the organs of state. But the modern nation-state owes much to political developments in the seventeenth century, and especially to the Peace of Westphalia in 1648. This political settlement was made up of two treaties signed successively at Osnabrück and Münster (both now in modern Germany). It marked the end of the Thirty Years' War in Europe, a protracted religious conflict between Catholics and Protestants that had entailed horrendous bloodshed and destruction. The peace required all parties to forget and forgive the atrocities that had preceded it; it defined the sovereignty and independence of European states; and at the same time it invited them to "a faithful neighborliness" in which each would seek the good of the others on the same terms as its own good – providing a model for the later idea of a family of nations. Only in the wake of that settlement did the state gain a developed and recognizably modern idea of its own sovereignty within its territories, and its right to freedom from interference by other similarly sovereign states. So the forms of political authority that make their appearance in the Old and New Testaments are not always clearly mappable onto our own. Neither are the feudal orders of medieval Christendom.

Despite these important historical developments, the nature of something like the "state" as it is sketched by Augustine in Book XIX of *The City of God* bears a striking resemblance to that characterized by the nineteenth-century English churchman and theologian John Henry Newman (1801–90) a millennium and a half later. Both actually tie their definitions of the "state" *closely* to their understanding of "society." For Augustine, the political entity in question is a *res publica*, a republic, and it is something like the sum of the values, or loves, of its individual members. Augustine takes Cicero's definition of the republic as an assemblage associated by:

1. a common acknowledgment of right; and
2. a community of interests.

Augustine then chooses to stress the second of Cicero's two criteria: the role played by a community of interests. So his own definition of a republic is: "an assemblage of reasonable beings bound together by a common agreement concerning the objects of their love." Augustine's definition deliberately focuses attention upon what his biographer Peter Brown calls "that 'middle distance' of human habits, values, and instincts which, far more than its [formal] structure, remains the greatest mystery of political society." We are linked to political society by something that somehow escapes our immediate consciousness (we do not, as in the terms of later myths of the state, *will* political society). This emphasis on the direction of one's love, concern, or esteem as the criterion of an organized society offered a way to explain the link between a given form of political structure and "what could be broadly called a civilization" (Brown): a set of traditionally accepted values. The state is not, for Augustine, an entity in itself; the state is the solidarity of the human beings of which it is composed, and its character is determined by the character of its citizens. Also implicit in his thought (and made explicit by the medieval thinkers who followed him) is the inference that the state in turn maintains specific values, and preserves the ends and loves to which its members attach themselves.

John Henry Newman shows the extraordinary durability of this Augustinian tradition when he writes:

> In every nation there will be found ... a certain assemblage of beliefs, convictions, rules, usages, traditions, proverbs and principles; some political, some social, some moral: and these tending towards some definite form of government and "modus vivendi", or polity, as their natural scope. ... This, then, is the constitution of a state: securing, as it does, the national unity.

Newman's stress, like Augustine's, is on the organic character of the state. It is the cumulative product of the assembled priorities and interests of the socially constituted human beings who make it up. A common thread running from one thinker to the other is the idea that individuals are not functionaries of a pre-existing state, nor is humanity's purpose to be understood reductively as service of the good of the state. To the contrary, the state is to serve the good of humanity, and it is to do so by serving the will of God. Here we may bring in John Calvin (1509–64) alongside Augustine and Newman. He would concur that if ever there are to be changes in the nature of the state, they are best achieved by changing the common agreement of the multitude as to what is good. None of these three thinkers questions the essentially social constitution of created humanity. For Calvin, the scriptural and natural law evidence are entirely united in their direction of human beings toward one another in *just* and *humane* relations (as in the second table of the Decalogue, or the Ten Commandments), as well as toward God in *piety* (as in the first table). For Newman, to be in Christ was a social principle. The church was not merely a philosophy or a book but actually enacted a new and living form of society – establishing the *koinonia* or fellowship wherein the individual found true fulfillment. Augustine, too, would have denied that social life was inherently an evil: God designed humanity in the Garden of Eden to be a social being.

What Augustine *did* argue, though, was that the Fall had corrupted that social life of free intercourse for which humanity was created. The state, or the city, was founded by Cain, and founded therefore on violence and robbery. At this point there enters the more critical side of what the mainstream Christian tradition has had to say about the state. As we saw in Chapter Four, Augustine drew a contrast between the City of God and the earthly city. They are not strictly speaking cities or even states, but realms of allegiance. But these two "cities," according to Augustine, do have *representatives*, whom in concrete terms he tended to treat as the Roman state (for the earthly *civitas*) and the church (for the divine society).

- The heavenly city follows the laws of the earthly city insofar as they do not hinder the service of Christ, but the condition of this is that the earthly laws (and the earthly peace) are radically relativized in relation to the heavenly laws and peace. The citizen of the heavenly city is primarily a pilgrim who makes use of earthly peace and laws as appropriate (thus revealing the properly provisional status of such laws), but regards heavenly peace as the only form of peace that really deserves the name.
- Earthly peace is not accorded any merit for itself, but only for its usefulness to the heavenly city. Indeed, there are polytheistic and pagan elements in the earthly city that are antithetical to the heavenly city, so that the laws of religion, particularly, cannot be the same in the two cities.

Some have argued that one practical effect of this doctrine is to acquiesce in the "fallen" injustices of the earthly city on the grounds that, as a pilgrim, it is barely worth seeking to change them whilst passing through: "The only thing that counts for man in this life is his relation to God: what matters it under what form of government a man lives – man with his brief life, man under the doom of death – provided only that he may serve his God?"

Augustine works in the tension between two traditions with scriptural roots:

1. Romans 13. Augustine is fully in the Pauline tradition that "there is no authority except from God, and those authorities that exist have been instituted by God" (Rom 13:1). In other words, God is sovereign even over the unrighteous earthly city. Coercive government has a place both punitive and remedial precisely to meet sin. As God used the Assyrians to punish and bring judgment on Israel, so also "victory, even when victory falls to the wicked, is a humiliation visited on the conquered by divine judgement, either to correct or to punish their sins." The godly have no place striving to *change* or to *reform* the state and its practices at any profound or structural level. That is God's business: God will raise up earthly powers, and bring them down again.

2. The Book of Revelation. At the same time, Augustine ruthlessly exposes the idolatrous pretensions of the earthly city – its vainglory, bloodthirstiness, and impiety. This means that he is working within another key tradition stemming from the New Testament: the Book of Revelation. Chapters 13–14 and

17–18 deal with the symbolic figures of the beasts (who represent the devil) and the Great Whore (who is identified with the unholy city of Babylon, a cipher for Rome), and in these figures the capacity of the Roman state to abuse power is displayed. In this context, Christians are warned not to get too cozy with any one order of worldly authority.

In this tension between seeing the "powers that be" as willed by God (Romans), and seeing them as impious (Revelation), it is again the case that much of the tradition has followed Augustine, and here too we may take John Henry Newman as an example. He seeks in a similar way what might be called the "perspective of eternity" on human social order (which he regards as basically no better in one age than in another). Earthly societies might shatter all things but they will inevitably perish before God. Therefore, the church's primary purpose in every age is essentially the salvation of souls. Changing the material condition of humankind does not fundamentally matter; it is a greater priority to minister to their spiritual needs in local situations. Newman shared, moreover, Augustine's profound pessimism about the roots of violence underlying the whole political order. Augustine had relished comparing earthly rulers with robbers and pirates. Even the "Roman virtues" of pride and the desire for glory, which he recognized as useful for the suppression of many vices and for effective government in the world, he nevertheless condemned as in essence lacking all true virtue, unable to make the Romans holy because not directed toward the highest and ultimate good of humanity. Newman echoes Augustine vigorously:

> Earthly kingdoms are founded, not in justice, but in injustice. They are created by the sword, by robbery, cruelty, perjury, craft, and fraud. There never was a kingdom, except Christ's, which was not conceived and born, nurtured and educated, in sin. There never was a State, but was committed to acts and maxims, which it is its crime to maintain and its ruin to abandon. What monarchy is there but began in invasion or usurpation? What revolution has been effected without self-will, violence or hypocrisy? What popular government but is blown about by every wind as if it had no conscience and no responsibilities? What dominion of the few but is selfish and unscrupulous? Where is military strength without the passion for war? Where is trade without the love of filthy lucre, which is the root of all evil?

Princeton theologian Eric Gregory (b. 1970) represents a different interpretation of *The City of God*, one which argues that an Augustinian politics need not lapse into pessimism or social disengagement. Instead, Gregory defends what he calls an Augustinian civic liberalism, centered on love of God and neighbor, that promotes a more just, egalitarian, and charitable society. For Gregory, this form of Augustinian politics "should offer a vision of citizenship open to social transformation by attending to virtue." He also insists on the fundamentally Christological shape of Augustine's thought; he maintains that the heart of Augustinian politics is to be found not in Book XIX but in Book X of *The City of God*, in which Augustine describes "the true worship of the crucified God and the charitable service of neighbor in collective *caritas* [love]." In his extension of Augustine's thought, Gregory offers a good example of someone whose approach weaves together universal, subversive, and ecclesial strands. His emphasis on citizenship in the earthly city draws on universal interests. He incorporates subversive insights by examining feminist critiques of Augustine and using feminist political theory to re-read Augustine's account of love and sin. And his insistence on the Christological character of Augustine's political ethic, as well as his consideration of virtue, points toward more ecclesial themes. His reading of Augustine has important similarities with that of Oliver O'Donovan, whose thought is considered in the ecclesial section below.

Gregory and Newman illustrate how important Augustine continues to be in modern political theory. It needs, however, to be emphasized that the Augustinian tradition is not the only influential one in Christian thought about the nature and role of the state, and of how Christians should relate to it.

Medieval Tradition

The medieval tradition has a generally more positive view. Its appeals to the natural law legitimized the idea of princely government, as in accordance with the hierarchical ordering of created nature for the promotion of social good. Monarchy, so Thomas Aquinas (1225–74) argued, accords with nature, and for this reason offers the best form of government. But at the same time, natural law thinking could be used to defend the independence of the church – even the sanctioning of political resistance in exceptional circumstances. This was because the same natural law that legitimized the state was also *above* the state, and was related to *divine* law. (For just this reason, the authority of emperors and kings could be constructed as subordinate to the authority of popes.) Overall, however, there was a strong presumption in favor of political authorities unless they seemed significantly to have forfeited their claim to legitimacy.

Reformed and Early Modern Tradition

Specific discussions of Martin Luther's and John Calvin's attitudes to earthly government can be found elsewhere in this volume (in Chapter Two and at more length in Chapter Four). Here we will notice Calvin in particular. The mainstream Reformed traditions did not abandon the medieval world's optimistic view of the state. Calvin tried to create a polity that would *not* be "committed to acts and maxims, which it [was] its crime to maintain and its ruin to abandon" (to recall Newman's gloomy words). To do so, he had in the first place to make his polity exclusively Christian. This was in accord with a belief, shared by Augustine and Newman, that a state must demonstrate the unity of commonly directed "loves." But Calvin had less sense than both Newman and Augustine that state and church necessarily had different priorities. And Calvin would admit far more concern for changing the material conditions of humankind within his polity than Newman ever would. For Calvin, there must be a profound harmony in the workings of divine sovereignty, and therefore a harmony between the form of "earthly" government established to administer the lives of humans in society, and the requirements of life in the church, preparing them for heaven. We know this because of the way in which Scripture itself lays down patterns of political behavior and outlines the nature of fundamental social institutions.

In the early modern period, as Christendom broke up into violently competing religious groups, a central political concern became how to manage these differences in a way that still allowed for collective human flourishing. It seemed necessary to try to prize people free from their deadly allegiances to religious viewpoints that could not be reconciled because they were of too great an import for the people who held them. So the idea of a "state of nature" was deployed, in which (it was argued) human beings exist as individuals, prior to any allegiances. The human individual is free. That freedom means equality with every other individual. The state of nature is a condition untrammeled by any claim of tradition, church, class, or location.

This became a critical principle for emergent liberal political theory. Thomas Hobbes (1588–1679) developed the idea that the power of the sovereign consists in the transfer to him (willingly, by all the people in a state) of their individual consent to being ruled. This they did for the sake of their own defense, security, and prosperity. John Locke (1632–1704) then developed the idea of *rights* as the property of individuals in order reciprocally to limit the power of the sovereign state over those individuals. (See Chapter Five for more on Hobbes and Locke.) The emergence of the modern nation-state has followed upon these early developments with a certain relentless logic, as it has seemed increasingly necessary for there to be strong "managerial" powers to enforce the ground rules that are needed if the play of individual interests and rights in modern societies is to run smoothly. Furthermore, the emergence of complex national (and, increasingly, international) problems that require large-scale action has seemed to demand executive authority with power to deal with them, and this power the state has consistently taken upon itself (as have, to some extent, certain large multinational bodies such as the League of Nations and the United Nations).

The Modern Period

Modern Protestant and Catholic traditions of ethics alike have sought to resist the onslaught of the modern secular state's claims for itself. Totalitarianism has left its mark, and both Catholics and Protestants have sought theological sanction for political resistance to tyranny more than ever before. Genocide, the crushing of opposition by terror, and the profound diminishment of human existence have been brought about in many parts of the world in the twentieth century through the huge power of the modern machinery of the state. The appalling nature of these experiences is perhaps only partially offset by attempts to turn the power and structure of the state to help the flourishing of human life through the provision of crucial services and systems of support to those in need.

The particular successes of Protestant churches in resisting the encroachments of overweening state power in modern times have in part been based on a greater readiness to see the state as a necessary remedy for the effects of sin rather than a positive part of an originally good creation. This has been especially true of thinkers in the tradition of the Radical Reformation, more wary as it has been of natural law bases for ethical judgments. At the extreme end of a radical Protestant spectrum, there is the view that the political order has no place in the life of redeemed freedom and is a bitter outcome of the Fall. On this account, the state lies only in the sphere of utility, and any sense it may have of its own ultimacy must be fiercely relativized. Although he wrote as a twentieth-century member of the French Reformed Church, a long time after the Radical Reformation, Jacques Ellul (1912–94) put this point of view well:

> The dialogue with the sovereign ... is conducted at every level of power by the voice and presence of each believer or group of believers so long as they are true ambassadors of the Wholly Other and not just participants in the power of the sovereign.

Karl Barth (1886–1968) and Emil Brunner (1889–1966) express points of view that are a little less stark. Brunner's use of a certain natural theology approach allowed him to say that the state had its place as a God-given order of creation, although with an authority severely limited by its dependence on more basic forms of human community like the family. While vehemently rejecting Brunner's use of natural theology, Barth developed his own argument that the power of the state is "God's ordinance for the security of the collective life of man even where the latter provides no scope for grace." It is God's patience that allows the state to exist, in order that there might be "time and freedom for the proclamation and knowledge of grace." And because the social life of those people who live apart from and contrary to the grace of God still has to be made possible, "grace itself must assume and maintain the form of a graceless order": a provisional and penultimate order which does not stand in contradiction to grace, but is precisely grace's expression in these particular circumstances.

It may be helpful, as we turn now to our threefold typology of universal, subversive, and ecclesial ethics of the state, to think of universal approaches as having a tendency to look to the doctrine of creation for their key reference points, and subversive attitudes as having a tendency to look to eschatology. The former tendency is perhaps the more dominant one in Christian tradition; the latter, however, has been a powerful voice in liberationist and other explicitly political theologies during recent decades (and also in some radical Christian movements in the past – like the Diggers and Levellers). In Richard Bauckham's typology:

- "The former tendency, with its backward-looking perspective, favours a conservative view of politics, in which the role of government is to preserve the good already given, though it can also support a reformist critique of corrupt governments which neglect and pervert the standards of the past."

- "The future-orientated perspective of the second tendency favours a more revolutionary outlook, in which the future can be expected to surpass the past and political action can effect radical changes for the better in human society."

There is an acknowledgment of the merit of both of these tendencies in a view which sees the kingdom of God – toward which history is moving and to which the church is a present and public witness – as the renewal of creation. This is typically the view of the ecclesial approach to politics.

Universal

The dominant Calvinist and Catholic approaches are universalist in their use of natural law arguments, which assume that the best form of government is one based on – and recognizable by – the reason and good will of all human beings, whether or not they are Christian. God's ordering of creation means that the church's pronouncements on the right ordering of society ought to be acceptable to human beings everywhere. The "common good" which the papal encyclicals advocate is thought to be genuinely that – the good common to all people created by God and placed in the world God has established and arranged (a world of harmonious proportion). This attitude underpins a remarkably sanguine Roman Catholic approach to the idea of international government, as we see in this quotation from the encyclical *Pacem in Terris* (On Establishing Universal Peace in Truth, Justice, Charity, and Liberty, 1963):

> Today the universal common good poses problems of world-wide dimensions which cannot be adequately tackled or solved except by the efforts of public authorities endowed with a breadth of powers, structure and means of the same proportions: that is, of public authorities which are in a position to act in an effective manner on a world-wide basis. The moral order itself, therefore, demands that such a form of public authority be established.

The public authority of the world, *Pacem in Terris* argues, must tackle problems of an economic, social, political, or cultural character that are posed by the "universal common good." There is no suggestion that there might in practice be problems in finding universal common assent to what the "good" *is*. The Roman Catholic Church's interests seem to be viewed as unproblematically coextensive with those of a world public authority.

Universalist principles also come into play, however, in seeking to limit the power of the state over the sphere of human self-determination. We see this, for example, in thought about Christianity's relation to the social order in a British theological tradition that had its heyday in the mid-twentieth century. "Human personality has a status, worth, and dignity quite independent of the State, and superior to that of the State itself" (William Temple). Archbishop Temple wrote *Christianity and Social Order* in 1942, in the face of the totalitarian Nazi state. He articulates what is a classically universalist ethical principle in relation to the state: that the human person, as intended by God, has her own intrinsic worth and dignity (characteristically expressed in her exercise of freedom and responsibility), which the state is not to take away. It is not membership in society as such that determines the worth of the human being, nor the requirements of the state that govern her. The action of the state is to be directed to an end determined by this moral and spiritual character of human nature.

The bishops at the 1948 Lambeth Conference of the Anglican Communion declared, in similar vein, that society exists to serve the needs of its members, not to enslave and possess them: "[B]oth the recognition of the responsibility of the individual to God and the development of his personality are gravely imperiled by any claim made either by the state or by any group within the state to control the whole of human life." For this reason they condemned the philosophy of what the Anglican leader W. R. Inge (1860–1954) called "the Wolf State": the aggrandizement of collectivism over the individual. Moreover, they added that a constant effort was needed to resist any encroachment by the state that might endanger human personality. The church was perceived to have a special role, in the modern state, as the guardian of personal freedom: a counterweight to the natural bias of the state towards totalitarianism – "a tendency of the state to encroach on the freedom of individuals and voluntary associations." This seemed to mean, among other things, that it should seek to preserve the spirit of voluntary social service alongside the state's provision of welfare. The Conference urged "Christians in all lands to guard such freedoms with vigilance and to convince public opinion that their preservation is essential to the maintenance of true democracy and personal and national wellbeing." There is very little to distinguish this attitude from that Roman Catholic view expressed in *Pacem in Terris*: "[E]very human being is a person, that is, his nature is endowed with intelligence and free will. By virtue of this, he has rights and duties of his own, flowing directly and simultaneously from his very nature." The sphere of human freedom and responsibility must be kept open, and in practical terms this led to arguments for various forms of what *Pacem in Terris* calls "intermediate groups and bodies" that have some degree of administrative autonomy.

This is in broad outline the principle of "subsidiarity," a precept according to which, to quote the Protestant thinker Emil Brunner writing in 1949, "[E]verything that free groups, anterior to the state, can do ought to be done by them, and not by the state. ... State intervention must always be the *ultima ratio* [the last resort]." The principle of subsidiarity celebrates the "associative quality" of social groupings like the family, the parish, the industrial union, and so on. They have an inherent life of their own; they are likely to feel responsibility for those who belong to them; those who belong to them are liable to feel and express more responsibility in return. Provided they have an eye also to the common interest, they should be allowed wherever possible to govern themselves.

Some modern-day Anglican thinkers, like Oliver O'Donovan, identify more with an ecclesial approach to the state. Others, such as Luke Bretherton (b. 1968), focus on the church's potential to contribute to "a common life politics" in religiously diverse societies. Bretherton, who has taught ethics at King's College London and at Duke Divinity School in North Carolina, understands Christianity – and all religions – as "one of the few corporate forms of life available for mobilizing and sustaining the ability of individuals to act together in defense of their shared interests." His book *Resurrecting Democracy* (2015) studies the role of religious groups, including the church, in community organizing, and he describes the potential of community organizing to nurture a "faithful, hopeful, and neighborly politics of a common life."

The modern Calvinist tradition – especially in the USA – has produced a range of thinkers who have been open to adapting social contractarian theory in ways they see as compatible with Christianity. Max Stackhouse (b. 1935), for example, defends modern liberalism (and human rights theory) by appeal to the biblical notion of covenant, seeing continuities between Puritan tradition and the thought of Locke in this regard. Richard Mouw (b. 1940) is an evangelical scholar who has advocated the importance of Christian engagement with public life in ways that respond to rather than dictate its terms of reference.

Subversive

It is unquestionably the case that since the Emperor Constantine's dramatic shift to the defense of Christianity after his victory at the battle of the Milvian Bridge in 314 CE, the church has had a long history of "establishment" of various kinds, in which it has been closely involved in the workings of official political authority. It is also the case, however, that it came to birth as a minority community of faith under a pagan power, and had its character forged in the fires of state persecution. Something of this spirit continues to inform traditions of subversive ethical reflection on the role and limits of state power.

In 1940, Bishop George Bell (1883–1958) wrote that, in his view,

> the citizen of a democratic State may be deprived of his freedom, by the subtle influence of the universal provision of social services, from ante-natal clinics to euthanasia couches, just as effectively as the German subject is robbed of his liberty by the system of spies and concentration camps.

His clear implication was that the democratic state is not free of all totalitarian tendencies simply by virtue of being democratic. Individual or group liberties can be restricted in many and various ways, and not merely the obvious ones represented by a Nazi or a communist regime. Jacques Ellul forcefully indicated the tendency of all modern states to want to become absolute in every field. "The state is totalitarian," he wrote, "not because of totalitarian doctrines, but because of the vast array of means, e.g., in planning, economic and administrative management, forecasting, investigation, control, research, inquiry, and psychological action." Individuals in society are inescapably bound up with a whole range of orders of necessity, of expectation and of obligation, simply by virtue of the fact that they are in society. Ellul was the advocate of a form of Christian anarchy which denied that there could be such a thing as a "theology of the state" at all. The political order does not belong to the realm of freedom; it belongs to the realm of necessity. That means that being a Christian will involve witness against the pretension of any society that thinks it can "act as a whole." The Christian will always question the legitimacy of such actions.

It is worth noting in this context that, for all their desire to check overblown state power, the arguments in favor of subsidiarity we looked at in the previous section do not in themselves go so far as to deny that the state is still the ultimate "court of appeal," or sovereign arbiter, in human affairs. For all that the state is prepared to give intermediary organizations a limited, subordinated, and superintendent legislative and judicial power by granting them public rights, the state nonetheless still stands over this domain of devolved responsibility, ever ready to intervene if there are abuses to be suppressed.

It is not clear how, ultimately, such a set-up differs from totalitarianism in the sense in which Ellul uses the term. Natural law approaches like those in Roman Catholic tradition may be unable to resist effectively the sort of heretical claims for "civil religion" that are made in the name of various nation-states (not least the USA). If problems of an economic, social, political, or cultural character are to be solved by the "public authority," then might not these include problems of a *religious* character too? "Civil government," or the state, will be inclined to enlarge its remit and become arbiter in matters of what it perceives as significant religious disagreement. This will require the churches (and indeed other religious traditions as well as Christian ones) to relinquish to civil agencies the authority to define God's commands – thus avoiding any ultimate clash of loyalties. Or, to put it another way, all churches' balloon strings will be available for handling by government. Robert Bellah and Phillip Hammond have shown how in the USA, the judicial system has assumed the right (independent of the churches) to judge their claims. A rationalized, generalized, predictable legal system, it is argued, fosters "better" social interaction, and therefore harmony. Bellah and Hammond demonstrate just how easy it is to turn the arguments of natural theology to the service of causes that very happily *deny* the church's allegiance to the higher sovereignty of God, and set up another god instead.

Theologies of liberation are characteristically reluctant to give endorsement to any such homogenizing management of religion by civil authorities. As we have noted in Chapter Six, the theology of liberation begins with a reality that confronts millions in the poorer parts of the world – the experience of poverty, appalling living conditions, malnutrition, and inadequate health care. What is then advocated on the basis of this attention to context is a theology in which the circumstances of the interpreters are given a primary importance in the articulation of an understanding of discipleship specifically relevant to the situation in which they find themselves. It is rare that these concerns sit comfortably with the interests of those in power. While on occasion, perhaps, forgetting that political activity on its own cannot establish the kingdom of God on earth, the European political theology of the 1960s and the theologies of liberation that sprang up in various parts of the less-developed world have brought to the fore a Christian imperative to oppose unjust political structures – as well as the social and economic interests that sustain them. North American black theology and the church-based opposition to apartheid in South Africa have added their voices to this chorus. The European political theologians were strongly influenced by philosophers who were themselves adapting and responding to Marxist ideas – for example, Ernst Bloch (1880–1959), Theodor Adorno (1903–69), Max Horkheimer (1895–1973), and Jürgen Habermas (b. 1929). Additional theologians were especially influenced by the Marxist emphasis on transformative praxis, including Johannes Baptist Metz (b. 1928), Jürgen Moltmann (b. 1926), and Dorothee Sölle (1929–2003). Chapter Six examined more closely the meaning of transformative praxis.

The South African theology that found expression in the *Kairos Document* in 1985 rejected "the theological justification of the [political] status quo with its racism, capitalism and totalitarianism" as a heretical "state theology." It asserted a "prophetic theology" in relation to the South African state; one that called for "repentance, conversion and change." This and other moral responses to state authority promote the idea that to be human is not to be part of a natural order so much as to be one who in partnership with others is engaged in shaping the future creatively.

Ecclesial

We will consider three examples of what an ecclesial ethics of the state can look like, in the thought of Karl Barth, William Cavanaugh (b. 1962), and Oliver O'Donovan (b. 1945).

1. Karl Barth: *Church as the basis of all true sociality.* For Barth, it is clear that Christians should participate in the work of the state, but despite this participation they retain a privileged standpoint over and against it. Their work in and for the state is merely a *part* of their higher service of God (a position that is an exact opposite of the "civil religion" position outlined by Bellah and Hammond). It is in obedience to the command of God that the state will properly be served. The fellowship of the church is in fact the true and real form of the world's fellowship: "In so far as this love is alive among Christians, in all its depth and reality, with all the joy and sorrow it brings … the Church is edified, the good work which God requires takes place, not only in the inner circle of Christians, but with the creation and maintenance of this circle for everyone and for the whole world."

    Barth makes the world subsidiary to the church, rather than the other way around. The world cannot claim a social foundation other than the church – which is the only true fellowship, because it is established in Christ: "The special fellowship of the Church, whose formation and preservation is the basic divine purpose, does not mean an absolute separation [between Church and worldly sociality], but is the basis of a worldwide fellowship." Christians' primary responsibility, then, is to conform to this "basic divine purpose," not seeing themselves as at war with the world. On the contrary, "in the sight of all men – whether the latter perceive it or not – they will work for the objective grace and the common weal of all," and this (for Barth, as for other ecclesial ethicists) will mean *being the church properly*, and nothing more. Barth does not pretend that the church and the state are separable: "The Church has a provisional character and is conditioned by the form of this world which, although it is overcome and abolished in principle, still has power over it. For this reason alone it cannot escape solidarity with the order of the State which rests upon the same presupposition."

But neither does he go along with the view of natural theology that *all* people are in a position to understand the proper function of the state. For him, it is supremely Christians who know what they are doing when they think and act as citizens. "For them it is not a matter of chance motives or personal inclinations, but the service of God. But they know, too, the limits and the provisional character of this matter."

2.   William Cavanaugh: *Church as the out-narration of the state.* A certain sort of modern secularity sees the state's role as simply managing conflict and keeping a lid on potentially violent difference. An ecclesial ethics like William Cavanaugh's responds critically to this essentially "tragic" account of human society. Cavanaugh argues that a belief in the Fall is actually a positive resource for Christian ethics, because if there was a Fall there must have been something to fall *from*, and thus conflictual plurality cannot have the ultimacy that some liberal accounts imply. The church must resist setting itself up as one more political interest group, or lobby, amongst many – which it does whenever it tries to translate its particular reasonings (formed through particular relationship to the person of Jesus and to his gospel) into "more universal and neutral terms." In Augustinian vein, it must think of itself as "greater" and not "smaller" than the state; as catholic (universal) and not like a territory "with boundaries that are policed." This gives it a political vocation that is neither total alignment with any existing political state nor withdrawal into a "sectarian" enclave. Its task is to "out-public" the state's claims to define the public realm – performing the reality of God's work of reconciliation as the key to the purpose of history.

3.   Oliver O'Donovan: *Church as the destiny of the state.* It is in just such an Augustinian tradition that Oliver O'Donovan operates, as he evokes for his readers an eschatological vision of ecclesial sociality as the context for all worthwhile reflections on politics. His works *The Desire of the Nations* (1996) and *The Ways of Judgment* (2005) push beyond considerations of the penultimacy of political institutions to the ultimate vision of the kingdom of God. The vision of the kingdom already guides the church in the historical realm, even though the church's response to its vision is often compromised. Temporary instruments of judgment are necessary, but they are provisional, and they will one day yield to a more perfect order of things, which at their best they gesture to and at worst

seek to substitute for. In this eschatological condition, God's own judgment will be enacted in the creation's complete and uncoerced fellowship with God, so that we can confidently defer our own judgment to the divine judgment. For the time being, the church models this "high mark of our calling"; it shows "the social humanity that the world is summoned by the Spirit of God to become." He goes on to say, "The church as the 'end' of political community is the matrix within which the created shape of human sociality emerges into view." This is how O'Donovan makes sense in the terms of his book of the peculiar dominical injunction "Do not judge, so that you may not be judged." He writes:

A society that refrains from judgment [by which he means the church] does so because it has the judgment of God to defer to. Living under God's judgment, then, and embracing it as the law of its life, it is free not to judge, since all human judgment is merely interim, waiting for the judgment that is to come. Such an earthly society is "unpolitical" in a helpful sense, because its politics of expectancy has gone to the heart of the political and emerged into life beyond judgment. Through the lens of this post-political society, political theology can view as in a mirror the pre-political society of God's creation, and can understand political judgment as a moment in parenthesis between the two.

It is the Holy Spirit who "does what the rulers of the nations do in their societies." The medium for its work of judgment, O'Donovan argues, is ultimately the human heart.

Justice and Punishment

There are, as conventionally outlined, a number of different types of justice:

1. **commutative justice**, which refers to that which is owed between individuals, e.g., in conducting business transactions;
2. **contributive justice**, which refers to what individuals owe to society for the common good;
3. **distributive justice**, which refers to what society owes to its individual members, i.e., the just allocation of resources;
4. **legal justice**, which refers to rights and responsibilities of citizens to obey and respect the rights of all and the laws devised to protect peace and social order; and, consequent on this,
5. **retributive justice**, which is concerned with the enforcement of appropriate punishment on those who have broken the law; and finally,
6. **restorative justice**, which has gained currency in recent thought on both sides of the Atlantic, and indicates the idea that criminal sanctions should not just punish, but serve the repair of the injury done, and in this way compensate for the wrong. One of its advantages is that it retains some sense of the importance and needs of the *victim*.

See Chapter Five's section on Right Relationships for an additional exploration of theories of justice.

Justice

In Christian tradition, justice has been recognized as involving the normative ordering and distribution of social benefits and obligations among citizens, but has always also meant a norm for human moral action that has its source in the being and action of God. Doing justice is a requirement indistinguishable from the requirement to honor the image of God in other people and foster it in one-self. We are to be just as God is just, and to let our justice mirror God's. This norm should find expression, according to mainstream Christian thought, simul-taneously in the virtue of individual moral agents and in those socially embodied patterns of regard for the neighbor that sustain such virtues. Especially impor-tant in the imaging of God's justice will be respect for the prophetic injunctions to care for widows, orphans, strangers, and the poor. Restitution is also a key principle, found throughout the Torah (e.g., in Exodus 22) as well as in Jesus' own teachings (e.g., Luke 19:8).

Dominant in the Roman Catholic tradition of moral theology has been the conception that the human doing of justice corresponds to a God-given justice that is encoded in God's good ordering of creation. We learn it as we see God's direction of all things to their proper ends. In Protestant tradition, the pattern of God's *salvific* action in imputing righteousness to the faithful has been regarded as the primary measure of justice. Christians are subsequently to imitate this sav-ing justice of God in their relations with one another.

There is a vigorous tradition of debate about the role of law in the Christian understanding of justice. We saw in Chapter Four how this worked itself out in the thought of Thomas Aquinas. Martin Luther (1483–1546) was dismissive of the importance of law for the community of the justified. It is to John Calvin that we have to turn for the most developed Reformation defense of law and its rela-tion to justice.

We saw earlier how law and gospel were not, for Calvin, fundamentally opposed.

> Man contains, as it were, two worlds, capable of being governed by various rulers and various laws. This distinction will prevent what the Gospel inculcates concern-ing spiritual liberty from being misapplied to political regulations, as though Christians were less subject to the external government of human laws because their consciences have been set at liberty before God, as though their freedom of spirit necessarily exempted them from all carnal servitude.

Calvin is basically true to Paul's injunction to be obedient to *all* earthly authori-ties as established by God. But he nevertheless retains clear ideas about what should in fact characterize good government as opposed to bad. As we have seen, his view that earthly government is naturally compatible with the life of sanctifica-tion leads him to allow it the power to enforce not only matters of *justice* and *humanity*, but matters of *piety* too: "to cherish and support the external worship of God, to preserve the true doctrine of religion, to defend the constitution of the Church." Civil government is not to *make* laws concerning religion and the worship of God, but it is to provide for the protection of such laws against violation and blasphemy. Kings and judges are to be the patrons and protectors of "the pious worshippers of God." The death penalty is readily acceptable because "an ill-advised lenity towards violent men may prove cruelty to the many who become their victims." Magistrates are "ministers of God to us for good."

In fact, his description of the ministry of magistrates as well as pastors indicates how he saw both as agents acting under instruction from God. The magistrate's duty was, of course, partly governed by Scripture, but the gaps in New Testament, and distinctively Christian, teaching required supplementation from the Old Testament and from Calvin's own contemporary understanding of the natural law. Magistrates are frequently left free to devise such laws and arrangements as they judge expedient. Although the law "has no place in believers' consciences before the tribunal of God," Calvin still felt it a congenial external measure of sanctification. For this reason, he felt, civil discipline and coercion by magistrates could be looked upon as an aid to such growth in holiness.

And the Christian's duty must lie in a conformity to rule: a willing conformity, certainly, but a conformity nonetheless. Rules are the proper way of concerning oneself with the external characteristics of actions, and no church could cope with offenses within itself without laws and arrangements to enforce them. The casuistry in which this inevitably involved Calvin at times (see the discussion of casuistry in Roman Catholic moral theology in Chapter Four) are an indication of the way that many of his political views and judgments were conventional ones. This is also true of his supplementation of these Christian "rules" from natural law sources. They only achieved their religious significance by being associated with his larger theological vision.

The modern period has marked a profound shift in understandings about the practice and application of the law, as about so many other areas of human activity. The administration of justice, it can be argued, has become increasingly procedural. This is because in the modern period the idea of justice as a guarantor of rights has been preferred to the idea of justice as embodying substantive agreements about what constitutes the good of both individual and community together, including about the end or goal of human life. Another way of putting this is to say that the idea of justice as a unitive force has receded before the idea of justice as a distributive force – i.e., one that oversees and regulates the pursuit of private goods or rival interests. The ascendancy of liberal political philosophies has played a key role in bringing about this fragmentation of ideas of "common good" into an acceptance that a plurality of competing private goods and interests is normal, and possibly, indeed, a positive thing. The language that has come to dominate liberal discourse about justice is not that of "the good," but of "rights," for which the law functions as a sort of police force. Such ways of thinking now influence the practice of the law in Western societies, as we saw in Chapter Five.

The shift in understandings of justice towards a predominantly rights-based model has provoked various Christian ethical responses, of which we identify three types here:

1. One type of response has been to embrace the idea of a God whose doing of justice is a promotion and protection of human rights of various kinds. The work of Nicholas Wolterstorff (b. 1932) has been especially significant in this vein. There is an evident implication here that justice is conceived as an external standard to which Christianity is accountable, and as something that makes sense apart from theological convictions and practices.
2. Some other responses accept the rights-based model of secular theories of justice, but argue for the need for a Christian theological supplement to it (e.g., the importance of tempering justice with mercy).
3. A third set of responses is far more critical of the whole rights-based discourse, and says that a recovery is needed of the idea that justice (after the pattern of God's own justice) is fundamentally oriented to redemption and reconciliation: in Daniel Bell's view, "Justice redeems; it does not enforce an economy of debt, dominion, and strict restitution. Justice is predicated on peace; it is not merely the regulation of conflict."

Punishment

Along with the profound shifts in understanding of the function of law in the modern period, it is inevitable that there should also be controversy about penal systems, and whether the principles of retributive justice they express should be held together with reformative ideals of punishment. The Western tradition has inherited some of these latter ideas from monastic traditions of penitential correction and restoration. In the early centuries of the church's existence there was often a marked contrast between its own penitential practices and those of its social environment, in which prisons barely existed, blood feuds were rife, and there was frequent recourse to torture or the death penalty. The monks preferred to use cells for the purpose of confinement in the service of reflection and a change of heart. This had the merit of keeping in play a concept of the good of the prisoner.

Two key approaches tend to characterize philosophies of punishment.

*   One is retributive, and justifies the punishment of a wrongdoer with reference to an objective wrong done, which an order of justice requires be punished. The concept of desert (i.e., just desert) is central to this notion; there is nothing arbitrary about what is done to the criminal on this account.
*   The second approach is utilitarian. The justification for punishment is that it will deter others, and/or reform and rehabilitate the wrongdoer. It was shaped in large measure in reaction to the capriciousness and savagery of many eighteenth-century criminal penalties.

Modern criminology has mainly concerned itself with the reformative ideal.

Universal

The medieval tradition exemplified by Thomas Aquinas begins with the classical principle "to each his [or her] due" (*suum cuique*). Aquinas follows the classical model in expounding the "virtue" of justice as one with two aspects – general and particular.

- "General" justice concerns itself with the unitive conception of the common good, and thus serves social solidarity.
- "Particular" justice concerns itself with questions of the contractual exchange and just distribution of goods.

So far so "universalist." But Aquinas departs from classical models in his suggestion that both sorts of justice have "charity" as their true end – and in this respect he lays the ground for what will become a prominent emphasis in "ecclesial" approaches to justice.

Christian approaches to justice that have adopted the modern paradigm of "rights" (with their focus on commutative and distributive models of justice) have usually taken statements that God is a God of justice to mean that God upholds or defends human rights. The implication here is that justice is some sort of pre-formed and external standard to which Christian theological ideas simply relate themselves. Apart from being historically inattentive, this claim has the practical effect of setting Christianity some sort of challenge to "prove itself" at the bar of secular accounts of what justice is – accounts that it may well feel leave certain crucial questions unanswered. Such questions might include the following: Who or what is the *source* of rights? Does human flourishing require more than the doing of social or individual justice? Does mercy have a place in the doing of justice?

Some Christian theories of justice adopt secular theories but seek also to adapt or supplement them, as, for example, when secular contractarian theories are defended on the basis of the biblical notion of covenant. A belief in the transcendental dignity of the human person as made in God's image is also a key plank in various modern theological defenses of human rights. It can be found as much in the natural law arguments of Roman Catholic thinkers as in many strands of liberation theology.

There are both deontological and consequentialist (specifically, utilitarian) theories of punishment to be reckoned with in recent times. Christian ethics of a universalist bent has tended to share the arguments of secular theorists.

- *Deontological.* Retributive justifications of punishment are deontological because of their adherence to the notion of desert. They are not so much concerned with any benefit that might arise from the punishment as with the simple fact that it has been imposed.

- *Utilitarian.* Justifications of punishment that focus on issues of deterrence or the reform of the criminal are utilitarian. They look for the benefits of punishment, either for the criminal or for wider society. Utilitarian approaches have been criticized in various ways.
  - It is argued that there is no clear evidence that rehabilitation or deterrence "work" very well.
  - Such approaches use criminals as a "means" to wider societal ends in a way that may be unjust.
  - If deterrence is to be achieved by making an example of someone, then a consequentialist argument taken to its logical extreme might advocate a disproportionately cruel punishment, as this would make it all the more effective *as deterrence*. This is where a retributivist's notion of desert can be helpful in safeguarding proportionality between crime and punishment.

In fact, a retributivist would say, all utilitarian arguments from deterrence actually imply some notion of retribution anyway. It is not clear why punishment should deter anyone *from* crime, unless it is in fact imposed *for* crime. Deterrence seems, to many people, meaningless without retributive considerations of this kind.

As in its general reflections on rights, so also in the specific domain of punishment the Roman Catholic Church has made important use of the principle of the created dignity of the person (in this case, the criminal). In recent years, the principle has provided the basis for opposition to capital punishment. Pope John Paul II challenged the traditional view that some crimes are commensurate with the death penalty. In the papal encyclical *Evangelium Vitae* (On the Value and Inviolability of Human Life, 1995) he acknowledged that there might be some exceptional cases in which it is necessary for there to be a judicial killing (e.g., the killing of unjust aggressors in cases where their death is the only way to defend innocent lives), but such killings ought not to be argued for as part of a *retributive* scheme of justice. The death penalty, on this account, is a part of a system of punishment only in the increasingly rare instances when it would not be possible otherwise to defend society.

Subversive

It might be fair to say that many of the traditions of Christian ethics we have broadly categorized as "subversive" for the purposes of this book in fact share many of the attitudes to justice that characterize more universalist positions. In few cases do they depart radically from the rights-based discourse of modern liberal politics. An intensifying concern to secure improvements in civil rights in many countries during the 1960s translated specifically into campaigns by minority groups of various kinds. Many of them had Christian voices. Martin Luther King Jr. (1929–68), called for the recognition of the civil and political rights of African Americans – as well as other victims of discrimination – on the basis of the Christian gospel. Feminist theology began to give a theological voice to movements for the equal rights of women in social, economic, and religious contexts. This included (and still does) a critical attention to the retention of sexist language in liturgy and church teaching. Liberation theology has used rights language forcefully to defend those who are victims of poverty and oppression in the developing nations of the world.

At the same time (like many universalists), subversive ethics may argue that there need to be supplementations of liberal discourse; that justice in a Christian sense needs to mean more than secular liberals mean by it (as, for Augustine, *true* justice was not to be found in the earthly city). So, for example, Latin American liberationists will acknowledge that forgiveness and mercy must always have the last word for Christians, even when it is acknowledged that justice is necessary. And feminist theologians have been increasingly critically alert to the individualism latent in certain liberal theories. The "feminine" strand of feminist ethics outlined in Chapter Six is a good example of this, in the way it affirms that women's ethical reasoning is generally relational rather than individual.

Ecclesial

Ecclesial accounts often begin with a highly embodied account of what justice is – and, in particular, are liable to claim that justice is displayed first and foremost in the person and life of Jesus Christ, and then bequeathed to a church that lives in his power. But what does it mean to say that justice is found in a person? The answer is that this person lives out of (and re-establishes by his actions) an "order of charity," in which both absolute truth and absolute mercy are displayed for the sake of the reconciliation of humans to each other and to God. This "redeemed justice" is intrinsically about serving "right relationship," and "right relationship" is about a great deal more than "rights." Atonement theories governed by imported legal concepts like retribution, debt, and equity are distorted to the extent that they forget this essential gearing of Christ's doing of justice to the restorative work of love. They separate justice and mercy. By contrast, in the words of Daniel Bell:

> making proper sense of Jesus as the justice of God entails recovering the atonement in its correct setting, the divine order of charity. Only then can we make sense of Augustine's extraordinary claim that true justice is found in Christ alone, or Thomas Aquinas's equally striking assertion that justice has as its end, charity, which is nothing less than friendship with God. Only such a repositioning promises not to pit justice against mercy but instead confirms that the beauty of justice is in complete accord with grace (Augustine), that mercy implements perfect justice (Aquinas), and the rule of God's justice is mercy (Anselm).

The reason it makes sense for Christians to speak of Christ's sacrifice on the cross as perfectly "just," therefore, is because it made it possible once again for human beings to render to God what was due (praise and worship), renewing the communion of humanity with God (and, in God, with each other). This is the basic connection between *justice* and *justification*. Because the church is the place where this justified life comes to expression, it is in the church that we should expect to find the "just" community – the community that knows what justice is because it has experienced it. This is why Augustine locates true justice in the City of God and not the earthly city.

Daniel Bell argues that medieval Christianity's traditional "works of mercy" are profound examples of how such justice can be expanded transformatively into the world.

- The seven corporal works involve caring for the hungry, the thirsty, the naked, the stranger, the sick, the prisoner, and the remains of the dead. They derive principally from the parable of the sheep and the goats in Matthew 25.
- The seven spiritual works involve the admonition of sinners, the instruction of the ignorant, the counseling of those who are doubting, the comfort of the afflicted, the patient bearing of wrongs, the forgiveness of injuries, and prayer for others (including the dead).

The sixth spiritual work in particular raises important issues for penitential practice; to conceive of forgiveness as a work of mercy is to seek to change a situation by *doing something* about it – "to liberate the offender from sin and effect reconciliation and the renewal of communion by means of confession, repentance, and satisfaction/reparation."

So here we turn to the question of punishment. One who does not believe that a criminal can repent and be reformed is likely to use punishment differently from one who does. Capital punishment and mandatory sentencing both express a mode of despair (though it might dress itself up as realism) about the possibilities for the reconciliation of criminals, and their reincorporation into the community. An ecclesial approach would argue that Christians who gather in the Eucharistic community – which is a community of radical reconciliation – have reasons to hope for more. They will be more equipped to re-envision punishment as a step on the way to the restoration of relationship. This is not to deny any place to ideas of penance. Christian ideas of justice generally require that, where possible, the offender make some form of reparation for her sin. This might involve returning someone's goods to him, or clearing his reputation, or paying some appropriate level of compensation for a loss. Conceived in the framework of reconciliation – which, it is argued here, is the proper framework for any Christian idea of justice – these sorts of reparation are called "satisfaction" or penance.

The ecclesial approach to punishment sees itself as in continuity with a classical Christian approach that has, in John Berkman's words, tended to focus on "the integral good (i.e., the reformation) of offenders with the specific victims of their offenses and/or the community which has been harmed." This reconciliation-based approach is seen as common to a tradition running through Augustine, Aquinas, Benedict, and others, and is wholly lost in "contemporary accounts of punishment, which emphasize 'deterrence' or 'a desire to protect society.'"

Retributive justifications of punishment may have receded in the modern period, but so too have reformative ones. Christians have too often ended up echoing this focus on deterrence and protection, and, it could be argued, need to recover a richer theological vision.

War

We saw in Chapter Two that in the earliest centuries of the church's life, Christian communities were notable for their commitment to peace. In addition to any aversion they may have had to taking the oaths of allegiance to Rome that were required of a soldier, it was widely taught that Christians should not fight or shed blood. The tradition contains within it the idea that the Christian is a "soldier of Christ" (*miles Christi*) within the "army of Christ" (*militia Christi*), but this metaphorical militancy functioned as an *alternative* to actual military service on behalf of the state rather than a justification for it. To be engaged in spiritual combat against the forces of evil may involve precisely a refusal to take up literal arms against other human beings. The case was made that praying for the emperor was indirect participation in the defense of the empire (indeed, it was justified as an even more effective form of service than fighting), but direct military service was shunned. Nonetheless, many Christians down the centuries have reconciled themselves to the need for armed conflicts in a fallen world that continues to await its full redemption – and some have positively advocated the vocation of Christians to take up arms and fight in causes that have been defined as "holy." For most of Christian history, the majority view has been that it is justifiable in Christian terms to fight in a just cause, out of concern for the peace, safety, or just treatment of others. Pacifism has thus been a minority view.

It is hard not to perceive some significant variation between Old Testament and New Testament attitudes to war. The writers of many Old Testament books are willing to claim that God not only enjoins the children of Israel to fight against their enemies, but actually fights alongside them. Paradigm cases of this include conflict with the Amalekites (see Exodus 17:8–16) and the conquest of Canaan narrated in the book of Joshua. In the New Testament, by contrast, Jesus Christ models an example of suffering love, and a call to forgive at radical personal cost that extends to the loss of one's life. This seems to imply that pacifism would be a better form of the *imitatio Christi* (imitation of Christ) than any endorsement of war could be. Having said that, even the New Testament is ambiguous on the carrying and use of arms. Jesus' admiration of the Roman centurion's faith in Luke 7 does not seem to suggest that his military status was a bar to his inclusion in the kingdom. And even though he tells Simon Peter to put away his sword in the garden of Gethsemane (John 18:11 and parallels), in Luke's Gospel he tells his disciples to equip themselves with arms (Luke 22:36–8). Meanwhile Paul defends the rights of government in Romans 13 – government that wields the sword both internally and externally.

Writing in 1960, Roland Bainton developed a threefold typology to try to capture these various stances: pacifism, crusade, and just war. They are not watertight categories, and some twelfth- and early thirteenth-century defenders of the Crusades clearly saw those violent adventures in just-war terms (and even as a sort of pilgrimage) on account of their authorization by popes. But in general, the concerns of the just-war tradition have been to limit and restrain the prosecution of conflicts while seeing them as (perhaps unavoidable) evils, whereas holy war ideas have positively justified conflicts as having a holy cause, divine participation (through guidance and aid of one side), and thus a clear demarcation between the godly and ungodly sides in the conflict.

Developing Bainton's categories we can speak of six kinds of war in ancient and modern guise.

Pacifism

(1) (a) Theological pacifism is rooted in the life, death, and risen life of Jesus, and the revelation Jesus thereby offers of the peaceful origins and ends of the whole creation. It understands creation as designed for the harmonious interplay of difference. In the light of Jesus' example, we see that the most powerful forces in history are not military, economic, or political forces but cross and resurrection. And so for Christians, the problem with the weapons of war is fundamentally not that they are too strong but that they are too weak – an argument developed by John Howard Yoder (1927–97) in *The Politics of Jesus*. (See also Chapter One's discussion of Jesus' passion and death as normative.) The way God redeems evil and makes differences not violently competitive but beautifully complementary is not by responding in kind but through self-giving, patient, open-hearted, non-resistant love.

The weakness of this position is that it is better at identifying what Christians should not do than what they actively should do. Moreover, a position that maintains its truth regardless of consequences is always going to be assaulted with a host of potentially dire consequences.

(b) Pragmatic pacifism is somewhat different. It often points to Jesus' injunctions to love our enemies, pray for those who persecute us, and turn the other cheek. But its commitments contrast subtly with those of theological pacifism. Pragmatic pacifism believes nonviolence is more effective than war as a means of attaining justice. Holding up figures such as Mahatma Gandhi and Martin Luther King Jr., it refuses to attain nonviolent ends through violent means, always seeking to make the means used worthy of the ends pursued. Whereas theological pacifism has a tendency to separate itself off from the world, renouncing the worldly structures and temptations of power, pragmatic pacifism is much more inclined to be active in seeking peace through conventional political arrangements; the work of the Quakers would be one example. Its weakness is that it assumes the oppressor has a moral conscience to appeal to, as Gandhi assumed in relation to the British in India. Where the opponent is ruthless, pragmatic pacifism is powerless.

Crusade

(2) If the pacifist tradition looks squarely to the New Testament, and specifically to the circumstances of Christ's passion, death, and resurrection, the crusading tradition draws from the warring narratives in the story of Israel, particularly the battles against great odds recorded in Joshua and Judges. Here what matters is that the battle is fought on God's behalf; the question of casualties and methods is secondary. Again we may suggest there are two forms of the crusade – the historic and the contemporary.

(a) The most notorious historic examples are the eight Crusades that followed the seizure of Jerusalem by the Turks in 1072, concluding in 1270. While in the Middle Ages these endeavors were considered formative for chivalry, today they are invariably cited as nadirs of Christian brutality.

(b) Nonetheless the contemporary era has seen many wars fought with similar conviction, wars in which the cause involved goes significantly beyond self-defense and assumes some desire to impose or introduce one's own culture to the party against whom one is at war. Some of these wars have shared the brutality of the historic Crusades, notably those fought when religious and ethnic hostility have also been in play. To introduce one's own culture by peaceful means to a people that has not sought it or requested it is generally described as colonialism. To do the same by forcible means may be described as a modern-day version of a crusade. Any contemporary war that is not simply a defensive response to an unprovoked attack could come under this broad definition.

Before we too quickly dismiss the crusade tradition as part of the misguided thinking of the medieval period, we might pause to consider recent examples of Western democratic countries justifying the invasion of other countries with the claim that they were bringing more advanced culture and values, such as democracy or the free market. The crusade is still a live option wherever people believe a war is a tool they can use to achieve the cultural enhancement of the body of people with whom they are at war. It is also a significant factor when the leaders of a country implore their people to strain every sinew to resist the attacker – as has been the rhetoric of the "war on terror." The language of crusade could be regarded as referring today to any war that is not restricted to members of the armed forces but requires wholesale civilian attention.

Just War

(3) The third tradition, that of the just war, can be seen as the way the pacifism of the early centuries of the church became adapted to the circumstances of the Christian empire and its successors. There had already been theories of just war in Greek and Roman times, but the crucial figure is Augustine, at the end of the fourth and the beginning of the fifth centuries. As we saw earlier in this chapter and in Chapter Four, Augustine talked of the earthly city in relation to the heavenly

city. While the church's ideals of pacifism made sense in the realm of the heavenly, eternal city, it was nevertheless currently living in the earthly, transient city. So it also had to come to terms with war as a part of human life. Augustine distinguished between unjustifiable individual acts of violence and killing, and those of collective or lawful authority:

> [T]he natural order which seeks the peace of mankind, ordains that the monarch should have the power of undertaking war if he thinks it advisable, and that the soldiers should perform their military duties on behalf of the peace and security of the community.

Just war tradition looks back to Augustine's formulation, but within it we may consider two versions of the theory, calling them just war and qualified just war respectively.

(a) The first systematization of just-war principles came with the *Decretum* of the Italian canon lawyer Gratian in 1148, which combined concern for the rights and wrongs of going to war in the first place (*jus ad bellum* – Augustine's main interest) with concern for the rights and wrongs of what is done within war (*jus in bello*). The former concern had as its hallmarks the need for war to be made only in a just cause, out of a right intention and authority, having a reasonable hope of success and a peaceful outcome, and doing a minimum amount of harm. The latter concern incorporated the desire to protect the immunity of the innocent. Just war theory then passed through the hands of a number of key figures. Another key twelfth-century thinker in this area was the Parisian Peter Lombard (ca. 1100–60). Thomas Aquinas then stressed the need for proportion between the means used and the ends intended, and introduced the notion of double effect into the tradition. Double effect acknowledges that when the principal intention and end of an action are good, then bad secondary effects of that action (sincerely unintended even if foreseen) are morally tolerable. (The section on consequentialism in Chapter Five explains the principle of double effect in greater depth.) With further important contributions from Martin Luther and the seventeenth-century Dutch jurist Hugo Grotius (1583–1645), Christian just-war theory emerged with around six or seven criteria for embarking upon a war.

- *Jus ad bellum.* The conventional criteria require a legitimate authority (i.e., a government, or in modern times the United Nations), a right intention (i.e., restoration of a suffered harm, such as a territorial invasion, or response to a grave public evil, such as the massive violation of the basic human rights of a whole population), and an overwhelming balance of injustice on one side. In such circumstances, such an authority, waging war as a last resort (i.e., having exhausted all diplomatic avenues) with a strong probability of success and a high expectation that the good to be achieved will outweigh the inevitable damage to be done may consider the declaration of a war to be just.
- *Jus in bello.* As to the conduct of a war, a just war should be pursued with due discrimination (i.e., avoiding non-combatants), with due proportionality

(i.e., avoiding reckless damage), and with minimum force. Some would argue that the greatest moral achievement of the modern era has been the accords through which since 1864 the international community has regulated the conduct of war, such as the four Geneva conventions concerning treatment of the shipwrecked, sick, and wounded, of prisoners of war, and of civilians; the Geneva protocol of 1925 banning biological weapons; and the Hague Conventions of 1899 and 1907 concerning military and naval conflict.

As to the ending of such wars, a more contemporary concern, just-war criteria seek to avoid revenge, restrain vindictive treatment of those not responsible for the hostilities, and prevent their exclusion from the international community. The criteria also promote processes such as apology, compensation, and war crimes trials.

(b) What is here called qualified just war is perhaps most famously expressed by the late Methodist theologian Paul Ramsey (1913–88). This is how he makes the case for just war:

> The western theory of the just war originated, not primarily from considerations of abstract or "natural" justice, but from the interior of the ethics of Christian love, or what John XXIII termed "social charity." It was a work of charity for the Good Samaritan to give help to the man who fell among thieves. But one step more, it may have been a work of charity for the inn-keeper to hold himself ready to receive beaten and wounded men, and for him to have conducted his business so that he was solvent enough to extend credit to the Good Samaritan. By another step it would have been a work of charity, and not of justice alone, to maintain and serve in a police patrol on the Jericho road to prevent such things from happening. By yet another step, it might well be a work of charity to resist, by force of arms, any external aggression against the social order that maintains the police patrol along the road to Jericho. This means that, where the enforcement of an ordered community is not effectively present, it may be a work of justice and a work of social charity to resort to other available and effective means of resisting injustice: what do you think Jesus would have made the Samaritan do if he had come upon the scene while the robbers were still at their fell work?

On this account, delivering other human beings from subjection to tyranny or protecting them from oppression are properly to be understood as merciful, loving actions. In certain situations, the only available means of coming to the aid of victims of injustice is to take action against the perpetrators: there is no choice. Sometimes this requires the use of force. So for a thinker like Ramsey it is possible to say that the justice of occasional uses of armed conflict originates from within the ethics of Christian love.

In his 2013 book *In Defence of War*, ethicist Nigel Biggar largely follows Ramsey's logic, accusing pacifism of "wishful thinking" and arguing that war, while always morally flawed, is sometimes necessary in order to punish grave injustice. In fact, moral demands can sometimes trump legal ones, such that a just (or justified) war may sometimes even transgress international law, as in the case of the North Atlantic Treaty Organization (NATO) intervention in Kosovo in 1999.

A war justly undertaken, however, must be conducted justly. If it is only in the cause of the innocent that Christians can have a rationale for the use of armed force at all, then they would be rendering that rationale senseless by deliberately killing innocents as a means of attacking the enemy. They must never resort to means that directly target non-combatants. So the principle that underpins the justification of war also underpins the restriction on certain military objectives. It enables a distinction between legitimate and illegitimate targets. Those "not closely cooperating in or directly engaged in the force that ought to be repelled" are amongst the innocent and helpless of the earth to whom Christians have a sacred responsibility.

On these grounds, there can be an unequivocal rejection of certain kinds of warfare as immoral. These would include:

- the dropping of the atomic bomb on Hiroshima; and by extension
- nuclear war against the civil centers of an enemy population; and
- the obliteration bombing perpetrated by both sides in World War II.

The Western tradition of restricted warfare, governed by limitations on the means and ends of war alike, is a product of reflection on the Christian calling to compassion. Christian compassion "always seeks if possible to wound none whom by His wounds Christ died to save," as Ramsey puts it. From his qualified just war point of view, the acts of war listed above are incompatible with all regulative norms in nineteen centuries of Western warfare.

All today's weapons of mass destruction fall foul of the same principle. This is because weapons of mass destruction are weapons that involve civilian populations in large numbers, and thus cannot fall within any traditional notion of a just war. In their guise modern people have to face the possibility of total war and of "mutually assured destruction." Modern methods of warfare have added biological and chemical weapons to nuclear ones, and the horror of war has increased in proportion to their massive destructive power. This enables the argument that because the destructive capacity of today's weapons is too great to be able to discriminate between military and civilian targets, they make the ill-effects of war disproportionate to any good end that could possibly be achieved, and in the face of them all the terms of reference of just war thinking fall apart. On the other hand, Ramsey himself (and some Catholic ethicists in recent decades) have held out some hope that technological advances that increase the precision of weapons-targeting, and a more developed capacity to control the collateral effects of weapons damage, could mean that just war principles will again make some sense in the context of modern warfare.

Another significant modern development is that warfare has become an activity that is far less the preserve of nation-states. Modern nomenclature includes the notion of rogue states, such as North Korea, pariah states such as Burma (Myanmar) and Zimbabwe, and failed (or fragile) states such as Somalia and Yemen. Other bodies have claimed to be engaged in fighting wars, in sometimes controversial ways. These have included rebel and terrorist groups, some of which operate international networks, such as the group that calls itself Islamic State or ISIS. International bodies like the United Nations also sponsor military activity and intervention, and it is harder than ever to define theoretically exactly what constitutes a war. The conventional categories of pacifism, just war, and crusade are not always helpful here. As the US and British intervention in Iraq showed, a foreign invasion can simply catalyze an inter-ethnic, inter-tribal, or inter-religious conflict with a host of warring parties that is hard to fit into any of the conventional approaches to war and peace.

Universal

There are a variety of pro- and anti-war stances in Christian ethics that can be identified as *deontological*. Typical of the anti-war strain is the view that war is wrong because it violates the commandment against killing. A Christian who participates in it, therefore, is committing a species of murder. He or she is also transgressing the command to love the neighbor. A key principle here is that it is never right to use force, even for good ends. By contrast, it is argued (by Paul Ramsey and Reinhold Niebuhr [1892–1971]) that involvement in one's country's defense and security is as much the domain of the responsible Christian citizen as it is of any other citizen until the eschaton is fully realized. If Christians participate in any aspect of the life of their society (including politics, trade, systems of education and health care, and so on), then on what grounds may they opt out of its warfare? Also, as we have seen, the just-war tradition has strong appeal to universalists as a means to draw both Christian and non-Christian perspectives into a common frame of reference when assessing the justice of particular wars or forms of warfare. In this sense, it is a paradigm example of universal ethics.

Consequentialist attitudes to war are equally universalist, but argue differently. A key principle here – as in relation to theories of punishment – is that of deterrence. Deterrence is the name given to the practice of discouraging aggressive action from another quarter by instilling fear of the retaliation that might follow. It is thus quintessentially consequentialist. The notion of deterrence has had its most developed use in relation to nuclear weapons, and was appealed to especially in the period of the Cold War between the USSR and the Western powers amongst whom the USA was foremost. Another consequentialist argument would argue that a pacifist policy on the part of one nation-state is irresponsible because the state in question thereby abandons any obligation to defend its values, and empowers less scrupulous states or parties to operate unchecked (thus making destructive military aggression more and not less likely).

A consequentialist defense of pacifism, on the other hand, asserts on the basis of an optimistic view of human nature that adherence to nonviolence, whether at an individual, group, or national level, will in the long run produce net good effects that outweigh bad effects.

Many would say that in the modern era the nature of weaponry itself (in particular, weapons of mass destruction) makes it insupportable to give any moral justification for their possession. Their enormous destructive power represents too great and uncontrollable a threat to human life on earth to be countenanced in any form, and the only moral course of action is disarmament. Others might argue that there is a moral distinction to be drawn between threatening a particular moral action (but not in fact intending to do it), and genuinely intending it when threatening it. In the context of deterrence, the decoupling of threat from intent (deterrence by "bluffing") may be considered acceptable, even if an actual strike would be immoral. There are also those who ground just war theory in the need for human life to have a basic order and structure, in the belief that justice cannot exist without such order, and that the order of justice must be protected through force. As we have seen, Ramsey argued that this is itself a form of love of one's neighbor.

Subversive

Subversive ethics, in its rejection of any claim to have identified a universal ground for moral argument or action, owes something to the revolutionary imagination that awoke in Europe in the late eighteenth century. If universal ethics sees military action against a background of fundamental continuity and stability – asserting, for example, the normal legitimacy of political institutions, and assuming that stable and benign government is a "natural" state – then political strife and violence (whether war, civil disobedience, or resistance to tyranny) have to be understood as temporary suspensions of the norm. Moreover, they occur *precisely in order to reinstate* the previously established but temporarily lost condition of legitimacy. But a genuinely revolutionary mindset denies the universalist pretensions of the "normal state of things," and can sometimes imagine a violent intervention that is not merely restoration or correction but the radical transformation both of individual consciousnesses and of social order – the creation of something genuinely new. Subversive ethics in this vein might appeal to Jesus himself as a figure of revolutionary resistance. As the philosopher and theologian James Childress (b. 1940) points out, "Jesus' use of 'force' in cleansing the temple, his entry into Jerusalem, the response of the people, the response of Jewish and Roman authorities, the mode of his execution, and the sign over the cross all have political overtones."

In borrowing the concepts of revolutionary praxis as the conscious and deliberate creation of new human institutions and patterns of relation, subversive ethics may also be open to borrowing some of the justifications of violent intervention that go with them. The use of force may be seen as an unavoidable way for politically passive peoples to be transformed into active political participants. Liberation theologians have pointed out that it is too easy to condemn revolutionary violence while overlooking the violence of the systems they oppose: the structural forms of violence that keep poor people poor, and uneducated people disempowered. The violence of the oppressed, on this account, is justified counter-violence.

Ecclesial

For John Milbank (b. 1952), the Augustinian commitment to the ontological priority of peace is enshrined in the practices of the church. Peace is embodied among Christians in the sacrament of the Eucharist. It is not simply the absence of conflict, nor should it be defined by reference to some notionally equal and opposite force (violence, or sacrifice), for this would be precisely to take away its character as genuine peace.

An ecclesial approach to the question of whether Christians may support or participate in violence might argue that it is inconceivable that a Christian could both share in the dynamics of the triune life through the sacraments of baptism and Eucharist and through the fellowship of the church, and at the same time fight and kill other human beings. The whole character of Christ's life is marked by his refusal to play the games of competitive aggression and fearful self-regard that mark the fallen human condition. He does not live by frantic attempts to shore up his own security or prolong his own existence at all costs. On the contrary, "[i]nstead of demonizing foreigners, he loved enemies. He offered security through generosity not hoarding, through risk but not through fear … [T]o eat from *this* table … and to call this life *the* very life of the triune God … is to implicate [oneself] in God's way of non-violent love" (so writes Gerald Schlabach). A Christian who fights is failing in the imitation of Christ, and in the requirement to be part of the suffering community in the world. Christ's death (conceived as exemplary) absolutely forbids the Christian to use coercion – let alone to take human life. The Christian's allegiance to the new kingdom inaugurated by Christ (a kingdom "not of this world," as Jesus says in John 18:36) precludes involvement in the military business of earthly kingdoms.

The faithful practices of Christian communities from day to day ought to instill in them a default preference for nonviolent approaches to personal or political threat – or so an ecclesial approach like that of John Howard Yoder or Stanley Hauerwas (b. 1940) would argue. This places the burden of proof on the shoulders of those who would justify warfare. In contrast to some strands of liberation theology, the ecclesial ethicist is more likely to contend that the conviction that God – and not us – is the one who "makes history come out right" should equip the Christian not to resort to violence in order to ensure that goodness and justice will prevail. Military options usually represent shortcuts to the solution of problems, which cannot ultimately work because they reinstate the practices of violence and fear that made them necessary in the first place.

Ecclesial ethics does not necessarily forfeit all sense of the tragic realities of the world in this confident affirmation of God's good purpose in God's good time. Indeed, it may well highlight the function of ecclesial practices (like the Eucharist) to display all the more painfully, acutely, and *by stark contrast*, the world's wounds and entrapment, and to make Christians more hungry for transformation.

Summary

This chapter has covered a good deal of ground, but its uniting theme has been how human life is to be framed in well-governed, well-disciplined, and well-protected political societies. In a tradition in which Augustine stands as a figure of towering influence, Christian ethics has tended to accept that the obligations of earthly government are unavoidable, including those that require the use of force to restrain evil, defend against threat, and enforce laws. But at the same time it has sought to refer such tasks to a higher measure: that of God's ultimate rule. More positive and often Catholic appreciations of the role of human government tend to see it as one of the orderings given by God in the creation of the world. More negative and often Protestant evaluations of the role of human government tend to see it as a mark of the Fall, which along with all other aspects of the created order must look for its redemption in a radical transformation at the end of days. Subversive traditions of ethics have been particularly good at sustaining an interrogation of the pretensions and complacency that tempt political power-mongers. We have seen that there is a lively and ongoing debate underway about whether states can claim the authority to "manage" complex and plural multi-religious societies, and whether religious traditions should accept such patronage.

In discussing justice, we have seen how Christian traditions are more ready to articulate issues of justice in *unitive* terms than merely *distributive* ones. The latter often reflect the individualistic tendencies of modern Western societies that are based on proprietorship and personal liberty. We have observed the creative influence that Christian practices and beliefs have had on the making and enforcing of laws. These have included a promotion of certain restorative forms of penal practice, as well as an influence upon international regulations like those that now govern conflict and cooperation between nations.

Finally, this chapter has looked at the fraught issue of how wars are categorized, authorized, and conducted. It has explored the implications of a radical theological appeal to the ultimacy of peace as the governing framework for human action. It has also looked at a variety of examples of Christian "realism" that advocate the use of regrettable but necessary instruments of human force to ensure a safe passage through the world of the penultimate on the way to God's kingdom.

References and Further Reading

The State

Augustine's greatest political work, as we saw in Chapter Four, is *The City of God* (Henry Bettenson, trans.; New York: Penguin Books, 1972, 1984); also available online in the Christian Classics Ethereal Library at www.ccel.org/ccel/schaff/npnf102.toc.html. We have made particular reference to Book XIX in this chapter. Augustine's definition of the state is given in *The City of God*, Book XIX, chapter 24, page 890. The quotation ("man with his brief life, man under the doom of death") is cited in Norman H. Baynes, *Byzantine Studies and Other Essays* (London: University of London, Athlone Press, 1955; New York: Greenwood Press Reprint, 1974), page 292. Augustine's statement on just war is taken from his *Reply to Faustus the Manichean*, XXII, 75 (printed in *A Textbook of Christian Ethics* [Robin Gill, ed.; London; New York: T & T Clark, 2006]). His comment about victory and divine judgment may be found in *The City of God*, Book XIX, chapter 15, pages 874–5.

One of the best introductions to Augustine's political thought is Peter Brown's *Religion and Society in the Age of Augustine* (London: Faber, 1972). The quotations of Brown in this chapter are from that book.

Another present-day expositor of Augustine is Oliver O'Donovan, whose works *The Desire of the Nations: Rediscovering the Roots of Political Theology* (Cambridge: Cambridge University Press, 1999), *The Ways of Judgment* (Grand Rapids, MI: Eerdmans, 2005), and (with Joan Lockwood O'Donovan) *From Irenaeus to Grotius: A Sourcebook in Christian Political Thought* (Grand Rapids, MI: Eerdmans, 1999) are especially relevant to this chapter.

For John Henry Newman's thought, the source used is the essay "Who's to Blame?" in *Discussions and Arguments on Various Subjects* (Notre Dame, IN: University of Notre Dame Press, 2004 [1873]), as well as *Sermons, Bearing on Subjects of the Day*, Sermon XVII ("Sanctity the Token of the Christian Empire") (London; New York: Longmans, Green, and Co., 1909). The excerpted section of Newman's analysis of the Augustinian tradition is from *Discussions and Arguments on Various Subjects*, page 315.

Eric Gregory's study of Augustine in modern political theory is in *Politics and the Order of Love: An Augustinian Ethic of Democratic Citizenship* (Chicago, IL: University of Chicago Press, 2008).

The source used for Calvin's thought is *Institutes of the Christian Religion*, with quotations from Book III.xix.15 and Book IV.xx.2–3.

The text by Jacques Ellul referred to in this chapter is *The Ethics of Freedom* (Grand Rapids, MI: Eerdmans, 1976). Quotations are from pages 386, 390, and 396.

To find out more about Emil Brunner's and Karl Barth's views of the authority of the state, in the larger context of their famous argument about the viability or otherwise of natural theology, look at Emil Brunner, *Nature and Grace: A Contribution to the Discussion With Karl Barth*, and Karl Barth, *No! Answer to Emil Brunner*. They are reproduced together in Karl Barth and Emil Brunner, *Natural Theology: Comprising "Nature and Grace" by Professor Dr. Emil Brunner and the Reply "No!" by Dr. Karl Barth* (Eugene, OR: Wipf and Stock, 2002). For some of Barth's mature reflections on the state, see *Church Dogmatics* II.2 (Edinburgh: T & T Clark, 1957); quotations in this chapter are from pages 719 and 722.

Richard Bauckham's useful typology of a creation-oriented ("conservative") political ethic and an eschatology-oriented ("radical") political ethic is outlined in *New Dictionary of Christian Ethics and Pastoral Theology* (David J. Atkinson and David H. Field, eds; Downers Grove, IL: InterVarsity Press, 1995), page 670.

William Temple is quoted from his book *Citizen and Churchman* (London: Eyre and Spottiswoode, 1941), page 29.

Quotations from the 1948 Lambeth Conference are from Resolutions 5 and 20 of the Conference, and can be found at www.lambethconference.org/resolutions/1948/.

The papal encyclical *Pacem in Terris* is available at http://w2.vatican.va/content/john-xxiii/en/encyclicals/documents/hf_j-xxiii_enc_11041963_pacem.html. A portion of the encyclical is also included in *Christian Ethics: An Introductory Reader*.

Emil Brunner's explanation of subsidiarity is from his *Communism, Capitalism and Christianity* (London: Lutterworth Press, 1949), page 13.

Luke Bretherton explores the role of the church in relation to community organizing in *Resurrecting Democracy: Faith, Citizenship, and the Politics of a Common Life* (Cambridge: Cambridge University Press, 2015).

Max L. Stackhouse and Richard Mouw are cited at the end of the section on "universal" ethics of the state. Stackhouse's thought on covenant can be followed up in his book *Covenant and Commitments: Faith, Family and Economic Life* (Louisville, KY: Westminster/John Knox Press, 1997). One example of Mouw's writing in this area is *Pluralisms and Horizons: An Essay in Christian Public Philosophy*, with Sander Griffioen (Grand Rapids, MI: Eerdmans, 1993).

George Bell is quoted in E. R. Norman, *Church and Society in England 1770–1970: A Historical Study* (Oxford: Oxford University Press, 1976), page 376.

The treatment of the thought of Robert Bellah and Phillip Hammond is based on *Varieties of Civil Religion* (San Francisco, CA: Harper and Row, 1980).

William Cavanaugh's theology of the state may be found in *Theopolitical Imagination* (Edinburgh: T & T Clark, 2003). Cavanaugh's thought in this chapter is drawn in particular from his essay in *The Blackwell Companion to Christian Ethics* (Stanley Hauerwas and Samuel Wells, eds; Oxford; Malden, MA: Blackwell, 2004).

Oliver O'Donovan's political thought is drawn from *The Desire of the Nations* and *The Ways of Judgment*; the longer quotation above is from *The Ways of Judgment*, page 238.

The following works on the state are quoted in the corresponding chapter in *Christian Ethics: An Introductory Reader*:

- *Quadragesimo Anno*: On Reconstruction of the Social Order (Encyclical of Pope Pius XI, May 15, 1931). Available online at http://w2.vatican.va/content/pius-xi/en/encyclicals/documents/hf_p-xi_enc_19310515_quadragesimo-anno.html.
- *The Kairos Document. Challenge to the Church: A Theological Comment on the Political Crisis in South Africa.* From Chapter Two, Critique of State Theology. http://www.sahistory.org.za/archive/challenge-church-theological-comment-political-crisis-south-africa-kairos-document-1985.
- *The Barmen Declaration.* From Arthur C. Cochrane. *The Church's Confession Under Hitler.* Philadelphia, PA: Westminster Press, 1962, pp. 237–42. http://www.sacred-texts.com/chr/barmen.htm.

Justice and Punishment

Nicholas Wolterstorff discusses justice and rights in *Justice: Rights and Wrongs* (Princeton, NJ: Princeton University Press, 2008).

Thomas Aquinas' conception of justice is in *Summa Theologica* (5 vols; Notre Dame, IN: Christian Classics, 1948), Secunda Secundae [Second Part of the Second Part], Question 58.

Quotations of Daniel Bell on the atonement and on the works of mercy are from *The Blackwell Companion to Christian Ethics* (Stanley Hauerwas and Samuel Wells, eds; Oxford: Blackwell, 2004); John Berkman's comments on punishment and the quotation "Justice redeems ..." are also in the same volume.

The following works on justice and punishment are in the corresponding chapter of *Christian Ethics: An Introductory Reader*:

- Oliver O'Donovan. "The Death Penalty in *Evangelium Vitae*." Pages 213–36 in *Ecumenical Ventures in Ethics: Protestants Engage Pope John Paul II'S Moral Encyclicals*. Reinhard Hütter and Theodor Dieter, eds. Grand Rapids, MI: Eerdmans, 1998.
- Daniel Berrigan: *Poetry, Drama, Prose*. Michael True, ed. Maryknoll, NY: Orbis Books, 1988. From Philip Berrigan et al., "Statement of the Catonsville Nine"; Daniel Berrigan, "Swords into Plowshares."

- Timothy Gorringe. *God's Just Vengeance: Crime, Violence and the Rhetoric of Salvation.* Cambridge Studies in Ideology and Religion 9. Cambridge: Cambridge University Press, 1996. From chapter 10, "Forgiveness, Crime and Community."

Roland Bainton's threefold typology of war is in *Christian Attitudes Toward War and Peace* (New York: Abingdon Press, 1960).

Paul Ramsey's classic work on just war is *The Just War: Force and Political Responsibility* (Lanham, MD: Rowman and Littlefield, 1986, 2002). Quotations are from Part Two: The Morality of War; Chapter 6, "Justice in War," selections from which are also included in the corresponding chapter of *Christian Ethics: An Introductory Reader.*

Nigel Biggar defends the necessity of war to combat grave injustice in his *In Defence of War* (Oxford: Oxford University Press, 2013).

Reinhold Niebuhr writes on just war theory in numerous places. One good source is his essay "Why the Church is Not Pacifist," reprinted in *The End of Illusions: Religious Leaders Confront Hitler's Gathering Storm* (Joseph Loconte, ed.; Lanham, MD: Rowman and Littlefield, 2004).

The quotation from James Childress on Jesus' use of force is from his article "Resistance," in *A New Dictionary of Christian Ethics* (John Macquarrie and James Childress, eds; London: SCM, 1986). See also his article "Pacifism," pages 446–8.

John Milbank's seminal work, containing the basis of his political theology, is *Theology and Social Theory* (Oxford: Blackwell, 1990).

Gerald Schlabach's theology of war is drawn from his essay "Breaking Bread: Peace and War," pages 360–74 in *The Blackwell Companion to Christian Ethics.*

Perhaps the most famous of John Howard Yoder's arguments for Christian pacifism is *The Politics of Jesus* (2nd edn; Grand Rapids, MI: Eerdmans; Carlisle, UK: Paternoster Press, 1993). See also Stanley Hauerwas, *The Peaceable Kingdom: A Primer in Christian Ethics* (Notre Dame, IN: University of Notre Dame Press, 1983).

In addition to the above, the following readings on war are included in the corresponding chapter of *Christian Ethics: An Introductory Reader:*

- John Gerassi, ed. *Revolutionary Priest: The Complete Writings and Messages of Camilo Torres.* New York: Random House, 1971.
- Dorothy Day. "Our Country Passes from Undeclared War to Declared War; We Continue Our Christian Pacifist Stand" (1942). In *The Power of Nonviolence: Writings by Advocates of Peace.* Howard Zinn, ed. Boston, MA: Beacon Press, 2002.

We have also drawn in this chapter upon Charles Curran's and James Childress's articles in *A New Dictionary of Christian Ethics* (John Macquarrie and James Childress, eds; London: SCM Press, 1986). Additional helpful readings include:

- J. Phillip Wogaman. *Christian Perspectives on Politics.* Rev. edn. Louisville, KY: Westminster/John Knox Press, 1988, 2000.
- Charles E. Curran. *American Catholic Social Ethics.* Notre Dame, IN: University of Notre Dame Press, 1982.

Chapter Nine
Good Life

Jesus proclaimed, "I have come that they may have life, and that they may have it abundantly" (John 10:10). But to ask about the character of a well-lived life is necessarily to ask about the networks of relations in which that life is held and by which it is sustained. These include the many forms of exchange and communication that constitute social life, and are developing at often dizzying speed in the modern world. This chapter deals with some of the aspects of such complex relational life, with special attention to money, work, and the media.

Economics, Wealth, and Poverty

Scripture and Tradition

Poverty is given a positive meaning in the New Testament as a mark of those who, in following Jesus, renounce earthly possessions. We might think of the rich young man whom Jesus tells to sell all he has (Mark 10:17–22), and Jesus' own statement that the Son of Man has nowhere to lay his head (Luke 9:58). Paul claims himself to be an example of apostolic poverty in this tradition (2 Cor 11:7–9, 26–27; Phil 4:16–18).

Nonetheless, this affirmation of poverty as a form of discipleship – though it was to be enshrined in the rules of life of many religious orders – does not override the general biblical view that unwilled poverty is neither desirable nor good. This view is particularly clear in the Old Testament. There is a great deal of concern about poverty in the Bible, and especially in the prophetic literature (cf. Amos 2:6–7; 4:1; Isa 3:15; Jer 2:34). Indeed, the prophets regarded the treatment of the poor and the weak as the test of a just society. The withholding of

Introducing Christian Ethics, Second Edition. Samuel Wells and Ben Quash with Rebekah Eklund.
© 2017 John Wiley & Sons Ltd. Published 2017 by John Wiley & Sons Ltd.

wages, and the failure to defend those who cannot maintain their own rights, are consistently condemned. Jesus' own message is presented as "good news for the poor," and there is an expectation that the kingdom he is initiating will transform the existing order so that the hungry may be fed and those without anything may be invested with much. In Christian history, there is a long and venerable tradition of *voluntary* poverty: we can see it in practices of Christian asceticism (or self-denying austerity), charity, and almsgiving. None of these things, however, detracts from Christianity's continued insistence that the poor must not be overlooked, as manifest in its historical condemnation of usury (the lending of money for interest) and its advocacy of just wages.

Wealth is also a perennial concern in Christian thought from the very beginning, and how property is used and distributed is generally seen as one of the tests of the command to love one's neighbor. Jesus' parable of judgment in which the righteous are welcomed by a king with the words "I was hungry and you gave me food, I was thirsty and you gave me something to drink, I was naked and you gave me clothing" (Matt 25:31–46) is often cited as a basis for a Christian ethic of philanthropy – along with the parable of the Good Samaritan (Luke 10:25–37). Just as in the Old Testament it is understood that the land belongs ultimately to God, and the people are merely tenants, so in the Christian tradition it is a fundamental conviction that the goods of the earth are God's, and are to be used on God's behalf for the promotion of the common good. This belief that money is to be used for the collective good, and not merely for one's own benefit, is one of the reasons why for centuries the church maintained the unlawfulness of usury – in the same way as Jews obeyed Torah by refusing to lend to other Jews for interest. The church reinforced its condemnation of usury further by drawing on Aristotle's argument that mere money was barren; it could not by any agency of its own be a maker of more money. The obligations of charity led strands of the patristic, medieval, and Reformed traditions to the strong assertion that those who have the means to give to the needy, yet do not do so, deserve the name "thief" as much as those who steal. (This has a tone to it that anticipates some of the concerns of subversive ethicists in the modern period; see Chapter Six.) And in parallel with these traditions of instruction about how wealth is positively to be used, there is also in constant play a negative concern about its power to corrupt. Thus, in the New Testament concept of Mammon (Matt 6:24), wealth is personified as an idol vying for allegiance with the Christian God.

Thomas Aquinas (1225–74) taught that private property ownership could be a part of positive human law even if not of natural law (these categories of law in Aquinas' thought are explained in Chapter Four), and saw in it certain advantages if rightly used (e.g., in practicing the virtues of almsgiving and generosity). Most mainstream Protestant tradition has shared this affirmative evaluation of ownership, with the exception of some of the radical sects like the Diggers and the Hutterites. On the whole, it has not preserved any equivalent to the outright renunciation of possessions that continued in the Roman Catholic monastic tradition. In general, Protestantism has preferred to think in terms of good stewardship of wealth rather than of radical religious poverty. At intervals, however, it has shared with medieval monastic orders the need to come to terms with the problems generated by prosperity. Eighteenth-century Quakers and nineteenth-century Methodists each faced the challenges (and acknowledged the spiritual dangers) of wealth.

John Locke (1632–1704) developed the idea that private property was a *right* that justified the possession of anything appropriated from the "abundance of nature" by one's own labor, regardless of whether it had any social usefulness or value for the common good. Taking its cue from this, early liberal capitalism exalted the freedom of individuals to pursue their own interests in a free market, in the expectation that the pursuit of self-interest could yield prosperity for all (this has come to be known as the "hidden hand" theory of market economics). It was only in this period (i.e., in the seventeenth and eighteenth centuries) that Western Christendom finally and formally abandoned its historic condemnation of usury, although in the meantime many actual forms of interest payment in trade had come to be accepted. Christian thinking in modern times has generally accepted the fact that interest is an established part of the machinery of modern life, though arguing frequently for controls on excessive borrowing and lending, and expressing concern for the damage done to vulnerable debtors by cynical lending practices.

Contemporary Debate

There are various ways in which trades unions, nationalized companies, different forms of welfare state, and the shift of control from capital to management have qualified the character of capitalist economies in the modern era. Nevertheless the ideology of capitalism generally resists government interventions in the economy, and many companies continue to operate with a high degree of freedom in the international arena.

The Christian socialist economic theorist R. H. Tawney (1880–1962) argued that such capitalist economics should be re-envisioned. "The rise of modern economic relations," he wrote, "which may be dated in England from the latter half of the seventeenth century, was coincident with the growth of a political theory which replaced the conception of purpose by that of mechanism." He meant that economic exchange was no longer seen as existing for some *higher good*, but was an enclosed system that simply needed to be allowed to function in as smooth a way as possible. This in its turn, he argued, could not have happened except for the fact that such a self-justifying economic system was accepted by certain strands of Reformation theology (especially Calvinism). In the thought of the Reformers and Puritans, he believed (following in the steps of Max Weber [1864–1920]), there was an unhealthy dichotomy set up between the earthly and the heavenly spheres. This was, in effect, a freeing of the earthly sphere to pursue its own interests, with a consequently diminished reference to a heavenly end or *telos* for the material goods it handled and owned. So for Tawney and others, the regaining of a proper *telos* in the economic sphere was a priority, and he called for a reappraisal of what economics and the social order were there *for*. He demanded a relativizing of its processes and a curbing of its assumed autonomy, attacking the philosophy of an industrial civilization which "assures men that there are no ends other than their ends, no law other than their desires, no limit other than that which they think advisable."

Tawney is thus a typically "left-wing" voice in Christian thought about economics in the modern period. Such a view is a counterpoint to influential "right-wing" defenses of capitalist economics like those of Friedrich Hayek (1899–1992), who claimed that now that human beings have moved beyond tribalism they can never again have shared or common ends. Hayek proposed a *laissez-faire* economy as the solution to this – believing that the market is a self-adjusting mechanism. Tawney, on the other hand, refused to abandon the principle that "free rights" to wealth and property should be subordinated to concerns for communal justice and well-being. When he argued that a purpose or *telos* is effectively a principle of unity, his point seems strikingly similar to that of Augustine, who (as we saw in the last chapter) defines a republic as "an assemblage of reasonable beings bound together by a common agreement concerning the objects of their love." A *telos* of this kind supplies a common end to which efforts can be directed, and it submits interests which would otherwise conflict with the judgment of an overruling aim. The pagan values of Mammon worship, Tawney claims, are the ones that dominate capitalist society. In the face of them he espouses an equality of consideration – in other words, the idea that every human being has an equal claim to respect. Society, as a consequence, should seek to cultivate this common humanity by putting stress on institutions and procedures that meet common needs, and are a source of common enlightenment and common enjoyment.

The vision of a genuine welfare state flourished at the time Tawney was writing, and especially in the immediate aftermath of World War II. The term probably originated with the English Archbishop William Temple (1881–1944), but the concept had been evolving for some time in reaction to a philosophy of possessive individualism derived from the thought of Adam Smith (1723–90). Its supporters believed that poverty was too often blamed on the poor themselves, and that private benevolence was not a reliable mechanism for its alleviation. In the words of Ronald Preston (1913–2001), who was in the middle years of the twentieth century one of the Church of England's leading voices on social ethics:

> A welfare state means that the community makes corporate provisions for its citizens by guaranteeing them a minimum standard of life as of right, below which they will not be allowed to fall. It is not a matter of merit or desert.

He argued that this should be made possible, even in cases of unemployment, by payments that guarantee subsistence, and by the provision of free education, health care, and sometimes housing. It is still insisted upon by its supporters that the welfare state embodies a more organic view of human society than free-market approaches, which dissolve social relationships into individual contracts and require the state simply to police those contracts.

The idea of comprehensive welfare provision by the state now seems to many to be less sustainable than it once did. There has been a renewed concern with how people can be encouraged to be more active in safeguarding their own well-being and that of their local communities, rather than passing all responsibility upwards to the instruments of government, and losing touch with any face-to-face sense of personal investment in the well-being of their neighbors.

Recent decades have witnessed the dramatic collapse of the communist experiment in most parts of the world. This too has given new impetus to questions about social justice in a contemporary context, and in particular about whether there is any viable alternative to economic systems based on self-interest. William F. May (1915–2011), the contemporary American moral philosopher who for two decades held the chair in Christian ethics at Southern Methodist University, points out that when self-interest is given free rein, then the weak person's only defense is to try to acquire more knowledge, shrewdness, and purchasing power. This flies in the face of the biblical notion of covenant (which, for him, founds true justice): for covenant relationships "oblige the more powerful to accept some responsibility for the more vulnerable and powerless of the two partners."

Universal

Christian economists working in a universalist mode have usually tried to commend their vision by finding terms that will be shared by a largely secular economic discourse on either left or right. The values and visions of justice of Tawney (and others in the same "left-wing" tradition) seemed to reconcile socialist principles with Christian faith relatively easily. Their socialist values, they argued, had their foundation in Christian visions of justice. But such a foundation is simply not generally accepted in most arguments for socialist economics. Left-wing theorists today usually claim a purely "rational" grounding and defense for their theories, by which they mean one without religious arguments. Thus (despite left-wing Christian hopefulness), there may in the modern period be little more than "coincidences" of Christian ideas with socialist economic principles. Likewise, free-market economic theory seems only accidentally convergent with theological arguments whenever such convergence can be found. This is because modern right-wing theorists too seek a grounding and defense for their theories that do not make any explicit appeal to ideas about God.

The challenge to Christian ethicists is that, when separated from any religious root to their values, both left- and right-wing positions tend to be largely materialist – and thus inadequate from a Christian point of view.

- The right-wing position argues for the absoluteness of the individual's right both to own and to determine the use of her personal property. It can seem uninterested in encouraging personal commitment to the voluntary service of fellow human beings.
- The left-wing position frequently assumes that if inequalities of ownership and material opportunity are eradicated then all conflict in society will disappear as

well. Particularly by its appeal to the state to effect this change, the left, as much as the right, ignores issues of charity and mutuality. It can forget the continuing importance of that personal initiative which contributes vitally to flourishing communities and which, arguably, the state cannot provide.

Tawney perceived the dangers of this materialism taking hold on both sides, amongst "haves" and "have nots" alike. When materialists feel social compassion or a sense of obligation to help others, they can think of nothing more original to do than to diminish poverty. This is because poverty, being the opposite of the riches that they value most, seems to them "the most terrible of human afflictions." They do not understand that "poverty is a symptom and a consequence of social disorder, while the disorder itself is something at once more fundamental and more incorrigible."

Many modern Christian responses to the stand-off between socialist materialism and free-market capitalism have involved the invocation of the deep purposes of human society. Those who support the idea of command economies envision the achievement by responsible authorities of complete economic power. Those who support capitalism want the pursuit of material wealth to be given a minimum of hindrance. But neither of these alternatives can even begin to create unity out of the dissension and mutual incomprehension of many modern societies. Faced with the global dominance of capitalist economic systems after the fall of Soviet communism, the churches have tended to seek to mitigate aspects of capitalist ideology, stressing principles of economic morality including:

- the social obligations that attach to ownership;
- the need to respect the dignity of workers (see the next section of this chapter);
- the importance of justice and the common good; and
- the social basis of economic regimes.

In papal encyclicals as well as in the work of the World Council of Churches, these principles have been held to apply at the international as well as at more local levels. Reasons for being concerned about the poverty of those in other parts of the world have been derived from a notion that there is a "natural law" that respects and binds *nations*.

Some of those working in a universalist vein make explicit appeals to scripture in order to promote an economic ethic that has universal validity. For example, the neighbor-ethic of the gospel ("you shall love your neighbor as yourself," illustrated most famously in the parable of the Good Samaritan in Luke 10:25–37) is used as an argument for why richer nations and individuals should stand in solidarity with the world's poor. There has also been a readiness to argue that discovery of the deep purposes of human society depends on the acknowledgment of God, and that the last word for economics will be a pessimistic one unless a beginning is made in demonstrating the true unity between human beings which is the gift of God. Only in submission to this vision can the other relations between people in society (including their economic ones) begin to find a proper foundation.

Subversive

"What is the proper Christian leaven in the lump of rich-nation politics: exemplary modest life-styles, or the hard political work of getting an entire affluent society to show preferential treatment to the world's poor?" asks Donald Shriver, a former president of Union Theological Seminary in New York City. The concern of subversive traditions of ethics to expose systemic injustices and abuses would tend toward the second option. Using tools of critical social and economic analysis that are frequently adapted from Marxist critique, it argues that the systems of export and import in contemporary international trade only perpetuate the historic injustices of Western imperialism. Thus, the liberation theologian José P. Miranda (b. 1946), following Marx, condemns "differentiating ownership" (in short, the difference between rich and poor), and Gustavo Gutiérrez (b. 1928) is highly critical of systems in which there is wealth for the minority at the expense of poverty for the majority. *At the very least*, poor countries in the world are owed the cost of their survival, since they are helping to pay the cost of the rich world's affluence.

The parables and the practice of Jesus are looked to by many liberation theologians as an anticipation of how the poor will be raised up in God's kingdom. There is a conviviality to this kingdom in the ways the parables depict it – and even though it is a conviviality into which everyone is invited, there is a preferential invitation to the least, the last, and the lost. This is seen as a display of God's own justice – a justice manifest in special care of those otherwise forgotten or wronged. Whereas a universal ethics might see Christ's love for these people as a paradigm case of the grace offered to all sinners, a subversive approach will be concerned not to allow this to occlude their actual status as *poor*.

The American Methodist Walter Wink (1935–2012) identifies the "principalities and powers" referred to in Ephesians with the forces involved in globalization, and argues that they must be engaged with by being unmasked (perhaps as Paul challenged the idols and idol-makers in Athens, in Acts 19). He suggests opposing to their imagined social reality what the British theologian Timothy Gorringe (b. 1946) calls the "counter-imaginary of the gospel." Meanwhile, feminist thinkers like Nel Noddings (b. 1929) and Fiona Robinson (b. 1966) have criticized the use of concepts like duty and rights in public reasoning about economic inequality, as well as the dominance of utilitarian approaches in seeking solutions to it. Working largely in the tradition that Chapter Six described as "feminine," they argue that these approaches are insufficiently relational to resource a proper ethical commitment to the alleviation of global poverty. Such approaches are abstract and cannot instill an ethic of care.

Ecclesial

The contemporary theologian and biblical scholar Stephen Fowl (b. 1960) argues from an ecclesial perspective that "one cannot treat matters of possessions apart from matters of Church unity, trust, truth-telling, forgiveness, and reconciliation." The challenge Christians face in the light of their practices is how "to hold our possessions in a way that bears witness to God's character."

For centuries of the church's life, it has been precisely communities of Christians who have built, run, and financed schools, hospitals, orphanages, and other charitable institutions. They have often been conceived as extensions of the church – organized around and permeated by its liturgical activity. There have been communities of mutual aid based on Acts 4:32 ("Everything they owned was held in common") – perhaps most evidently in the monastic traditions, in Franciscan practices of living on the free-will offerings of others (mendicancy), and in certain Anabaptist (e.g., Mennonite and Hutterite) and Quaker experiments in systems of reciprocal voluntary care. Voluntary participation by Christians in associations or communities of mutual aid in cases of need provided a model for insurance and welfare programs in the later history of the West.

According to ecclesial ethics, we do not engineer the justice of the kingdom; we seek it. It is received from God as a gift, not constructed by us. Nonetheless, it is essentially involving and relational, and in this sense it means nothing unless it is embodied in actual communities, by those who find in the *gift* of justice that there is also a *call*. According to the Scottish theologian Duncan Forrester, writing in 2001, "Those who seek God's righteousness are called to walk in the ways of justice, to anticipate in their practice the justice of the coming Kingdom. Justice is pervasively relational. It has to do with the proper structure of relationships between God and people and among people." This includes, centrally, *economic* justice.

For Stanley Hauerwas, the justice of God is displayed in the practices of the church:

> The task of the church [is] to pioneer those institutions and practices that the wider society has not learned as forms of justice. (At times it is also possible that the church can learn from society more just ways of forming life.) The church, therefore, must act as a paradigmatic community in the hope of providing some indication of what the world can be but is not … The church does not have, but rather is, a social ethic. That is, she is a social ethic inasmuch as she functions as a criteriological institution – that is, an institution that has learned to embody the form of truth that is charity as revealed in the person and work of Christ.

From an ecclesial point of view, the Eucharist proclaims that we are not to accept poverty and its grim companions of hunger, disease, and death as a necessary or final feature of God's plan for the creation. The miracle of the feeding of the 5000 (Matt 14:15–21 and parallels) has certain resonances with the Eucharist, and may be about more than answering physical hunger with bread, but the actual distribution of real food is clearly a central and daily part of the story, as it was in the church's life right from the beginning. In the miracle, bread is not just a symbol for something else.

Kelly Johnson (b. 1964) accepts that the notion of intercessory prayer may conjure for some the specter of an infinitely rich God, seated on a throne of glory, allowing a dribble of wealth to be transferred to poor human petitioners. For ecclesial ethics a truer picture would center on the theme of the church's unity in intercession, which has as its correlate its unity in possession of goods. Christian prayer belongs within a set of wider practices that include those of the distribution and use of material resources. Johnson writes:

> [T]o pray for each others' needs is to take the other's need on as one's own because it is taking part in Christ's intercession and this is what he does. ... Temptation to despair of God's goodness in the face of human misery meets its antidote in the right practice of intercession, which is Christian solidarity.

This ought to lead to a recovery of the proper meaning of "charity," which is not just the patriarchalism of the rich that patronizingly dispenses favors to the poor, but is fully integrated with concepts of justice and neighbor-regard. Practices of almsgiving, in this light, are, according to the British theologian Robert Song (b. 1962), "fundamentally about friendship and personal encounter between rich and poor." Supporting fair trade, meanwhile, might witness to a belief that "it is possible to engage in ... trade as a witness to a new economic order, one that expresses the idea of eucharistic community."

Ecclesial ethics seeks to resist the reduction of economic ethics to a sort of "procedural" morality designed only to provide minimal ground rules to keep the system running – avoiding insider trading, for example, and making sure the accounts are in order. It does not take as a "given" the assumption that the struggle for virtue is a waste of time because it has no correlate in economic success. It may not tinker with the existing system of exchange, but it envisions an altogether different one that has the distinctive and radical character of Eucharistic communion; which *is*, indeed, Eucharistic communion extended to encompass and redeem monetary exchange. It believes that this model – unlike the present system – is one which ultimately has a future, because it is grounded in God's life and purposes.

Work, Business, and Management

Work

Scripture

Work is a basic social reality. Unless we work, we starve. In complex societies, there is always a correlatively complex division of labor, and work thereby becomes a key part of the interdependence and mutual obligation that allow common human living. Many Protestant thinkers have viewed work as one of the divinely implanted "orders" or "mandates" of creation (e.g., Emil Brunner [1889–1966]).

Overall, the texts of Scripture are affirmative of work. Human beings in Genesis are given tasks and responsibilities by God for the shaping and ordering of their environment, and although Adam's punishment when he is cast out of the garden is *hard* labor amongst thistles and thorns, this does not detract from the fact that making, forming, building, and planting are also ways of imaging God's own activity. The texts of the New Testament view work as capable of being a medium not only of the service but also the praise of God. In the New Testament, we encounter Paul emphasizing that the Christian ought not to be idle, and calling for a cheerful spirit in work (1 Thess 4:10–12; 2 Thess 3:6–13). "Whatever your task, put yourselves into it, as done for the Lord and not for your masters, since you know that from the Lord you will receive the inheritance as your reward; you serve the Lord Christ" (Col 3:23–4). This establishes the possibility that one's work might at the same time be a vocation – though a subversive ethicist might point out that this is actually an argument that slaves should work hard!

While Scripture affirms the value of work, it also insists on the sacred necessity of rest; indeed, while work is commended, rest is *commanded*, in the form of the Sabbath day on which even animals and slaves must not be forced to labor (Deut 5:12–15). In the New Testament the book of Hebrews pictures eternal life with God itself as an endless form of perfect Sabbath rest. Similarly some Christian ethicists have turned their attention to the counterpoint of an ethics of work and considered the ethics of play, especially in the form of sports, wondering to what extent the biblical narrative of creation, work, and rest might both resonate with and challenge the ethos of contemporary sports.

Tradition

The idea that vocation was not only to be found in the monastery or in the ordained ministry was given vital impetus by the Reformers. On the basis of 1 Corinthians 7:17, 24, and other key passages, they developed the idea that Christians should do their best to shoulder worldly work. By working to the best of one's ability, one is being Christ to one's neighbor. The key thing is to seek to make the state of life to which one is called a pleasing offering to God. This position was intended to contrast with a tradition that had evolved in patristic and medieval theology that made the "active life" of work a commendable but less-exalted alternative to the "contemplative life" of piety. Both Augustine and Thomas Aquinas used a "double standard" to endorse but at the same time relegate to a second order the work of common human living. Contemplation for them is "loved"; the work of farmers, merchants, and craftspeople is merely "endured." There was a recognition here that ordinary trades do not *in themselves* bring us to heaven – and to the blessed and eternal vision of God – even if they are an essential prop on the journey. Augustine's way of relating human work to the blessed state of being in God's presence resonates here, in his distinction between "use" and "enjoyment" (see Chapter Ten's section on "Friendship" for more on this distinction). Only God is truly enjoyed; other things are to be used for the purpose of entering into that enjoyment more completely.

A necessary counterbalance to the Christian tradition's affirmative statements about work is its conviction that the work of human hands needs divine grace to "prosper" it; without this blessing, it can become demonic (as in the story of the Tower of Babel) or simple drudgery – and in neither case will it bring redemption. Work does not achieve salvation: it does not reconcile God and humankind, it does not heal or forgive sin, and it does not restore creation. Moreover, too great an emphasis on work can obscure the fact that human beings are also created to worship, to rest, and to play. It has been a fundamental assertion of some Christian ethics that a theological account of work must always be ordered to a theology of the Sabbath, which for Christians came to be celebrated not on Saturday (as for Jews) but on Sunday, the day of Christ's resurrection. The Sabbath is celebrated by Christians on the first day of the week, not the last. In this light the enjoying of Sabbath rest can be seen as having priority over the doing of mundane tasks – a logical priority reflected in its temporal priority. Christians celebrate it before any tools are taken up for the week's work. Karl Barth (1886–1968) wrote with especial eloquence on this theme, stressing that the Sabbath rest is not just the absence of work, and thus something defined negatively; it is a positive reality rooted in the goodness and being of God, without which we cannot begin to understand or relate well to work at all.

Contemporary debate

The conviction that humanity is meant for more than work alone has constituted a bulwark in Christian theology against the pretensions of both Marxism and Western materialism. The former has claimed that world history is "nothing but the creation of man by labor." The latter's vision exhaustively defines the human person at each moment by whether she is a producer or a consumer. An older model of work that involved *employing persons* is replaced by one in which one *buys units of their skill and time*. The idea of vocation evaporates on such an account. The modern ideologies of both left and right have demonstrated an infatuation with work with a fundamental contradiction at its core. They think it will deliver us from "bondage," making us people of means with choices and spending power. Their aspiration and expectation is that peace and freedom will derive from plenty. But plenty in turn derives from *work*. So at the same time as longing for the idealized leisure of a consumer lifestyle, they prize constantly increasing production and productivity. And paradoxically, this has the effect of reintroducing bondage again: a bondage to work.

Christian ethicists, like other social reformers with whom they have often made common cause, have been acutely aware that some sorts of work – in the modern as in the ancient world – are wearisome and can serve only to break a person's spirit. The work of slaves was something from which God delivered the children of Israel, and in the wake of the Industrial Revolution and the advent of mass production, work can often give little or no opportunity to the worker for self-expression or pride in the tasks accomplished. There are also many in the modern world who do not have work at all. It has generally been the concern of a Christian social ethics to call for humane working conditions and to advocate support and opportunities for the unemployed. This is done in the service of a social order in which there is positive interdependence and mutuality, and a concern to encourage human fulfillment.

Business and Management

Scripture and tradition

Business, or trade, is as old as human life. By it, humans get things that they either need or want in exchange for other things of which they have a surplus. The regard of Christians toward trade and commerce has covered the full range from deep suspicion to wholehearted endorsement. Both views look back to the creation account. The positive view sees God as the archetypal artisan. By contrast the negative view dwells on the account of the Fall in Genesis 3, where work seems to be a form of punishment. Such a view is reflected in the Latin words *otium* (leisure) and *negotium* (business, literally non-leisure). There is also the traditional ban on usury found in Exodus 22:25. This was ardently maintained through the medieval period, such that usurers were punishable with excommunication.

Some of the ambiguity of Christianity's relationship to business is expressed in Acts 16, when Paul and Silas are thrown into prison for interfering with some slaveowners' profit margins by healing their spirit-possessed prophetess, and again in Acts 19 when Paul causes the craftsmen of Ephesus to riot because of his preaching against idols. Mainstream Christian tradition may have accepted the existence of market activity, but always with strict provisos about the wrongness of the unrestrained pursuit of profit, and the illegitimacy of business interests that capitalize on error or sin. Patristic and medieval thought was always more favorable toward the work of producing and transporting commodities than toward the mercantile activity that sold them.

The tradition of the just price held that it was wrong to gain financially without actually creating something, and in particular immoral to take advantage of market conditions of scarcity. In Thomas Aquinas' words:

> If someone would be greatly helped by something belonging to someone else, and the seller not similarly harmed by losing it, the seller must not sell for a higher price: because the usefulness that goes to the buyer comes not from the seller, but from the buyer's needy condition: no one ought to sell something that does not belong to him.

The Crusades, along with the growth of medieval trade fairs, made transporting large quantities of money an issue of importance. The transportation of money was difficult. Such difficulties encouraged the rise of banking. Banking was not regarded as usury, and the papal banks became particularly influential. Jews had the same scriptural restrictions on lending for interest as Christians did – but they did not see those strictures as limiting their interactions with Gentiles. They were pushed to marginal professions such as collecting rents and taxes and lending money at interest: their role was needed as much as it was reviled.

Henry VIII's Act in Restraint of Usury (1545) marks a symbolic transformation in the attitude to trade and commerce brought about by the Reformation. The act allowed the charging of interest on any sum lent to a person or business. The focus of attention shifted from usury itself to the charging of excessive rates of interest. The Reformation brought a significant change from the limited medieval view of human endeavors to the more positive perception that everyday occupations genuinely fell within the bounds of God's kingdom. Both Luther and Calvin saw trade and commerce, rather than simply works of mercy, as part of an economy of grace. Luther in particular extended the notion of vocation beyond the strictly "religious" roles of priest, monk, or nun to previously "secular" roles, thus bringing the world of commerce within the boundaries of what could be considered as godly life.

Contemporary debate

The Christian churches through the centuries have insisted that trading relationships are precisely that – *relationships* – and should therefore be governed for Christians by the same considerations that govern their other relationships: practices of truth-telling and kindness, and not naked self-interest. There is no place for Friedrich Hayek's principle (see above) that amorality and anonymity are good things because they are beneficial to trade in modern large-scale societies. The community should limit the risks that trade may harm the weak or the ignorant, and foster a sense of mutual regard between sellers and buyers.

Management is a more recent invention than business. It is a largely secular theory drawing on a mixture of sources (including behavioral psychology) and is often closely allied with business, which it tries to make more efficient and therefore more profitable. Its insights and techniques have, however, been extended to nearly all other areas of organized human endeavor.

In relation to the emergent discipline of management, there have been various Christian responses, both welcoming and critical.

1. Welcoming responses have attempted to see in the Genesis accounts of Adam's commission to *subdue* the earth – often rendered by recent theologians as *responsible stewardship* – a prototype for a positive ethic of management. This is extended to include the management of both non-human resources and people. It is said by some Christian ethicists that Jesus' parables teach us the benefits of good forward planning and good budgeting (Luke 14:28–31). The instruction to church leaders in the Pastoral Epistles gives further material that seems to dovetail with modern theories of what makes a good manager of people: as the South African Christian businessman John A. Temple (b. 1941) puts it, "leading by example, coaching, encouraging, motivating, empowering and challenging."

2. Critical responses have been many, and have focused on management theory's prioritization of the *efficiency* of an activity over any assessment of the intrinsic and particular value of what that activity *is*. As we noted in passing in Chapter Three, management techniques are open to serving any master – and are in practice more likely to recognize and serve an economic master, whose "good" is the maximization of profit. In line with this, there often seems to be an overly

pragmatic concern with the "outputs" of the management process at the expense of what Christians might see as the valuable "inputs" *to* that process: righteousness, diligence, humility, compassion, and so on. There can often too be a naïve presumption that human beings will act rationally in all circumstances.

A paradigm case of the use of business and management concepts in an area of acknowledged ethical complexity comes in relation to environmental ethics (of which there will be more discussion in Chapter Twelve). Cost–benefit analysis has presented itself as a natural option when approaching questions of how to treat the environment, and this is because it handles all human moral convictions (that is to say, perceptions of what is true, good, and beautiful, and thus worthy of respect) as "preferences." The effect of this is that very different entities – like a rare bird species, or a wilderness – are measured in the same calculus alongside our desire to fly in airplanes (for example) or have air conditioning. The neatness of such an approach might be welcomed by ethicists trying to cut a way through a jungle of knotty issues.

But the difficulties this approach faces are that innumerable things for which humans instinctively have an ethical regard do not have a "social value" in a way that can be priced and compared with (say) a person's preference for running two cars. For example, we might think of our grandchildren's future, or the cleanness of the world in which they will live. The cost–benefit analyst finds herself unable to justify the moral values typically expressed in many areas of Christian ethics (namely, that certain things are "pricelessly" valuable, or have an absolute claim to respect). Such analysis does not recognize that there are different *kinds* of good, different *kinds* of interest, and different *kinds* of entitlement in play in ethical decision-making (as the British thinker Michael Banner [b. 1961] argues). All values can be reduced to mere preferences. For instance, the alleged preference of native peoples for their rainforests can be set against the alleged preference of logging companies and their consumers for the trees. This will seem to permit calculations based by analogy on economic valuation. All values will seem capable of being measured against one another, as like with like.

A contemporary holy grail in much self-styled "ethical" business practice is getting the balance between growth and sustainability. It commonly arises when businesses take account of the effects of their practices on the human or natural environment in which they operate – partly because they understand the need for stable and favorable conditions that will enable their own continued smooth functioning. Sustainability also shapes the discussions of environmentalists and government planners when they discuss how to respond to business proposals. Ideally, sustainable practices seek to balance the following requirements:

- development (by which wealth is created);
- equity (by which injustice is avoided and the few do not benefit at the expense of a disadvantaged majority); and
- protection, or conservation, of the environment.

At best, it is hoped that a way will be found to enable these three concerns to serve one another – and at this point, again, the agency of management is usually invoked to do the work.

But management models in all their forms, even in their best form, are frequently seen by Christian thinkers as not up to the tasks given to them. They are seen as vulnerable to criticism in at least two ways. They are prone to treat the human or natural creatures they deal with as objects (like pieces on a chess board) – even to instrumentalize them (like tools in a tool box). And they depend on a human capacity to predict the future and the consequences of human interventions and plans. This capacity is questionable, given the extraordinary complexity of what is often being dealt with. The truth is that the detail of the universe is largely beyond our grasp, and the extraordinary combination of factors and relationships that constitute it is rarely something we have a secure hold on. Meanwhile, when we are in management mode we risk over-manipulating the things for which we have assumed responsibility, as though they had independence of us, and no countervailing interests. As John Milbank (b. 1952) points out: "The danger is that claims to have identified 'optimum' environments ... will often mask the ruses of human power and ambition."

Work, business, and management are major features of our daily lives. They shape the material world we live in, order our use of time (both *taking* our time and claiming to *save* our time), and influence many of our habits of thought. We now look at how they are thought about by universal, subversive, and ecclesial traditions of Christian ethics, respectively.

Universal

Recent Roman Catholic discussion of the theme of work is led by the 1981 encyclical *Laborem Exercens* (On Human Work), in which there is a hopeful account of work as divinely given for the fulfillment of human beings. People thrive on purposeful activity, and work is a constitutive part of human life in the world. In claiming to identify fundamental drives in human nature, this is an argument from natural law, but it also draws on the exegesis of passages from Scripture like Genesis 2:15 ("The Lord God ... put [the man] in the garden to till it and keep it"). The two values of work that are highlighted in the encyclical are that it makes us more human, and that it draws us closer to God by involving us as "co-creators" who share in God's activity: the church's role is to develop a spirituality of work that will "help all people to come closer, through work, to God, the Creator and Redeemer, to participate in his salvific plan for man and the world and to deepen their friendship with Christ."

There have been criticisms that this approach to the ethics of work is not a particularly scriptural one, and that it is based instead on a questionable personalist philosophy. Personalism is a philosophical school that rejects both the non-relational individualism of liberal political thought and the collectivism of Marxist political thought, and centers on the value of human persons and their fulfillment in freedom and relationship.

Other accounts of the nature and purpose of work may have a more cautious tone than *Laborem Exercens* (being less celebratory of work as a created good) but will also operate in natural law terms, and may be every bit as "universalist" in intent as the 1981 encyclical. The more modest claim that work is a necessity because it gives us a way of making a living, of being of service to others, and of keeping occupied is still basically universalist in character. The description may not be saying anything distinctively Christian, but for some traditions of Christian ethics, it is saying something important nonetheless.

Laborem Exercens also takes the opportunity of fielding general principles to defend the rights of workers to a fair wage. The argument for the just remuneration of a worker with responsibility for a family, for example, is made by reference to the fact that on any reasonable account he or she must have sufficient means to "establish and properly maintain" that family, and "provide security for its future."

International business practices depend upon certain commonalities existing across many societies and cultures, regimes, and tribes – and at the most basic level they depend upon trust, without which business cannot be carried on in a sustainable way. Once again, it is the natural law tradition that has offered itself as the most obvious candidate within Christian thought for explaining the possibility of these commonalities, and fostering their promotion. As the Reformed theologian Max Stackhouse (b. 1935) points out, "It is not only interests that reach across boundaries, ethics does so as well." The recognition of certain minimal human conditions of *virtue*, which is where ethics most obviously emerges as a concern internal to the practice of business and to the discipline of economics, also opens the door to some classical consequentialist reasoning. If people are not straight with each other, the system does not work and everyone suffers. Principles of fair exchange, transparency, the rejection of insider dealing, and so on are made necessary principles because without them the mechanisms of business exchange simply cannot function.

A universal approach can also argue that economic life (including business practice) is part of a collective human project, in which nature is positively transformed (even, perhaps, for redemptive purposes). The alliance of business growth to technological advances permits the belief that ethical business, like technology, can ameliorate the lot of fallen humanity – assisting in its gradual perfection. Technological change allied to economic activity can be seen as a moral good, which human beings have a duty to support for the betterment of humankind. This too is a consequentialist argument, and has continuities with an optimistic theological framework that had its heyday in the nineteenth century.

In relation to management, principles derived from Scripture are sometimes invoked to support management theory. The marks of a good steward of God's gifts that can be identified in various biblical passages are seen as being every bit as useful to a budding manager in today's world as they were in Old and New Testament times. Such lessons in good management will be seen as universally useful, *whether or not* a modern manager is Christian. In either case, management of the natural order should be exercised with justice (Prov 14:34; Mic 6:8), diligence (Prov 10:4), fairness (Amos 8:5–6), and faithfulness (1 Cor 4:2). Those who manage people are offered the "biblical principle" that "because they are made in God's image, men and women possess dignity and must be treated with respect," blessed as they are with "creativity, initiative, personality, morality, individuality, intellect, knowledge, wisdom, power, authority, and the ability to work" (John A. Temple). The manager's job is to harness and direct these innate qualities of the human person.

Subversive

Universal approaches to work tend to emphasize its dignity by reference to the order of creation, and to celebrate it as a medium for "co-creation" with God. This might be summarized as a view that *work equals vocation*. A subversive approach, by contrast, might be more inclined to the view that *vocation judges work*, and maybe that *vocation reforms work*. There will be evil in the workplace. Organizations that employ people – like all corporate bodies – have dynamics and embedded interests that can foster corrupt practice and structural oppression. Christians committed to the transformation of their environment will be concerned to expose and reconstitute that environment in the face of such institutional sin.

Many contemporary Christian ethicists criticize contemporary economic and business practice. In this area it is often hard to make a distinction between subversive and ecclesial styles of ethics (although a subversive approach will be more likely to focus on issues such as equal pay for women and sexual harassment in the workplace). Such thinkers identify the fact that the market's goals (e.g., productivity and wealth) represent rival "ultimate goods" to those of Christian tradition (e.g., worship and service of others). Indeed, they say, contemporary business makes all goods into only *market* goods – by transforming land, for example, into "real estate" and people into "human resources." This Christian critique sees business practices habitually prone to:

- the prioritization of self-interest over the just distribution of wealth (by contrast with the "school for sharing" which, in Timothy Gorringe's phrase, is the church); and
- the promotion of consumption over a Christian disciplining of desire.

It is also a critique that seeks to expose the alliance between business interests and military power: the fact that the so-called "hidden hand" of the market needs a "hidden fist" to keep the world safe so that business can carry on without disruption.

The way the elderly, the disabled, and the dying are regarded in society raises what is superficially an unrelated matter, in that it does not immediately seem to belong in a discussion of work or business. However, the treatment of the elderly, the disabled, and the dying is increasingly seen as a management issue. A subversive ethics that keeps in mind the needs of such groups will be particularly hostile to the use of "management" language and "management" techniques in relation to them. A view of the world centered on management sees everything as a *problem* that must be made more efficient, or eradicated altogether. But elderly and disabled people may show us important aspects of our human nature by challenging our desire to make everything function smoothly or profitably – in this sense they may be not problems but prophets. Subversive approaches challenge the tendency of modern management discipline to describe the infirm and the dying as a drain on resources as opposed to being humanly valuable. They also challenge our widespread tendency (at least in the West) to entrust care of the infirm and dying to what Michael Hanby (b. 1966) describes as "new industries operated by strangers," the use of these care industries being justified "on the tenuous … grounds that a happy worker, one unburdened with guilt over the neglect of … a dying parent, is a productive worker." Management cannot be a quasi-therapeutic force in every domain of life in the way it sometimes likes to pretend it can. We are to resist the ways it encourages the idolization of ourselves and our own power, and makes invisible everything that offends or interrupts that fixation.

Ecclesial

A key ecclesial emphasis has been on the way that work can exist to serve the true worship of God. "To be baptized," writes the contemporary North American theologian Rusty Reno (b. 1959), "is to be placed into a divine workplace." The bread and wine offered in the Eucharist "complete" the labor that began with planting and harvesting. The transformation of material substance – wheat and grapes – shows that all matter has a vocation, but *work* – the work of tending them – should be understood as being elevated too. What is offered at the altar is "the fruit of the earth *and* the work of human hands," to quote a prayer often used liturgically when bread and wine have been brought to the altar along with the monetary offerings of the people. And the book of Isaiah gives the church resources to describe even paradise, where we have union with God, in the images of transfigured work: the joy of Jerusalem will include the building of houses and the planting of vineyards (Isa 65:17–21).

In a line of thought inspired by John Milbank and Oliver O'Donovan (b. 1945), the British theologian John Hughes (1978–2014) asserts the quasi-liturgical character of work, in the face of the utilitarian accounts of it that are typical of modern capitalism. Capitalism has lost contact with any sense of transcendent value that might give work meaning and dignity. Hughes wants to explore the potential of work as a beautifying creative activity which is valuable in its "useless" but significant praise of God. He argues that the Romantic thinkers with whom he interacts (like John Ruskin [1819–1900] and William Morris [1834–96]) were able to preserve something of such a sense, in their belief that work and human productive activity have a more ultimate end than simply profit-making. They resisted the general reduction of the worker to a mere means to produce more profit.

Latent in an ecclesial approach to business is the idea, expressed by Timothy Gorringe, that "the whole inhabited earth" is "our shrine and altar," and that there is not a separate domain in which the business of the world may go on without reference to worship or the common good. It can be argued that business adopted a quintessentially Christian social format (and, in origin, a highly relational one) in evolving "corporations." The prototype of the modern, non-governmental corporation is derived from the religious institutions of the West, and the word "corporation" (a *body-like* entity) itself reflects an incarnational Christian sensibility. Examples of Christian corporations include independent religious orders, guilds, hospitals, colleges, and schools – all with a degree of self-governance, and the right to own property and to buy and sell goods and services. The process by which business corporations took on this inherited social form had its most dramatic period of growth in the nineteenth century. Some Christian ethicists argue that a moral theory of the corporation is one of the key areas in which business has things to relearn from the Christian tradition today. Ecclesial ethicists in particular are likely to argue that, in the end, any human corporation will be judged by the extent to which it lends itself to the divine praise. Human associations will have all kinds of purposes, but in pursuing these purposes they should allow their forms of human solidarity and exchange to be transparent to a more ultimate human vocation. The "summit" of the human vocation is shown in the church's practices, and consummately in Eucharistic sharing and gift-giving.

Management techniques, meanwhile, must be challenged by Christian practices of intercessory prayer, which are in some ways their opposite because they are about acknowledging our dependency and limits, and are not just about the efficient use of power. As Rowan Williams (b. 1950) puts it: "intercession acknowledges the reality of the need of others and one's own powerlessness in respect of their future." In management terms, intercession (like worship more generally) is profligate with time – and in particular it "squanders" time on those who often seem least likely to have a productive future – the disabled, the elderly, the dying. Michael Hanby writes:

> Truthfully naming and waiting amidst the reality of pointless suffering and death, intercessory prayer has a share in the grief and powerlessness that inevitably attends our lives in time. Yet in commending this powerlessness to the eternity of God, this prayer has a share in the hope that God offers in offering himself. This grief and this hope, which are denied by managerial discipline, then characterize how we most fully live out our identity as creatures and how, as creatures called to witness to the goodness of both God and the world, we embody God's commitment to the world in Jesus.

Media

Because most forms of the media are modern inventions, this part of the chapter does not begin as others do with what Scripture and tradition have to say. Scripture and tradition do not speak explicitly about the ethics of mass communication – although, as we shall see, there is much relevant material about good communication in the Bible and church teaching, and this wisdom can be transferred to new contexts. Moreover, the Holy Spirit has been understood by many Christians as the profoundest medium of communication there is: the source of the church's common life, and the inspirer and purifier of its speech.

Although there may be little traditional material about this fast-developing area of human life, there is nevertheless plenty of lively contemporary debate about media ethics, among Christians and non-Christians alike.

Contemporary Debate

Through newspapers, magazines, radio, television, mobile phones, and the Internet we communicate with one another, and are communicated with, by large and powerful organizations – commercial and governmental – from around the world. It is a largely uncontroversial assumption that we are also *influenced* by these media, and that our beliefs, values, and standards take on new shapes as a result. While in earlier times a palace revolution would focus on the royal household, in the modern era a coup d'état shifted its attention to the radio or television headquarters – and more recently to online forums and social media platforms. Control of the media has come to mean control of the state, as was vividly illustrated in the links between Twitter and the Arab Spring.

Our choices of clothes, holidays, and political parties (to name but a few) are all heavily influenced by television, radio, and the Internet. So a key question for Christian ethics is whether the organs of communication that shape us should be accountable to public standards that can be imposed upon them, or whether they may be left alone as relatively unregulated channels through which private enterprise can do what it likes. The danger on the one hand is that a minority dictates the restrictions that are placed on the material that is made available to a mass audience. This is a form of paternalism. A corrupting lowering of standards (intellectual or moral) is the danger perceived on the other hand, for example when newspapers become part of the entertainment industry, distorting or sensationalizing human life and experience.

Jesus himself seems to have chosen a mode of communicating the truths of the kingdom of God that was a sort of "indirect communication" – not propaganda, but teaching through parables. Jesus' parables make listeners work hard to discern their meaning (e.g., even the disciples do not immediately "get" the parable of the sower in Mark 4:13), while suggesting at the same time that in the end only God can reveal their truths ("to you *has been given* the secret"; Mark 4:11). This is sometimes seen by Christians as contrasting with the glib generalizations of the mass media, with their appeal to shallow emotions, their avoidance of controversy and complexity, and their reluctance to display or interact with the full range of human life and experience.

Rather than dealing exhaustively with all the varieties of modern communication that there are today (including email, web-based social networking sites, text messaging, and so on), we will look in what follows at just a sample of the dominant media in the contemporary world. Many of the conclusions drawn in relation to these will have wider applicability to other parts of the world of modern media.

Advertising

Advertising today is virtually a social science, basic to competitive capitalism. It uses creativity to sell products which may benefit consumers, but may also exploit them. Advertising is one of the most all-pervasive and powerful communicative media of the modern developed world, whether we like it or not. In no time an image created in one continent to market goods made in another appears on a cinema screen in a third, or on a television screen in a fourth.

It has been estimated that an ordinary American is exposed to 1600 advertising messages a day. Advertisements are the places where questions of the good are most insistently and popularly posed in our daily lives, and for this reason cannot be ignored by contemporary ethicists.

Some advertisements are masterpieces of creative skill. They are funny, slick, superbly filmed, brilliantly acted, full of the best special effects money can buy. They may even have certain useful functions. If you genuinely have a product that can make people's lives better, and they are unaware of it, then advertising is the most effective means of telling them it is there. But in the end, advertisements are not just seeking to *serve* desire, they are seeking to *stimulate* it. We do not turn to advertising out of desire for the good; advertising seeks us out in order to make its goods desirable. Advertising is the business of what one writer calls "The Want Makers."

There are, of course, a huge number of ways to make a person feel their "want" of something. There are roundabout ways of provoking desire. Fear, for example, can have the effect of making you want to avoid certain consequences. Fear that you will be despised or laughed at by your peers can generate an extremely strong desire to acquire an article of clothing, or behave in a certain way. And there are many more motivations than fear – so many, and so complex, and so variable from individual to individual, in fact, that scholars who have devoted all their energies to studying consumer motivation cannot untangle them all. We do not even understand what motivates *ourselves* – as St. Paul once pointed out, a long way ahead of the psychologists ("I do not understand my own actions"; Rom 7:15). If the human mind (to quote a parody of Freudian theory) is "a dark cellar in which a maiden aunt and a sex-crazed monkey are locked in mortal combat, the affair being refereed by a rather nervous bank-clerk" (Donald Bannister [1924–86]), then how can we possibly hope to make sense of the way it motivates us? The advertisers, though, are undaunted by this. They are practical people, and sufficiently good at isolating broad and basic trends that they can bypass a lot of the technical studies and go for the sale. In the marketing world, the desire to be beautiful and free from pain can be regarded as universal and limitless. People spend money out of fear, envy, vanity, health, utility, profit, pride, love, and entertainment – no more and no less.

Celebrity

Advertising and the news media are just two of the organs of publicity that tower over modern Western societies, in alliance with the cult of celebrity. It can be argued that all of these abuse our basic need to *appear* before one another (to be acknowledged; to have recognition) by commodifying and packaging human beings and displaying them to us in a way that is largely non-reciprocal. Publicity is a distinctively modern way in which we are supposed to become known to one another; but Oliver O'Donovan describes it as a "roaming spotlight" that selects its subjects with apparent arbitrariness and makes tokens or fictions of them. Those who look at them *spy* on them: it is one-way looking – intimacy without any self-bestowal. Its subjects die of it – sometimes quite literally when the levels of scrutiny they experience place them under intolerable pressure. The state of publicity is too lonely for them. Others cynically use it to hide the truth about themselves for their own short-term advantage. And yet we are all under pressure to join in the game of publicity. Recognition of "celebrities" has become (in Oliver O'Donovan's words) "a kind of civic discipline." One's social competence is tested by whether one recognizes celebrity names.

The massive growth of social media platforms like Facebook, Twitter, and Instagram bears some comparison with the way that modern societies can celebrate celebrity. Every individual person is given the opportunity to design and manage his or her public appearance, and it can often be very enticing to "show" oneself as though in the whirl of a celebrity-style social life. Here too there is a risk that the selves we present online are untruthful constructs of ourselves, and therefore incapable of opening genuinely reciprocal relationship with others.

The Mobile Phone

In his 2001 book *Heidegger, Habermas and the Mobile Phone*, philosopher George Myerson (b. 1957) undertakes a critique of contemporary culture through a comparison of some twentieth-century philosophers of communicative action, on the one hand, and the cell phone industry, on the other. Heidegger and Habermas are of interest to Myerson because they have things to say about the conditions and disciplines human beings need in order to communicate well. "Both the philosophers and the mobile campaigners," he writes, "are interested not just in routine communication, but in the road to utopia. For all their differences, the two 'discourses' share the view that modern utopia will be about ideal communication." But their respective ideas about what such "ideal communication" actually is differ markedly.

The comparison turns out to center on questions of how we relate best to our temporality – how best to conceive time, and how best to act in it. Myerson depicts the "fast world" of the cell phone marketers alongside the "slow world" of the philosophers. By examining the press releases of the cell phone companies, Myerson shows them attempting to conjure up a vision of the contemporary world in which:

> Old slow-moving "talk" is being pushed aside by its faster cousin "communication" … all that talk is making the traffic move too slowly, a kind of communicative gridlock is setting in. We will need, the implication is, some better way to communicate in the future. The destiny of the mobile is to take us beyond the "world of talk," into some other world where "communication" means something … far quicker.

And Myerson's points about the cell phone are applicable to other fast-evolving modes of communication like email, text messaging, and Twitter (which we consider in more depth below).

As Myerson points out, there is nothing Martin Heidegger (1889–1976) or Jürgen Habermas (b. 1929) would disagree with in a general commendation of the importance of "communication." For them, being human is something that emerges precisely in reciprocal relationships with others, and in meaningful conversation. But beneath this superficial agreement on a general principle there lies a profound difference between them and the architects of the world of the cell phone – a difference to which time is central. For the inhabitants of the fast world, "dialogue is pushed aside by the term 'exchange.'" The painstaking search for meaning, understanding, and agreement is too slow. It could not ever be an "ideal" form of communication or interaction.

> In mobile terms, the responses are often too slow, and perhaps the requests aren't clear enough. In philosophical terms, the responses are too fast, and there isn't enough time given to achieving understanding. Here is the real crunch. Both schools (let's call them that) regard ordinary communication as imperfect, or, more positively, as having the potential to be improved. Mobilisation seeks to improve ordinary communication by giving it new channels, clarifying the real meaning of the message, speeding up the response time, whereas the philosophers want communication to be more gradual, more weighted by the search for understanding.

Myerson's most basic criticism of the culture represented by the mobile phone, then, is that it is impatient with the fact that living in human societies takes time, and impatient with the time needed for human growth. The zappy world of the cell phone is constructed as a world of atomized users whose principal forms of utterance are expressions of want. The individual's present moment exercises a kind of tyrannous sway in the realm of communication. It is not conversation at all. "If mobilisation were completed, the prime example of communication would not be *two people* – it would be *one* person, set in the context of millions of other separate people."

The Smartphone and Social Media

It is possible to argue that the transition to mobilization *has* been completed – or at least has advanced much further – in the advent of the smartphone, which places the global Internet literally under a person's thumb. On the one hand, the smartphone and its instant access to rapidly evolving social media platforms has been enthusiastically embraced for its capacity to link those otherwise isolated (e.g., people in remote parts of Africa) into global communication networks, or for its role in galvanizing social and political revolutions like the Arab Spring and the Occupy movements. But observers have disagreed about whether the smartphone has greater capacity to increase or to overcome isolation, to create or to hinder true community. Some have raised alarms over the similarities of smartphone use to addictive behavior, or wondered why, in the words of Sherry Turkle, "we expect more from technology and less from each other." Political writer Evgeny Morozov (b. 1984) has launched fierce critiques of what he calls "the folly of technological solutionism," or the dominant and naïve belief that technology, particularly the Internet, can solve all our problems. The last chapter of his 2013 book *To Save Everything, Click Here* is aptly titled "Smart Gadgets, Dumb Humans."

Christian ethics tends to call for a cautious embrace of social media and other digital technologies. As early as 1957, Pope Pius XII welcomed the new technological advances represented by films, radio, and television, but also insisted that the church must exercise "vigilant care" due to the potential dangers of these new media (*Miranda Prorsus*, On Mass Communications). More recently, in 2015, Pope Francis offered a similar note of concern regarding media and the digital world when he wrote, "Today's media do enable us to communicate and to share our knowledge and affections. Yet at times they also shield us from direct contact with the pain, the fears and the joys of others and the complexity of their personal experiences." Yet rather than calling for the abandonment or curtailment of these new media, Pope Francis urges their thoughtful shepherding: "Efforts need to be made to help these media become sources of new cultural progress for humanity and not a threat to our deepest riches" (*Laudato Si'*, On Care for Our Common Home). In the words of Albert Borgmann (b. 1937), technology for the church is neither foe nor merely friend; "we can restrain it and we must redeem it."

Community in a Virtual Age

How can people maintain a quality of true community in the midst of such pressures? For Christian ethics, modern media have the potential to serve good ends, when used rightly. They can foster a broad and informed view of the world around us – and thus be aids to high-quality *attention*, which is for Christians a condition of obedience to God's will. They can give more informed insights into the deliberations of government. From the point of view of mission, they can offer unprecedented opportunities for the intelligent proclamation of the Christian gospel. They can, for example, fulfill the high ideals set (specifically for television) by the founders of the BBC: to inform, educate, and entertain – and not make the first two into mere servants of the last. All of this can be affirmed, despite the threats of checkbook journalism, or the abuses of power that arise when the strings of mass communication media pass through the hands of too few individuals. There are encouraging examples of how the media can equip listeners, viewers, or readers to make their own judgments about important issues, rather than simply make up their minds for them.

At the same time, it will be a likely Christian response that the more the organs of media communication multiply, the more need there is for high-quality face-to-face communication without the props of technology. Dietrich Bonhoeffer (1906–45), in his book *Life Together* (1939), argued for what we might call a clear-eyed and mutual "ministry of presence." He argued that recognition and acknowledgment of the truth about ourselves and our condition as human beings were the only ways to achieve this presence to one another. Without this presence to one another there can be no true and godly community. Only by being present to one another in the light that God's truth sheds on us do our forms of human community progress beyond being what Bonhoeffer calls mere "hot-house flowers" liable to wither away in an instant. Truly Christian life together, Bonhoeffer says, grows "healthily in accord with God's good will in the rain and storm and sunshine of God's outdoors." The pressing question is what forms of media might enable such a ministry of presence – or whether they are fundamentally unable to foster genuine community. In other words, must true community be *embodied*, and if it must, can any form of digital media ever approximate bodily presence?

Universal

A universal approach may argue that the church must embrace electronic media if it is not to place itself at a serious competitive disadvantage in the contemporary world of fast and prolific communication. On this account, the church must become as attractive as secular forms of entertainment or face its own demise. It must be as gripping as major sports events, as current as the latest hits on YouTube, and as inventive as the latest plot on *Lost*. This is to buy into the terms of an existing discourse, and make the church a player in that discourse on its own unchallenged terms.

Another universalist approach is to accept the basic state of play in relation to the domination of mass media communication, and work instead to reform and improve its operations by summoning either its providers or its consumers to certain ideals of good practice. Principles of truth and discipline are commonly fielded, as part of God's requirement of and command to humankind. Advertising should not exaggerate or misrepresent, and all media should be held to high standards of integrity. The Bible's words about the dangers of idle or careless speaking may be invoked, as also the sin of bearing false witness (Matt 12:36; John 18:37). "To trifle with the truth, to trivialize great issues and to spread falsehood are manifestly contrary to the will of God. A biblical and Christian critique of the media would call them to account in the areas of truthfulness and seriousness in handling great issues" (David Winter [b.1929]). The two papal encyclicals cited above are also, at least in part, a universal approach in that they consider the role of media in the flourishing of human society as a whole.

Subversive

A subversive ethicist might ask: how do films and television reinscribe or challenge dominant cultural narratives of masculinity, femininity, and racial identity? Whose voices are heard and whose stories go untold in the mass media? What role could new forms of digital technology play in unveiling and combating injustice at home and abroad – or, conversely, in encouraging cynicism and fear in the face of such staggering global challenges?

Subversive and ecclesial ethicists alike agree that media such as films have tremendous capacity to shape our moral imaginations. Ethicists operating in a subversive mode are more likely to interrogate media's ability to warp the moral imagination by identifying (for example) mass media's aversion to the on-screen portrayal of people with disabilities, its repeated identification of young women as princesses needing rescue by handsome princes, its tendency to depict Muslims as terrorists, or its addiction to certain standards of racially encoded beauty. Others have noted the troubling link many people unconsciously make between physical attractiveness and intelligence or skill, and the way the mass media rarely challenge that connection. These are concerns shared more broadly in popular culture, but Christian ethics will ask specifically how they intersect with the formation of Christian identity and with Christian principles such as justice, care for the vulnerable, and a commitment to seeing the image of God in all people.

Rhetorical critic Kristy Maddux focuses on the roles of popular media and gender norms (which have always been influenced by Christianity) in shaping models of civic engagement. In her study of four Christian-themed films (*The Passion of the Christ*, *Left Behind*, *Amazing Grace*, and *The Da Vinci Code*) and one TV show (*7th Heaven*), she concludes that their competing models of civic participation reflect their ideology of gender while typically urging either moral reform or social justice, which she identifies as the two competing modes of civic engagement within American Christianity. For example, while she notes that both *The Passion of the Christ* and *Left Behind* depict Christian civic participation under a repressive regime, she sees the former as valorizing a form of "feminine" submission to the regime (exemplified by both Mary and Christ), whereas the latter valorizes "brutish masculinity." *The Da Vinci Code* embraces the "privatization of faithfulness" and therefore a form of civic non-participation that is also, in her view, more "feminine." She concludes by suggesting that Christianity, as a countercultural space that is neither state nor market, can offer a wider range of creative, alternative possibilities for civic participation to both men and women, particularly if it remains alert to avoiding paternalism – a common problem in media portrayals of civic engagement.

Finally, there is a vigorous scrutiny of popular media content by those who doubt the adequacy of "universal" or "common" paradigms for selecting it. They ask whether enough access is given to, or guaranteed for, under-represented groups and voices in society. When mass audiences are a prime concern, broadcasting and publishing can lose their ability to be of "public service," if genuinely public service involves attending to the needs and interests of minority groups. And when the mass media are closely aligned with Western orientations and biases, then they can too easily peddle gender and ethnic stereotypes, and promote a sort of cultural imperialism.

Ecclesial

For ecclesial ethics, it is primarily in the church and its practices that Christians are constructed in their experiences and understandings so that when they are in the media arena they bring with them a conviction about what is really *good*. They are then able to ask the question whether what the media present as good is *really* good – more than just good for us, but good in itself. Likewise, they can question whether what the media offer as desirable is *really* to be desired.

Ecclesial ethics recognizes that we never, of course, act without any desire at all. As philosopher Alasdair MacIntyre argues, if a person growing out of childhood is to become more than an intelligent animal, who directs itself "towards the immediate satisfaction of felt bodily wants," he or she must learn desires that are not just urgently felt wants. We become – if we mature properly – more open instead to what MacIntyre calls "considerations regarding our good." We begin to distinguish between the answers to the question "What do I want?" and the answers to the question "What is it best for me to do?" All this is to say that our passions and desires become transformed. We act less often from badly flawed motivation.

Rowan Williams, former Archbishop of Canterbury, is one proponent of such an approach. Myerson's criticisms of the culture of fast communication, described above, show him to have a lot in common with Williams, who in his 2000 book *Lost Icons* examines those "time-taking" practices and disciplines that constitute the self, help the self to flourish with others, and, ultimately, play a part in the self's salvation. These include contemplation, deliberation, conciliation, and long-term care for others. He attacks the fantasies (prevalent in modern North Atlantic culture) that selves are "timeless desiring and deciding mechanisms." These fantasies, he argues, explain the waning of ideas like honor, remorse, and charity, all of which are bound up with the idea that one has a character not reducible to momentary self-dispositions or self-descriptions. Rather, one's character is conserved in some way "outside" oneself, in one's relationships to others, to one's past, and to God. Only in the recognition that this is true can we become "actual and not abstract subjects."

He pays determined attention to the fact that such human realities exist in time, and *take* time; and to the related fact that (viewed individually) they are always partial and incomplete. This is where we begin to appreciate what the soul might be. For Williams, it is *selfhood-in-relation*, and cannot be considered apart from its aspect of *duration*. What we are called to as human creatures is "a material life that somehow *represents* the duration in which it lives." In line with this, Williams' book is a plea for a renewed concern with *discipline* and *discipleship* – in other words, and in a fully Christian sense, with *learning*. Its model of learning is situated firmly within a description of the embodied character of humanity, its relational obligations, and its call to be shaped in the *imitatio Christi* (the imitation of Christ). A link can be made here with the embodied, remembering learning process that liturgy is.

Liturgies, or specific patterns and rites of communal Christian worship, are forms of discipline that take time, and that also remind those participating in them of the fact that in seeking to shape our lives well as human creatures we need to be acted upon as well as to act. We may call these the wisdom of receptivity and the wisdom of temporality:

- *The wisdom of receptivity.* By the wisdom of receptivity, learnt in liturgy, we are brought before something that is "outside" ourselves, and that sifts and reads us over time: God's self-communication. Liturgical participation is not reducible to the activity of our egos and their strivings, nor of our particular preconceptions and preferences at any one moment.
- *The wisdom of temporality.* By the wisdom of temporality, we learn that there can be a significantly counter-cultural dimension in what superficially looks like the wasting of time for a purpose that is not reducible to human interests. This has been discussed much more fully and effectively by writers like Stanley Hauerwas and Jean Vanier. Liturgy is a time-taking activity in which character is formed. It is in relation to many features of liturgy that this is the case: reciting the psalms; being exposed to the texts of Scripture through the lectionary in yearly and seasonal cycles; as well as the celebration of the sacraments. Moreover, as Oliver O'Donovan has remarked, to pray well is to have to pay close attention to one's social surroundings and to the *time in which one is*, and then to think hard about what prayers it needs.

Liturgy's role as something that weans us from the compressions and destructive accelerations of Myerson's "fast world" can thus be seen as something that helps us to make the most of our temporality. Something along these lines is also acknowledged by Pope Pius XI's (1857–1939) reported description of the liturgy as "the most important organ of the Church in the ordinary exercise of its teaching office." "Ordinary teaching" requires time and regularity; it requires day-to-day continuity. The liturgy can be seen as a model of *catechesis* (or church instruction) because over time it initiates its recipients into a living faith, and helps them to live out the mystery of salvation. It is induction, not the delivery of instantaneous information.

In both areas of wisdom, according to ecclesial ethics, liturgy teaches us about what is good in a way that must be brought correctively to bear on our media-saturated culture. Methodist theologian D. Brent Laytham (b. 1962) takes on just such a task in his 2012 book *iPod, YouTube, Wii Play*, in which he places specific liturgical acts in conversation with various aspects of Western entertainment culture, including the media. For example, he considers (among other topics) the iPod in relation to the hymnal and the practice of singing communally; YouTube together with baptism as processes of identity construction; and Twitter alongside the practice of ceaseless prayer. Like Pope Francis, Laytham does not urge the abandonment of technology. Instead, he writes, Christians must think far more thoughtfully and theologically about how habitually using media might form character in ways that run counter to the Christian story.

Summary

The very disparate issues treated in this chapter are united by one theme: they are about social bonds and social interchange. At the turn of the twenty-first century, other related challenges began to emerge that will increasingly require ethical attention: to name two, urban planning and the flourishing of cities, as the world's population continues to flow from rural contexts into large urban centers; and the related issues of migration and immigration, which juxtapose the motif of social bonds in this chapter alongside themes such as justice and the role of the state from the previous chapter (Good Order), and the environmental considerations of the final chapter (Good Earth).

The section on economics, wealth, and poverty looked specifically at different views on the left and the right about how human societies should be justly ordered, and the effects of such views on the way that wealth is distributed and redistributed. It noted that there are some who believe that financial transactions can be regarded as serving a higher purpose than the smooth functioning of markets in the service of profit (whether this "higher purpose" be an ideal of equality of ownership and opportunity, or a more explicitly Christian ideal of communion in shared possession). But at the same time it recognized that many others believe that the market is its own justification and its own regulator. It observed that dominant economic theories of today are barely theological, if at all, and that attempts by universalist Christian ethicists to converse with such theories tend to require them to make their theological reasonings invisible.

The middle part of the chapter dealt with economics (on the one hand), and the topics of work, business, and management (on the other) – two areas that overlap significantly with one another. Modern capitalist practices set powerful terms for how these topics can be understood and interpreted in the modern world. Subversive and ecclesial voices on these themes have to work hard to get a hearing and often have the character of being minority or prophetic voices when they talk about community as one of the highest human callings, and about the claims of the weak and afflicted on those who are strong and well.

The economic themes of commodification and consumption are also prominent in the final section on the media, which looked at how, for many modern media, time itself is a commodity that must be "saved" or "spent." The deliberative processes by which a wise view is formed about how to save or spend time are often not nurtured by a high-speed media environment, which is perhaps one of the reasons why the church seems to struggle to adapt to it, and why (for some ecclesial ethicists) it needs to draw deeply upon its liturgical habits to offer an alternative: an economy of grace whose origin is the deep wisdom and inexhaustible abundance of God.

References and Further Reading

Economics, Wealth, and Poverty

John Locke's discussion of private property is from *Two Treatises of Government* (New York: Dutton, 1924), pages 131–41.

R. H. Tawney's major critical works on capitalist economics are *The Acquisitive Society* (London: Longman, Green, and Co., 1921) and *Religion and the Rise of Capitalism* (Gloucester, MA: P. Smith, 1962). His is a left-wing perspective that can be contrasted effectively with that of the right-wing thinker Friedrich Hayek (also cited in this chapter), for example in Hayek's work *The Road to Serfdom* (Chicago, IL: University of Chicago Press, 1994). Specific quotations are from *The Acquisitive Society*, pages 10 and 33. The later quotation from Tawney about poverty is from *The Acquisitive Society*, page 5.

Archbishop William Temple's *Christianity and Social Order* (New York: Penguin Books, 1942) is one of the key texts in which he develops the theological rationale for a welfare state.

Ronald Preston's key works on economics are *Religion and the Persistence of Capitalism* (London: SCM Press, 1979) and *Religion and the Ambiguities of Capitalism* (Cleveland, OH: Pilgrim Press, 1993).

William F. May's covenantal thought can be followed up, for example, in *Beleaguered Rulers: The Public Obligation on the Professional* (Louisville, KY: Westminster/John Knox Press, 2001), as well as in his earlier *The Physician's Covenant: Images of the Healer in Medical Ethics* (2nd edn; Louisville, KY: Westminster/John Knox Press, 1983, 2000). Both books are relevant to the discussion of professional ethics in Chapter Three.

Donald Shriver's comment about "rich-nation politics" can be found in his article on "World Hunger," in *A New Dictionary of Christian Ethics* (John Macquarrie and James Childress, eds; London: SCM Press, 1986), page 286.

José P. Miranda offers one of the most influential accounts of what Christian ethics might have to learn from Marxist thought in his book *Marx and the Bible: A Critique of the Philosophy of Oppression* (Maryknoll, NY: Orbis Books, 1974). Gustavo

Gutiérrez also has much to say on economic justice from the point of view of liberation theology; see *Gustavo Gutiérrez: Essential Writings* (James B. Nickoloff, ed.; Minneapolis, MN: Fortress Press, 1996).

Many of Walter Wink's writings deal with issues of power, justice, and resistance. See, for example, *Unmasking the Powers: The Invisible Forces That Determine Human Existence* (Philadelphia, PA: Fortress Press, 1986).

Nel Noddings' influential work on an ethics of care is *Caring: A Feminine Approach to Ethics and Moral Education* (Berkeley, CA: University of California Press, 1984), and Fiona Robinson's publications include *Globalizing Care: Ethics, Feminist Theory and International Relations* (Boulder, CO: Westview Press, 1999).

Stephen Fowl's discussion of the ecclesial context for the use of possessions may be found in his essay "Being Blessed: Wealth, Property, and Theft," in *The Blackwell Companion to Christian Ethics* (2nd edn; Stanley Hauerwas and Samuel Wells, eds; Oxford; Malden, MA: Blackwell, 2004).

Duncan Forrester's account of justice and the kingdom is from "Social Justice and Welfare," in *The Cambridge Companion to Christian Ethics* (Robin Gill, ed.; Cambridge: Cambridge University Press, 2001).

Stanley Hauerwas' famous remark about the church not *having* but *being* a social ethic can be found in *Truthfulness and Tragedy: Further Investigations in Christian Ethics* (Notre Dame, IN: Notre Dame University Press, 1977), pages 142–3.

Kelly S. Johnson writes about intercessory prayer in her essay "Praying: Poverty," pages 225–36 in *The Blackwell Companion to Christian Ethics*. The extended quotation is drawn from pages 230 and 234. Robert Song discusses poverty and economic justice in "Sharing Communion: Hunger, Food, and Genetically Modified Foods," pages 388–400 in *The Blackwell Companion to Christian Ethics*. As well as the explicit quotations of Song, we are also drawing on his work when discussing the importance of actual bread in the feeding of the

5000. Timothy Gorringe, Michael Hanby, and Rusty Reno also have important contributions in the *Blackwell Companion to Christian Ethics* which touch on issues of business and management, and which we have drawn upon in this chapter.

For an analysis of contemporary economic theory from a Christian perspective, see John E. Stapleford, *Bulls, Bears and Golden Calves: Applying Christian Ethics to Economics* (Downers Grove, IL: InterVarsity Press, 2002), which interacts with seven standard introductory economics textbooks from the perspective of Christian ethics and especially through the lens of Scripture.

The following works on economics and the church are in the corresponding chapter of *Christian Ethics: An Introductory Reader*:

- Adam Smith. *An Inquiry into the Nature and Causes of the Wealth of Nations.* Vol. 1. R. H. Campbell and A. S. Skinner, eds. Oxford: Clarendon Press, 1976, 1979. From Book I, chapter 2, "Of the Principle which gives occasion to the Division of Labour"; Book IV, chapter 2, "Of Restraints upon the Importation from foreign Countries of such Goods as can be produced at Home." http://www.econlib.org/library/Smith/smWN.html.
- Medellín document. "'The Church in the Present-Day Transformation of Latin America in the Light of the Council' (August 26–September 6, 1968)." In *Liberation Theology: A Documentary History.* Alfred T. Hennelly, ed. Maryknoll, NY: Orbis Books, 1990. From "Document on the Poverty of the Church."
- Martin Luther King Jr. "I See the Promised Land." www.mlkonline.net/promised.html.

Work, Business, and Management

For explorations of the ethics of sport, see Lincoln Harvey, *A Brief Theology of Sport* (Eugene, OR: Cascade Books, 2014); and Patrick Kelly, *Catholic Perspectives on Sports: From Medieval to Modern Times* (Mahwah, NJ: Paulist Press, 2012).

For Karl Barth's understanding of the Sabbath, see *Church Dogmatics* III.4 (Edinburgh: T & T Clark, 1957), pages 47–72.

Thomas Aquinas treats buying and selling in *Summa Theologica* (5 vols; Notre Dame, IN: Christian Classics, 1948), Secunda Secundae [Second Part of the Second Part], Question 77, Article 1.

John A. Temple's comment on "leading by example" and his remarks about biblical principles and management are taken from his article "Management," in *New Dictionary of Christian Ethics and Pastoral Theology* (David J. Atkinson and David H. Field, eds; Downers Grove, IL: InterVarsity Press, 1995), page 564.

The British theologian Michael Banner offers an acute critique of the problems with cost–benefit analysis when dealing with many complex moral issues. We drew on his book *Christian Ethics and Contemporary Moral Problems* (Cambridge: Cambridge University Press, 1999) when discussing management models in ethics, and he will reappear in Chapter Twelve.

John Milbank's quotation about management and "optimum environments" is in his essay "Out of the Greenhouse," in *The Word Made Strange: Theology, Language, Culture* (Oxford; Malden, MA: Blackwell, 1997), page 262.

The 1981 papal encyclical *Laborem Exercens* (On Human Work) is on the Vatican's website at http://w2.vatican.va/content/john-paul-ii/en/encyclicals/documents/hf_jp-ii_enc_14091981_laborem-exercens.html. The quotation is from Part V, "Elements for a Spirituality of Work," section 24, "A Particular Task for the Church."

Max Stackhouse's discussion of how ethics reaches across boundaries is from "Business, Economics and Christian Ethics," in *The Cambridge Companion to Christian Ethics.* An excerpt from Stackhouse's book *Public Theology and Political Economy: Christian Stewardship in Modern Society* (Commission on Stewardship, National Council of Churches; Grand Rapids, MI: Eerdmans, 1987) is also included in the corresponding chapter of *Christian Ethics: An Introductory Reader*.

The categories "work equals vocation," "vocation judges work," and "vocation reforms work" used in the section exploring subversive responses to work are taken from Michael Moynagh's article on "Vocation," in *New Dictionary of Christian Ethics and Pastoral Theology*, page 882.

Michael Hanby's treatment of the care of the infirm and dying, and intercessory prayer, are from his chapter "Interceding: Giving Grief to Management," pages 237–49 in *The Blackwell Companion to Christian Ethics.*

Rusty Reno explores the themes of work and baptism in his chapter "Participating: Working Toward Worship," pages 319–31 in *The Blackwell Companion to Christian Ethics.*

John Hughes discusses work and liturgy in his *The End of Work: Theological Critiques of Capitalism* (Oxford: Blackwell, 2007).

Rowan Williams' words about intercession are in his *On Christian Theology* (Oxford: Blackwell, 2000), page 12.

Another helpful resource for this section of the chapter is Michael Northcott, *Life after Debt: Christianity and Global Justice* (London: SPCK, 1999).

The following works also appear in the corresponding chapter of *Christian Ethics: An Introductory Reader*:

- Miguel de la Torre. *Doing Christian Ethics from the Margins.* Maryknoll, NY: Orbis Books, 2004. From Part IV: Case Studies on Business Relationships; Chapter 13, "Corporate Accountability."
- Alasdair MacIntyre. *After Virtue: A Study in Moral Theory.* 2nd edn. Notre Dame, IN: University of Notre Dame Press, 1984, 2003. From Chapter 7, "'Fact', Explanation and Expertise."

Media

The opening remarks of the section on media draws upon the helpful article by E. J. Tinsley, "Ethical Issues in Media," in *A New Dictionary of Christian Ethics.* We are also indebted to David Winter's article on "Media," in *New Dictionary of Christian Ethics and Pastoral Theology*, page 580; and to Michael Budde's chapter, "Collecting Praise: Global Culture Industries," in the *Blackwell Companion to Christian Ethics*, pages 123–38.

The quotation from Donald Bannister is taken from Eric Clark's book *The Want Makers* (New York: Viking, 1989).

Oliver O'Donovan discusses publicity in his essay "The Concept of Publicity," in *Studies in Christian Ethics* 13, no. 1 (2000): 21–2.

George Myerson's thoughts on communication and the cell phone are in *Heidegger, Habermas and the Mobile Phone* (Duxford, UK: Icon; USA: Totem Books, 2001).

Sherry Turkle's exploration of "why we expect more from technology and less from each other" is the subtitle of her book *Alone Together* (New York: Basic Books, 2011).

Evgeny Morozov criticizes what he sees as the dominant ideology of Silicon Valley in *To Save Everything, Click Here: The Folly of Technological Solutionism* (London: Penguin, 2013).

The 1975 encyclical *Miranda Prorsus* (On Mass Communications) by Pope Pius XII may be found at http://w2.vatican.va/content/pius-xii/en/encyclicals/documents/hf_p-xii_enc_08091957_miranda-prorsus.html; see especially sections 1–4.

Pope Francis comments briefly on the media in the 2015 encyclical *Laudato Si'* (On Care for Our Common Home), 1.IV.46–47, 1.V.49; available at http://w2.vatican.va/content/francesco/en/encyclicals/documents/papa-francesco_20150524_enciclica-laudato-si.html.

Albert Borgmann argues for restraining and redeeming technology in *Power Failure: Christianity in the Culture of Technology* (Grand Rapids, MI: Brazos Press, 2003).

Dietrich Bonhoeffer explores a "ministry of presence" in *Life Together* (London: SCM Press, 1954); the specific quotation is from page 24. For another thorough discussion of "being with" one another, see Samuel Wells, *A Nazareth Manifesto: Being With God* (Oxford: John Wiley and Sons, 2015), especially chapter 8.

David Winter's quotation on the dangers of media comes from his article "Media" (see above).

An example of a subversive approach to media is Kristy Maddux's *The Faithful Citizen: Popular Christian Media and Gendered Civic Identities* (Waco, TX: Baylor University Press, 2010).

The discussion of Alasdair MacIntyre in the media section is from his book *Dependent Rational Animals: Why Human Beings Need the Virtues* (London: Duckworth, 1999).

Rowan Williams explores "time-taking practices" in *Lost Icons* (Edinburgh: T & T Clark, 2000), pages 142 and 159.

Pius XI's spoken description of the liturgy and the teaching office of the church is reported in Irénée Henri Dalmais, *Principles of the Liturgy* (Vol. 1 of *The Church at Prayer: An Introduction to the Liturgy*, Collegeville, MN: Liturgical Press, 1987), page 274.

D. Brent Laytham reflects on the intersection of entertainment media and liturgical practices in *iPod, YouTube, Wii Play: Theological Engagements with Entertainment* (Eugene, OR: Cascade Books, 2012).

In addition to the above, the following works addressing media are in the corresponding chapter of *Christian Ethics: An Introductory Reader*:

- *Aetatis Novae*: On Social Communications on the Twentieth Anniversary of *Communio et Progressio*. http://www.vatican.va/roman_curia/pontifical_councils/pccs/documents/rc_pc_pccs_doc_22021992_aetatis_en.html.
- Mary E. Hess. "Growing Faithful Children in Media Cultures." Chapter 5 in *The Ministry of Children's Education*, Professors of Christian Education at the ELCA Seminaries, Philadelphia, PA: Fortress Press, 2004.
- Michael Budde. *The (Magic) Kingdom of God: Christianity and Global Culture Industries.* Boulder, CO: Westview Press, 1997.

For further reflections on the media, consult Jolyon Mitchell's *Media Violence and Christian Ethics* (Cambridge; New York: Cambridge University Press, 2007) and Michael Budde's article "Collecting Praise" (see above).

Chapter Ten
Good Relationships

No scriptural passage sums up the seamless connection between the nature of God, the person of Christ, and the character of Christian discipleship more succinctly than 1 John 4:7–12.

> Beloved, let us love one another, because love is from God; everyone who loves is born of God and knows God. Whoever does not love does not know God, for God is love. God's love was revealed among us in this way: God sent his only Son into the world so that we might live through him. In this is love, not that we loved God but that he loved us and sent his Son to be the atoning sacrifice for our sins. Beloved, since God loved us so much, we also ought to love one another. No one has ever seen God; if we love one another, God lives in us, and his love is perfected in us.

The questions addressed in this chapter derive from this explicit link between God's love and human love. They cover three broad areas.

1. What is the purpose and what is to be the nature of regular and sustained human interaction? This involves a discussion of friendship.
2. What is the purpose and what is to be the form and quality of intimate and passionate human interaction? This involves a discussion of the family, marriage, and sex.
3. Are there specific kinds of relationships that may only ever be the former, and may never be the latter? This involves a discussion of same-sex relationships.

Introducing Christian Ethics, Second Edition. Samuel Wells and Ben Quash with Rebekah Eklund.
© 2017 John Wiley & Sons Ltd. Published 2017 by John Wiley & Sons Ltd.

Friendship

Scripture

In some ways Scripture as a whole is the story of what it means for Israel and the church to be God's friends. Perhaps the key verses of Scripture are Jesus' words to his disciples in John 15:12–15:

> This is my commandment, that you love one another as I have loved you. No one has greater love than this, to lay down one's life for one's friends. You are my friends if you do what I command you. I do not call you servants any longer, because the servant does not know what the master is doing; but I have called you friends.

The Old Testament offers several examples of notable friendships, including Ruth and Naomi, David and Jonathan, and Esther and Mordecai, together with warnings against false friends. The New Testament offers the fundamental commands to love God and to love one's neighbor as oneself (Matt 22:34–40), but there remains a tension around whether these two loves are in any sense the same and whether the notion of neighbor challenges or supplants the notion of friend. The New Testament also suggests that the kinship bonds created between "brothers and sisters" in Christ are stronger and more enduring than those created by marriage or biological family, raising another kind of tension for Christian ethics. For certain New Testament texts, especially the letters of Paul, Christ's resurrection and the inauguration of God's new age means that singleness is a valid form of faithful Christian discipleship – opening up the possibility that friendship, and not marriage, may be the primary form of human relationship for some Christians.

Ancient Philosophical Tradition

Friendship is a significant theme in classical literature.

1. Plato's dialogue the *Lysis* defines love as desiring happiness for the beloved. (Happiness is the life of a dignified and honorable citizen.) Unlike many Christian theologians, Plato held *eros* (desire) in high esteem, since *eros* forms the wings that lift human attention to the transcendent ideals of goodness, truth, and beauty. In the *Phaedrus* Plato suggests it is well for *eros* to settle upon another (male) person, but that the path to happiness lies in restraining the urge to consummate such love physically, instead maintaining harmonious self-control and mutual friendship. The philosopher (literally, "lover of wisdom") maintains this friendly love or *philia*. In his *Symposium* Plato portrays this asceticism as a ladder, ascending from love of a beautiful body through love of a beautiful soul and on to abstract beauty in customs and laws, culminating in the form of Beauty itself.

2. For Aristotle, *philia* is the virtue that holds the city-state together. Friendly love for one another differs from love for inanimate objects because in the case of objects there is no returned love and no regard for the object for its own sake. Friends are those who are in a consciously mutual relation of returned love and regard for their own sake. Friendship depends on *koinonia* (community) – such as kinship, citizenship, a common project, or simple common humanity. There are three kinds of friendship – the noble, the pleasant, and the useful.

    a. Perfect friendship arises where each person is so noble that loving them for their own sake is the same as loving them as good persons.

    b. Imperfect friendship arises where the partners merely love one another out of some benefit they can get from one another. These friendships cease when the partners' needs or tastes change.

    c. Useful friendship does not assume the partner is pleasant, nor does it seek the partner's company very much. Such friendships can include business partnerships and fleeting erotic attractions. Perfect friendships are both pleasant and useful.

Aristotle is the first to consider what it might mean to be one's own friend. He recognizes that love of others is like love for oneself. It may be that all love derives from self-love; whether or not this is so, self-love is a model for other kinds of love, for a friend is "another self." Likewise parents and benefactors love that which they have created as an extension of themselves. Because friendly love is always love of the good as well as love of the other person, evil persons not only cannot rightly love others, they cannot even rightly love themselves.

3. In the Roman era, Cicero (106–43 BCE) regarded friendship (*amicitia*), along with wisdom, as to be desired above all things, for through friendships come all the constituents of the happy life – fame, glory, joy, and peace of mind. There is a natural bond known as *societas* that holds humankind together. Within this bond may emerge intimate friendships resting on *caritas* (love), which itself rests upon *benevolentia* (good will). Thus, friendship is "an accord in all things, human and divine, conjoined with mutual good will and affection." Cicero sees friendship as arising from nature and not from need: in this he reflects his sympathies with the Stoic tradition and his antagonism to the Epicurean tradition. (See Chapter Three for a discussion of Stoicism and Epicureanism.) It is natural, Cicero argues, to be attracted to a person of virtue and congenial character, just as it is natural to be drawn to a light. Friendships based on need (rather than virtue) are never permanent.

    Cicero is also notable for the way he sees friendship as arising from self-sufficiency, in contrast to Plato who sees friendship as rooted in *eros* (desire). Like Aristotle, Cicero sees a friend as "another self," and the love one bears for a friend is an analogy of the love one has for oneself. Since self-love means being ruled by virtue rather than passion, one becomes a friend by first becoming good and then finding that rare person who holds within themselves the reason why they should be loved. One difference from Aristotle is that Cicero sees equality as a consequence rather than a prerequisite of friendship. For Aristotle, one could not truly be a friend of a person who was of a higher or lower social standing, whereas for Cicero, a true friendship should seek to equalize the partners' social standing.

Ancient and Medieval Christian Thought

From the time of the early Church Fathers through the medieval era, Christian thinkers adapted classical thinking on friendship within a Christian framework, reshaping notions of friendship especially around the concept of friendship with God. Other challenges emerged, such as whether men and women could form genuine friendships with one another – a possibility largely rejected by the classical tradition and by some (but not all) Christian thinkers as well. The option of celibate life provided by monasteries for both men and women opened up avenues for friendships not generally available in wider society. Several famous male–female friendships in the pre-Reformation church include Jerome and Paula in the early fifth century and Francis and Clare of Assisi in the early thirteenth century.

We may take three pre-Reformation figures as significant in the shaping of thought about friendship and Christian love: Augustine (354–430 CE), Aelred of Rievaulx (1110–67), and Thomas Aquinas (1225–74).

1. In Augustine it becomes clear that the question of friendship is at heart the question of the nature of Christian love. Augustine faced a number of problems in relation to friendship, few of which he fully resolved despite repeated treatments of the question.
   a. One ambivalence concerns self-love. Is love of self the opposite of loving God, or is it the same as loving God? (In the *City of God* Augustine suggests the heavenly city – the church in pilgrimage – was created by love of God, while the earthly city was created by self-love or contempt for God.)
   b. A second ambivalence concerns the relative significance of friend and neighbor. Is it right to love some especially, or is one to love all equally? (He points out that Jesus chose as his friends not senators, but fishermen – he chose the weak to confound the strong.)
   c. A third ambivalence lies in relation to those who do not love God. Do they therefore lack the capacity to be a friend? (In his *Confessions*, Augustine suggests that true friendship is not possible without the bond created by the Holy Spirit.)
   d. A fourth ambivalence concerns other Christians. Is another Christian a brother (or sister) or a friend? (Calling an enemy a brother helps to explain why one can experience hatred but nonetheless be called to love. It therefore could seem a more fundamental category than friend.)

Because Augustine sees God as complete within the Trinity, and is reluctant to see human beings as free agents, he does not dwell on what it means for Christians to be friends of God. In general *amicitia* (friendship) is absorbed into *caritas* (love), and the latter is entered into primarily with God, love of neighbor being a fruit or reflection or perhaps a step toward love of God. Thus, we love God for God's sake and we love all else – ourselves, our neighbors, and our bodies – for God's sake too. Book IV of the *Confessions* is largely devoted to friendship. The love of friends is good, but a friend must be loved in God. It is only God who does not perish or change; friends cannot therefore be loved for themselves alone.

One very significant distinction Augustine makes is between *uti* (use) and *frui* (enjoyment). To use something is to treat it as a means to an end. To enjoy something is to regard it as an end in itself. Only God is truly to be enjoyed as an end in this sense. As ever with Augustine, there remains an ambivalence about whether other people are to be enjoyed for their own sake or to be used – that is, to be loved for God's sake. This does not just apply to friendship; the same ambivalence applies to marriage.

2. Aelred of Rievaulx was a Cistercian abbot in Yorkshire, England, who, in common with many writers from the Benedictine monastic tradition, saw strict asceticism as a voluntary sharing in Christ's suffering in order to learn his way of love, and regarded the Song of Songs as the definitive allegory of mystical love. His treatise *Spiritual Friendship* was inspired by Cicero's philosophical dialogue *On Friendship* and examines the question of friendship through the lens of faith in Christ. Like Augustine, Aelred proposes that true friendship is oriented around fellowship in Christ, but he explores the capacity and beauty (or "excellence") of human friendship in a more sustained way than Augustine.

For Aelred, charity (love) and friendship were perfectly united before the Fall and will be reunited in God's future kingdom. Until the eschaton, friendship occurs in three main types: carnal (physical), worldly, and spiritual. The first two kinds are temporary and are not genuine friendship. Carnal friendship seeks pleasure and is guided by passion; worldly friendship seeks advantage and depends on a person's usefulness. Spiritual friendship, on the other hand, is true friendship, which is guided by the virtues and always seeks the good of the other. It is not the same thing as charity (love), since one is commanded to love one's enemies as well as one's friends. Through the healing power of Christ's grace, the love of friends can mirror the love of God.

The three loves – of self, of neighbor, and of God – are inseparable and complementary in Aelred's thought. "Each love is found in all, and all in each, nor can one be had without the other," although the love of God comes first. Unusually for his time, Aelred notes: "How beautiful it is that the second human being [Eve] was taken from the side of the first [Adam], so that nature might teach us that human beings are equal and, as it were, collateral, and that there is in human affairs neither a superior nor an inferior, a characteristic of true friendship." Reflecting Cicero's contention that friendship is wisdom, Aelred transposed the language of 1 John 4:16 with the words, "God is friendship." If it were not for the Fall, which introduced avarice and envy, friendship would be evident as humankind's nature and destiny.

3.   Thomas Aquinas explores the various Latin words for love – *concupiscentia* (acquisitiveness), *dilectio* (selfless love), *amor* (desire), *benevolentia* (good will), *concordia* (peace), and *beneficentia* (generosity) – and concludes that *caritas* (love) is summed up in *amicitia* (friendship). He perceives three levels of friendship:

- *amor*, which mainly concerns the senses;
- *dilectio*, which includes the will; and
- *amicitia*, in which loving companionship becomes a habit.

God is intimately present to all creatures, and God's love takes the form of willing their inherent good to emerge from them. Aquinas seems to use the terms lovers, friends, and children of God interchangeably. God's goodness attracts us toward our true purpose and flourishing, and then God gives us friendship as a gift. Like Aelred and Augustine, Aquinas is clear that friendship with God is prior to human friendship: the neighbor is loved for God's sake. Just as we love the children of a friend (whether they are friendly to us or not) because we so much love our friend, so we love our enemies because we so much love God.

Love is "to will good to someone," and this means there are two kinds of love – friendship-love (for the friend themselves) and desiring-love (for the goods we seek to acquire for the friend). But Aquinas insists these two loves are complementary. Our love for God is more the former than the latter, because God is greater than any of the benefits God brings us. In other words, we love God more than ourselves. But love of self is next to love of God, and comes before love of neighbor. But here it is vital to note that our selves are not identical with our physical bodies: hence we may and sometimes must jeopardize our physical bodies for a friend, but we may *not* jeopardize our spiritual selves for a friend. Our first duty is to save our own soul. Our body is still a true object of love, but it ranks below God, self, and neighbor.

These are among the most significant theological sources that inform the contemporary discourse on friendship and neighbor-love. Among less theological sources, notable is Michel de Montaigne (1533–92), who in his essay *On Friendship* wrote: "What we ordinarily call friends and friendships are nothing but acquaintanceships and familiarities formed by some chance or convenience, by means of which our souls are bound to each other." He added: "In the friendship I speak of, our souls mingle and blend with each other so completely that they efface the seam that joined them, and cannot find it again."

This rich discourse on friendship and its relation to other forms of love largely falls quiet in the post-Enlightenment period. There are a number of reasons for this, not least the anxiety that all friendships are fundamentally erotic in nature. As previously noted in other chapters, the Protestant Reformation undercut the monastic model of faithful Christian life, thus excluding not only the option of celibacy but also the setting in which intimate but non-sexual friendships were often formed and tested. And several influential theologians dispensed with the notion of preferential friendship in favor of non-preferential neighbor-love (see below). Changing social norms in the mid-twentieth century tended to focus the church's attention on the relationship between stable marriages and families and a well-functioning society, rather than on the bonds of friendship, which were increasingly relegated to the private sphere or minimized in favor of family commitments. But as Western societies in the twenty-first century have shifted away from a model in which the majority are married and have children, some Christian ethicists have begun anew to consider the meaning and purpose of both singleness and friendship in a theological framework.

Universal

Friendship is a theme that has tended to be neglected in universal ethics. This is largely because it is not a question that can be reduced easily to actions or outcomes – the conventional territory of value-free description. Neither is it an area where government or legislation appear to have any significant bearing. Even though right relationships are an important dimension of universal ethics, friendship is seldom seen as a "public" relationship upon which ethical reflection should dwell.

For those thinkers, particularly from the Reformed tradition, who tend to distribute issues between family, work, state, and church, there is no obvious location for a discussion of friendship. Three key figures, all shaped by Lutheranism, may be taken as representative of this abiding lack of consensus regarding the place of friendship.

1. For Immanuel Kant (1724–1804), in his *The Metaphysics of Morals* (1797), there is a greater role for friendship than one might assume if one were to restrict one's view of Kant to his categorical imperative alone. He sees ethics as about love (benevolence expressed in generosity, gratitude, and sympathy) and about respect (which permits the other their dignity and space). Friendship, at best, refers to union through equal and mutual love and respect. There is a universal duty of friendship, although this duty is somewhat impractical, and thus we should aspire to be a friend of humankind, seeking the welfare of all and never disturbing that welfare without profound regret.

    Because equality was such a foundational notion for Kant, he excluded patronage from friendship. Friendship is thus more than philanthropy. It is the desire to be everyone's brother under one universal parent. Perfection means being everyone's friend.

2.   Søren Kierkegaard (1813–55) expressed reservations about all forms of exclusive love, including friendship, in the starkest terms. For Kierkegaard, especially in his *Works of Love* (1847), there is an absolute distinction between selfish love and self-denying love. Divine love, otherwise known as love for the neighbor, is universal and eternal and is the moral and spiritual demand from which arise all other commitments. The neighbor is every person, and every person is to be loved without reserve. Since this is immensely demanding, it rests on God implanting this love in each person. Kierkegaard assumed Christianity had abolished distinctions between different kinds of love. He saw classical friendship with an "other self" as simply self-love: it was exclusive, sentimental, and based on chance. His contrast between neighbor-love and self-love is crystallized in this distinction: "We human beings speak about finding the perfect person in order to love him, whereas Christianity speaks about being the perfect person who boundlessly loves the person he sees."

3.   This contrast reaches its definitive expression in the Swedish Lutheran Anders Nygren's (1890–1978) immensely influential *Agape and Eros* (two volumes, 1930, 1936). Nygren was writing at a time when there was a tendency to distinguish between the Hebraic idiom of the early disciples and the Hellenistic vocabulary of later patristic theologians. Hence Nygren identified one Greek word for love, *agape*, with the divine, selfless love of sacrificial giving, and the other Greek terms, notably *eros* (desire) but also *philia* (friendly love), with the self-serving, acquisitive egocentrism of desire. Nygren recognized that this contrast was not found in John's Gospel, but held that it was maintained throughout the first three gospels and in Paul. His severe distinction between *agape* and *eros* is rooted in Luther's emphasis that justification comes by grace alone through faith alone, and thus the Lutheran skepticism toward any suggestion that humans can find righteousness before God on their own merits. However, more recent linguistic analysis has come to question whether the distinction between the different terms has any serious grounding in the patterns of first-century Greek, or whether in fact terms like *agape* and *philia* were more or less interchangeable.

The legacy of Kierkegaard and Nygren is threefold. They strengthened the tendency to regard friendship as outside the regular roster of ethical issues. (The most common conclusion has been to channel dimensions of neighbor-love into notions of justice.) They rendered Christian love an almost impossible ideal. And they made marriage and family problematic as expressions of distinctively *Christian* love.

Subversive

Subversive critiques of friendship fall broadly into two aspects of the threefold pattern outlined in Chapter Six. There are those who seek to revise the paradigm and those who reject the paradigm.

1.   *Revision.* When one reads C. S. Lewis' description of friendship in his *Four Loves* (1960), it is not hard to depict a male world of genial camaraderie, tweed suits, warm beer, pipe-smoking, hearty walks, and rarefied conversation that is largely true to the Aristotelian ideal but nonetheless begging to be deconstructed along the lines of class, gender, and race. A revision of this kind of false universal paradigm is often pursued in Kantian terms of equality and the convergence of love and respect. Thus, for example, Jürgen Moltmann (b. 1926), a longstanding member of the Evangelical (Lutheran and Reformed) faculty at Tübingen in southwestern Germany, suggests that rather than concentrate on Christ as prophet, priest, and king, he should be seen first of all as friend. Moltmann's language of friendship reflects Kantian themes of love and respect, but insists that friendship must retain the openness of the messianic banquet, always reaching across lines of class and propriety, and never restricted to those who look or sound the same.

   In her *Models of God* (1987) Sallie McFague uses the three Greek words for love to suggest a Trinitarian configuration of God as mother (*agape*), lover (*eros*), and friend (*philia*), thus equating friendship with the role traditionally played by the Holy Spirit. In characteristic "liberal" fashion (a model described in Chapter Six), McFague sees friendship as resting on freedom, inclusiveness, and mature responsibility. Other feminist theologians point to the patriarchal tendency to identify *agape* (self-giving love) and altruism with submissive virtues in women. In this context the movement in John 15:15 from servants to friends has much to offer as the evocation of a free community without constricting gender roles. These issues are not simply about gender: liberation theologians have recognized the danger of abstraction in their identification of the class struggle in Latin America. Thus, friendship becomes a way of ensuring solidarity is about real people, not notional social groupings.

2.   *Rejection.* For some feminists the historic discourse of friendship is overshadowed by a pervasive assumption that friendship is a secondary category alongside the dominant model of marriage and family (institutions that rejectionists tend to see in exclusively patriarchal terms). Here there is some discussion about whether or not the erotic is fundamentally sexual, or whether it better refers to deep human connection more broadly. In this way the line between friendship (generally assumed to be non-sexual) and marriage/cohabitation may be blurred, especially for lesbian women who sometimes regard their relationships as a form of female friendship. For some feminists, like radical thinker Mary Daly (1928–2010), the prevailing model of friendship is so irredeemably patriarchal that it must be abandoned in favor of a new one, rooted in the self-understanding and experiences of women.

Ecclesial

Friendship has been a significant theme in recent ecclesial ethics, largely because it fits so neatly into the recovery of Aristotelian virtue ethics. Aquinas, and to a slightly lesser extent Aelred and Augustine, have been eagerly reclaimed as thinkers who relocate ethics toward character, commitments, and convictions shaped by communities over time within traditions and grounded in habits and practices. Paul Wadell (b. 1951), for example, describes friendship as "the crucible of the moral life" and argues that growth in virtue *requires* the kind of relationships that Aelred calls spiritual friendships. In addition to these emphases some particular themes have emerged in recent ecclesial approaches.

1.   *Hospitality.* If friendship is to be rescued from stuffy partiality, it needs renarrating in such a way that it recasts the conventional distinction between intimate friend and needy but distant neighbor. The practice of hospitality has emerged as a key theme in showing how the nuclear family and corresponding notions of exclusive friendship are turned inside out by openness to see the neighbor, the stranger, and the needy as a gift. For example, the practice of taking in refugees from political and religious oppression (such as Jews fleeing the Holocaust) has proved a defining moment in the identity of many Christian communities. Meanwhile some point out that Luke's account of Jesus' birth suggests his life was from the first open to the elements and to strangers. Thus, marriage and family are not basic to Christian identity in the way baptism and Eucharist are.

Hospitality offers a very different model for the recognition and understanding of difference compared to the widespread language of tolerance. Tolerance refers to the acceptance of religious, moral, or ethnic differences that one would normally, as an individual or community, discourage, dislike, or even abhor. This acceptance is grounded in the limits and fallibility of human knowledge, the importance of respect for judicial process and authority (including the assumption of an impartial state), and the explicit good of individual autonomy. By contrast ecclesial thinkers ground respect for difference elsewhere. Alasdair MacIntyre grounds it in *misericordia* (compassion), which he sees as a universal capacity. Those who begin with Scripture point out that eating with "sinners" was a key feature of Jesus' ministry. Those who focus on sacraments point out that Christian witness is at heart an invitation to a banquet. The emphasis of Acts is that purity now lies not in keeping clean from other people or animals but in Christ alone, and that the Christian life is a perpetual interplay of discovering that one is first a host, then a guest. The work of the L'Arche communities in transforming relationships between those with severe developmental disabilities and those who care for them, and the witness of Dorothy Day (1897–1980) and the Catholic Worker movement in care of and with the poor, are frequently cited as iconic examples of this guest–host dynamic of Christian hospitality.

2.   *Singleness.* For those who are not married, friendship may be experienced as the primary form of relationship. Ecclesial ethicists often point out that the New Testament appears to regard singleness, rather than marriage, as the norm, and assumes the church is to grow through regeneration (conversion

and baptism) rather than conventional sexual generation. But leaving monastic and other forms of community life aside, this leaves the discussion of singleness somewhat quiet. It cannot be claimed that friendship absorbs all the positive aspects of singleness. Nonetheless the recovery of the tradition of friendship demonstrates the way ecclesial ethics has developed an ethic rooted in vocation rather than simply creation. This is one of the ways in which it differs from universal ethics. Singleness is thus seen less as sexual renunciation, and more as the forfeiting of heirs – the only hope of survival beyond the grave – and the placing of all one's hope in Christ. It is also seen as a way of embodying in practice the theory that the church provides a family for those not otherwise set in nuclear families through marriage. Wesley Hill, for example, draws on Aelred's writings to argue that Christians should resist viewing friendship through the modern lens of personal autonomy as "a relationship of minimal obligations and maximal liberty" and instead reconfigure it as one more akin to the enduring bonds between spouses or siblings.

3. *Common life.* Acts 2 and 4 give vivid descriptions of the ways the dynamism of Pentecost created new forms of social relationships founded on cross and resurrection.

> All who believed were together and had all things in common; they would sell their possessions and goods and distribute the proceeds to all, as any had need. Day by day, as they spent much time together in the temple, they broke bread at home and ate their food with glad and generous hearts, praising God and having the goodwill of all the people. (Acts 2:44–7)

While universal approaches have tended to regard these accounts as utopian, a long tradition of both monastic and lay communities has sought to put them into practice. The monastic experiment is narrated in Chapter Two. As to lay initiatives, perhaps the most influential account is Dietrich Bonhoeffer's *Life Together* (1939). Here Bonhoeffer grounds community in divine reality rather than human striving and lays practical proposals alongside theological reasonings.

The Family, Marriage, and Sex

Our discussion of friendship considered sustained relationships with some, several, or even all people. We now turn to intimate and passionate relationships with a few people, or possibly only one person. A host of issues arise. They may be broadly grouped under three headings: when marriage and family go well, the boundaries of marriage and family, and when marriage and family go wrong.

1. *When marriage and family go well.*

    Reflection in the tradition on constructive views of marriage and the family falls into four general areas:

    a. whether male and female are complementary identities, whether such complementarity is a reflection of the nature of God, to what extent such complementarity is and should be realized in marriage, and whether such questions need to be revisited in the light of the changing roles of women and men in church and society;

    b. the ways marriage and family life can be means of grace and points of entry to the kingdom of God;

    c. sexual intercourse, dwelling on whether and to what extent sex and sexual desire are gifts to be enjoyed or forces to be reckoned with; and

    d. the nature, the best nurture, and the particular qualities of childhood.

    The most-cited scriptural references in this regard begin with Genesis 1–3, which sees sexual difference as good and designed for both reproduction and partnership, and inequality of male and female resulting not from creation but from the Fall. Jesus grounds his understanding of marriage in the creation account of the making of the male and the female (Mark 10:6). The New Testament includes the grand analogy between marriage and the relationship of Christ to the church, and the emphasis on mutual submission (Eph 5:21–33), as well as the more prosaic collections of "household codes" modeled on the three ancient relationships governing the hierarchy of the home: slave–master, husband–wife, and father–children. However, it is hard to find in Jesus a model for marriage or conventional family life – as his words about "hating father and mother" in order to follow him illustrate (Luke 14:26). Jesus prizes children by insisting they be allowed to come to him and describing a child's faith as a model for all disciples. But in general the New Testament is oriented to the coming kingdom of God and not so much to the specifics of healthy marriages and families. Paul, for example, suggests that it would be better *not* to be married so as to attend more single-mindedly to the things of the kingdom of God (1 Cor 7:25–35).

2. *The boundaries of marriage and family.*

    The degree of desire and passion evoked by intimate and familial relationships and the ways self-deception can cloud judgment mean particular attention is given to where the boundaries of such relationships should be drawn and what should be the consequences of transgressing those boundaries. The questions include the following. Should sexual expression begin with and be limited to marriage? (These issues include pre-marital sex, cohabitation, promiscuity, autoeroticism, adultery, further marriage after divorce, polygamy, and practices surrounding prostitution.) Should these judgments be based on relationships or commitments in themselves, or are they relative or subject to other roles such as parenthood? May marriages end and, if so, in what circumstances?

While the Old Testament includes strict rules concerning marriage, with uncompromising punishments, it also includes the Song of Songs, which portrays plenty of sexual desire but no mention of children or marriage. Some Old Testament practices seem to accept polygamy, but none condone adultery or sex before marriage. In 1 Corinthians 7 Paul offers the New Testament's only extended treatment of sexual boundaries. Marriage limits sexual passion, but celibacy is preferred. The key issue is what builds up the church. Fornication, prostitution, adultery, and incest are all forbidden. Jesus overturns the Old Testament's acceptance of divorce (Matt 5:31–2; 19:9; Mark 10:11–12; Luke 16:18; 1 Cor 7:10–11), although whether adultery might provide a possible grounds for divorce has frequently been a matter of dispute.

3.   *When marriage and family go wrong.*
Marriage and family have never been straightforward matters: the New Testament includes several accounts of troubled households. However, changing social conditions have made this third set of issues particularly prominent in recent decades. Greater acknowledgment of the rights of women has drawn attention to patterns of domestic violence. Amid increasing awareness of child abuse and neglect there is the question of whether children have rights and, if so, whether, how, and in what circumstances any bodies outside the family can or should intervene when family life has gone wrong.

Jesus is explicitly critical of those who misuse children, saying it would be better for a millstone to be put around that person's neck and they be thrown into the sea (Mark 9:42; Matt 18:6; Luke 17:2).

The early church was ambivalent toward the family. On the one hand Christian households were becoming vital institutions for embodying and disseminating the faith and modeling God's care of creation. The archbishop of Constantinople John Chrysostom (ca. 347–407 CE) sought in what we might call ecclesial ways to locate the family within the worship and mission of the church. On the other hand, a deep strain of theological writing saw family life in general and sex in particular in largely negative terms. For example, the Greek theologian from Asia Minor Gregory of Nyssa (ca. 335–94 CE) described marriage and family as institutions created out of a fear of death; and Jerome (347–420 CE), famous for first translating the Bible into Latin, perceived sex, even within marriage, as intrinsically evil. Hence the significance of Augustine's commitment to portray both marriage and singleness as legitimate vocations.

Augustine described singleness as the greater good, and marriage as the lesser good. Marriage is the lesser good, because since the Fall, sex is a matter not so much of the will as of involuntary *concupiscentia* (lust). The divided will, no longer able to control its desire and its body, results in sex becoming a matter not of delight and fellowship but of shame. Thus, marriage is like the journey of a lame man: the things a lame man walks toward are not any less good because his journey to them is impeded, but his disability is not made good because his destination is worthy. Thus, procreation is not bad because lust is evil, but lust is not made good because procreation is good. Augustine outlines three goods of marriage: children, faithfulness between the partners, and the sacramental mirroring of Christ's union with the church. Marriage directs human lives, loves, and bodies more into line with the shape of living God desires for the creation. While marriage was necessary to bring humanity to the time when God's full revelation appeared in Christ, since then marriage is not essential and singleness is the best witness to the promise of Christ's return. While Adam's original sin is passed from parent to child through procreation, Christ's salvation is not passed on in this way but must be received anew in each generation by baptism. Thus, Augustine dismantled ideas about perfecting humanity through selective breeding and progressive improvement – ideas that were influential in imperial Rome and have remained so to the present day.

The medieval consensus around the family, marriage, and sex converged around three themes.

1. Marriage is a matter of natural law, and is designed for procreation: adultery and fornication are ruled out.
2. Marriage is a contract that undergirds social stability and therefore a concern of civil law. It is a public institution constituted by consent and vows and invalidated by degrees of consanguinity or disability.
3. Marriage is a means of grace – a sacrament and thus a concern of spiritual law: it is not simply concerned with the redemption of lust but with friendship between spouses and care of children.

The third understanding, together with the analogy between marriage and the bond between Christ and the church, meant not just that marriage should not be dissolved, but that now it could not be; if divorce took place, further marriage was ruled out until one party died. In practice greater social mobility and devastating plagues meant the conjugal family (of grandparent, parent, and child) came to replace the manorial household (with its large extended families) as the normal social structure.

Martin Luther (1483–1546) regarded marriage as a gift – to allay lust – and a duty – to raise children as Christian servants. No longer was marriage to be seen as a sacrament or singleness to be regarded as superior to marriage. Marriage was part of the order of creation, and had no role in the order of redemption; it properly belonged therefore under the jurisdiction of the magistrate rather than the church. Divorce was in some cases inevitable, and had been sanctioned by Moses and (in Luther's view) acknowledged by Christ; time had shown that adultery was not the only grounds for divorce, and invariably further marriage avoided temptation and misconduct.

Meanwhile John Calvin (1509–64) saw marriage less in terms of creation than of covenant. A marriage was not just between two persons, but the roles of parents, witnesses, magistrate, and minister are crucial to the ceremony and the institution itself. The purposes of marriage were mutual love, procreation and childrearing, and protection from sin. Divorce was accepted in cases of adultery or abandonment. The church might have an active role to play in investigating, admonishing, or even excommunicating wayward spouses. The English Puritan Richard Baxter (1615–91) builds on Calvin and describes in great detail the relationships of the household: husband to wife, parent to child, and master to servant. Servants (a term broader than domestic staff) are to be treated with "tenderness and love." Thus, the family serves not itself but a whole social order oriented to sacrificial mutual love.

Entering the modern era, the three areas concerning family, marriage, and sex with which we began our discussion – the goods, the boundaries, and the failures – are largely taken up by the three main strands of ethical discourse, respectively: universal ethics tends to concentrate on boundaries, subversive ethics is largely taken up with failures, and ecclesial ethics tends to look toward rearticulating goods.

Universal

Universal ethics tends to concentrate on identifying and seeking to resolve anomalies and ambiguities concerning the appropriate boundaries of sexual relationships.

Preliminary to this enquiry is the question of whether male and female genders are *essential* or *external* dimensions of the self.

- Those theologians who see the key element of the human person as the soul are less inclined to emphasize the fundamentally gendered character of human existence, and thus more likely to take an *external* view of sexuality. For the external view, sexuality is something we *do* (perhaps even something we *choose*), rather than something we *are*. In this view sexual expression may, but need not, communicate a fundamental aspect of the self.

  For some externalist views, gender identity is not fixed or given but operates on a "sliding scale" and may even change over time – that is, one is not male or female, but may have characteristics of both, and may identify with either at different times in the course of a lifetime.

- Those who place a higher value on the human body as integral to the notion of being a person are more likely to reflect on the fact that the human body is a gendered entity, and thus take an *essential* view. Yet the human body created by God in Genesis 1 seems in the judgment of some theologians to be androgynous, since division into male and female is only a second step. Those who tend toward an essentialist view often point out that the body–soul dichotomy is a Greek and not a Hebrew distinction, and that the resurrection of the body affirms the permanent unity of body and soul.

  Some essentialist views maintain that besides the genitalia and the role each sex performs in intercourse and reproduction there is no fundamental difference between the sexes; other essentialist views are more far-reaching and extend the significance of sexual differentiation into many, perhaps all, aspects of human life. The claim that men are from Mars and women are from Venus is a well-known example of such an essentialist view.

The notion of transgendered identity blends elements from both an essentialist and externalist view. That is, transgendered people may understand gender as an essential but not *bodily* form of identity, such that they feel they have been born into a gender that is not their true identity. Thus, gender may be changed (by altering the body's chemistry or physical attributes through surgery and hormones, as well as through socially encoded markers such as clothing, hairstyle, and makeup) in order to match a felt sense of one's true gender identity.

While there are a host of issues discussed in this literature, they may be grouped into three areas.

1. Promiscuity, pre-marital sex, and cohabitation. These three terms cover the issues sometimes grouped under the traditional language of "fornication."

    Cohabitation is the consistent sharing of a residence and a bed on the part of a heterosexual couple over a significant period of time as a preparation or substitute for marriage. It is advocated on deontological and consequential grounds.

    The deontological arguments are that a committed relationship depends on love, rather than contract, and that it offers an opportunity to model less conventional and restrictive social roles. The deontological arguments fit quite comfortably within an essentialist view of sexuality. They sometimes originate from subversive sources, which may be especially inclined to highlight the shortcomings in conventional marriage roles.

    The consequential arguments are that cohabitation is sometimes considered easier to begin and end than marriage, and thus advantageous when commitment for perhaps sixty years together seems daunting; it may be less expensive, particularly regarding social expectations of a lavish wedding; and it promises the intimacy of marriage while preserving the autonomy of singleness. These arguments tend to assume more of an external view of sexuality, which is less inclined to see a person's whole being as taken up within the cohabiting relationship. Like many arguments that rely on an external notion of sexuality, they become harder to uphold in the face of childbirth. Children, and their conception and need of care, represent the most intractable counter-argument to external views of sexuality. Most sympathetic treatments of cohabitation treat it as a *de facto* marriage when and if children are born.

    Pre-marital sex is a less specific term that refers to sexual relations between heterosexual partners who see themselves as having a level of commitment to one another that exceeds promiscuity but falls short of marriage (although it can include intercourse between engaged couples). Because of the difficulty in defining terms, such relationships are most easily divided into those that largely resemble cohabitation, and thus come under the considerations examined above, and those that largely resemble promiscuity, and thus come under the considerations examined below.

Promiscuity refers to acts of intercourse with serial partners with little or no particular regard toward the partner beyond the maximization of sexual pleasure and the minimization of emotional manipulation or distress. The arguments supporting promiscuity tend to rest increasingly on an external view of sexuality that relies on the ability to separate one's bodily actions from one's true identity. However, arguments against promiscuity are notorious for overstating their case.

Deontological arguments rest on the conviction that sexual intercourse belongs within marriage, and thus to engage in it elsewhere diminishes marriage, diminishes sex, and diminishes the parties involved. (It is seldom made clear whether the issue that binds sex to marriage is primarily about respect for and fostering of intimacy or about the need for a trusting environment in which to nurture children.) These arguments, however, are often (unhelpfully) augmented by associations with purity, which not only tend to be disproportionately concerned with female over male chastity, but run counter to the New Testament tendency to revise prior assumptions about purity.

Moreover a host of consequential arguments, by no means all theologically grounded, are often introduced, citing surveys that provide data both for and against the practice of promiscuity, including reports of later marital longevity, sexual disappointment, and experience of loneliness – that seldom enhance the deontological claims. Advocates for permissive attitudes to promiscuity or premarital sex understandably spend much or most of their time questioning or rejecting the weaker of these arguments, rather than proposing constructive alternatives.

2. *Autoeroticism.* In the case of cohabitation and promiscuity, the social changes occasioned by increasing longevity and the equality of women offer a backdrop to many of the arguments. In the case of autoeroticism (often known as masturbation), the social changes largely concern the reduction of the concern to avoid population decline. The logic of the ancient discouragement of masturbation (the stimulation of one's own sexual organs for pleasure), still officially upheld in Roman Catholic circles, is that every sexual act should be open to procreation. In premodern times it was widely believed that male semen contained the embryonic new person, and thus the waste of semen was on a moral level with abortion. This historical note may continue to have some bearing on these questions. For those traditions that do not share this deontological presupposition, there are few if any deontological grounds for objecting to the practice.

Plenty of consequential grounds are cited. The practice sometimes evokes profound guilt, particularly when associated with primal notions of purity (discussed under promiscuity above). It can become obsessive. It can become part of a pattern of the objectification of others, most often women, as no more than sources of sexual gratification, particularly when associated with the use of or addiction to pornography. And it can be part of a pattern of withdrawing sexual activity from a place where it might be seen to belong, notably marriage: some thus fear that it risks weakening the marriage bond, or is a symptom of such weakening. Yet it is sometimes condoned or even tacitly encouraged as an alternative to adultery for the unhappily married or fornication for the unhappily single.

However, perhaps the most significant question about autoeroticism is whether it is "sex" at all. If sex is not inherently tied to reproduction, then not only do the (Roman Catholic) strictures on being open to reproduction come into question, but many external notions of sexuality become relevant. Yet if sex is inherently tied to reproduction, and there are activities (including autoerotic and same-sex practices) that are without possibility of reproduction, then does it still make sense to describe these activities as sex? And if not, would these activities come under the same strictures as those heterosexual practices traditionally considered under "fornication"? These are the most provocative questions raised by autoeroticism.

3.   The third boundary area concerns issues surrounding marriage itself. These include adultery, divorce, further marriage after divorce, polygamy, and practices surrounding prostitution.

Adultery. The deontological argument against adultery rests squarely on the commandment that explicitly forbids it (Exod 20:14). The last of the Ten Commandments also forbids a man coveting the wife of his neighbor (Exod 20:17), and Jesus extends this theme in pointing out the extent and hiddenness of adultery: "everyone who looks at a woman with lust has already committed adultery with her in his heart" (Matt 5:28). Adultery is generally considered a profound offense against all three conventional purposes of marriage – desire, friendship, and children. The deontological tradition against adultery is so strong that consequential arguments (for or against) or deontological arguments for the practice are seldom aired. Possible exceptions might be the open marriage or the use of surrogates in sex therapy. But these are in fact both consequential attempts to affirm monogamy, inasmuch as such practices are intended to enrich, stabilize, or otherwise save the marriage.

Divorce has often been accepted on the grounds of two scriptural texts:
- "Anyone who divorces his wife, except on the ground of unchastity, causes her to commit adultery" (Matt 5:32 – sometimes known as the "Matthean exception"). This is a somewhat puzzling text, since if the grounds are unchastity then the man's wife has committed adultery already. For some, it does not appear to support the uses to which it has often been put, that is, justifying divorce on the grounds of adultery. Moreover, it may encourage a climate in which, following adultery, divorce seems inevitable, which is not always the case.
- "If the unbelieving partner separates, let it be so; in such a case the brother or sister is not bound" (1 Cor 7:15 – sometimes known as the "Pauline privilege"). This text provides grounds for divorce that is initiated by the non-Christian partner in a marriage after the conversion of their spouse.

When sexuality is seen in essentialist terms, however, together with Jesus' words that "the two shall become one flesh" (Matt 19:5), the deontological case against divorce is almost unassailable. Attempts to make a deontological case on scriptural grounds are fragile. The only course is to reduce the significance of the New Testament material by arguing that it was offered in a context where the end of the world was thought to be imminent.

Thus, arguments in favor of permitting divorce are largely confined to consequential grounds. In circumstances of adultery, desertion, or cruelty there may seem to be no point in upholding a deontological ideal (although there are many examples of reconciliation in these circumstances). In the case of irretrievable breakdown, realism inclines many people to accept that a marriage has died rather than attempt extensive social machinations to pretend otherwise. People simply live much longer than in biblical times, and their expectations of their "quality of life" have changed significantly: some suggest these changes alter the playing field dramatically. Some argue that the rise in divorce rates is not a bad development, since it indicates, among other things, that fewer women are tolerating domestic abuse and exploitation. However, consequential arguments are also made against condoning divorce: in a time of rising expectations for personal fulfillment and the maintenance of autonomy in marriage, a relaxed approach to divorce is seen by some as encouraging people to leave marriages in which their forebears may have remained. It is generally assumed in such arguments that the benefits to society and especially children that accrue from staying in such (non-abusive but nonetheless in some way unsatisfactory) marriages outweigh the disadvantages. Consequentialist arguments tend to be divided on which harms children more: divorce or unhappy marriages.

Further marriage after divorce. The issues concerning further marriage after divorce are somewhat different from the issues concerning divorce, although they are often considered together. There is no evidence that Jesus condoned let alone commended further marriage: his disciples responded to his firm line with the words "then it is better not to marry" (Matt 19:10). This creates a very high degree of pastoral pressure in social circumstances where the proportion of divorced people of marriageable age is large and growing. Deontological approaches to this challenging situation tend to be of three kinds.

- One is to argue that the first marriage was not a real marriage, because it lacked one or more of the vital constituents of marriage, and thus seek an annulment. This is the approach most often found in the Roman Catholic Church, which prohibits divorce (and bans the divorced from taking the Eucharist) but allows for annulment in certain cases; this is not intended to be an argument for *further* marriage. Pope Francis's 2016 apostolic exhortation *Amoris Laetitia* (The Joy of Love), while it calls for a more welcoming attitude to divorced and remarried Catholics, stops short of instructing that they be welcomed at the Eucharist. Orthodox churches take a similar approach; while marriage is viewed as a permanent union, Orthodox rites allow for the dissolving of the first marriage in some limited cases.

- The second deontological approach is to investigate and prove which party was the innocent in the divorce and to absolve that party of the strictures that might apply to the "guilty party." This is not a process that can claim scriptural warrant but is practiced by some Protestant churches.
- The third and most common deontological approach is to contrast Jesus' merciful approach to the least, the last, and the lost, and simply to see those seeking further marriage (in general, and sometimes with exceptions) as in need of compassion rather than condemnation.

The argument concerning further marriage is largely held on deontological territory, because the scriptural deontological prohibitions are so strong. However, the third of these approaches, the compassionate one, often blends into consequential (or ecclesial) thinking. In practice much or most anxiety tends to concern the marital separation and divorce itself, and further marriage, should it arise, is often treated in largely consequentialist terms – especially regarding the welfare of any children involved. The widespread practice of conducting further marriages across North American Protestant denominations bears this out. In practice, such denominations tend to focus on the adults as individual decision-makers and regard the children involved as secondary factors subsequent to the decision to remarry or not.

Polygamy is usually a euphemism for polygyny – the practice of one man having several wives. There is ample evidence of polygyny in the Old Testament, with Gideon, David, and Solomon notable practitioners – despite the principle of the husband and wife becoming "one flesh" in Genesis 1:24. By contrast, Jesus' use of the term "one flesh" (Matt 19:5) seems to exclude the practice, and leave no deontological space to accommodate it. Thus, consequential criticisms, such that it can lead to jealousy, while often made, seem superfluous. When polygyny has been encountered in missionary contexts, its tolerance has more recently been advocated on humanitarian (consequentialist) grounds.

Prostitution. The general approach to prostitution (sexual activity offered in return for immediate monetary or similar compensation) has been similar: deontological opposition accompanied by consequential acceptance resulting in legal tolerance. Thomas Aquinas, citing Augustine, memorably described the role of prostitutes in towns as like the role of sewers in a palace: "take away the sewers and the palace becomes an impure and stinking place." The magisterial Reformers upheld the criminalization of prostitution, largely on consequential grounds, including the spread of venereal diseases. Likewise the practice is illegal in almost the entire United States. Contemporary ethics differs from this consensus only in expanding the range of deontological arguments against prostitution and of consequential arguments in favor of nonetheless not outlawing it, and in broadening those under ethical scrutiny to include not just the prostitute but the client and especially the broker – the pimp or brothel-keeper. Thus, those investigating the circumstances that give rise to prostitution have sometimes maintained that legalizing the practice is in fact likely to reduce the exploitation of women.

Subversive

The ways in which feminist ethics began with the rejection of conventional gender roles within marriage and the family have already been surveyed in Chapter Six. Subversive ethicists are not all agreed on whether sexuality is external – and that humans are fundamentally androgynous – or essential. Those who take the essential line are inclined to see the essential elements as limited to roles in conception and birth and not to wider roles in childrearing and work beyond the home. Some, however, would defend a thoroughgoing essentialist distinction that sees men and women as profoundly different and truly complementary, only resisting the depiction of that complementarity in hierarchical terms.

Subversive ethicists have significantly influenced many if not all of the issues described above under universal ethics. However, their particular contribution has perhaps been most explicitly seen in considering what may go wrong in the area of family, marriage, and children. In this respect it may be helpful to make a distinction between domestic abuse and child abuse, and then to recognize a racial dimension.

1. *Domestic violence.* This concerns the abuse or manipulation of power in relationships where the parties share a household – usually between men and women. It can include battering or rape on the part of the man or violent self-defense on the part of the woman. While many responses to domestic violence are made in deontological terms (violence is always wrong and can never be justified), and reference is frequently made to rights, particularly the rights of women, there is also much awareness of the significance of context. Questions of domestic violence have been close to the heart of attempts to redraw or abandon the contours of marriage, since violence seems to arise from male jealousy, a male assumption that a woman's body is his possession, and a male desire to assert dominance, sometimes in the face of supposedly emasculating circumstances such as unemployment or a woman's greater economic independence. Texts such as 1 Peter 3:1–9 that urge wives to be submissive have often been cited as problematic. The emergence of women's (and family) shelters has redirected attention to therapies for surviving such abusive relationships and avoiding repetition in the next generation. Others have noted that the recipients of domestic violence are not exclusively women, and that care as well as preventive measures must attend to male victims as well.

2. *Child abuse.* This involves physical, emotional, or sexual abuse of children, or their neglect, by a parent or by another who fails to honor the trust placed in them. It is only within the last 100–150 years that the commonly accepted notion of childhood has emerged, as a state of innocence and discovery, requiring attentive practices of nurture grounded in trust. In this light, child abuse comes to seem more than ever a breach of an ideal. The intensity of public response to egregious cases, such as child prostitution and sex trafficking, highlights how widely the ideal is now held. These are matters that appear deontologically clear, and need no consequential examination. Jesus' words "It would be better for you

if a millstone were hung around your neck and you were thrown into the sea than for you to cause one of these little ones to stumble" (Luke 17:2) have often been read in this light.

Closer enquiry, however, reveals some degree of cultural variation. In the West, not sending one's child to school might be regarded as neglect; in nations where child education is not universally available, this might not be so. In nations such as Thailand where child prostitution is sometimes regarded as the only form of income for a household in desperate straits, even this most nefarious form of abuse might come to be relativized in consequential terms. Consequential arguments have tended to emerge more explicitly when it has come to deciding how to alleviate or reduce the risk of abuse in households known to be vulnerable; for example, it is not clear that simply removing a child from his or her home is always the best strategy for the child, and the alternatives available, while they may preserve life, may in some cases have little else to commend them.

Perhaps most controversial of all has been the question of the resettlement and rehabilitation of known and proven pedophiles. Here the Christian logic of forgiveness and reconciliation runs up against Christian notions of justice and the protection of the vulnerable, as well as psychological studies of the intractability of damaging behavior. The unveiling of widespread (arguably endemic) abuse in church circles across denominations has highlighted these issues and the deeply troubling legal, emotional, and theological difficulties they raise.

3. *Hagar.* The construction of race in America has sometimes been portrayed, notably by Presbyterian womanist theologian Delores Williams (b. 1937), as one in which black men are perpetually considered a threat to white women's bodies, while the access of white men to black women's bodies has been considered of less account. This portrayal identifies the metaphorical sense in which America itself has sometimes been seen as a white woman's body at risk of a black (or minority immigrant) population's invasion, while the original conquest of the "colored" Amerindian body by the white male invader continues to go largely unnoticed. Hagar, Abraham's concubine (Gen 16:1–16 and 21:9–21), emerges as a model for oppressed women in a domestic setting. She suffered along the lines of class (as a slave), race (as an Egyptian), and gender (as a raped woman) – but she met God in the wilderness and her son Ishmael could not be entirely excluded from God's story.

Ecclesial

Ecclesial approaches to the family, marriage, and sex emerge in response to the tendency of universal approaches to concentrate on boundary issues and to be somewhat blind to the cultural and social locations of their definitions. Ecclesial writers are principally concerned to advocate for the church (rather than the family, marriage, or the state) as the primary focus of Christian identity and loyalty. They also strive to renarrate fundamental Christian convictions about marriage and family in the light of relatively recent transformations in social structure and gender roles. Two questions may illustrate the kinds of issues raised in ecclesial ethics and the ways they differ from the quandaries that have generally been the focus of universal ethics.

1. Is the family a church, and is the church a family? For all the analogies between family and church, ecclesial ethicists largely insist that the two are separate entities that should not be confused. There are exceptions – Pope John Paul II (1920–2005) is among those who have described the family as a domestic church, and this view is a frequent component of Catholic ethics. Likewise Orthodox ethics has a strong tendency to elevate marriage and the family as the primary sites for the upbuilding of the church, even suggesting that the family models the self-giving love of the Trinity. Elsewhere the family has tended to be described in the language of creation, vocation, and providence. All owe their existence to some form of family, many are called to be parents themselves, and involving human agency in sustaining human life is generally seen as God's providential way of interweaving divine purpose and human freedom. By contrast the church is primarily an eschatological entity, rooted not in generation and birth but in regeneration and baptism, inherently (rather than secondarily) open to the stranger and sustained not by biological logic but by the Spirit alone. While the Eucharistic table and the family dining table are both locations for significant meals, those meals, even though they profoundly inform one another, are not the same.

    Jesus' words "Whoever comes to me and does not hate father and mother, wife and children, brothers and sisters, yes, and even life itself, cannot be my disciple" (Luke 14:26) are sobering reading for those who seek congruity between family and ecclesial commitments. And yet so much of the language of faith – of father and child, brotherly love and sisterly care – arises from familial contexts. Likewise Jesus' response to the Sadducees' question about marriage in heaven, "When they rise from the dead, they neither marry nor are given in marriage, but are like angels in heaven" (Mark 12:25), is not encouraging news for those who see sex and marriage as a dimension of salvation. Ecclesial ethicists are usually seeking to counter not only universal approaches that make the church invisible, but individualistic accounts of Christian faith that accommodate the family as an extension of the individual, but sometimes see little or no role for the church – even on occasion replacing it with the state. Emphasizing the priority of church can point out the possible idolatries of state or family.

2. If marriage is an analogy for the relationship of Christ and the church, is it a unique and/or indispensable analogy? While universal ethics has tended to

emphasize the explosive nature of sexual attraction, and thus the need to set boundaries around its expression, and subversive ethics has tended to dwell on the destructive potential of sexual relationships, and thus the need to protect the rights of the vulnerable parties involved, ecclesial ethics has tended to downplay the role of sexual excitement and place the "sprint" of ecstasy within the "marathon" of mundane fidelity. There remains, therefore, an ambivalence in ecclesial ethics concerning whether the relationship between husband and wife is a (or the) fundamental human relationship.

Another area of uncertainty is whether the profound change in the status and role of women in recent generations renders the language of submission unacceptable – even the language of mutual submission as found in Ephesians 5:21. For some, the language of partnership and friendship needs to replace that of submission; for others, Christians should beware of giving in to the expectations of autonomy, and the language of mutual submission is an important way of safeguarding this.

While eager not to claim more for the household than can be sustained without diminishing the notion of church, ecclesial ethicists tend to see the household as a place of hospitality and an aspect of mission, rather than simply a haven from the storm of life. In this way they tend to overcome the severe distinction between marriage and singleness by seeing both as complementary settings for the development of discipleship, ministry, and friendship.

Ecclesial ethics tends not to stress deontological arguments. This is significant in areas of sex and sexuality, where deontological arguments tend to dominate the field. Because ecclesial ethicists tend to put a greater emphasis on community and communal discernment, they sometimes come to more flexible judgments on questions such as divorce and further marriage than some universal ethicists, particularly deontologists, do. For example, a deontological approach to marriage may well become fixed on the notion of a couple becoming "one flesh," and thus see marriage as indissoluble. An ecclesial approach may be more likely than a deontological approach to explore questions of forgiveness and bearing one another's burdens, and may be more open to asking why divorce seems to be regarded in some quarters as the one unforgivable sin. Meanwhile an ecclesial perspective may be more ready than a consequential view to go beyond considering the likely outcomes for the couple involved, and insist that the process is open to the support and scrutiny of members of the church. The key difference is that marriage "belongs" not so much to the couple as to the church and the community. Thus, divorce may not be out of the question in some circumstances. It may well be possible to see how further marriage might build up the church and foster virtues of courage, patience, and hope through an overriding commitment to mercy. But the involvement of members of the church may make such an approach sufficiently rigorous to offset fears that a gentler line on divorce might lead to fewer couples persisting in marriage through difficult times.

Same-Sex Relationships

Issues surrounding same-sex relationships are divisive in many churches for one central reason: they appear to be, more than perhaps any other issue, questions where the apparently broad, inclusive generosity and humanity of Jesus' ministry seem to conflict with the explicit witness of the scriptural text. Thus, the question of same-sex relationships is invariably also the question of the use of the Bible in Christian ethics. Meanwhile it is not clear whether the practices explicitly prohibited and condemned in the New Testament are identical to the practice and expression of same-sex relationships today, particularly in the West. Thus, the question of same-sex relationships is invariably also a matter of history and social location. Finally, given the passionate nature of the disagreements within denominations on this question, the issue is also one of how churches and congregations sustain life in the face of disagreement, and thus is one of ecclesiology. These three questions tend to be the respective (though by no means exclusive) concerns of universal, subversive, and ecclesial ethics, as we shall shortly see. An introductory treatment needs at least to address the biblical and historical questions in brief.

1. *Biblical texts.* There are a limited number of scriptural texts that are regarded as speaking directly to this issue.
    * Leviticus 18:22 states: "You shall not lie with a male as with a woman; it is an abomination," an admonition repeated at Leviticus 20:13. These texts come from a purity code that includes a number of other strictures not considered to have abiding significance today (such as intercourse during a woman's menstruation) and that seems to arise at least in part from concerns about maintaining population growth and asserting national identity.
    * The story of Sodom and Gomorrah (Gen 19), in which there is a vivid threat of homosexual rape, has historically been very visible in this discussion. However, when the story is addressed elsewhere in scripture (Ezek 16:49; Amos 4:1, 11; Isa 1:10–17), it is regarded as more concerned with pride and breaches of hospitality than with same-sex behavior more specifically.
    * 1 Corinthians and 1 Timothy include *malachoi* (1 Cor 6:9) and *arsenokoitai* (1 Tim 1:10) under a general list of lawlessness and profanity. The translation of these terms is disputed. Some have assumed they refer to anal intercourse. Others have taken them to refer to pedophilia or homosexual rape. It is sometimes pointed out that in the Roman context homosexual relations were not regarded as consensual because of differences in age and wealth. Thus, the assumption that these general terms refer to same-sex behavior alone (or even at all), or are in any significant way transferable to a contemporary context, is sometimes questioned today.

- Perhaps the key text is Romans 1:18–32, which locates same-sex behavior as a form of idolatry. Paul argues that, even without the Law of Moses, the Gentiles still stand under judgment. He tells how God "gave them up to degrading passions. Their women exchanged natural intercourse for unnatural, and in the same way also the men, giving up natural intercourse with women, were consumed with passion for one another. Men committed shameless acts with men and received in their own persons the due penalty for their error" (Rom 1:26–7). This has proved an influential text because it invites the prospect of homosexual behavior invoking direct earthly punishment: a theme that was controversial in the early years of the AIDS crisis in the 1980s.

There is no reference to homosexuality in the gospels; it is not clear how significant this omission might be. Some argue it is significant indeed and point out that Jesus never explicitly condemns same-sex relations; others note that his strict teachings on marriage and divorce assume the restriction of sexual activity to a man and a woman within the marriage covenant.

2.   *Historical context.* A number of social changes have altered the context in which the issue of same-sex relationships arises. David Greenberg, in his book *The Construction of Homosexuality* (1988), makes a sustained case that homosexuality is not a uniform phenomenon across history and that beliefs widely held about homosexuality are largely traceable to identifiable features in the societies in which they are found.

For example, children were once seen not only as a biological inevitability but as a life assurance policy: they alone provided income and care for the elderly, and they alone provided material security against attack, famine, or infirmity. Marriage and family life were therefore not optional, and attraction and fulfillment within the marital relationship were not the primary issues. Allowing for the flaws of generalization, Greenberg identifies four very broad historical periods in the light of this overarching assumption about domestic necessity.

a.   The first we may call the time of *distraction*: that is to say, the tendency in the Roman Empire and in the early medieval period was of nominal condemnation of certain forms of homosexual behavior coinciding with general tolerance. The distinction between orientation and behavior was unknown – same-sex behavior was regarded as a distraction from heterosexual necessity, in some ways like masturbation.

b.   The second may be termed the time of *perversion*: from the fourteenth century (according to the influential historical anthropologist John Boswell) there was a turn against minorities of many kinds, and the Reformation only enhanced the climate of hostility and state persecution.

c.   The third era, perhaps beginning in the nineteenth century, may be identified as the time of *illness*. It is no coincidence that this was a time in the West when economic necessity was no longer the fundamental basis for marriage.

In the late nineteenth century the term homosexuality, newly coined, began to denote a condition seen more as a failure of health than of morality or will. Various behavioral, genetic, and circumstantial explanations and diagnoses began to be put forward (notably the "overbearing mother" theory), often with relatively little empirical evidence. The treatment of homosexuality (often then known as "inversion") as a pathology, while often resisted today, was at the time widely experienced as a relief for those who had previously seen their orientation and behavior regarded as degenerate.

d.   From 1967 same-sex relations were no longer outlawed in the UK; they have only been legal nationwide in the USA since 2003. In 1973 homosexuality ceased to be regarded as a pathology by the American Psychiatric Association. Same-sex relations had entered the era of limited but growing social acceptance as a *variation* on heterosexuality. Likewise attitudes toward same-sex marriage in the West changed with remarkable rapidity in the first two decades of the twenty-first century, a social reality increasingly mirrored in civil law. However, Christian stances toward same-sex relations in the non-Western world have largely remained opposed to the blessing of same-sex marriages or behavior.

One change that might at first sight have little relevance to same-sex relations is the acceptance at the 1930 Lambeth Conference of Anglican Bishops of the practice of contraception. This is the most tangible element in an emerging consensus in some parts of the Christian world that procreation is not the only, or perhaps even the most significant, purpose and dimension of sexual interaction. (This emerging consensus is shared neither by the Orthodox churches nor by the Roman Catholic Church – it is a view that was firmly rejected by Pope Paul VI in his 1968 encyclical *Humanae Vitae*, On the Regulation of Birth.) Once this recognition had been made, and the companionable as well as the passionate aspects of marriage thus became more prominent, the logic of dismissing same-sex relationships came to focus less on the way they excluded childbearing than on whether and on what grounds the manner of intercourse involved was inherently inappropriate.

Universal

As with other issues of sexuality, the heat of the battle is on deontological territory. Consequential arguments seldom seem to have the intellectual or moral authority to play a decisive role. One curious feature of the debate is that the arguments against homosexuality have varied considerably across time and context; meanwhile the arguments defending or advocating homosexual activity have also adopted significantly different grounds. It is not a static debate. In what follows we shall consider the ten arguments most frequently heard in these conversations, stretched across four broad categories. They may appear to be a spectrum but in fact, as we shall see, they may more nearly resemble a circle, since the more extreme views have surprising (and ironic) elements in common with one another.

1. *Same-sex orientation does not exist.* This is perhaps the most fascinating category, because it includes people of what might be conventionally regarded as diametrically opposite views. Three kinds of arguments fit this category, which is squarely on deontological territory.

   a. All humans are heterosexual, and gays and lesbians are either deluded or willfully perverted. While this is not a view that tends to pay close attention to empirical research, it is arguably a more logical view than some that take a more conciliatory line. It rests on a natural law perspective and an essentialist view of sexuality that sees sexual behavior as an embodiment of clearly defined rules and roles linked directly to procreation and the joining together of opposite but complementary genders.

   b. There is no such thing as fixed orientation. What this has in common with the previous view is a move away from the consensus surrounding the notion of orientation. However, it comes to an opposite conclusion: assuming an external view of sexuality, it maintains there is no essential sexual identity (as heterosexual, bisexual, or homosexual), and tends to enjoy terms such as "experimentation" and "discovery." It attracts opposition on consequential grounds from both sides: from those who take an essential view of sexuality it seems to trivialize sex and ignore the procreative dimension altogether, thus jeopardizing marriage as an institution and the welfare of children; while those advocating acceptance of same-sex behavior are nervous about public suggestions that sexual orientation is not a fixed state. Because it does not assume stability, this view is extremely alarming to many Christian eyes. It is not offended by the suggestion that same-sex attraction and relationship are inherently unstable. But the price of this sanguine approach is equal equanimity on the subject of the inherent stability of heterosexual love and relationships. And this is the point at which anxieties about marriage are raised.

   c. Gay and lesbian sex is not sex. A third approach arose in our earlier discussion of masturbation. If the procreative dimension of sex is regarded as fundamental, then sex that has no possibility of being procreative must be one of three kinds: it is analogous to procreative sex (as in the sexual relations of a married couple in their sixties); it is wrong; or it is, in fact, not sex at all. Few have argued this last perspective, but it has some logic on its side, particularly from a Roman Catholic perspective that ties sex so closely to procreation. Hence gay and lesbian sexual behavior would be judged not on sexual grounds but according to other criteria, such as the Kantian commitment always to treat others as ends rather than as means.

   These three approaches all appear extreme in different ways, but their deontological nature highlights how profound are the deontological assumptions made by most parties in contemporary debates.

2. *Same-sex orientation exists but same-sex behavior is wrong.* This is the view that has achieved consensus in "conservative" Christian circles (outside fundamentalist churches, which sometimes favor 1a above). It is also the official teaching of the Roman Catholic and Orthodox traditions. For example, the Roman Catholic apostolic exhortation *Amoris Laetitia* (The Joy of Love, 2015) affirms the traditional Catholic teaching on the indissolubility of marriage between one man and one woman while also urging more pastoral care and empathy for gay couples. This view has two principal (but not entirely overlapping) deontological aspects, both of which assume an essential view of sexuality.

  a. The Bible regards same-sex behavior as idolatrous and disruptive of the created good of marriage. This view has several dimensions. It stresses the positive dimension of marriage as the formation of one flesh between male and female. This is a feature of the good creation, to which Paul also appeals in Romans 1. The Ten Commandments appear to rule out sex outside marriage (although whether same-sex activity constitutes adultery is not explicitly stated). The reference in 1 Corinthians 6:9 incorporates an eschatological perspective, concerning who will inherit the kingdom of God. Thus, the argument is consistent through creation, covenant, and consummation.

  b. Natural law insists sexual intercourse must serve its created purpose. Thomas Aquinas and almost all Roman Catholic moral theology after him assume human beings are physically and essentially ordered toward heterosexual reproduction. Thus same-sex behavior goes against natural law. Karl Barth (1886–1968) and many others from a Protestant perspective emphasize the complementarity of male and female in creation and in the conjoining of one flesh. Those who have sought extra empirical justification for their deontological scriptural argument against same-sex behavior have sometimes strayed into natural law territory, citing surveys or scientific research, but these forays have invariably weakened their arguments by tying them to evidence that has often come to be contradicted in subsequent studies.

These two arguments constitute the conservative case against gay and lesbian sexual expression. It is a formidable deontological case. However, the concession that homosexuality exists is a significant one. What is the cause of same-sex orientation? Some argue that if God *made* people to be gay and lesbian, then these two arguments falter – or a distorted picture of God emerges. Hence the attractiveness of seeing homosexuality as a pathology – not as serious as pedophilia, but a pathology nonetheless – which, in the view of a few vocal proponents of this view, can be healed. Others see heterosexual desire as part of the original created order and same-sex inclinations as a result of the Fall – that is, as one form of warped or malformed desire among many others. Thus, while acknowledging that same-sex orientation exists, it treats it as an element of the fallen rather than the good creation.

Advocates of same-sex relationships have been divided on whether to mount a case on deontological or consequential grounds. Some dismiss the second argument above by rejecting natural law arguments entirely. This still leaves Scripture. Some strive to relocate and renarrate each of the celebrated texts in social contexts, arguing that what Paul opposed was more akin to prostitution and thus not the same-sex relationships that today present themselves, about which he expressed no opinion. This is a way of upholding the authority of Scripture while coming to a more open view on permanent same-sex relationships. Others regard the distinction between orientation and behavior as unsustainable in theory and unliveable in practice, except for those called to celibacy. This often leads to highlighting the prevalence of homophobia, and the deontological argument that gay and lesbian people have the right to be left in peace. The common acceptance of the distinction between what some might regard as immoral and what all must treat as illegal (between sin and crime) is a relatively new development in this area, and is displayed clearly in the debates over gay marriage. There are also consequential questions to be faced: one of these is whether it is better to encourage stable gay and lesbian relationships than invite the personal and social consequences of same-sex promiscuity.

3.   *Same-sex orientation exists but same-sex behavior is a lesser good.* This is a view that few would defend publicly but may well be widely held (often under the label of "tolerance"). It comes in two theologically distinct but pastorally interrelated forms, both of which are largely consequential in nature.

   a.   Kingdom urgency. This view expresses ambivalence concerning same-sex relationships themselves, but certainty that, in relation to other issues facing the church and the world, the question is of relatively minor importance. It often objects to the prominence of sex in the popular public and conservative Christian imagination. Jesus, it seems, was more concerned with use of wealth, loving God with all one's heart, soul, mind, and strength, loving one's neighbor as oneself, and simply following him. This view, however, lacks a constructive proposal. It is hard to celebrate a lesser good.

   b.   Pastoral patience. This is a very widespread view that recognizes that in the "time between the times," many human relationships, to use a celebrated term from the Church of England House of Bishops, "fall short of the ideal." It recognizes the changing social climate and the assumption that sexual relationships are much more closely connected to personal fulfillment and expression than once was normal. It often rails against the apparent inconsistency of interpretation that upholds the scriptural injunctions on this issue but ignores them on so many others where often they are more incontrovertible (e.g., usury). It points out that a disproportionate amount of suffering is caused by a conservative line on this issue, and little of this suffering seems to be felt directly by those most ardently promoting it. It recognizes the way divorce and further marriage have become increasingly accepted, despite (in the view of some) having no more explicit justification in Scripture than homosexual expression. It points out that many other aspects of life, such as the eating of meat, might not fit comfortably into an ideal Christian lifestyle but seem to fit reasonably comfortably into a pragmatic ethic. And it casts an ironic eye at the wonders God can do in unexpected places. All these are, at root, consequential arguments. Because the debate is largely held on deontological territory they are sometimes dismissed as irrelevant. In addition it deplores the lack of basic tolerance shown to those who are different – a deontological argument that is harder to ignore.

4. *Same-sex orientation and behavior are good – as good as heterosexual orientation and behavior.* While perhaps less widely held in mainstream churches of all denominations than the previous view, it has become much more common in "mainline" or liberal Protestant churches in the West, and has gained prominent (if comparatively few) advocates in the evangelical Christian community. This view is a more substantial challenge to the conventional conservative approach (2 above) because it sets its stall out in deontological terms, where questions of sexuality historically have been almost exclusively debated and where the conservative argument is strongest. As the structure of this chapter makes clear, Christianity has understood two forms of stable sexual expression: either singleness, accompanied by chaste, non-exclusive friendships, or marriage, being the union of man and woman, generally with the expectation of procreation. Thus, advocates of same-sex relationships must adapt either of the existing models or propose a third. Constructive proposals come in three forms, which overlap very little.

a. Same-sex relations are a good to be expressed in a marriage resembling or mirroring a heterosexual marriage. This tends to assume God created people to be gay or lesbian. Once one has moved away from seeing same-sex attraction as a pathology and begun to see it as a variation, there needs to be a good lifestyle to be aspired to. There is little precedent to be found in discussions of Scripture or natural law. Nonetheless the logic is that of creation: if God created it, it must have a purpose congruent with the rest of what God has created; and that must be to join the chorus returning the gifts of creation to God in praise, restoring the broken, and seeking out the lost. Marriage is the time-honored way in which this is done in a domestic setting, and while direct procreation is not possible, adoption is another time-honored way in which the lost and the broken are restored to God's company. Adoption seems, to many, particularly suited to the challenging context of gay and lesbian marriage. Additionally, reproductive technologies are making it increasingly possible for same-sex couples to conceive and raise children to whom they have a biological connection, at least in part (the ethical challenge of many of these technologies are discussed in the next chapter). This capacity raises especially pressing questions regarding whether same-sex marriages can therefore fulfill the same three goods as heterosexual marriage – including that of procreation.

b. Same-sex relations are a good to be expressed sexually in an exclusive friendship. While similar in many respects to the argument for same-sex marriage, this view tends to see the procreational dimension as intrinsic to marriage. As noted above, it is clinically possible for lesbians and gays to conceive children in different assisted ways, but this view tends to see marriage as a heterosexual phenomenon, and to seek to develop an understanding of friendship that can expand to include intimate, permanent, and exclusive gay and lesbian partnerships. One possible strength of this view is that it makes clear same-sex relationships are not a threat to heterosexual marriage. One weakness is that the New Testament seems to assume that the whole church will be involved in the business of raising and nurturing children, potentially loosening the link between marriage and procreation and thus lessening the need to reconfigure same-sex relationships under the umbrella of friendship rather than marriage. And the possibility of same-sex couples conceiving or adopting children raises related questions about whether friendship or marriage is the most suitable context for raising children.

   Another weakness is that marriage continues to have an enduring social significance and status that friendship lacks, leading many gay and lesbian couples to wonder why they should be barred from the considerable social, emotional, and legal advantages of marriage. An alternative form of this view argues for the separation of civil unions from Christian marriage and suggests that same-sex couples ought to have full access to the first but not to the second.

c. Same-sex relationships are a good to be expressed in a new form of relationship. Some would recognize the flaws in adapting marriage or friendship to a new context, and seek a model that might include impermanent relationships, partners of more than one gender at different stages of life, and even "open" relationships where conventional fidelity is not expected. People who identify as bisexual or queer might especially fall into this rubric. This radical view raises all the worst fears of those who uphold the deontological claims of the conservative line (2 above) for largely consequential reasons – that is, to preserve marriage and social stability. But it is still rooted in the deontological, if perhaps sometimes unnuanced, view that people should be true to the way they have been created. It has significant features in common with some views described among the first group of approaches above. It therefore demonstrates our earlier claim that these ten views constitute a circle rather than a spectrum.

Subversive

In many ways the "universal" treatment of same-sex relationships has been a debate led by heterosexuals for the benefit of heterosexuals. Subversive treatments of the issue make visible aspects or identities that the conventional universal debate is inclined to suppress or ignore. Four dimensions, in particular, are significant.

1. *Oppression.* Opposition to same-sex expression often leads to homophobia, and homophobia can involve various forms of discrimination and sometimes violence. Thus, sexual identity often takes its place alongside gender, race, and class as a type of social exclusion and oppression. Subversive ethicists highlight and protest against cases of oppression; but they also speculate about the sources of homophobia. One noted source is that much fear of gay people arises from a fear of being oneself gay. Sometimes more far-reaching speculation involves the assumption that sexual penetration symbolizes being "on top" in every social and domestic dimension of power relations, and homophobia arises from panic at the idea of men being penetrated, and thus potentially socially and domestically subservient.

2. *Diversity.* Subversive ethics points out that heterosexuality and homosexuality do not represent the only options in the conversation. For some, bisexuality is not simply a variation on homosexuality but an identity in itself. Meanwhile some children are born with organs relating to both genders, making them intersex. It is not clear how such identity is best to be negotiated – by medical resolution or by personal and social accommodation. In some cases a person believes his or her true identity lies in the other gender, and this may result in surgery that renders him or her transgendered. Here the impulse to encourage self-expression and self-fulfillment can conflict with the need to undergird other responsibilities – such as sustaining the role of being a father.

3. *Equality.* Some would go so far as to say gay and lesbian relationships are not just equivalent to heterosexual marriages, they are superior. This tends to be grounded on the greater role of equality perceived or portrayed in these relationships. Lesbian feminism can be particularly inclined to this view (see Chapter Six for more on lesbian feminist ethics). A similar but perhaps more far-reaching point is that universal ethics is too obsessed with what people do with their genital interactions, and that such represents a diminished notion of sexuality. If homosexuality is principally an identity rather than a behavior, gay and lesbian love is about a quality that extends well beyond the bedroom into every aspect of human companionship and cherishing. The question then becomes one of how to foster and express sustainable love, not simply what genital relations are legitimate.

4. *Rereading Scripture.* Subversive readings of Scripture question conventional interpretations of familiar texts and highlight the significance of less familiar ones. Sodom is a story about hospitality; Leviticus is concerned with not replicating the temple prostitution cults of the Canaanite tribes; Romans argues it is wrong to change one's nature, thus if one's nature is LGBQT (lesbian, gay, bisexual, queer, transgender) it is equally wrong to give up that nature; 1 Corinthians and 1 Timothy refer to pederasty, a very common phenomenon in Hellenistic culture, or male prostitution.

Among the new texts brought into the debate, the most commonly cited is the intimate relationship between David and Jonathan (described at various moments from 1 Sam 18 to 2 Sam 1). The account of their beauty, their kissing, Saul's jealousy, and their deep love reads differently when extricated from heterosexual assumptions, and has invited speculation about whether homosexual practice existed in Israel in the way it did in Greece. (It has also raised questions of whether this interpretation imports modern Western cultural norms into an ancient Near Eastern context.) The story of Ehud and Eglon (Judges 3) again appears differently when references to secrecy, reaching under the garment with the left hand, bringing out a long knife, and stabbing in the king's fat area are read through new eyes. In the New Testament attention is drawn to Jesus' curious saying "there are eunuchs who have been so from birth, and there are eunuchs who have been made eunuchs by others, and there are eunuchs who have made themselves eunuchs for the sake of the kingdom of heaven" (Matt 19:12) – words that are sometimes figuratively read as affirming gay or lesbian identity. Finally the debate over whether Gentiles could join the early church without being circumcised and becoming Jews inspires some to suggest that gays and lesbians may join the church without first becoming straight.

Ecclesial

Like subversive ethics, ecclesial ethics is reluctant to discuss same-sex relationships as an "issue" abstracted from gay and lesbian people and the context of the society in which they live. It also resists the narrowing of the issue to what individuals do or do not do with their genitals, but seeks to broaden the question to one of the purpose of sex and the nature of discipleship. Among many themes, three may be taken as representative.

1. *Vocation.* Many ecclesial ethicists would be suspicious of the now conventional distinction between same-sex orientation (which is affirmed) and same-sex behavior (which is rejected). The reason is that marriage and singleness are both typically understood as vocations, rather than injunctions. Thus, commanding a gay or lesbian person to celibacy is like commanding a person to have a vocation to the priesthood. It is a category mistake. Vocation only makes sense in the context of election. What is a gift should not be demanded as an *a priori* point of recognition as a disciple. Thus the tendency in ecclesial ethical circles is to look to LGBQT people themselves, in conversation with the church as a whole, to articulate and model what it might mean for them to live a holy life.

    In this sense some in ecclesial ethics regard the issue of same-relationships as a gift from God to the church in this generation to find out what sex means and what it means to be the church. Part of the reason the question of same-sex relationships is so difficult to resolve is that it seems hard to justify such a severe line on this one sexual issue when such laxity (or pastoral caution) abounds on so many others, yet a transformation on this issue would seem to catapult forward the less rigorous line on every other issue, and hence seems symbolic and terrifying to many. Nonetheless, these issues go to the heart of the church and the heart of society, and discussing them through the lives of LGBQT people ensures the issues are always about people and not about abstractions. Sometimes it is only in retrospect that what seemed for so long to be a problem can be discovered to have been a gift.

2. *Ministry.* The Episcopalian theologian Eugene Rogers, who teaches at the Greensboro campus of the University of North Carolina, is among those who distinguish between the purpose of marriage and the goods of marriage. Rogers is inspired by Anglican Rowan Williams' description of the purpose of sex. For Williams and others, sexuality is centrally about learning to be desired by God. Sexual encounter is a gift when it becomes a context in which we learn how much God desires us, where we have the privilege and great responsibility of showing the beloved how much God desires them. The traditional view has been that the explosive dynamism of sexual touch can only be properly embraced within the loving permanence of lifelong marriage between a woman and a man. But as Rogers points out, the *goods* of marriage include the practice of hospitality and the strengthening of ministry; these build up the church and, as is invariably the case, what builds up the church is the key question in ecclesial ethics. Thus, the real question becomes: What kinds of relationships amongst its members make the church best able to act justly, love mercy, and walk humbly with its God? Do the relationships in question build up the church in its mission to and presence with the hungry, the thirsty, the homeless, and the stranger? Rather than trying to get back to an idealized era of faithful marriages and domestic bliss, Rogers proposes the churches should set their eyes and hearts on a future society of generosity to the outsider and hospitality to the outcast, a society that some might suggest looks remarkably like Jesus' ministry.

By contrast, Joel James Shuman seeks to refocus debates about sexuality in ecclesial terms by considering the body in reference to liturgical practices. For Shuman this means rejecting the narratives of post-industrial consumer capitalism that regard the body merely as an instrument for satisfying desire: it means instead attending carefully to the Christian story with its attendant practices, especially the Eucharist. It is through gathering bodily at the table of the Eucharist that Christians learn to be friends of one another and of God, and that they learn "properly to value the gifts that are [their] bodies." In his insistence that friendship with one another and with God is prior to the gift of sexual love, Shuman returns us to the theme with which we began this chapter. While Shuman is less confident than Rogers that same-sex relationships can or should fulfill the same goods as marriage, he seeks like Rogers to center the debate firmly in the life of the church as it anticipates and bears witness to the kingdom of God.

3.   *Communion.* A vexed question is that of whether differing attitudes toward same-sex behavior should constitute a reason for splitting denominations or churches. It is increasingly common in ecclesial ethics to focus on the significance of worship, in particular the shared communion expressed in the Eucharist. Thus, a proposal for sustaining communion might go like this. The communion embodied in the Eucharist indicates that Christians:

a.   believe they have a *place at God's table*, along with the members of the Trinity;

b.   sit at God's table *with one another*;

c.   recognize the sacramental and moral *discipline and order* required for this special act of sharing bread and wine and in doing so are aware of the presence of Christ's body and blood;

d.   share in the *practices* of this special act of sharing in Christ's body – the other particulars of the liturgy.

This is a hierarchical and sequential series designed to sustain unity. Most problems that arise in a community engage one or more of these understandings of communion. Problems with one of the series do not invalidate the rest – on the contrary, the others help to overcome a problem in one of them. It is only when there is no shared understanding in any of the four areas that communion seems lost. The first understanding, the invitation to eat with God at God's table, is the purpose of creation and redemption. But if Christians cannot meet the terms of the second understanding they risk being excluded from enjoying the fellowship of God eternally. The purpose of the third and fourth understandings should help Christians carry out the second one, rather than make it more difficult.

While profound differences may jeopardize sharing in every aspect of the fourth understanding, ecclesial ethicists see the severing of communion as a drastic step, which should only be accepted if consensus on all four understandings has collapsed. The 2016 decision of Anglican bishops worldwide temporarily to suspend the Episcopalian Church in the United States from decision-making and representative roles within the Anglican Communion due to its support of same-sex marriage and the ordination of openly gay priests – but nonetheless to remain in communion with one another – is a poignant example of the complex issues around church unity and ethical disagreements. This example also highlights the divisive nature of many contemporary ethical issues along the lines of race and geography – given that many Christians in Africa and in the non-Western world more broadly have views on same-sex marriage that differ significantly from many of their Western counterparts.

Summary

This chapter has explored the ethics of love, when love is an intimate matter between two people. It did not begin by assuming such relationships are inherently sexual, and so it began with friendship. Several complex areas arose, including whether one could be a friend of God, how being a friend compared with being a sibling or being a neighbor, and whether there is a class or gender dimension to friendship.

Turning to marriage, the family, and sex, the line between the three kinds of ethics appeared clearer than usual. Universal ethics dwells on exceptions and boundary issues relating to appropriate circumstances for cases such as divorce or sex outside marriage. Subversive ethics tends to identify the victims and the suppressed voices within these debates. Ecclesial ethics has sometimes been more comfortable articulating constructive models of marriage and intimate relationship. The distinction between essential and external views of sexuality – between sex as something you are and sex as something you simply "do" – proved very significant.

Same-sex relationships and marriages are a current topic of considerable debate. Here we suggested that the spectrum of views in fact is best regarded as a circle, since the more extreme views of each side have surprising elements in common. This issue shows, as well as any, the importance of exploring Scripture, history, and philosophy (including, in this case, science) in order to understand the sources of universal, subversive, and ecclesial ethics.

References and Further Reading

Friendship

Plato's definition of love is from *Lysis*, available in print (*Plato's Dialogue on Friendship: An Interpretation of the Lysis* [David Bolotin, trans.; Ithaca, NY: Cornell University Press, 1979]) or online through the Internet Classics Archive (http://classics.mit.edu/Plato/lysis.html). For his discussion of *eros* and *philia* see *Phaedrus* (Christopher Rowe, trans.; London; New York: Penguin Books, 2005) or online at http://classics.mit.edu/Plato/phaedrus.html. For the description of the "ladder" and the form of Beauty see the *Symposium* (Robin Waterfield, trans.; Oxford; New York: Oxford University Press, 2008) or online at http://classics.mit.edu/Plato/symposium.html.

Aristotle describes the three kinds of friendship in Book VIII of *Nicomachean Ethics* (Roger Crisp, ed.; Cambridge: Cambridge University Press, 2000).

One may find Cicero's consideration of friendship in *De Amicitia* ("On Friendship") in *Other Selves: Philosophers on Friendship* (Michael Pakaluk, ed.; Indianapolis, IN: Hackett, 1991), pages 86–7. Further exploration of the views of Cicero and other philosophers on friendship can be found in *Philosophy and Friendship* by Sandra Lynch (Edinburgh: Edinburgh University Press, 2005).

The discussion of male–female friendships in the church is drawn from Rosemary Rader, *Breaking Boundaries: Male/Female Friendships in Early Christian Communities* (New York: Paulist Press, 1983).

Augustine contrasts self-love and love of God in *City of God* (Henry Bettenson, trans.; London; New York: Penguin Books, 1972, 2003), Book XIV, chapter 28. Augustine's thoughts on friendship are mainly in his *Confessions* (Gary Wills, trans.; New York: Penguin Books, 2006), especially Book IV. Augustine's distinction between *uti* (use) and *frui* (enjoyment) is made in *On Christian Doctrine*, Book One, chapters 3 and 4 (available in the Christian Classics Ethereal Library at www.ccel.org/a/augustine/doctrine/doctrine.html).

Aelred of Rievaulx explores friendship in his *Spiritual Friendship* (Mark F. Williams, trans.; Cranbury, NJ; London; Mississauga, Ontario, Canada: Associated University Presses, 1994). His note about equality in friendship is on pages 77–81; and he quotes "God is friendship" on page 41. Portions of *Spiritual Friendship* are included in the corresponding chapter in *Christian Ethics: An Introductory Reader*.

Love and friendship are explored by Thomas Aquinas throughout his works: see Liz Carmichael, *Friendship: Interpreting Christian Love* (London; New York: T & T Clark, 2004), pages 105–26.

Michel de Montaigne's essay *On Friendship* may be found in the volume *Complete Essays* (Stanford, CA: Stanford University Press, 1958); the particular quotation is from page 138.

Wesley Hill summarizes Benjamin Myers' research on the eclipse of friendship in modern Western societies in *Spiritual Friendship: Finding Love in the Church as a Celibate Gay Christian* (Grand Rapids, MI: Brazos Press, 2015).

Contemporary Christian ethicists who have written on the significance of friendship and singleness for ethics include Jana Marguerite Bennett, *Water is Thicker than Blood: An Augustinian Theology of Marriage and Singlehood* (Oxford: Oxford University Press, 2008) and Lauren Winner, *Real Sex: The Naked Truth about Chastity* (Grand Rapids, MI: Brazos Press, 2005).

Immanuel Kant's discussion of friendship may be found in *Metaphysics of Morals* (Mary Gregor, trans.; Cambridge; New York: Cambridge University Press, 1996), pages 215–17.

Søren Kierkegaard explores self-love and neighbor-love in his *Works of Love* (Howard and Edna Hong, trans.; New York: Harper, 1962); the specific quotation about the distinction between them is from page 170.

Anders Nygren's work *Agape and Eros* (Philip S. Watson, trans.; Philadelphia, PA: Westminster Press, 1953) famously draws a sharp distinction between these two terms for love.

C. S. Lewis' description of friendship in his *Four Loves* (London: Geoffrey Bles, 1960) is found in chapter 4, and is also quoted in the corresponding chapter in *Christian Ethics: An Introductory Reader*.

Jürgen Moltmann's language of Christ as a friend may be found in *The Church in the Power of the Spirit* (Margaret Kohl, trans.; New York: Harper and Row, 1977), pages 114–21.

Sallie McFague's exploration of friendship and the Trinity is from *Models of God* (Minneapolis, MN: Fortress Press, 1987), especially pages 78–90, 157–80.

For a radical feminist ethic of friendship, see Mary Daly, *Gyn/Ecology: The Metaethics of Radical Feminism* (Boston, MA: Beacon Press, 1978), chapter 9; and Mary E. Hunt, *Fierce Tenderness: A Feminist Theology of Friendship* (New York: Crossroad, 1991).

Paul Wadell's makes a case for the importance of friendship in an ethical life in *Friendship and the Moral Life* (Notre Dame, IN: University of Notre Dame Press, 1989) and *Becoming Friends: Worship, Justice, and the Practice of Christian Friendship* (Grand Rapids, MI: Brazos Press, 2002).

Alasdair MacIntyre's treatment of difference and *misericordia* is in *Dependent Rational Animals: Why Human Beings Need the Virtues* (Chicago and La Salle, IL: Open Court, 1999, 2001), pages 123–8.

In his book *Spiritual Friendship*, Wesley Hill is particularly interested in deeper, Christian models of friendship for celibate gay Christians.

Dietrich Bonhoeffer's influential account of life in Christian community is in *Life Together* (London: SCM Press, 1954).

In addition to the above, the following is included in the corresponding chapter of *Christian Ethics: An Introductory Reader*: Mary Daly, *Gyn/Ecology: The Metaethics of Radical Feminism* (Boston, MA: Beacon Press, 1978); from chapter 9, "Sparking: The Fire of Female Friendship."

For additional further reading see Gilbert Meilaender, *Friendship: A Study in Theological Ethics* (Notre Dame, IN: University of Notre Dame Press, 1981). Liz Carmichael's book *Friendship* (see above) has also been an important source for the "Friendship" section of this chapter.

The Family, Marriage, and Sex

John Chrysostom's views on the household can be found in *St. John Chrysostom on Marriage and Family Life* (Catherine P. Roth and David Anderson, trans.; Crestwood, NY: St. Vladimir's Seminary Press, 1986). See also Vigen Guroian, "Family and Christian Virtue in a Post-Christendom World: Reflections on the Ecclesial Vision of John Chrysostom," *St. Vladimir's Theological Quarterly* 35, no. 4 (1991): 327–50.

Gregory of Nyssa's views on marriage and fear of death are in his treatise "On Virginity," available online in the Christian Classics Ethereal Library at http://www.ccel.org/ccel/schaff/npnf205.toc.html.

Jerome's views on sex may be found in parts of his treatises *Letter XXII to Eustochium* and *Against Jovinian*; see *St. Jerome: Letters and Select Works* (W. H. Fremantle, trans.; Select Library of Nicene and Post-Nicene Fathers, Ser. 2, Vol. VI; Edinburgh, 1892); also available in the Christian Classics Ethereal Library at www.ccel.org/ccel/schaff/npnf206.v.XXII.html and www.ccel.org/ccel/schaff/npnf206.vi.vi.html, respectively.

Augustine's three goods of marriage are in section 3 of his treatise *On the Good of Marriage* (available online in the Christian Classics Ethereal Library at www.ccel.org/ccel/schaff/npnf103.v.ii.html).

Martin Luther's views on marriage are summarized in Brent Waters, *The Family in Christian Social and Political Thought* (Oxford; New York: Oxford University Press, 2007), pages 28–30.

For John Calvin's views on marriage, as drawn from a variety of his writings, consult Waters, *The Family in Christian Social and Political Thought*, pages 31–2; and John Witte, *From Sacrament to Contract: Marriage, Religion, and Law in the Western Tradition* (Louisville, KY: Westminster/

John Knox Press, 1997), pages 94–126. Richard Baxter builds on Calvin's views in his 1830 work *A Christian Directory* (part 2); see Waters, *The Family in Christian Social and Political Thought*, pages 32–8.

Thomas Aquinas compares the role of prostitutes to that of sewers in Bartholomew of Lucca and Thomas Aquinas, *De Regimine Principum (On the Government of Rulers)* (James M. Blythe, trans.; Philadelphia, PA: University of Pennsylvania Press, 1997), Book IV, chapter 14, page 254.

Delores Williams explores the construction of race and gender in America in *Sisters in the Wilderness: The Challenge of Womanist God-Talk* (Maryknoll, NY: Orbis Books, 1993).

Pope John Paul II refers to the family as a domestic church in his 1981 exhortation *Familiaris Consortio* (Of the Christian Family); see, e.g., sections 21 and 49–51. Available online at the Vatican's website at http://w2.vatican.va/content/john-paul-ii/en/apost_exhortations/documents/hf_jp-ii_exh_19811122_familiaris-consortio.html.

For an Orthodox ethic of marriage and family, see Vigen Guroian, *Incarnate Love: Essays in Orthodox Ethics*, 2nd edn (Notre Dame, IN: University of Notre Dame Press, 2002) and John and Lyn Breck, *Stages on Life's Way: Orthodox Thinking on Bioethics* (Crestwood, NY: St Vladimir's Seminary Press, 2005), chapter 2.

In *Christian Ethics: An Introductory Reader*:
- J. I. Packer. "Personal Standards." *Churchman* 111, no. 1 (1997): 19–26. [This article is a reprint of two chapters from Packer's Commentary on the Montreal Declaration of Anglican Essentials.] www.churchsociety.org/churchman/documents/CMan_111_1_Packer.pdf.

- Rosemary Radford Ruether. *Christianity and the Making of the Modern Family.* Boston, MA: Beacon Press, 2000. From chapter 9, "Reimagining Families: Home, Work, Gender, and Faith."
- Vigen Guroian. *Incarnate Love: Essays in Orthodox Ethics.* Notre Dame, IN: University of Notre Dame Press, 1987. From chapter 4, "An Ethic of Marriage and Family."

Further reading on issues surrounding marriage and family include:

- Lauren Winner. *Real Sex: The Naked Truth About Chastity.* Grand Rapids, MI: Brazos Press, 2005.
- Rodney Clapp. *Families at the Crossroads.* Downers Grove, IL: InterVarsity Press, 1993.
- Brent Waters. *The Family in Christian Social and Political Thought* (see above).

Homosexuality

David Greenberg traces views on homosexuality throughout history in his book *The Construction of Homosexuality* (Chicago, IL: University of Chicago Press, 1988).

Thomas Aquinas discusses natural law and heterosexuality in *Summa Theologica* (Notre Dame, IN: Christian Classics, 1948), Secunda Secundae [Second Part of the Second Part], Questions 153–4.

Karl Barth's views on the complementarity of male and female are in section 54, "Freedom in Fellowship," in *Church Dogmatics* III.4 (G. W. Bromiley and T. F. Torrance, eds; Edinburgh: T & T Clark, 1961); see especially pages 116–18 and 150–81.

Eugene Rogers' views on sexuality and marriage are explored in "Sanctification, Homosexuality, and God's Triune Life," pages 217–46 in *Theology and Sexuality: Classic and Contemporary Readings* (Eugene F. Rogers Jr., ed.; Oxford; Malden, MA: Blackwell, 2002); an excerpt of this essay is also included in the corresponding chapter of *Christian Ethics: An Introductory Reader.* Rogers draws significantly on Rowan Williams' essay "The Body's Grace," pages 309–21 in *Theology and Sexuality.* Rogers further explores the issue of homosexuality in his book *Sexuality and the Christian Body* (Oxford: Blackwell, 1999).

Another ecclesial approach to same-sex relationships in the church is Joel James Shuman, "Eating Together, Friendship, and Homosexuality," pages 453–65 in *The Blackwell Companion to Christian Ethics*, 2nd edn (Stanley Hauerwas and Samuel Wells, eds; Oxford: Wiley-Blackwell, 2011), quotation from page 457.

For a discussion of ethical disagreements and the unity of the church from a predominantly Catholic perspective, see Michael Root and James J. Buckley, eds, *The Morally Divided Body: Ethical Disagreement and the Disunity of the Church* (Eugene, OR: Cascade Books, 2012).

In addition to the essay by Rogers, the following are quoted in the corresponding chapter of *Christian Ethics: An Introductory Reader*:

- Stephen J. Pope. "Scientific and Natural Law Analyses of Homosexuality: A Methodological Study." *Journal of Religious Ethics* 25, no. 1 (Spring 1997): 89–126.
- John Boswell. *Christianity, Social Tolerance, and Homosexuality: Gay People in Western Europe from the Beginning of the Christian Era to the Fourteenth Century.* Chicago, IL: University of Chicago Press, 1980.

Chapter Eleven
Good Beginnings and Endings

However short the shortlist of conventional ethical issues, abortion and euthanasia are always on it. They are perhaps the two most celebrated ethical questions of modern times. The reason is twofold. In the first place they concern the two most mysterious moments in human life – its beginning and its ending. Anyone who has attended a birth or a death will recognize the air of wonder and the visceral sense of the unknown that surround these profound transitions. In the second place they are issues not just for Christians but for every member of society – and yet they are questions on which outspoken Christian views have been influential and sometimes highly controversial, evoking contrary views, sometimes involving high legal drama and even murderous violence.

While questions of the beginning and ending of life are sometimes considered in isolation from one another, some have attempted to identify a single principle, such as the sanctity of life, that can guide moral decision-making on all of these fraught issues – and on others such as capital punishment that are not usually considered under the rubric of medical ethics or bioethics. For example, Roman Catholic Cardinal Joseph Bernardin (1928–96) insists on a "consistent ethic of life" that protects the sanctity of life beginning with conception and ending with death.

These debates take place not just in the context of human contingency and the relationship of Christianity to democracy; they also find an extra dimension in the light of technological developments that alter both the human capacity to know more of what were previously mysteries and to alter and choose what could previously only be hoped for or feared. Thus, the issues involved are not just abortion and euthanasia but a wider range of matters where research and technology change the possible and the imaginable.

Introducing Christian Ethics, Second Edition. Samuel Wells and Ben Quash with Rebekah Eklund.
© 2017 John Wiley & Sons Ltd. Published 2017 by John Wiley & Sons Ltd.

Contraception, Assisted Conception, and Genetic Engineering

At first glance it might seem surprising to group these three issues together. Yet they all converge on a single theme: the desire to have children, to have them at the right time, and to have children who have the greatest possible expectation and opportunity of flourishing and fulfillment in adult life. The ethical questions are similar in each case: while these are understandable desires, are they legitimate ones, and are there limits to the methods employed to attain them?

1.   *Contraception*. There is little explicit reference to contraception in the Bible. The story of Onan describes how, after the death of his elder brother Er, he was asked by his father Judah to sire a son by Er's wife Tamar to be regarded as Er's heir. "But since Onan knew that the offspring would not be his, he spilled his semen on the ground whenever he went in to his brother's wife, so that he would not give offspring to his brother" (Gen 38:9). God put him to death for doing so. In general, childbirth is seen as an unqualified blessing.

Throughout history, those committed to natural law, such as Stoics, have tended to see procreation as the purpose of sexual intercourse. Augustine's view was colored by his rejection of his Manichean past; he saw the rejection of procreation as the characteristic conviction of the Manichees – one countered by the Christian endorsement of procreation. The tendency remained in church history to see marriage (with children) and singleness as the two vocations, with contraception offering a threateningly ambiguous third option, often associated with prostitution and other forms of fornication.

From the nineteenth century onwards arguments began to be made in Protestant circles that contraception was a blessing to family life, rather than a threat to it. In 1930 the Lambeth Conference of Anglican Bishops accepted that when the limiting of a family's size was an obligation or a necessity, contraception could be used as an alternative to abstinence. Later the same year Pope Pius XI issued the Catholic papal encyclical *Casti Connubii* (On Christian Marriage), which reaffirmed the natural law opposition to contraception in uncompromising terms. Gradually thereafter contraception became accepted in Protestant circles, and procreation ceased to be the principal purpose of marriage. In 1968 Pope Paul VI issued the encyclical *Humanae Vitae* (On the Regulation of Birth). This appeared to reiterate the outright ban on contraception, but some Catholics interpreted it as simply banning prophylactic methods during the four-day fertile period of the menstrual cycle.

Four methods of birth control have emerged.

a.   Surgery. In men this refers to vasectomy, which severs the sperm ducts; in women to severing the fallopian tubes. Both result in sterilization. In addition a surgical procedure may insert an inter-uterine device (IUD or coil) into the uterus for a five- to ten-year period.

b. Devices. For women this refers to the diaphragm, which fits over the cervix. For men it refers to the condom.

c. Medication. Chemical contraception is sought through the hormones progestin and estrogen, either ingested (the combined oral contraceptive pill, more commonly known as "the Pill") or injected (in drugs such as DMPA and NET-EN).

d. Restraint. Three methods have long been known and tried, with mixed results: abstinence, *coitus interruptus* (male withdrawal before climax), and the rhythm method (restriction of intercourse to avoid the four fertile days per month). The latter is the only accepted method of "contraception" in the Roman Catholic Church.

2. *Assisted conception.* While the desire to have a child, and the desire to overcome congenital health adversities, might both be considered perennial human concerns, the range of technologies available in relation to these issues has expanded enormously in recent generations. The search for scriptural prooftexts is once again in vain: while childlessness is a regular theme in the Bible, from Sarah and Abraham to Hannah and Elkanah, this seems to be a debate beyond the imagination of the scriptural world.

Around 10–15 percent of couples in the West experience involuntary infertility. Assisted conception refers to a variety of reproductive technologies through which infertility on the part of prospective parents may be overcome, including the following.

a. Straightforward rectification of malfunctioning organs. This may involve, for example, repairing fallopian tubes or restoring regular ovulation.

b. Artificial insemination. This simply means inserting semen into the woman's vagina by technological, rather than conventional, means. The semen may come from a husband (AIH), or from a "donor" (AID), usually an anonymous party. When the semen inserted is from the husband or partner of another couple, where the intention is for the latter couple to raise the child, the process is known as surrogacy. When both the egg and the sperm come from another couple it is known as full surrogacy. Surrogacy is becoming a more common option (and alternative to adoption) for same-sex couples who wish to raise children from infancy.

c. *In vitro* fertilization (IVF). This process stimulates the production of several eggs in a woman's ovary, then surgically removes them, and fertilizes them in a laboratory (the glass test tube yielding the term *in vitro*, which is Latin for "in glass"). The fertilized egg is known as a zygote. A number of things can then happen. One or more zygotes can be reinserted into the woman's uterus. One or more zygotes can be inserted into a woman other than the original egg donor, for the eventual "motherhood" of either woman. One or more zygotes can be genetically altered whether before being reinserted into a uterus or not. It is thus this method that provides the connection between assisted conception and genetic engineering, because it invariably produces more zygotes than are needed simply for conception, and the surplus zygotes are either a problem or an opportunity. A related procedure is gamete intrafallopian transfer (GIFT), where the fertility process is similar, but the meeting of sperm and egg actually takes place inside the fallopian tube.

3. *Genetic engineering.* It is not clear whether the scriptural ban on incest was a deontological concern about close relatives or a consequential concern about the likelihood of physical or developmental disability. Either way, this is the closest the Bible gets to explicit concern about the causes and consequences of human difference. Since then a number of areas of work and possibility have emerged as research and technology have developed. They fall into three areas.

    a. Social eugenics. Gregor Mendel (1822–84), the pioneer of genetics, and Charles Darwin (1809–82), the pioneer of evolutionary theory, were contemporaries. Speculation on the social implications of their findings was not slow to arise. A host of measures, such as restricted immigration and sterilization, were accordingly pursued in many countries at a government and public policy level throughout the twentieth century. By far the most notorious of these was the extensive eugenics program of Nazi Germany.

    b. Pre-birth genetics and embryology. Many genetically informed methods are used to ensure the birth of a healthy baby. Genetic screening identifies genetic disorders and those at high risk of transmitting them, and seeks to counsel those likely to give birth to severely disabled children; it is liable to cause distrust on racial grounds and there is much debate over whether such screening should be voluntary or required. Pre-natal screening refers to the detection of unusual diseases or conditions including Down syndrome, spina bifida, cleft palate, sickle cell anemia, and cystic fibrosis. This can be done by invasive means (such as amniocentesis) or non-invasive means (such as ultrasound examination). Parents may abort the fetus, investigate adoption, or proceed with pregnancy and raising the child. Controversy surrounds not only the option of abortion, but also the definition of what constitutes a "severe disorder," and the use of such tests for other purposes, such as identifying unwanted female progeny.

    When a zygote is created in a laboratory but not subsequently inserted into a woman's uterus, and when a fetus is aborted or miscarried, embryonic stem cells become available. Stem cells in blastocysts (four- to five-day-old embryos) can differentiate into any of the specialized embryonic tissues. They therefore seem highly promising candidates for being developed in a laboratory for use in medical therapies of various kinds – although none has yet emerged. Many have serious misgivings about developing therapies from stem cells derived from some or all of these sources. The use of adult stem cells (undifferentiated cells that occasionally occur among the differentiated cells in a certain tissue or organ) tends to be less controversial, since in theory they can be extracted from a human patient, stimulated to differentiate, and then reintroduced back into the same patient.

c.   Post-birth genetics. Gene therapy for children and adults is still a fledgling phenomenon. It refers to the practice of inserting genes into a person's cells and tissues to treat a disease – for example, in the case of a hereditary disease where a mutant gene is replaced by a regular one. There are two varieties. In somatic cell gene therapy a defective gene from a vital organ or tissue is replaced by a healthy one, thereby treating a serious condition but not preventing the condition being passed on to a descendant. In germ-line gene therapy a germ from the sperm or eggs is altered, in the attempt to eradicate the condition from future generations. The former procedure has not yet yielded permanent alleviation of any condition. The latter procedure is not currently legal.

The complexity of genetic possibilities and challenges is bewildering to most of the non-scientific community, and responses are often made on a gut level. Yet for those affected by conditions that genetic interventions and therapies offer to resolve, the attractions are obvious. The same is to a lesser extent true of assisted conception. For those parties opposed to active contraception, notably the Roman Catholic Church, the question has been complicated by the HIV/AIDS pandemic, and its connection to sexual vulnerability and promiscuity. The question could be phrased in these terms: is the Catholic opposition to contraception an ecclesial claim or a universal one, and, if the former, can an ecclesial argument ever be trumped by a universal consequential need, such as the need to reduce the spread of HIV?

Universal

The Roman Catholic view is a consistent deontological natural law approach derived originally from Aristotle: that the purpose of sexual intercourse is procreation; that every instance of sexual intercourse should be open to procreation; that conception outside this context (e.g., in a laboratory) undermines the sacredness of this context; and that any use of embryos for purposes other than their own well-being is a sign of the disasters that await when natural law goes unheeded and sex and babies become unhinged from one another. Thus, most of the methods and technologies listed above would be ruled out except such practices as rectification of malfunctioning organs. Pre-natal screening is not inherently wrong but is suspicious because it is so closely linked with the option of abortion. The rhythm method of contraception is positively encouraged.

Protestants have tended to be divided, depending crucially on different notions of fallenness. Some see sin as perversity, and root human shortcomings in the Fall and thus in original sin. Others see sin more in terms of immaturity, and see human weakness as resembling the ignorance of a child.

1. Those who perceive sin as perversity tend to welcome contraception but become suspicious regarding some dimensions of reproductive technology and genetic engineering. These reservations are often along Kantian lines, following the categorical imperative to treat people always as ends, never as means. If a baby is being created by artificial means simply to fulfill the wishes of its parents, or if an embryo is being used to research a cure for a disease carried by others, Kant's categorical imperative appears to be broken.

2. By contrast those who perceive sin as largely about immaturity and ignorance tend wholeheartedly to welcome technological advances that offer new dawns in human progress and especially the alleviation of infertility and suffering. These latter approaches tend to be consequential ones and concentrate on issues such as the anonymity of sperm donors in AID procedures. Thus, Joseph Fletcher (1905–91) regarded assisted conception as "more human" than conventional conception, since he saw overcoming "natural" obstacles to human flourishing as central to human identity. For him, parenthood is not primarily a biological matter but an emotional bond; and marriage rests on the quality of relationship between the couple rather than their ability to have children of their "own." While Fletcher applauds the parents' perspective as "willed, chosen, purposed, and controlled," many have pointed out on deontological grounds that in IVF procedures the embryo can become a toy in the hands of parents, physicians, or researchers. There seems to be no autonomy for the product of assisted conception: the embryo.

More nuanced views have emerged from those committed to a universal perspective. The contemporary Lutheran writer Gilbert Meilaender (b. 1945) recognizes that:

> It cannot be right to rule out all human intervention in the procreative process – as if we were finite beings who ought never to seek to transcend and control what is naturally given. The use of reason and will to free ourselves from some of the constraints of nature is itself part of our God-given nature.

Meilaender also points out that:

> The pre-modern English-speaking world, impressed with the world as given by a Creator, used the term "pro-creation." We, impressed with the machine and the gross national product (our own work of creation), employ a metaphor of the factory, "re-production."

With Kantian logic, Meilaender doubts if the happy results of artificial reproduction justify the means that "destroy the intimate connection between the love-giving and life-giving aspects of the one-flesh marital union." The process of IVF, he feels, cannot ignore the question of what happens to the surplus zygotes: while "we need not suppose that every couple setting foot on this path will come to think of their child as a product for which they must exercise quality control," the drift is toward seeing the embryo as made rather than begotten.

Referring to embryo experimentation, Oliver O'Donovan (b. 1945) summarizes this line of concern thus:

> If we should wish to charge our own generation with crimes against humanity because of the practice of this experimental research, I would suggest that the crime should not be the old-fashioned crime of killing babies, but the new and subtle crime of making babies to be ambiguously human, of presenting to us members of our own species who are doubtfully proper objects of compassion and love. ... Unless we approach new human beings, including those whose humanity is ambiguous and uncertain to us, with the expectancy and hope that we shall discern how God has called them out of nothing into personal being, then I do not see how we shall ever learn to love another human being at all.

In summary there are four prominent deontological themes and three consequential ones. The deontological arguments are as follows.

1. *Purpose.* This is the natural law argument that sex is for babies, and that babies should emerge only from sex. It is mainly used in relation to contraception. In relation to assisted conception the argument becomes one that non-sexual reproduction seems somehow less than truly human. As O'Donovan puts it, "The primary characteristic of a technological society is not the things it may *do* with the aid of machines, but the way it *thinks* of everything it does as a kind of mechanical production. Once begetting is acknowledged to be under the laws of time and motion efficiency, then its absorption into the world of productive technique is complete."
2. *Dignity.* This is the Kantian argument that people should never be used as a means to an end, and that embryos appear to have no dignity in the more technological processes of assisted reproduction. Children become a product rather than a gift.
3. *Choice.* When individual choice and autonomy become key values in society, the recognition that an embryo has no choice – for example, in the use of surplus zygotes in IVF – is a telling one. On the other hand, the choice of the parents is enhanced.
4. *Resources.* There is no doubt that artificial conception can be immensely expensive, and its availability is likely to be restricted to a small segment of the world's population for some time to come. These two issues evoke deontological objections, in a world where so many lack the material necessities of life.

The consequential arguments tend to be more sympathetic to technological intervention – although not entirely. Here are the most prominent ones.

1. *Control.* Whether or not control over nature is seen as a good thing in itself, its results are often taken to speak for themselves. Contraception has revolutionized the role and status of women, limited the HIV/AIDS virus, and arguably increased both the standard of living and the quality of domestic

life by limiting family size and reducing unwanted pregnancies. Assisted conception has simply brought into the world many deeply desired people who would otherwise never have been born. Genetic engineering promises to limit or eradicate several damaging and troubling conditions. It is a formidable list of achievements.

Control obviously evokes objection on deontological grounds, on the grounds of "playing God" (see Meilaender's response to this above). But control also elicits consequential objections. Technological control appears to risk loosening the social structure that has broadly accommodated the vagaries of nature hitherto – the family. Not all things can be solved in the laboratory. New technologies invariably bring unforeseen effects, and these could be very damaging.

2.   *The wedge (or slippery slope)*. Those who advocate genetic engineering and reproductive technologies communicate excitement about the ability of humanity to overcome constraint and create a new kind of society. But those who oppose such developments on consequential grounds sometimes do so because the *telos*, or end, is so frightening. It seems to be the thin end of a wedge. The new world of manufactured humanity is the stuff of science fiction. On a modest level, the promise of anonymity in the case of procedures such as AID is by no means watertight and the psychological effects of discovering one's own true biological identity can be complex. More dramatically, the prospect of creating different kinds of people – perhaps even clones – raises fears of a new apartheid between "real" and "constructed" individuals. Meanwhile the legacy of eugenics, particularly in the Nazi era, offers the specter of such technology falling into the wrong hands.

3.   *Gender balance*. More interference in the regenerative process has led in some cases to the birth of a higher proportion of males than females, an outcome that many see as problematic for a range of reasons. In China, for example, there are currently 33 million more men than women. Many worry that continued interference will lead to the same result in other places, particularly in more traditional societies.

Subversive

Every aspect of subversive ethics discussed in Chapter Six above – class, race, gender, disability, and age – is significant in this debate.

Just as in some circumstances the bearing of many children is the only insurance against poverty in old age, so in other circumstances the tyranny of perpetual pregnancy is a guarantee of intractable poverty. Despite the fact that conception and birth (and even infertility) are universal phenomena, this is a prime area where context is highly significant – and thus a field where subversive ethics is very prominent. The class issues include the following. Assisted conception can be very expensive, and seems to offer hope to a small minority of (fairly affluent) couples seeking to have a child. Meanwhile economic pressures (e.g., to raise funds to pay for a college education) may lead a woman to donate eggs (or even a womb), or a man to donate sperm, and thus become part of the complex web of relationships assisted reproduction sometimes involves. When it comes to genetic engineering, ethicist Amy Laura Hall, a United Methodist theologian at Duke University in North Carolina, has pointed out that the quest for the perfect baby in twentieth-century America was a profoundly race- and class-shaped one, with a host of efforts at public education through various media promoting a particular (white middle-class) social location as the ideal.

Most of the issues of class in this debate transfer also to race. Reproduction is one of the most, if not the most, obvious ways in which the dominant social group has striven to overcome the limitations of its own bodies, if necessary by employment of the bodies of less dominant social groups. In Chapter Six we noted the way the story of Hagar, mother of Ishmael, in Genesis 21 can be seen as the use and rejection of the body of a woman of a different race and class by a man and woman of the dominant group. Perhaps the most significant area where race is crucial is that of genetically transmitted diseases that are largely or wholly limited to one racial group – such as sickle cell anemia, which in the USA occurs mainly among African Americans. The distribution pattern of resources in relation to diseases of this kind is a telling indication of the role of race in an unjust social system.

Perhaps most obviously, gender is never more significant than in questions of reproduction. One could argue that feminism is born in the struggle to overcome the social disadvantage women have historically been under when their role in reproduction has been allowed or made to dominate their social status in damaging ways. The greatest argument for contraception is that it restores to women an important degree of autonomy in regard to when they may (or at least may not) anticipate becoming pregnant. Thus, to advocate for the widespread availability and permissibility of contraception seems to many to be a statement that the role of women in society is about a very great deal more than reproduction. The issues surrounding assisted reproduction are more complex, because women find themselves in such a variety of locations – for example, as a person longing for a child or as a person in a position to be a donor. Here questions of class sometimes seem more significant. Nonetheless a number of reflections on gender continue to suggest themselves – for example, that male analyses of these questions tend to focus on techniques and procedures, whereas female ones are more centered on personal dimensions such as the physical and psychological costs to women of various procedures. Likewise some feminists have concluded that family law is more suitable than contract law for settling conflicts over reproductive rights, because family law seems more concerned with what will benefit the child. Family law concerns the variety of issues that arise around the formation, conduct, and termination of marriage and similar relationships. By their very nature these issues are concerned with supporting the vulnerable, rather than declaring a victorious or guilty party. Contract law, on the other hand, is generally more concerned with enforcing legally binding promises and agreements with less regard for personal consequences.

Disability will take a more prominent role in the discussion of abortion, below. Here it is worth noting the way questions of assisted reproduction and genetic engineering highlight existing ambivalences about the place of disability in the contemporary social imagination. On the one hand novel techniques might be thought to risk a higher incidence of disability, and thus seem questionable on utilitarian grounds. On the other hand genetic engineering offers to reduce the incidence of disability. This latter promise seems to be one of real progress – but not in the eyes of those who see the questions of disability as lying in the eye of the beholder rather than in the body of the holder. As for age, these issues arguably highlight where the dynamics of power genuinely lie in modern Western societies: not with the elderly, and certainly not with the unborn. The struggle, as often, for subversive ethics is whether the language of rights empowers disadvantaged groups or simply sets their needs and aspirations in opposition to one another.

Ecclesial

As ever, ecclesial responses to these questions are a mixture of critique (which in some cases has significant overlaps with universal and/or subversive treatments) and constructive argument (which tends to be unique).

Thus, in relation to the status of children and new life, a perennial question for Stanley Hauerwas (b. 1940) is why people have children at all. He points out that children never turn out as expected and always bring with them problems (and opportunities) that could never have been foreseen. Parenthood is therefore not so much a right or a consumer expectation as a vocation and a gift that one learns how to receive – and a responsibility no one can carry out adequately without the support of a wider community. It is not possible to enter into arguments about rights and wrongs of contraception and assisted reproduction without wider questions of community and interdependence coming into play.

When it comes to genetic engineering some ecclesial ethicists share the kinds of criticisms found in subversive and some universal treatments. So, for example, some perceive that biotechnology is an industry that, like any other, is in search of a market. The habit of advertising is to make many people feel impoverished without this new product, and to encourage them to imagine the joy to be had if only it were purchased. The real beneficiaries are likely to be not the public but the shareholders. Such a critique gains a theological dimension when attention is given to what is really driving the quest for genetic improvement – or perfection. For some, the issue at stake is the understanding of salvation as "the redemption of our bodies" (Rom 8:23). The desire for bodily redemption is urgent both because the body is limited and because it is contingent. It is limited because it cannot do everything one may want it to do and it is subject to disease and decay.

It is contingent because the final eschatological redemption (apparently so imminent in the New Testament) seems endlessly delayed. Thus, there is always a temptation to bypass the body in search of a secret knowledge that guarantees redemption – a pattern of belief known as Gnosticism. There is a parallel temptation to perfect human bodies and postpone decay and death as long as possible, thereby achieving a salvation insulated from God. Ecclesial ethics tends to locate genetic engineering within these kinds of theological impulses.

As for the more constructive dimensions of ecclesial responses to these issues, they tend to focus on two general areas: the nature of regeneration and the nature of medicine.

- Assisted reproduction goes to the heart of the question of what reproduction means theologically. Most ecclesial ethicists would stress that reproduction (or regeneration) is fundamentally a sacramental action and only secondarily a biological one. In other words, the church reproduces not primarily by sexual intercourse, conception, and birth but by evangelism, conversion, and baptism. (This is the kind of claim that universal ethicists tend to struggle with, since the language of sacrament seems to rule out participation by those outside the sphere of faith.) If people face quandaries over assisted reproduction, it would be related to a lack of clarity over the true significance of baptism. For example, adoption becomes a more integral theological response to infertility when one believes that baptism embodies the conviction that all Christians are in fact adopted and thus that no parents have children "of their own."
- Turning to the nature of medicine, ecclesial ethics tends to linger on questions of why limiting and enhancing fertility is considered a "medical" issue at all. For example, Joel Shuman is a member of the Assemblies of God who teaches at King's College in Pennsylvania, and Therese Lysaught is a Roman Catholic and a professor at Loyola University Chicago. These two scholars and others have pursued the roots of medical ethics and have identified core themes that reach back to the medieval period and beyond, themes that are in danger of being neglected in a technologically and consumer-driven culture. For example, the term "patient" refers to one who waits in a particular way with a particular virtue: waits both for the physician and for the grace of God. Meanwhile the term "care" is a very different term to "cure," and yet care is perpetually in danger of being obscured by the pressure for cure. Likewise a "hospital" should rightly be a place not of consumer demand or of manufactured solutions but above all of hospitality.

Abortion

There is no explicit word in Scripture on the matter of abortion. That is not to say Scripture is not cited in the contemporary debate, but there are no supposedly "knock-down" texts (as there are sometimes taken to be for same-sex relationships or divorce, for example). The whole thrust of the Old Testament treatment of conception and childbirth is to see them as a demonstration of providence and blessing. In Matthew and Luke, God is intimately involved in Jesus' conception (Matt 1:18; Luke 1:35), and John the Baptist leaps in the womb when Elizabeth and Mary greet one another (Luke 1:44).

From earliest times the new Christian communities became known for their condemnation of abortion, in contrast to the prevailing Roman mores. The early documents the *Didache* and the *Letter of Barnabas* condemn abortion. One development is the distinction between the "formed" fetus, which has a soul (in Augustine's view from the 46th day), and the "unformed" fetus, which does not, although justification for killing even the unformed fetus is rare, and the life of mother and fetus are often considered equal in early Christian texts.

A clear distinction between Catholic and Protestant views begins to emerge. Catholic views seldom begin with the context and aspirations of the mother. They tend to have high expectations that there are clear rules that are rationally identifiable and apply in all circumstances. The natural law tradition not only yields confidence in a congruity between the disclosures of revelation and the conclusions of secular reason, it also assumes this congruity can be carried over into the field of public legislation. And that, of course, is where the sparks fly. Protestant views tend to have a more sober estimation of the ability of reason to identify clear rules and the ability of human beings to keep them. Some Protestant strands have adapted more readily than the Catholic Church to the changing social role and expectations of women. There is generally – though not universally – less of an assumption that the civil law is an appropriate instrument for exercising moral conviction, and often (but not always) more willingness to condone unwelcome results of what are commonly seen as tragic predicaments.

In what follows it will become clear that the tendency in universal ethics has been to focus somewhat narrowly on the fetus and its competing claims *vis-à-vis* its mother, while subversive ethics seeks to restore the mother's perspective, and ecclesial ethics generally seeks to portray this classic "decisionist" issue against a backdrop of wider concerns without which it is unintelligible and insoluble.

Universal

The contemporary debate about abortion can be resolved into two broad areas: the rights and wrongs of the issue itself, and the degree to which it is appropriate for Christians to seek to resolve those rights and wrongs through civil legislation. In regard to the issue itself, the debate has three main ingredients: the fetus, the mother, and the other interests concerned, including the father, the community, and the church.

1. *The fetus.* There are two deontological strands relating to the fetus itself.
    a. Killing. The deontological issue, usually known as the "sanctity of life," in fact refers to the prohibition, rooted in the Ten Commandments,

against taking innocent life. It is not usually considered a prohibition against taking all human life, since many who ardently oppose abortion consider capital punishment and killing in war to be legitimate in appropriate circumstances. (It is arguable that only pacifists take a completely consistent line against abortion, since only they refuse to make a distinction between innocent and other life.) The deontological question is therefore not whether the fetus is innocent, which it obviously is, but whether it is life, at least whether it is life in the sense that a person living outside the womb is. If it is human life in the same sense as infant life (as the term "unborn child" assumes), at what point does it become so?

- John Calvin's view was that the fetus (what would today be called a zygote, or fertilized egg) is ensouled at conception. This also tends to be the Eastern Orthodox view. Some look to the words of God to Jeremiah ("Before I formed you in the womb I knew you," Jer 1:5) to underline this claim. Yet 40 percent of zygotes never make it to become a fetus: this weakens the emphasis on conception as decisive.
- For others, birth itself is the key moment of transition; this tends to be the Jewish view.

Between conception and birth, a variety of staging posts appear as significant or crucial:

- *implantation*, when the zygote (technically now known as a blastocyst) attaches to the womb;
- development of the primitive streak, which marks the beginning of bilateral symmetry and arguably the capacity to feel pain (around fourteen days);
- *quickening*, when the fetus first moves in the womb;
- detectable *brain waves*, disclosing consciousness;
- or *viability*, when the fetus could survive as a child outside the womb (somewhere over twenty weeks).

The Reformation emphasis on the necessity that a person come to a faith on their own, and the Enlightenment concentration on individual autonomy, both contribute to the notion of personhood as more significant than life itself. Thus conscience, rather than conception, heartbeat, or consciousness, emerges as a key threshold beyond birth; yet some consider this to jeopardize the lives of some of the developmentally disabled by opening the door to infanticide.

b. *Rights*. A second approach, which focuses on the fetus as a subject, argues that abortion violates the fetus' right to life. Similar issues arise in relation to when the fetus is taken to be "alive" in a sense comparable to fully fledged human life – whether at conception, when blood first appears, later in pregnancy, at fourteen or twenty-two weeks, or at birth.

The key question is whether and when the fetus is a "person." There is, of course, no agreed definition of what constitutes a person. Some would say the possession of DNA, and thus of being human in species; others would suggest brain activity is required; others again would argue for the ability to live independently of the mother; others would speak of having a soul, whenever that is taken to begin. The significant aspects of the shift to rights language are that it directs the debate in constitutional directions and that it immediately sets the rights of the fetus in tension with the rights of the mother (and perhaps of others, such as the father). Being a person does not automatically settle legal questions: some non-persons, such as animals, are legally protected, and the law could not necessarily enforce one body to support another, if both were regarded as persons.

2.   *The mother.* There are four strands in relation to the mother, all of which tend to put the mother's perspective and rights in conflict with those of the fetus. Only the last of them is truly a deontological approach.

   a.   Extreme circumstances of conception. Many who take a firm deontological stand against abortion would make exceptions in cases where conception has arisen after rape or incest. The argument is that it is unreasonable to expect a woman to bear in her body the result of her violation unless she expresses a clear willingness (perhaps a vocation) to do so. It has the force of a deontological argument but is largely a consequential argument grounded in the psychological well-being of the mother.

   b.   Disability. Again, many would make an exception on behalf of parents who find they are expecting a child with multiple or complex patterns of disability. This is sometimes defended as being a decision made on behalf of the child (rather than the parents), though this is hard to argue conclusively. It appears to be a deontological argument but, like the previous argument, it is largely put forward in consequential terms – of the resources and disruption to life such a birth would bring about. Disability advocacy groups are among those highly skeptical of such reasoning.

   c.   Every child a wanted child. The theory here is that no child should come into the world unless it is wanted and likely to be cherished by its parents. Adoption is ruled out as requiring unreasonable commitment from the birth mother and offering unsatisfactory psychological security to the child. Yet again this seems to be a deontological argument, but is in fact a consequential argument hinging on the psychological well-being of the mother and the child.

   d.   A woman's body. This is the only genuinely deontological argument of the four. It maintains that a woman has complete rights over her own body, and that she should be able to have an abortion at any stage she sees fit. Advocates often point out that women who take such a step invariably do so with great reluctance. But the principle is that others (usually men) should no longer have the right to dominate the process of reproduction and the social roles that result. Civil law does not in fact recognize anyone's complete rights over their own body (hence seatbelt legislation). Nonetheless abortion becomes an explosive social issue when this deontological rights argument runs up against the deontological arguments made on behalf of the fetus, in the context of prospective legislation, particularly when churches or pressure groups have made the issue a litmus test of faithfulness or identity.

3. *Other parties and interests.* The tendency of universal ethics is to see only two significant contexts – the individual and the state. In this case there may well be more than one individual involved, but the two fundamental contexts remain the same.

    a. The father and the family. The role of the father is ambiguous. The ambiguity parallels that over whether the assumed context for abortion is within a marriage or outside one. On the one hand the lack of a supportive father and a secure domestic setting is sometimes cited as a reason why abortion is necessary. On the other hand a father who wishes a pregnancy brought (or not brought) to term is seldom seen as having the right to overrule the wishes of the mother, either morally or legally. Likewise one reason frequently cited for abortion is to avoid impoverishing other children in the family, but there is seldom any question of their views being gauged.

    b. The civil law. There are three broad legal issues.

        i.   One is whether the law is the best mechanism for establishing a moral order. One of the most significant reasons why abortion was legalized in the UK in 1967 and in the USA in 1973 was the consequential issue that the prevalence of back-street abortions was doing untold harm. Such laws as a blanket ban on abortion, it is argued, being likely to punish some of the most vulnerable people in society, and being unlikely to be kept, bring the whole legal system into disrepute.

        ii. Another issue is the degree to which it is appropriate for religious bodies to seek to influence legislation – particularly in avowedly secular polities such as the USA.

        iii. A third question is one of public policy. In 2001, 1.3 million children were born in Russia, while 1.8 million abortions were performed. When abortions exceed live births, many believe something is seriously wrong.

Subversive

The key terms in feminist perspectives on abortion tend to be context and power. In relation to context, feminists tend to be skeptical of the assumption that these issues can be settled by a team of (usually male) experts detached from specific contexts. The context that most matters is that of how women come to face unwanted pregnancies. This may be for a variety of reasons:

- becoming sexually active before grasping the methods of contraception;
- facing resistance from a partner, or scruples or carelessness in themselves;
- when contraception fails; or
- in being subject to sexual violence.

Thus, the real question is not so much abortion alone as greater economic opportunity and social security. What is needed are policies that will largely eradicate abortion by facilitating procreative choice.

What purports to be dispassionate theological, moral, or political reasoning is identified as an exercise in ecclesial or social power. Thus, feminists tend not to tackle the deontological argument against abortion head on, but instead question whether deontological arguments are sustainable in isolation, given the invariably prejudicial social location of their origin.

In general feminist arguments tend to make two key moves. The first is to shift attention away from the fetus alone. Not only is there no question of any life or well-being for the fetus that does not presume a prior life and well-being of the mother, but, as we have seen, the question of whether the fetus is a human being, in the same sense as the mother, is by no means clear. Assumptions that a zygote, blastocyst, fetus, or embryo is equivalent to a baby are rooted in an Aristotelian notion of potentiality that assumes that the true identity of an organism lies in what it is one day going to be. "Killing" only applies if this notion of potentiality is accepted.

The second move is to stress that there is no inherent antagonism between woman and fetus, only a common need to realign the relationships that shape the world in which both exist. In an ideal world, says Beverly Wildung Harrison (who taught for many years at Union Theological Seminary in New York; 1932–2012), there would be safe and reliable means of contraception; men and women would share responsibility for procreative choices and children's well-being; and there would be no sexual violence or abuse. In such a world saving the mother's life would be the only criterion for abortion. However, given that this world is far from ideal, "safe, surgical, legal abortion is a moral blessing." The current stand-off between pro-life and pro-choice activists will only end when the "pro-life" advocates "link their concern for fetal life with an ethically adequate concern for the well being of women and the children they bear."

Welcome as initiatives to help a woman embrace her pregnancy may therefore be (provided they are not covers for manipulation), they do "not address women's well being as a caste." Like many efforts at charity, such efforts are responses to others "as isolated individuals apart from the social reality that creates their dilemmas."

Ecclesial

Ecclesial ethics sets out to expose why this most archetypal of ethical quandaries is insoluble in the decisionist terms in which it is conventionally framed, and to propose a more suitable context in which Christians may understand the challenge of abortion. It therefore has both a critical and a constructive approach.

Each conventional aspect of the debate tends to be found wanting.

1.   The question is not about when life (or personhood) begins. The term "sanctity of life" too easily becomes detached from its theological moorings. As Stanley Hauerwas says, "Christians do not believe that life is sacred. Christians took their

children with them to martyrdom rather than have them raised pagan. Christians believe there is much worth dying for. We do not believe human life is an absolute good in and of itself. To say that life is an overriding good is to underwrite the modern sentimentality that there is absolutely nothing in this world worth dying for. Christians know that Christianity is simply extended training in dying early." Instead Christians should be in the business of forming and fostering communities in which unexpected life is welcomed as a gift rather than a threat. This should have a personal cost: rather than say simply "there should be greater government support for parents," Christians should be able to say "come and live with me."

The issue of personhood is significant because it was at the center of the *Roe v. Wade* judgment that legalized abortion in the USA in 1973. Ecclesial ethicists tend to be deeply suspicious of attempts to distinguish between rational and non-rational human beings, a distinction rooted in assumptions about autonomy that justifies aborting disabled fetuses and is occasionally extended to proposals for genetic screening and selective infanticide. If churches are to be formed to welcome all human life as a gift, there is no justifiable distinction between "normal" and "abnormal" life.

2. The question is not about rights. Most ecclesial ethicists welcome the notion of rights, provided those rights stand alongside appropriate duties, responsibilities, and goods. Many follow Nicholas Wolterstorff's (b. 1932) conviction that the origin of the notion of natural rights lies with the church's canon lawyers of the twelfth century and not in the Enlightenment. But the notion of *inalienable* rights, rooted in John Locke's (1632–1704) account of the natural right to life, liberty, and property, is seen by most ecclesial ethicists as a denial both of human existence as a contingent creature and of the renunciation of autonomy that takes place in baptism. So the question becomes not whose rights, the fetus' or the mother's, should prevail, but what kind of community can live out the promise of baptism to enjoy life as a gift to be received and not as an achievement to be attained. Such a community aspires not to independence from one another but to modes of mutual dependence that enhance the body that most matters, the body of Christ.

3. The question is not about compassion. Stanley Hauerwas regards the slogan "every child a wanted child" as especially dangerous. He says, "Too often we assume compassion means preventing suffering and think that we ought to prevent suffering even if it means eliminating the sufferer." He suggests it is vital for the church to challenge this ethic of compassion. To do so it needs to offer a radically different perspective on the ways Christians respond to suffering.

4. The question is not a medical one. Ecclesial ethicists often point out that lawyers and doctors have become the priests of the contemporary era, because they are the ones understood to have the real power. But the term "abortion" is a moral description (one that assumes Aristotle's notion of potentiality) very different from the medical description "termination." The real questions for

ecclesial ethicists lie in more fundamental areas such as why people have children at all, and whether they expect any child to be a product of their best genetic and nurturing efforts.

Thus, ecclesial ethicists find it very hard to comprehend abortion, not on deontological grounds, but because it is hard to see in what circumstances an abortion might be said to build up the church. They share much of the critique made by subversive ethicists that deontological approaches mask issues of power, but they are usually reluctant to seek women's autonomy as a solution to misuse of (largely male) power.

Euthanasia and Suicide

The question of a good death is driven less by technological developments than by theological transformation. For much, perhaps most, of church history, the overriding concern was that one's life and one's death be such as to fit one for heaven. With the decline of belief in hell from the nineteenth century onwards and the consequent diminishing anxiety concerning the precarious nature of any afterlife, attention shifted gradually away from death in general and more toward dying in particular. The availability of anesthesia from the early nineteenth century onwards coincided with these theological developments. Euthanasia and suicide emerge more prominently than they had before because they emphasize two significant themes of the modern age: they highlight individual autonomy, the desire to be in control of the most bewildering force of all, one's own mortality; and they offer a response to that most abiding of questions, human suffering.

There are a number of scriptural accounts of suicide. Abimelech's suicide is assisted by his armor bearer (Judges 9:50–5). Saul falls upon his sword after his armor bearer refuses to help him kill himself (1 Sam 31:4). Ahithophel hangs himself in 2 Samuel 17:23. Judas Iscariot's suicide is recorded in Matthew 27:5 and Acts 1:18–20. None of these accounts is endorsed by the narrator, but there is no unequivocal denunciation of suicide or euthanasia in the Bible: traditional condemnation is grounded more in the notion of God's sovereignty over life and death, affirmed in verses such as Ecclesiastes 8:8, "No one has power over the wind to restrain the wind, or power over the day of death."

Euthanasia is a term used to cover a spectrum of at least four distinct practices.

1.   The exposure or abandonment of unwanted infants or the execution of elderly or disabled members of society whose well-being for a variety of reasons is considered of no concern to the rest of society. This ancient practice has almost no advocates today. It gained modern prominence during the Nazi period in Germany when a great many people, particularly children, with developmental or physical disability or deformity were exterminated. It remains unclear whether infanticide meets any definition of euthanasia.

2.   Killing without explicit consent. The terms used tend to be involuntary
     (when consent is given by a third party – a relative, physician, or state judiciary)
     or non-voluntary (when the patient is not considered to have the mental facul-
     ties required for such a decision, for example because of infancy). The phrase
     "mercy killing" is often used, particularly in the latter circumstance. Here a
     distinction is often made between active methods (killing) and passive (allow-
     ing to die). A common citation is the principle of the nineteenth-century
     English poet Arthur Hugh Clough: "Thou shalt not kill; but needst not strive
     officiously to keep alive."
       Three celebrated cases illustrate this distinction.
     • Karen Ann Quinlan (1954–85) lapsed into a persistent vegetative state at
        the age of 21. Her Roman Catholic parents asked the hospital to allow her
        to die. The hospital refused, resulting in a celebrated legal battle that signifi-
        cantly influenced the establishment of formal ethics committees in hospitals
        and the development of advance health directives. Life support was indeed
        removed in 1976 but she lived on in a coma until dying of pneumonia in
        1985.
     • Tony Bland (1970–93) was a supporter of the Liverpool soccer club and
        attended the FA Cup semi-final in 1989 at Hillsborough in Sheffield, UK.
        The crush at the Leppings Lane end of the ground killed 96 people and left
        Bland with two punctured lungs, which interrupted the oxygen supply to
        his brain, leaving him in a persistent vegetative state. The brain stem
        remained intact, but there was no cortical activity. The Airedale General
        Hospital, with his parents' support, applied to the courts to let him "die
        with dignity." He thus became the first patient in England to die by court
        order through the withdrawal of life-prolonging treatment.
     • Terri Schiavo (1963–2005) collapsed in her home in St. Petersburg, Florida,
        after complications perhaps arising from bulimia and after respiratory and
        cardiac arrest. She experienced brain damage that resulted in a persistent
        vegetative state. A seven-year battle through the courts ensued between her
        husband, who sought permission to remove her feeding tube, and her par-
        ents, who argued that she was still conscious – and who received the sup-
        port of the Florida and United States governments. Eventually her husband
        won the right to remove her feeding tube on the grounds that Terri would
        not wish to continue life-prolonging measures.
   In the case of both Tony Bland and Terri Schiavo a "passive" argument for involuntary euthanasia was sustained.

3.   Voluntary euthanasia. Despite high-profile cases of the second kind, it is in
     this third area where the majority of the debate tends to lie. It combines the
     presupposition that extreme suffering is intolerable with the assumption that
     autonomy in life should naturally be extended to autonomy in the timing of
     death. Related to this is the existence of advance directives, or "living wills,"
     which are relatively common in the United States. In a litigious culture they

appear to offer a way to preserve patient autonomy even in circumstances where the patient is unconscious or mentally unreachable, and to avoid court battles on occasions when third parties disagree over the patient's wishes.

In the United States the Armenian American pathologist Jack Kevorkian (b. 1928) has become famous for assisting 130 patients to die and championing physician-assisted suicide, succeeding in having such legislation passed in Oregon in 1994. From 1999 to 2007 he was incarcerated for second-degree murder. He is well known for saying "dying is not a crime." Physician-assisted suicide was decriminalized in Holland in 1993 and in Belgium in 2002.

In Britain the most prominent case was that of Diane Pretty (1958–2002), who attempted to change British law so she could end her own life because of the pains that she endured due to motor neurone disease. The disease made it impossible for her to move or communicate easily even though her mental faculties remained normal. She was entirely dependent on her husband and nurses, and thus could not take her own life, which she claimed she would have done had she been able to. She asked that her husband should be able to assist her in ending her life. Her case failed at every level up to and including the European Court of Human Rights. She eventually died from lung and chest problems.

4.   Double effect. In distressing circumstances it is relatively common for a physician to administer medication such as a strong dose of morphine, which may seriously or even fatally damage one of the patient's vital organs in order to alleviate pain or other symptoms from another organ of an even more pressing nature. While such a practice may be regarded as euthanasia by some, it is seldom described as such, and a distinction is conventionally made between medication whose intent is analgesic and medication whose intent is lethal.

Suicide comes in three broad forms.

1.   *Pathological.* The first form is generally considered a dimension of some kind of illness, most commonly depression. The historic condemnation of suicide has been softened by an increasing recognition that many, perhaps most, suicides should be understood as arising from psychological pathologies rather than be regarded as straightforward self-murder. Thus, in 1961 suicide was decriminalized in the UK such that those who failed in the attempt would no longer be prosecuted.

2.   *Deliberate.* This refers to the taking of one's own life after careful reflection, rather than as an aspect of a clinical condition. There are significant overlaps here with the debate over euthanasia. The 1961 Act in the UK that decriminalized suicide acknowledged that those who found their life intolerable had the right to end their existence. Contemporary suicides in the face of likely future pain, shame, or distress fall into this category. So also do political acts such as Bobby Sands' death in 1981 by hunger strike during the Northern

Irish Troubles and Emily Davison's death under the hooves of the king's horse in the Epsom Derby in 1913 during the women's suffrage campaign. The traditions of suttee (where a Hindu Indian woman would immolate herself on her husband's funeral pyre) and seppuku (or hara-kiri – where a Japanese samurai would die by ritual disembowelment) are similar, although they emerge from cultural conditions where assumptions differ significantly from those currently pertaining in most parts of the contemporary West.

3. *Purposeful.* There are a number of circumstances where people take their own life as part of a larger project of publicity or war. Two examples are suicide attacks, where a person blows himself up along with many other people (the most notorious being September 11, 2001), and mass suicides, which sometimes take place among religious cults. Bobby Sands' and Emily Davison's deaths could be regarded in this category, although the designation is usually reserved for those whose suicides entailed the deaths of others.

In addition there are two areas that are not usually considered suicide but have common features. One is sometimes known as parasuicide. Parasuicide refers to the attempt at suicide, which nonetheless bears many signs that it was designed to be a failed attempt. Perhaps only one in ten apparent suicide attempts results in a death. Another is a range of behavior including self-harm and unhealthy eating which, though not explicitly intended to result in death, may in some cases be considered to be on a lengthy continuum.

Universal

The debate is dominated by one consequentialist argument and one deontological argument. The former is the slippery slope argument as applied to euthanasia – that permitting voluntary euthanasia would lead to all kinds of involuntary euthanasia becoming possible or even acceptable. The latter concerns the by-now familiar deontological commitment to the sanctity of life.

The deontological arguments are as follows.

1. *The commandment not to kill.* Throughout Judeo-Christian history there has been debate over the circumstances in which it was possible to kill, given the commandment not to do so. Judicial killing and killing in war have often been considered legitimate. But euthanasia has generally been regarded as murder, and suicide as self-murder – that is, killing without legitimate authority. There is a consequential dimension to this argument – that is, if suicide and euthanasia were to be regarded as permissible, other forms of non-judicial killing might become harder to outlaw.

2. *The sovereignty of God.* The most common theological argument is that life is God's to give and God's to take away. To take a life – one's own or someone else's – is a kind of theft: it is taking something that does not belong to you. Though suffering can be terrible, it is a denial of providence to suggest that

even a deeply troubled life is of no value. John Locke took the view that human life belongs to God: it is our duty to use it to its best effect, but our control over it is on trust, and does not extend to absolute ownership and the consequent right of disposal. However, in modern times, many have taken Locke's logic concerning property and assumed that the body is indeed one's own to dispose of how one wishes. The argument on the grounds of property rights is thus ambiguous.

3. *The categorical imperative.* Kant argued that if the principle of one's action should be a universal moral law, one could not rationally endorse suicide or euthanasia because that would imply the extermination of all people. While Kant's argument may seem exaggerated, it is helpful in highlighting the difference between suicide – which requires the right to end one's life when life seems intolerable – and euthanasia – which seems to invoke a right to be allowed to kill a person, which seems absurd when expressed in such terms. Kant's argument discourages terms such as "assisted suicide" that make euthanasia and suicide seem similar if not identical.

The consequential arguments include two against and one in favor:

1. *The wedge/slippery slope.* The most frequently repeated anxiety about voluntary euthanasia is that it would open the door to involuntary euthanasia. How can one be sure that the patient really wants to die *at the moment of death*? An advance directive might have been made long before in very different circumstances; it might have been made while under pressure from depression or the desire to please family members. It does not guarantee patient autonomy. The specter of children hastening burdensome parents and parents hastening challenging children to early deaths on the utilitarian grounds that it is hard to see their quality of life or benefit to society is frequently taken to be a likely and frightening one.

2. *Loss of trust.* A closely related concern is that the vulnerable lose trust not only in close relatives but in the medical profession too. Once the merest hint is allowed to develop that medicine is about something other than cherishing and prolonging life, and may also be concerned with ending life, the vital bond of trust may be inhibited.

3. *Double effect.* In practice the most influential argument in the contemporary hospital ward or domestic bedside is that of double effect: the stated intention of a particular medication or of the withdrawal of treatment may be the well-being of the patient. Over time, the course of action may be a significant factor in the patient's death; but, provided that the patient's death was not the intention of that course of action, it may be regarded as legitimate. The distinction between killing and letting die is vital to this argument. While it is possible to be cynical about motives, this approach is widely regarded as a humane practice of not striving "officiously to keep alive." Those cases where it does not easily apply, such as the Diane Pretty case, are thus the most

troubling to the public conscience. (See Chapter Five for a more thorough exploration of the principle of double effect.)

Subversive

Since subversive ethics tends to articulate the voices of those marginalized by conventional hegemonies, it is not hard to see why the subversive literature in the area of suicide and euthanasia is small. Those at most risk from involuntary euthanasia – the very young, the very sick, and the very old – are not likely to be in a position to voice their concerns about anything. Nonetheless the vulnerability of the newborn and the very frail is frequently pointed out by many parties in the debate. The paradox is that voluntary euthanasia is propounded precisely for the benefit of the very same people who seem most vulnerable in the face of involuntary euthanasia – those whose age, disability, gender, race, and class make their lives, in the face of distress, seem to others not worth living.

Ecclesial

There are two dimensions to ecclesial responses to suicide and euthanasia. The first is to challenge the assumptions that make personal autonomy and elimination of suffering seem so compelling. Gilbert Meilaender does this especially clearly.

> Because we are inclined to overemphasize our freedom and forget the limits of our finite condition, inclined to forget that life comes as a gift, death becomes the great reminder of those limits. ... The principle which governs Christian compassion is not "minimize suffering." It is "maximize care." Were our goal only to eliminate suffering, no doubt we could sometimes achieve it by eliminating *sufferers*. But then we refuse to understand suffering as a significant part of human life that can have meaning or purpose. ... The suffering that comes is an evil, but the God who in Jesus has not abandoned us in that suffering can bring good from it for us as for Jesus. We are called simply to live out our personal histories – the stories of which God is author – as faithfully as we can.

Meilaender's principle is "always to care, never to kill." As he points out, it has been "precisely our deep commitment not to abandon those who suffer" that has driven the development of modern medicine. When we cannot relieve suffering, "we must remember that God does not really 'solve' or take away the problem of suffering: rather, God himself lives that problem and bears it." Good physicians "can help us avoid the notion that there is any 'technological fix' for the fundamental human problems of suffering and death." Meanwhile it is often pointed out that prolonging life at all costs can be a form of an idolatry – that is, an idolizing of life itself, disregarding a God of resurrection.

The second dimension is the establishment, support, and active promotion of alternatives to suicide and euthanasia. Many of these have been and often continue to be explicitly rooted in self-consciously theological and ecclesial convictions, however broadly articulated. Thus, in the case of suicide, the Anglican parish priest Chad Varah (1911–2007) founded the charity Samaritans in 1953. Varah's first service as an assistant curate in Lincoln in 1935 had been for a fourteen-year-old girl who committed suicide because she had begun to menstruate and feared she had a sexually transmitted disease. Samaritans is staffed by volunteers who receive phone calls, letters, and emails and respond in attentive, non-judgmental, and non-sectarian ways.

In the case of euthanasia, the Anglican nurse Cicely Saunders (1918–2005) founded St. Christopher's Hospice, the world's first purpose-built hospice, in 1967. The hospice movement that traces its roots to her is founded on the principles of combining expert pain and symptom relief with holistic care to meet the physical, social, psychological, and spiritual needs of its patients and those of their family and friends. In 2005 more than 1.2 million individuals and their families in the USA and over 250,000 in the UK received hospice care. Ecclesial ethicists tend to regard hospices as embodying the kinds of virtues required to withstand the otherwise compelling logic of personal autonomy and the elimination of suffering.

Reformed theologian Allen Verhey (1945–2014) considers what it might be like to die a "good death" in *The Christian Art of Dying*, written while facing his own final illness. He draws on the medieval tradition of the *ars moriendi*, the good death, to imagine an alternative model for dying that is rooted in the Christian virtues, including the three theological virtues of faith, hope, and love, but also those of patience, humility, letting go, and courage. For him, these virtues are exemplified in the death of Jesus, who provides a model for a good death even in the midst of great suffering.

Summary

The issues discussed in this chapter all raise the theme of compassion. On first glance, they each seem to be about whether a person should be given what they dearly want or feel they cannot continue without – a child, an abortion, a painless death. In a society that has elevated freedom and choice to the highest status, it is hard to identify a logic that justifies withholding from people what they dearly want or feel they desperately need. To do so seems patriarchal or paternalistic, or both.

But quickly a host of reasons to pause cluster in. Some of these concern the understanding of "nature" and of "interference," two apparently simple but in fact very complex subjects. Others concern the question of whether medicine, so shaped by its dedication to preserve life, is damaged when harnessed to the cause of terminating life. Others again center around whether human life is in the process of being turned into some kind of product, shaped by mechanized procedures that make it seem something to be summoned up and disposed of at will.

Behind all of these questions lie some of the greatest human mysteries of all – of the origin of life and of the destiny of death. It is these shadowy moments that give this chapter a profile perhaps sharper than any of the others in this part of the book. However strident or subtle the arguments, there continue to be moments when those on all sides must simply wonder at the fragile gift of life itself.

References and Further Reading

Cardinal Joseph Bernardin's thoughts on a consistent ethic of life for Catholic moral theology are found in *The Seamless Garment: Writings on the Consistent Ethic of Life* (Maryknoll, NY: Orbis Books, 2008).

Contraception, Assisted Conception, and Genetic Engineering

The papal encyclicals *Casti Connubii* and *Humanae Vitae* are available on the Vatican's website at www.vatican.va/phome_en.htm. A portion of *Humanae Vitae* is included in the corresponding chapter of *Christian Ethics: An Introductory Reader*.

Joseph Fletcher's views on assisted conception may be found in the article "Ethical Aspects of Genetic Controls," *New England Journal of Medicine* 285 (1971): 776.

Gilbert Meilaender reflects on the procreative process in chapter 2 of *Bioethics: A Primer for Christians* (2nd edn; Grand Rapids, MI: Eerdmans, 1996, 2005). Specific quotations are drawn (in quoted order) from pages 16, 10, 18, and 20.

Oliver O'Donovan discusses embryo experimentation in *Begotten or Made?* (Oxford: Clarendon Press; New York: Oxford University Press, 1984), chapter 5. A portion of this work is also in the corresponding chapter of *Christian Ethics: An Introductory Reader*.

Amy Laura Hall examines genetic engineering and twentieth-century American religious history in *Conceiving Parenthood: American Protestantism and the Spirit of Reproduction* (Grand Rapids, MI: Eerdmans, 2008).

The question of why people have children appears in Stanley Hauerwas, *Truthfulness and Tragedy* (with Richard Bondi and David B. Burrell; Notre Dame, IN: University of Notre Dame Press, 1977), pages 147–83; and *A Community of Character* (Notre Dame, IN: University of Notre Dame Press, 1981), pages 155–95.

Another resource is the chapter on conception in Michael Banner, *The Ethics of Everyday Life* (Oxford: Oxford University Press, 2016).

In addition to the above, the following work is quoted in the corresponding chapter of *Christian Ethics: An Introductory Reader*: Margaret A. Farley, "Feminist Theology and Bioethics," pages 238–54 in *Feminist Theology: A Reader* (Ann Loades, ed.; Louisville, KY: Westminster/John Knox Press, 1990).

For further reading on the roots of medical ethics, see Joel Shuman and Brian Volck, *Reclaiming the Body: Christians and the Faithful Use of Modern Medicine* (Grand Rapids, MI: Brazos Press, 2006), and M. Therese Lysaught, "Love Your Enemies: Toward a Christoform Bioethic," pages 307–28 in *Gathered for the Journey: Moral Theology in Catholic Perspective* (David Matzko McCarthy and M. Therese Lysaught, eds; Grand Rapids, MI: Eerdmans, 2007).

Abortion

Abortion is condemned in the *Didache* (chapter 2, verse 2; see www.thedidache.com) and *The Letter of Barnabas* (chapter 19, verse 5; see http://www.earlychristianwritings.com/text/barnabas-lightfoot.html).

Beverly Wildung Harrison addresses abortion in her article (with Shirley Cloyes), "Theology and Morality of Procreative Choice," pages 213–32 in *Feminist Theological Ethics: A Reader* (Lois K. Daly, ed.; Louisville, KY: Westminster/John Knox Press, 1994); selections from this article are in the corresponding chapter of *Christian Ethics: An Introductory Reader*.

Stanley Hauerwas explores the Christian conception of life and dying in "Abortion, Theologically Understood," pages 603–22 in *The Hauerwas Reader* (John Berkman and Michael Cartwright, eds; Durham, NC: Duke University Press, 2001);

see pages 614–16. An excerpt of this essay is included in the corresponding chapter of *Christian Ethics: An Introductory Reader*. His thoughts about preventing suffering are in *Suffering Presence: Theological Reflections on Medicine, the Mentally Handicapped, and the Church* (Edinburgh: T & T Clark, 1988), pages 23–4.

Nicholas Wolterstorff's claims about the origins of natural rights may be found in his book *Justice: Rights and Wrongs* (Princeton, NJ: Princeton University Press, 2008), pages 10–13, 32–8.

In addition to the above, a selection from the following essay is quoted in the corresponding chapter of *Christian Ethics: An Introductory Reader*: James M. Gustafson, "A Protestant Ethical Approach," in *The Morality of Abortion: Legal and Historical Perspectives* (John T. Noonan Jr., ed.; Cambridge, MA: Harvard University Press, 1970).

Euthanasia and Suicide

Arthur Hugh Clough's principle is in his poem "The Last Decalogue," available online at http://theotherpages.org/poems/clough01.html.

John Locke's view that human life belongs to God is expressed in his *Second Treatise on Civil Government*, chapter 2, par. 6 (see www.constitution.org/jl/2ndtreat.htm).

Gilbert Meilaender explores issues related to suicide in chapter 6 ("Suicide and Euthanasia") of his book *Bioethics* (see above), a section of which is also included in the corresponding chapter of *Christian Ethics: An Introductory Reader*. The extended quotation ("Because we are inclined…") is drawn from pages 62–3.

Allen Verhey considers the Christian tradition of the good death in *The Christian Art of Dying: Learning from Jesus* (Grand Rapids, MI: Eerdmans, 2011).

Another helpful resource is the chapter on euthanasia and suicide in Michael Banner, *The Ethics of Everyday Life*.

In addition to Meilaender, the following works are quoted in the corresponding chapter of *Christian Ethics: An Introductory Reader*:

- Richard A. McCormick. "The New Medicine and Morality." *Theology Digest* 21, no. 4 (Winter 1973): 308–21.
- Jennifer A. Parks. "Why Gender Matters to the Euthanasia Debate: On Decisional Capacity and the Rejection of the Woman's Death Request." *Hastings Center Report* 30, no. 1 (2000): 30–6.

Further reading on the issues treated in this chapter include:

- Allen Verhey. *Reading the Bible in the Strange World of Medicine*. Grand Rapids, MI: Eerdmans, 2003.
- Joel James Shuman. *The Body of Compassion*. Boulder, CO: Westview Press, 1999.

Chapter Twelve
Good Earth

Speaking of the "natural world" as something apart from us, and the "non-human creation" as something from which we humans are by definition distinct, can reinforce a dualism between humans and something we have chosen to call "nature." Meanwhile, speaking of the "environment" can play into an anthropocentrism that denies proper respect to other living things and complex systems in their own right. Whose "environment" is "the environment"? The answer is, inevitably, "human beings." Talk of the environment can make it sound as though everything in the world exists merely as the scenery for human activity. How do we decide whether that is true or not? How should the human relationship to nature be construed? What policies and practices ought to be developed not only to meet immediate crises but to foster longer-term visions of flourishing? These are some of the questions this chapter sets out to address.

Thought about the human relationship to the natural world tends to work itself out in the tension between two modern perceptions: the freedom and self-direction of human agents on the one hand, and the existence of determining forces outside our control on the other. The former emphasis tends to enforce the idea that we are "not-nature"; it is perhaps corrected by the latter's reminder that in crucial ways we *are* (as the Christian tradition itself affirms, drawing on the creation accounts in the book of Genesis, and as Charles Darwin, Karl Marx, and Sigmund Freud have shown us in other ways). But there can be distortions the other way too. The latter emphasis can enforce the idea that we are not free (and therefore not responsible), and needs its own correction by the former. This dialectic does not dissolve the tension between freedom and determinism – it may not be soluble in the terms currently available within a modern "story" about who human beings are and what they ought to do. But managing this tension

Introducing Christian Ethics, Second Edition. Samuel Wells and Ben Quash with Rebekah Eklund.
© 2017 John Wiley & Sons Ltd. Published 2017 by John Wiley & Sons Ltd.

presents modern thinkers with some of their most acute problems – and this is certainly so in the area of environmental ethics.

Several categories help to order the broad types of response given to the question of how we are to treat the non-human world. The first is one whose specter we have already raised in these opening remarks: *anthropocentrism*. These are some features of an anthropocentric approach:

- it will often work within a personalist ethical framework, valuing human persons more than anything else, and locating morality solely in human consciousness;
- it will often make ethical judgments about aspects of non-human reality only with the criterion of how they affect conscious persons (individually or in aggregate);
- it may be prone to elevate function or utility over relationship – in other words, to accord respect to aspects of the natural world for "what they have done for us" (or might yet do), not because we are related parts of a single whole, the other parts of which have their own moral standing.

Personalism is a twentieth-century philosophy with origins in France and the USA (see the discussion of Borden Bowne [1847–1910] in Chapter Four). As Michael Northcott (who teaches at the University of Edinburgh, b. 1955) has pointed out:

> It was, and continues to be, in relation to such personalist concerns that appeals to environmental conservation are principally made and environmental regulations and laws are framed. Thus the important report of the United Nations Commission on Environment and Development *Our Common Future* frames its appeal for a more environmental form of economic growth, or "sustainable development," in terms of the interests of presently existing humans and their progeny.

Pope Francis's 2015 encyclical *Laudato Si'* (On Care for Our Common Home) likewise derives its urgency in part from a similar appeal to the present and future generations of humanity, but it also criticizes anthropocentrism as a misunderstanding of humanity's place relative to nature.

What is seen as anthropocentrism's tendency to assume manipulative hegemony over the things of the earth is a position variously countered in the name of *zoocentrism*, *biocentrism*, and *ecocentrism* (and even, occasionally, in the name of theology, as in *Laudato Si'*).

- Zoocentrism claims that the higher animals are also, alongside humans, proper objects of moral concern.
- Biocentrism extends this concern to all living things.
- Ecocentrism extends this concern to whole ecosystems.

Arguing that the brutal, instrumentalizing use of non-human life for the satisfaction of human wants has to be checked, however, may not necessarily lead one to the complete abandonment of an anthropocentric position – or at least a position that recognizes that we have no other perspective from which to attribute value and make ethical judgments than one grounded in our humanity. The truth is that it is *as humans* that we do our valuing. Even the most sympathetic and "self-less" valuing of the non-human world happens *as human* valuing. On occasions when we admit that other animals (snakes, for example) have interests, and value aspects of *their* environments in ways that have no reference to humanity, we nevertheless cannot step out of our own natures.

One prevalent response that seeks to arbitrate between different "claims" in environmental debate uses the modern legal language of "rights" claims (beginning with an assumed proprietary right of human beings over their possessions and over their own acts). The extension of this assumed proprietary right can lead to the attribution of "rights" to non-human creatures (animals, plants, and even whole ecological systems), as though they too could be construed as proprietary wills, as rights-bearing subjects. We will look in more detail at how "rights" language is used in the sections that follow.

The various ways outlined above of thinking about the good of the earth, and the *goodness* of the earth, influence and inform Christian ethics. This chapter looks at how Christian environmental ethics works itself out in three particular areas:

1. *Animals.* The question here is the relationship of humans to animals, including the questions of whether people ought to use animals for food, entertainment, or experiment.
2. *Crops.* An examination of crops involves the agricultural system from start to finish – the production, potential modification, distribution, and consumption of food from the earth.
3. *Ecology.* This term encompasses a variety of related issues, including climate change, biodiversity, and sustainable development.

Animals

Scripture

Biblically derived accounts of the moral status of animals may appeal to Genesis 1, in which God blesses the animals and gives them the same command to "be fruit-ful and multiply" that is later given to humanity. They are preserved in the Flood for new life, and share in the covenant (and thus, it can be argued, the hope) given to Noah afterwards (Gen 9:8–17). Also in Genesis we learn that God requires a "reckoning" for every animal that is killed for food, on the grounds that all life belongs to him (Gen 9:4–5). They are included in the prohibition against work on the Sabbath day (Deut 5:12–14). A series of visions of eschato-logical peace and plenty in Scripture involves an anticipation of the peaceful coex-istence of all creatures (Hos 2:18; Isa 11:6–9). At the end of the story of Jonah, in a way that may surprise and amuse the modern reader, the Lord clearly takes notice of and cares for the well-being of the cattle (Jonah 4:11)! And in the New Testament Jesus preaches God's providential care for animals and of all creation (Matt 6:26; Luke 12:24).

These scriptural texts have been appealed to because they say things about *animals*. There are also texts that are interpreted as specifying the responsibilities of *humans where animals are concerned*. These are texts that are interpreted as being about "stewardship," a concept that has become a popular theme in many areas of environmental ethics. Human beings are made in God's image, and the God in whose image we are made is creator of all things. We are given to share in God's "dominion" over the animals but, in the light of the *imago Dei* (image of God), should understand our "dominion" not in terms of the selfish exploitation and abuse of animals, but as a responsible, creative, and careful relationship, which (as use of the word stewardship implies) involves accountability. Thus, for example, the farmer is instructed not to "muzzle the ox when he is treading the grain" (Deut 25:4). But there is a risk of building too much on the resonances of the English word "stewardship," which does not have a direct equivalent in many languages, and in fact appears in only one passage of William Tyndale's sixteenth-century English translation of the Bible, in Jesus' parable about the shrewd manager (Luke 16:1–9).

Tradition

The premodern history of Christian moral philosophy does not treat animal welfare as a distinctive topic, but deeply rooted strands in the Christian liturgy, as in the words of Scripture, highlight the importance of God's inalienable relation to non-human creatures. For example, we see this in the canticle *Benedicite, Omnia Opera* ("Bless [the Lord], all works," which is traditionally used in the Roman Catholic office of Lauds and in the Anglican Book of Common Prayer's service of Matins (see also Psalm 103:22; The Prayer of Azariah 36 [Dan 3:57]). In verse tumbling over verse, the panoply of created things is addressed directly, as though possessed of its own subjectivity: "O all ye works of the Lord, bless ye the Lord: praise him, and magnify him for ever." The sky, the rain, the sun and the moon, stars, winds, fire and frosts, night and day, light and darkness, mountains, hills, green things upon the earth, seas, whales, birds, beasts, cattle, and finally human beings – all are summoned to do exactly the same thing: "praise him, and magnify him for ever." They are shown to be orientated to the disclosure of the glory of God, and to be known and loved by God in a way that does not always need to make reference to human beings – though we *are* encouraged to see ourselves as in relationship (in *fellowship*) with them. They can speak to God, and be spoken to by God, directly, just as we can. The Franciscan tradition has incorporated this sensitivity to the independent agency of natural things – for example, in the "Canticle of the Sun" attributed to St. Francis of Assisi himself, which declares, "Be praised, my Lord, through all your creatures," including Brother Sun and Sister Moon.

Contemporary Debate

In recent decades there has been a growing attention to the moral status of animals. This has been true both in Christian and in secular traditions of ethical thought. The issues tend to present themselves in one of three connections:

- Should we use animals for food, and if so, how?
- Should we use animals for sport, and if so, how?
- Should we use animals for experimentation, and if so, how?

A further question might be this: to what extent is the term "animal" a moral description that attempts to distinguish humans from others among God's creatures?

One of the most vivid examples of the human tendency to elevate function over relationship with regard to animals is the undoubtedly efficient (in a limited, technical sense) but at the present time brutal and ugly mass production of animals for food. At the same time, even for a strict vegan, it is virtually impossible to avoid benefiting in some way from other people's exploitation of animals – often indirectly or unwittingly. For example, a plastic used instead of leather may contain substances that at some point in the past were tested on animals. Then there is sport. Intuitively, the pursuit, baiting, or harnessing of animals for sport can seem considerably less justified than their use for food or experiments, as the goods that result for humans (principally, entertainment) seem relatively trivial compared with sustenance or advances in scientific knowledge. The carefully regulated use of animals for certain medical procedures (e.g., using their heart valves to save human lives) can seem more tolerable because the goods in view are more evident.

A key step for some modern thinkers who are frustrated or repelled by anthropocentrism in relation to the ethics of animal welfare has been to go back to the utilitarian tradition of Jeremy Bentham (1748–1832), who was introduced in Chapter Five. In particular, they have taken his moral principle that pain is to be minimized and pleasure maximized, and extended it to apply to what are manifestly also sentient beings: animal organisms. It is now widely judged to be "morally considerable" that many animals are capable of experiencing pain. This new respect for sentience in non-humans has worked itself out in a number of ways, some of which we will examine below.

Universal

Philosophical varieties of the universalist approach have both denied and adopted the idea that animals have rights. (Note, though, that as so often the use of rights language is also a feature of the sort of ethics we will label *subversive* in this area – see below.)

Animal rights deniers

- At one extreme, those who have denied the idea of animal rights have invoked a natural law principle, namely, that it is hard-wired into the created order that some animals (including ourselves) should hunt and/or use other animals. The British philosopher Roger Scruton (b. 1944), for example, has been a determined defender of fox-hunting on this basis. To echo the Victorian poet Alfred, Lord Tennyson, in his 1850 poem *In Memoriam*, nature is "red in tooth and claw," and we sentimentalize and work against the grain of it if we deny that.
- Others who deny the idea of animal rights have concentrated mainly on the specifically human issues of human obligations to each other, of right motivation and of good conduct when using animals – these being features of an anthropocentric perspective (see above). Questions to do with the ethical status of the animals themselves do not usually emerge as very important in such a perspective.

Animal rights endorsers

Those who have adapted the language of rights for application to animals as well as to humans are often working within a deontological framework. As we have just seen, they have often taken animals' sentience (or ability to feel pain) as a key moral factor.

The rights-centered approach of some ethicists (e.g., the work of the American philosopher Tom Regan [b. 1938]) is intended to awaken an enhanced sense of relationship with animals, and duty toward them.

- In their strong form, such approaches will admit of no exception to their judgment that animals possess the same moral rights as humans. Centrally this has included the right not to be experimented upon, or to be killed before their lives naturally end, because they are capable of experiencing pain and have memories and some sense of identity.
- In weaker forms, the claim that animals have rights has not absolved its advocates from the utilitarian need to balance such rights against the competing claims of humans – and, indeed, of other animals – and in some cases to allow that it is proper to take an animal life in order to save a human one. In this form it is also widely accepted even by those who oppose euthanasia that it is sometimes right and merciful to end an animal's life in order to end its suffering – admitting a moral distinction between the rights of a suffering human (who can often express her wishes concerning the end of life) and those of an animal (who cannot).

Consequentialist approaches

At this point, there is a shading into more obviously consequentialist approaches, like that of the Australian philosopher Peter Singer (b. 1946), whose book *Animal Liberation* (1975) was a landmark in this field of debate and who is highly critical of Christianity.

- A consequentialist principle is in play when experimentation on animals is justified for the sake of significant *medical* progress that will be of benefit to humans (though it can be affected by the numbers of animals involved, and the degree and nature of the pain inflicted). But it is equally in play when, for example, people dismiss the value of experimentation on animals for the sake of developing *cosmetic* products. Health and beautification are here valued differently, and these valuations are then reflected in different consequentialist judgments.
- Another consequentialist approach argues that raising animals for meat is an inefficient use of scarce resources, since the use of land and agricultural products to produce feed grains for animals is highly inefficient when compared to the production of vegetable protein. At a time when many people are starving, it is often argued, the change to a vegetarian diet is imperative.

Subversive

Subversive ethics may choose to defend the interests of animals (as a notional group) in ways that are analogous to the defense of other minority or oppressed groups, and thus (as we have already noted) they may use the language of rights. In a way that shares much with the "strong" version of the deontological approach outlined above, subversive ethics may refuse the sort of utilitarian calculus that justifies certain sorts of animal experimentation; it will hold that the rights of individual animals are not expendable. Peter Singer may be identified in this camp as well as in the universal one, when he compares certain attitudes to animals with racism. Just as racists violate the principle of equality by giving priority to the interests of members of their own race, so human "speciesists" do not accept that pain is as bad when it is felt by a primate or a mouse or a bird as when it is felt by a human.

Certain subversive approaches promote the idea that exclusion of humans from nature is the only means of controlling their inherent tendencies to abuse and degrade their environment. A good example of this is the insistence by advocates of a radical animal-rights position that humans should not be involved with the keeping of animals in any way.

Ecclesial

After making the animals, God spoke to them: "Be fruitful and multiply and fill the waters in the seas …" (Genesis 1:22). The verbs are in the imperative form so they belong to the language of address, not just of *statement about* something in the world. By speaking to creation in this way, God seems to establish the possibility of reciprocal address. We may conclude that the non-human creatures that surround us are in their own right objects of God's love and regard, and can relate and respond to God independently of humans.

Psalm 104 tells us that the Lord rejoices in all created things. If there is to be a serious recognition that the *lex orandi* (rule of prayer) should be allowed to shape the *lex credendi* (rule of belief), then maybe the liturgy ought to teach Christians that they should not seek to shape and direct the ends of other animals unless there is first a recognition that they are fellow creatures in relationship to God (even, potentially, friends). "The Church has been singing and praying for centuries in terms that clearly specify that all things have a voice; why not take that seriously?" asks Stephen Clark (b. 1945; Professor Emeritus of the University of Liverpool).

This might lead an ecclesial ethics to commend vegetarianism as a proper form of Christian discipline, as it is for Stephen Clark – particularly given the feasibility today of finding equivalent nutrition from other non-animal sources: "Vegetarianism is now as necessary a pledge of moral devotion as was the refusal of emperor-worship in the early Church. … Those who still eat flesh when they could do otherwise have no claim to be serious moralists." For some, the point here is the conviction that sacrifice has come to an end in Christ, and there is thus no need for the ritual slaughter by which animals lay down their lives so that humans may live.

On the other hand, some ecclesial approaches would argue, Christians know that God intends their use of creaturely goods, and it is not possible this side of the eschaton to live without incurring some expense to the lives of others (non-human and – inevitably – human as well). We cannot pass through the world and leave no footprint. This was the instinct that seems to have informed Karl Barth's (1886–1968) attitude: yes, there will be no more killing of non-human animals by human ones in the eschatological state, but until then we have to accept that we live fallenly, and we cannot be too precious about that. But in the light of the doctrine of the resurrection this is not a paralyzing thought, for Christians know from the proclamation of Christ's resurrection that God's power can transform and restore all of God's creatures in a life that does not end, and they rejoice that this hope has been bestowed on all matter, not just human mammals.

Crops

Even an ethic extended to incorporate sentient creatures like animals will risk leaving out of the picture the non-sentient forms of life that surround us. These include trees and microorganisms, vegetables and coral. Again, and perhaps even more than in relation to animals, there is a tendency to value them only insofar as they are of use to humans – and it is to counter this that the principles of biocentrism and ecocentrism have been proposed, to encompass more in the circle of what is regarded as having a moral status. Nonetheless this section concerns primarily the land and its edible plants – in other words, the complex and inevitable human project of agriculture. While humans can survive without eating animals, they cannot survive without the bounty of the earth.

Scripture and Tradition

Just because Christianity seems to imply a special position for humanity, this does not imply that it devalues the rest of creation. They are inseparably linked. One of the characteristics of the environmental crisis is that it has caused the destruction of traditional ways of life of peoples as well as the spoiling of the earth. It can be argued that greater respect for human beings and human life, as created in the image of God and dignified by the incarnation of Christ, ought for Christians to lead to an increased rather than diminished view of the importance of the non-human creation.

Biblically derived attitudes to the land and its output affirm the goodness of the earth – in its plant life just as in its animal life – but regard the Fall as bringing a curse on the ground, making human food-producing activity frustrating and burdensome (Gen 3:17–19). The hope for a restored creation has room in it for a vision of a new quality of untrammeled joy in the fruitfulness of the land. The prophet Isaiah's vision of the new heavens and new earth that God promises includes restoration of the fruits of labor to the workers: "they will plant vineyards and eat their fruits" (65:21).

Old Testament scholar Ellen Davis (b. 1950), professor at Duke Divinity School, has shown how concern for the care of the land is deeply embedded throughout the Old Testament. She argues that the biblical writers are pervasively agrarian – that is, they are always interested in how the flourishing of the community "is based on the health of the land and of living creatures." Indeed, the fruitfulness of the land is inextricably linked to Israel's faithfulness: if Israel does not obey God, "Your land will not give its produce, and the trees of the land will not give their fruit" (Lev 26:20). Particularly in the Old Testament, the Bible teaches that the justice people embody or disregard in their dealings with one another – and thus the health or ill-health of the human community – is deeply connected to the health or ill-health of the whole creation. To take one example from many that might be chosen, here are some words from Isaiah:

> Ah, you who join house to house, who add field to field, until there is room for no one but you, and you are left to live alone in the midst of the land! The Lord of hosts has sworn in my hearing: surely many houses shall be desolate, large and beautiful houses, without inhabitant. For ten acres of vineyard shall yield but one bath, and a homer of seed shall yield a mere ephah. (Isa 5:8–10)

For this reason, many discussions of how to grow and sell crops ethically in the Christian tradition come under the broad purview of discussions of economic justice. These themes are discussed at greater length in Chapter Nine.

Contemporary Debate

Agriculture has, thus, always been a part of business. But modern agriculture has become *big* business. The products of agriculture are traded on world markets; the producers can be huge multinational corporations – and increasingly so in this era of genetically modified (GM) crops, which are intended to produce greater and more reliable yields. Supporters of GM crops will argue that there is more to them than a desire to manage agricultural outputs more effectively and make them more lucrative; they argue that they will be a benefit to poor farmers whose crops are vulnerable to disease or adverse weather conditions, and who cannot afford to lose a harvest. Critics of GM foods say:

1. that they reduce biodiversity;
2. that the world can produce enough food already to feed the poor, so that the problem lies with our systems of justice, not with our crops in themselves (richer countries protect their agriculture and export domestic surpluses on the world market, making it difficult for poor countries); and
3. that the science is not yet well enough understood for us to know what the long-term effects will be – whether effects on other plants or on consumers – of releasing new strains of GM plant life into circulation.

The fact remains that, alongside expanding agricultural giants in the modern world, there remain countless tiny subsistence growers who are extremely vulnerable. The rising cost of fertilizers, high-yielding seeds, and irrigation projects, all tied to Western technology, are often beyond the reach of farmers in the developing world; they are frequently the monopoly of agribusiness.

The issue of world hunger has emerged into stark prominence as a problem for world economics in recent decades, its starkness matched only by its complexity. Surplus and famine are world economic facts, and, as we have just noted, international markets seem incapable of appropriate sensitivity to the needs of national and local economies – many of them subsistence economies. Hunger is also sometimes the result of short-sighted patterns of land use by local populations. Forests are cut down for fuel or to satisfy the land needs of expanding populations. The results of this include erosion of topsoil during the rains and consequent desertification.

One of the areas of controversy in relation to world hunger is what level of responsibility the richer nations should (or can afford to) have for the poorer ones. Most Christian ethicists, believing that world hunger is the world's largest solvable health problem – because of the food surpluses that exist and the powers of planning that are available – hold that the world's rich should be finding more creative ways to defend the needs of the world's poor. It is generally agreed that outdated models of "aid" will not do. There needs also to be empowerment of those in the poorer countries, whose choice of which crops to grow – both historically (from as far back as missionary times) and today – has too often been dictated from outside by the desires of a more affluent West.

In Chapter Nine we saw how certain strands of Christian ethics (like that represented by William F. May) use the biblical notion of covenant as a basis for advocating truer kinds of economic justice. Covenant relationships require those in the more powerful position of a covenant partnership to assume some responsibility for those who are more vulnerable in the partnership. Attempts to promote fair-trade practices in agriculture, as in other areas of trade, seem on this basis to embody much that is covenantal, based as they are around establishing economic partnerships for mutual benefit. *Relationship* is at the heart of this model – and especially the relationship between the grower of food and the buyer of food. This contrasts the fair-trade model with models that emphasize a more impersonal and contractarian exchange of money for goods. The latter model ends up instrumentalizing the producer.

As we noted in the previous section of this chapter, there is also an important link between the way humans relate to their crops and the way humans relate to animals. The assumption that there is a right (or even a necessity) to kill animals for food may prevent a proper attention being given to the ways in which a sufficient variety of plant foods can fully substitute for such a diet. Humans in most parts of the world can be delivered of the need to get nutrition from animal flesh; they could invest in vegetarian agricultural systems on a much larger scale than they do, and at the same time dispense with the need to use land inefficiently to grow fodder for the animals being farmed for food. A comparable issue may be emerging today in relation to a market for biofuels. These too promise to be land-greedy, and could fail to serve the need of the poor to eat whilst pandering to the desire of the rich to burn energy.

Universal

There are two main areas in which a universal approach operates in this sphere of ethics. One has to do with the economics of food production and distribution, and is therefore focused on the just actions of people. The other is to do with the intrinsic value and nature of crops and the land they grow in, and is thus a subset of discussions about the ethical status of plant life and the earth more generally.

1. *Crops and justice.* Christian ethicists apply principles of justice to the production of plants for food just as they do to other areas of economic activity. Encouraging fair trade is often promoted on the basis of equity; food aid from areas of plenty to areas of need is seen as an imperative on the basis that the human community has a basic obligation to preserve the dignity and life of the most vulnerable. If modern technology has made it possible for a small percentage of people to produce enormous quantities of food and for agriculture to be almost independent of weather shocks, then (on the principle of neighbor-love if nothing else) it is argued that Christians should work for the transference of such skills and technology to needy areas. Poor countries should be assisted to develop productive agricultural systems that can be sustained by indigenous skills and resources, so that they are not perpetually reliant on aid, and are not kept dependent on Western technology that sells them their fertilizers, irrigation systems, and GM seeds.

Some Christians call for a simpler lifestyle in affluent countries, as a response to the needs of hunger and economic development in poor countries. Again the principle here is often that of solidarity with the vulnerable neighbor, whose rights to food and health and opportunities for self-direction are the same as the more affluent neighbor. Those who recognize that the impact of such a response will be minimal unless it is combined with political action (the promotion of more just trade relations, for example, or discouragement of the arms trade in which many of the governments of poor countries invest in preference to agriculture) are adopting a subversive stance but nonetheless often also relying on universalist appeals to fairness.

2.   *Crops and the earth.* We saw in our discussion of management ethics in Chapter Nine how the tool of cost–benefit analysis is often used as a way of trying to quantify and balance the tension between immediate land use for exploding populations and long-term needs of conserving the environment. Underlying this attitude, however, is an intuition that organic life of all kinds can be ascribed some sort of ethical status. As we have seen, it usually comes down in practice to (changeable) sets of human preferences, but some ethicists would argue that plants of all kinds (crops included) have a value that is not reducible to their bare use-value for us. Some would argue that the diversity of plants is a good thing in itself – an achievement of a fecund and generative earth which is to be treasured.

Consequentialist varieties of approach to crop production are evident in those who argue for:

a.   the dangers of a reduction in biodiversity on the grounds that having fewer genetic strains of any particular plant will result in it having a diminished base from which to resist as yet unforeseen diseases; and

b.   the dangers of human over-reliance on a small number of food types or sources, in case one of them fails.

The example is often given here of the Irish potato famine in the mid-nineteenth century, during which a breed of potato blight wiped out the majority of that country's potatoes at a stroke and caused untold deaths from starvation.

Similar consequentialist arguments will be used in relation to the long-term dangers of over-intensive farming. The land cannot be "flogged to death," it is argued; at some point it will go on strike or even bite back if it is driven too hard. We need a more developed sense of the delicate reciprocity of our relationship with it, and with what grows on it, and this will evolve sensitivity and responsiveness.

Arguments both for and against GM crops also tend to be consequentialist in character, the former highlighting the positive benefits of GM crops especially to poorer parts of the world, and the latter warning of anticipated and unintended consequences such as irreversible damage to non-modified crops or unforeseen dangers to human health.

Subversive

From the 1970s through to the end of the twentieth century, the apparent increase in numbers of those in absolute poverty (despite the focus on developmental aid in the 1960s and beyond) helped fuel a new focus on changing the underlying exploitative structures that appeared to be perpetuating the poverty gap in the modern world, and keeping millions of people hungry. Some pointed out that hunger often results less from scarcity of food per se and more from the ravages of war and unjust distribution of land and wealth. The Millennium Development Goals adopted by the United Nations in 2000 focused not only on poverty but also on underlying issues such as maternal health and primary education, especially for girls. These goals seemed to have had some success, since by some measurements absolute poverty worldwide fell significantly between 1990 and 2015.

In the course of these changes, theological categories like justice and righteousness have replaced those of compassion and benevolence at center stage, and voices from the developing world itself have been more assertive in making themselves heard. The notion of liberation has come increasingly to the fore; the Exodus paradigm of escape from slavery is more often cited; and the powerlessness of the poor has become the heartbeat of theological reflection (see Chapter Six). There is passionate, and sometimes revolutionary, critique that attacks the vested interests it sees in the present world system of land use: Michael Northcott highlights "the corporate and inter-governmental calculus which sets as a price for international debt repayment the systematic clear-cutting of ancient forests and the environmental exclusion of peasant farmers and tribal peoples from their ancestral lands."

The ecofeminist work of Rosemary Radford Ruether (b. 1936; see the "Gender" section of Chapter Six) argues for a profound rethinking of the way in which even "domestic" or cultivated land is used to grow things so as to link such land use more explicitly to issues of justice. The church should be an exemplar of this radical approach, she argues:

> The vision … needs to flow out in our stewardship of the land and the church buildings, as well as through a community praxis of recycling and conservation of energy. It can be expressed in the transformation of our lands from wasteful overwatered lawns to natural grasses and permaculture gardens to help feed the poor. And it needs to be communicated through the public policy advocacy of church members and bodies seeking ecological health together with social justice.

Ecclesial

In the Orthodox liturgy the cross is printed on the loaf that is used in the Eucharist (just as it often is on Eucharistic wafers in traditions where wafers are used). If the bread is a sign of creaturely reality and of human beings' work with the things of creation, then the sign of the cross shows their proper dedication to God. "With this sign," Dumitru Staniloae (1903–93) writes, "the priest blesses the water of Baptism, and also the holy water with which he sprinkles the house, the fields and the whole world in which the Christian lives and works – all is covered with the sign of the cross."

Christians see that all living things – plants as well as animals – have an origin in God's goodness and a direct relationship with God. Their value is real, and irreducible, inasmuch as it springs from God's love and regard. The things of the earth are known and recognized as gifts; they do not become just things in themselves without any meaning as signs of God's love. Neither are the things of the earth valued for the mere usefulness that human beings have from them.

From an ecclesial point of view, the handing over of created things at the offertory (not just money, but bread and wine too) is a way of letting them be what God wants them to be, rather than what human beings wish to make them. But it is manifestly not a losing of all relationship with those goods (though it is, it may be argued, a surrender of the proprietary will). The gifts come back in a way that is miraculously new, and nourishing. If Christians have learned to see in the offertory gifts the symbols of the whole creation, then they receive the creation back too – not as what they wish to make it, but as a creation that God has a relationship with (it is God's more than it could ever be ours; it is ours only inasmuch as we too relate to God). This does not eliminate human agency. Human beings still have responsibility. The offering itself is something they genuinely do; the gifts are in their charge even if they are not theirs by some entitlement. And although God relates to the things of creation in their own right, they are nevertheless restored to people for their good. The nourishment people receive from them is intended for them, and, nourished in this fashion, they are to live in changed and responsible ways.

Hope in the resurrection means that Christians are less bound, in their attitude to the things that grow in the earth they inhabit, by a determination to survive at all costs and grab what can be grabbed – or hoard what can be hoarded. They are more ready to give things up and set aside their immediate preferences (for, as Staniloae says, "attachment to the things of this world is felt particularly strongly by those who do not believe that there is any further transformation of this world after the life which we now know"). If there appears to be scarcity, the worshipping practices of Christians ought to teach them "to want only what can easily and justly be obtained, to live in a way that is alert to our dependence on a fruitful world, and on the grace of God" (Stephen Clark). This too is a habit learnt in the offertory.

For Samuel Wells (b. 1965), the Eucharist is the central Christian practice by which Christians learn to distribute and share food. Wells notes that God is already in the business of "modifying" food, by transforming bread and wine into the body and blood of Christ. Thus, the morality of GM crops is to be tested by asking whether they "prefigure the kingdom by enabling a greater sharing of food and power among all God's people," therefore creating more just communities. Or, do GM foods represent a rival form of the transformation of food, one which perpetuates injustice and "dismantles the social relations made possible by the Eucharist"? For ecclesial ethics, these are the true tests for determining how Christians should approach GM crops.

Ecology

Scripture and Tradition

It can be argued that specific focus on an ethics of the environment, and the idea that ecological systems may be objects of ethical regard, is a distinctively modern phenomenon made more acute by the sense of environmental crisis that now prevails. There is therefore less that can be pointed to directly in Scripture and tradition that deals with "ecology." It is a concept that has been developed and refined in a contemporary context. Nevertheless, as we already noted in our section on animals, Jesus in the New Testament preaches God's providential care for all creation (Matt 6:26; Luke 12:24). Scripture also indicates that the entire created order participates in the worship of God, when the psalmist writes that "The heavens are telling the glory of God; ... their voice goes out through all the earth" (Psalm 19:1, 4); when the prophet Isaiah declares that the mountains and hills shall burst into song, and the trees of the field clap their hands, to welcome Israel home from exile (Isaiah 55:12); and when Jesus claims that the stones would shout God's praises if his disciples remained silent (Luke 19:40). And when the New Testament's vision expands to its most cosmic scale, it seems clear that the sacrifice of Christ is for the redemption of the whole of groaning creation, human and non-human alike: for everything that lives (Rom 8:19–22; Col 1:20; Eph 1:10). The eschaton, or the new age in which humans dwell face to face with God, is described not as a disembodied heaven but as a re-creation, a new heavens and a new *earth* (Rev 21:1).

Contemporary Debate

Something in the order of a mass extinction of plant and animal species is underway across the globe. This is the latest of several mass extinctions in the earth's history, but it is distinctive in that an animal – *Homo sapiens* – is playing a key role in bringing it about.

1. The rate of extinction of species is at around 10,000 per year. Biodiversity – as we remarked in the previous section – has been drastically reduced by deforestation, deep sea fishing, destruction of coral reefs, and use of pesticides.
2. Climate change is accelerating, and is especially being caused by the burning of fossil fuels for heating, transportation, and electricity production. This is leading to rising sea levels, increasing numbers of cyclones, and the melting of the Antarctic ice shelf.

3.   Pollution is widespread in oceans, rivers, air, and soil – clear indicators of its coming effects are a plunging reduction in the frog population and the reduced growth rate of trees. Chlorofluorocarbon (CFC) emissions have led to an expanding hole in the ozone layer and consequent skin cancers in humans and mammals, especially in countries like Chile and New Zealand, which are close to the Antarctic ozone hole.

4.   As we also noted when discussing crops, soil erosion and desertification have been steadily increasing, linked to overgrazing, industrial tillage, and the use of inappropriate land (e.g., hillsides) for arable production.

That is how environmental ethicist Michael Northcott summarizes the present state of play. The Christian philosopher Stephen Clark has, if anything, an even bleaker summary, drawing on the work of the scientist E. O. Wilson:

> We do not know – and probably will not know until it is far too late – if too many key species are being eliminated for the whole to survive in any form hospitable to us. "One planet, one experiment." ... Sometime in the next century, we will have pulled so many threads out from life's tapestry that the whole begins to fray. We have already made inevitable a climate change that is likely to drown millions and starve millions more. The bacterial and invertebrate population of the planet will no doubt adjust. Human beings have been trying to live "at the top of the food chain," as if they were large carnivores, despite the obvious truth that carnivores are always scarcer than their prey. We have been trying to secure things for ourselves despite the obvious truth that everything we have and relish is the product of a system that we do not understand and cannot replace. The only sort of species that has much hope of survival is one without delusions of grandeur ...

Many of the "stories" that purport to orientate people in relation to these issues leave much to be desired. Two key ones rehearse the freedom–determinism dialectic that we outlined in the opening part of this chapter – that is, the tension between regarding humans as self-directing agents and humans as determined by forces beyond their control. The story of freedom largely plays into an ethics of management, whereas the determinist story is the product of an immanentist outlook.

1.   *Freedom (= Management)*. In the terms of the freedom–determinism dialectic, much ecological decision-making operates with the idea that the natural world needs *management*. The idea of management was discussed in Chapter Nine, where we touched briefly on its use in relation to ecological issues, and it has already appeared a little earlier in this present chapter. A management approach to ecological issues does not necessarily view nature's "uncontrolled forces" as a threat to human freedom, but it at least views these forces as a problem that needs to be dealt with. There is no language here for the basic goodness of creation.

The management model of response can take a variety of forms. At one extreme there is a fatalism about the impossibility of changing the voracious and destructive human demand for more and more goods and services, whatever the cost to ecosystems and the species that depend on them. The best hope humans have is to trust that their technological skills will permit them to adapt if and when they make the planet a desert. Human beings may, in other words, have to make for themselves artificial environments when they have destroyed their "real" one. Perhaps these will be in space, or in carefully sealed bubbles on the earth. A side effect of this imagined future might well also be gross inequality between those who can afford to inhabit these carefully engineered spaces, and those who must face the worst consequences of a consumption they barely, if ever, had a chance to participate in. Like the residents of present-day "gated communities," only the relatively powerful and wealthy will be able to afford the security and privilege of comfortable survival.

At the other extreme there is a utopian vision, with all its attendant implausibility, that foresees a new visionary state of affairs in which there are radical changes in the way that people treat each other and the world around them, and large corporations behave with impeccable ethical accountability. A few environmentalists hold to this paradigm as realizable, at least in principle; but, as more and more people in some of the largest countries in the world (China and India, in particular) seize with enthusiasm their first opportunities to drive their children to and from school, thus at long last tasting the way of life so long envied in the developed West, the odds seem stacked against a sudden, worldwide change of heart. Corporations anxious to market the products associated with such a "successful" way of life simply and ruthlessly exploit such desires.

2.   *Determinism (= Immanentism)*. Another dominant "story" by which a non-theological environmental ethic frequently tries to orientate itself is what we might call the immanentist one. Immanentism is the stance that no evaluation of natural goods or natural rights is permitted to make appeal to anything outside the material world itself, and humans are viewed as wholly embedded in its processes. The inexorable processes of the material world can be described as the "world-system." This is therefore more on the determinism side of the freedom–determinism dialectic, since humans cannot resist or rise above the processes of the natural world.

Immanentist stories can variously assume scientific and mystical guises, and sometimes represent a mixture of the two. The more hard-line scientific versions of immanentism are well known and often polemical: for example, those of the British atheist biologist Richard Dawkins (b. 1941), who upholds a resolutely Darwinian evolutionary account of the world and its processes. The more mystical extremes echo the habits of mind of the Romanticism of a previous era, and counsel an effacement of human concerns before the oracular, self-regulating wisdom of Mother Nature. Her "utterances" represent the only viable source of both spiritual and aesthetic value for contemporary humanity.

These latter appeals can seem intellectually unsustainable. Critics argue that one cannot have it both ways – both denying any transcendent source of value, form, and meaning, and at the same time wanting to keep goodness, beauty, and truth in play. And one cannot presume a secure basis for honoring human persons (and individual creatures) and their projects and desires when ultimately everything is "world-process" inexorably unfolding toward its own end. Rather, the honest logical conclusion of this immanentism must be what is sometimes called "eco-fascism": a pejorative term that describes a state of affairs in which individuals are required to subject themselves to, or even sacrifice themselves for, the sake of the land. As John Milbank (whose work we considered in Chapter Seven) notes, even if we are the strongest and cleverest of animals, we are bound "to gloriously submit ourselves to the yet stronger, the planet as such, the self-maintaining totality." The danger of pure immanentism is resignation to death and redundancy, to the "natural law" of competition. "Exactly what, for such an outlook, inhibits an ecological fatalism of the kind which assumes that humanity's gloriously natural self-vaunting is doomed to an equally natural demise, although the planet will continue, at least for aeons?" asks Milbank.

The Christian story seems to contrast with the immanentist one, because the immanentist has no reason to anchor the truth, goodness, or beauty of any individual being (or relation) anywhere other than in the immanent processes and struggles of the "world-system." This means that the immanentist can only believe in particular interests or preferences, not in absolute value. Inasmuch as there is any arbiter of value, it is the "world-system" itself, but this is only to say that what will be will be, which is to enthrone fate – a Stoic policy (see the discussion of Stoic ethics in Chapter Three). Human perceptions of what is right or glorious, human loves and attachments to things of the creation, can be no different from the interests or preferences of any other life-form competing to survive. So the immanentist's enjoyment of material goods is shadowed by the acute sense of their transitoriness, and the belief that the enjoyment itself is at best a "phenomenon" generated largely accidentally by a process that has not the slightest regard for the happiness of persons.

Universal

Part of the problem afflicting present environmental decision-making, as the British ethicist Michael Banner (b. 1961; Dean of Trinity College, Cambridge) points out in a 1999 essay, is a crisis in *how* to value the environment – before any particular practical decisions get made about what to do in this or that situation. There is genuine confusion at the present time about where the environment's complex values derive from and how they are to be measured. This is part of a larger modern debate, and a variety of matrices for the attribution of value have been put forward (cost–benefit analysis being one somewhat unsatisfactory one, as we have seen; an earlier one was Marx's, in which labor determined all value).

A relatively optimistic outlook on environmental challenges hopes that policy interventions by benign governments, and the introduction of internationally agreed regulatory frameworks and planning processes, will temper human greed and avert the worst consequences of our current excess. This depends on governments actually sticking to the frameworks upon which they agree, and being prepared to accept the consequences of electoral unpopularity for measures that restrict consumer freedom. (It also risks a more bureaucratic and state-interventionist world.) One example of this approach is the 2015 Paris Agreement, in which 195 nations agreed to take specific actions aimed at reducing global warming. Meanwhile the notion of "sustainable development" seems to rest on a similarly optimistic assessment of the ability of businesses (or governments) to rein in their own self-interest.

Christian ethicists working in a universal vein may promote modified versions of the managerial (free) or immanentist (determined) positions outlined above. Christian ethicists are less likely to adopt a version of the immanentist position, since (as noted above) immanentist views tend to clash with Christian understandings of creation, truth, and divine transcendence. A Christian version of the determinist pole will be anxious to stop short of anything that might be mistaken for eco-fascism, but *will* be open to more "holistic" or organic understandings of the whole natural order in its complex interrelatedness. The moral claims of "nature-as-a-whole" are argued on the basis that it is "a creative, life-sustaining process, the well-functioning of which is not only vital to but constitutive of human and non-human well-being"; so says the contemporary American theologian Richard Fern.

Fern calls nature-as-a-whole "sentiotic," by which he means that, as an inter-related totality, it is productive and purposeful. He describes the sentiotic character of nature in this way: "Affirming the sentiotic goodness of nature does not depend on a belief in God, let alone a theodicy. All that it requires is a belief that wild nature has an inherent proclivity to well-being." But it is seen by some ethicists as wholly compatible with a Christian outlook, and with the idea that God endowed nature with an order and a self-correcting agency that are part of its original God-given goodness. There are ways to live with or against the grain of this self-regulating whole, and a consequentialist argument will say that to live against it is against our own species' interests, because we will become the problem that the system has to correct – in a sort of ecological "judgment."

Meanwhile some Christian ethicists have promoted modified versions of the managerial (free) position. Their version of the freedom pole will incline less to "management" and more to a concept we have already introduced in the section on animals: stewardship. This principle of "stewardship" is commonly assumed to be one that has a general applicability in non-theological discourses, even though its roots are traced to the divine charge in Genesis to live close to the earth and exercise appropriate dominion over it. Its advantage over a strong management model is that it is less a celebration of the omnicompetence of human ingenuity and organization, and more a matter of responsiveness and care. Stewardship is often assumed to be a more palatable concept than dominion, which people tend to think of as domination or abusive exercise of power. But "dominion" in a biblical sense does not necessarily imply any of the baggage of individual "proprietary right" – and therefore possessive domination – that has established itself in the modern period; it may be something far more like the shared possession of the first-century Christian communities described in Acts 2. Old Testament scholar Ellen Davis proposes that humans are meant to have "mastery among" the rest of creation rather than "dominion over" creation in Gen 1:28, with mastery connoting the role of a shepherd who travels along with his flock to guide and protect it. And the concept of stewardship itself has its dangers. A steward looks after someone else's chattels, or personal possessions, and to view the non-human parts of creation as God's chattels is perhaps to make them less fully the object of a loving and relational divine regard than they should be. Other terminology has become more common, including "creation care," responsibility, and interdependence or mutuality.

Another universal approach especially found in Catholic social teaching is an appeal to the concept of the common good. Pope Francis gave his 2015 encyclical *Laudato Si'* the English title "On Care for Our Common Home" and addressed it to "every person living on this planet." In its appeals to the common good and the social mortgage, its calls for dialogue at the local and international levels with science and with people of all religions or faith commitments, and its claim that access to fresh water is "a basic and universal human right," it draws on various universalist concepts. Yet it also gestures to subversive commitments when it observes that environmental degradation harms the poor the most, and when it issues a plea to hear "both the cry of the earth and the cry of the poor." Finally, the encyclical also has an ecclesial element. Its Latin title is drawn from Francis of Assisi's "Canticle of the Sun": *Laudato Si'* means "Praise be to you," and it invokes Francis's view of nature "as a magnificent book in which God speaks to us and offers us a glimpse of his infinite beauty and goodness" in order to claim that the world is not "a problem to be solved" but rather "a joyful mystery to be contemplated with gladness and praise."

Subversive

The American historian Lynn White Jr., writing in 1967, described Western medieval Christianity as the most anthropocentric religion the world has ever seen. This is a strong statement of an evaluation that is nonetheless widely held: that Christianity's anthropocentrism has underwritten a domineering and exploitative attitude to the non-human world, and that its preoccupation with linear historical progress has led it to prize technological advances over attunement to the cyclical rhythms of the earth. Evangelical Christian ethics particularly has struggled against the notion sometimes present in fundamentalist thought that this present earth is dispensable because it will be destroyed by divine fire at the end of history and then re-created *ex nihilo* by God.

Some Christian ethicists have aligned themselves with just these criticisms of their own tradition – and thereby also the criticisms of the ecological attitudes of a Western world. Other Christian ethicists working in a subversive vein would temper White's claims, finding within the Christian tradition itself resources of justice and liberation that may be applied not only to the oppression of humans but to the oppression of the earth *by* humans.

A central example of a subversive approach to the environment is "ecofeminism," a term that covers a broad and diverse global movement. Despite this diversity, however, it can be pointed to as having taken a lead role in subverting accepted models of ecological thinking. These include even those of other sorts of subversive ethics. Race- and class-based theologies of liberation, for example, have not always led the way in addressing ecological issues – although this is beginning to change as ecowomanism takes shape (more on that below). In parts of India and Latin America, women have used ecofeminist theology to critique the ecological inadequacies of such male-dominated liberation theologies, as well as of secular environmental policies. Ecofeminists are committed to the interconnectedness of living beings, often described by images such as the "web of life." The movement thus pushes the boundaries of the liberation movement to include all earthly life.

Ecofeminism has argued that there are disturbing connections between the abuse of the earth (which is often described in feminine terms, as Mother Earth) and the abuse of women. In practical terms, it claims that women are often those first affected by environmental change, for example, when they have to walk further to collect water. But it also sees a deeper ideological connection between the habits of mind that promote the exploitation of nature and those that foster the domination of women. In both cases a dualistic mindset has been at work – one that has set human beings in hierarchical opposition to non-human nature just as men have set themselves in hierarchical contradistinction to women.

One of the most influential representatives of ecofeminism is the North American theologian Sallie McFague (b. 1933), who asserts provocatively in the title of one of her books that the earth is *The Body of God*. But ecofeminism has roots in a variety of religious and spiritual traditions in different parts of the world.

Just as womanism adds issues of race to feminist thought, and challenges feminism to take the experiences of black women into account, so also ecowomanism comes alongside ecofeminism to include questions of race in its examination of gender and the environment. As with ecofeminism, it is shaped both by elements of the Christian tradition and by African and Native American cosmologies, which it often views as more adaptable to feminist and womanist concerns. Ecowomanist writers have been at the forefront of identifying the complex intersection of race, class, and gender in environmental issues – for example, by unearthing examples of environmental racism, or the phenomenon that low-income and minority communities are much more likely to dwell in proximity to toxic waste and to polluted air, water, and soil. (See Chapter Six for a longer discussion of ecofeminism and ecowomanism.)

Ecclesial

An ecclesial approach looks for ways in which what goes on inside the church may address, judge, and offer resources for repairing the relationship between human agents and their natural environment. The church uses physical things to convey God's grace, and this use has a significance for the way Christians look on the natural world. They cannot ignore the fact that the water that is used to incorporate people into the church through baptism is the same water that human beings pollute; that the bread eaten in the Eucharist is denied to many in the world while others are overfed; that countries go to war over oil while Christians use it to anoint – and so on. Every act of sacramental worship makes an ecological statement about the proper ends to which Christians put the resources of the natural world.

We have already noted the instructiveness of the offertory for an ecological ethics when talking about crops. Bread and wine are brought to the altar in procession, from amongst the people, in the same way that collection money is. This liturgical action stresses that fact that bread and wine are also, like money, the product of human labors in the context of God's gracious provision (God's provision of the conditions we need for the work of our hands to prosper). The words said over the bread and wine in some traditions make this even more explicit:

> Blessed are you, Lord God of all creation; through your goodness we have this bread to offer, which earth has given and human hands have made. It will become for us the bread of life. Blessed are you, Lord God of all creation; through your goodness we have this wine to offer, fruit of the vine and the work of human hands. It will become for us the cup of salvation.

And in each case the people respond: "Blessed be God forever." In these liturgical exchanges the congregation learns to think about the whole creation (in connection with these specific gifts of the creation) as belonging to God ("Lord God of all creation"). It learns in appropriate humility to acknowledge that it "has" these gifts only because of life-giving forces wholly in excess of its own control ("through your goodness"; "which earth has given"). The congregation learns to make its offering in the trust that God's goodness will reciprocate in ways that amaze it and confound normal expectations ("it will become for us the bread of life"; "it will become for us the cup of salvation"). And it learns to set this whole interaction in the context of divine praise ("Blessed be God"), so that the focus is never on the objects of exchange in their own right, but on the God who is the divine subject of this giving and receiving. The Orthodox theologian Dumitru Staniloae is alert to this danger of focusing only on the objects and not their source, because it threatens to affect the way that human beings handle all the things of the earth:

> The world is a gift of God, but the destiny of this gift is to unite man with God who has given it. The intention of the gift is that in itself it should be continually transcended. When we receive a gift from somebody we should look primarily towards the person who has given it and not keep our eyes fixed on the gift. But often the person who receives a gift becomes so attached to the gift that he forgets who has given it to him.

The offertory is a powerful antidote to this tendency to forget the giver.

Perhaps more than anywhere in Christian liturgy, this moment of the "presentation of the gifts" highlights the possibilities latent in material things – the things of the earth, God's non-human creatures. They are themselves to be the vehicles of "life" and "salvation." They are treated with reverence (carried in procession, no less) and placed on the altar. And the overriding emphasis is that they are not our servants, they are God's blessings, and it is by God's relation to them (not our manipulation of them) that they bring life. This is the way ecclesial ethics disciplines what it sees as the pretensions of management approaches.

If God's work in Christ, made present in the Eucharist, is a work of reassembly – the display of a surprising ordering of things – then just as at Christmas God reassembles man and woman, kings and working people, stars and animals, heaven and earth in a way that makes Christmas thoroughly eschatological, just so in the Eucharist God reassembles the dispersed characters of creation in a way that shows their true relations in the light of their ultimate end. In the Eucharist's ordering of creation, humanity is shown to be that part of creation that does not wield supreme manipulative mastery over it, but that brings creation's fruits to the altar in a Eucharistic act that is humanity's highest calling (the offering of praise and thanksgiving). Humanity has to nurture, foster, care for the creation precisely so that it can fulfill this specially human task in the context of the creation's whole ecology of praise – the task of offering creation at the altar to be blessed. In this perspective, humanity does not nurture, foster, and care for the creation because otherwise humanity would die out (the consequentialist move); it does so because otherwise humanity (and through it the world) could not fully realize its Eucharistic calling – could not fully celebrate the Eucharist.

For ecclesial ethicists, there is a particular sort of humility to be learnt in seeing oneself as part of such an ecology. Moreover, Christians are cautious about making claims about their own knowledge of the future. God lets Christians live with a strong awareness of where things have come from originally (from God's goodness) and of what their "end" is (God's glory), but they are ready to be surprised by what happens in the interim. What God does with the gifts placed on the altar is not a mechanical function of cause and effect, it is an act of grace. This is the way an ecclesial ethics disciplines the fatalism of immanentist approaches. What God will do with the creation, even in the manifest crisis in which it is now embroiled, is not wholly predictable by the faithful believer. Christians should perhaps be ready to live with uncertainty, though not with despair, about specific outcomes in relation to the immediate or even medium-term future of the environment. They can be realistic about the seriousness of present circumstances and the limits of their ability to change them (we are humans, not deities), yet deeply hopeful that God can make all things new, and utterly committed to doing what they can to make that hope visible in the present.

An acute part of the difficulty facing environmentalists at the moment is the near-impossibility of making decisions that are in common. The uniting factor is often little more than an agreement to survive. Some Christian ethicists, notably Pope Francis in *Laudato Si'* and Yale theologian Willis Jenkins, call on diverse religious traditions to bring their own resources to bear cooperatively on the ecological crisis, without requiring any prior agreement on the metaphysical nature of the created world. Others argue that it is only with such a common mind that we can approach the physical environment in a coherent way, shaping it for justice and beauty, but also for "convenience" – that is, for *conveniens*: for its fittingness, its supreme suitability to its true purpose, including the flourishing of the human that takes place in reciprocal and responsible relation to the flourishing of other creatures. Justice, beauty, and convenience "reflect and embody a common civic life: constitute, materially, a mode of human reciprocity collectively affirmed" (John Milbank). By God's grace, an ecclesial ethics will say, Christians have this common life in the form of the church, and should seek to foster it there for the sake of the world's salvation. God has given the church a form of life whereby it can identify objectives and goods "which technocratic and expert thinking cannot themselves determine" (Michael Banner). This form of life teaches Christians that the whole world belongs to God. It gives them the understanding, moreover, that the whole world has been (and is being) renewed in Christ, whose resurrection is the restoration of creaturely moral order. By the power of the Holy Spirit, who educates them in the church, they can learn how to use and enjoy it aright.

Summary

This chapter has considered the questions Christian ethics faces about the environment in three areas: animals, crops, and ecology. We noted that although there is material in the Bible that treats the relationship between human beings and the non-human creation, it does not emerge with full force as a distinct area of ethical thought until the twentieth century (with precursors in nineteenth-century Romantic thought). There are nevertheless rich resources in the church's liturgical tradition that suggest good ways of thinking and acting toward the environment. Liturgy often suggests that non-human creatures have an independent and reciprocal relation to God that is not reducible to human utility. The concept of human stewardship of natural goods makes best sense in the context of this sort of understanding – an understanding in which non-human creatures are first known as under *God's* dominion such that human beings' concern with them is related at every point to the natural world's final end in God's purposes. God's purposes are increasingly seen by recent Christian ethicists as being the mutual fellowship of the whole created order, within which human beings are just one interdependent part.

We outlined a number of ways in which contemporary thought about the environment maps its range of moral consideration: focusing variously on humans alone (in their relation to the natural world); on animals too; on all biological life; and on whole ecosystems. We tested the limits of the language of rights as it is borrowed from modern political and economic theory to do justice to these various levels of organic interdependence, noting that rights theory is a somewhat "thin" solution to a set of problems that is both intensely pressing and that requires a greater common mind about how and why the natural world should be respected, protected, and valued.

References and Further Reading

Michael Northcott's comments about personalism and environmentalism in the introduction to this chapter come from his essay "Ecology and Christian Ethics," in *The Cambridge Companion to Christian Ethics* (Robin Gill, ed.; Cambridge; New York: Cambridge University Press, 2001), page 217.

The papal encyclical *Laudato Si'* (On Care for Our Common Home) is available at https://laudatosi.com/watch; for the critique of anthropocentrism, see especially section 116.

Animals

David Atkinson offers a helpful outline to a Christian view of the right treatment of animals in the *New Dictionary of Christian Ethics and Pastoral Theology* (David J. Atkinson and David H. Field, eds; Leicester: InterVarsity Press, 1995), pages 745–7, which this chapter draws on in its introduction to the "Animals" section. We have also drawn on Andrew Linzey's contributions to *A New Dictionary of Christian Ethics* (John Macquarrie and James Childress, eds; London: SCM Press, 1986), pages 28–33, especially his points about the difficulty even scrupulous vegans face in avoiding indirect benefits from animal testing.

Tom Regan's work in this area can be found in *The Case for Animal Rights* (2nd edn; Berkeley, CA: University of California Press, 1983, 2004), and Peter Singer's important discussions from a non-Christian viewpoint are in *Animal Liberation* (rev. edn; New York: Avon Books, 1990).

Roger Scruton's principal work in this area is *Animal Rights and Wrongs* (3rd edn; London: Metro in association with Demos, 2000).

Stephen R. L. Clark is a Christian philosopher who has written passionately and sharply about the claims of the natural world upon us – and especially of animals. He is quoted several times in this chapter, from *Biology and Christian Ethics* (Cambridge Studies in Christian Ethics; Cambridge: Cambridge University Press, 2000). The extended quotation in the "Ecology" section of this chapter is from page 114 of that book.

Karl Barth's attitude toward animals is expressed in *Church Dogmatics* III.1 (Edinburgh: T & T Clark, 1975), pages 205–12.

In addition to the above, selections from the following works are included in the corresponding chapter of *Christian Ethics: An Introductory Reader*:

- Andrew Linzey. *Animal Theology*. Urbana and Chicago, IL: University of Illinois Press, 1995.
- Carol J. Adams. *Neither Man Nor Beast: Feminism and the Defense of Animals*. New York: Continuum, 1994.
- Stephen H. Webb. *Good Eating*. Grand Rapids, MI: Brazos Press, 2001.

Crops

Ellen F. Davis explores the agrarian view of the Old Testament writers in *Scripture, Culture, and Agriculture: An Agrarian Reading of the Bible* (Cambridge: Cambridge University Press, 2009); see pages 1 and 61 for specific citations.

Robert Song, drawing on William F. May, is our source for the discussion of *fair trade as covenantal*, from his essay "Sharing Communion: Hunger, Food, and Genetically Modified Foods," pages 388–400 in *The Blackwell Companion to Christian Ethics* (Stanley Hauerwas and Samuel Wells, eds; Oxford: Blackwell, 2004).

As in Chapter Nine, we have drawn on Michael Banner's book *Christian Ethics and Contemporary Moral Problems* (Cambridge: Cambridge University Press, 1999) when discussing cost–benefit analysis.

Michael S. Northcott's book *A Moral Climate: The Ethics of Global Warming* (London: Darton, Longman and Todd, 2007) is an important intervention in this area. It is included in the *Introductory Reader*. We have also drawn in this chapter on his essay in *The Cambridge Companion to Christian Ethics* (see above). The quotation "the corporate and inter-governmental calculus …" is from his essay "'Behold I have set the land before you' (Deut. 1.8): Christian Ethics, GM Foods and the Culture of Modern Farming," in *Re-ordering Nature: Theology, Society and the New*

Genetics (Celia Deane-Drummond, Bronislaw Szerszynski, and Robin Grove-White, eds; London: T & T Clark, 2003), page 106.

Rosemary Radford Ruether has written widely on ecological questions, and her works include *Gaia and God: An Ecofeminist Theology of Earth Healing* (New York: HarperCollins, 1994). We have also drawn in this chapter from her article "Ecojustice at the Center of the Church's Mission," IAMS, *Mission Studies* 16 (1999): 1–31.

Orthodox theologian Dumitru Staniloae's short book *The Victory of the Cross* (2nd edn; Fairacres, Oxford: SLG, 2001) was an additional source for material in this chapter. The extended quote "The world is a gift of God…" is from page 1.

Samuel Wells discusses GM crops from an ecclesial perspective in *Improvisation: The Drama of Christian Ethics* (Grand Rapids, MI: Brazos Press, 2004), chapter 14; quotations are from page 211.

The following works on crops are in the corresponding chapter of *Christian Ethics: An Introductory Reader*:

- Derek Burke. "Genetic Engineering of Food." In *Christians and Bioethics*. Fraser Watts, ed. London: SPCK, 2000.
- Wendell Berry. *What Are People For?* San Francisco, CA: North Point Press, 1990.

Ecology

The source for Michael Northcott's summary of the current state of ecological debate is his essay "Ecology and Christian Ethics" (see above).

John Milbank writes about environmental ethics in *The Word Made Strange: Theology, Language, Culture* (Oxford: Blackwell, 1997). The relevant

chapter is "Out of the Greenhouse" (pages 257ff.).

Richard Fern, as we have seen in this chapter, has developed an original and engaging language for talking about nature's moral status as "sentiotic," and his major study is called *Nature, God and*

Humanity: Envisioning an Ethics of Nature (Cambridge: Cambridge University Press, 2002).

For Ellen Davis's discussion of the translation "mastery among" in Gen 1:28, see her *Scripture, Culture, and Agriculture*, page 55.

The discussion of *Laudato Si'* draws specific material from sections 3, 30, 49, 93, and 12.

Lynn White Jr.'s comment about Christianity as an anthropocentric religion is in his essay "The Historical Roots of Our Ecologic Crisis," *Science* 155 (March 10, 1967): 1203–7.

Sallie McFague's influential work in the area of ecofeminism is exemplified by her book *The Body of God: An Ecological Theology* (Minneapolis, MN: Fortress Press, 1993), a selection from which is included in the corresponding chapter of *Christian Ethics: An Introductory Reader*.

Ecowomanist resources include Melanie Harris, "Ecowomanism: An Introduction," *Worldviews: Global Religions, Culture, and Ecology* 20, no. 1 (2016): 5–14; and Delores S. Williams, "Sin, Nature, and Black Women's Bodies," in *Ecofeminism and the Sacred* (Carol J. Adams, ed.; New York: Continuum, 1993), pages 24–29; see also Willis Jenkins, *The Future of Ethics: Sustainability, Social Justice, and Religious Creativity* (Washington, DC: Georgetown University Press, 2013), chapter 5.

Willis Jenkins calls for a practical response of mutual responsibility and cooperation among all religious traditions in his *The Future of Ethics*.

In addition to McFague, the following works on ecology are also in *Christian Ethics: An Introductory Reader*:

- Jürgen Moltmann. *God in Creation: An Ecological Doctrine of Creation*. Margaret Kohl, trans. London: SCM Press, 1985.
- Laura Ruth Yordy. *Green Witness: Ecology, Ethics, and the Kingdom of God*. Eugene, OR: Cascade Books, 2008.

Additional reading includes Michael Northcott, *The Environment and Christian Ethics* (Cambridge: Cambridge University Press, 1996). For resources that draw on Catholic social teaching, see David Cloutier, *Walking God's Earth: The Environment and Catholic Faith* (Collegeville, MN: Liturgical Press, 2014) and Christiana Z. Peppard, *Just Water: Theology, Ethics, and the Global Water Crisis* (Maryknoll, NY: Orbis, 2014). For a more evangelically oriented approach, see Steven Bouma-Prediger, *For the Beauty of the Earth: A Christian Vision for Creation Care* (Grand Rapids, MI: Baker Academic, 2010).

Timeline

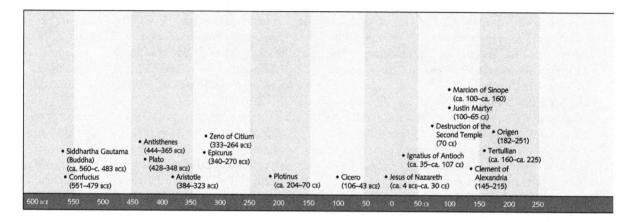

- Siddhartha Gautama (Buddha) (ca. 560–c. 483 BCE)
- Confucius (551–479 BCE)
- Antisthenes (444–365 BCE)
- Plato (428–348 BCE)
- Aristotle (384–323 BCE)
- Zeno of Citium (333–264 BCE)
- Epicurus (340–270 BCE)
- Plotinus (ca. 204–70 CE)
- Cicero (106–43 BCE)
- Jesus of Nazareth (ca. 4 BCE–ca. 30 CE)
- Ignatius of Antioch (ca. 35–ca. 107 CE)
- Clement of Alexandria (145–215)
- Marcion of Sinope (ca. 100–ca. 160)
- Justin Martyr (100–65 CE)
- Destruction of the Second Temple (70 CE)
- Origen (182–251)
- Tertullian (ca. 160–ca. 225)

600 BCE   550   500   450   400   350   300   250   200   150   100   50   0   50 CE   100   150   200   250

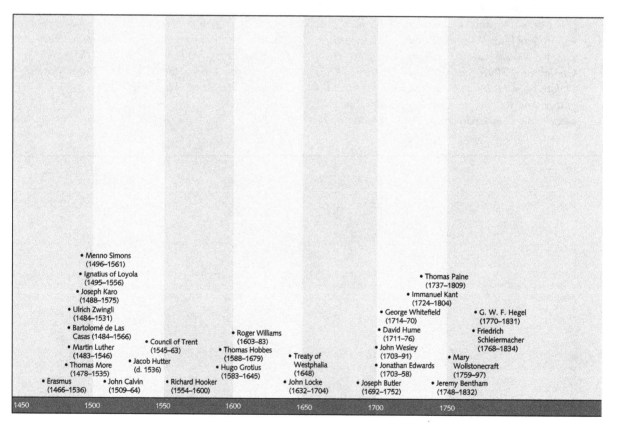

- Menno Simons (1496–1561)
- Ignatius of Loyola (1495–1556)
- Joseph Karo (1488–1575)
- Ulrich Zwingli (1484–1531)
- Bartolomé de Las Casas (1484–1566)
- Martin Luther (1483–1546)
- Thomas More (1478–1535)
- Erasmus (1466–1536)
- John Calvin (1509–64)
- Jacob Hutter (d. 1536)
- Council of Trent (1545–63)
- Richard Hooker (1554–1600)
- Roger Williams (1603–83)
- Thomas Hobbes (1588–1679)
- Hugo Grotius (1583–1645)
- John Locke (1632–1704)
- Treaty of Westphalia (1648)
- George Whitefield (1714–70)
- David Hume (1711–76)
- John Wesley (1703–91)
- Jonathan Edwards (1703–58)
- Joseph Butler (1692–1752)
- Thomas Paine (1737–1809)
- Immanuel Kant (1724–1804)
- G. W. F. Hegel (1770–1831)
- Friedrich Schleiermacher (1768–1834)
- Mary Wollstonecraft (1759–97)
- Jeremy Bentham (1748–1832)

1450   1500   1550   1600   1650   1700   1750

Introducing Christian Ethics, Second Edition. Samuel Wells and Ben Quash with Rebekah Eklund.
© 2017 John Wiley & Sons Ltd. Published 2017 by John Wiley & Sons Ltd.

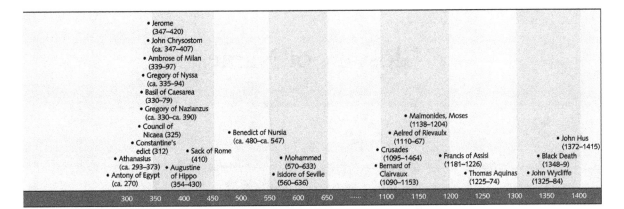

• Jerome
(347–420)
• John Chrysostom
(ca. 347–407)
• Ambrose of Milan
(339–97)
• Gregory of Nyssa
(ca. 335–94)
• Basil of Caesarea
(330–79)
• Gregory of Nazianzus
(ca. 330–ca. 390)
• Council of
Nicaea (325)
• Constantine's
edict (312)   • Sack of Rome
• Athanasius   (410)
(ca. 293–373)   • Augustine
• Antony of Egypt   of Hippo
(ca. 270)   (354–430)

• Benedict of Nursia
(ca. 480–ca. 547)

• Mohammed
(570–633)
• Isidore of Seville
(560–636)

• Maimonides, Moses
(1138–1204)
• Aelred of Rievaulx
(1110–67)
• Crusades
(1095–1464)   • Francis of Assisi
• Bernard of   (1181–1226)
Clairvaux
(1090–1153)   • Thomas Aquinas
(1225–74)

• John Hus
(1372–1415)

• Black Death
(1348–9)
• John Wycliffe
(1325–84)

300 350 400 450 500 550 600 650 ...... 1100 1150 1200 1250 1300 1350 1400

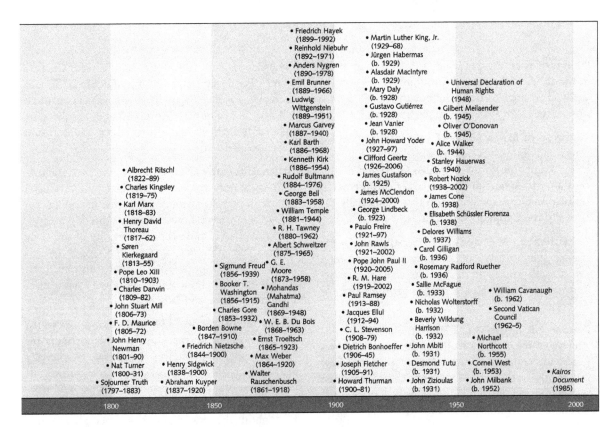

• Friedrich Hayek
(1899–1992)
• Reinhold Niebuhr
(1892–1971)
• Anders Nygren
(1890–1978)
• Emil Brunner
(1889–1966)
• Ludwig
Wittgenstein
(1889–1951)
• Marcus Garvey
(1887–1940)
• Karl Barth
(1886–1968)
• Kenneth Kirk
(1886–1954)
• Rudolf Bultmann
(1884–1976)
• George Bell
(1883–1958)
• William Temple
(1881–1944)
• R. H. Tawney
(1880–1962)
• Albert Schweitzer
(1875–1965)

• Albrecht Ritschl
(1822–89)
• Charles Kingsley
(1819–75)
• Karl Marx
(1818–83)
• Henry David
Thoreau
(1817–62)
• Søren
Kierkegaard
(1813–55)
• Pope Leo XIII
(1810–1903)
• Charles Darwin
(1809–82)
• John Stuart Mill
(1806–73)
• F. D. Maurice
(1805–72)
• John Henry
Newman
(1801–90)
• Nat Turner
(1800–31)
• Sojourner Truth
(1797–1883)

• Sigmund Freud
(1856–1939)
• Booker T.
Washington
(1856–1915)
• Charles Gore
(1853–1932)
• Borden Bowne
(1847–1910)
• Friedrich Nietzsche
(1844–1900)
• Henry Sidgwick
(1838–1900)
• Abraham Kuyper
(1837–1920)

• G. E.
Moore
(1873–1958)
• Mohandas
(Mahatma)
Gandhi
(1869–1948)
• W. E. B. Du Bois
(1868–1963)
• Ernst Troeltsch
(1865–1923)
• Max Weber
(1864–1920)
• Walter
Rauschenbusch
(1861–1918)

• Martin Luther King, Jr.
(1929–68)
• Jürgen Habermas
(b. 1929)
• Alasdair MacIntyre
(b. 1929)
• Mary Daly
(b. 1928)
• Gustavo Gutiérrez
(b. 1928)
• Jean Vanier
(b. 1928)
• John Howard Yoder
(1927–97)
• Clifford Geertz
(1926–2006)
• James Gustafson
(b. 1925)
• James McClendon
(1924–2000)
• George Lindbeck
(b. 1923)
• Paulo Freire
(1921–97)
• John Rawls
(1921–2002)
• Pope John Paul II
(1920–2005)
• R. M. Hare
(1919–2002)
• Paul Ramsey
(1913–88)
• Jacques Ellul
(1912–94)
• C. L. Stevenson
(1908–79)
• Dietrich Bonhoeffer
(1906–45)
• Joseph Fletcher
(1905–91)
• Howard Thurman
(1900–81)

• Universal Declaration of
Human Rights
(1948)
• Gilbert Meilaender
(b. 1945)
• Oliver O'Donovan
(b. 1945)
• Alice Walker
(b. 1944)
• Stanley Hauerwas
(b. 1940)
• Robert Nozick
(1938–2002)
• James Cone
(b. 1938)
• Elisabeth Schüssler Fiorenza
(b. 1938)
• Delores Williams
(b. 1937)
• Carol Gilligan
(b. 1936)
• Rosemary Radford Ruether
(b. 1936)
• Sallie McFague
(b. 1933)
• Nicholas Wolterstorff
(b. 1932)
• Beverly Wildung
Harrison
(1932)
• John Mbiti
(b. 1931)
• Desmond Tutu
(b. 1931)
• John Zizioulas
(b. 1931)

• William Cavanaugh
(b. 1962)
• Second Vatican
Council
(1962–5)
• Michael
Northcott
(b. 1955)
• Cornel West
(b. 1953)
• John Milbank
(b. 1952)

• Kairos
Document
(1985)

1800   1850   1900   1950   2000

Glossary of Names

Aelred of Rievaulx (1110–67). A Cistercian monk at the abbey of Rievaulx in Yorkshire who was eventually appointed to be the abbot there. He is best known for his treatise on spiritual friendship.

Ambrose of Milan (339–97 CE). Bishop of Milan renowned for his preaching (his sermons helped bring **Augustine** to the Christian faith) and for his resistance to **Arianism**. He was also instrumental in translating Greek theology into Latin, especially the works of the **Cappadocian Fathers**.

Antisthenes (444–365 BCE). A student of the philosopher Socrates, who highlighted his master's dutiful self-possession in even the most trying circumstances, thus helping lay the groundwork for **Stoicism**.

Antony of Egypt (ca. 270 CE). Also known as Antony of the Desert or one of the Desert Fathers (and Mothers), Antony was a monk who withdrew into the desert to live a solitary, ascetic life. He is often considered the father of monasticism. His life was recounted by **Athanasius** in *The Life of St Antony*.

Aquinas, Thomas. *See* **Thomas Aquinas**.

Aristotle (384–323 BCE). Ancient Greek philosopher and student of **Plato**. A component of his work that is important for later philosophical ethics is his understanding of the four causes (see Chapter Three). His thought significantly influenced Christian theology, particularly in the medieval era through scholars like **Thomas Aquinas**, and has become important again in the virtue ethics tradition and thus in ecclesial ethics.

Athanasius (ca. 293–373 CE). Bishop of Alexandria who vigorously opposed **Arianism** and produced several important theological works, including *The Life of St Antony* (about the desert monk **Antony**), *To Serapion* (which defends the divinity of the Holy Spirit), and *Discourse against the Greeks* (which argues against paganism). Athanasius lived in Alexandria just under one hundred years after **Origen** had lived and taught there.

Augustine of Hippo (354–430 CE). Key Christian thinker born in northern Africa who recounts his spiritual pilgrimage in his *Confessions*. Originally attracted to **Manicheism**, Augustine turned to Christianity and became bishop of Hippo. His great work *The City of God* has played an influential role throughout the church's history, especially in terms of the church's relationship to society. He was also an important opponent of **Donatism** and **Pelagianism**.

Barth, Karl (1886–1968). Perhaps the most influential theologian of the twentieth century, Barth was

Introducing Christian Ethics, Second Edition. Samuel Wells and Ben Quash with Rebekah Eklund.
© 2017 John Wiley & Sons Ltd. Published 2017 by John Wiley & Sons Ltd.

a pastor in the Reformed Church of Switzerland whose thinking was significantly shaped by what he saw as the failure of liberal Protestant theology in Germany at the onset of World War I. In response, he sought to make central the concepts of divine revelation and divine transcendence. Barth's school of theology is sometimes called dialectical or neo-orthodox theology: dialectical for its emphasis on the utter difference between the human being and God, and neo-orthodox for its rejection of liberalism and recovery of patristic and classical Christian thought. His key work is the fourteen-volume *Church Dogmatics*. Barth is the most important background figure in ecclesial ethics.

Basil of Caesarea (330–79 CE). Also known as Basil the Great or one of the **Cappadocian Fathers** (along with his brother **Gregory of Nyssa** and his friend **Gregory of Nazianzus**), Basil was a central figure in the development of Trinitarian doctrine.

Bell, George (1883–1958). Anglican theologian who was dean of Canterbury and later bishop of Chichester; he was also a member of the House of Lords and was president of the World Council of Churches from 1945 until his death. Bell is considered to be one of the founders of the ecumenical movement, and is also known for his courageous opposition to carpet-bombing during World War II.

Benedict of Nursia (ca. 480–ca. 547 CE). Central figure in Western monasticism whose *Rule* is a founding document for monastic discipline and practice.

Bentham, Jeremy (1748–1832). English legal and social reformer and a key proponent of **utilitarianism** along with his student **John Stuart Mill**. Bentham proposed the "greatest happiness principle," or the seeking of the maximum amount of pleasure among the maximum number of people.

Bernard of Clairvaux (1090–1153). Bernard founded and served as abbot of the Cistercian monastery at Clairvaux in northeast France. He was an influential theologian who took part in several controversies, including a political one (defending the disputed election of Innocent II to the papacy) and a theological one (arguing against the immaculate conception of Mary).

Bonhoeffer, Dietrich (1906–45). German theologian and pastor in the Confessing Church (the church that rejected the official German Church's support of Nazi Germany). Bonhoeffer was hanged for his participation in a plot to assassinate Adolf Hitler. His best-known works are *The Cost of Discipleship*, in which he contrasts the "costly grace" of discipleship with "cheap grace," and *Life Together*, which captures his vision of the church as a serving, worshiping, and witnessing community.

Bowne, Borden (1847–1910). A lay Methodist theologian and educator who taught philosophy at Boston University and introduced the notion of **personalism** or personalist idealism.

Brunner, Emil (1889–1966). Pastor and Reformed theologian who taught dogmatic theology at the University of Zurich. Despite similarities with fellow Swiss theologian **Karl Barth**, his understanding of **natural theology** (among other things) brought him into sharp conflict with Barth.

Bultmann, Rudolf (1884–1976). German Protestant theologian and New Testament scholar whose historical-critical study of the Bible left him skeptical of the possibilities of uncovering the "real," historical Jesus through the gospels. In his effort to make the New Testament relevant to the twentieth century, he sought to "demythologize" it by emptying it of all its "primitive" or unscientific features, focusing instead on Jesus' radical call to decision and on the essential "kerygma" (preaching) of the gospel.

Butler, Joseph (1692–1752). Bishop first of Bristol, and later of Durham, Butler opposed **Thomas Hobbes'** view of **natural law**. Butler dismissed Hobbes' claim that selfish impulses are the basic motivation for most human actions and argued instead that concepts of moral duty and self-interest need not be in conflict with one another. Butler was also an opponent of **Deism**.

Calvin, John (1509–64). One of the great theologians of the Protestant Reformation. Calvin, who was born in France, eventually settled in Geneva, where he sought to transform the city into a model of Christian civilization. He developed his theology in the *Institutes of the Christian Religion*, which emphasizes knowledge of God, especially knowing God in order to glorify God. The branch of theology known as Reformed developed from Calvin's thought.

Cavanaugh, William (b. 1962). A Catholic theologian and student of **Stanley Hauerwas** who teaches theology at DePaul University in Chicago. His work, which focuses on the church, politics, and the nation-state, falls under the umbrella of ecclesial ethics.

Chrysostom, John (ca. 347–407 CE). Patriarch of Constantinople whose preaching earned him the nickname "Chrysostom," which means "golden mouth." The bulk of his work consists of homilies on biblical texts, which are still widely regarded as some of the greatest expositions of the Bible produced by the church. Chrysostom became embroiled in controversy and was exiled toward the end of his life, but he is best remembered for his eloquent sermons.

Cicero (106–43 BCE). Marcus Tullius Cicero was a Roman orator, philosopher, and politician. He was sympathetic to **Stoicism** but tended to oppose **Epicureanism**.

Clement of Alexandria (145–215 CE). Theologian born in Athens who converted from paganism to Christianity. Clement lived briefly in Alexandria, but was forced to flee because of persecution. One of his important works is *Who is the Rich Man That Shall Be Saved?* Clement admired classical philosophy and was an important influence on **Origen**'s theology.

Cone, James (b. 1938). Professor of systematic theology at Union Theological Seminary in New York. Cone is also an ordained minister in the African Methodist Episcopal Church. He is the key figure in the emergence of black **liberation theology**.

Confucius (551–479 BCE). Founder of the Chinese philosophy known as Confucianism. The life of Confucius (or Kongzi) is known mainly through tradition and legend; the influence of his teachings on Chinese thought is extensive.

Daly, Mary (1928–2010). Self-described radical elemental feminist. Daly taught for most of her career at Boston College. She is sometimes called a post-Christian feminist for her rejection of the Bible and Christian tradition as irredeemably patriarchal.

Darwin, Charles (1809–82). English naturalist who pioneered the theory of natural selection and evolution in his 1859 work *On the Origin of the Species.*

Du Bois, W. E. B. (1868–1963). William Edward Burghardt Du Bois was a civil rights activist, scholar, poet, and educator who helped found the National Association for the Advancement of Colored People (NAACP) in 1909. He is recognized as the leading African American intellectual of his time.

Edwards, Jonathan (1703–58). Sometimes known as "America's theologian," Edwards was a philosophical theologian deeply influenced by **John Locke** and **John Calvin**. His work centers around God's sovereignty and holiness; he is also associated with the religious revivals of the first **Great Awakening**.

Ellul, Jacques (1912–94). Social activist and lay theologian in the French Reformed Church. He taught law and politics at Bordeaux University in southwest France. In his book *Anarchy and Christianity*, Ellul examined the Bible as a source of political anarchy. He defined anarchy as the "nonviolent repudiation of authority."

Epicurus (340–270 BCE). Greek philosopher who asserted that the highest good is pleasure, but for Epicurus pleasure is the absence of pain in the body and trouble in the mind, not the sensual indulgence that has come to be associated with his name (see **Epicureanism**).

Erasmus (1466–1536). Desiderius Erasmus of Rotterdam was a Dutch humanist and theologian of the Renaissance era. He is an important contributor to the Catholic humanist tradition.

Fiorenza, Elisabeth Schüssler (b. 1938). Harvard Divinity School professor and pioneer of feminist theology. Her work has focused on issues of feminist biblical interpretation and theological education.

Fletcher, Joseph (1905–91). American professor and Episcopalian priest who later rejected Christianity. Fletcher promoted **situation ethics**, a kind of consequentialist ethic that resists moral rules or laws and argues that Christian *agape* (or love) is the only guideline for making ethical decisions.

Francis of Assisi (ca. 1181–1226). Born to a wealthy merchant family, Francis renounced his riches and gave himself to the bride he called "Lady Poverty," going on to found the Franciscan Order. Francis is renowned for his joyful dedication to voluntary poverty and his reverential attitude toward nature (expressed in his "Canticle of the Sun"). The saint's life is heralded as an inspiration for environmental ethics, as well as for liberation ethics, because of his commitment to being among and serving the poor.

Francis, Pope (b. 1936). Jorge Mario Bergoglio made history when he was the first Latin American elected to the papacy in 2013, taking the name Francis from **Francis of Assisi**. His 2015 encylical *Laudato Si'* (On Care for Our Common Home) made an urgent appeal for a Christian environmental ethic.

Freire, Paulo (1921–97). Brazilian educator whose book *Pedagogy of the Oppressed* remains a central text for **liberation theology**. A key theme associated with Freire's work is **conscientization**.

Freud, Sigmund (1856–1939). Born in Moravia (then in Austria; present-day Czech Republic) but raised in Vienna, Freud is the founder of the practice of psychoanalysis. He is particularly associated with his theory of the way in which human beings are subject to unconscious drives within themselves.

Gandhi, Mohandas (Mahatma) (1869–1948). Spiritual and political leader of the Indian independence movement and adherent of Hinduism who advocated nonviolent resistance. Gandhi was a significant influence on **Martin Luther King Jr.** and the civil rights movement in the United States.

Garvey, Marcus (1887–1940). Jamaican-born social and political activist who worked in Jamaica and the United States. He founded the Universal Negro Improvement Association as a way of uniting all people of African descent, and advocated the return of blacks in America to Africa.

Geertz, Clifford (1926–2006). Cultural anthropologist who founded a field of study known as interpretive or symbolic anthropology, which studies the symbols (rituals, belief systems, and so on) that give meaning to human life.

Gilligan, Carol (b. 1936). Feminist thinker and psychologist who spent most of her career at Harvard University. Her book *In a Different Voice* critiqued the work of developmental psychologist Lawrence Kohlberg. Gilligan has been a pioneer in gender studies, especially in the study of the development of young girls.

Gore, Charles (1853–1932). Anglican priest with socialist commitments who was bishop of Worcester, Birmingham, and Oxford. In 1892 Gore founded the Community of the Resurrection, which trained a number of black Anglican priests in South Africa, including **Desmond Tutu**.

Gregory of Nazianzus (ca. 330–ca. 390 CE). Known as one of the **Cappadocian Fathers**, along with **Gregory of Nyssa** and **Basil of Caesarea**. Gregory was, reluctantly, bishop of Nazianzus and patriarch of Constantinople, but devoted himself primarily to study and theological reflection. He opposed **Arianism** and was important in the development of Trinitarian doctrine.

Gregory of Nyssa (ca. 335–94 CE). One of the great Cappadocian theologians, along with his brother **Basil of Caesarea**, his sister Macrina, and **Gregory of Nazianzus**. Gregory opposed **Arianism** and was instrumental in the development of Trinitarian doctrine. Gregory also contributed to the theology of the resurrection (in *On the Soul and the Resurrection*, in which he claims to record his sister Macrina's teachings) and to later mystical theology.

Grotius, Hugo (1583–1645). A Dutch Calvinist (with sympathies for **Arminianism**) and a political theorist who is often held to be the founder of modern **natural law** and international law theory. His works were influential on evolving Christian views on just war and on natural law in ethics.

Gustafson, James (b. 1925). An ordained United Church of Christ pastor who has taught at Yale University, the University of Chicago, and Emory University. His work in theological ethics is from what he calls a "theocentric perspective," i.e., the grounding of ethics in understanding God's purposes for all creation.

Gutiérrez, Gustavo (b. 1928). Peruvian Catholic priest who is one of the foremost figures in Latin American **liberation theology**. He contributed substantially to the documents of the Medellín Conference in Colombia in 1968, which laid out for the first time some of the guiding principles of liberation theology. A key phrase for Gutiérrez is God's **"preferential option for the poor."** His 1973 book *A Theology of Liberation: History, Politics, and Salvation* is the most influential work in liberation theology.

Habermas, Jürgen (b. 1929). German philosopher whose work in theories of knowledge and communication has influenced the field of biblical interpretation.

Hare, R. M. (1919–2002). English moral philosopher who developed the ethical theory of **prescriptivism**, sometimes called universal prescriptivism. His key work is his first book, *The Language of Morals*.

Harrison, Beverly Wildung (1932–2012). Feminist theologian and long-time professor of ethics at Union Theological Seminary in New York, notable in particular for her work in social ethics and medical ethics.

Hauerwas, Stanley (b. 1940). Self-avowed Texan, prolific writer, and Methodist theologian who has taught at Notre Dame University and Duke University. He is a key figure in ecclesial ethics. His wide-ranging work in ethics centers on issues of the church's relationship to the state and civil society, on the practices of the church, and on the recovery and transformation of a virtue ethics tradition stemming from **Aristotle**.

Hayek, Friedrich (1899–1992). Austrian economist and political theorist whose book *The Road to Serfdom* was a warning against what he saw as the dangers of socialism.

Hegel, G. W. F. (1770–1831). Prominent nineteenth-century German philosopher who saw the pursuit of absolute reality as an unfolding historical process of **dialectic**. Hegel's thought influenced **Karl Marx** and Latin American **liberation theology**.

Hobbes, Thomas (1588–1679). Seventeenth-century English philosopher whose work centered on politics and **natural law**. Hobbes was a thoroughgoing materialist – that is, he took only that which is material to be real. In his *Leviathan*, he lays out his views of the social contract and the necessity of civil government.

Hooker, Richard (1554–1600). Anglican clergyman whose principal and massive work is *Of the Laws of Ecclesiastical Polity*. Hooker was influenced by the **scholasticism** of **Thomas Aquinas**.

Hume, David (1711–76). A Scottish-born philosopher and an empiricist – that is, he held that true knowledge is based solely on experience. His mode of moral reflection came to be known as **emotivism**.

Hus, John (1372–1415). Teacher, pastor, and Reformer in Prague who admired the teachings of **John Wycliffe**. Under threat of discipline by the Catholic Church, Hus moved to Bohemia. He was later tried and executed as a heretic.

Hutter, Jacob (d. 1536). Anabaptist leader born in northern Italy who spent much of his life in Moravia, where there was more tolerance for Anabaptist views than in other parts of Europe. The Hutterite Brethren arose in Moravia from Hutter's work.

Ignatius of Antioch (ca. 35–ca. 107 CE). Bishop of Antioch in Syria. He was executed under the Emperor Trajan sometime between 98 and 117 CE. His seven letters (written on his way to Rome where his martyrdom awaited) are important early witnesses to the Christian faith and to early understandings of Christian martyrdom.

Ignatius of Loyola (1495–1556). Founder of the Society of Jesus, also known as the Jesuits. His *Spiritual Exercises* remains one of the classic works on spiritual discernment and Christian spirituality.

Irenaeus of Lyons (d. ca. 202 CE). Important Greek-speaking theologian who defended the church against **Gnosticism** and against **Marcion**, and who laid out an early version of the "rule of faith" or *regula fidei*, a summary statement of essential Christian beliefs that guide the interpretation of Scripture.

Isidore of Seville (560–636 CE). Bishop of Seville in Spain considered to be the last of the great Latin Fathers of the church. Isidore was instrumental in passing on the heritage of the classical philosophical tradition (especially **Aristotle**) to the church of the Middle Ages.

Jerome (347–420 CE). Jerome lived and taught in Rome, Antioch (where he was ordained a priest), and Constantinople, but spent the last thirty-five years of his life in Bethlehem in Palestine. His most long-lasting accomplishment was his translation of the Bible into Latin; this translation is known as the Vulgate.

John of Damascus (ca. 670–749 CE). Considered to be the last Father of the Eastern (Orthodox) Church. He served as a priest in Palestine and is well-known for his defense of the veneration of icons.

John Paul II (1920–2005). Born Karol Wojtyla in Poland, John Paul II was pope from 1978 until his death in 2005. As a cardinal, he took part in the **Second Vatican Council**. During his twenty-seven-year-long pontificate, he encouraged dialogue with Jews and members of other religions, and authored a number of significant papal encyclicals endorsing the dignity of the human person.

Kant, Immanuel (1724–1804). Eighteenth-century German philosopher from Königsberg in Prussia (present-day Russia) who has had widespread influence on subsequent philosophy and on modern theology. Key concepts for Kant are the **categorical imperative** and the principle of **universalizability**.

Karo, Joseph (1488–1575). Spanish-born Jewish scholar who spent much of his life in Turkey. In order to make the **Halakhah** available to every Jew, he wrote the *Shulchan Arukh* (the Prepared Table) as a simple guide for what a Jew was supposed to do in every circumstance of life.

Kierkegaard, Søren (1813–55). Danish Lutheran theologian who published an extensive collection of writings, some of them under pseudonyms such as "Johannes *de silentio*." He emphasized the otherness of God and the unique vocation of the church, and in his later years attacked what he saw as the failings of the Danish Lutheran Church.

King, Martin Luther, Jr. (1929–68). African American Baptist pastor and civil rights leader who famously advocated nonviolent resistance (drawn in part from the teachings of **Gandhi**) as a means to lasting social change. King strove toward the creation of the "Beloved Community," an inclusive community of reconciliation and solidarity.

Kingsley, Charles (1819–75). Anglican clergyman and social reformer who promoted the Christian socialist movement in England.

Kirk, Kenneth (1886–1954). Anglican priest, professor, and bishop of Oxford whose book *The Vision of God* explored the relationship between ethics and worship.

Kuyper, Abraham (1837–1920). Dutch Calvinist theologian, statesman, and pastor who broke with the State Church and formed the Reformed Church of the Netherlands.

Las Casas, Bartolomé de (1484–1566). Dominican friar and bishop of Chiapas in southeast Mexico who rejected the forced evangelization of indigenous peoples and instead advocated for their self-determination and natural right to freedom.

Leo XIII (1810–1903). Vincenzo Gioacchino Raffaele Luigi Pecci was born near Rome and was pope from 1878 to 1903. His lasting influence on Catholic social teachings came through his initiation of the tradition of writing papal encyclicals, beginning with his 1891 encyclical *Rerum Novarum* (On Capital and Labor).

Lindbeck, George (b. 1923). Lutheran theologian and long-time Yale University professor with strong ecumenical interests. Lindbeck is one of the main figures of **postliberal theology**.

Locke, John (1632–1704). British philosopher and political theorist who is often considered the father of empiricism – the doctrine that true knowledge is based on experience and rational reflection. Locke explored the limits of human understanding and the nature of government, and was instrumental in developing the notion of natural rights.

Luther, Martin (1483–1546). German church Reformer whose vigorous disagreements with elements of Catholic theology and practice sparked the Protestant Reformation. A key component of Luther's thought is his stress on the doctrine of justification by faith. Another lasting contribution is his translation of the Bible into colloquial German. Luther's theology is often called a "theology of the cross" because of the way it centers on the hidden or concealed revelation of God's power in the suffering and shame of the cross.

MacIntyre, Alasdair (b. 1929). Scottish moral and political philosopher who has taught for most of his career in the United States. MacIntyre is an important figure in ecclesial ethics, in part for his revival and revision of **Aristotle**'s virtue ethics.

Maimonides, Moses (1138–1204). Moses Maimonides, or Rabbi Moses ben Maimon, is widely held to be the greatest Jewish philosopher of the Middle Ages. He was born in Cordoba, Spain, but lived most of his life in Egypt. His most prominent works include a commentary to the **Mishnah** and *The Guide for the Perplexed*, which seeks to harmonize Jewish teachings with **Aristotle**'s philosophy.

Marcion of Sinope (ca. 100–ca. 160 CE). Theologian from Sinope in Pontus (modern-day Turkey) who drew a sharp distinction between the God of the Old and New Testaments. He was vigorously opposed by the theologians **Irenaeus of Lyons** and **Tertullian**, among others, for his rejection of the Old Testament and great parts of the New Testament (with the exception of portions of the Gospel of Luke and 10 Pauline letters). Marcion was declared a heretic in 144 CE.

Martyr, Justin (100–65 CE). Sometimes known simply as Justin, he was a second-century Greek apologist (defender of the Christian faith, to both Jews and pagans). Justin was a native of Palestinian Syria who later taught in Rome, where he was martyred.

Marx, Karl (1818–83). German economic and political theorist. Together with Friedrich Engels, he developed a socialist system of thought that came to be known as Marxism, which centers on the material conditions of human life and means of production. Marxism was an influential philosophy in the development of Latin American **liberation theology**.

Maurice, F. D. (1805–72). Frederick Denison Maurice was an Anglican theologian whose thought inspired the Christian socialist movement in England. He was later forced to resign his teaching post at King's College London for denying the doctrine of eternal punishment.

Mbiti, John (b. 1931). Anglican theologian from Kenya whose work studies the interplay of African culture and Christianity. Mbiti has sometimes been called the father of contemporary African theology. He is also a leader in the ecumenical movement and has been prominent in the World Council of Churches.

McClendon, James (1924–2000). Baptist theologian whose work falls broadly into the stream of Anabaptist thought. His three-volume *Systematic Theology* established him as a prominent figure in ecclesial ethics.

McFague, Sallie (b. 1933). American feminist theologian who teaches theology at Vanderbilt University. She is known for her work on Christianity and ecology, including an ecological model for understanding God's relationship to the world.

Meilaender, Gilbert (b. 1945). Lutheran theologian who teaches ethics at Valparaiso University. He is portrayed in this volume as a bridge figure between universal and ecclesial ethics.

Milbank, John (b. 1952). Anglican theologian who has taught at the University of Cambridge, University of Virginia, and University of Nottingham. He is the principal figure in a contemporary theological movement known as **Radical Orthodoxy**, and is also associated with ecclesial ethics.

Mill, John Stuart (1806–73). Nineteenth-century economist and philosopher indebted to the thought of **Jeremy Bentham** and **John Locke**. Mill coined the term "**utilitarianism**" in his work of the same title.

Moore, G. E. (1873–1958). British philosopher who taught at the University of Cambridge. Moore criticized **naturalism** for committing what he called the **naturalistic fallacy**. He proposed instead the theory of **intuitionism**.

More, Thomas (1478–1535). English author remembered for his book *Utopia* (a description of a fictional island society). His opposition to Henry VIII's divorce and subsequent remarriage led to his beheading.

Newman, John Henry (1801–90). English theologian, philosopher, and cardinal of the Roman Catholic Church. Newman was a key figure in the founding of the Oxford Movement, which revived Catholic traditions within the Church of England.

Originally an Anglican, Newman taught at Oxford until his conversion to Catholicism.

Niebuhr, Reinhold (1892–1971). Influential American theologian whose thought has had a lasting impact on American theology and politics. His distinctive strand of theology is often called Christian realism. **Postliberal theology** and ecclesial ethics have emerged in part as criticisms of Niebuhr's thought.

Nietzsche, Friedrich (1844–1900). Late nineteenth-century German philosopher born into a Lutheran family. Nietzsche portrayed Christianity as a religion for the weak.

Northcott, Michael (b. 1955). Anglican priest and theologian who teaches ethics at the University of Edinburgh. He is best known for his work on environmental ethics.

Nozick, Robert (1938–2002). Harvard University philosopher who defended free-market libertarianism in his *Anarchy, State, and Utopia*. Nozick and **John Rawls** were colleagues at Harvard.

Nygren, Anders (1890–1978). Ordained minister in the Lutheran Church of Sweden who taught theology and ethics, and who played an active role in the ecumenical movement. He is best known for his work *Agape and Eros*, which draws a strict distinction between the *agape* that is Christian love and the *eros* of Platonic philosophy.

O'Donovan, Oliver (b. 1945). A priest in the Church of England and a professor of theology and ethics at the University of Edinburgh. O'Donovan has emerged as one of the most influential political theologians of the current era. He is portrayed in this volume as a bridge figure between universal and ecclesial ethics.

Origen (182–251 CE). A creative thinker and prolific writer, Origen was born in Alexandria, spent time in Caesarea, and died in Tyre. He is often considered the finest theologian of the church to that date, although some of his theories were later declared to be heretical. His theological influence remained powerful for the next several centuries.

Paine, Thomas (1737–1809). Revolutionary and Deist philosopher in England who supported the revolutions in France and the United States.

Plato (428–348 BCE). Athenian philosopher whose work has had one of the greatest lasting impacts on Western thought. He was a student of Socrates and predecessor to **Aristotle**. Plato's and Aristotle's thought are the most significant elements of what is often described as the classical tradition.

Plotinus (ca. 204–70 CE). The last great classical Greek philosopher. Plotinus was born in Egypt and studied in Persia, but developed his school of philosophy in Antioch and Rome. His philosophy is known as Neoplatonism for its blending of Plato's thought with elements of Pythagoras, **Aristotle**, and mysticism.

Ramsey, Paul (1913–88). Prominent American Methodist theologian who taught at Princeton University. His work in ethics impacted American moral reflection, politics, and medicine. Ramsey and **Joseph Fletcher** both used Christian love (*agape*) as the guiding principle of their ethics, but Ramsey's emphasis on moral norms and principles placed him in opposition to Fletcher's **situation ethics**.

Rauschenbusch, Walter (1861–1918). American Baptist pastor who inspired the **Social Gospel** movement in the late nineteenth and early twentieth centuries. The followers of the Social Gospel sought to bring the gospel to bear on issues of social justice and social transformation. **Reinhold Niebuhr** and **Martin Luther King Jr.** were influenced by Rauschenbusch's thought.

Rawls, John (1921–2002). One of the most important American political philosophers of the twentieth century. A prominent aspect of his work is his notion of justice as fairness. Rawls' book *A Theory of Justice* remains the most influential contemporary work on the subject of justice.

Ritschl, Albrecht (1822–89). Lutheran theologian and New Testament scholar. He was a leading figure in German liberal Protestantism. His conception of the kingdom of God influenced American theologian **Walter Rauschenbusch** and the **Social Gospel** movement.

Ruether, Rosemary Radford (b. 1936). American Catholic feminist thinker, writer, and activist. Ruether is a pioneer of feminist theology whose book *Sexism and God-Talk* is a classic example of a feminist critique of Christian theology.

Schleiermacher, Friedrich (1768–1834). German Reformed preacher, theologian, and philosopher; born in Breslau, Silesia (present-day Poland). He spent most of his life teaching and preaching in Berlin. For Schleiermacher religion centers around a "feeling [i.e., an immediate self-consciousness] of absolute dependence." Perhaps the most influential figure in nineteenth-century German liberal Protestant theology, he is often called the father of modern theology for his role in re-envisioning theology after the challenge of the Enlightenment in general, and **Immanuel Kant** in particular.

Schweitzer, Albert (1875–1965). German pastor, physician, concert organist, and theologian. In his book *The Quest of the Historical Jesus*, he portrayed Jesus as an eschatological prophet who preached the imminent end of the world; Jesus' ethic was therefore meant for a brief, interim time before the coming of the end. Schweitzer was awarded the Nobel Peace Prize in 1952 for his medical missionary work in Lambaréné in French Equatorial Africa (present-day Gabon in west central Africa).

Siddhartha Gautama (Buddha) (ca. 560–ca. 483 BCE). Founder of Buddhism who was born in present-day Nepal. "Buddha" means Enlightened One or Awakened One.

Sidgwick, Henry (1838–1900). English utilitarian philosopher following in the tradition of **Jeremy Bentham** and **John Stuart Mill**. He advanced the notion of ethical hedonism, by which every individual should seek the common good and happiness of all.

Simons, Menno (1496–1561). Sixteenth-century Dutch Anabaptist leader. His crucial leadership of the Anabaptist movement in the Netherlands prompted Dutch and later Swiss Anabaptists to adopt the name of Mennonites.

Stevenson, C. L. (1908–79). Charles Leslie Stevenson was an American analytic philosopher who studied under **G. E. Moore** and **Ludwig Wittgenstein** at Cambridge. He taught for many years at the University of Michigan. Stevenson developed the work of **David Hume** alongside that of the **logical positivists**. His book *Ethics and Language* proposes that ethics is a matter more of feeling than

of reason or propositions (an ethical system known as **emotivism**).

Tawney, R. H. (1880–1962). Richard Henry Tawney was a British Christian socialist who taught at the London School of Economics and Political Science. He was a friend of Anglican Archbishop **William Temple** but came to be critical of the Church of England as an institution. His most famous book is *Religion and the Rise of Capitalism*. Tawney's socialist thought is a counterpoint to that of capitalist-minded contemporary **Friedrich Hayek**.

Temple, William (1881–1944). Anglican priest and one of the foremost Anglican theologians of the twentieth century. Temple was archbishop of Canterbury from 1942 to 1944. He promoted reforms in Anglican church polity and supported social and economic reforms in England. His book *Christianity and Social Order* articulates his vision of a just post-war society.

Tertullian (ca. 160–ca. 225 CE). First of the great Latin theologians; he became a **Montanist** in the later part of his life. Tertullian was born Quintus Septimius Florens Tertullianus in Carthage, Tunisia (present-day Tunis). He is well known for his **rigorism**, and for his opposition to incorporating classical philosophy into Christian theology.

Thomas Aquinas (1225–74). Aquinas, often known simply as Thomas, was a theologian from Aquino in Italy who joined the newly formed Dominicans (the "Order of Preachers") and became one of the most influential scholars of the church. His most famous work is the magisterial *Summa Theologiae* (also known as the *Summa Theologica*), written as a systematic summary of Christian doctrine. Thomas is important, among other reasons, for his incorporation of classical philosophy, especially **Aristotle**'s, into Christian theological reflection.

Thoreau, Henry David (1817–62). American poet, essayist, and philosopher from Massachusetts. His essay "Civil Disobedience" was a crucial influence in the later civil rights movement in the United States.

Thurman, Howard (1900–81). Baptist pastor and African American theologian. He was Dean of the

Chapel first at Howard University in Washington, DC, and later at Boston University. Thurman's meeting with **Gandhi** in India exerted a lasting influence on his theology. His book *Jesus and the Disinherited* influenced **Martin Luther King Jr.** and other civil rights leaders.

Troeltsch, Ernst (1865–1923). German theologian whose work concentrated on the philosophy and history of religion. A key aspect of Troeltsch's thought that continues to be influential today is his classification of religious expressions intro three types: church, sect, and mysticism.

Truth, Sojourner (1797–1883). African American woman born into slavery in New York as Isabella Baumfree. Sojourner Truth spoke extensively for women's suffrage and for the abolitionist movement. Her most famous speech "Ain't I a Woman?" was delivered at a women's rights convention in Ohio in 1851.

Turner, Nat (1800–31). African American born into slavery in Virginia. Turner led a revolt of slaves known as Nat Turner's Rebellion that resulted in fifty-five deaths and in his subsequent execution.

Tutu, Desmond (b. 1931). Former Anglican archbishop of Cape Town, South Africa. Tutu was awarded the Nobel Peace Prize in 1984 for his work opposing apartheid and promoting reconciliation. He chaired the Truth and Reconciliation Commission (1996–8), which sought to establish the truth about South Africa's apartheid past.

Vanier, Jean (b. 1928). Founder of the L'Arche communities, which are homes for people with developmental disabilities. Vanier was born in Geneva, Switzerland, to a French-Canadian family. He still lives at the first L'Arche community in Trosly-Breuil in northern France. L'Arche is the French term for Noah's ark.

Walker, Alice (b. 1944). African American author who describes herself as a womanist, a term she uses to name the distinctive experiences of women of color. Womanist theology or **womanism** has come to be an important strand of feminist theology.

Washington, Booker T. (1856–1915). African American intellectual born as a slave in Virginia.

Washington became principal of Tuskegee Institute in Alabama, and is often recognized as the foremost black educator in American history.

Weber, Max (1864–1920). German social theorist. Weber is a forefather of the sociology of religion and modern social science. Weber's book *The Protestant Ethic and the Spirit of Capitalism* proposed that the Calvinist work ethic helped give birth to the development of capitalism.

Wesley, John (1703–91). Anglican preacher who founded the Methodist movement with his brother Charles. Along with **George Whitefield**, Wesley was a famous open-air preacher who traveled and preached widely throughout England. In 1738 he had a significant conversion experience where he felt his heart "strangely warmed" by a reading of Martin Luther's Preface to the Epistle to the Romans. Methodism began to spread throughout Scotland, England, and the United States when Wesley started ordaining lay preachers. Wesley is also associated with the notion of Christian perfection – a process of sanctification or becoming like Christ and having the mind of Christ. For Wesley, perfection was not sinlessness, but perfection in love.

West, Cornel (b. 1953). African American intellectual and philosopher who has taught at Union Theological Seminary, Yale, Harvard, the University of Paris, and Princeton University. He has written extensively on racism (particularly in his book *Race Matters*) and on democracy.

Whitefield, George (1714–70). Anglican priest and eloquent preacher who figured prominently in the evangelical movement of the eighteenth century. He studied at Oxford, where he was befriended by brothers Charles and **John Wesley**. Whitefield's Calvinism distinguished him from John Wesley's **Arminian** commitments.

Williams, Delores (b. 1937). African American womanist theologian. Williams taught feminist theology for many years at Union Theological Seminary in New York.

Williams, Roger (1603–83). English theologian who dissented from the Church of England and founded the colony of Providence, Rhode Island, in

1635. He advocated for freedom of religion and for the separation of church and state.

Wittgenstein, Ludwig (1889–1951). Key philosopher of the early twentieth century. Wittgenstein was born in Vienna, Austria, and taught at Cambridge University. His work in the philosophy of language has influenced a number of Christian theologians, including **Stanley Hauerwas**.

Wollstonecraft, Mary (1759–97). London-born Anglo-Irish writer and early feminist. Her 1792 book *A Vindication of the Rights of Woman* advocated for the equality of the sexes. She also spent time in Paris during the early days of the French Revolution.

Wolterstorff, Nicholas (b. 1932). Professor of philosophical theology at Yale University. Wolterstorff's work has dealt with the areas of metaphysics, aesthetics, the philosophy of religion, and political philosophy. He previously taught at Calvin College in Michigan.

Wycliffe, John (1325–84). Wycliffe taught theology at Oxford University. His thought is considered to be a precursor to the later Protestant Reformation; thus he is sometimes called the "morning star" of the Reformation. One of Wycliffe's achievements was the translation of the Vulgate (Latin translation of the Bible) into English.

Yoder, John Howard (1927–97). American Mennonite theologian and historian who taught at Goshen Biblical Seminary and Notre Dame University. He is best known for his Christian pacifism and for his contributions to ecumenical dialogue. Yoder's work is a key influence on the thought of **Stanley Hauerwas**.

Zeno of Citium (333–264 BCE). Hellenistic philosopher from Citium in Cyprus. Zeno is the founder of the school of thought known as **Stoicism**.

Zizioulas, John (b. 1931). Eastern Orthodox theologian and Metropolitan (bishop) of Pergamon in Turkey. His most famous work is *Being as Communion*.

Zwingli, Ulrich (1484–1531). Ulrich (or Huldrych) Zwingli was a leader in the Protestant Reformation in Switzerland. Along with **John Calvin**, he is often considered one of the founders of the Reformed tradition. Like Calvin, he emphasized Christian influence on civil society, but he was more like **Martin Luther** in his stance on the centrality of the Scriptures. His main difference from both these Reformers was his view of the Lord's Supper not as a sacrament but as a memorial act that remembers Christ's sacrifice on the cross and celebrates his spiritual presence.

Glossary of Terms

Albigensians: The Albigensians were a Christian sect arising in the eleventh century in southern France (they are named after the French city of Albi) that had affinities with **Gnosticism** and **Manicheism**. They were vigorously and sometimes violently opposed by the Catholic Church.

antinomianism: From the Greek for "against law," antinomianism is the ethical position that resists prescribed rules. Within Christianity, it is specifically a stance against adopting the Jewish law (**Torah**) as binding on Christians. Augustine's oft-quoted phrase "love and do you what you will" has sometimes been understood in this way. Most forms of **consequentialist** ethics may be seen as antinomian.

apocalyptic: A genre of literature that typically uses vivid symbolism and metaphors to portray cosmic events, especially those related to the end of the world. In Jewish literature, the book of Daniel has apocalyptic elements; in the New Testament the book of Revelation is the prime example of a Christian apocalypse.

Apocrypha: Biblical books written between approximately 300 BCE and 100 CE that are included in the Greek version of the Old Testament (known as the Septuagint). They are excluded from the Jewish and most Protestant Christian canons but included in the Roman Catholic Church's canon. Apocryphal books are sometimes also known as Deuterocanonical (from the Greek for "second canon").

Arianism: Theological heresy named after the Christian priest Arius, who was opposed by **Athanasius** and was declared to be a heretic at the Council of Nicaea convened by the Roman Emperor Constantine in 325 CE. Arius was condemned for teaching that Jesus was a created being rather than eternally co-existent with God the Father. The debate between the supporters of Arius and Athanasius led to the writing of the Nicene Creed (at the Council of Nicaea, and later at the Council of Constantinople in 381 CE) and to a more thorough development of the doctrine of the Trinity. Arianism, which denies the full divinity of Christ, may be seen as theologically opposite to the earlier ideas of **Docetism**, which denied his full humanity.

Arminianism: School of theology named after its founder, Dutch Reformed theologian Jacob Arminius (1560–1609). Arminianism is characterized by its position that salvation is through free acceptance of God's grace extended to all sinners, rather than God's predestination of humanity to salvation or damnation. Arminianism has come to be associated with Wesleyan Methodism and as a theological opponent to five-point Calvinism (see **Synod of Dort**).

Introducing Christian Ethics, Second Edition. Samuel Wells and Ben Quash with Rebekah Eklund.
© 2017 John Wiley & Sons Ltd. Published 2017 by John Wiley & Sons Ltd.

asceticism: The practice of denying oneself physical pleasures or necessities for spiritual benefits.

canon: In general terms, a list of books considered to be authoritative sacred scripture. In Judaism, this means the books called the Hebrew Bible or Jewish Scripture. The Protestant Christian canon most often includes the sixty-six biblical books of the Old and New Testaments, while the Roman Catholic Church canon includes the **Apocrypha** as well.

Cappadocian Fathers: Common nickname for the theologians **Basil of Caesarea**, **Gregory of Nazianzus**, and **Gregory of Nyssa**. Macrina, sister of Basil and Gregory of Nyssa, is also often considered one of the great Cappadocian theologians.

categorical imperative: **Immanuel Kant**'s influential principle that a moral law is binding regardless of context or outcome; this is also known as **universalizability** (that a moral law must be capable of being universally applied), and includes the principle that people are always to be treated as ends, never as means.

catholicity: The word "catholic" traditionally refers to the universal church that adheres to the faith believed always, everywhere, and by all the faithful. When Christians say in the Apostles' Creed that they believe in "the holy catholic church," this is what they mean. Catholicity thus refers to a trait of the church or of theology that is orthodox (non-heretical or non-schismatic) and universal to Christianity. When capitalized, Catholic refers to the Roman Catholic Church.

cenobitic monasticism: This refers to a variety of monasticism that emphasized communal living, rather than solitary practice (which is known as **eremitic monasticism**). St. **Basil of Caesarea** and his sister St. Macrina, St. Benedict and his sister St. Scholastica, and St. **Francis of Assisi** and St. Clare are important figures in cenobitic or communal monasticism.

coherence notion of truth: This is the position that there are no free-standing facts, but that all truth is like a piece of a jigsaw puzzle that is evaluated by whether it fits with other recognized truths.

conscientization: A key component of educator **Paulo Freire**'s thought, conscientization or "critical consciousness" is the process of analyzing the socio-economic, political, and cultural forces that shape one's life, so that one may transform these forces through **praxis**. **Liberation theology** has drawn significantly on Freire's work.

consequentialism: A family of ethical theories that rejects **deontological ethics**, consequentalist ethics focuses on achieving good results or outcomes.

correspondence notion of truth: This is the assumption that statements describe states of affairs that are real and true whether the statement had been made or not; truth is thus regarded as an objective matter.

Council of Trent: Council convened by the Roman Catholic Church and that met periodically between 1545 and 1563 to define Catholic doctrine, partially in response to the Protestant Reformation.

Counter-Reformation: Also known as the Catholic Reformation, the Counter-Reformation was a response to the Protestant Reformation within the Roman Catholic Church. It included apologetics (defense of the Catholic faith), reaffirmation of Catholic doctrines, and reforms of Catholic life and practice. The **Council of Trent** was a key component of the Counter-Reformation.

declension narrative: The identification of a point in history at which a more faithful form of life or philosophy was lost, and an account of the consequences of that "fall" or decline.

deduction: Deductive reasoning is a type of logic expressed in premises (propositions) and a conclusion. In deduction the conclusion is certain and is contained within the premises. In inductive reasoning, on the other hand, the conclusion is *probable* and is based on the premises but may go beyond them (see also **induction**).

Deism: A religious philosophy that adheres to belief in a creator God or supreme being on the basis of reason alone. Deism, as a natural religion, stands in contrast to revealed religions (such as Christianity, Judaism, or Islam), which are based on revelation from God to human beings. Deism is also generally associated with belief in a God who does not intervene directly in human affairs or human history.

deontological ethics: Derived from the Greek noun *deon* meaning duty or obligation, deontology refers to any ethic that focuses on right action and/or right intention. Deontological ethics includes **divine command**, **natural law**, and **Immanuel Kant**'s **categorical imperative**.

determinism: The view that individual choice is not the primary cause of the outcome of events, but that the outcome lies outside human volition.

Deuteronomistic history: Name given by biblical scholars to the biblical books Deuteronomy, Joshua, Judges, 1–2 Samuel, and 1–2 Kings, which are often assumed to have been compiled by the same editor and which share a similar theological outlook.

dialectic: Threefold process, associated with **G. W. F. Hegel**, of proposing a concept (thesis), recognizing plausible contradictory arguments (antithesis), and seeking to overcome those incompatibilities (synthesis). Hegel conceived of dialectic as a continually unfolding process leading to greater truth.

***Didache*:** Also known as the *Teaching of the Twelve Apostles* (*didache* means "teaching" in Greek), the *Didache* is an early Christian document thought to be written between 50 and 120 CE. It contains some of the earliest Christian instruction on baptism and the Eucharist.

Diggers: Mid-seventeenth-century social revolutionaries in England who advocated economic equality and a return to the land. Also known as the True Levellers, the Diggers established small rural communes. Many later ecological and social movements looked back to the Diggers and their leader Gerard Winstanley for inspiration.

divine command ethics: The ethical theory that actions are required, good, permissible, or evil simply because God decrees them so.

Docetism: The belief, judged to be a heresy by the early church, that Christ was fully divine but only appeared to be human and to suffer. Docetism, which denies the full humanity of Christ, is the theological opposite of views that deny Christ's full divinity (see, for example, **Ebionism** and later **Arianism**). Docetism was especially prominent among Gnostics in the second century (see **Gnosticism**).

Donatists: A sect of Christians in North Africa in the early fourth century that lasted until the Muslim conquest of North Africa in the seventh century. Donatism is named after the bishop Donatus, a key figure in the Donatist controversy. Donatists believed that sacraments were invalid if administered by clergy who renounced their faith under persecution. Donatism is a form of **rigorism** for its views that the church and her ministers must remain holy. A form of Donatism persists today whenever people believe that the efficacy (validity) of the sacraments depends on the virtue of the minister.

double effect: Recognition that an action may promote some good while at the same time cause harm as an anticipated side-effect. Under this principle, an action is acceptable if it is good or at least indifferent, if it brings about a good outcome, if the good outcome is not the direct outcome of the bad side-effect, and if the resulting good exceeds the incurred harm.

dualism: The belief that good and evil are two equal, opposing forces. Dualism is also reflected in the belief that flesh (considered to be evil) and spirit (considered to be good) are opposed to one another, as in **Gnosticism**. **Manicheism** is another dualistic philosophy.

Ebionites: Early Jewish Christian sect that practiced **asceticism**, continued to observe the Jewish law, and denied the full divinity of Christ. Ebionism continued for about 200 years after the time of Jesus Christ.

emotivism: Strand of **non-cognitivist** ethics promoted by **David Hume** that saw morals as a matter of the heart and the emotions rather than of reason or proposition.

Epicureanism: School of thought of the ancient Greek philosopher **Epicurus**, who concentrated solely on material reality and asserted that the highest good was pleasure. For Epicurus, pleasure was not sensual indulgence but the calm serenity that abides when the soul is at peace.

eremitic monasticism: A variety of monasticism that focused on a solitary, ascetic existence; it is often associated with a single monk living alone in the desert. St. **Antony of Egypt** is a key example of eremitic monasticism. **Cenobitic monasticism**, on the other hand, refers to forms of communal monasticism.

eschatology: The study of the last things (from the Greek *eschatos*, "last" or "final") and the future kingdom of God; or the section of Christian theology devoted to the doctrines surrounding death, judgment, heaven, and hell.

Essenes: Jewish group in Palestine active from the second century BCE to the second century CE who lived in ascetic and separatist communities. The Dead Sea Scrolls community at Qumran is thought by many scholars to be an Essene community.

Euthyphro's dilemma: The question, drawn from **Plato**'s *Euthyphro*, "Does God command this particular action because it is right, or is it right because God commands it?" Plato's *Euthyphro* is the record of a conversation between Socrates and Euthyphro.

Gemara: Commentaries on the **Mishnah**, the written form of Jewish oral traditions. There are two Gemaras that correspond to the two compilations of the **Talmud**: the Jerusalem Gemara, published in Palestine around 350 CE; and the Babylonian Gemara, compiled by Jewish scholars in Babylon in the fifth century CE. The Babylonian Gemara together with the Mishnah comprise the Babylonian Talmud, and vice versa.

Gnosticism: Religious movement influential on the development of early Christianity that viewed the material as evil, taught that salvation depended on special or secret knowledge (*gnosis*), and held a dualistic view of the world (see **dualism**). Forms of Christianity influenced by Gnosticism tended to believe that Jesus was not fully or truly human or bodily (see **Docetism**).

Great Awakenings: Religious revivals throughout American history that emphasized emotional response to God and visible conversion. The First Great Awakening occurred from approximately the mid-1720s to the mid-1740s in colonial New England and is associated with preachers **Jonathan Edwards** and **George Whitefield**. The Second Great Awakening is dated to the end of the eighteenth and beginning of the nineteenth centuries; and a third revival is sometimes identified in the period 1875–1914, coinciding roughly with the birth of the Pentecostal movement at the turn of the century.

Halakhah: Halakhah means "conduct" (or literally "to go"). It is a large body of Jewish moral instruction, or classical Jewish religious law.

Hasidism: A mystical Jewish revival movement founded in Poland in the eighteenth century by Israel ben Eliezer, the Baal Shem Tov ("Master of the Good Name"). Hasidism emphasizes serving God with joy, inner devotion, and communion with God.

Haustafeln: Also known as the "household codes" found in the New Testament books Ephesians and Colossians, the *Haustafeln* contain teaching on the three traditional household relationships in the ancient world: husband and wife, father and child, and master and slave.

Hellenistic: An adjective broadly referring to the embrace of Greek language and culture, and more specifically to the wide and pervasive spread of Greek culture after Alexander the Great's conquest of the Persian Empire in the fourth century BCE. Hellenistic values were seen as a threat to Judaism by some Jews (particularly during the Maccabean revolt of 168–165 BCE) but tended to be adopted somewhat more readily by early Jewish Christians.

hermeneutic of suspicion: A form of biblical interpretation that begins with a mistrust of both the social location of a text's author and the dominant historical ways such a text has been read. This method of reading the Bible is associated with subversive ethics.

historical materialism: **Karl Marx**'s understanding that human existence is an unfolding drama whose driving dynamic is human relationship to the means of production.

ideal observer: Within a relativist ethical position, the ideal observer is the person who is fully informed, wholly rational, and yet suitably compassionate and imaginative; the concept of the ideal observer is thus an attempt to counter the most obvious dangers of relativism.

immanentism: In immanentist philosophy, God is so much absorbed in nature or humankind that there is little or no notion of a God beyond those phenomena. Specifically in regards to environmental ethics, immanentism implies that nature contains its own values, without the need for reference to any source or order beyond itself.

induction: Inductive reasoning is a kind of logic that begins with particular premises (propositions) and infers general conclusions from them. It is often contrasted with **deduction** or deductive reasoning.

intuitionism: A strand of **consequentialist** ethics developed by **G. E. Moore**. Intuitionism holds that there are objective truths and falsehoods that are self-evident to every human being through common sense.

Jainism: A religion that arose in India in the sixth century BCE and adheres to five basic principles, the achievement of which will free one from the cycle of rebirth: nonviolence (*ahimsa*), truthfulness, not stealing, non-possessiveness, and chastity.

Jewish War: The Jewish–Roman War (66–70 CE), a Jewish revolt against Roman rule, ended with a decisive Jewish defeat and the destruction of the Jerusalem temple by Roman troops.

Levellers: Early seventeenth-century political movement in England that employed **natural law** arguments in service of a strongly egalitarian political vision but (unlike their later contemporaries the **Diggers**) did not undermine property rights.

liberation theology: Branch of Christian theology originating in Latin America in the 1960s that emphasizes liberation from oppression, God's special care for the poor and vulnerable, and the central role of **praxis** in theology.

logical positivism: An influential **non-cognitivist** philosophical movement from the late 1920s that assumed philosophy is concerned simply with verifying the truth or falsehood of propositions. Because ethical statements are neither analytic (inherently true) nor synthetic (requiring empirical evidence), they are unprovable. Logical positivism is also known as logical empiricism.

Mahayana Buddhism: Reform branch of Buddhism that has been most active in northern Asia; Mahayana means "Greater Vehicle."

Manicheism: Religion founded by Mani of Persia in the late third century CE with roots in the ancient Persian religion Zoroastrianism and with some similarities to Christianity. Manicheism preached asceticism and, like **Gnosticism**, the **dualism** of good and evil. **Augustine** was briefly associated with Manicheism before his conversion to Christianity. Manicheism lingered in the West until about the seventh century.

Mishnah: The Mishnah (meaning "instruction" or "repetition") is a collection of Jewish oral traditions and doctrines compiled around 200 CE. The Mishnah comprises part of the larger body of work known as the **Talmud**.

Montanism: Christian group originating in the mid-second century CE that practiced **asceticism** and was led by Montanus, who preached that the Holy Spirit was giving new revelations to the church beyond those contained in the Bible. Montanism was marked by intense eschatological expectation, asceticism, and an emphasis on the Holy Spirit's presence in phenomena like ecstatic prophecy. The theologian **Tertullian** became a Montanist toward the end of his life; the sect persisted for several centuries.

natural law: Ancient and modern belief that the principles of human action are in accord with nature and therefore have universal validity. Natural law is a major stream of thought within universal ethics.

natural theology: Strand of theology that claims knowledge of God is available through reason and observation of the natural world, not through revelation alone. **Karl Barth** was a vigorous opponent of natural theology.

naturalism: The assumption that ethical systems should be based only on properties or characteristics in the natural world that can be discovered by observation, experience, or experiment.

naturalistic fallacy: The error of assuming it is possible to derive an "ought" (a moral statement) from an "is" (an observation of a phenomenon in the natural world). This was **G. E. Moore**'s criticism of **naturalism**.

neo-scholasticism: Revival of medieval **scholasticism** sometimes called neo-Thomism after key figure **Thomas Aquinas**. Neo-scholasticism flourished especially in the second half of the nineteenth century.

non-cognitivism: A twentieth-century moral philosophy that shares **G. E. Moore**'s belief that ethics cannot be derived from the natural world (see the **naturalistic fallacy**), but which has also abandoned the claim that ethical judgments can be simply true or false. **Emotivism** and **logical positivism** are two influential forms of non-cognitivism.

non-realism: Strand of philosophy, significant within **consequentialist** ethics, that regards truth not as a matter of tangible, objective realities but instead as a subjective result of human cultural construction.

pagan: A term used by Christians to describe people in the Roman Empire who participated in the worship of local deities and the imperial cult; it was also used to refer more generally to a person of a religion other than Christianity, Judaism, or Islam.

Pastoral Epistles: The New Testament books 1 and 2 Timothy and Titus are known as the Pastoral Epistles for their attention to the life and ministry of the church.

Pelagianism: A theological heresy named after the early fifth-century theologian Pelagius, who denied the doctrine of original sin and believed in the fundamental ability of humanity to do good. Pelagianism tends to stress human effort rather than God's grace as the key to achieving a good or moral life.

personalism: Personalism is a late nineteenth-century philosophy with origins in France and the USA. It was articulated by Methodist **Borden Bowne** in his 1905 book *The Immanence of God*. In personalism, personality or personhood is the central philosophical concept. Jesus Christ is the embodiment of God as an infinite person and is therefore the model for personhood.

Pharisees: Jewish party in Palestine that developed around the third century BCE. Pharisees are the precursors to rabbinic Judaism, and are best known for their devotion to the Jewish law or **Torah**, both oral and written. The Pharisees and **Sadducees** were the two main expressions of Judaism at the time of Jesus.

Pietism: A seventeenth-century renewal movement that originated in the German Lutheran Church. Pietism emphasized personal scriptural study and a faith that lives in the heart and not simply in the intellect. When not capitalized, pietism also refers in a more general sense to an emphasis (sometimes an over-emphasis) on personal or emotional religious experience.

positivism: A materialistic philosophy developed by Auguste Comte in the early nineteenth century that argues all genuine knowledge is based on that which can be received through the senses. **Logical positivism** is a later cousin of positivism.

postliberal theology: Late twentieth-century strand of theology that resists the emphasis of liberal Protestant theology on reason, human experience, and common religious experience, and focuses instead on the practices of Christian communities, understanding theological language as the "grammar" of faith and the cultural embodiment of Christian doctrine. Postliberal theology is deeply indebted to **Karl Barth**'s theology and has often been associated with Yale Divinity School and theologians there, including **George Lindbeck** and Hans Frei.

praxis: From the Greek for "practice," the term praxis has been adopted in contemporary theology to mean action to transform or liberate from oppression. In **liberation theology**, theological reflection is always grounded in praxis – in human experience and a commitment to God's **preferential option for the poor**.

preferential option for the poor: The conviction, held particularly by **liberation theologians**, that God is on the side of the oppressed and the poor, and that the church should share this commitment.

prescriptivism: A type of **non-cognitivist** ethics developed by **R. M. Hare** in the mid-twentieth century. For Hare, ethical statements are either descriptive or non-descriptive/evaluative. Prescriptivism is like **emotivism** in its claim that ethical statements cannot be statements of fact. On the other hand, it is similar to **Immanuel Kant**'s **universalizability** principle when it claims that evaluative (non-descriptive) statements are genuine imperatives for all times and places.

prevenient grace: To believe in prevenient grace or prevenience is to believe that God's grace "comes before" (the meaning of "prevenient") to prepare the heart of a person to accept God's offer of salvation. Prevenient grace is especially associated with **John Wesley** and with **Arminianism**.

proportionalism: A development in late twentieth-century Roman Catholic moral theology that seeks to steer a path between **deontology** and **consequentialism**. It accepts **natural law** (rather than divine command), and affirms that acts should be evaluated by outcome as well as intention. Proportionalism was developed by Bernard Hoose in his 1987 work of that name, and was decisively rejected by Pope **John Paul II** in his 1993 encyclical *Veritatis Splendor* (The Splendor of Truth).

Radical Orthodoxy: A postmodern theological movement centered around British Anglican theologian **John Milbank**. Radical Orthodoxy rejects modern secularism and liberalism and seeks a return to orthodox Christian doctrine as represented particularly by figures such as **Augustine** and **Thomas Aquinas**.

Radical Reformation: The branch of the sixteenth-century Reformation characterized by a rejection of infant baptism in favor of adult or believer baptism. It is sometimes called Anabaptism (anabaptism means "re-baptism"). The Radical Reformers (such as **Menno Simons** and **Jacob Hutter**) also had an aversion to hierarchical church authority and tended to emphasize the clear distinction of the church from the world.

realism: School of thought that regards morality as an objective matter – that is, the notion there is only one unchanging moral truth. All **deontological** theories and some **consequentialist** theories of ethics fall into the realist camp.

rigorism: A strand of Christian thought that accepts no compromise between Christian practice and secular culture. It tends to reject involvement in cultural activities outside the church and is inclined to be suspicious of accommodation to societal or cultural mores. **Tertullian** and Novatian were notable early Christian rigorists.

Sadducees: Jewish party in Palestine active from the second century BCE until the destruction of the temple in 70 CE. The Sadducee party largely represented the aristocracy and high priests. Sadducees embraced the incorporation of Hellenism (Greek culture) into Judaism. They rejected the validity of the oral law, and insisted instead on the sole use of the written **Torah**. The **Pharisees** and Sadducees were the two main expressions of Judaism at the time of Jesus.

scholasticism: School of thought within medieval Christianity that sought to build a philosophical system that reconciled Christian doctrine with ancient philosophy. **Thomas Aquinas** is a key scholastic theologian.

Second Vatican Council: Also known as Vatican II, this influential council of the Roman Catholic Church was convened by Pope John XXIII in 1962 and concluded by Pope Paul VI in 1965. Among its important achievements were several key changes in Catholic liturgy, including authorizing the use of the vernacular (mother-tongue languages such as English) rather than Latin in the Mass. Vatican II also heralded a new era in ecumenical relations between the Roman Catholic Church and other expressions of Christianity.

situation ethics: Strand of **consequentialist** ethics presented by **Joseph Fletcher** in the 1960s that is sometimes associated with moral relativism and has some resemblances to **proportionalism**. Situation ethics attempts to find a mean between legalist (**natural law** and **divine command**) ethics and **antinomian** (spontaneous and unprincipled) ethics by proposing that any law is useful inasmuch as it brings about greater love of neighbor as its result.

Social Gospel: Early twentieth-century movement in American theology led by Congregational pastor Washington Gladden and Baptist pastor **Walter Rauschenbusch**. The Social Gospel concentrated on the earthly realization of the kingdom of God through human action and progress.

Stoicism: Influential ancient Greek philosophy that sees the natural world as broadly identical with the divine mind. It thus emphasizes submitting to the laws of nature and is especially associated with the rejection or reasoned use of the emotions.

subsidiarity: The political principle that as much as possible ought to be done by smaller and less centralized authorities rather than by larger or more centralized ones. Subsidiarity is a key principle of modern Catholic social thought. It was introduced in the 1931 encyclical *Quadragesimo Anno* ("On Reconstruction of the Social Order").

supersessionism: The belief, judged by the church to be heretical (false), that the church has replaced or superseded Israel in God's plan of salvation.

syllogism: A type of **deduction** or deductive logic expressed in three propositions: a major premise (a general statement), a minor premise (a specific statement), and a conclusion based on the two premises. For example: 1. God loves the world; 2. The world is full of sinners; 3. Therefore, God loves sinners.

Synod of Dort: The Synod of Dort was held 1618–19 by the Dutch Reformed Church in response to **Arminianism**. The Synod adopted what has become known as the five points of Calvinism (total depravity, unconditional election, limited atonement, irresistible grace, perseverance of the saints).

Synoptic Gospels: Common term for the New Testament books Matthew, Mark, and Luke, which are grouped together for their similarities against the more unique Gospel of John (the Greek roots of "synoptic" mean "to see together").

Talmud: Corpus of Jewish writings that includes the **Mishnah** (the written form of Jewish oral traditions) and the **Gemara** (commentary on the Mishnah); the Talmud is the basis for Jewish legal and ethical instruction in addition to the **Torah**. Two compilations exist: the Jerusalem or Palestinian Talmud, thought to have been completed in Palestine around 350 CE; and the Babylonian Talmud, compiled by Jewish scholars in Babylon in the fifth century CE.

teleological ethics: Ethics that is concerned with a final end, or *telos*. *Telos* is the Greek word for "end" or "goal." **Consequentialist** ethics is sometimes referred to as teleological. In ecclesial ethics, however, teleology means focus not simply on an outcome, but on a final end such as the coming kingdom of God and/or the building up of the church.

theodicy: Attention to the paradox that, in the face of God's love and sovereignty, evil and suffering nonetheless exist. The "problem" of theodicy is sometimes expressed as the question, if God is all-good and all-powerful, why does suffering exist? Theodicies are theories intended to justify the ways of God in the face of the experience of suffering.

theosis: The Eastern Orthodox teaching that Christ's incarnation – his uniting of the human and the divine – enables humanity to take on the likeness of God and achieve union with God.

Theravada Buddhism: School of Buddhism that has flourished in Southeast Asia; Theravada means "Doctrine of the Elders."

Torah: The Torah (meaning "instruction" or "Law") refers to the first five books of the Jewish or Hebrew Bible (Genesis, Exodus, Leviticus, Numbers, Deuteronomy), which are also known as the Pentateuch. Torah is one of the three major sections in the Hebrew Bible, alongside the Prophets and the Writings.

Tosephta: Jewish teachings that supplement the **Mishnah** and were probably compiled around 300 CE. The Tosephta are sometimes included in the larger body of work known as the **Talmud**.

universalizability: Fundamental principle of **Immanuel Kant**'s **categorical imperative** that states that one should act only according to that maxim whereby one can at the same time will that it should become a universal law. For Kant, every action that could not be universalized should be avoided; e.g., it is never permissible to break a rule one expects others to keep, such as lying – even if the lie serves to protect a life.

utilitarianism: Ethical theory developed by **Jeremy Bentham** and **John Stuart Mill** (who coined the term) in the early nineteenth century. Utilitarianism grounds morality on the "greatest happiness principle," or on achieving the greatest happiness for the greatest number. Somewhat like **Stoicism**, utilitarians distinguish between the lower, bodily pleasures and the higher, intellectual pleasures. Most subsequent **consequentialist** views define themselves in relation to utilitarianism.

womanism: A branch of feminism that focuses on the experiences of non-white women, especially African American women. The term is often said to originate in an essay by **Alice Walker**. *Mujerista* ethics is an outgrowth of womanism that centers on the experiences of Latina women.

Zealots: The Zealots were nationalistic Jewish revolutionaries in first-century Israel who were given their name for their fierce loyalty to the Jewish law and the Jewish nation, and who sought the establishment of an independent Jewish monarchy, by violent means if necessary.

Name Index

Aelred of Rievaulx, 306–8, 311–13
Ahn, Ilsup, 176
Ambrose of Milan, 45, 46, 94
Antisthenes, 68
Antony of Egypt, 43–7
Aquinas, Thomas, *see* Thomas Aquinas
Aristotle
  on friendship, 305, 306
  and Islam, 75
  and Lindbeck, George, 203–4
  and MacIntyre, Alasdair, 204–6
  and Maimonides, 73
  on natural law, 347
  and potentiality, 358, 359
  and praxis, 161–2, 165
  and Thomas Aquinas, 97, 130–1
  and usury, 271
  and virtue, 2, 49, 208, 216–19, 226
Athanasius, 17, 43–5
Augustine of Hippo
  and abortion, 354
  on church and state, 47, 96, 207–8, 236–40, 248, 255, 256, 273
  on family and sexual ethics, 42, 95, 180, 315–16, 322, 344
  on friendship, 306–7
  and Milbank, John, 207–8
  monastic order of, 47
  and penitential manuals, 48
  and Plato, 69
  and the Reformers, 51
  on Scripture, 7
  theology of, 45, 94–6, 114, 233
  and Thomas Aquinas, 98, 99
  and virtue, 212, 217
  on war, 259–60, 265
  on work, 279–80

Bainton, Roland, 258
Banner, Michael, 193–4, 283, 386, 392
Bantum, Brian, 171–2
Barth, Karl
  on animals, 376
  on church and state, 242, 247–8
  and divine command, 17
  and Hauerwas, Stanley, 208
  and Herdt, Jennifer, 211, 212
  on the Sabbath, 280
  on sexual ethics, 331
  theology of, 17, 108–9, 201–4, 227
Basil of Caesarea, 45, 93–4
Bauckham, Richard, 242
Baxter, Richard, 317
Bell, Daniel, 252, 255–6
Bell, George, 245
Bellah, Robert, 246, 247
Bentham, Jeremy, 137–9, 152, 165, 205, 373
Bernard of Clairvaux, 42, 143
Bernardin, Joseph, 343
Berryman, Jerome, 194
Biggar, Nigel, 261
Bland, Tony, 361
Boff, Clodovis, 163
Boff, Leonardo, 163
Bonhoeffer, Dietrich, 59, 106, 294, 313
Borgmann, Albert, 293
Bowne, Borden, 110, 370
Bretherton, Luke, 213, 244–5

Subject Index

abortion
  ethics of, 215, 353, 360
  and legislation, 84
  and liberalism, 181, 205
  in the modern era, 81
  and pre-natal screening,
    346, 347
  and sanctity of life, 148
advertising, 185, 290–1, 294, 352
African American theology, 117,
  167–73, 351
  see also womanism
African theology, 64, 75, 173–7,
  247, 389
agape, see love
agency, 48–50, 146, 175, 176,
  212, 216, 369, 382, 384–5
Albigensians, 49
Amoris Laetitia, 321, 331
Anabaptists, *see* Radical
  Reformation
Anglican traditions
  on contraception, 329, 344
  on incarnation, 206
  on Scripture, 5, 7
  social ethics of, 150–1, 244
  in South Africa, 173

themes in, 109–12
unity of, 338
animals, 130, 131, 133, 206,
  279, 296, 370–6, 379
antinomianism, 10, 35, 144
Arminianism, 107
asceticism, 38, 43, 45, 93, 271,
  304, 307
Asian American ethics, 176, 192
assisted conception, *see*
  conception, assisted
autonomy
  and abortion, 348, 349, 355,
    359, 360
  and aging, 193
  and contraception, 351
  and euthanasia, 361–2, 364–6
  and Kant, 91, 134, 135, 207
  in relationships, 313, 321, 326

Bible, *see* Scripture
birth control, *see* contraception
Black Lives Matter, 172–3
Buddhism, 75–7, 166
business and management,
  78–80, 249, 281–8, 377–8
Byzantine Church, 44, 47, 50

Calvinism, 51, 53, 84, 100–1,
  107–9, 243, 245, 272, 317
  see also Calvin, John
canon, canonical criticism, 5, 7,
  9, 10, 22
canon law, 111, 359
capitalism, 53, 86, 148, 163, 170,
  173, 184, 204, 247, 272,
  275, 287, 290, 336
capital punishment, 53, 86,
  148, 163, 170, 173, 184,
  204, 247, 272, 275, 287,
  290, 336
Caribbean theology, 176–8
Casti Connubii, 344
casuistry, 112–13, 213, 251
Catholic Church
  on abortion, 354
  on capital punishment, 254
  on contraception, 319, 329,
    344, 345, 347
  on divorce, 321
  and justice, 250
  and liberation theology, 57,
    161, 165
  on marriage and family, 325,
    330, 331

Introducing Christian Ethics, Second Edition. Samuel Wells and Ben Quash with Rebekah Eklund.
© 2017 John Wiley & Sons Ltd. Published 2017 by John Wiley & Sons Ltd.